Tube and Pipe Design

Autodesk® Inventor® 2024

November 2023

Trademarks

The following are registered trademarks or trademarks of Autodesk, Inc., and/or its subsidiaries and/or affiliates in the USA and other countries: 123D, 3ds Max, Alias, ATC, AutoCAD LT, AutoCAD, Autodesk, the Autodesk logo, Autodesk 123D, Autodesk Homestyler, Autodesk Inventor, Autodesk MapGuide, Autodesk Streamline, AutoLISP, AutoSketch, AutoSnap, AutoTrack, Backburner, Backdraft, Beast, BIM 360, Burn, Buzzsaw, CADmep, CAiCE, CAMduct, Civil 3D, Combustion, Communication Specification, Configurator 360, Constructware, Content Explorer, Creative Bridge, Dancing Baby (image), DesignCenter, DesignKids, DesignStudio, Discreet, DWF, DWG, DWG (design/logo), DWG Extreme, DWG TrueConvert, DWG TrueView, DWGX, DXF, Ecotect, Ember, ESTmep, FABmep, Face Robot, FBX, Fempro, Fire, Flame, Flare, Flint, ForceEffect, FormIt 360, Freewheel, Fusion 360, Glue, Green Building Studio, Heidi, Homestyler, HumanIK, i-drop, ImageModeler, Incinerator, Inferno, InfraWorks, Instructables, Instructables (stylized robot design/logo), Inventor, Inventor HSM, Inventor LT, Lustre, Maya, Maya LT, MIMI, Mockup 360, Moldflow Plastics Advisers, Moldflow Plastics Insight, Moldflow, Moondust, MotionBuilder, Movimento, MPA (design/logo), MPA, MPI (design/logo), MPX (design/logo), MPX, Mudbox, Navisworks, ObjectARX, ObjectDBX, Opticore, P9, Pier 9, Pixlr, Pixlr-o-matic, Productstream, Publisher 360, RasterDWG, RealDWG, ReCap, ReCap 360, Remote, Revit LT, Revit, RiverCAD, Robot, Scaleform, Showcase, Showcase 360, SketchBook, Smoke, Socialcam, Softimage, Spark & Design, Spark Logo, Sparks, SteeringWheels, Stitcher, Stone, StormNET, TinkerBox, Tinkercad, Tinkerplay, ToolClip, Topobase, Toxik, TrustedDWG, T-Splines, ViewCube, Visual LISP, Visual, VRED, Wire, Wiretap, WiretapCentral, XSI.

NASTRAN is a registered trademark of the National Aeronautics Space Administration.

All other brand names, product names, or trademarks belong to their respective holders.

Disclaimer

THIS PUBLICATION AND THE INFORMATION CONTAINED HEREIN IS MADE AVAILABLE BY AUTODESK, INC. "AS IS." AUTODESK, INC. DISCLAIMS ALL WARRANTIES, EITHER EXPRESS OR IMPLIED, INCLUDING BUT NOT LIMITED TO ANY IMPLIED WARRANTIES OF MERCHANTABILITY OR FITNESS FOR A PARTICULAR PURPOSE REGARDING THESE MATERIALS.

Published by:

ASCENT Center for Technical Knowledge
630 Peter Jefferson Parkway, Suite 175
Charlottesville, VA 22911
866-527-2368
www.ascented.com

Contents

Introduction

The *Autodesk® Inventor® 2024: Tube and Pipe Design* learning guide is designed for use in Authorized Training Centers (ATC) locations, corporate training settings, and other classroom settings. Although this courseware is designed for instructor-led courses, you can also use it for self-paced learning.

This introduction covers the following topics:

- Course Objectives
- Prerequisites
- Using This Learning Guide
- Downloading and Installing the Exercise Files
- Setting Up the Project File
- Feedback

This learning guide is complementary to the software documentation. For detailed explanations of features and functionality, refer to the Help in the software.

Course Objectives

After completing this course, you will be able to:

- Describe the tube and pipe environment and why you would use it.
- Set up routes and runs and place the initial fittings in your tube and pipe design.
- Create, edit, and manage routes for rigid pipe, rigid tube, and flexible hose designs.
- Manage content libraries, publish custom content to content libraries, and create new styles that use custom content.
- Document tube and pipe designs through the creation of 2D drawings and parts lists and export the 3D design data.

Prerequisites

This learning guide is designed for experienced users of the Autodesk Inventor software. The following is recommended:

- Users should have completed the *Autodesk® Inventor® 2024: Introduction to Solid Modeling* learning guide, or have an equivalent understanding of the Autodesk Inventor user interface and working environments.
- Knowledge of part modeling, assembly modeling, and drawing view creation and annotation is recommended.

Using This Learning Guide

The lessons are independent of each other. However, it is recommended that you complete these lessons in the order that they are presented unless you are familiar with the concepts and functionality described in those lessons. Each chapter contains:

- **Lessons -** Usually two or more lessons in each chapter.
- **Exercises -** Practical, real-world examples for you to practice using the functionality you have just learned. Each exercise contains step-by-step procedures and graphics to help you complete the exercise successfully.

Downloading and Installing the Exercise Files

The Exercise Files page in this learning guide contains a link and instructions to download and install all of the data required to complete the exercises.

Setting Up the Project File

Most users work on several projects at a time, and each project might consist of a number of files. You can use Autodesk Inventor projects to organize related files and maintain links between files. This guide has a project file that stores the paths to all the files that are related to the exercises. When you open a file, Inventor uses the paths in the current project file to locate other required files. To work on a different project, you make a new project active in the Project Editor. Follow the instructions below to locate the Tube and Pipe Design project file for this courseware and make it active.

1. Start Autodesk Inventor.
2. On the Home page, select ⋮ (Projects and Settings) > Settings or you can also click on (Projects) in the Quick Access Toolbar at the top of the interface.
3. At the bottom of the Projects dialog box, click Browse.

   Browse to *C:\Autodesk Inventor 2024 Tube and Pipe Design Exercise Files*.

   Click *Tube and Pipe Design.ipj*.

   Click Open.
4. Click Done to close the Projects dialog box.

Feedback

We always welcome feedback on the learning guides. After completing this course, if you have suggestions for improvements or want to report an error in the learning guide or with the exercise files, please send your comments to *feedback@ASCENTed.com*.

Exercise Files

To download the exercise files for this learning guide, use the following steps:

1. Type the URL ***exactly as shown below*** into the address bar of your Internet browser, to access the Course File Download page.

   Note: If you are using the ebook, you do not have to type the URL. Instead, you can access the page simply by clicking the URL below.

   https://www.ascented.com/getfile/id/scopulorumPF

2. On the Course File Download page, click the **DOWNLOAD NOW** button, as shown below, to download the .ZIP file that contains the exercise files.

3. Once the download is complete, unzip the file and extract its contents.

   The recommended exercise files folder location is:
   C:\Autodesk Inventor 2024 Tube and Pipe Design Exercise Files

Note: It is recommended that you do not change the location of the practice files folder. Doing so may cause errors when completing the practices.

Chapter 1

Introduction to Tube and Pipe

This chapter introduces you to the tube and pipe environment in the Autodesk® Inventor® software. Using the tube and pipe environment, you can create rigid pipe, bent tube, and flexible hose runs between your assembly components.

Objective

After completing this chapter, you will be able to:

- Describe the tube and pipe environment.

Lesson: Introduction to Tube and Pipe

Overview

This lesson describes the tube and pipe environment and the creation of rigid tube, pipe, and flexible hose routes for fluids and gases in a machine assembly.

The tube and pipe environment enables you to easily create and optimize tube, pipe, and hose runs, saving design time and streamlining the process of creating and distributing more accurate models. Typical uses for the environment include routing fluids and gases through mechanical assemblies, and creating project designs using rigid tube, pipe, or flexible hose segments.

The following image shows a typical tube and pipe design in which rigid pipe, bent tubing, and flexible hoses are used to route air and oil between components.

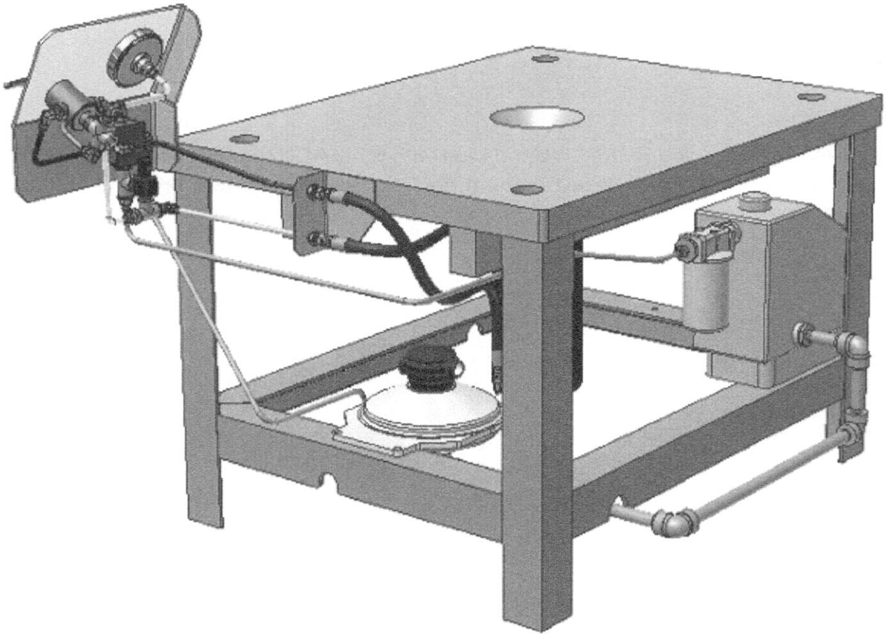

Objectives

After completing this lesson, you will be able to:

- Describe the purpose and characteristics of a tube and pipe design.
- Describe how the tube and pipe environment is integrated into Autodesk Inventor.
- Explain the basic steps involved in creating tube and pipe runs.

About Tube and Pipe Designs

The Autodesk Inventor Tube and Pipe environment includes features for setting tube and pipe styles, adding runs and routes to mechanical assemblies or product designs, populating selected routes with library components, and adding optional fittings. When a tube and pipe run is complete, the tube and pipe information can be represented in drawings and presentations.

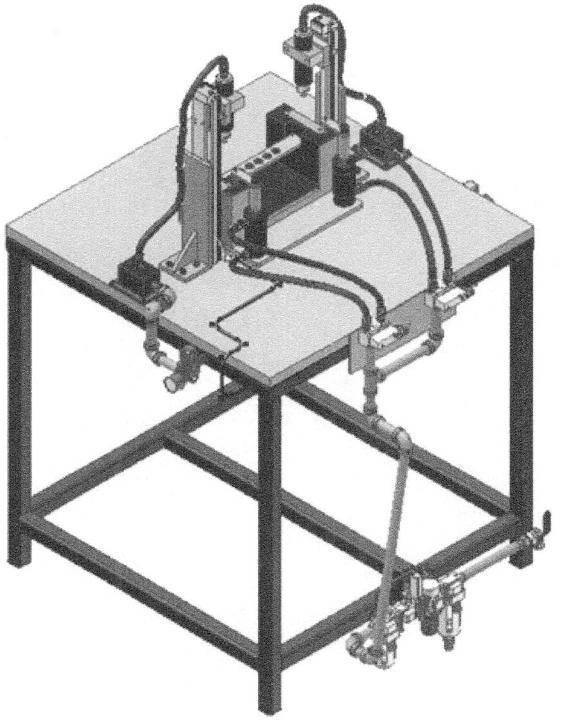

Definition of Tube and Pipe Designs

Pipes, tubing, and hoses are common in a variety of machinery. You use the tube and pipe environment to model rigid pipe, bent tube, and flexible hose runs between assembly components. As your design changes, the runs automatically update to match changes in the positions of related assembly components.

The tube and pipe environment is designed to create pipe, tube, and hose runs for industrial machinery. The tube and pipe environment is not intended for large process piping designs.

Example of a Tube and Pipe Design

In the following image, an example of how you can use tube and pipe designs to help finalize your prototype is shown. As you can see, you can use various styles to represent your design.

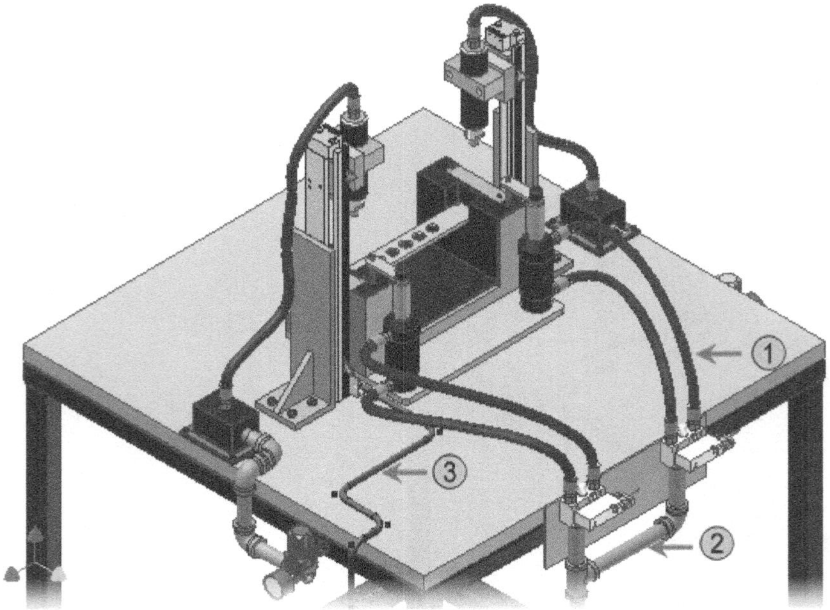

1. A flexible hose is routed between two components.

2. A rigid pipe design is connected by optional fittings.

3. A bent tube design.

Tube and Pipe Environment

Tools for creating tube and pipe designs are available from the assembly environment on the ribbon through the Tube and Pipe tab, Pipe Run tab, and Route tab.

Ribbon Tabs in the Assembly Design

As you switch design tasks and environments, the tabs and panels on the ribbon change accordingly.

Tube and Pipe Tab

The Tube and Pipe tab displays when you create or activate a primary runs assembly. The Tube and Pipe tab contains tools you use to work with tube and pipe assemblies.

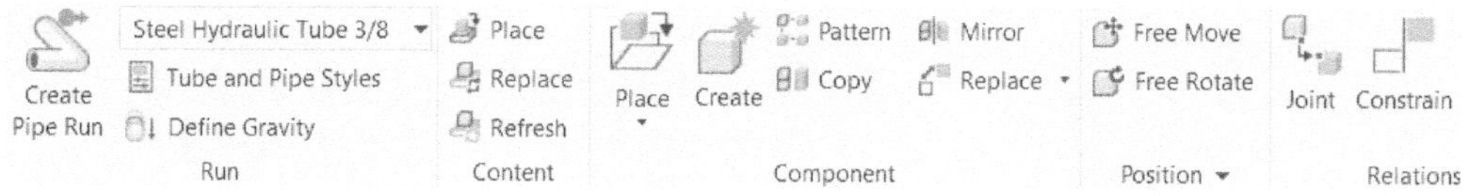

Pipe Run Tab

The Pipe Run tab displays when you activate a pipe run. The Pipe Run tab contains tools you use to create pipe runs.

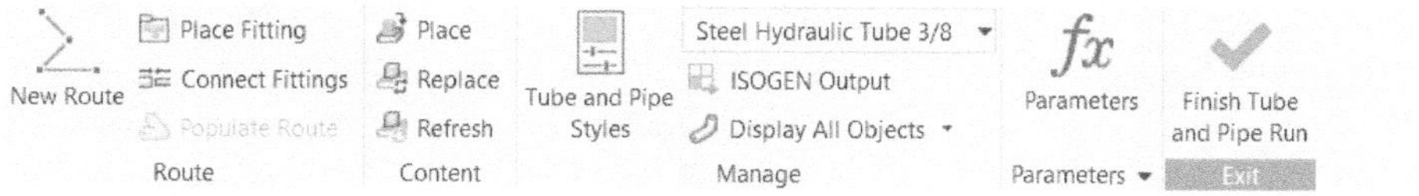

Route Tab

When you activate a route, the Route tab displays. This ribbon tab contains tools specific to routing.

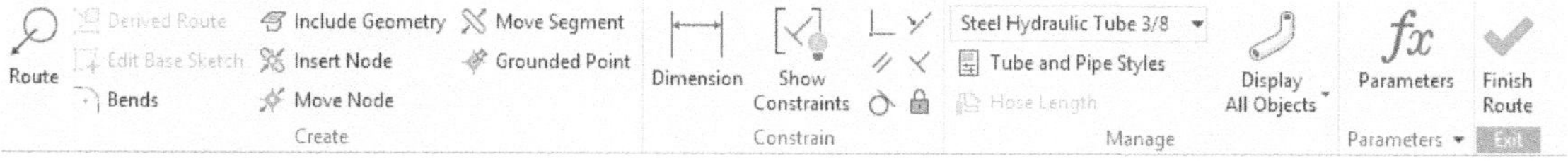

Browser

When you add tube and pipe runs to a design, a tube and pipe subassembly is created. This subassembly contains the model data for all tube and pipe runs in the model. Each run is automatically placed in a separate subassembly. The following image shows a tube and pipe design with various components expanded, illustrating the organization of the design data.

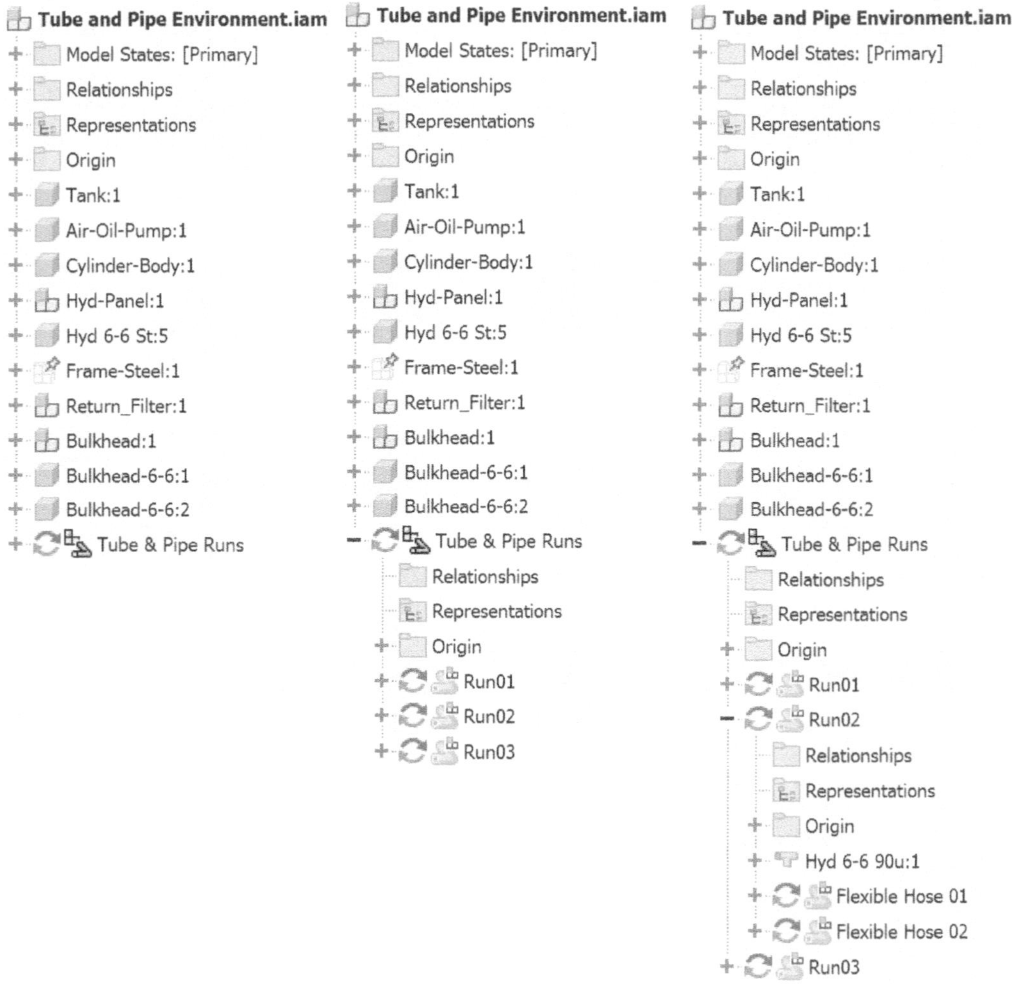

Part Environment

The tube and pipe environment provides an authoring tool to create custom fittings and components. This authoring tool enables you to prepare either an iPart or a normal part for publishing to the Content Center Library. The authoring tools are found in the Manage tab>Author panel, as shown in the following image.

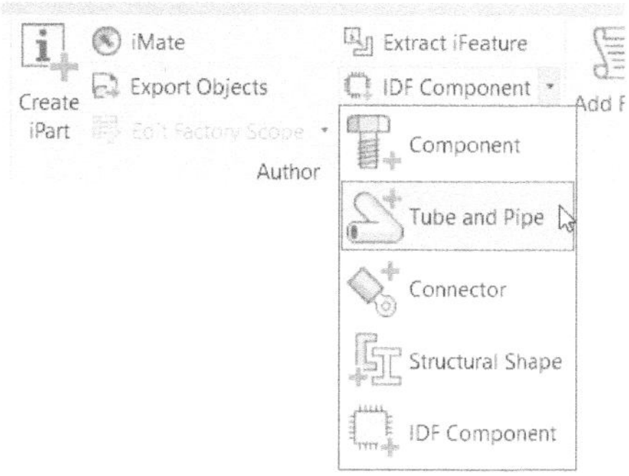

Creating Tube and Pipe Runs

Just as there are many tasks and procedures to follow when creating an assembly design and the parts in the assembly, there are multiple tasks and procedures to follow during the creation of a tube and pipe design. To learn how to create a tube or pipe design, you should first understand the basic steps involved in creating tube and pipe runs.

The following image shows a completed run that is populated with pipe segments, elbows, and couplings that are automatically placed along the route based on the current style used.

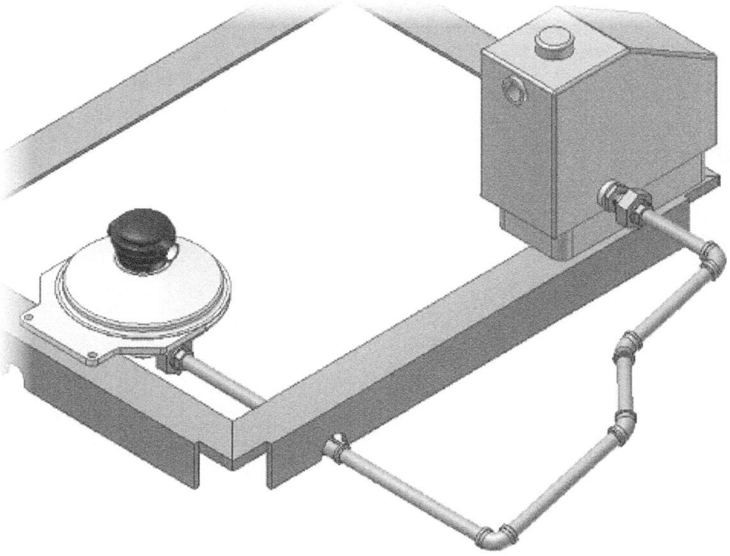

Process: Creating Tube and Pipe Runs

The following diagram gives an overview of creating tube or pipe runs.

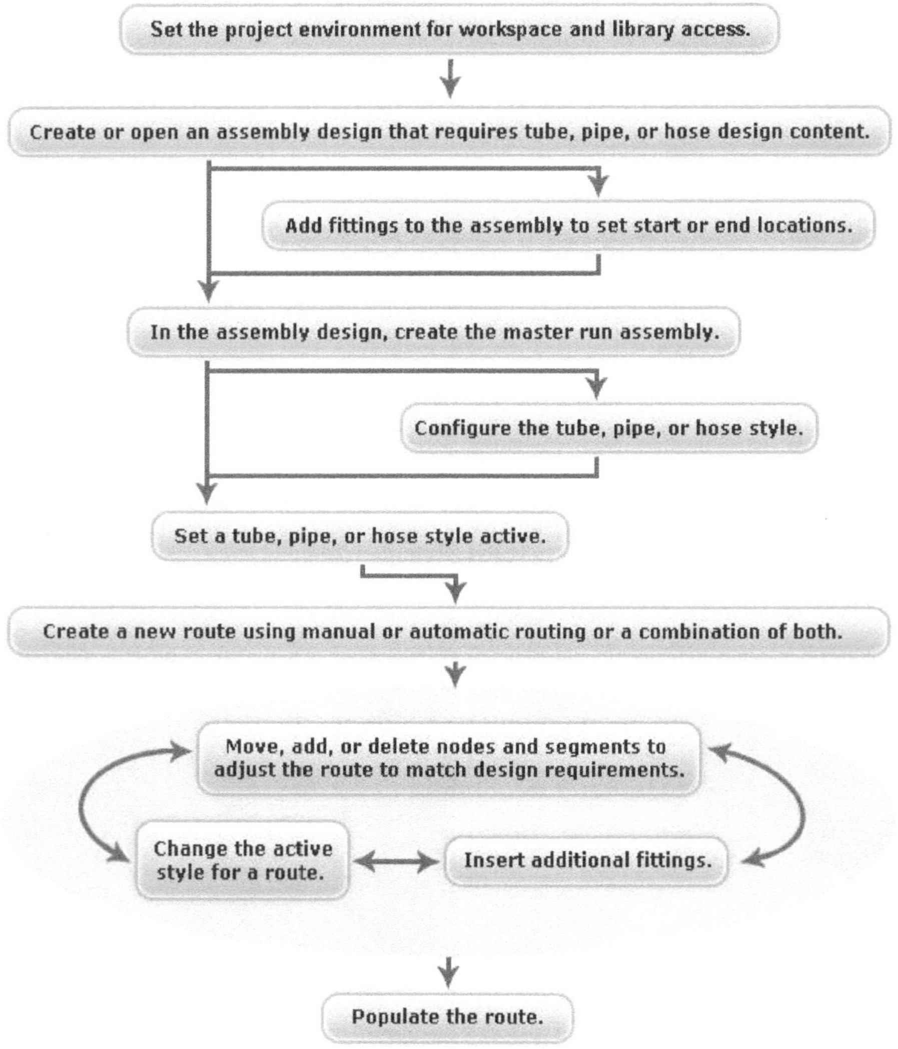

Primary Runs Assembly and Tube and Pipe Runs

When you select to create a tube or pipe run, a single primary subassembly is added to the overall assembly, if the primary runs subassembly does not already exist. The default browser name for this primary subassembly is Tube & Pipe Runs. Every run you create in the overall assembly is added to this primary runs subassembly. The number of runs you include depends on your design and manufacturing requirements.

Each run can include one or more individual routes that can share the same style or use different styles. Because you have the ability to choose unique styles, it is possible for you to have all three route types, each with different size diameters in a single run. Routes can start and end on assembly model geometry or an initial fitting dropped on the route to create a branch or fork.

In the following image, the browser shows that the primary runs assembly Tube & Pipe Runs consists of three unique tube or pipe runs.

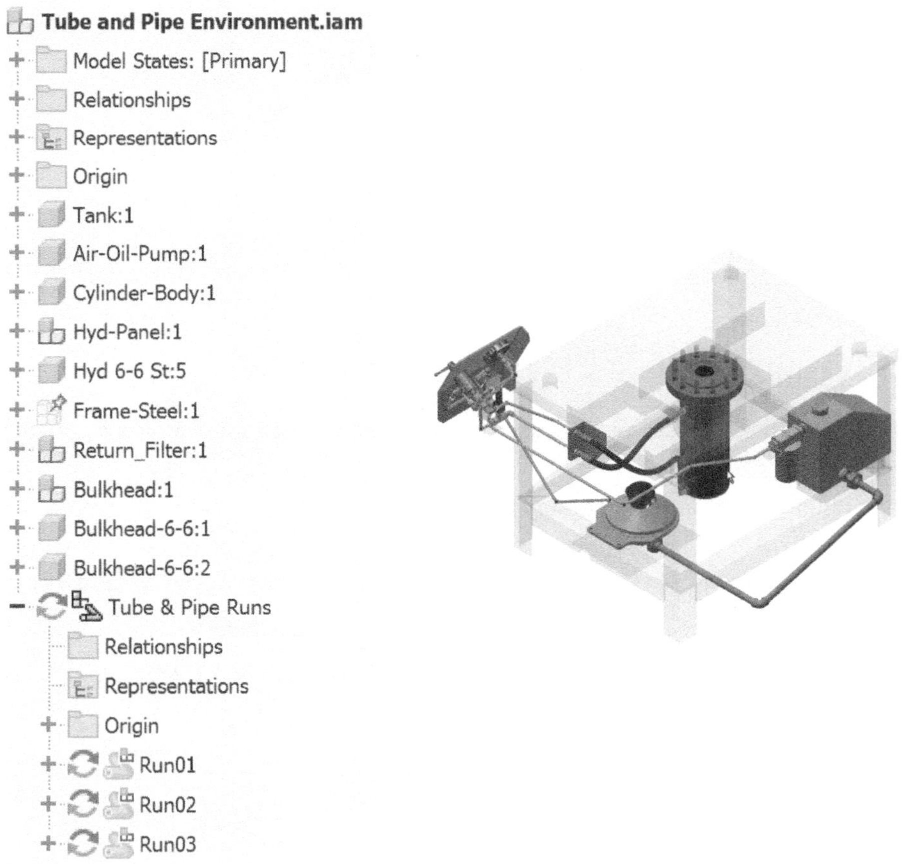

Exercise: Examine a Tube and Pipe Design

In this exercise, you will open a model that contains rigid pipe, rigid tubing, and a flexible hose. You will examine the tube and pipe environment including the ribbon and browser.

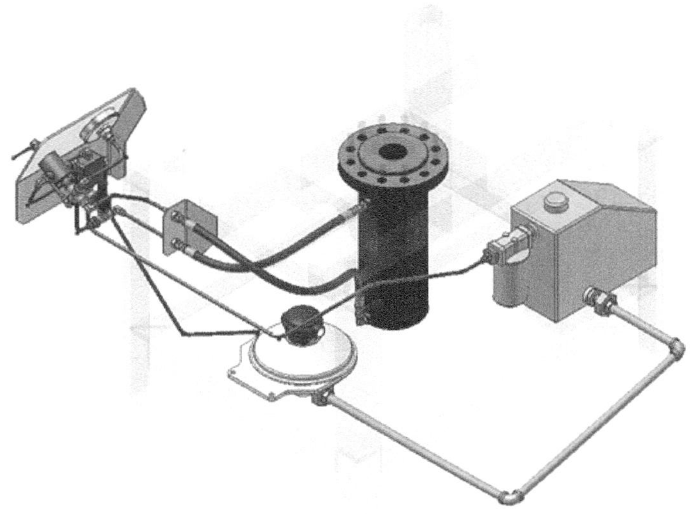

The completed exercise

Exercise Setup

Before you start this exercise, you must activate the Tube and Pipe Design project associated with this course.

1. Start Autodesk Inventor Professional.

2. On the Home page, select ⋮ (Projects and Settings) > Settings or you can also click on (Projects) in the Quick Access Toolbar at the top of the interface.

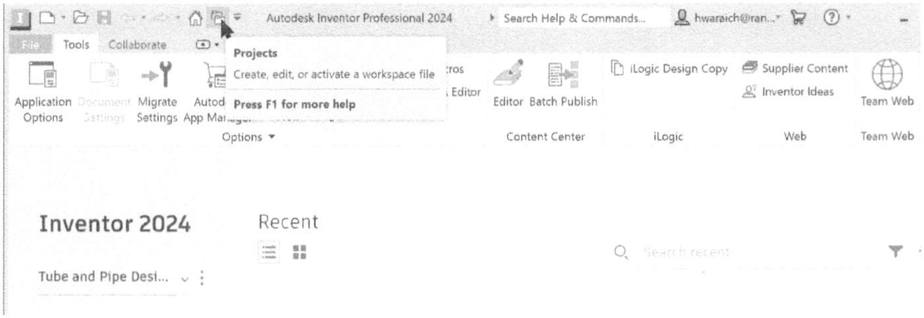

3. At the bottom of the Projects dialog box, click Browse:
   - Browse to the saved location of the data set, for example *C:\Autodesk Inventor 2024 Tube and Pipe Design Exercise Files.*
   - Click *Tube and Pipe Design.ipj.*
   - Click Open.
   - Click Done.

Examine a Tube and Pipe Design

1. Open *Tube and Pipe Environment.iam.*

   The assembly includes several runs including rigid pipe, bent tubing, and flexible hose.

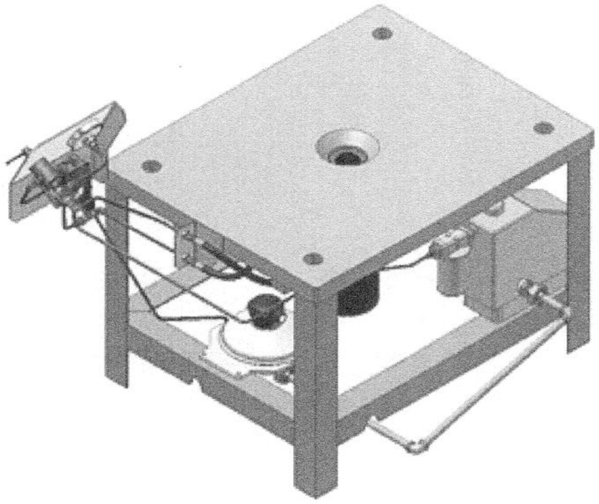

2. In the Browser, click Bulkhead:1 to highlight the component in the assembly.

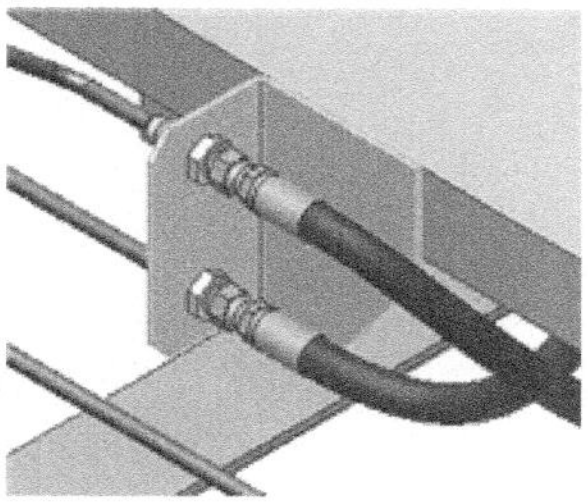

3. In the browser, expand Bulkhead:1. While observing the component in the assembly, change the offset for the Flush15 constraint to **220 mm**.

   The tube and pipe runs update to reflect changes you made to the position of the bulkhead.

4. In the browser, right-click on Frame-Steel:1. Click Enabled to toggle off this option so that you can see the tube and pipe runs.

5. In the browser, right-click on Tube & Pipe Runs and click Edit.

   In the ribbon, the Tube and Pipe tab displays and the Tube and Pipe Run is now active. In the Tube and Pipe tab, the tools and the tube and pipe style list display.

6. In the Run panel, review the available styles.

   The document includes styles for rigid pipe, tube, and flexible hose.

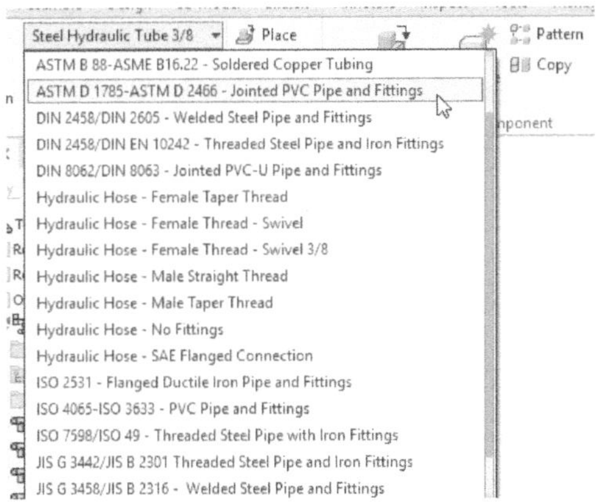

7. In the browser, expand Run01.

   The run subassembly contains two routes. Route01 defines the path for the rigid pipe with fittings. Route02 defines the path for the tubing. The run subassembly also contains the parts for both routes. The fittings above Route01 in the browser are the start and end connections that were placed before the routes were created.

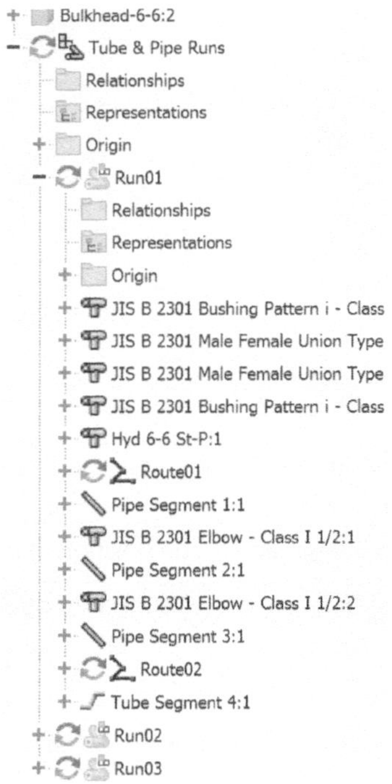

8. In the browser, double-click on Run01 to edit the run. The Pipe Run tab displays.

9. In the browser, double-click on Route01 to edit the route. The Route tab displays.

10. In the browser, expand Autoroute 1.

The route contains two manually placed route points that define the start and end points for the route. The four points in the Autoroute 1 group define the points that were created using the Autorouting tool.

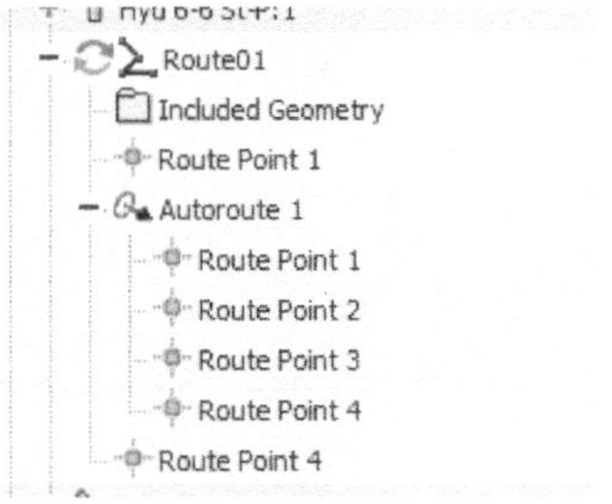

11. In the Route tab, in the Create panel, click Move Segment. Move the cursor over the segment shown in the following image. When the drag handles display, drag the segment away from the frame.

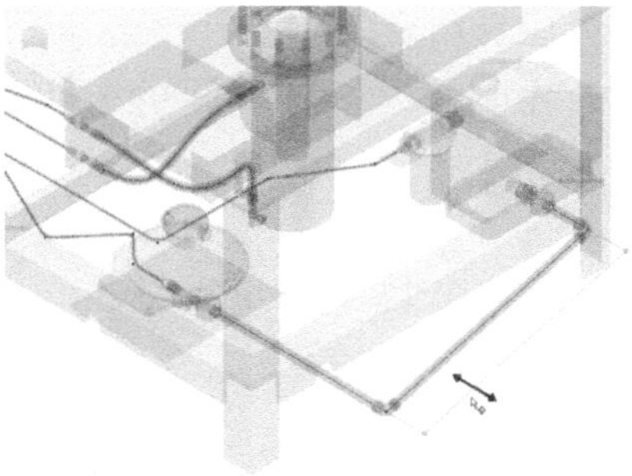

12. Right-click in the graphics window and click Done.

13. In the Route tab, in the Exit panel, click Finish Route to return to the Run01 subassembly. The rigid pipe run updates based on the changes you made to the route.

14. In the browser, double-click on Route02 to edit the tube route. Zoom in to the route.

The route consists of linear segments with rounded corners. In this route, most of the linear segments are dimensioned because their route points were placed manually.

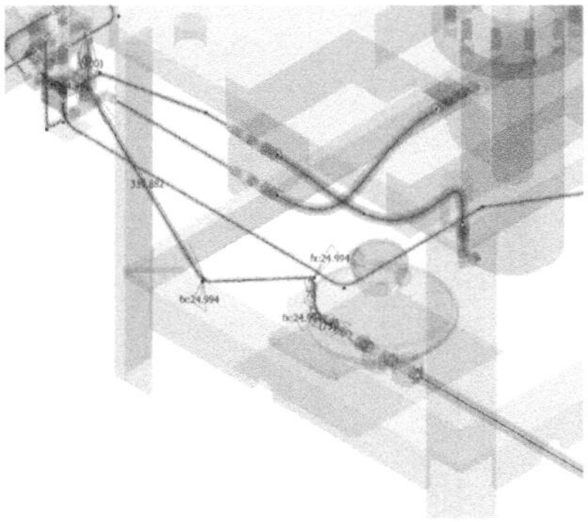

15. In the browser, double-click on Run02 to edit the subassembly that contains the flexible hose runs. Each flexible hose is contained in its own subassembly.

16. Expand Flexible Hose 02. Double-click on Hose02 to edit the route. The route contains two points: the start point and end point.

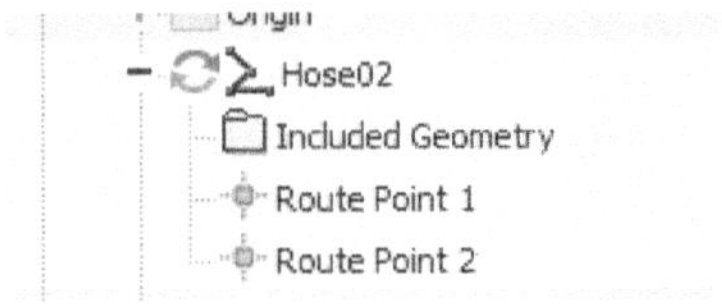

17. In the model, examine the route. A flexible hose route consists of a single spline that passes through the route points.

18. Return to the top-level assembly.

19. Close all files without saving changes.

Chapter Summary

This chapter introduced you to the tube and pipe environment in the Autodesk Inventor software. Using the tube and pipe environment, you can create rigid pipe, bent tube, and flexible hose runs between your assembly components.

Having completed this chapter, you can:

- Describe the tube and pipe environment.

Chapter 2

Setup for Routes and Runs

In this chapter, you learn how to plan and set up your routes and runs, and how to place and connect the initial fittings in your tube and pipe designs.

Objectives

After completing this chapter, you will be able to:

- Set the active tube or pipe style and create a tube and pipe runs subassembly.
- Place and connect fittings to assembly components before creating a route.

Lesson: Setup for Routes and Runs

Overview

This lesson describes the planning and setup for routes and runs and how tube and pipe styles control the type and size of tubes and pipes in a route.

When you have a good understanding of how to create a tube and pipe assembly, how tube and pipe content is structured, and the structure for how the files are stored, you can work more efficiently when creating and modifying your designs. To create routes and runs with the types and sizes of pipes and fittings you require, you need to have an understanding of tube and pipe styles and how to set them active for use.

The following image shows a number of pipe, tube, and flexible hose routes in an assembly.

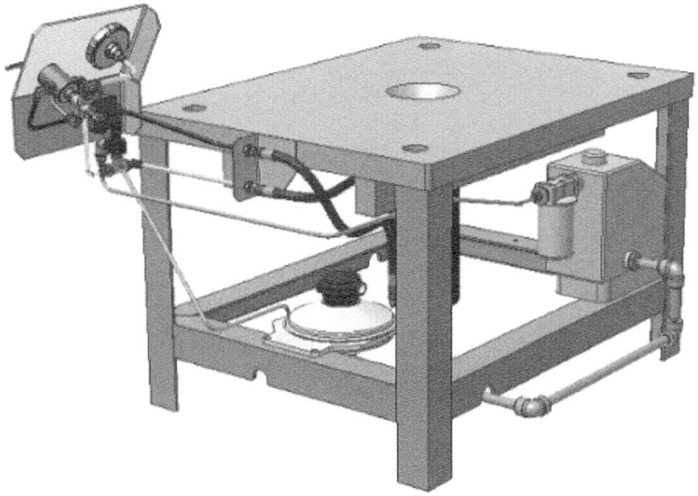

Objectives

After completing this lesson, you will be able to:

- Describe the file structure for tube and pipe routes and runs.
- Create a Tube & Pipe Runs subassembly.
- Describe how a style controls the components and rules for a route.
- Set the active tube or pipe style for different runs.

Tube and Pipe Files

A tube and pipe design contains one or more runs. Each run can consist of a number of routes, conduit segments, and fittings. The final design consists of multiple parts and subassemblies. A moderately complex tube and pipe design can generate a large number of files in various locations. To effectively work with and manage your tube and pipe designs, you need to understand the file structure for tube and pipe routes and runs.

The following image shows an instrumentation assembly with a number of fittings and routes. All of the fittings and routes are contained in a single run subassembly.

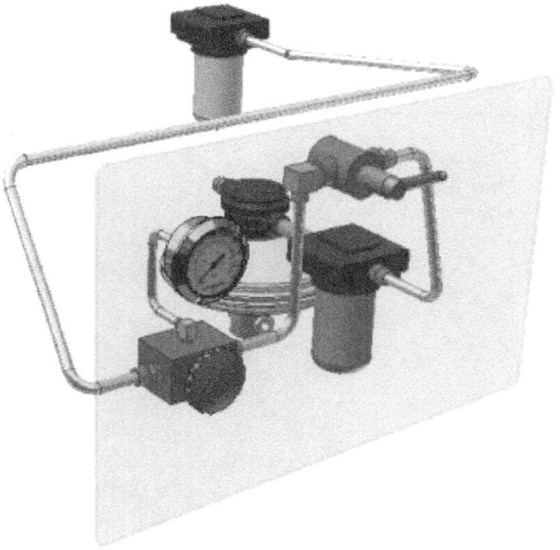

About Tube and Pipe Files

The conduit segments and fittings for pipe, tube, and hose routes are saved to locations defined by the active project file. Most of the fittings you use in your tube and pipe designs are placed from the Content Center. Subassemblies and parts generated by the tube and pipe application, and the individual conduit segments, are stored in folders relative to your workspace.

Files names and locations of the primary runs assembly, runs, and routes can be determined upon creation, but cannot be later modified. By default, multiple routes and runs are incrementally numbered based on file naming convention. Display names of tube and pipe documents in the browser differ from file names in your project workspace. You can use the Design Assistant to rename display names in the browser.

When conduit parts are placed into a tube and pipe assembly from the Content Center using AutoDrop, they are stored in the corresponding pipe run folder and either the Content Center file name schema or a custom name is used. When conduit parts are used to populate routes, the tube-and-pipe-specific naming convention of a 13-digit number is automatically assigned based on the current time that your computer is used. The naming also specifies pipe, tube sweeping, or hose. When fittings are placed from the Content Center using AutoDrop, or used to populate routes with tube and pipe styles, they are always stored in the Content Center Files location in your workspace. The Content Center file name schema is respected. By default, Content Center file naming is in the *<NOMINAL_SIZE>.ipt* format.

Tube and Pipe File Structure

You can create routes and runs in any assembly but you must first open the assembly in a separate window. You cannot edit a subassembly in-place and then create or edit routes and runs in the subassembly. When you create the first run in the assembly, a Tube & Pipe Runs subassembly is generated. This subassembly contains run subassemblies that hold route parts and the conduit parts generated for each route. It is important to note that a unique part is generated for each conduit segment, even if two segments in a route or run are identical in length.

The files are, by default, stored in a set of folders below the workspace defined in the active project file. Although you can specify a different folder for the Tube & Pipe Runs subassembly and for each run during creation, the default file locations provide a structured set of folders that match the hierarchy of the runs and routes in your design.

The following image shows the relationship between runs and routes in the browser and their default locations relative to the workspace of the active project file.

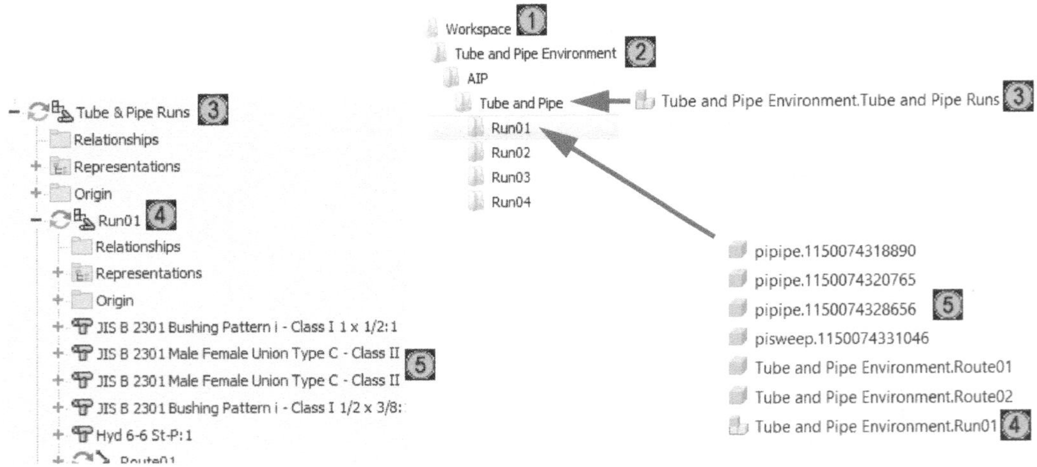

(1) Workspace folder.

(2) Default Tube and Pipe Runs subfolder matches top-level assembly name.

(3) Tube & Pipe Runs subassembly.

(4) Run subassembly (Note the separate folder matching the name of the run).

(5) Route part and conduit parts in a run.

Content Center Parts

Most fittings along the length of a route, such as elbows, tees, and couplings, are placed from the Content Center. These parts are generated and saved below the Content Center files folder specified in the active project file. If you do not use the Autodesk® Vault software to manage your work in progress data, you can save the Content Center files to a common server to make them available to all team members. If you use the Autodesk Vault software to manage your work in progress, you can map the Content Center files library in your vault to either a common drive or to a local folder on each computer. When you check in your design, the fittings are saved to the vault and can be checked out to any team member along with the route or run.

The following image shows how the location of generated Content Center parts is controlled by the active project file.

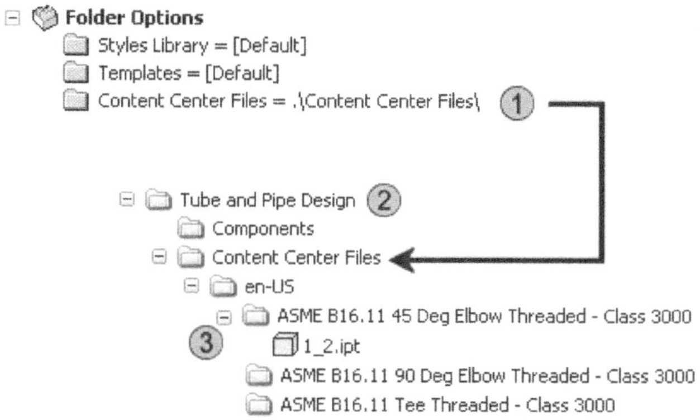

1. In this project file, the Content Center files location is mapped to a folder relative to the workspace.
2. Workspace folder.
3. Content Center part located in family folder.

> Editing a tube and pipe route can generate a number of new conduit parts and change any number of existing conduit parts. If possible, check out the Tube & Pipe Runs subassembly and all children from the vault prior to editing any route or run. Check the files back into the vault only when you have completed all required edits.

Example of Tube and Pipe Files

In the following example, you see how the folder structures are related to the Autodesk® Inventor® model, including the main run subassembly and the Content Center files.

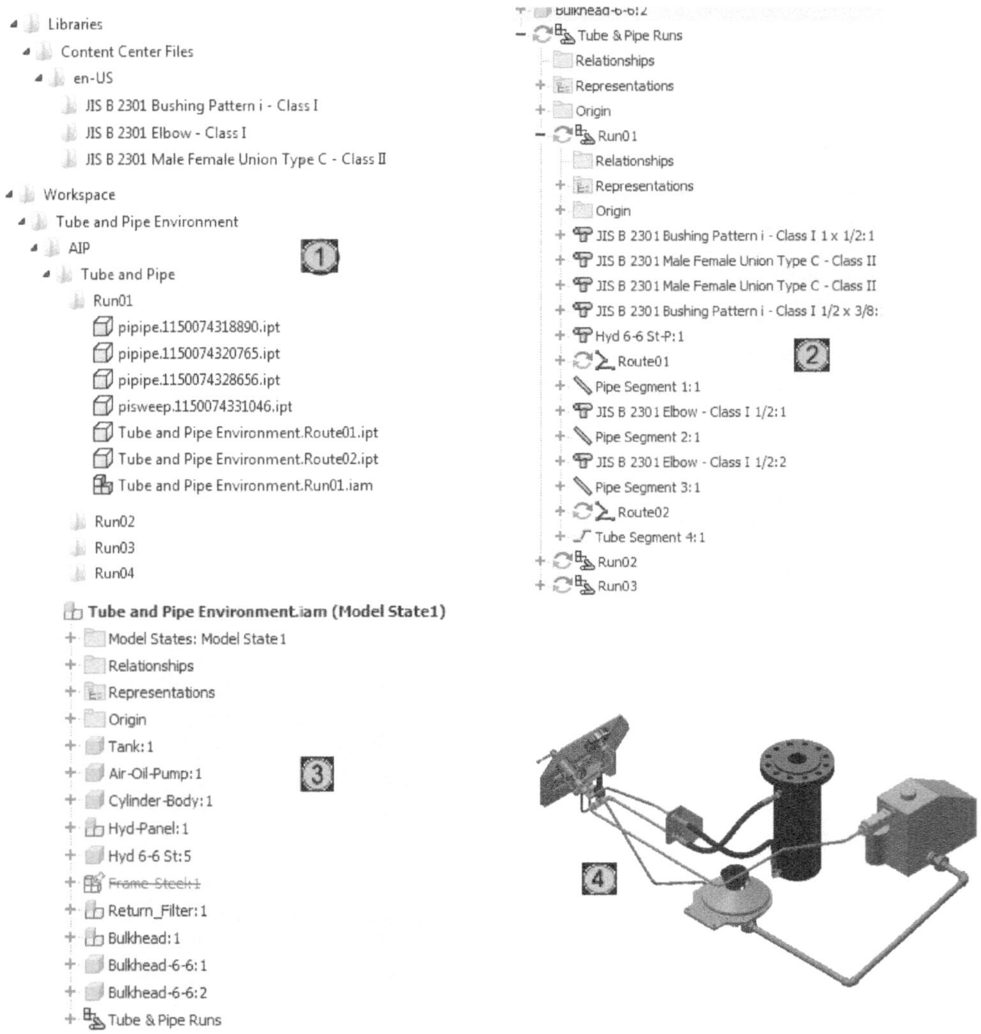

1. This is the folder structure that is created when the Autodesk Inventor model is created. Note the locations of the *Workspace* folder, the *Content Center Files* folder (under the *Libraries* folder), and the *Run01* folder.

2. This view from the browser shows the run subassembly, and the route parts and pipe parts in the run. This includes parts from the Content Center.

3. This view from the browser shows some of the parts that were placed directly into the assembly.

4. The Autodesk Inventor tube and pipe assembly model is shown.

Creating a Tube and Pipe Assembly

Before you create or modify a rigid pipe, tube, or hose style, you must create a Tube & Pipe Runs subassembly, which contains the pipe, tube, and hose runs and routes for all levels of the assembly. This subassembly is created the first time you use the Tube and Pipe tool located in the Environments tab, in the Begin panel. All pipe, tube, and hose runs are subassemblies in the Tube & Pipe Runs subassembly.

Primary Runs Subassembly

When an assembly file is first opened, the assembly environment displays and you can begin adding pipe runs. For the first pipe run added, the system creates the primary runs assembly along with an individual run. The primary runs assembly is a container for all pipe runs added to the assembly. The number of runs you include depends on your design and manufacturing documentation needs. Each run can include one or more individual routes. All routes in a run can use the same or different styles. With the capability to assign unique styles, it is possible to have all three route types, each with different size diameters in a single run. Routes can start and end on assembly model geometry or on an initial fitting dropped on the route to create a branch or fork.

When you create the first pipe, tube, or hose run in an assembly, the following events occur:

- You are prompted to save the first pipe run assembly. The Create Tube & Pipe dialog box shows the name and location of the file. The Tube & Pipe Runs subassembly is automatically named and placed in a folder created in the project workspace. If your project file does not have a workspace or workgroup search path, the default is the folder containing the parent assembly.
- The pipe run subassembly is created in the folder containing the Tube & Pipe Runs subassembly.

> Because you edit only the run subassemblies in place in the assembly, never change the folder names from the names generated automatically. All runs are given a generic name in the browser. You can rename the run in the browser for better identification.

Process: Creating a Tube and Pipe Assembly

The following steps outline the process to create the Tube & Pipe Runs subassembly and the first run subassembly in the Tube & Pipe Runs subassembly.

1. Configure your project file and vault (if used) to manage the files generated in the tube and pipe design. Ensure that all team members have access to the same Content Center files.

2. Assemble the components to be connected by pipe, tube, or flexible hose routes and runs. You can add hangers and other supporting components in the top-level assembly, a subassembly, or in the Tube & Pipe Runs subassembly or one of the runs after you create them.

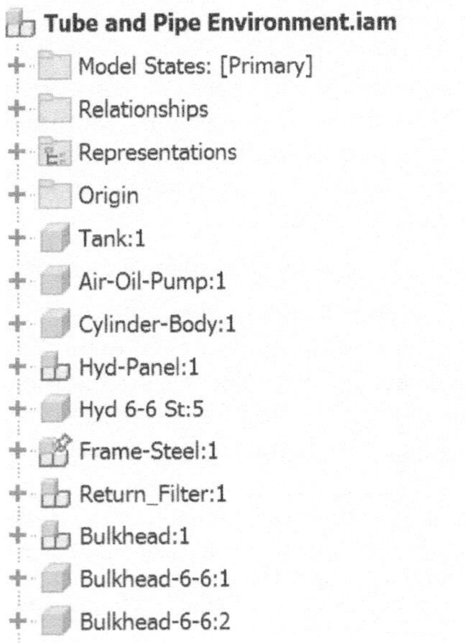

3. Create the first run in the top-level assembly. If required, rename or relocate the Tube & Pipe Runs subassembly and/or the run subassembly.

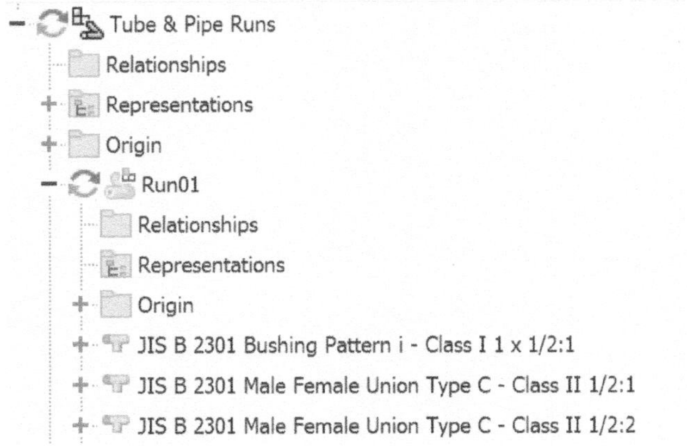

Guidelines for Tube and Pipe Routes and Runs

The following list outlines guidelines for working with tube and pipe routes and runs:

- Enter a descriptive name for each run you create. The run name is used in both the folder structure and the browser and can help you navigate complex, multi-run tube and pipe designs.
- If you are not using the Autodesk Vault software, specify a shared folder for Content Center files in the project file. This shared folder is required to enable all team members to access all generated fittings.
- Use the tools in the tube and pipe application to create and edit routes and runs. Do not use the Place Component or Create Component tools to create or place runs or routes.

Tube and Pipe Styles

Tube and pipe styles describe the characteristics for tube, pipe, and hose routes. These styles are key to controlling the design of the routed system as it evolves from prototype to manufacturing.

Styles determine the properties of rigid pipe, tube, hose paths, and components, such as the size and material of the pipe, tube, or hose segments and the specifications for the default fittings. The active style defines the characteristics of both the route and run.

A route is a defined path in the assembly that, at a minimum, connects the start point and endpoint. A run is a subassembly that contains one or more routes, including the segments and fittings placed along the routes. Each route in a run can be associated with a different style. Although it is common for all routes in a run to be the same type (pipe, tube, or hose), you can include routes with any mix of styles. For example, you can define an inlet run that includes a rigid pipe route to a distribution node, and flexible hose routes from the distribution node to a number of devices.

The style defines a set of segment length rules that are maintained during route creation and editing. Minimum and maximum segment lengths ensure that the run can be constructed with available materials, and an increment length enables engagement between segments and fittings while maintaining measurable segment lengths. The Autodesk Inventor Professional software includes default styles for common ANSI, ISO, DIN, and JIS tube and pipe standards, and flexible hose styles based on standard Parker hoses and fittings. You can use one of these styles, create your own style based on one of the existing styles, or create your own style based on published conduit parts and fittings.

The following image shows a rigid pipe run, a rigid tube run, and a flexible hose run. Each run and its underlying route is controlled by a separate style.

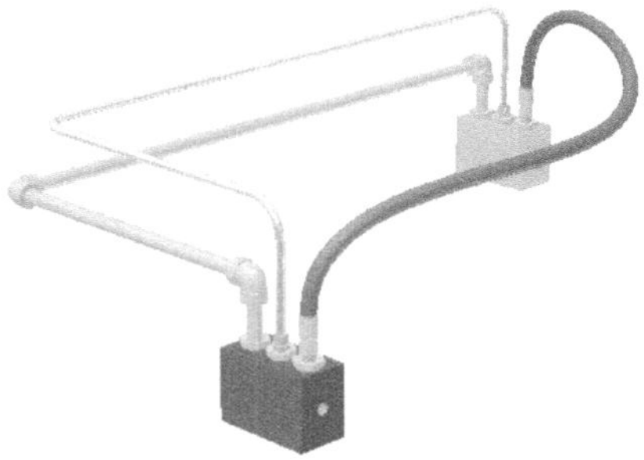

A style specifies settings for a single nominal diameter. You must create a new style for each size. To simplify the process, you can create a new style based on an existing style and change the diameter property of the new style. It is possible to define a style with which you are unable to create a route, such as if you select fittings that do not have compatible end treatments. While the Tube & Pipe Styles tool enables styles to be defined in this way, routes cannot be created using such a style.

Rigid Pipe Styles

A rigid pipe style defines the rules and properties for a series of rigid pipe segments connected by elbows and couplings. The directions a route can change are governed by the settings for the elbows in the style. All rigid pipe styles must include a 90° elbow. A rigid pipe style can also be configured to include 45° elbows and custom published elbows that have custom angles. The use of custom angled elbows is important for a pipe style that is set to create self-draining routes that apply a target slope or runoff angle.

When you are creating a route using a rigid pipe style, along with adding elbows to change directions, you can also create custom bends in a rigid pipe route. When you create a custom bend, a formed pipe segment is used in place of an elbow fitting.

If a straight route segment is longer than the maximum segment length defined in the style, the coupling that is defined in the style is added to the route to join multiple pipe segments.

The following image shows a rigid pipe run. The pipe, fittings, and routing rules are all defined in the active style.

Rigid Tube Styles

Styles for rigid tube routes differ from rigid pipe styles in that a tube route does not contain elbows. The default bend radius for the tube is defined in the style, and you can override the radius of any bend after you create it. Couplings connect tube segments that are longer than the maximum segment length defined in the style.

The following image shows a simple rigid tube route. All bends share a common radius defined in the style.

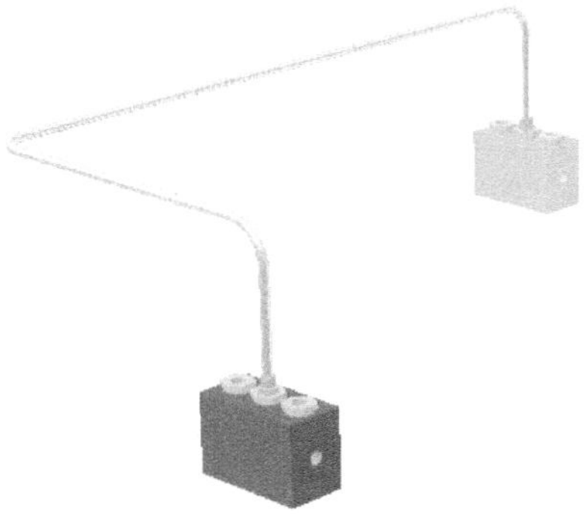

Flexible Hose Styles

A flexible hose style defines the rules for a spline-based route between a start and end point. A single hose segment connects either the start and end fittings, or start point and endpoint defined in the route if the style suppresses the fittings. The style defines a minimum allowable bend radius for the spline and a round-up value for the length of the hose segment. The round-up value generates a useful hose length value from the actual length of the spline path.

The following image shows a flexible hose route. The fittings, hose type and length, and minimum allowable bend radius are governed by the active style.

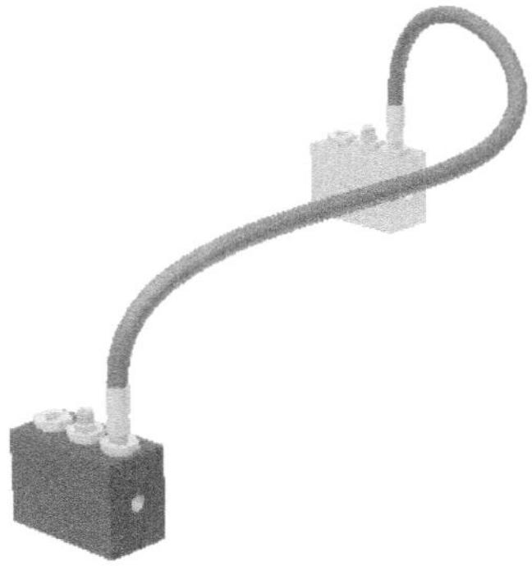

Example of Tube and Pipe Styles

Many times designers leave a lot of the details to the installers or machine builders. This is very common with tubes and pipes. Being able to use all of the different Tube and Pipe styles enables designers to complete the design and digital prototype themselves. Instead of the builders having to bend and measure the tubes on site or as they go, these items can be made ahead of time. In some cases, automated machinery can be used with the code output by the Autodesk Inventor software, saving time and avoiding mistakes.

In the following image, you see the use of tubing with bends to connect different parts of a system. One of the bent tube routes is also shown in a run in an Autodesk Inventor assembly design.

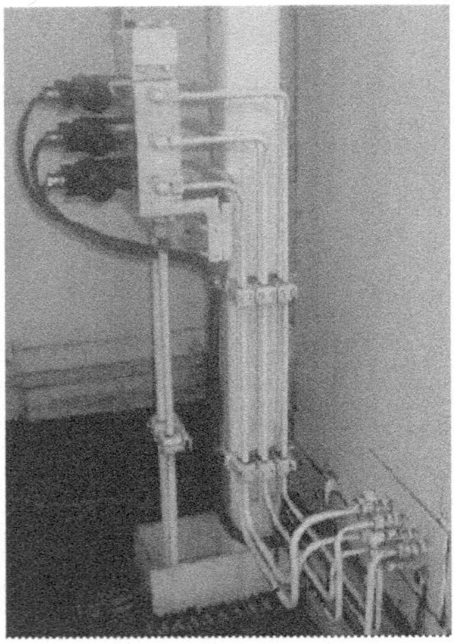

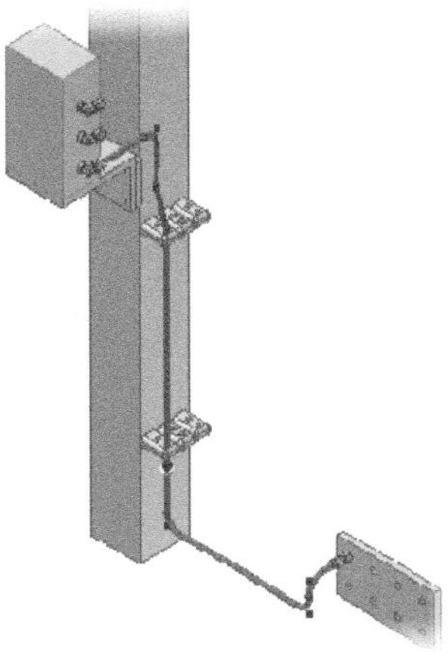

Activating a Style

Before you begin working with routes and runs, examine the style settings, choose or make a style, and then set that style active. The active style controls the design of the routed system and determines what type of tube or pipe is used and what content parts are used. The point at which you change or make a style active affects how the route is constructed.

There is a list of system-supplied tube and pipe styles in the Autodesk Inventor Professional software. You can use one of these styles, create your own style based on one of them, or create your own style based on published conduit parts and fittings.

In the following image, the process of creating a new Tube and Pipe style based on an existing Flexible Hose Style is shown. To access the Tube & Pipe Styles dialog box, click Tube and Pipe Styles on the Pipe Run or Tube and Pipe tab.

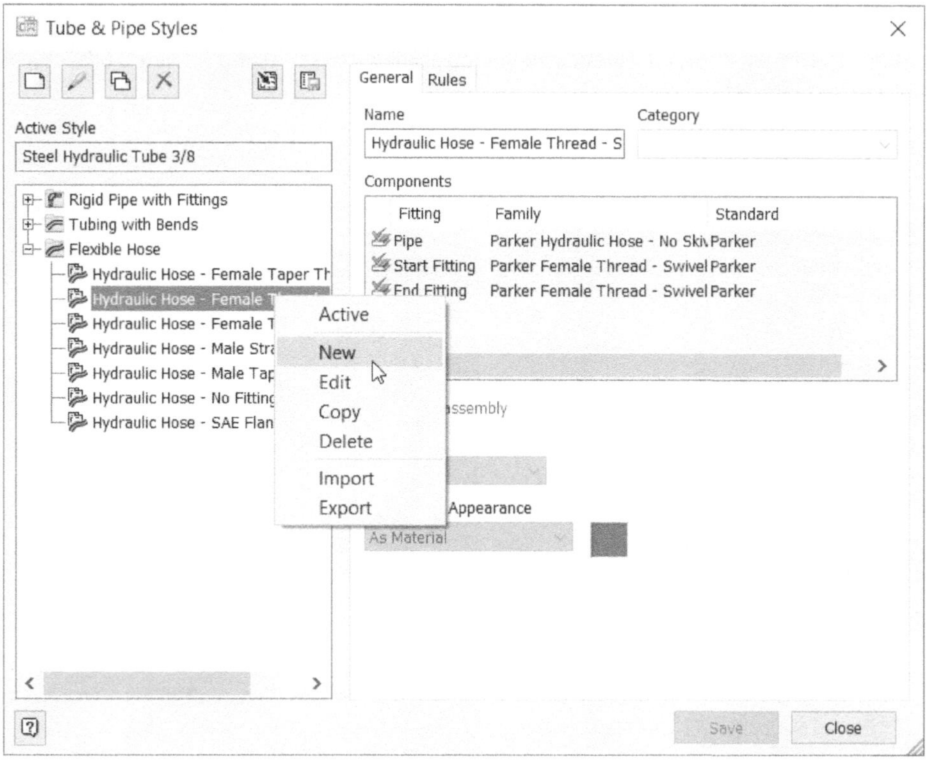

Access for Activating a Style

You set the active style by selecting it in the Tube and Pipe tab, in the Run panel or in the Tube & Pipe Styles dialog box. To activate the style in the Tube & Pipe Styles dialog box, right-click on the style in the list and then click Activate.

The following image shows the list of styles being accessed to select and activate a different style from the Tube and Pipe tab.

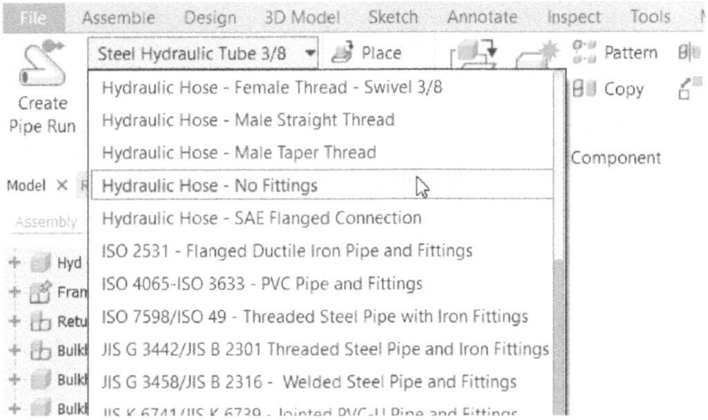

In the following image, a portion of the Tube & Pipe Styles dialog box is shown, with a tube style in the process of being set as the active style.

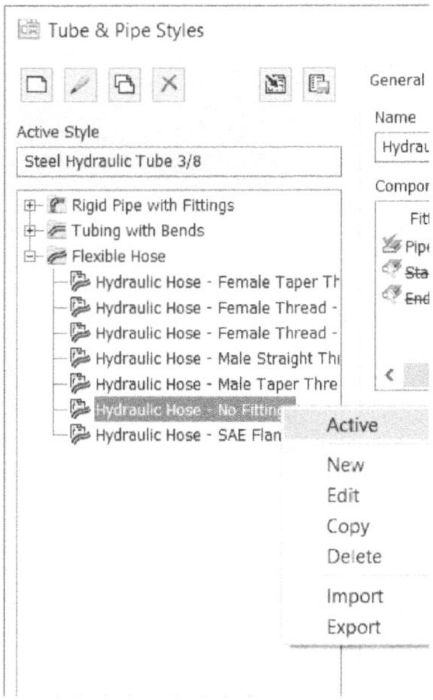

Impact of Changing or Editing Styles

Although it is best to set styles before creating routes or placing fittings, you can create styles at any time. Style changes can be applied to new and existing routes throughout the design process. With styles you can:

- Set style defaults for all new routes you create.
- Change the active style for the tube and pipe assembly.
- Change the style for the active route.
- Modify settings for all routes that use the same style.

When you create a new route, it takes on the active style. You can also go back and edit existing routes and change the active style. When you finish the edit, the route automatically updates. When creating multiple routes with different styles, you change to the required style before selecting the New Route command.

> You cannot apply a rigid type style to an existing flexible hose route and vice versa. To change between a rigid style and flexible hose style, you must delete the route and create a new one using the flexible hose style.

Procedure: Activating a Style for a Route

The following diagram gives an overview of activating a style in a new or existing route.

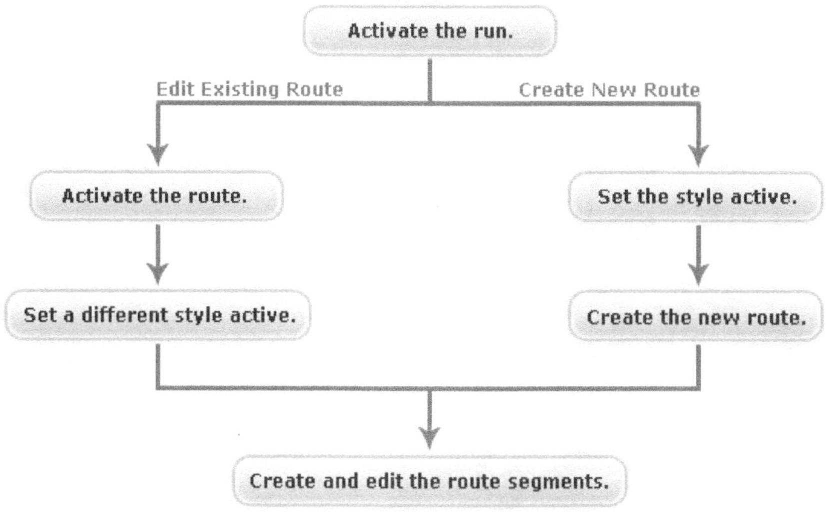

Exercise: Activate a Tube and Pipe Style

In this exercise, you will first create a new run and then change the active style to be associated with that run. You will then edit Run01 and change the styles associated with two of the hose routes, demonstrating how the runs automatically update and change with the style.

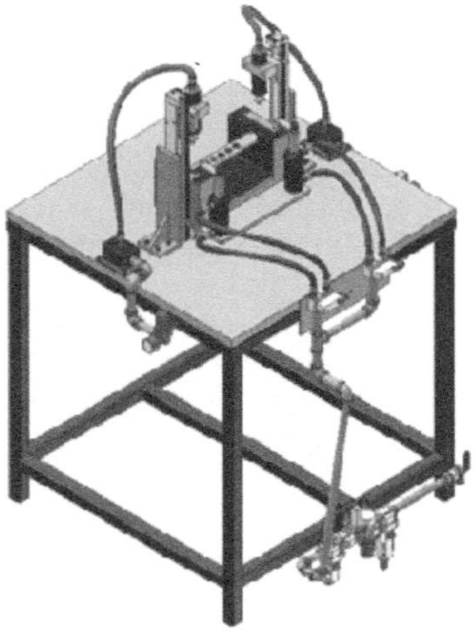

The completed exercise

1. Open *Activate A Tube and Pipe Style.iam*.

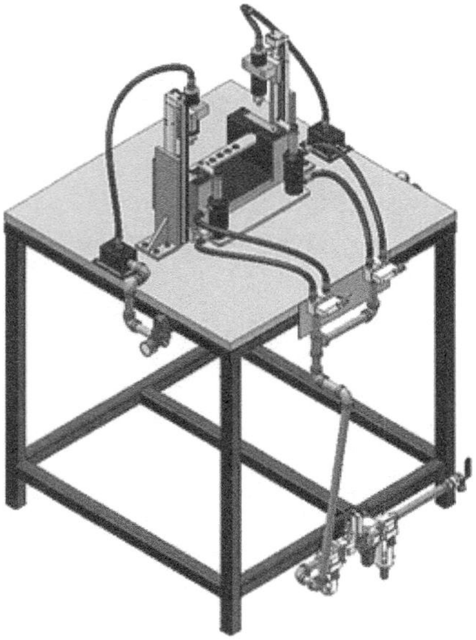

2. To create a new run subassembly:
   - In the Environments tab, in the Begin panel, click Tube and Pipe.
   - In the Create Run dialog box, click OK to accept the default file names and locations.

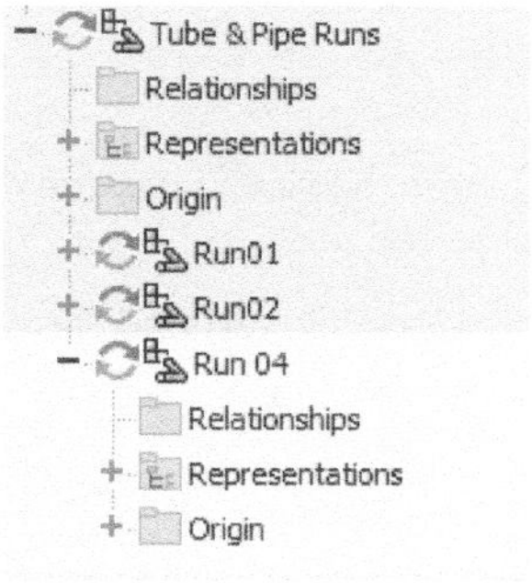

3. To begin setting the active style, in the Pipe Run tab, in the Manage panel, click Tube and Pipe Styles.
4. In the Tube & Pipe Styles dialog box:
   - In the list of styles, expand the Flexible Hose folder.
   - Right-click on 5/16" Blue Hose-Male Taper Thread. Click Active.
   - Click Close.

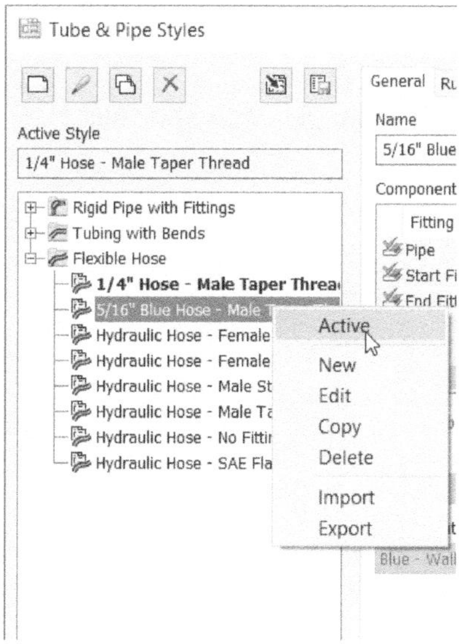

5. To create a new route that is set to use the style you just set as active:
   - In the Pipe Run tab, in the Route panel, click New Route.

   In the Create Hose dialog box, click OK to accept the default name for the new route.

6. In the styles list on the Route tab, review the active style for the route you just created.

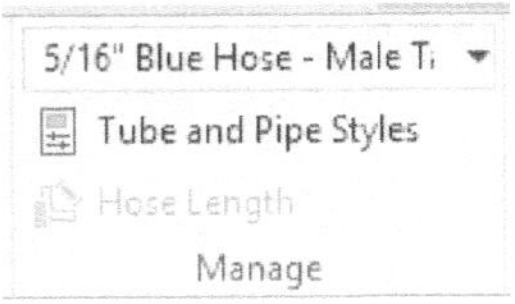

7. In the Route tab, in the Exit panel, click Finish Route. Then, in the Pipe Run tab, in the Exit panel, click Finish Tube and Pipe Run to finish editing the route and run.

8. To begin changing the active style in an existing route, expand Run01 and Flexible Hose 05. Double-click on route Hose05 to edit the route.

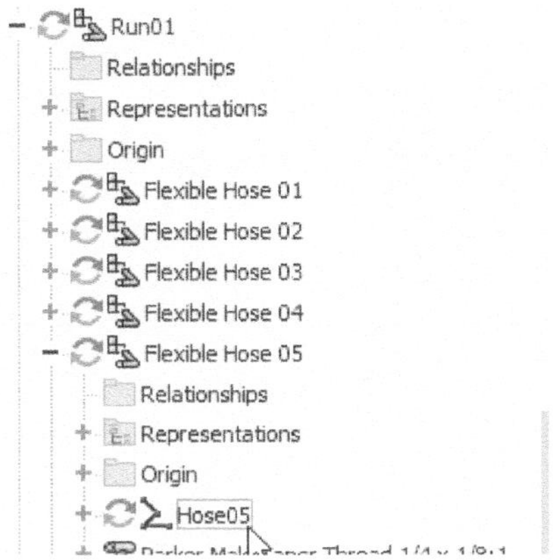

9. In the Route tab, in the Manage panel, in the style list, select the 5/16" Blue Hose - Male Taper Thread style.

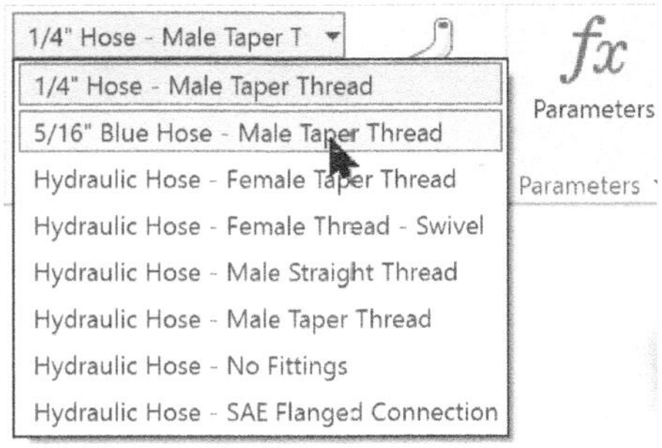

10. In the Route tab, in the Exit panel, click Finish Route.

11. Repeat the steps to change the active style in the route for Flexible Hose 06.

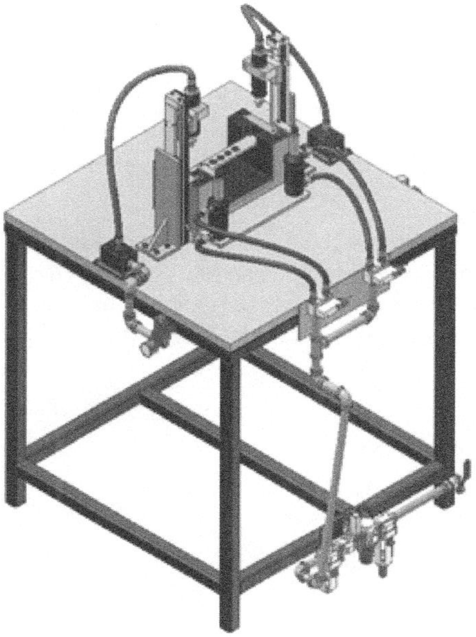

12. Close all files without saving changes.

Lesson: Placing Initial Fittings

Overview

This lesson describes how to place and connect fittings to assembly components before you create a route.

Fittings are selected from either the Content Center or the active project workspace and inserted in both populated and unpopulated routes in the assembly. You can also select any non-library fitting in the assembly using the Place Fitting tool. Fittings inserted in routes enable the pipe run to branch off a primary route to create multiple routes in a single run. You can also insert fittings in routes to build groups of adjacent fittings.

In the following image, a bushing is shown ready to connect to a valve body. Additional fittings, or a route, can start from the open connection on the bushing.

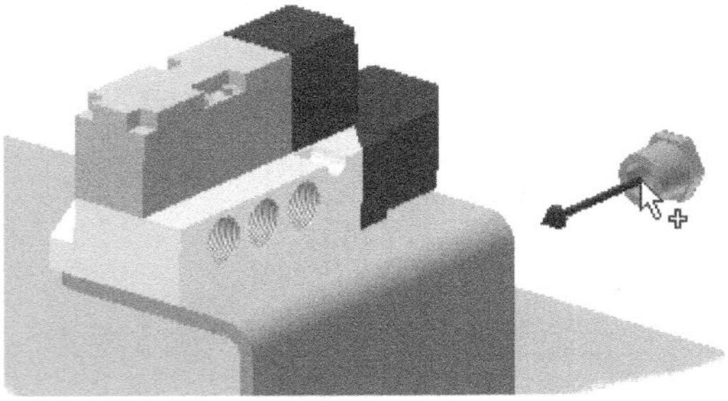

Objectives

After completing this lesson, you will be able to:

- Describe how library and authored fittings are used in routes and runs.
- Place initial fittings in a run from the Content Center.
- Place initial fittings in a run from saved authored parts.
- Connect fittings to other fittings or standard parts during their initial placement.
- Connect existing fittings to other fittings or standard parts.
- Edit the engagement for a fitting connection.

About Tube and Pipe Content

A variety of fittings for different standards are stored in the default Content Center libraries. You can also publish your own fittings to a custom Content Center library. You can place standard fittings from the Content Center or authored parts stored outside the Content Center in your design. You can then use these fittings as start and end fittings for different routes.

You typically know the fittings that are required at each end of a route to connect conduit segments to assembly components. You must place and connect these fittings in the run subassembly before you create the route. You can create any number of run subassemblies in the Tube & Pipe Runs subassembly, and then place and connect the required fittings in each run before you create routes in any run. You can reposition, replace, or remove a fitting at any time.

In the following image, a number of fittings were required to create the assembly design. To visually highlight the fittings, the parts display as opaque.

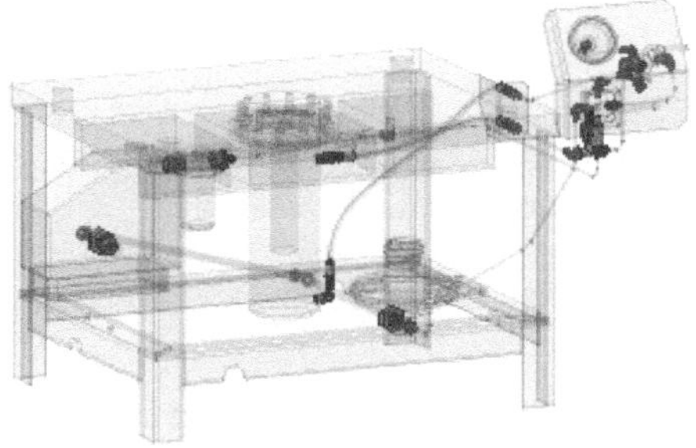

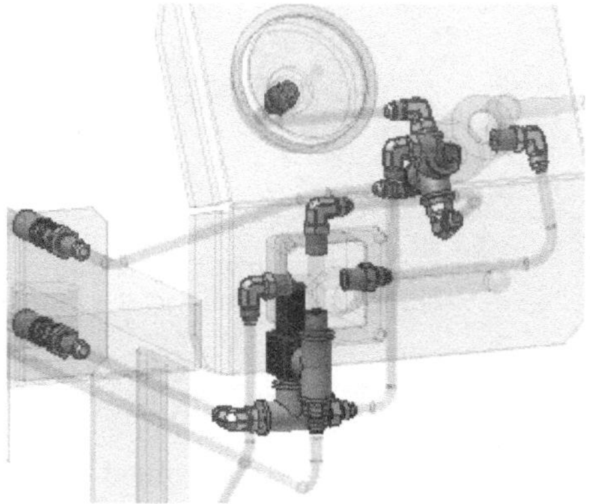

Content Center Fittings

The Content Center libraries include a Tube and Pipe category. This category contains common fittings for a number of rigid pipe, tube, and hose standards. You can insert fittings from the library into a run assembly and connect the fitting to another fitting or to a standard part. Before you create a route, you can place end fittings and any other fittings required at endpoints of the route. All fittings placed from the library contain connection information so that the fitting can automatically connect to other fittings or to a hole in a standard part.

The Content Center also provides the default conduit (pipe, tube, or hose) and fittings for a tube and pipe style. Conduit segments are not placed directly from the library. They are generated by the tube and pipe application when you create or edit a route.

The following image shows some of the tube and pipe fittings available in the default Content Center libraries. To access the Content Center, click Place in the Content panel in the Pipe Run tab.

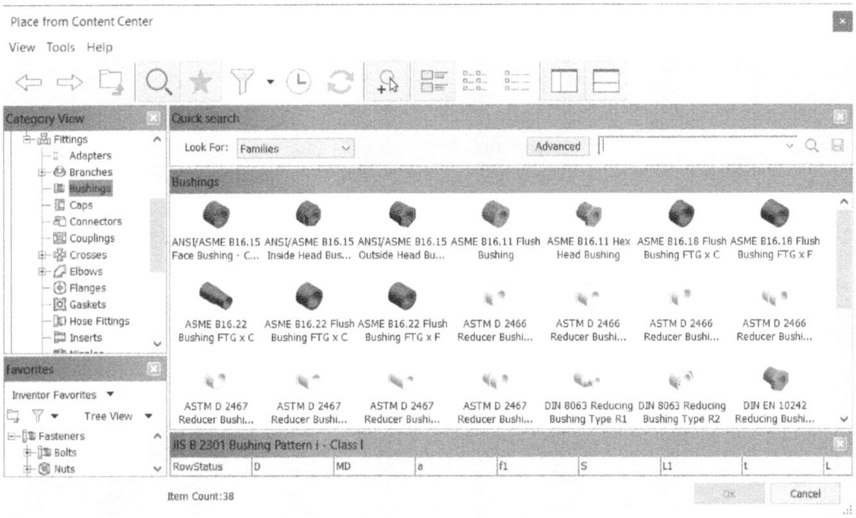

> Activate the run subassembly before you place a fitting from the Content Center. Fittings placed outside of a run subassembly cannot be easily restructured into the assembly.

Custom Tube and Pipe Content

The standard libraries in the Content Center are read-only. You cannot edit or add fittings or new conduit parts to these libraries. You can copy any portion of the standard library to a new library and then add to or edit the content in the new library. You can also publish your own fittings and components to a custom library and use those fittings in future routes and runs.

The following image shows a custom valve published to the Content Center.

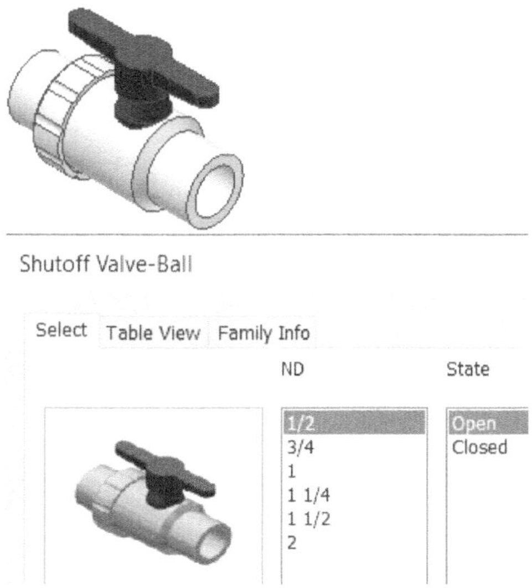

Authored Fittings

You do not have to publish all custom tube and pipe fittings and components to the Content Center. You can add connection information to a standard component and save it as an authored part. You can place an authored fitting in your assembly design, either inside or outside of a pipe run assembly. The connection information stored in the component is used to automatically place fittings and route nodes.

Example of Tube and Pipe Content

Tube and pipe routes and runs connect assembly components. All route types connect to the components with one or more fittings. For most rigid pipe and tube runs, you must place and connect start and end fittings before you create the route. You may have to place multiple fittings in combination to support the active style. For example, both a pipe nipple and a union may be required at the connection between a component and a rigid pipe route. Flexible hose styles can include a start and an end fitting, but you may need to place additional fittings to facilitate a connection to the components.

In the following image, some of the fittings that are required to complete this design have been identified. Without these fittings, the pipe route could not complete the connection to the other components.

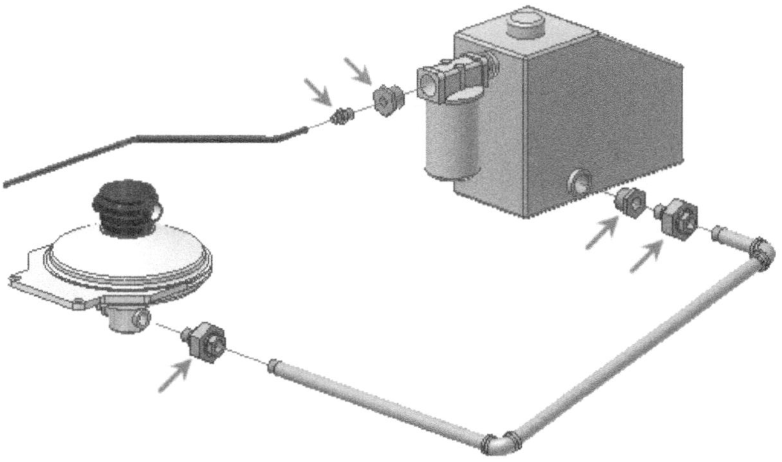

Placing Library Fittings

Most initial fittings share the piping standard of the conduit and fittings generated for a route. You can place initial fittings such as bushings, reducers, and bulkhead connectors from the supplied Content Center libraries. You can also publish your own custom fittings or other components such as valves or filters to a custom Content Center library and place them in your runs as initial fittings. When you place a fitting from the Content Center, the generated part is saved to the Content Center Files folder specified in the active project file. The storage location is a library path and can be located on the local computer or on a network drive. No limit exists for the number of fittings you can place in your design.

In the following image, a fitting from the Content Center library is shown being placed and connected to another part in the assembly design. The results of the placement and connection are shown on the right.

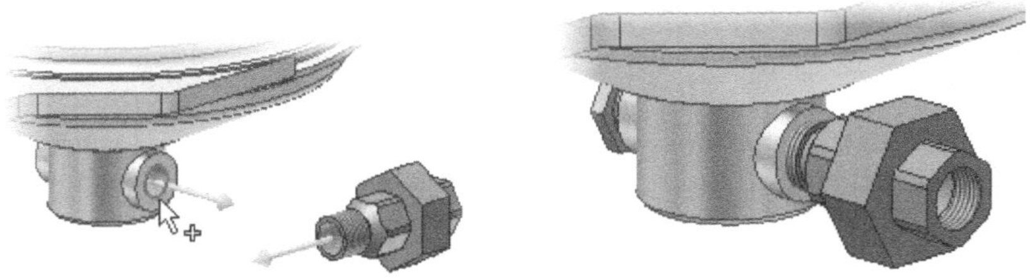

Access

Ribbon: Tube and Pipe tab>Content panel

Ribbon: Pipe Run tab>Content panel

Ribbon: Tube and Pipe tab>Component panel

Procedure: Placing a Fitting from the Content Center

The following steps outline how to place a fitting from the Content Center into an existing run.

1. Create or activate a run subassembly in the Tube & Pipe Runs subassembly.

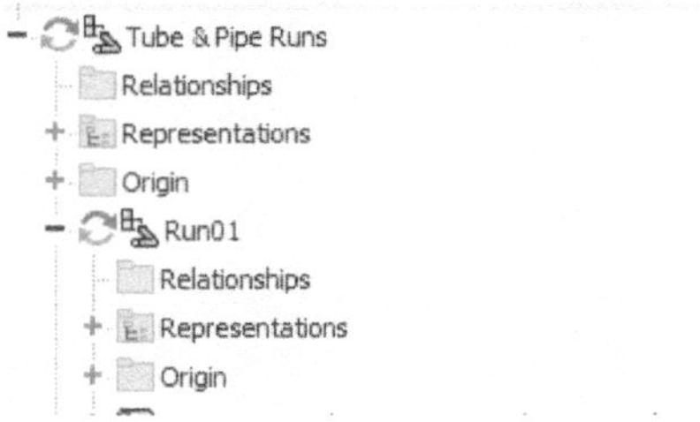

2. Start the Place from Content Center tool in the Content panel. Expand the Tube and Pipe Category and browse to the folder for the required fitting type.

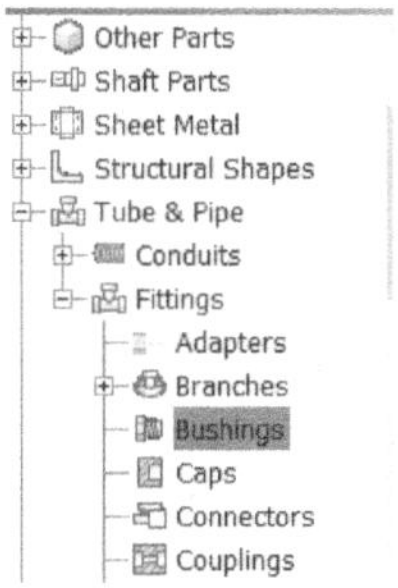

3. Select the required fitting family. Click OK.

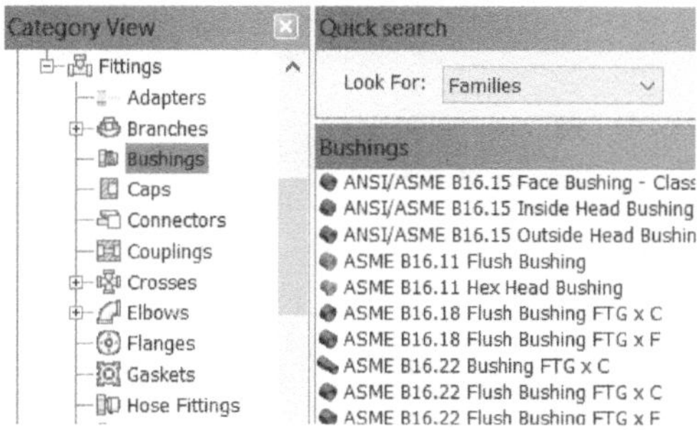

4. Select the nominal diameter and any other keys to define the placed fitting. Click OK.

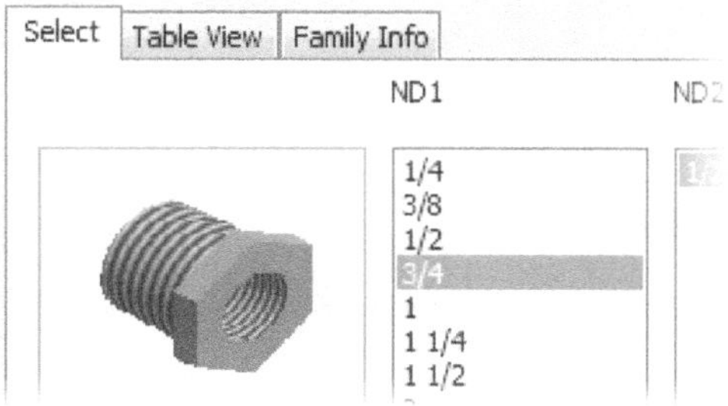

5. Do one of the following:

- To place an instance of the fitting, click the graphics window background.
- To connect the fitting to another fitting or geometry on a standard part, right-click on the graphics window background. Click Connect Fitting.

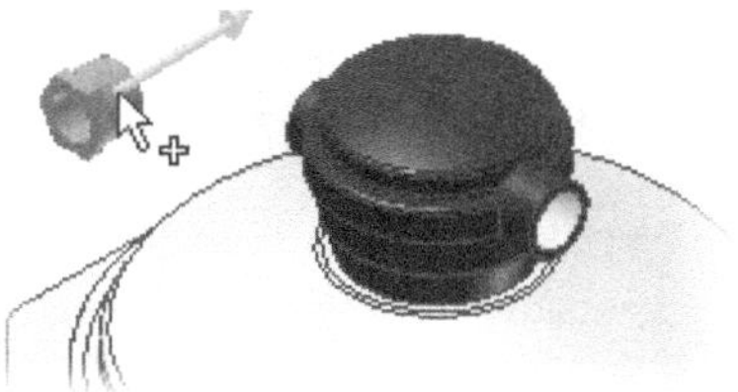

Placing Authored Fittings

You can place authored fittings in a run subassembly and connect them to other fittings, parts, and route segments. Each authored fitting represents a single nominal diameter. You cannot place different versions or sizes of an authored part as you can with a component from a Content Center library. You can however author different versions of the part for different nominal diameters and then place them in runs. You can connect the authored part to other fittings or to part geometry. You can reorient the authored fitting after placement and edit or delete the connection.

In the following image, a previously authored fitting was placed in the design and is now in the process of being connected to the valve.

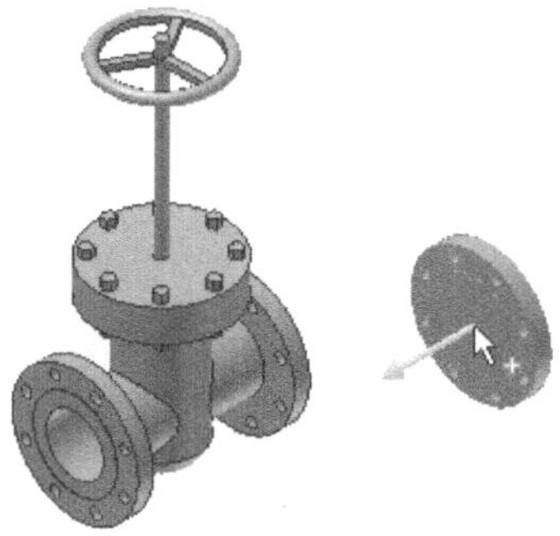

Access

Ribbon: Pipe Run tab>Route panel

Procedure: Placing an Authored Fitting

The following steps outline how to place an authored fitting in a run subassembly.

1. Create or edit a run subassembly in the Tube & Pipe Runs subassembly.
2. Start the Place Fitting tool.
3. Browse to the folder containing the authored part. Select the authored part and click Open. The authored part is previewed and attached to the cursor.
4. Do one of the following:
   - To place an instance of the fitting, click the graphics window background.
   - To connect the fitting to another fitting or geometry on a standard Autodesk Inventor part, right-click on the graphics window background. Click Connect Fitting.

> You cannot use the Place Fitting tool to place standard parts. A warning displays if the selected part is not an authored part.

Connecting Fittings During Placement

Library fittings and authored parts can have multiple connections. Each connection contains information on how the connection engages with another fitting, conduit segment, or part geometry such as a hole. When you place an authored part or a fitting from the Content Center, you can use this information to connect the initial fittings to assembly components or other fittings.

When you place library or authored fittings, connections can be created only when an individual run is the active subassembly.

Placement Options for Fittings

When you are adding an authored or library fitting to an active run, you have three options for placing the fitting. You access these options on the shortcut menu when the fitting preview is in the graphics window at the cursor. The three options are Place Fitting, Connect Fitting, and Insert Fitting. When you are adding an authored or library fitting to the overall assembly or the Tube & Pipe Runs subassembly, only the Place Fitting option is available.

Option	Description
Place Fitting	The default option. Use to add a component to the assembly without applying a connection to another part. Click an existing fitting to replace that fitting with the current fitting type and size.
Connect Fitting	Use to add the component and apply a connection to another fitting, a conduit part, or a normal Inventor part in the assembly.
Insert Fitting	Use to insert and connect the fitting between two connected fittings in a run.

The following image shows an example of the placement options being accessed on the shortcut menu.

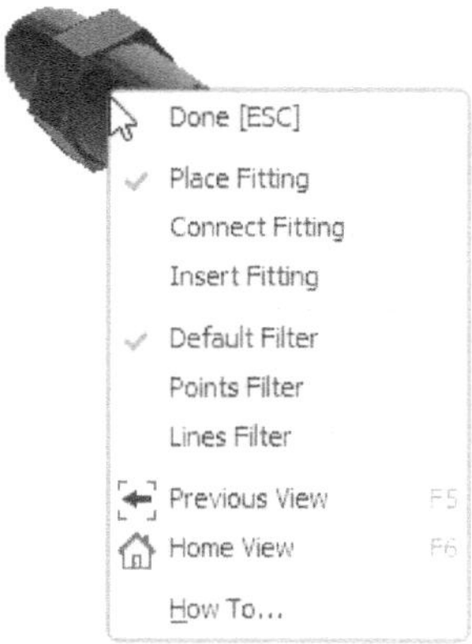

Procedure: Connecting a Library or Authored Fitting

The following steps outline how to connect a library or authored fitting to an assembly component or existing fitting during placement.

1. Create or edit a run subassembly.
2. Insert the Content Center fitting or authored fitting. Ensure that it is previewed and attached to the cursor.
3. Right-click on the graphics window background and click Connect Fitting. An arrow previews the connection point and direction. Press SPACEBAR to cycle through the fitting's connection points.
4. Move the cursor over an open connection point on an existing fitting in the same run or over a circular part edge. The fitting snaps to the connection point or circular edge.
5. Click to connect the fitting and activate the Edit Orientation tool.
6. Do one of the following:
   - Drag the arrows on the Edit Orientation tool to rotate the fitting about the connection axis.
   - Click an arrow and enter a precise rotation angle.
7. Right-click in the graphics window background. Click Done.

Connecting Existing Fittings

When you place library and authored fittings into a run subassembly, you can place them without connecting them to other fittings or parts. To use the defined connection information to assemble the fitting, you need to know which tool to use and the options for connecting existing fittings to other fitting or standard parts.

In the following image, a fitting that was placed but not connected is shown being connected on the left, and the results of the connection on the right.

In the following image, a fitting that was placed but not connected is shown on the left being inserted between an existing fitting and a section of pipe, and the results of the insertion on the right.

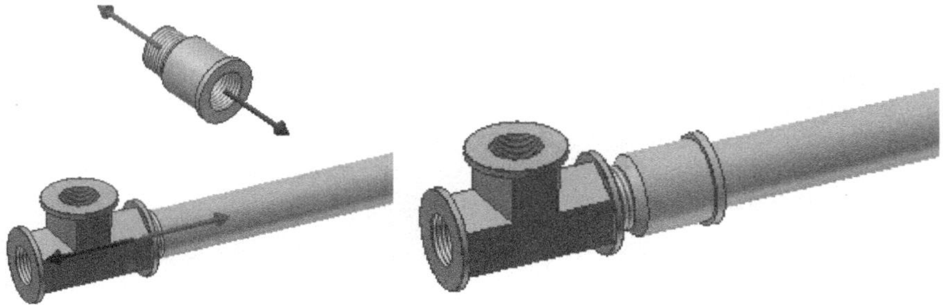

Access

Ribbon: Pipe Run tab>Route panel

Options for Connecting Fittings

You use the Connect Fittings tool to connect two components relative to one another in a tube and pipe assembly. This tool utilizes the connection information contained in the fitting to set the orientation of the fitting and to determine the engagement distance at the connection. The Connect Fittings tool is available only when an individual run is active. You can use the Connect Fittings tool to connect a free fitting to a location, or you can use the tool to insert and connect a fitting between two connected fittings. When using the option to insert the fittings, the free fitting must have its defined connections colinear so that it can be inserted between the currently connected parts.

To connect a fitting, the fitting to connect must be a free fitting and must be in the active run. A free fitting is a fitting that is not already connected to another part. Along with specifying the free fitting, you must have a base fitting or fittings to connect to. After selecting the free and base fittings, you specify the engagement value between the parts. The engagement is either the defined value as set in the free or base fitting or a custom value.

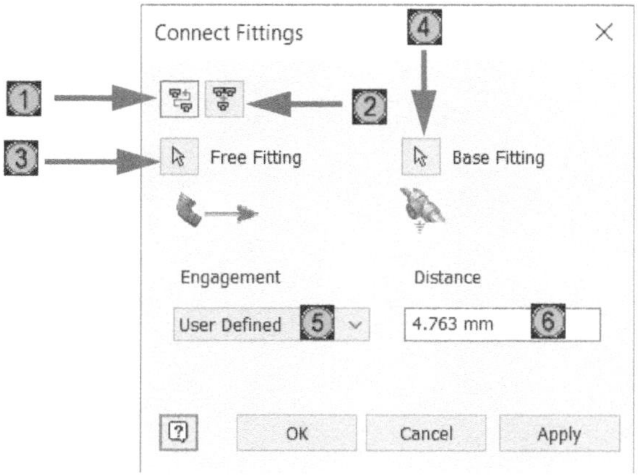

1. Connects two components relative to one another in a tube and pipe assembly.

2. Inserts and connects a fitting between two connected fittings in a tube and pipe assembly.

3. Selects the free fitting. You can select a fitting or a normal Autodesk Inventor part in the active pipe run assembly that is not driven by a free fitting node in a route or by any other fitting. When inserting a fitting between an existing fitting connection, the fitting must be colinear. After the free fitting is connected to the base component, it is always positioned relative to the base fitting during updates and other operations.

4. Use to select the base fitting. You can select a fitting, a conduit part, or a normal Inventor part that is located anywhere in the assembly. The base fitting specifies the connection that constrains the position and routing of the free fitting.

5. This list contains the name of the parts selected as the free and base fitting and the User Defined option. Select the fitting to use the engagement value that is set in that part, or select User Defined to enter a custom engagement distance.

6. Indicates the engagement distance used for the connection between fittings and components. You can edit the value only if you select the User Defined engagement type.

Procedure: Connecting Existing Fittings

The following steps give an overview of connecting an existing fitting to other fittings or standard parts.

1. Activate the run that has the fitting that requires connecting.
2. Start the Connect Fittings tool.
3. In the Connect Fittings dialog box, select either the Connect Fittings option or the Insert Fitting option.
4. Select the free fitting that you want to connect.
5. Select the base fitting that the free fitting needs to connect to.
6. If required, change the engagement distance.
7. Apply the connection.

Editing Fitting Connections

The initial engagement of the placed fitting may not match your final requirements. Most connections are made between one male and one female connection type. The initial engagement between the two components is determined by the engagement length of the female connection. Because holes in unauthored parts have no connection information, a zero engagement length results when a male connection on a placed library fitting or authored part is connected to a hole or cylindrical cut feature on a standard part. The female connection's engagement length also determines engagement when both connections have connection data.

You can edit the engagement after completing the placement of the fitting or authored part. You can select the male connection to supply the engagement length, or enter a custom engagement length value.

Fitting Connection Engagement Options

The following images show the different connection engagement types. In the drop-down list under Engagement, you can choose which fitting you want to extract connection information from. This information determines the distance of engagement between the two components. The User Defined option enables you to enter a custom engagement length.

This image shows that component 1 is selected in the Engagement list and is controlling the distance of 15 mm.

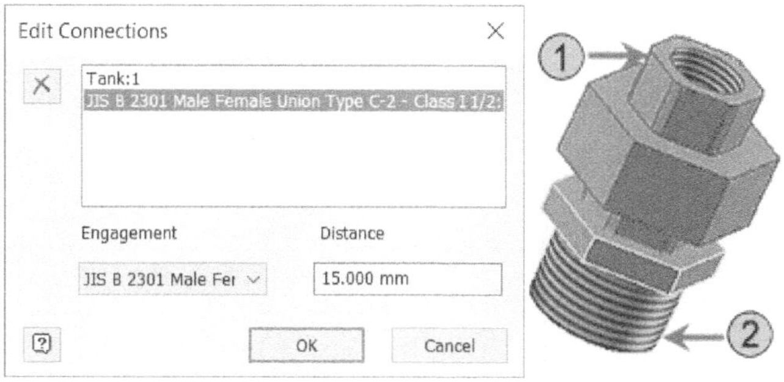

This image shows that component 2 is selected in the Engagement list and is controlling the distance of 11 mm.

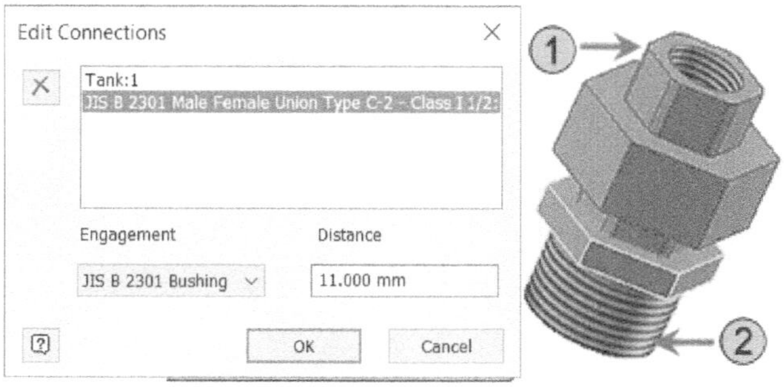

This image shows that User Defined has been selected from the list and is controlling the distance of 5 mm. This distance value can be changed as required.

Procedure: Changing Engagement Depth

The following steps outline how to change the engagement of a placed and connected library fitting or authored part.

1. Right-click on the fitting or authored part. Click Edit Fitting Connections.
2. In the Edit Connections dialog box, click the connection that you want to edit.
3. Select the engagement option that you want from the Engagement list.
4. Click OK.

Exercise: Place Initial Fittings

In this exercise, you will place and connect multiple fittings to a tank and pump. You will place library fittings from the Content Center and authored parts stored as separate files. You will also learn how to connect fittings during and after placement.

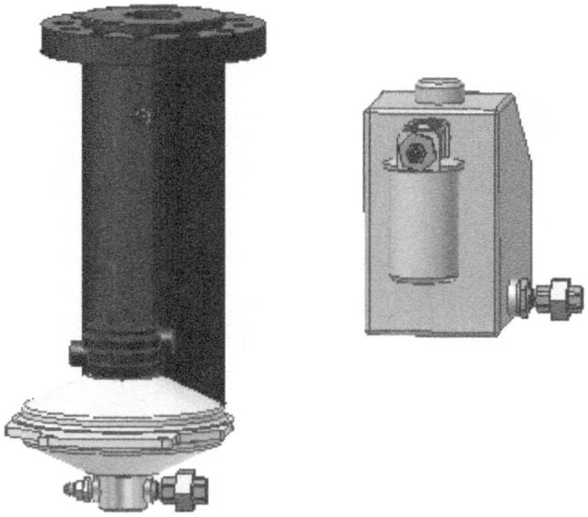

The completed exercise

Place Content Center Fittings

In this portion of the exercise, you will place and connect fittings from the Content Center.

1. Open *Place Initial Fittings.iam*.

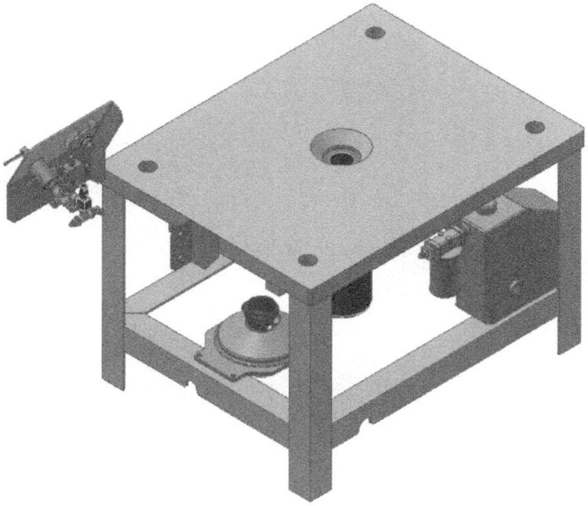

2. In the browser, expand Representations.
   - Expand View: Primary.
   - Right-click on Hydraulics and click Activate.

3. In the browser, expand the Tube & Pipe Runs subassembly. Double-click on Run01.
4. In the Pipe Run tab, in the Content panel, click Place.
5. In the Place from Content Center dialog box:
   - Under Category View, expand Tube and Pipe.
   - Expand Fittings.
   - Click Bushings.

   The family list shows all bushing families in the Content Center.

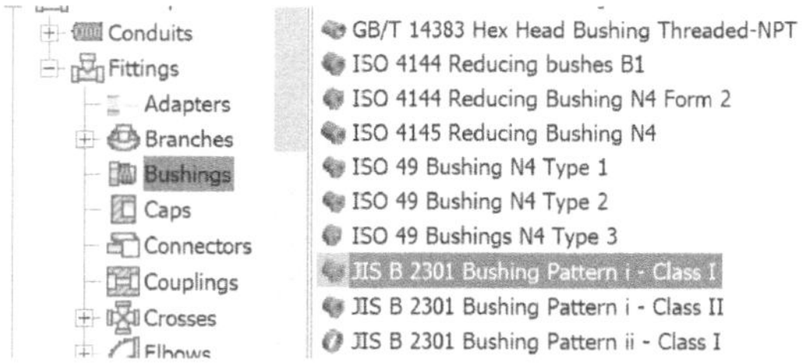

6. In the family list, double-click on JIS B 2301 Bushing Pattern i - Class I.
7. In the JIS B 2301 Bushing Pattern i - Class I dialog box, under ND1 (nominal diameter one), select 1. Under ND2, select 1/2.

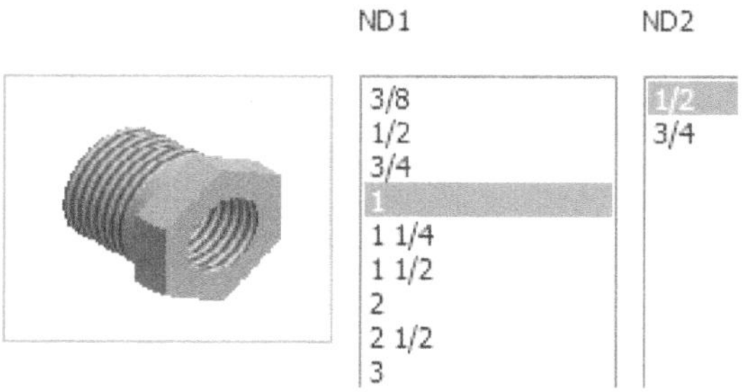

8. To generate the bushing and attach it to the cursor in the graphics window, click OK.

9. Right-click in the graphics window and click Connect Fitting.

10. Move the fitting over the opening in the tank. The male end of the bushing snaps to the circular edge. If it does not engage in the correct direction, press <Spacebar> to cycle through the available connections. Click to connect the bushing to the tank once it is in the correct orientation.

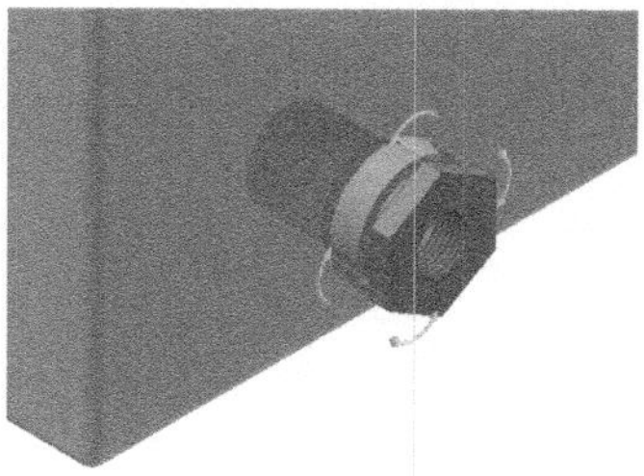

11. Right-click in the graphics window and click Done.

12. In the Pipe Run tab, in the Content panel, click Place. Under Category View, browse to Tube & Pipe>Fittings>Unions.

13. In the family list, double-click on JIS B 2301 Male Female Union Type C-2 - Class I.

14. In the Content Center family dialog box:
    - Under ND, select 1/2.
    - Click OK.

15. In the graphics window:
    - Click near the tank to place an instance of the fitting without connecting it to another fitting or component.
    - Click near the pump to place a second instance of the fitting.

16. Right-click in the graphics window and click Done.

17. In the Pipe Run tab, in the Route panel, click Connect Fittings.

18. Move the cursor over the union that you placed near the tank. When the connection preview arrow for the male thread connection displays, click to select the connection.

19. Click the bushing that you connected to the tank.

    A direction arrow extends from the open connection on the fitting.

20. In the Connect Fittings dialog box, click Apply.

    Note: The default engagement depth is the maximum engagement depth of the female connection.

21. With the Connect Fittings dialog box open, click the male end of the union near the pump.

22. Click the circular edge of the threaded hole in the base of the pump.

23. In the Connect Fittings dialog box, from the Engagement list, select User Defined.

24. For Distance, enter **10 mm**. Click OK. The union engages the hole to the specified depth.

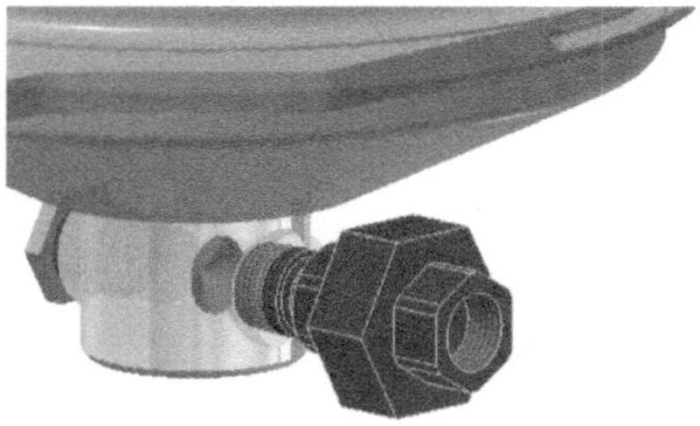

Place Authored Fittings

In this portion of the exercise, you will place and connect an authored part that is not saved to the Content Center.

1. Reorient your view as shown in the following image.

2. In the Pipe Run tab, on the Route panel, click Place Fitting.
3. Open *Hyd-6-6 St-P.ipt*. The fitting displays in the graphics window, attached to the cursor.
4. Right-click in the graphics window and click Connect Fitting. Click the bushing connected to the outlet of the pump.

5. Right-click in the graphics window. Select Done. The engagement length is controlled by the connection information of the female fitting, the bushing in the pump.
6. In the graphics window, right-click on the hydraulic fitting and click Edit Fitting Connections.
7. In the Edit Connections dialog box, select Bushing-8-6:1.

8. In the Engagement list, select Hyd-6-6 St- P:1. Click OK. The engagement depth changes to match the connection information in the hydraulic fitting.

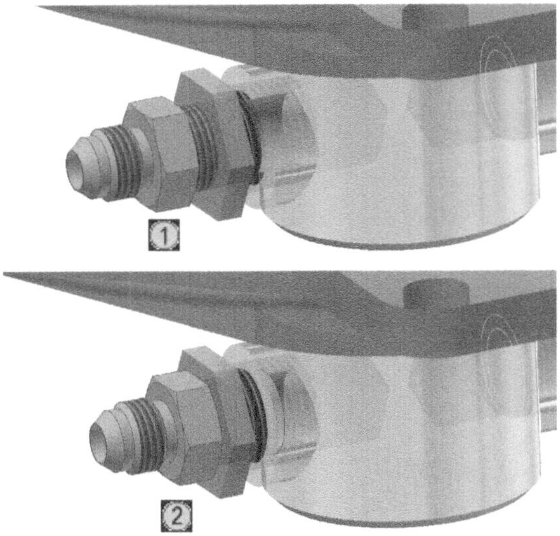

1 Female connection controls engagement

2 Male connection controls engagement

9. Close all files without saving changes.

Chapter Summary

In this chapter, you learned how to plan and set up your routes and runs, and how to place and connect the initial fittings in your tube and pipe designs.

Having completed this chapter, you can:

- Set the active tube or pipe style and create a tube and pipe runs subassembly.
- Place and connect fittings to assembly components before creating a route.

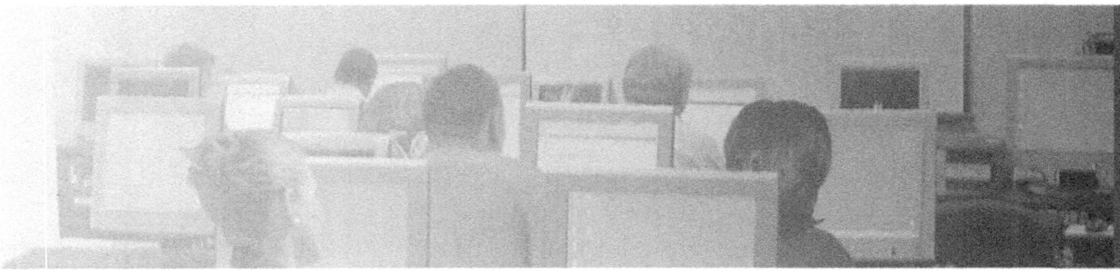

Chapter 3

Routes and Runs

In this chapter, you learn how to create and edit rigid pipe and tube routes, and identify and use different fittings in rigid routes. You also learn how to create and edit flexible hose routes, and how to successfully manage routes and runs.

Objectives

After completing this chapter, you will be able to:

- Create rigid routes for tube and pipe designs.
- Create rigid routes by using the sketching tools and techniques.
- Edit rigid tube and pipe routes.
- Edit fittings and modify styles.
- Create and edit flexible hose routes.
- Reuse tube and pipe routes and runs, and configure tube and pipe run subassemblies in different versions of an iAssembly.

Lesson: Creating Rigid Routes

Overview

This lesson describes how to create rigid tube and pipe routes.

A route defines a path for the pipe segments and their associated fittings. A route can be as simple as a start point and endpoint related to geometry in the assembly, or a complex, multi-segment path associated to many components in an assembly. Most rigid pipe routes contain a number of user-defined intermediate points, called nodes. In addition to user-defined nodes, the tube and pipe application can automatically add nodes to create a valid path between user-defined nodes, or to match the requirements of the current style. You can use the 3D ORTHOgonal Route tool to specify the locations of node points in a rigid pipe route, or you can derive the route from an existing 3D sketch.

The following image shows a simple rigid pipe route. The route nodes and segments determine the position of elbows and couplings along the route, and the length of pipe segments between the fittings.

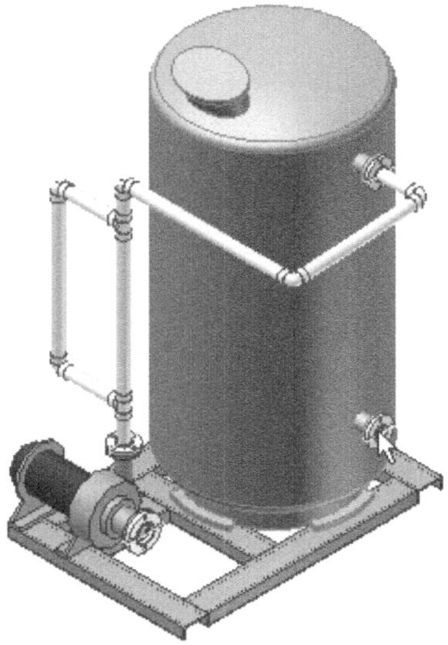

Objectives

After completing this lesson, you will be able to:

- Describe common workflows for creating rigid routes.
- List the geometry you can use to start a rigid route.
- Explain the process and options for creating sketched route segments and controlling their size and position.
- Describe the difference between sketched route segments and autorouted regions in a route.
- Describe how to use a standard 3D sketch to define a rigid route.
- Set the direction of gravity for a self-draining route.

Creating Rigid Routes

The path that a rigid pipe with fittings or tubing with bends traverses through your design is set by the route you create. To create designs of rigid pipe or bent tubing that meet your requirements, you need to know the methods and tools for creating rigid routes and how to populate the routes with components.

The following image represents a rigid route made up of sketched segments and autoroute regions.

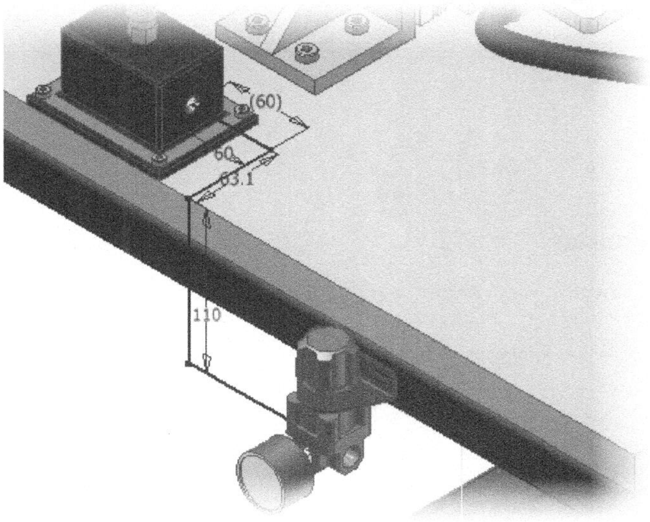

Description of Rigid Pipe Routing

All routes are created in the active run, and all runs are contained in the Tube & Pipe Runs subassembly. The active tube and pipe style specifies a route type that can be rigid pipe segments connected by elbows and couplings, rigid tube segments that have bends in place of elbows, or flexible tubing with or without fittings. A rigid pipe style can include both 45° and 90° elbows, be limited to 90° elbows only, or set to be self-draining and include custom angled elbows.

You create a rigid pipe route with a series of nodes placed in 3D space. A route always contains at least two nodes, a start node and end node. You can place any number of intermediate nodes to arrange the route relative to components or work geometry in your design. The tube and pipe application adds geometric and dimensional constraints to these sketched route segments. You can edit, delete, and add to these constraints to control the position and orientation of the route relative to components in your design.

The creation of segments between nodes and the behavior of these nodes depends on the workflow you use to create them. Route segments are either created one at a time using the 3D ORTHOgonal tool or automatically between two specified points. The specified point can be a connection point, circular edge, vertex, or the last sketched node using the 3D ORTHOgonal tool. Many rigid pipe routes consist of both autoroute regions and sketched route segments. The nodes and segments in autoroute regions automatically update when you edit your design.

The following image shows a rigid pipe route with both sketched route segments and an autoroute region.

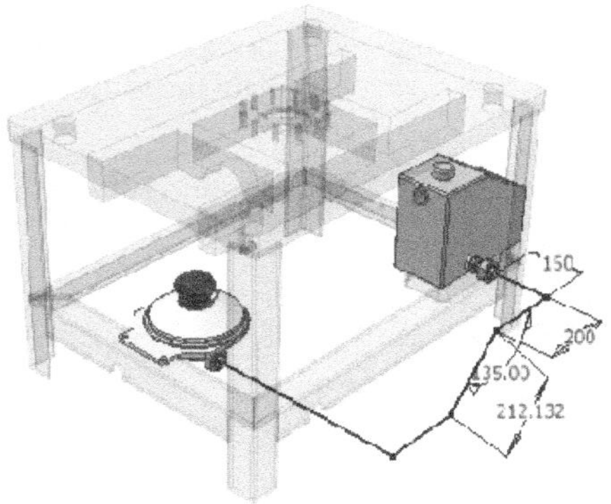

Process: Creating Rigid Routes

The following diagram gives an overview of creating a rigid route.

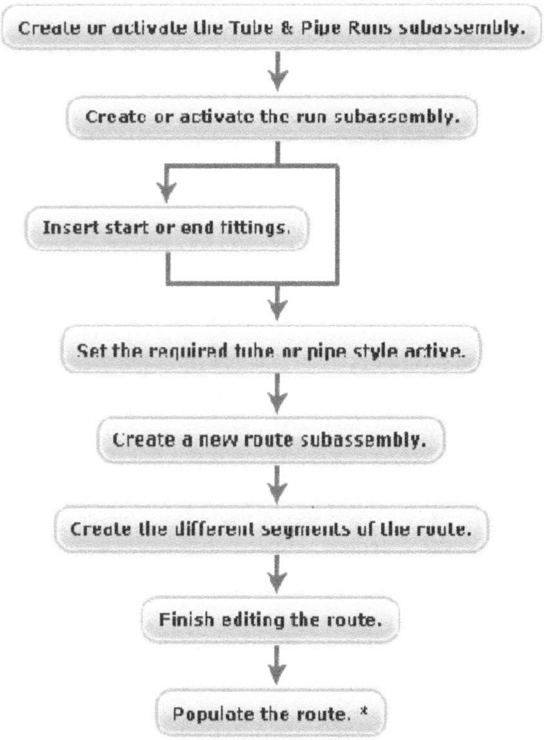

Populate the route only when you are ready. Populating the route early in the design process increases the number of parts being loaded in the assembly design.

Sketched Route Segments

You can precisely control the position of a node relative to the previous node, or to other geometry in your design, with the 3D ORTHOgonal Route tool. The tube and pipe application automatically adds geometric and dimension constraints to route nodes and segments as you create them. You can include any geometry from existing components in a route, and constrain sketched route segments and nodes to the included geometry. The sketched route segments remain associative to the referenced geometry and update if the underlying components are moved or modified.

The following image shows a rigid pipe route where all route segments are sketched route segments. The position and orientation of the nodes and segments are controlled by geometric and dimension constraints.

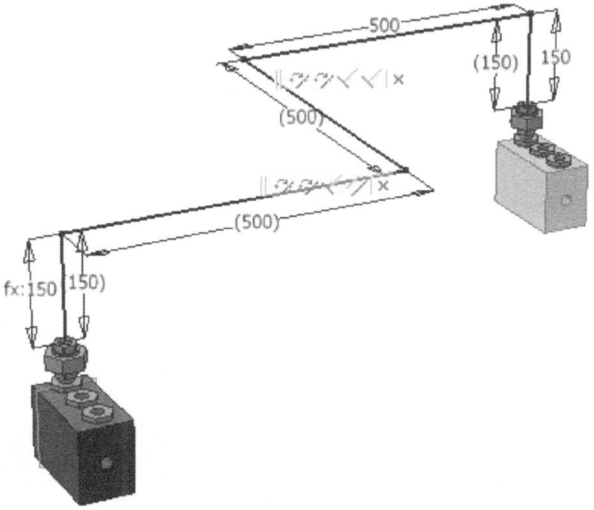

Autoroute Regions

You generate an autoroute region when you select a start and end point for all or a portion of a route. These points are circular or arc edges, vertices, or most often connection points on two different fittings. One or more route solutions are generated automatically. You can cycle through a preview of each route and select a solution. Intermediate nodes and segments are automatically placed, based on the rules in the active style. The nodes for these automatically generated route sections are grouped in the browser as an autoroute region.

You can display alternate route solutions for an autoroute region at any time and select from any of the presented routes. If edits to your design change the position of the start or end node, the tube and pipe application automatically calculates new solutions for all autoroute regions and presents the new solutions for selection.

You can convert autoroute regions into sketched route segments, but you cannot convert sketched route segments into autoroute regions. Because sketched route segments are constrained, they update in a more predictable fashion. When you are confident about the general configuration of the route, you can consider converting autoroute regions to sketched route segments.

In the following image, the first two route segments from the right-side block are sketched segments and the remainder of the route is an autoroute region. Two of the available route solutions are shown.

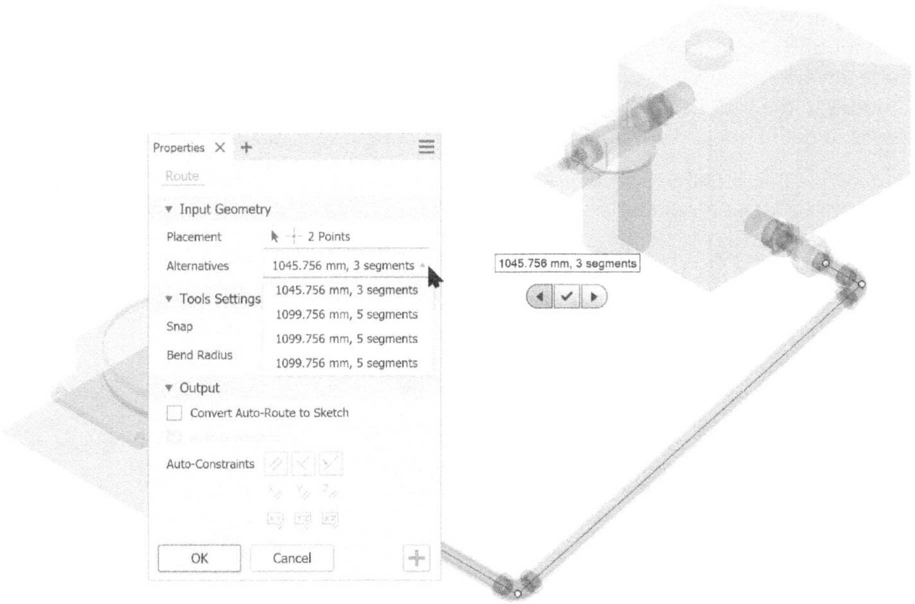

Joining Route Sections

Route nodes can be placed in any order. You are not required to create the route as a continuous set of nodes from start point to endpoint. It is often practical to create part of the route from the start point, and then place nodes starting at the end point back to the open interior route node.

In the following image, a route is completed from both ends to accommodate design requirement near the start and end fittings.

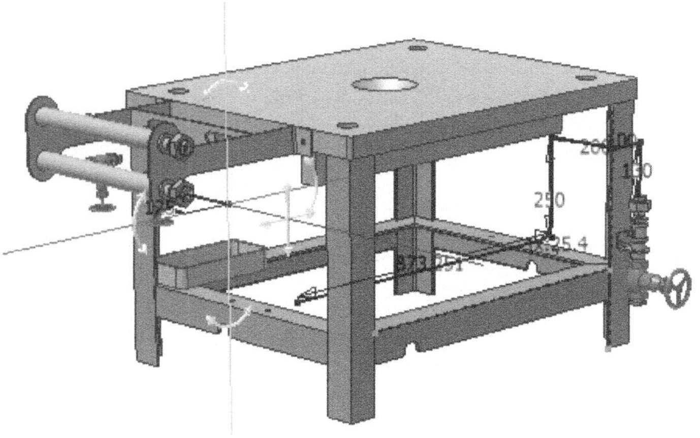

Route Direction Through a Node

When you hover the cursor over geometry to select a start, end, or intermediate node, a vector arrow displays at that location. The direction that the arrow points indicates the direction the route enters into that point. If the vector arrow is not pointing in the direction you require, before clicking that point, press the SPACEBAR to toggle the vector direction.

In the following image, the vector direction arrow is shown on the left with the resulting automatic route on the right. When connecting to a fitting, you cannot change the direction.

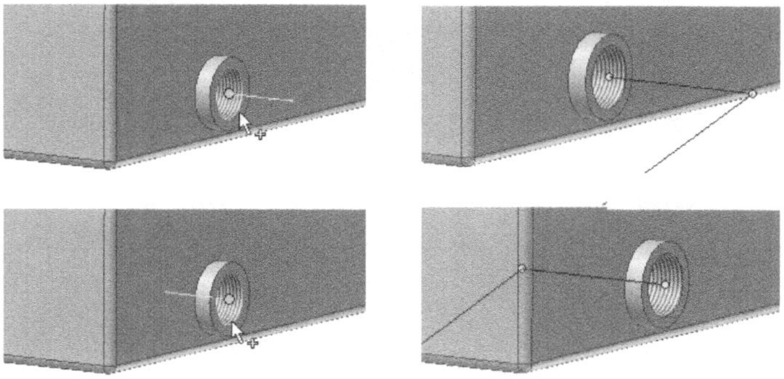

Finishing a Route

A rigid pipe route typically ends at a fitting constrained to an assembly component or at a threaded hole. After you define the last route node, click an arrow in the Select Other tool to cycle through the possible route solutions. When the required route displays, click the checkmark in the center of the Select Other tool to accept it, or right-click and click Continue. Alternatively, you can also pick the options under Alternatives drop-down list in the Route Properties window. Pressing ESC or Done in the context menu will cancel the route creation. You can edit and continue an existing route at any time in the design process, even after the route has been populated with conduit segments and fittings.

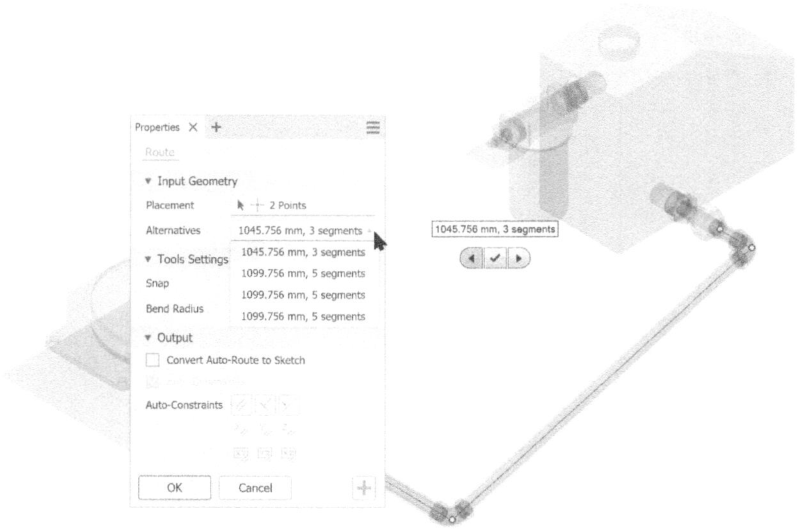

Populating a Rigid Pipe Route

You can terminate a route at any time and return to the run subassembly. When you populate a rigid pipe route, elbows are placed at direction change nodes, except at nodes with custom bends. Couplings are placed at interior nodes where there is no change in route direction. Pipe segments are placed between the fittings and engage the fittings as defined by the current style and the fitting's connection information. Routes are populated automatically or the route population can be done using the Populate Route option in the Pipe Run tab.

The following image shows an unpopulated rigid pipe route on the left. The same route is populated with conduit segments and elbow fittings in the right-side image.

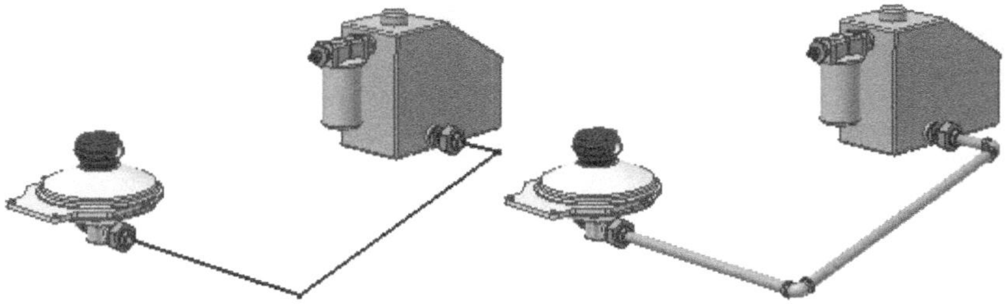

> If you need to create multiple routes, consider leaving them unpopulated until you have defined all the routes. Populated routes can contain many components and require more resources than unpopulated routes.

Route Start Point

Where and how you start a route for a rigid tube and pipe depends on your design requirements and the current state of the design. In most cases, the starting point for a route is a defined connection point on an existing fitting or the circular edge of a part feature such as a threaded hole. Because of this, before you begin creating the route segments, you typically place and connect fittings and other components in the run. To create the exact route start point where you require it, you need to know and understand the options for selecting and creating a start point for any tube, pipe, or hose route.

The following image shows three different start point options.

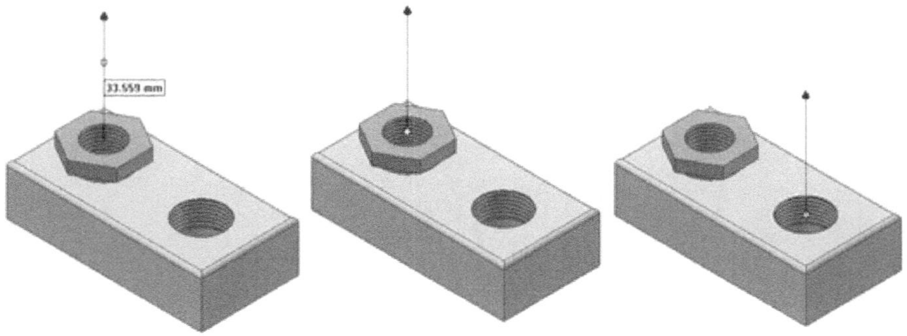

Starting a Route

All routes start from a defined point. This point is also known as the start point (node). The three primary methods you use to set the start point for a new route are:

- At a fitting connection.
- At a circular edge.
- Offset from a circular edge.

> When you place a node either at or offset from a connection point or a circular edge center point, on a part vertex, or on a part or assembly work point, the node is associative and moves to match any change in the position of the underlying geometry. Additional nodes might be automatically added to the route when the node adapts to the new position of the referenced geometry.

Starting at a Fitting Connection

A common route start point is a defined connection point in a placed library fitting or authored part. As you move the cursor over a library fitting or authored part, the nearest unconsumed connection point is highlighted and a direction axis displays. When the connection point is highlighted, click to place the start node at the connection point.

The following image shows a rigid pipe route started at a fitting. The connection information in the fitting controls the engagement of the pipe segment and the fitting.

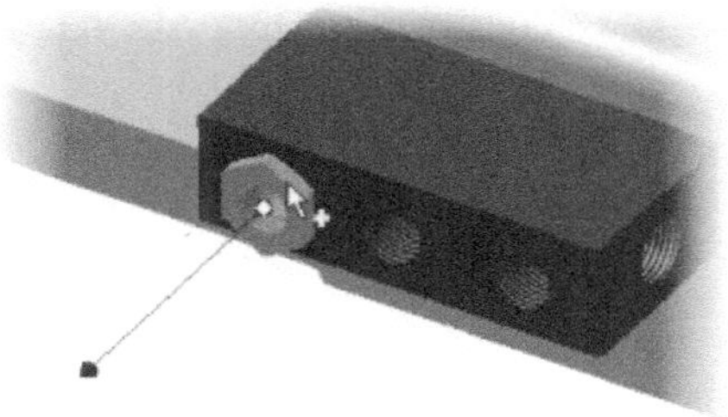

> When you select a connection point on a library fitting or authored part, the conduit segment extends into the fitting. The engagement length is defined when the part is authored.

Starting at a Circular Part Edge

When you move the cursor over a circular or arc edge of an unauthored part, the edge and center point become highlighted. When the edge and center point are highlighted, you can click to place the start node at the center point.

The following image shows a rigid pipe route started at a circular edge on a part.

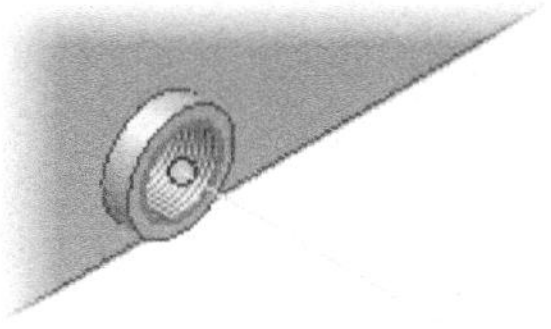

Offset Start Point

You can also move the cursor along the direction arrow normal to the connection or center point. You can click to place the route node at a distance from the edge center point. A tooltip displays the offset from the connection or center point. The arrow lies on the axis of the opening and indicates the direction that the route takes to approach the point. You can switch the arrow direction either by pressing SPACEBAR or by right-clicking and then clicking Select Other Direction.

In the following image, the route start point is offset along the axis from a fitting connection point.

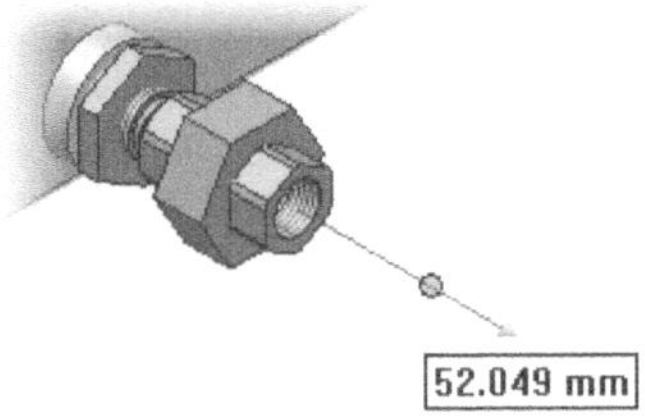

Precise Offset Start Point

You can also enter a precise offset from the connection point or edge center point. While the cursor is over the direction arrow, enter a number. The Enter Distance dialog box opens as you begin to enter the value. You can also activate the Enter Distance dialog box from the shortcut menu.

In the following image, the start point for a rigid pipe route is precisely offset from a fitting connection point.

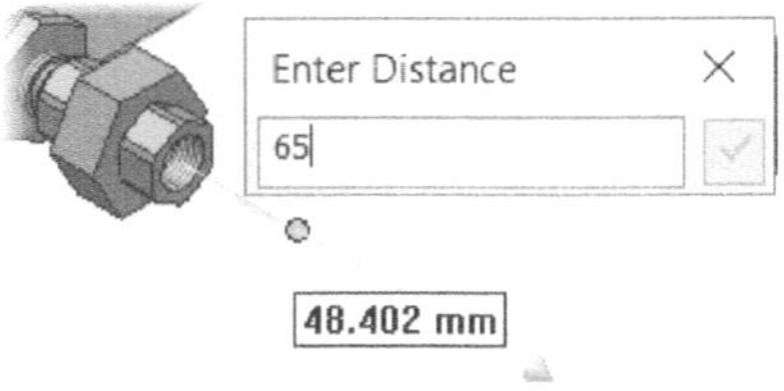

Other Start Points

Other valid selections for route start points are part vertices and part or assembly work points. You can offset the start point from a work point, but only along one axis that is determined by the method used to create the work point. You cannot offset the start point from a part vertex.

The following image shows a route started at a work point. The orientation of the route axis is determined by the geometry used to create the work point.

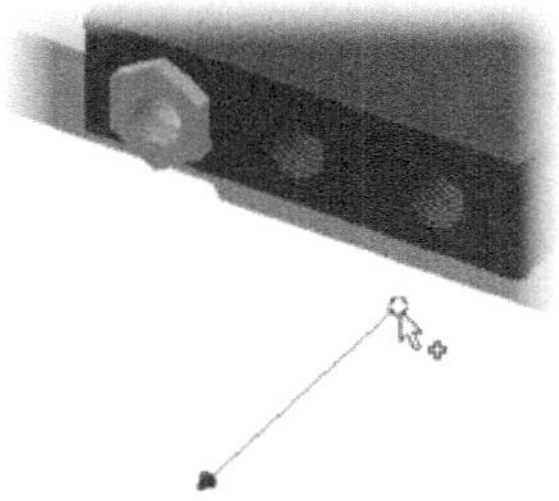

Sketching Route Segments

A tube and pipe route often needs to go through an assembly design in different directions to get from its start point to its end point. To get the route to follow the exact path you require, you must sketch the route. To learn and use the tools and techniques for sketching a route, you need to understand the process and options for creating sketched route segments and how the route segments' size and positions are controlled.

In the following image, a new route is in the process of being sketched. A few of the common key items in a sketched route have been called out for identification.

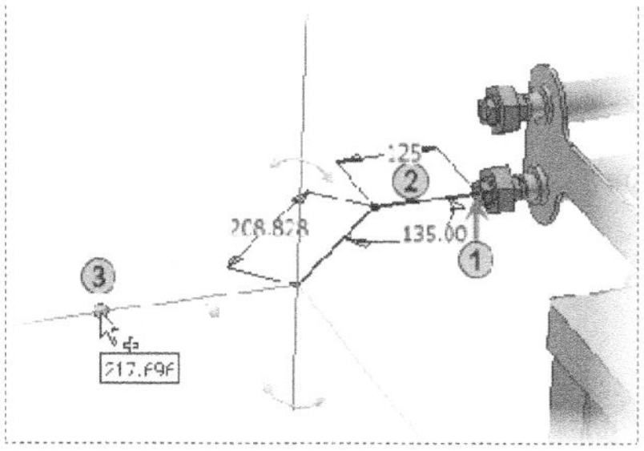

1. Route start point (first route node).

2. The first route segment aligned with the axis through the fitting at the first node.

3. A route node placed along one of the axes of the 3D ORTHOgonal Route tool.

Description of Sketching Route Segments

After you specify a starting point for a rigid pipe route, you can create subsequent nodes using the 3D ORTHOgonal Route tool. By using this tool, you can create points along one of the route's axes, set a different bend radius for the next created point in the route, or change the rotation angle of the axis and thus change the bend or fitting angle at that node.

The first node you place after selecting the start point must lie on the route axis that extends from the start point. Further nodes can be placed along any axes of the tool. You can also reference geometry in the assembly to help align the tool axes and to help position nodes. The tube and pipe application automatically adds geometric constraints and dimensions to the nodes and route segments. The result is a parametric route that you can edit by changing dimensions. Add or delete constraints between route segments or between a route segment or node and the geometry in your design.

It is not required to create associations between all route nodes and the adjacent faces, edges, and vertices of assembly components. You can use the 3D ORTHOgonal Route tool to place route nodes and segments that meet the requirements of the current style and are constrained only to other nodes and segments in the same route.

If you know the route requires references to specific geometry, before sketching route segments, include the geometry before you create route nodes. You use the Include Geometry tool to manually include any existing vertex, linear edge, planar face, or work feature in the route. When you select geometry to be included in the route, one or more adaptive work features are added as references in the route. The work features are placed in the Included Geometry folder below the route node in the browser.

Access

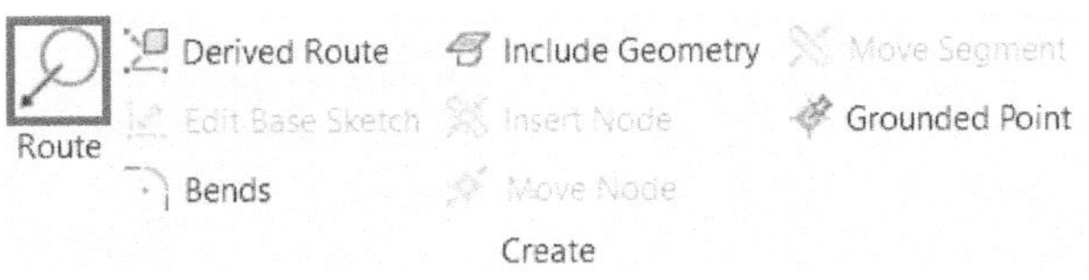

Ribbon: Route tab>Create panel

The Tube and Pipe Route command uses a property palette UI. As you make selections, each of the actions to define the route populate in the palette as well. You can also use the right-click menu to define the routing options.

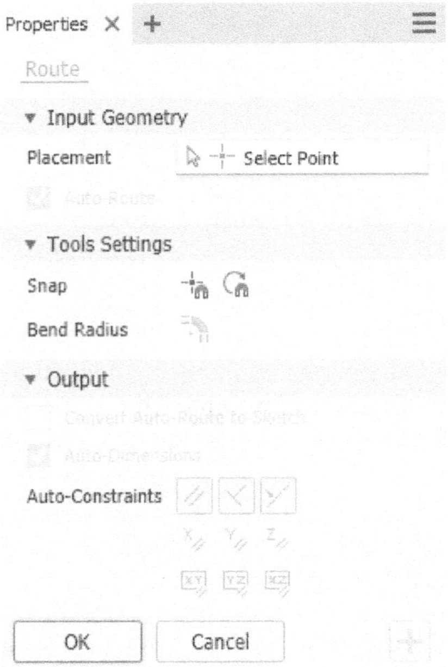

Process: Sketching Route Segments

The following image gives an overview of sketching route segments.

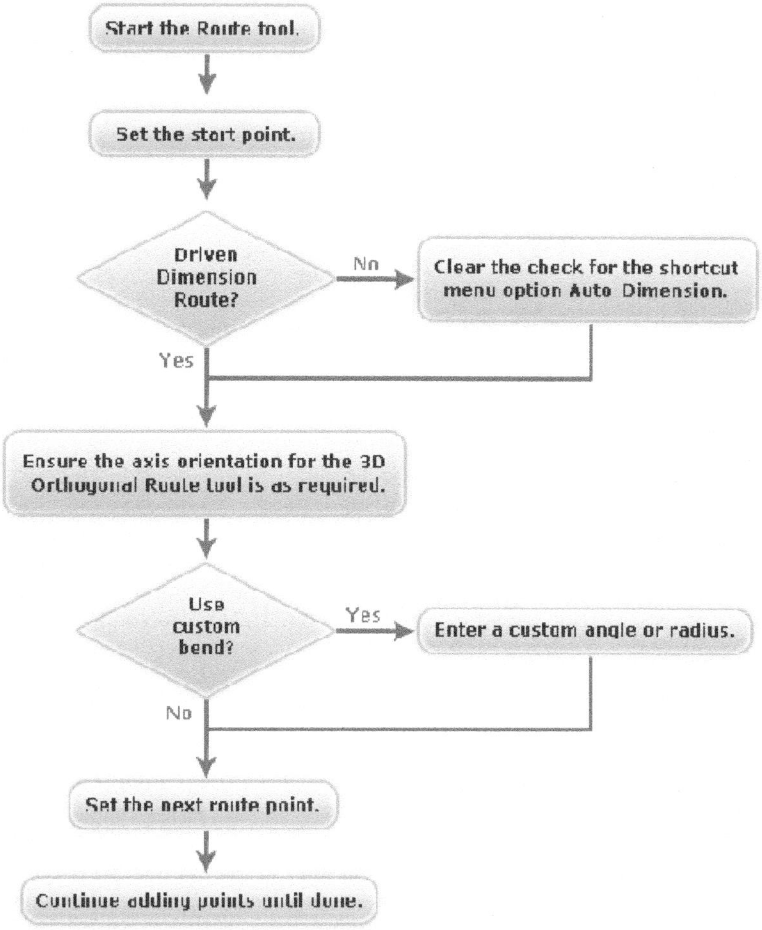

Autoroute Regions

An autoroute region is created by selecting valid geometry as start and end route points and can have any number of continuous autoroute segments that are controlled by autoroute points. Multiple solutions can exist for an autoroute segment, and you have the ability to cycle through these solutions and select the one that best fits your design. To achieve the benefits of automatically routed regions, you need to understand the characteristics of autoroute regions and their differences from sketched route segments.

The following image represents a three-segment autoroute region finishing the rigid route.

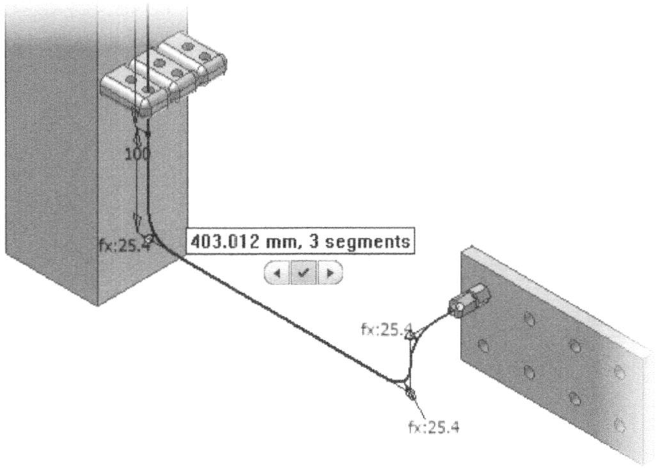

Definition of Autoroute Regions

An autoroute region is a section of a route that is managed by the tube and pipe environment. You create an autoroute region when you select a connection, circular edge, or vertex that does not lie along one of the 3D ORTHOgonal Route axes. The tube and pipe environment generates any intermediate nodes required between the current node and the selected endpoint to meet the rules of the active style.

You can generate a complete rigid pipe route by selecting only the start point and endpoint for the route. You can create any number of autoroute regions in a route in combination with sketched route segments generated by the 3D ORTHOgonal Route tool. When an autoroute region is required, a valid route is previewed between the start point and endpoint. If there are multiple valid route solutions between the points, the Select Other tool opens. Autoroute solutions are evaluated and prioritized based on length and number of segments. The length and segment information is included in a tooltip as you consider available solutions. Click the arrows in the Select Other tool to cycle through the solutions. Click the middle green button to make your selection. Your solution is typically selected upon route creation; however, you can also use the Alternate Route Solution tool in the shortcut menu of an autoroute region to change the solution at a later time.

Segments in an autoroute region can always dynamically update when changes are made to associated geometry. The system automatically calculates the new autoroute region solution so that segments might be added or removed. Sketched route segments must be manually edited or deleted. The system dynamically adjusts segment length and orientation unless they are fully constrained, but no segments are added or removed.

All route nodes in the autoroute region are listed under an Autoroute node in the browser. You can delete the entire autoroute region, convert it to sketched route segments, or switch between valid autoroute solutions. A rigid pipe route often has a mix of autoroute regions and sketched route segments.

Managing Autoroute Regions

Autoroute regions enable you to speed up the creation of rigid routes. It can be difficult to align a route to mid-route supports such as hangers, or to the end fitting with the 3D ORTHOgonal Route tool. If the component or fitting has a circular edge or contains connection information, an autoroute region can quickly generate an accurate path to it. You can drag the position of some segments and nodes in an autoroute region to modify the selected route solution.

An autoroute segment is automatically constrained to adjacent segments or associated terminal geometry using constraints, which are represented with a specific symbol. Use the Show Constraints tool in the Route Panel or the Show All Constraints tool in the shortcut menu to display the client constraint symbol.

The client constraint blocks all regular 3D sketch constraints and dimensions. You cannot apply geometric constraints or dimensional constraints to an autoroute segment. Autoroute regions use their own logic and dynamically change the geometry as the assembly changes.

If you want to directly control an autoroute segment with constraints or dimensions, you can either convert the autoroute region to sketch route segments, or delete client constraints on individual segments. Applying the Convert to Sketch tool to the autoroute region is equivalent to giving the segments in the autoroute region the same constraints as a manually sketched region. Deleting client constraints manually results in the following behaviors:

- If an autoroute constraint on an intermediate segment is deleted, the region is split into two regions.
- If constraints on terminal autoroute segments are deleted, the segment remains colinear or perpendicular.

When an edit to your design affects the route, the tube and pipe environment examines the autoroute regions and might recalculate the number and position of nodes and segments in each. To prevent undesired updates to your routes, convert autoroute regions to sketched route segments as soon as possible. When you convert an autoroute region to sketched route segments, geometric and dimensional constraints are automatically added to the converted route nodes and segments.

In the following image, the two route segments in the left-side image are in an autoroute region. In the right-side image, the autoroute region is converted to sketched route segments that are automatically constrained and dimensioned to other route geometry.

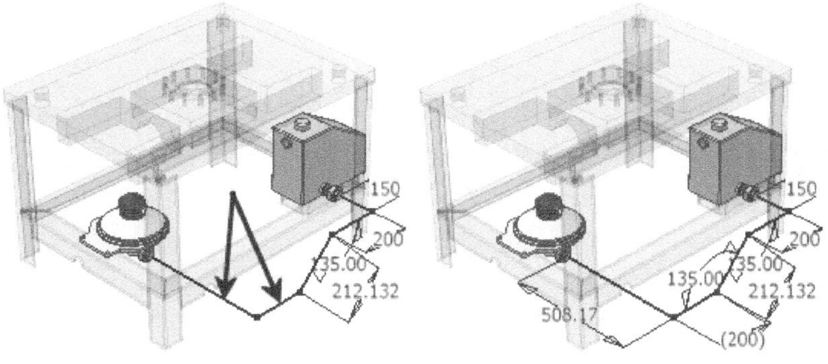

Self-Draining and Autorouting

The autorouting functionality of the Routing tool supports custom angled fittings. It supports these fittings by obtaining the correct angle and fitting information from the active tube and pipe style. It then applies the angle to the required members in the route. The tool also has the intelligence to place the correct elbows in the correct places. Custom angle elbows are placed at the transition from vertical to sloped, and 90° elbows are placed at the transition between two sloping segments.

In the following image, the position and orientation of the custom elbow were automatically rotated into the correct location.

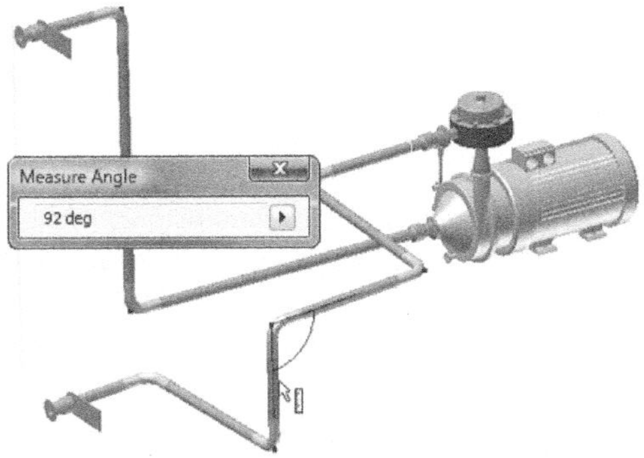

Example of Autoroute Regions

There are many situations where you can use a combination of different methods for creating a route. In the following image, an autoroute region is generated from an intermediate route node to the end fitting for the route.

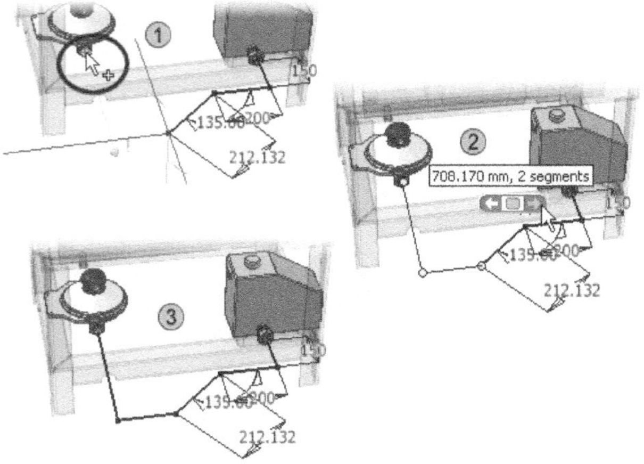

1. End fitting connection point is selected. It does not lie along any of the axes of the 3D ORTHOgonal Route tool. The start point is from the end of the sketched route.

2. Alternate route solutions are previewed.

3. The selected route solution is generated.

Creating Derived Routes

You can derive rigid pipe and tube routes from all or part of an existing 3D sketch in the assembly. You can use this workflow to create routes and runs in previously created assemblies where 3D sketches outline conduit paths outside of the tube and pipe environment. The route is associative to the 3D sketch, and any changes to the sketch geometry are reflected in the derived route. You cannot create a derived route for flexible hose.

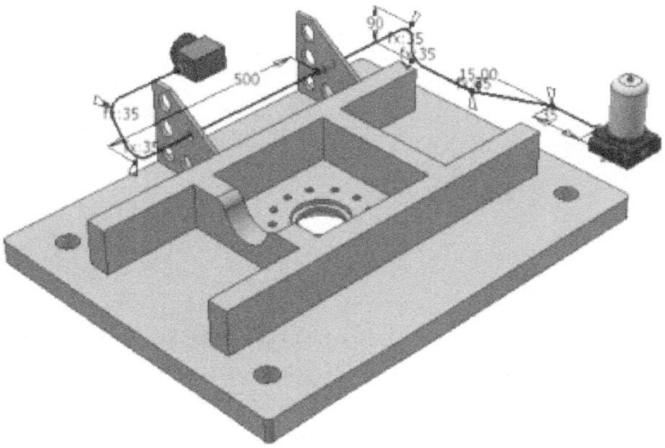

Requirements for 3D Sketches for Derived Routes

When you create a 3D sketch for a derived route, you should consider the style of the resulting route. Because routes for rigid pipes have more restrictions than tube routes, the 3D sketches for these routes must meet stricter requirements.

All 3D sketches used in derived routes have the following general requirements:

- The 3D sketch cannot be contained in an existing route. The sketch can be contained in a part in the top-level assembly or in any of the subassemblies below the top-level assembly. You can also include the 3D sketch in the Tube & Pipe Runs subassembly, but it must be located outside of any routes defined in the runs. You can create the sketch with the Autodesk® Inventor® software.
- The 3D sketch must approach end fittings or points perpendicular to the openings. Derived routes do not recognize connection points or the requirement that the adjacent segment be colinear with the connection axis.
- The 3D sketch does not need to be continuous. A single 3D sketch can describe the route for multiple conduit segments.
- There are no restrictions on how you create the 3D sketch. You can use any combination of associative work points, grounded work points, and freehand sketch points.
- If the start point and endpoint of each chain in the 3D sketch are associated to circular edges of fittings, you do not need to position the points to engage the fittings. You can use the Trim or Extend Pipe tool to define the engagement at each fitting after you create the route.

The following image shows a route derived from a 3D sketch. The 3D sketch line starts at the center point of a circular edge on a fitting.

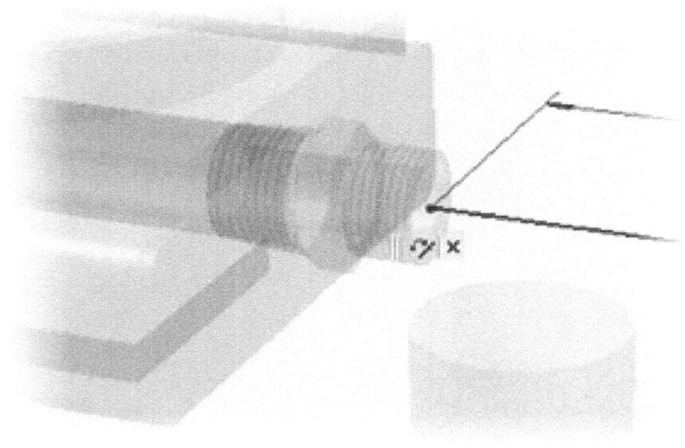

Derived Route or Sketched Route

When you start a new route, you can sketch the route with the 3D ORTHOgonal Route tool, or select start and end points to generate an autorouted route. Optionally, you can derive the entire route from an existing 3D sketch. If you derive the route, you cannot add nodes and segments to the route with the 3D ORTHOgonal Route tool. You can break the link between the 3D sketch and the route and then use the 3D ORTHOgonal Route tool to edit the route.

> Only 3D line and arc segments can be derived into a route. You can use the Include Geometry tool to create 3D sketch entities from part edges, but included segments that are splines are ignored when the 3D sketch is derived into a route.

3D Sketches for Rigid Pipe Routes

A 3D sketch for a rigid pipe route must conform to the settings for the active style. If the pipe style has only 90° elbows, all line segments in the 3D sketch must be perpendicular to the adjacent segments. You can apply perpendicular and parallel constraints in the 3D sketch to control 90° direction changes. If the style includes 45° elbows, you can add angular dimensions between sketch segments to create valid angles.

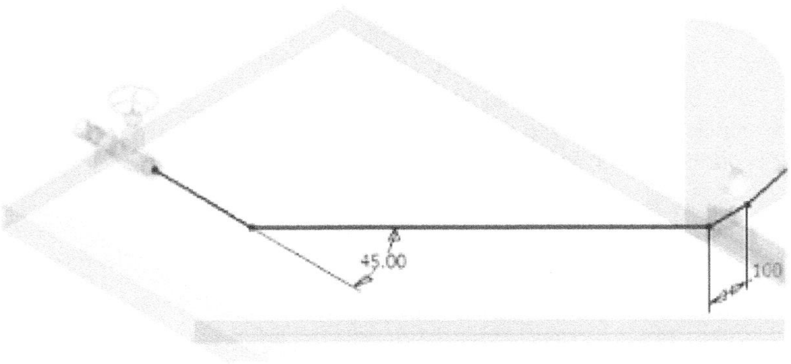

3D Sketches for Tube Routes

You can derive a 3D sketch into a route when the active route type is tubing with bends. You can orient adjacent lines in the sketch at arbitrary angles, and you can include bends in the 3D sketch. If two adjacent lines are not connected with a bend in the 3D sketch, a default bend radius is added when the 3D sketch is derived into the route.

You can use equations in sketch dimensions to create parametric bends. For example, you can create a 180° bend in a 3D sketch that maintains the bend angle when the bend radius is changed.

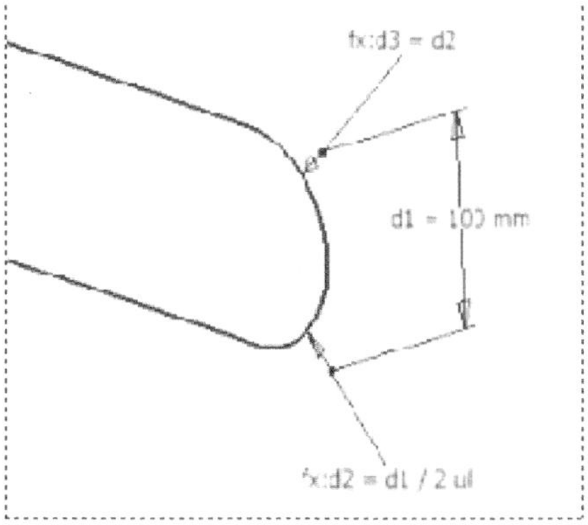

Bends in 3D Sketches

Toggle off automatic bend placement when you create a 3D sketch for a rigid pipe route. You can add individual bends at sketch points where a custom pipe bend is required. A custom bend is automatically placed in the derived route at each radius in the 3D sketch. Use dimensions on the 3D sketch to control segment lengths and angles between adjacent segments.

Route Violations

When you initially derive a route from a 3D sketch, each route segment is compared to the minimum and maximum length rules of the active style. Any violations display in the Show Violations dialog box. Click any listed violation to select the segment in the graphics window. You can either cancel creation of the route or accept the route and edit the base sketch or active style to eliminate the violations.

If you accept the route, the route icon in the browser indicates that the derived route includes segments that violate the current style. To reopen the Show Violations dialog box, right-click on the route node in the browser and click Show Violations.

Other 3D sketch problems might either not be reported or might cause the derived route to fail. Adjacent lines that are not connected with a bend can violate the elbow requirements of the active pipe style. This problem is not identified when you derive the route. When you populate the route, the two pipe sections are not joined with a fitting. If you select three line segments in the sketch that share an endpoint, the derived route succeeds but you must add a tee or other fitting and trim or extend the conduit segments with the Trim or Extend Pipe tool to engage the fitting.

Access

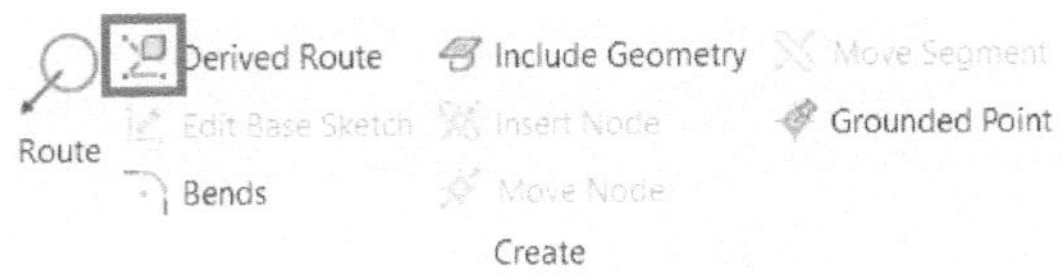

Ribbon: Route tab>Create panel

The Tube and Pipe Derived Route command uses a property palette UI.

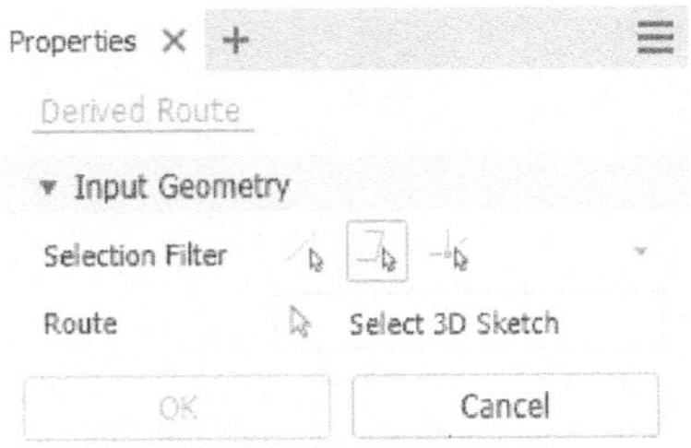

3D Entity Selection

After you start the Derived Route tool, you select the 3D geometry to derive from using one of three selection options. You change which selection option to use by right-clicking in the graphics window and clicking the option in the shortcut menu or by selecting one of the Selection Filters under Input Geometry in the Derived Route palette. The selection options are:

Option	Description
Single	Select individual line or arc segments.
Chain	Select a continuous set of line and arc segments connected to the selected entity. Selection stops at intersections of three or more valid entities.
Whole Sketch	Select all line and arc entities in the 3D sketch.

The following image shows the three options for entity selection in a 3D sketch.

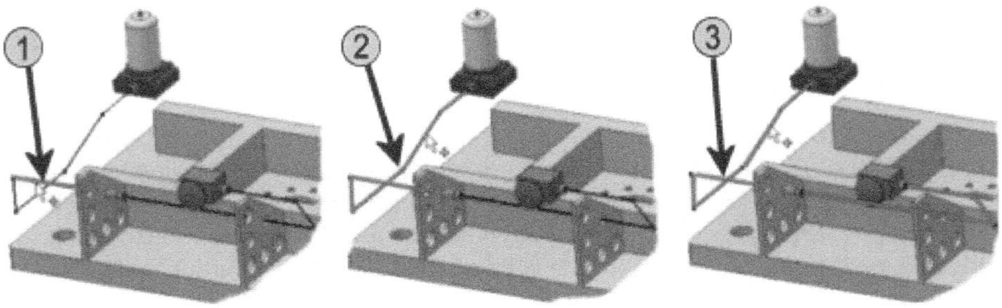

1 Single selection

2 Chain selection

3 Whole sketch selection

Procedure: Creating a Derived Route

The following steps give an overview of deriving a rigid pipe or tube route from a 3D sketch.

1. Create a new run in the Tube & Pipe Runs subassembly or edit an existing run.
2. Start the Derived Route tool.
3. Use the required selection method to select the lines and arcs you want to derive from a single 3D sketch.

> If the 3D sketch includes a few segments that are not required in the route, select a chain or the whole route. Switch to Single selection mode, press SHIFT, and click entities to remove them from the selection.

Defining Gravity for a Self-Draining Route

In order for a tube and pipe run to be self-draining, gravity must be set and defined in your design.

Defining Gravity

Gravity is an option in the Tube and Pipe tab, in the Run panel. When a self-draining tube and pipe style is made active, Inventor does not create any routes until gravity is assigned.

To enable and define gravity, you activate the Tube & Pipe Runs assembly and then access the Define Gravity tool in the Tube and Pipe tab, in the Run panel. After selecting the Define Gravity tool, you select a face or an axis in the assembly. The gravity vector is previewed in the graphics area. If required, the vector direction can be reversed.

In the following image, the direction of gravity is defined for a pipe run.

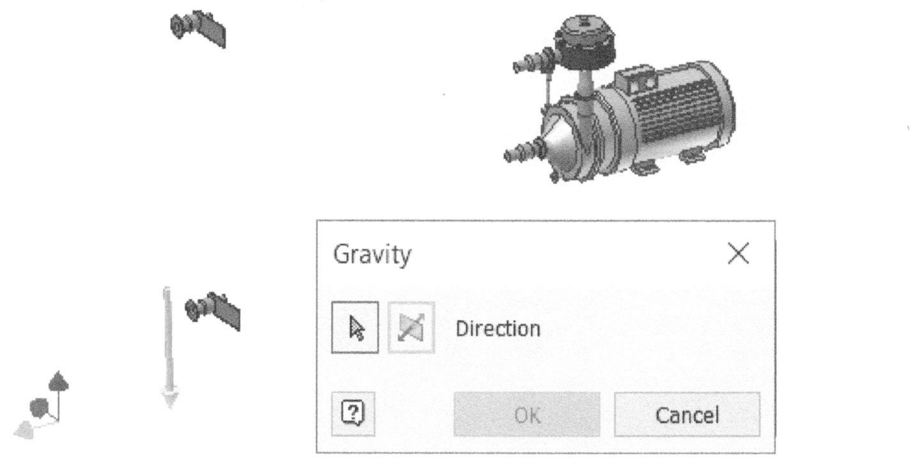

Access

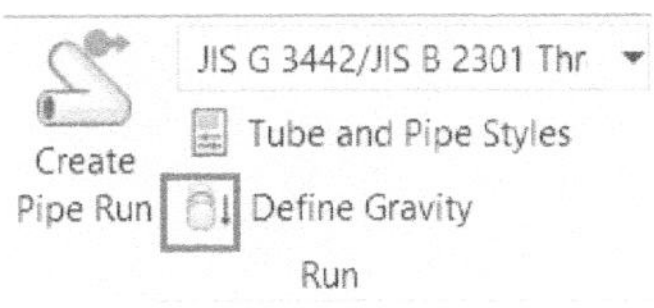

Ribbon: Tube and Pipe tab>Run panel

Procedure: Defining Gravity for a Self-Draining Route

The following steps give an overview of defining the direction of gravity for a self-draining route.

1. Double-click on the Tube & Pipe Runs subassembly in the assembly browser to activate the Tube and Pipe tab in the ribbon.
2. Start the Define Gravity tool.
3. Select an axis, linear edge, circular edge, or a cylindrical or planar face to set the vector direction.
4. Accept the vector direction. If required, reverse the vector direction before clicking OK.

> Gravity defined in Tube and Pipe is separate from the gravity definition in Dynamic Simulation and Stress Analysis.

Exercise: Create a Simple Route

In this exercise, you will create a simple pipe route using autorouting, cycle through route solution options, and select a solution option.

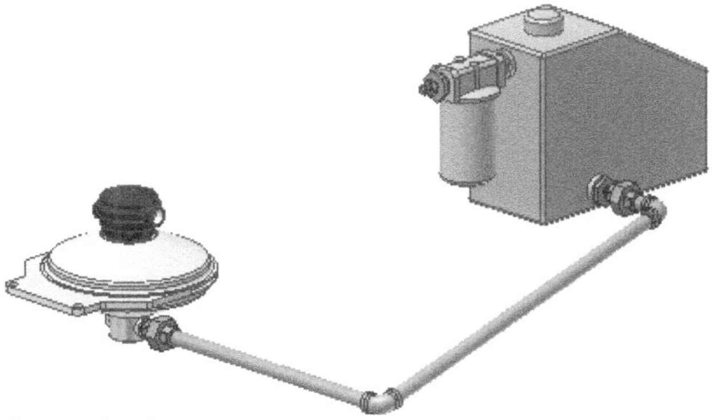

The completed exercise

1. Open *Simple Route.iam*.

2. In the browser, expand the Tube & Pipe Runs subassembly. Double-click on Run01.

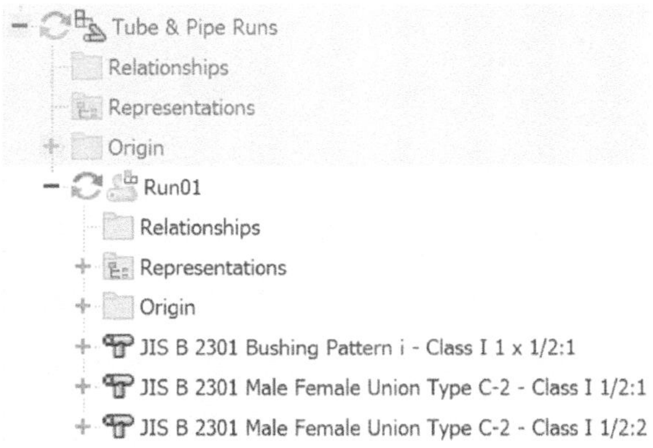

3. In the Pipe Run tab, in the Manage panel, select JIS G 3442/JIS B 2301 Threaded Steel Pipe and Iron Fittings from the Styles list.

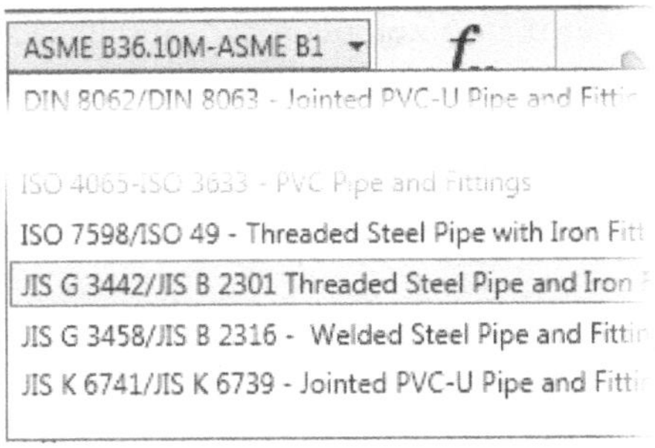

4. In the Pipe Run tab, in the Route panel, click New Route. Click OK to accept the default route name (Simple Route.Route01) and file location.

5. To begin creating a new rigid route, in the Route tab, in the Create panel, click Route.

6. To set the start point:
   - Move the cursor over the union connected to the tank to have the open connection point highlight.
   - Click to place a node at the connection point.

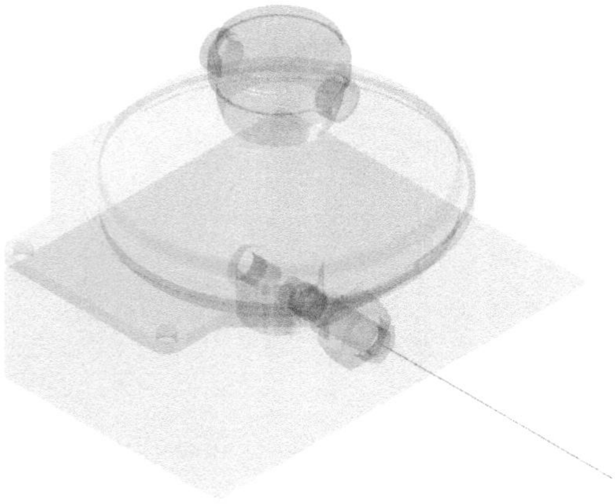

7. To set the endpoint:

- Move the cursor over the union connected to the pump.
- When the connection arrow is shown, click to place the end node.

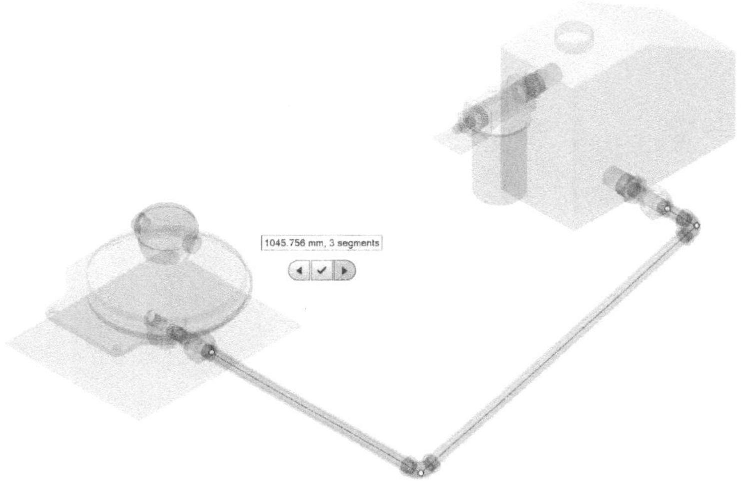

8. To cycle through the route solutions, click an arrow in the Select Other tool or you can also pick the options under Alternatives drop down list in the Input Geometry section of the Route Properties palette.

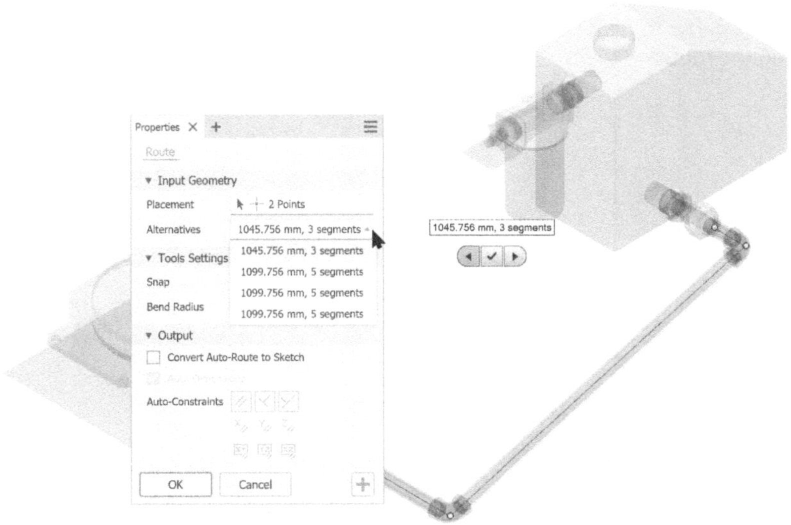

9. When the route with three segments displays, click the checkmark in the center of the Select Other tool to accept it.

10. In the graphics window, right-click on one of the route segments. Click Alternate Route Solution.

11. Use the Select Other tool to cycle through the alternate route solutions.

    Additional alternate solutions are previewed. In addition, the alternate route solution is shown along with the current route for comparison.

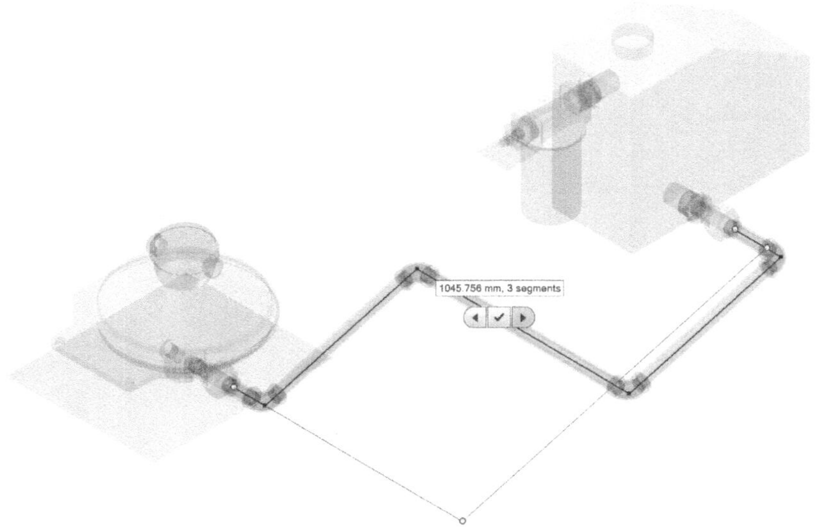

12. When the route with three segments is shown, click the checkmark in the center of the Select Other tool.

13. Right-click in the graphics window. Click Finish Edit. Alternatively, click Finish Route in the Route tab. The route is populated automatically, and pipe segments and elbows are added along the route.

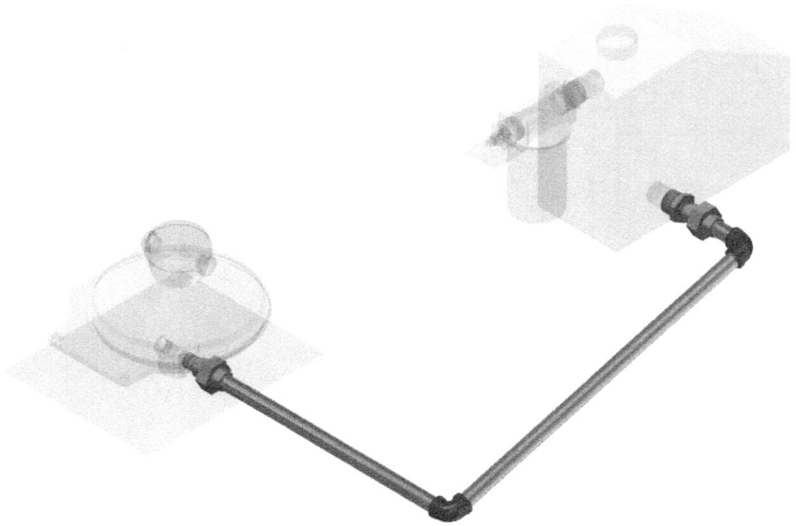

14. Close all files without saving changes.

Lesson: Sketching Rigid Routes

Overview

This lesson describes the tools and techniques for sketching new rigid tube or pipe routes.

A rigid tubing or piping route is typically a mixed set of autoroute regions and sketched route segments. Sketched route segments are manually created so that they are the size, location, and direction that you require. As you create a sketched route, you use the 3D ORTHOgonal Route tool and its options to ensure the sketched route meets your requirements. To create rigid routes that meet your requirements, you need to know how to use the sketching tools and techniques.

The following image shows a number of tube routes at a control panel.

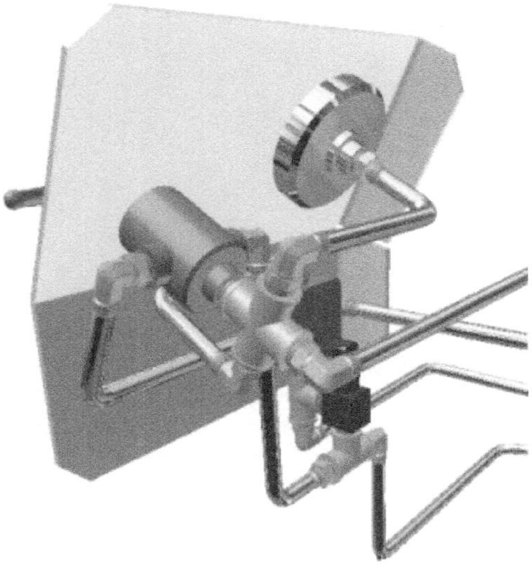

Objectives

After completing this lesson, you will be able to:

- Explain when the 3D ORTHOgonal Route tool is accessible and what it is used for.
- Place intermediate points along an axis of the 3D ORTHOgonal Route tool.
- Explain how to create a rigid route with bends for 45-degree pipe fittings, or bends in any angle for tubes or pipes.
- Add a bend with a custom radius to a pipe or tube route.
- Use Point Snap and Rotation Snap to precisely locate node points for a rigid route.
- Set an axis of the 3D ORTHOgonal Route tool parallel or perpendicular to model geometry.
- State the use of construction lines in a route, and how you initiate the creation of a construction line.

3D ORTHOgonal Route Tool

With the 3D ORTHOgonal Route tool, you can create or reposition points in a rigid route, or place nodes for flexible hose routes. The tool also serves to place or reposition fittings. You can also use the tool to create construction lines in the parametric regions during forward route creation or later edits. To efficiently use the 3D ORTHOgonal Route tool when sketching a rigid route, you must understand when it is accessed and its options for use.

The following image shows the 3D ORTHOgonal Route tool.

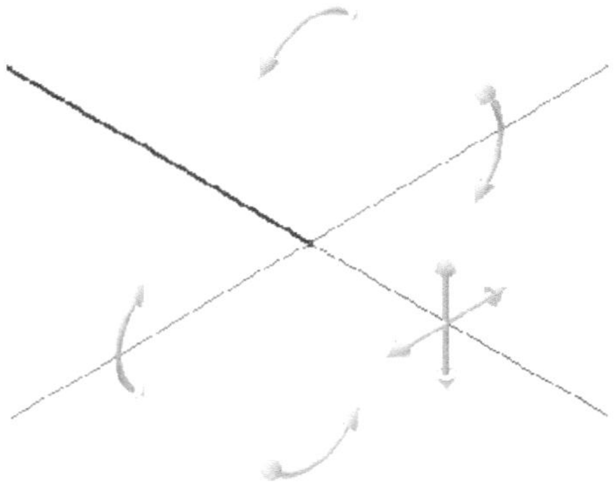

3D ORTHOgonal Route Tool Access and Options

The 3D ORTHOgonal Route tool displays when you create and edit route points in rigid routes, or place nodes for flexible hose routes that do not contain start or end fittings. It is also activated when you place or reposition fittings, unless the placement is fully defined by the connection data. When you are creating a route, the display and controls in the 3D ORTHOgonal Route tool depend on the active tube or pipe style, and whether the start point has been specified or the active node is at the end of a route segment. The initial orientation of the axes is based on the axes orientation for the active route point. Only the extender axis displays when the active node is the starting node for the route.

In the following image, on the left, because the route consists only of a start point, only the line extender axis of the 3D ORTHOgonal Route tool displays. After a second node has been created, the 3D ORTHOgonal Route tool displays all of the axes and additional handles, as seen on the right. The handles that display depend on whether the active style is for tubes or pipes.

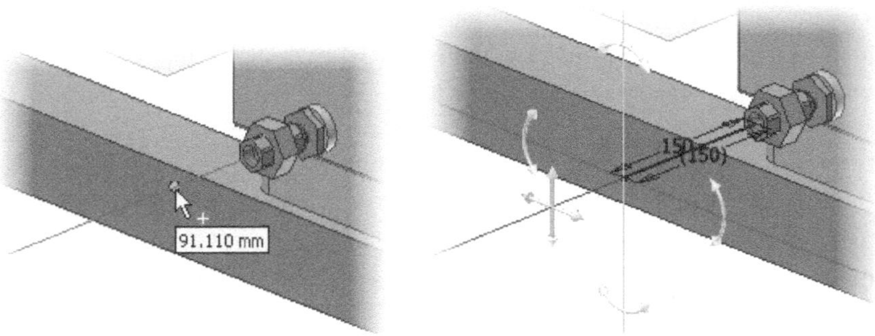

When the tool is active, depending on the active style and which node in the route was just created, tasks you can accomplish include:

- Adding a route node along a direction axis or line extender.
- Rotating the direction of the axes.
- Aligning an axis to model geometry.
- Snapping to intersection locations between an axis and other model geometry.
- Setting a radius for a bend.
- Toggling on and off the automatic dimensioning of created route segments.

Parts of the 3D ORTHOgonal Tool

The following image shows two different display configurations of the 3D ORTHOgonal Route tool. The 3D ORTHOgonal Route tool shown on the left is for rigid pipe routes. The route angle control handle is absent if the active style does not include 45° elbows. The 3D ORTHOgonal Route tool on the right shows the unique tube route handles on the 3D ORTHOgonal Route tool. The tool also displays in this manner for rigid pipes when a custom angle has been entered.

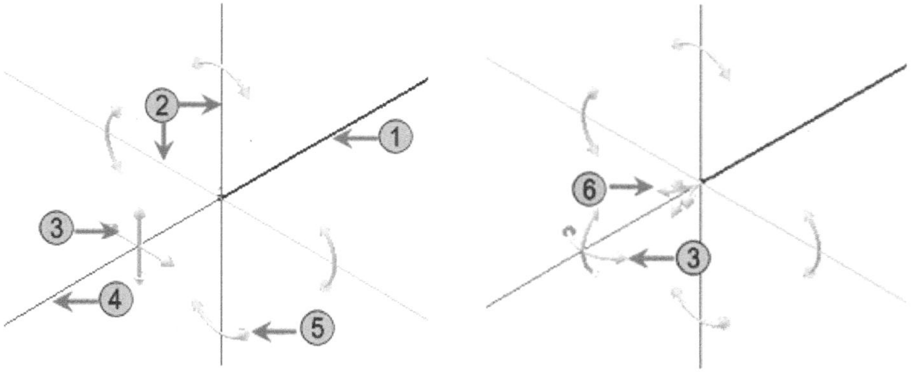

1 **Existing Route Segment** - The last created segment of the route or the segment associated with the node where the route extends.

2 **Direction Axes** - The Y and Z axes.

3 **Angle Control Handles** - Use to set the angle of the line extender axis relative to the existing route segment. Straight arrow increments the angle every 45°. Arcing arrows enable any angle.

4 **Line Extender Axis** - The axis extending from the node away from the last segment. Initially colinear to the existing route segment.

5 **Rotation Handles** - Use to rotate the tool around the line extender a dynamic amount or enter an exact angle.

6 **Radius Handles** - Displayed when creating a tube route or a pipe route with a custom bend. Use to set the radius of the bend.

The colors of the axes correspond to the colors of the 3D Indicator for assembly and part models. Having the axes display in different colors helps you identify which axis is which. This is especially helpful if you rotate the axes.

- Red is the X axis.
- Green is the Y axis.
- Blue is the Z axis.

> Use the + and - keys to enlarge or reduce the size of the 3D ORTHOgonal Route tool.

Self-Draining Angle

The 3D ORTHOgonal Route tool provides dynamic support for self-draining lines. As you create a route for a self-draining route, the Z axis automatically adjusts to include the slope as defined in the style. Clicking the rotation arrows flips the direction of the slope of the axis. The vertical axis of the Routing tool is always parallel to the gravity vector. The route that is created reflects the current self-draining style's custom elbow angle.

In the following image, two different viewing directions for the creation of a self-draining route are shown. On the left, the first segment in the route is created and the next point needs to be created. On the right, the Z directional axis has the defined slope for the style factored into it. Adding a point to this axis creates the route segment with the correct slope.

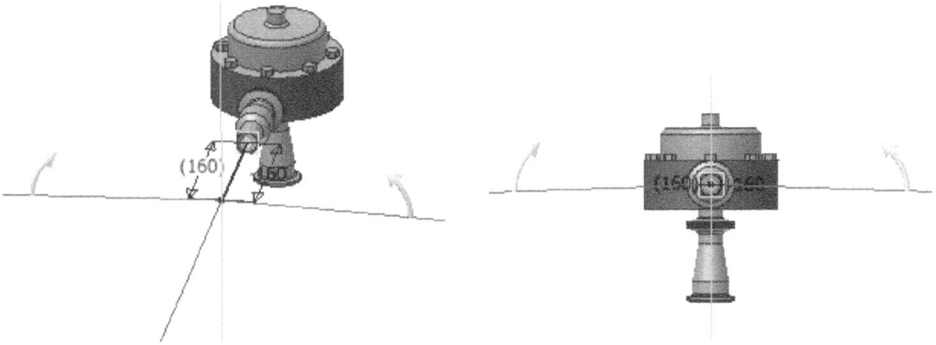

In the following image, a section of self-draining pipe is being dynamically edited.

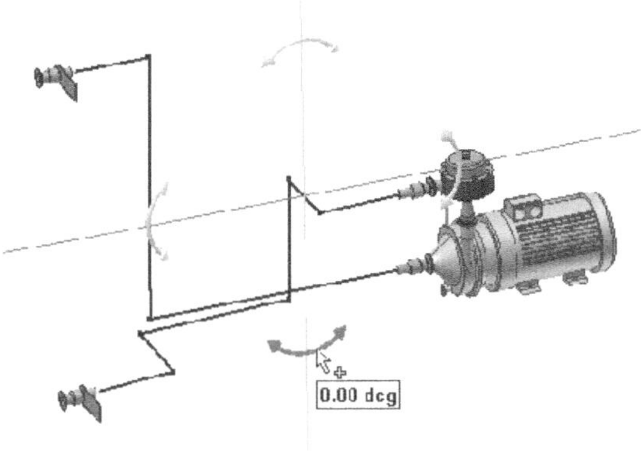

Placing Points Along An Axis

You can sketch a custom route path by creating points that are relative to the last route point and that fall along one of the axes on the 3D ORTHOgonal Route tool. You have two primary options for positioning a point along an axis, you can pick the point location or enter an exact distance. To create the route points along an axis of the 3D ORTHOgonal Route tool where required, you need to know your options and the procedure to follow.

The following image shows an example of entering in a precise distance to place the node on the axis.

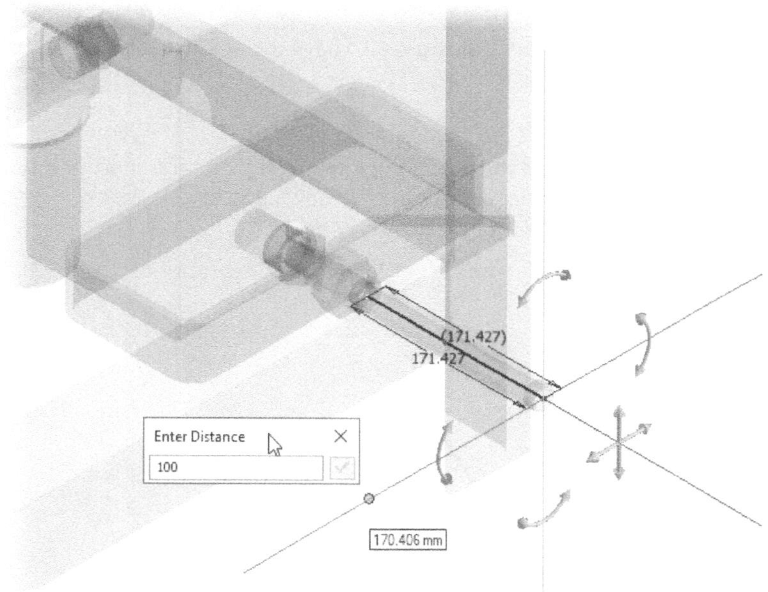

Procedure: Selecting a Point Along an Axis

The following steps give an overview of creating a point in a route by selecting a point along an axis of the 3D ORTHOgonal Route tool.

1. When the 3D ORTHOgonal Route tool is displaying all three axes or just the extender axis, hover the cursor over the axis you want to create a point along.
2. Move the cursor along the axis until the green dot displays in the required location. If the axis does not extend out as far as you need it, press + to increase the display of the 3D ORTHOgonal tool.
3. Click to create the point at the previewed location.

Create a Point a Precise Distance

When the 3D ORTHOgonal Route tool is active, you can create a point at a precise distance from the last point and along an axis of the tool. You have two options for initiating the entry of the distance value. You can either hover the cursor over the appropriate axis and then enter the distance value, or you right-click on the axis, click Enter Distance, and then enter the distance value. After entering the distance, you can accept the value displayed in the Enter Distance dialog box and the point is created.

Procedure: Placing Points a Precise Distance

The following steps give an overview of placing a point at a precise distance from the current point in the route.

1. When the 3D ORTHOgonal Route tool is displaying all three axes or just the extender axis, hover the cursor over the axis you want to create a point along.
2. Enter distance value to activate the Enter Distance dialog box with that value displayed. You also can right-click on the axis, click Enter Distance, and then enter the value in the Enter Distance dialog box.
3. Accept the value in the Enter Distance dialog box to have the point created at that distance.

Valid Route Nodes

A blue dot opens at the cursor location if the resulting segment might be too short to support an elbow at its other end. Avoid placing nodes in this zone whenever possible. A green dot indicates that the indicated node location meets all rules of the active style.

The following image demonstrates the feedback for valid node locations.

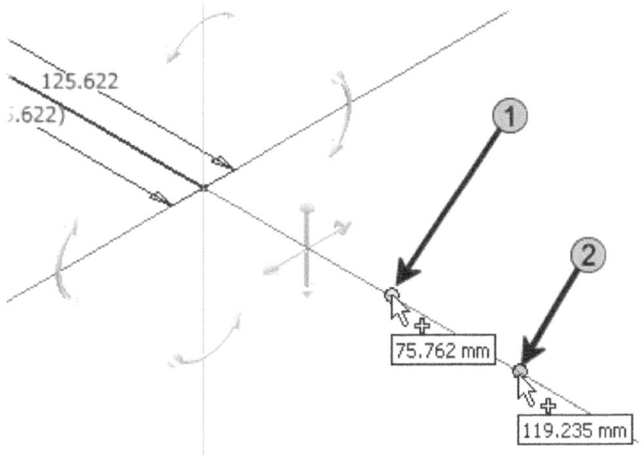

1 **Blue dot -** Node location might generate a segment that does not meet the minimum conduit segment length in the active style.

2 **Green dot -** Node location meets all rules for the active style.

> The length of a route segment is not the same as the length of the corresponding pipe segment in the populated route. The pipe segment length is less than the node- to-node distance to enable for fittings. Therefore, the minimum acceptable distance between route nodes is greater than the minimum segment length in the active style.

Creating Bends in Routes

When you are sketching a route and you place a point on the Y or Z 3D ORTHOgonal Route tool axis, a 90° bend is automatically added to the route. For pipe routes, a 90° fitting is added when the route is populated. For bent tubes, a 90° bend is created. In many designs that use rigid tubes, route bends or fittings are required that are at angles other than 90°. To create a design that meets these requirements, you must understand how to create a rigid route with bends for 45° pipe fittings, and bends in any angle for tubes or pipes.

In the following image, the same route was populated using a pipe style and a bent tubing style. The pipe style contains elbow fittings at each angle change of the route, while the tubing is bent to follow the direction of the route.

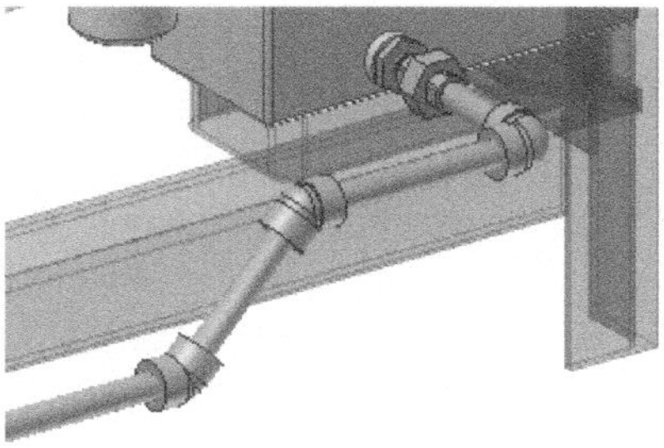

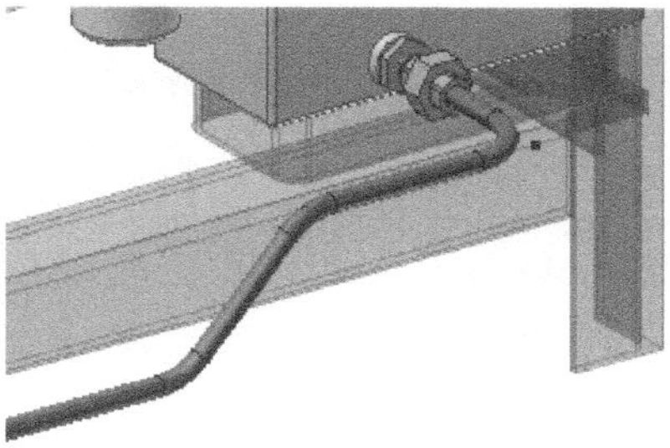

Bends in Routes

A bend in a route occurs when two connected route segments are not colinear. An angle can be measured between the segments where the bend occurs. The route angle handle on the 3D ORTHOgonal Route tool enables you to create a route with a bend by changing the angle from the extender axis. Using this handle, you can easily add a 45° bend in a pipe route that uses 45° elbow fittings or add a custom angle to a pipe or tube route. The custom angle can be any value greater than 0 and less than 180.

The following image identifies the two different states of the tool based on the style in use. Note the difference in the two angle handles.

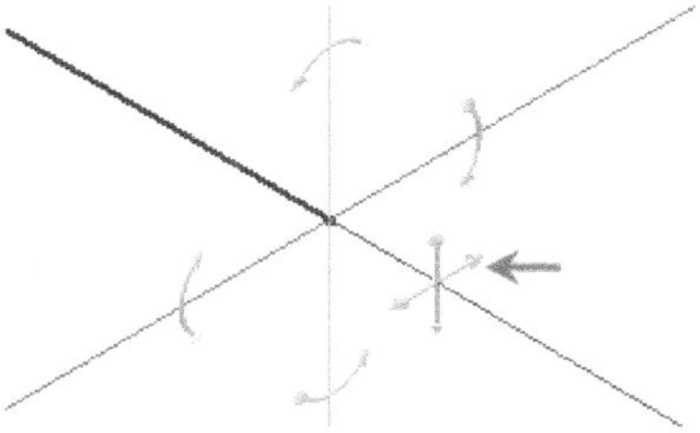

Rigid Pipe Style

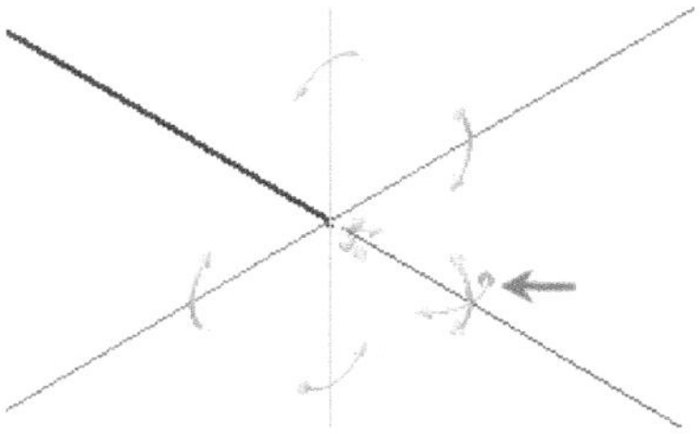

Rigid Tube Style

When you are creating a route for a rigid pipe, you add a 45° angle to the route by clicking the angle handle arrow that points in the direction you want to angle the route toward. To add a custom bend to a tube route, you either click and drag the arrow handle to the required angle or enter a specific angle value. You add a custom bend to a pipe route in the same manner as a tube route after right-clicking in the graphics window and then selecting Custom Bend. Clicking Custom Bend switches the 3D ORTHOgonal Route tool to have the angle handles and radius handles that are used for bent tubing routes.

When you create a custom bend angle by dragging the angle handle on the 3D ORTHOgonal Route tool, the angle the handle increments is based on the 3D Angle Snap setting. You set this increment value in the current document in the Document Settings dialog box, Modeling tab, Angle Snap field.

After you have set the angle of the 3D ORTHOgonal Route tool, to create a segment at that angle with a bend to the previous segment, you must place a point on an axis.

The default minimum segment length for a tubing style is 0 document units, so that the straight line segment between two bends can be consumed. You can use this behavior to place two 90° bends together to create a 180° bend.

> Create a compound bend in a route by using the rotation handles to rotate the 3D ORTHOgonal Route tool about the extender axis, and then use the angle handle to change the direction of the extender axis.

Angling the Route Direction for 45° Pipe Elbows

If a pipe style definition includes 45° elbows, the angle control handles are visible on the 3D ORTHOgonal Route tool. To rotate the line extender 45° from the previous route segment, click one of the angle control arrows.

The following image shows the creation of the second segment in the route. The second segment is angled down 45° relative to the first segment.

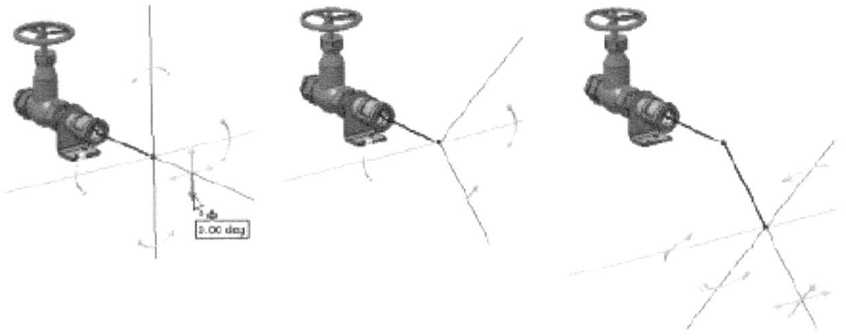

In the following image, the same route is shown before and after populating with fittings and pipe segments. This route includes both 90° and 45° fittings.

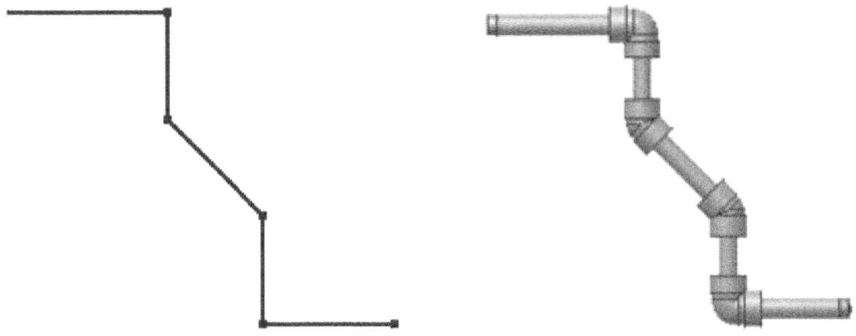

Procedure: Angling Routes for Pipe Elbows

The following steps give an overview of rotating the 3D ORTHOgonal Route line extender 45° to change the route direction and permit for the population of a 45° elbow fitting.

1. With the 3D ORTHOgonal Route tool active, click and drag the route angle handle arrow to rotate the line extender in that direction.

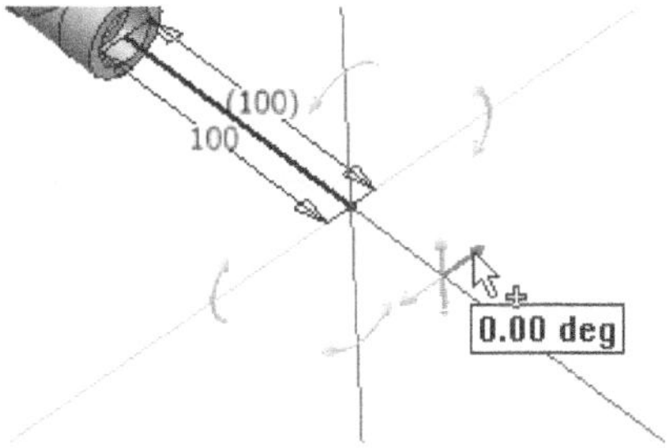

2. Place a point on a 3D ORTHOgonal Route axis an approximate or exact distance.

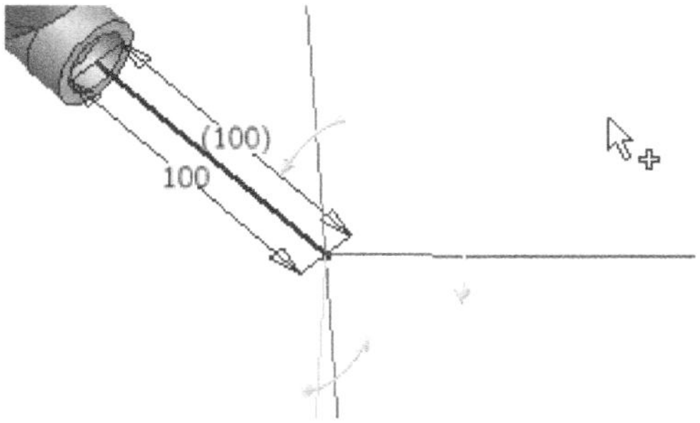

Angling the Route Direction for Custom Pipe Elbows

A custom angled elbow can be added to a rigid pipe run.

When a style with custom elbows is activated, select the Custom Elbows option in the Route dialog box and use either the curved arrow manipulators or type a value to angle the elbow relative to the current position.

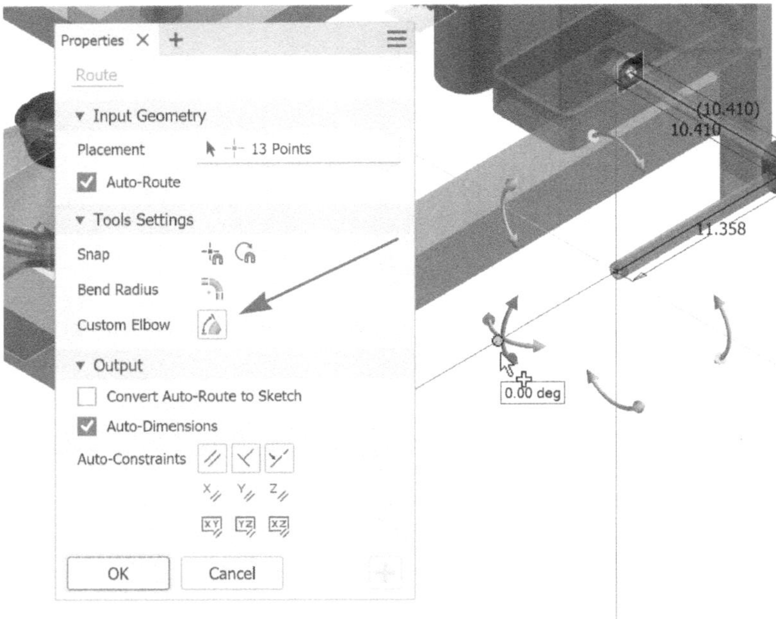

When dragged to 45° or 90°, the route is populated with a rigid elbow. The rigid elbow is placed as a **Standard** part.

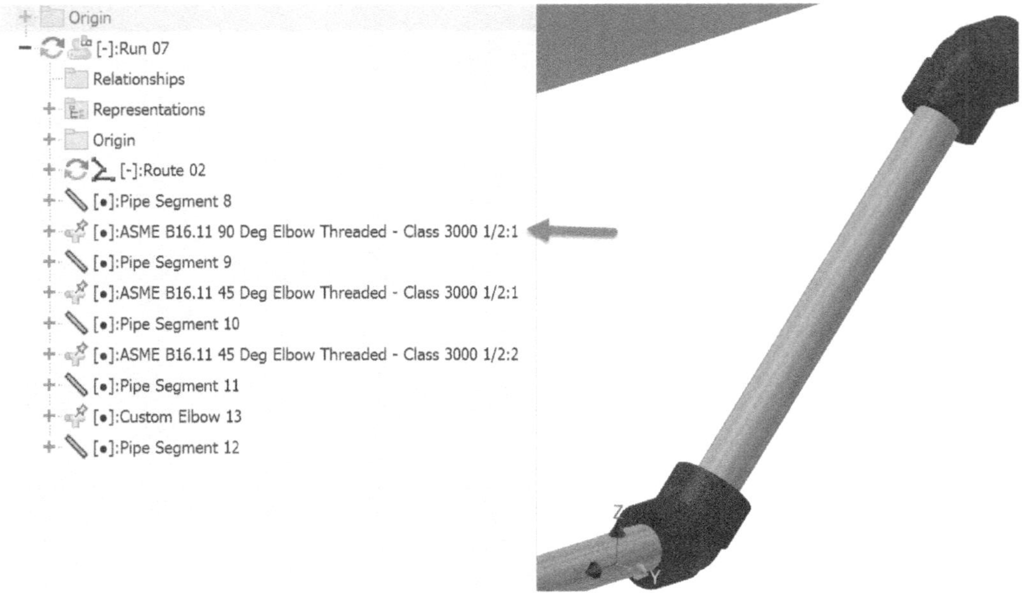

When dragged to other than 45° or 90° degrees, the route is populated with a custom elbow. The custom elbow is placed as a **Custom** part.

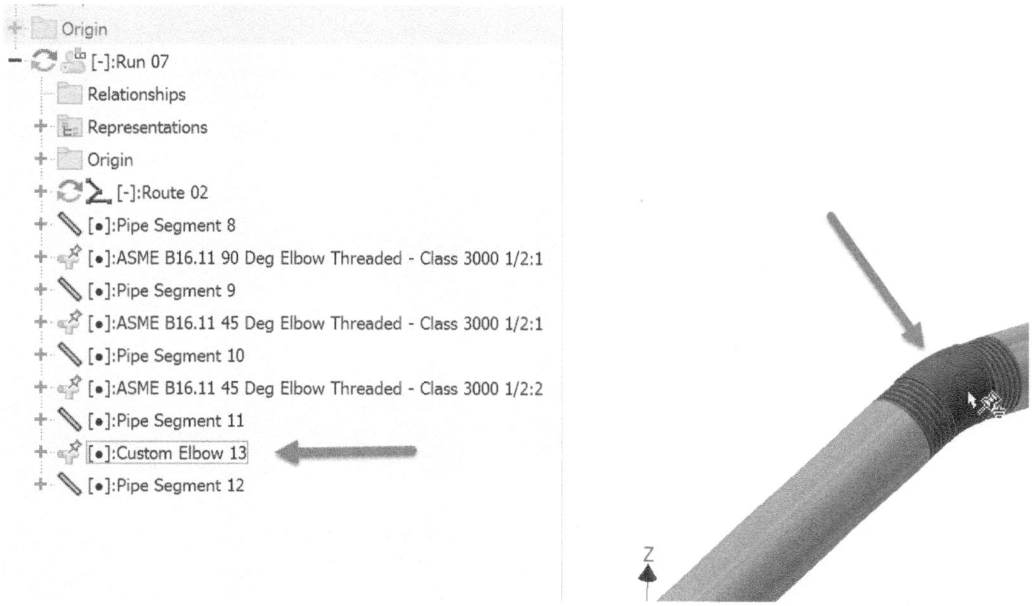

Angling the Route to Create Bends in Tube Routes

When you are creating a route for bent tubing, you can add bends ranging from small angles to large angles and even compound bends. The procedure for creating bends with small to large angles is the same. You change the angle and then add a point along an axis. To create compound bends, not only do you change the angle the extender axis points from the last node, you also rotate the 3D ORTHOgonal Route tool around the extender axis.

In the following image, a route for bent tubing is being created that has a bend with an angle greater than 90°. Based on the current axes alignment, placing a point on the extender axis creates a compound angle from this last node.

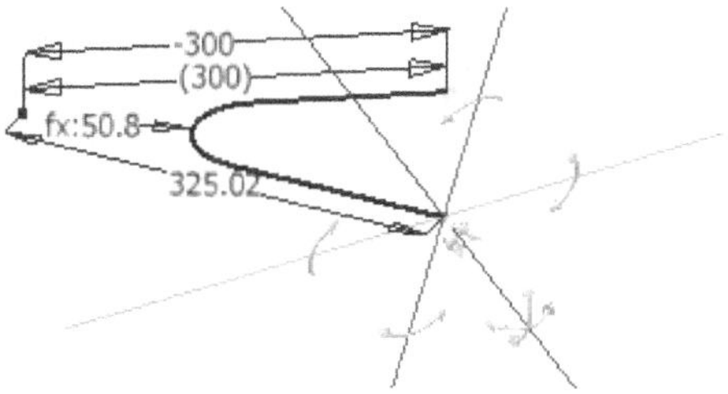

Procedure: Angling Routes for Tube Bends

The following steps give an overview of creating a bend in a route for bent tubing by angling the route axes.

1. With the 3D ORTHOgonal Route tool active, set the angle direction and distance by clicking and dragging the route angle handle until the extender axis aligns as required. Or, hover the cursor over the angle handle arrow that points in the direction you want to rotate toward and then enter the angle value.

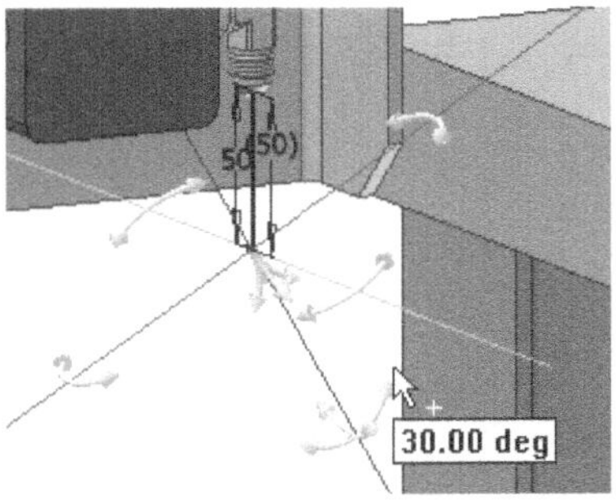

2. Place a point along one of the axes by selecting a location or entering a specific distance.

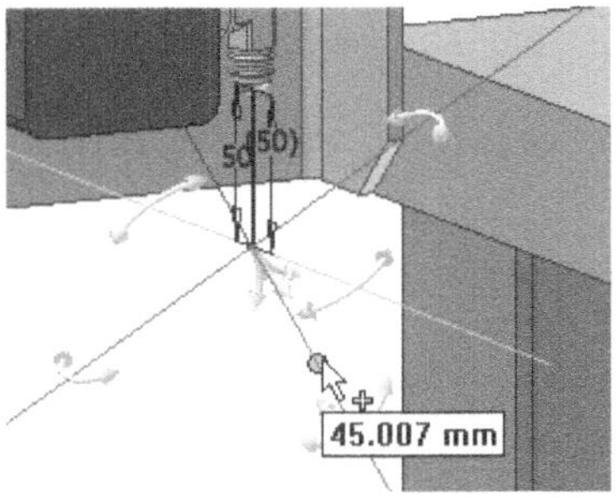

Procedure: Creating a 180° Bend

The following steps give an overview of combining two 90° bends to create a 180° bend in a rigid tube route.

1. Place a node on one of the direction axes. Enter a precise distance that is twice the distance of the default bend radius.

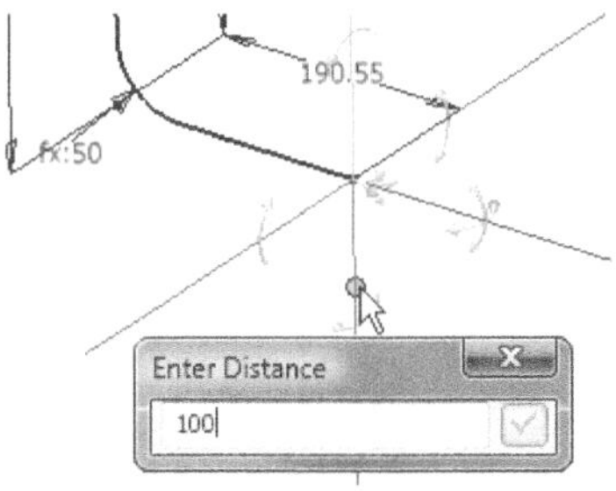

2. Place a second node along the axis parallel to the segment adjacent to the just-completed bend. The new bend consumes the segment between the two bends and generates a 180° sweep consisting of two 90° bends.

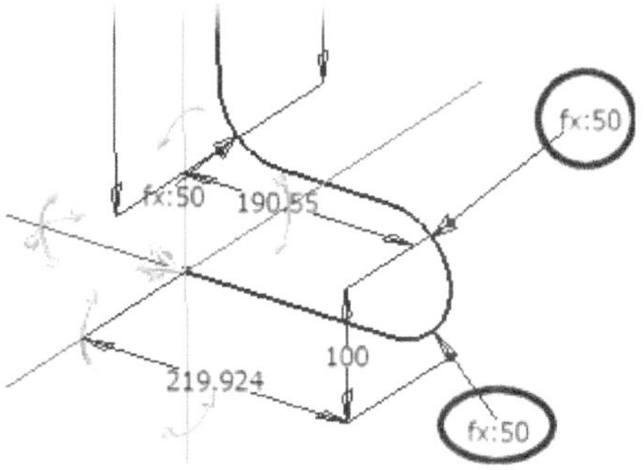

> If you later edit the route and move a node or segment that affects the position of one or both of the bends, the continuous 180° sweep might be disrupted. You might need to make additional edits to recover the continuous bend.

Custom Bends in a Rigid Pipe Run

You can add a custom bend to a pipe route other than the 45° and 90° elbows associated with rigid pipe styles. With the 3D ORTHOgonal Route tool active, right-click on and click Custom Bend to activate the angle and radius handles in the 3D ORTHOgonal Route tool. Set the required angle for the pipe in the same manner you do for bent tubing.

When you populate the route, the two adjacent segments in the run are combined into a single segment that includes the custom bend.

The following image shows a custom bend in a rigid pipe route and the resulting conduit segment in the populated route.

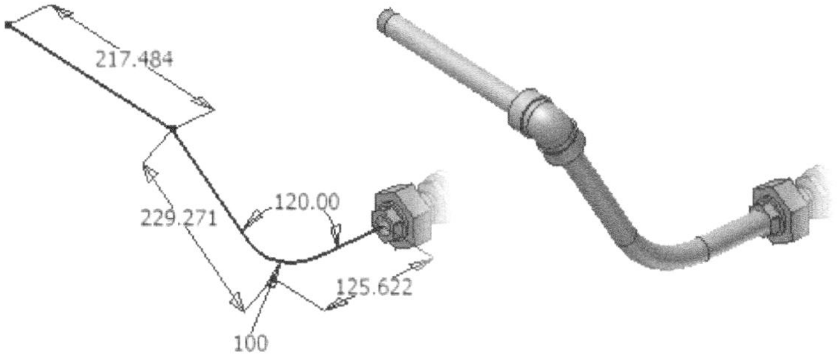

> A bend requires a certain length on the route segment. If the route is already populated or being populated, the system checks whether the remaining route segment conforms to the minimum segment length.

Adding a Custom Bend Radius

As you add bends to a route, a common radius value is applied to each bend. In some design situations, you might require the radius to be a different value from the default. To create a custom bend in a route for bent tubing or a rigid pipe, you need to learn how to add a bend with a custom radius.

The following image shows a route for bent tubing before and after populating it. This route consists of three bends. Two of the bends have dimensions with formulas that reference the default value, while the third bend is a larger custom value.

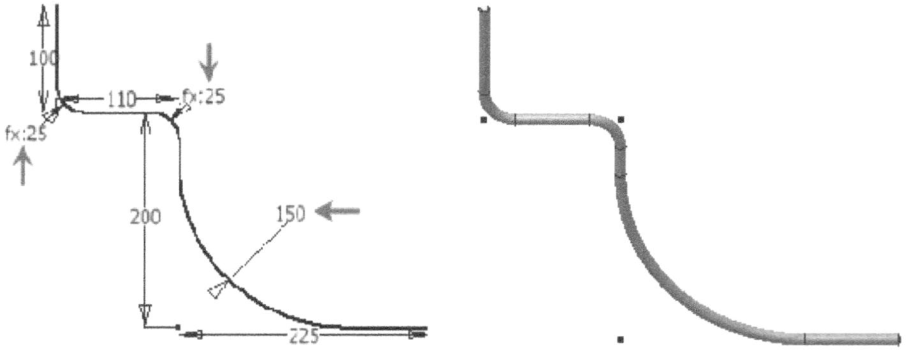

Default Bend Radius and Setting a Custom Radius

The active tube style specifies a default bend radius for the route. As you place nodes along the axes of the 3D ORTHOgonal Route tool, adjacent route segments are joined with a bend. A user parameter is added to the part with the default radius. You can override the value of the bend at the current node with the radius handles on the 3D ORTHOgonal Route tool. After you place the next point in the route and the bend with that custom radius is added, the radius value for the next bend returns to the default. In the following image, hovering over the radius handle on the 3D ORTHOgonal Route tool shows the default radius value. Clicking this handle displays the Enter Radius dialog box, where you can enter a custom radius value and override this default value.

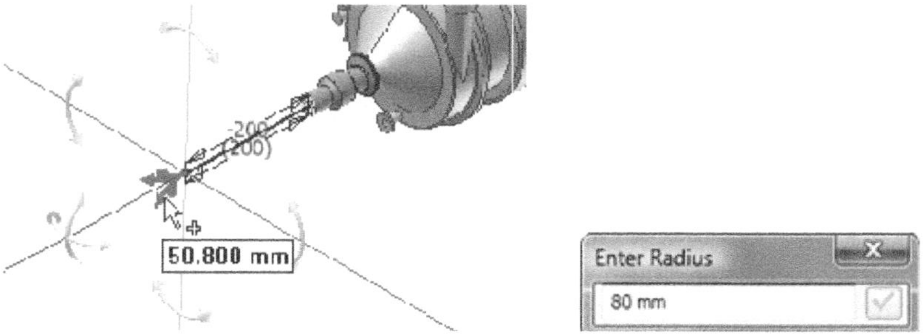

The following image shows a rigid tube route with a custom bend radius. The radius of the other bend is controlled by an equation linking it to the default bend radius for the active style.

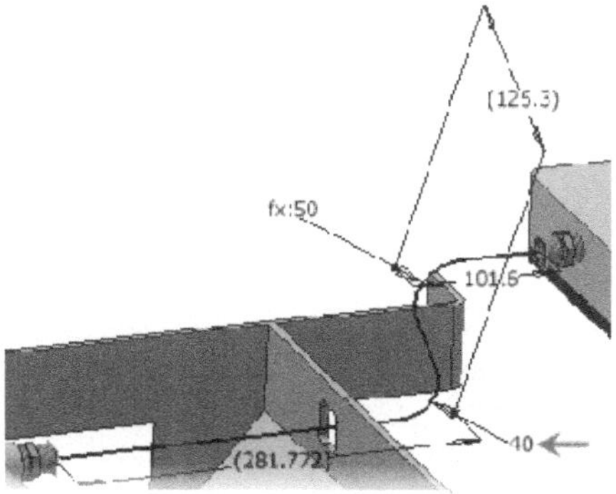

Another way to set a bend in a route to have a custom radius is by editing the sketch dimension after you create the bend.

Procedure: Adding a Custom Bend Radius

The following steps give an overview of adding a bend in a route with a custom bend radius.

1. With the 3D ORTHOgonal Route tool active, click the radius handle. In the Enter Radius dialog box, enter a custom radius value.

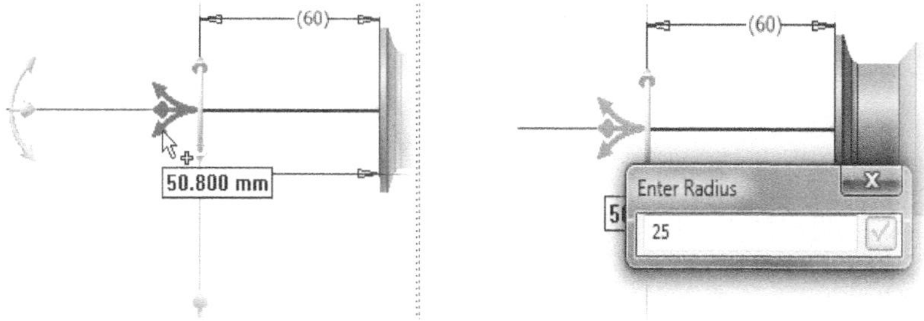

2. Place a point along one of the axes by picking a location or entering a specific distance.

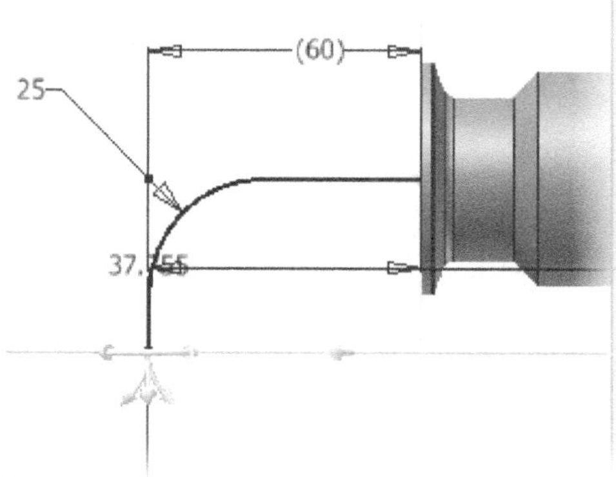

Snapping to Points and Rotations

When sketching a rigid route, you might often need to route directly to a set location or to align with an axis through an opening. To place a node at a precise location relative to existing geometry, or to align the axes of the 3D ORTHOgonal Route tool with geometry in the assembly, you need to know how to use the Point Snap and Rotation Snap options that are associated with the 3D ORTHOgonal Route tool.

In the following image, a route point is being defined at the location where the selected work plane intersects the axis of the 3D ORTHOgonal Route tool.

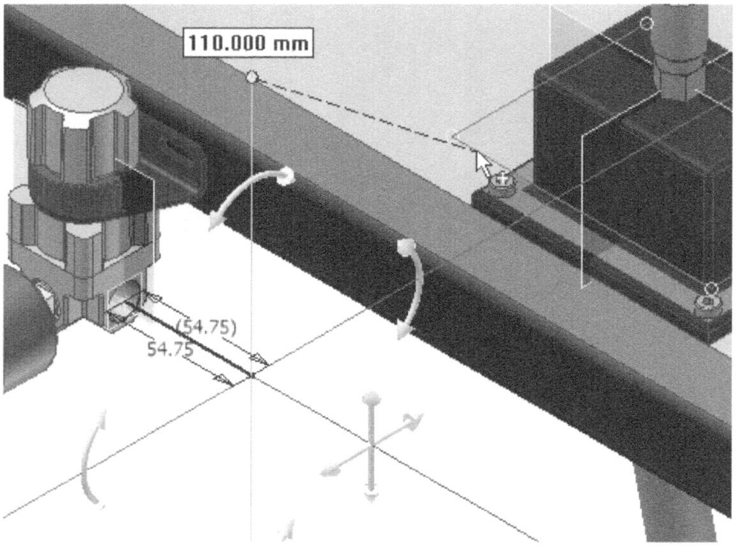

Point Snap

The Point Snap option for the 3D ORTHOgonal Route tool enables you to precisely locate points along the tool axes relative to planar faces and work planes. As you move the cursor over a planar part face or work plane, the intersection of the plane and one of the tool axes is previewed as the next route node. Click in the graphics window to create the node when the preview of the intersection point displays. Use Point Snap for accurate routing around components in an assembly.

The following image shows how the Point Snap option helps you position route nodes. On the left, a route node is previewed at the intersection of a selected face and the route axis. On the right, the route continues from the node generated at the intersection.

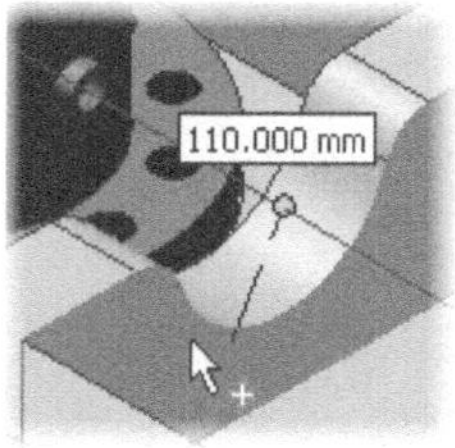

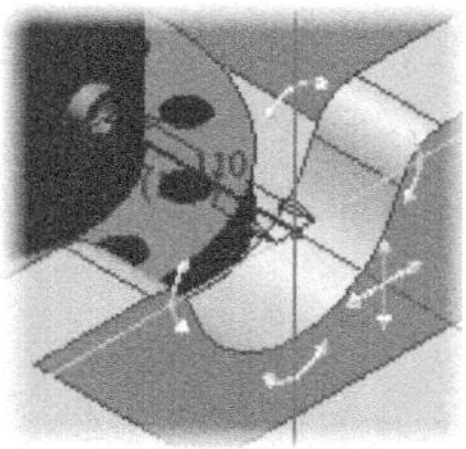

You can also specify a precise offset value along the axis from the intersection point. Both negative and positive offsets are permitted. A positive offset places the node farther along the axis from the previous node. A negative offset places the node closer to the previous node. To offset a distance from an intersection point, enter the offset distance when the preview of the intersecting point displays.

In the following image, the Point Snap previews the point at the intersection of the selected face and the route axis. The positive value of the entered offset results in a route node 50 mm beyond the intersection point.

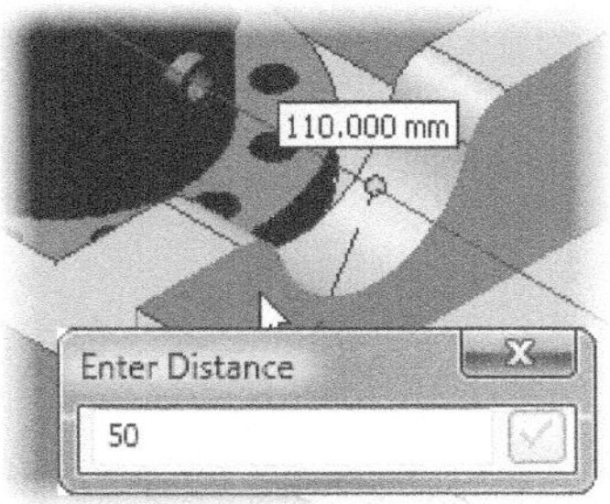

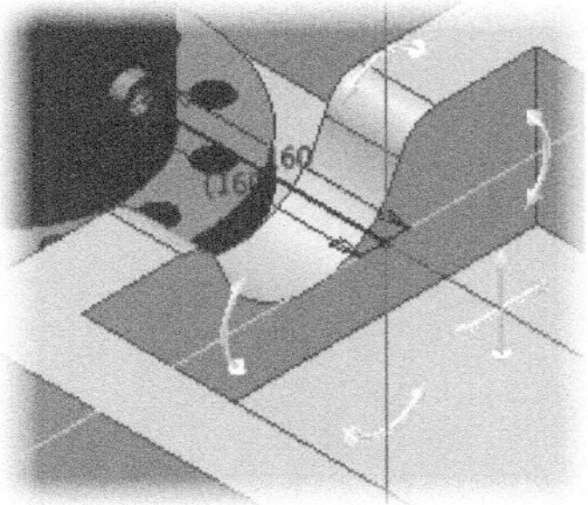

If the selected plane intersects more than one tool axis, you can right-click and click Select Other Snap to cycle through the projected intersections of the plane and the tool axes.

The following image shows how you can cycle through solutions when the selected face intersects two route axes on the 3D ORTHOgonal Route tool.

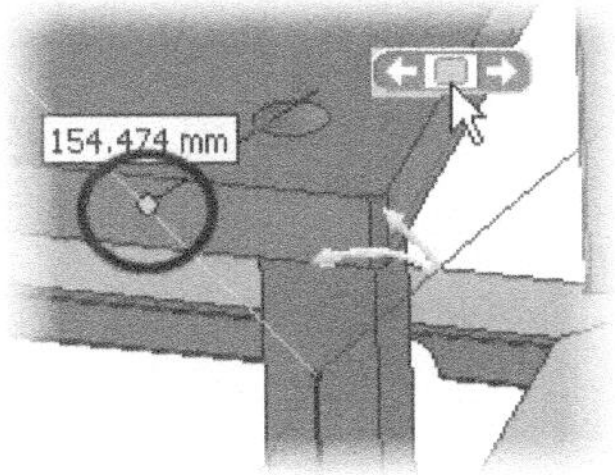

Rotation Snap

You use the Rotation Snap option to point one of the direction axes of the 3D ORTHOgonal Route tool to its intersection with a linear edge, route construction line, or axis. In a rigid pipe route you drag one of the angle handles, and as you move over geometry the direction axis snaps to the projection of the geometry. In addition to edges and axes, you can drag over fitting connections, circular part edges, vertices, and work points. The implied route axis from these points is used to define the rotation snap angle.

The Rotation Snap option can help you complete a route with a minimum number of segments. As you approach the endpoint of the route, you can use Rotation Snap to align one of the axes of the 3D ORTHOgonal Route tool with the implied axis from the fitting or circular edge.

In the following image, a direction axis is rotated and snaps to its implied intersection with the axis through a circular edge.

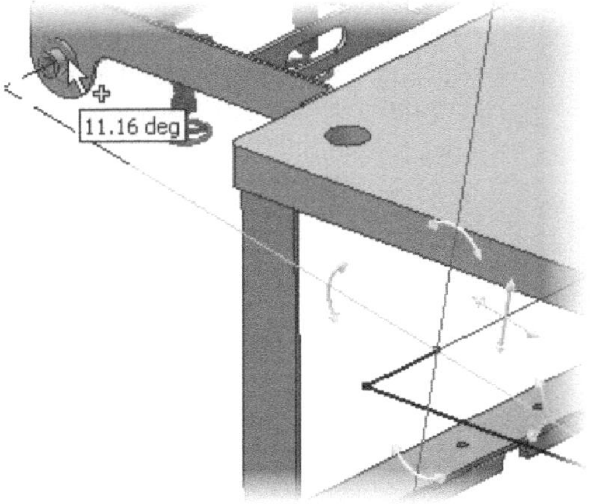

Use Rotation Snap to align routes with existing geometry such as clamps and bulkhead openings.

Accessing Point Snap and Rotation Snap

You toggle the options Point Snap and Rotation Snap on and off in the shortcut menu when you are actively creating a route and the 3D ORTHOgonal Route tool is displaying. A checkmark to the left of the option indicates the option is already on. After you have enabled the option, you can use it as required as you sketch the route. The option stays on for subsequent nodes until you toggle it off. Alternatively, you can select the options under Tools Settings in the Route palette.

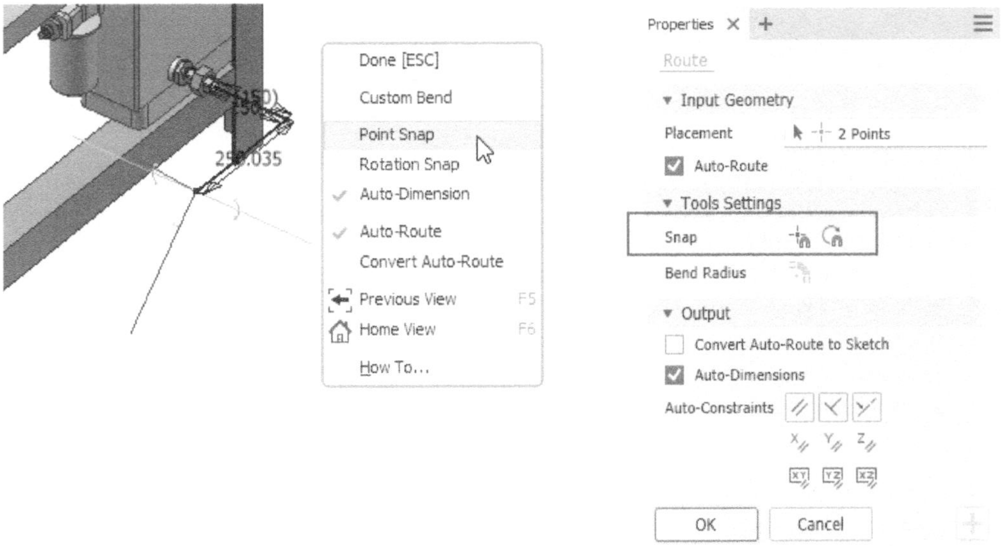

Procedure: Snapping to Points and Rotations

The following steps give an overview of using Point Snap and Rotation Snap to precisely locate node points during the creation of a rigid route.

1. While you are creating a route, right-click in the graphics window. In the shortcut menu, click Point Snap. A checkmark indicates that Point Snap is on. Use the same process to toggle on Rotation Snap.
2. With Rotation Snap selected, click and drag a rotation arrow on the 3D ORTHOgonal Route tool. Move the cursor over a circular edge along the route path. Release the mouse button when a dashed line indicates that the tool axis intersects the axis through the circular edge. Do not click the circular edge. If you click when the circular edge is highlighted, the route continues to the edge center point.

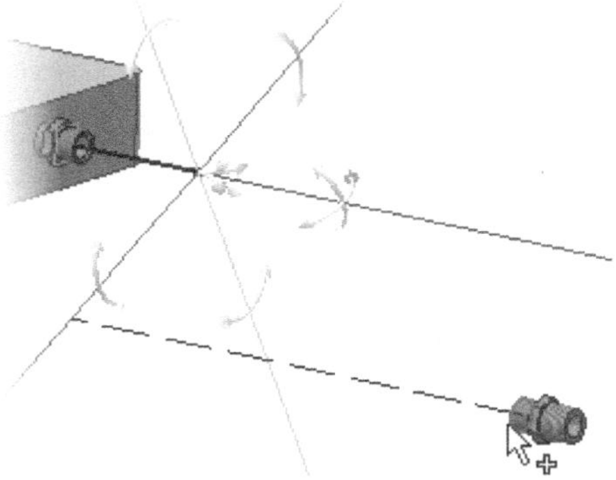

3. With Point Snap selected, right-click on the same circular edge and click Select Other Snap.

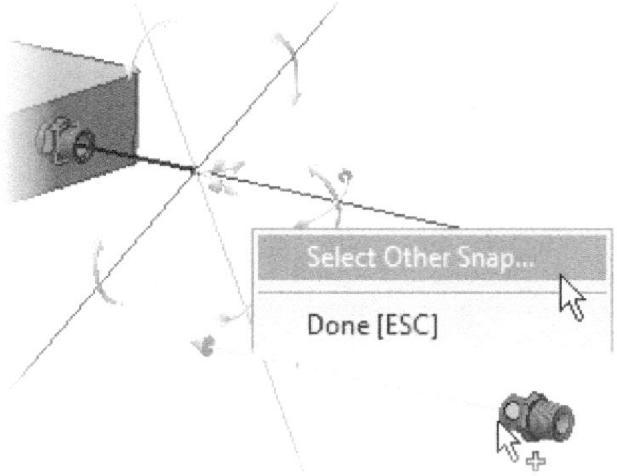

4. A dashed line and green dot preview the single node to be created. Click the checkmark on the Select Other tool to create the node.

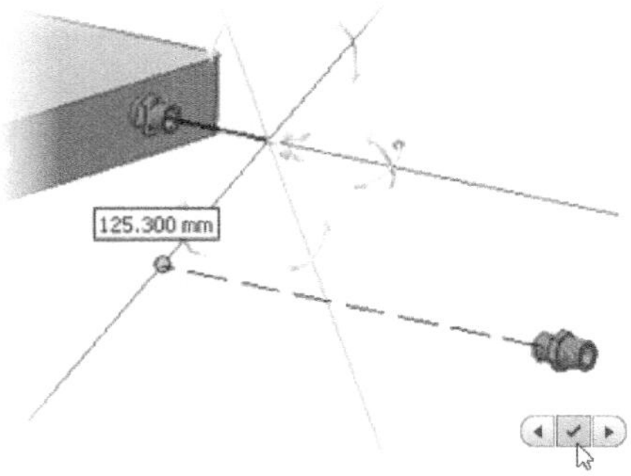

5. A single route segment is added, ending at the node. Note that one of the axes is now colinear with the axis through the circular edge.

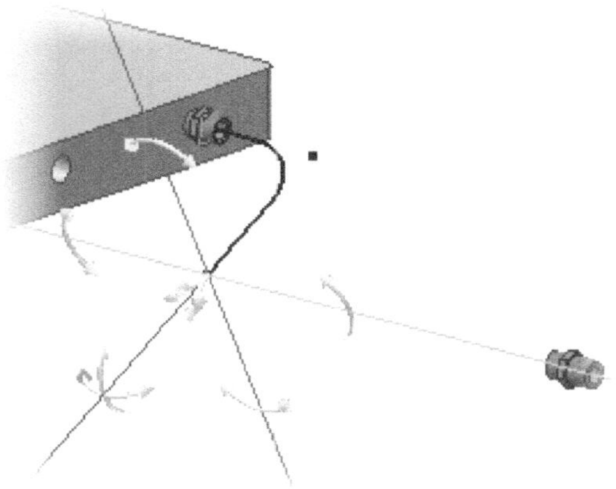

Using Point Snap or Rotation Snap to create route nodes does not create a relationship between the selected geometry and the node. To associate the node with the geometry, you can include the geometry in the route and then dimension or constrain the route node to the reference work plane.

Aligning the Axes

When the direction axes of the 3D ORTHOgonal Route tool do not align with the required geometry or your design, you can align them by using the rotation and angle handles to rotate around the extender axis and from the extender axis. There are some design situations where you need to align an axis of the 3D ORTHOgonal Route tool to be parallel to an edge or perpendicular to a face. In those situations, you need to know how to access and use the Parallel with Edge and Perpendicular to Face options.

In the following image, a 3D ORTHOgonal Route tool axis is shown being aligned parallel with a model edge. After aligning the axis and adding a point for the next segment, the edge of the model was automatically projected to the current route for future reference by that segment.

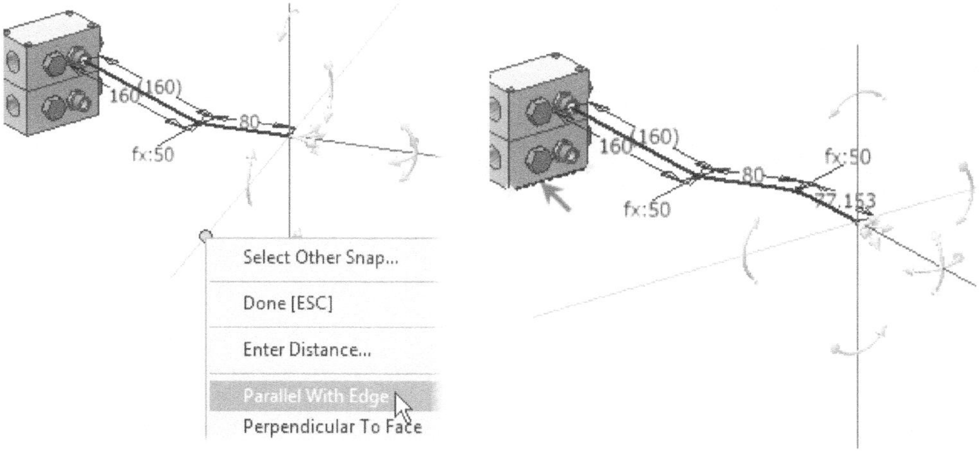

Rotating the Direction Axes

To rotate the tool around the line extender, click and drag one of the rotation arrows. As you drag, the axes snap in increments based on the 3D Angle Snap setting in the active document. To specify a precise angle, select a rotation arrow and begin to enter an angle value. The Enter Angle dialog box opens, and you can finish entering the angle value. The axes rotate in the direction of the selected arrowhead. You can also right-click on one of the rotation arrows and click Enter Angle to open the Enter Angle dialog box.

In the following image, to set the next point 90° right and 30° down from the last point, the alignment of the Z direction axis was rotated down 30° by dragging the rotation handle of the 3D ORTHOgonal Route tool.

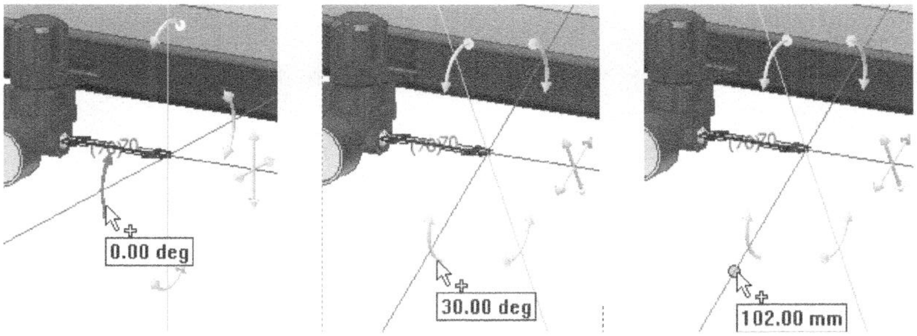

Align Route to Geometry

When you place a new node in a rigid pipe route, the 3D ORTHOgonal Route tool aligns with the previous route segment. If the segment is at an angle to other route segments or geometry, you often need to set the next segment so that it aligns with an edge or a face of an assembly component. You can realign the tool axes perpendicular to a planar face or work plane, or parallel with a linear edge or work axis. The selected geometry is automatically included in the route. If you complete a segment without reorienting the 3D ORTHOgonal Route tool, an appropriate perpendicular or parallel constraint is added between the new segment and the included geometry. You access the Parallel with Edge and Perpendicular to Face options in the shortcut menu after right-clicking on the 3D ORTHOgonal Route tool direction axis you want to set parallel or perpendicular to other geometry.

The following image shows the Y axis of the 3D ORTHOgonal Route tool aligned to be perpendicular to the selected face.

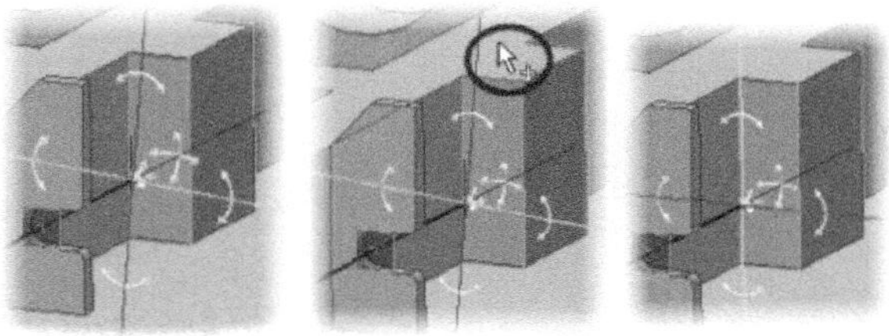

① ② ③

1. Route axes are not aligned to the part edges.

2. 3D ORTHOgonal Route tool realigned perpendicular to the top face of the bracing.

3. Realigned route axes.

> When the Parallel with Edge or Perpendicular to Face options are applied to reorient the axis, it might create an angle other than 45° or 90° to the preceding route point. If the route is for a rigid pipe, a custom bend is created, and the 3D ORTHOgonal Route tool changes to display the radius and angle handles for additional control.

Procedure: Aligning the Route to Geometry in the Assembly

The following steps give an overview of aligning the tool axes parallel with a linear edge.

1. Identify the axis to align and the geometry to align it.
2. Right-click on the axis to align. In the dialog box select the method to use: Parallel with Edge or Perpendicular to Face.
3. Select the geometry to align to. If you chose Perpendicular to Face, this can be a planar face or work plane. If you chose Parallel with Edge, this can be a linear edge or axis.
4. Review the results.
5. Continue placing points along the axis.

Construction Lines

Some of your tube or pipe route designs might require more complex positioning or control than just rotating or aligning the axes of the 3D ORTHOgonal Route tool. In those situations, you might benefit from the creation of construction lines in the route. To achieve this benefit, you need to learn how to initiate the creation of a construction line and learn the characteristics of construction lines.

In the following image, a construction line was drawn in the route and then later used to position a point of a route segment along that construction line.

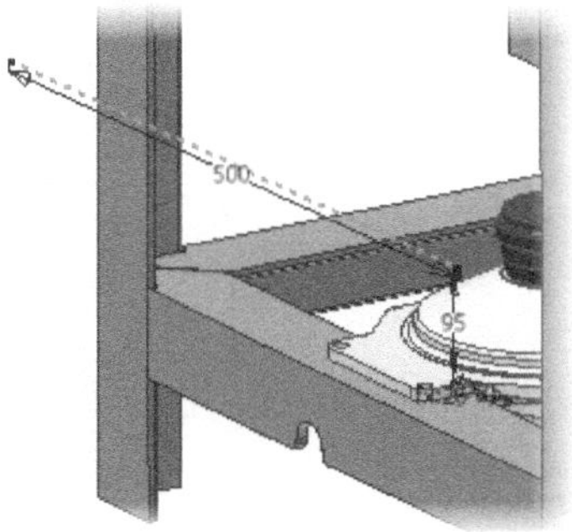

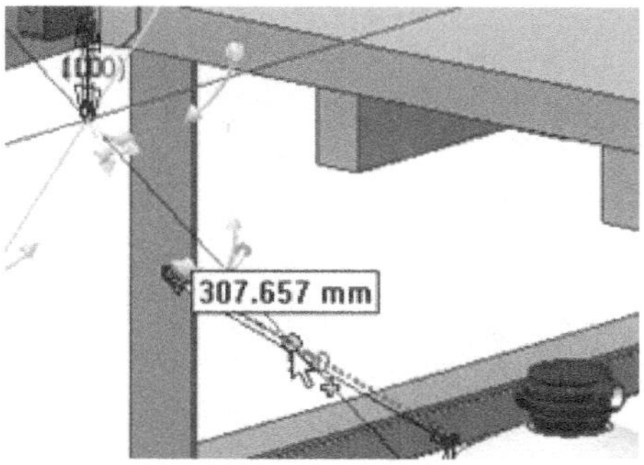

Using Construction Lines

To create a construction line, with the route active for editing but no tool active, in the browser or graphics window, right-click on a sketched route point. Click Draw Construction Line. The 3D ORTHOgonal Route tool then displays at that point. use the options of the 3D ORTHOgonal Route tool to position another point. A construction line is then drawn from the point you initially selected to the newly created point. The 3D ORTHOgonal Route tool also finishes so you can continue creating or editing route segments.

You can use the 3D ORTHOgonal Route tool to draw a construction line from any route node. You can start more than one line from the same node, but you cannot continue with other lines from the end of the construction line. You can constrain the construction geometry to route segments and included geometry in the route to help position and orient route segments and nodes.

In the following image, a construction line controls the angle of a route segment. The construction line is constrained to other route segments and included geometry.

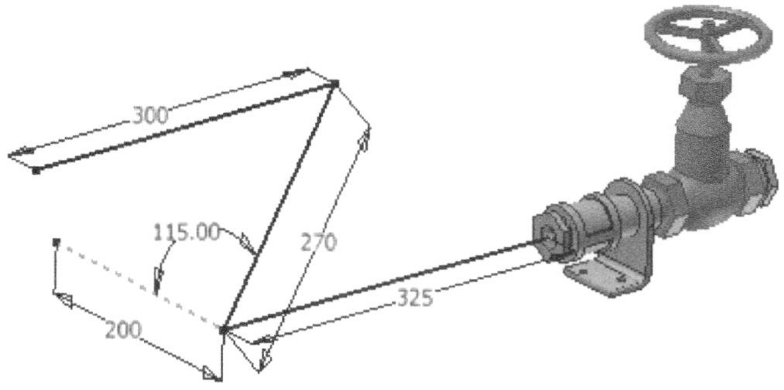

Exercise: Create a Rigid Pipe Route

In this exercise, you will create a new pipe route for a low- pressure feed from the tank to the pump. You will use the 3D ORTHOgonal Route tool to place route nodes between the start and end fittings. This exercise demonstrates fundamental tools and workflows in the tube and pipe environment.

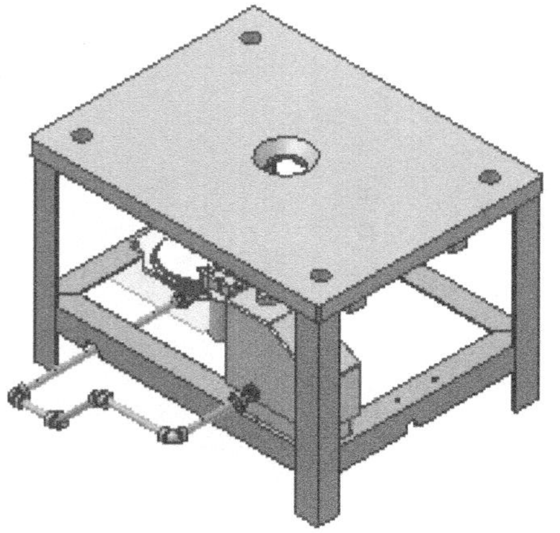

The completed exercise

Create a Route

In this portion of the exercise, you will create a rigid pipe route with sketched and autoroute sections.

1. Open *Rigid Pipe Route.iam*.

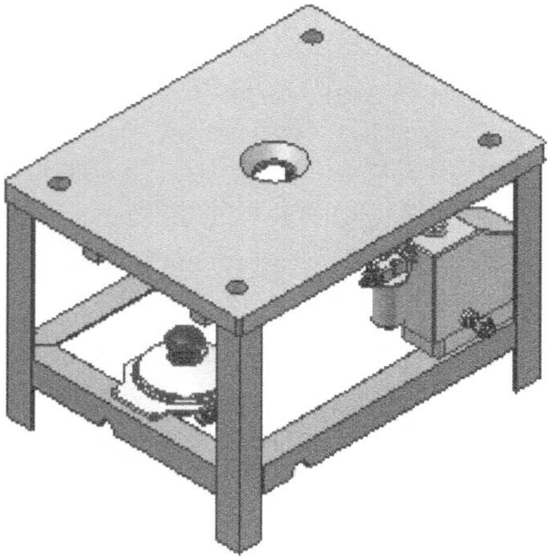

2. Rotate the model as shown in the following image. Check if the user-defined work plane is already showing in the model as shown in the image below. If it is not showing, toggle on the visibility of user-defined work planes that will assist in positioning route nodes, press ALT +].

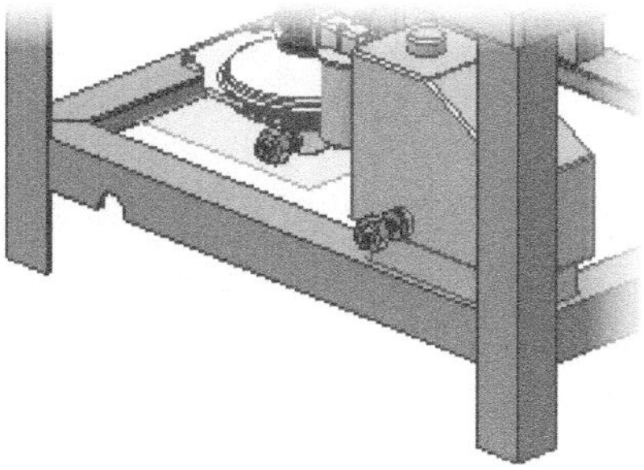

3. In the browser, expand Tube & Pipe Runs. Double-click on Run01.
4. In the Pipe Run tab, in the Route panel, click New Route. Click OK to accept the default route name and file location.
5. In the Route tab, in the Create panel, click Route.
6. Move the cursor over the union connected to the tank. Click when the connection point is highlighted.

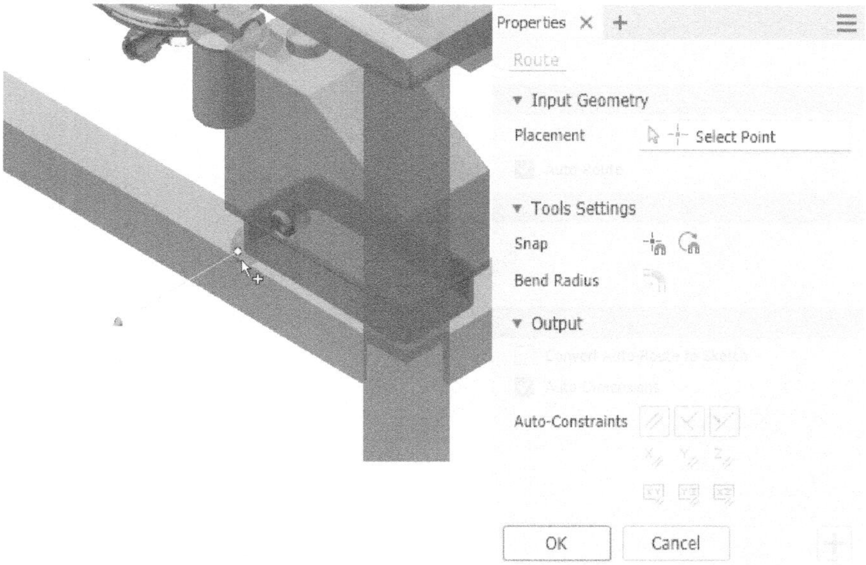

7. Move the cursor along the route axis. Note the feedback at different locations along the axis. The green dot indicates the current location and the tooltip the offset location. Do not select the line.

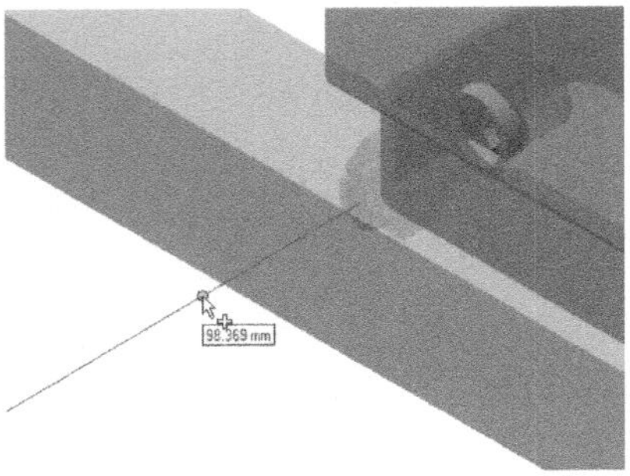

8. Place a second node a precise distance along the route axis. With the cursor over the axis, enter **150** to open the Enter Distance dialog box.

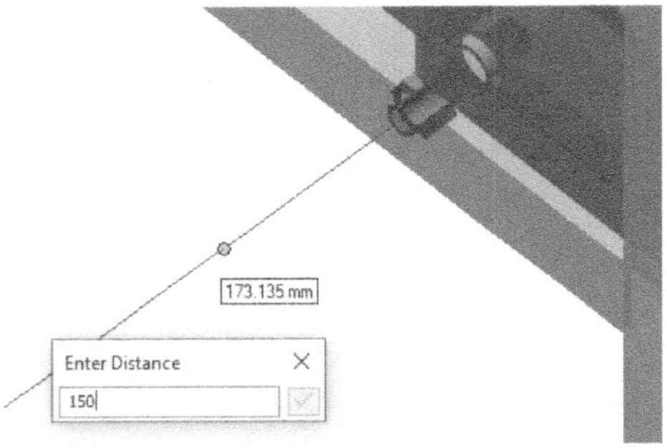

9. To generate the node and segment with constraints relative to the start node, press ENTER.

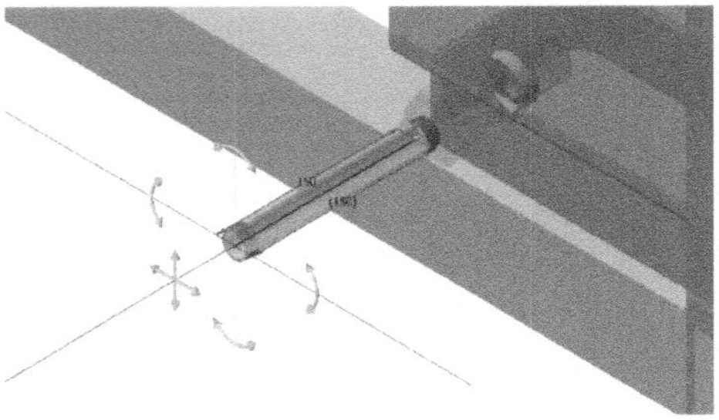

10. To create a node along an axis an approximate distance:

- Move the cursor over the horizontal direction axis. Review the maximum approximate distance that previews.
- Press the + key to increase the length of the tool axes.
- Move the cursor until the tooltip indicates a distance of approximately 250 mm from the previous node.
- Click to place a node.

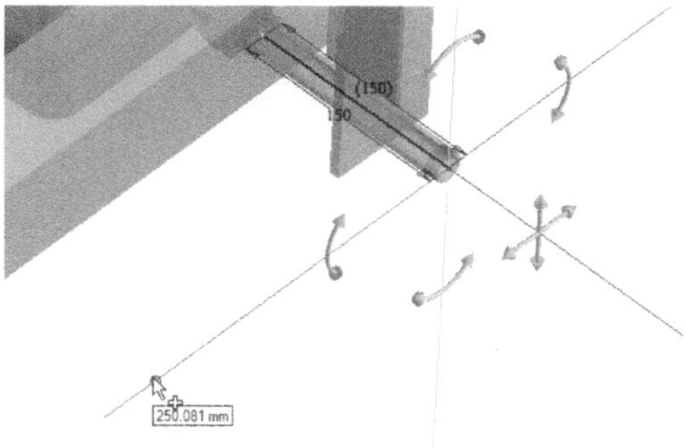

11. To create a 45° bend, click the route angle control arrow as shown in the following image.

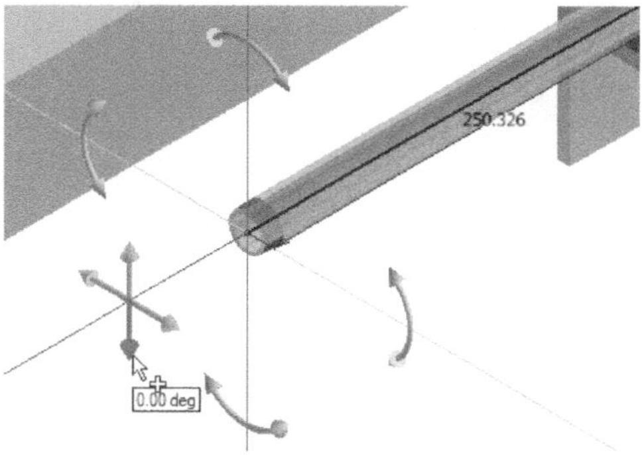

12. Right-click on the graphics window. Click Point Snap to toggle on Point Snap. Alternatively, you can select the Point Snap option () under Tool Settings in the Route palette.

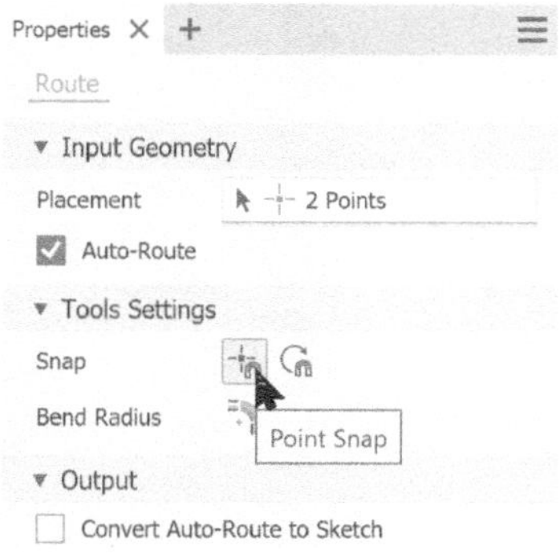

13. Move the cursor over the horizontal work plane through the pump. When a dashed line indicates the intersection of the plane and the line extender, click to place the node.

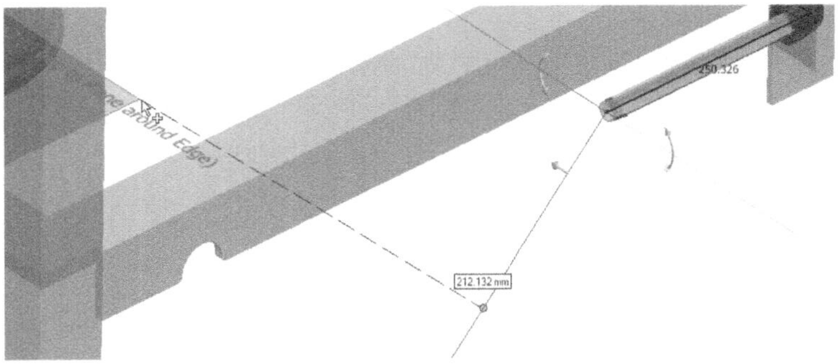

14. Click the upper route angle control arrow to return the line extender to a horizontal orientation.

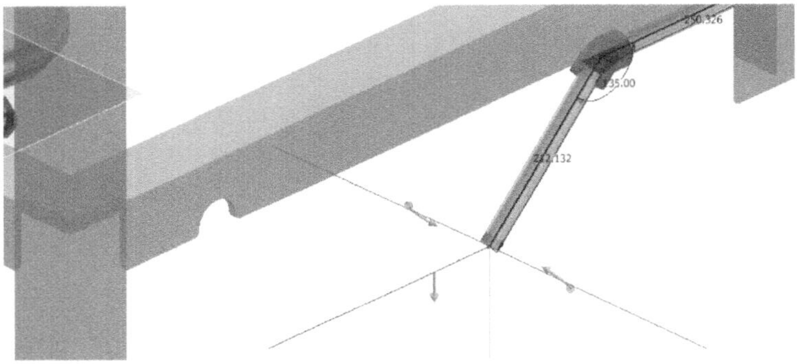

15. Move the cursor over the circular edge on the adjacent frame rail. Right-click in the graphics window. Click Select Other Snap.

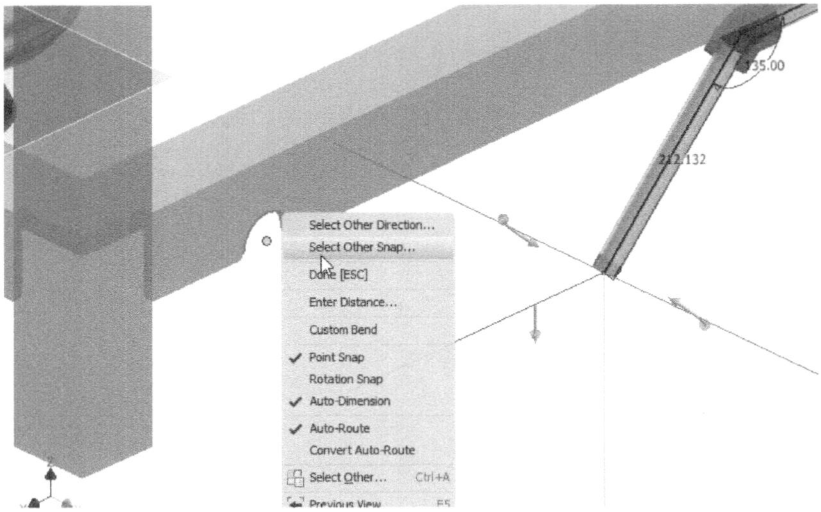

16. When a dashed line extends from the center of the edge to the line extender, click the checkmark in the Select Other tool.

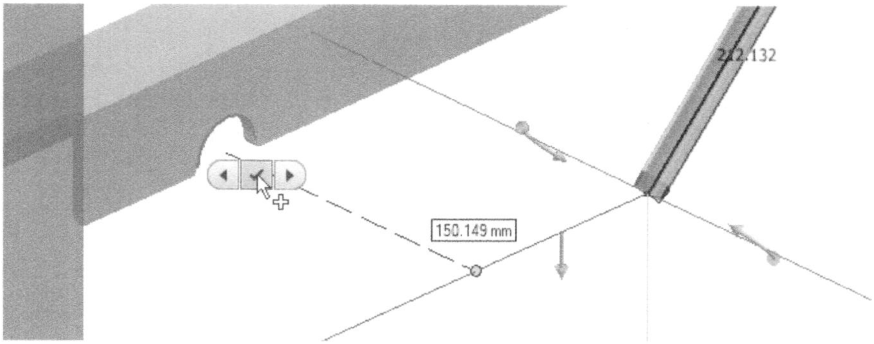

17. To set the endpoint for the route:

- Move the cursor over the union connected to the pump.
- When the connection point is highlighted, click to place the end node for the route.

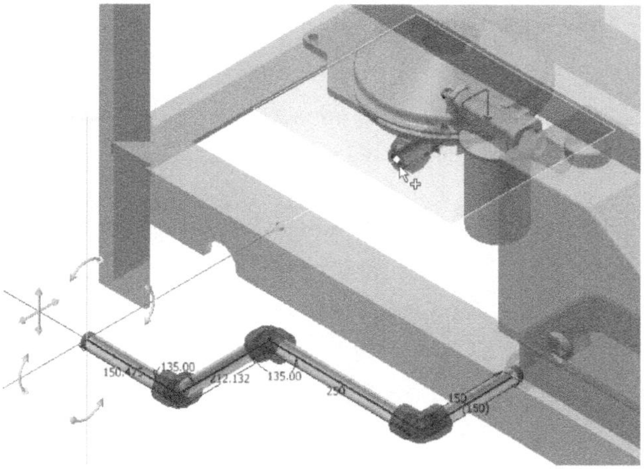

18. Click OK to close the Route palette.

Use Sketched and Autoroute Route Sections

In this portion of the exercise, you will change between autoroute and sketched route sections, and populate the completed route.

1. Examine the browser. Route01 contains a number of route points representing the sketched (dimensioned) nodes in the route. The last segment in the route is not dimensioned and is represented by Autoroute1 in the browser. Route points 5 and 6 are listed under Autoroute 1.

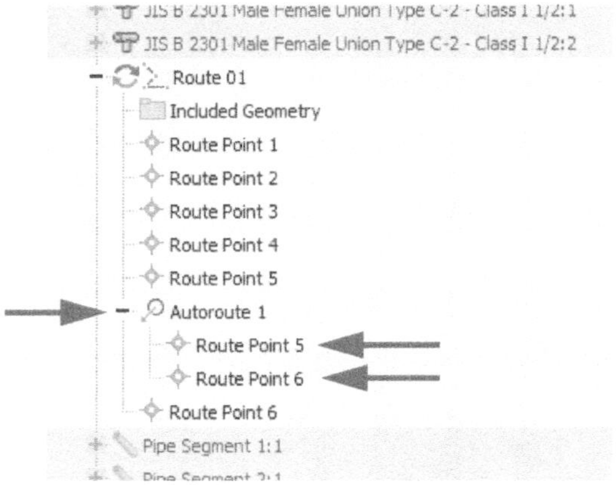

2. To begin making an edit to the route to see the impact on the route, double-click on Route 1:
   - In the graphics window, double-click on the 150 mm dimension associated with the first route segment.
   - In the Edit Dimension dialog box, enter **200 mm** as the new segment length.
   - Click the green checkmark to apply the dimension.

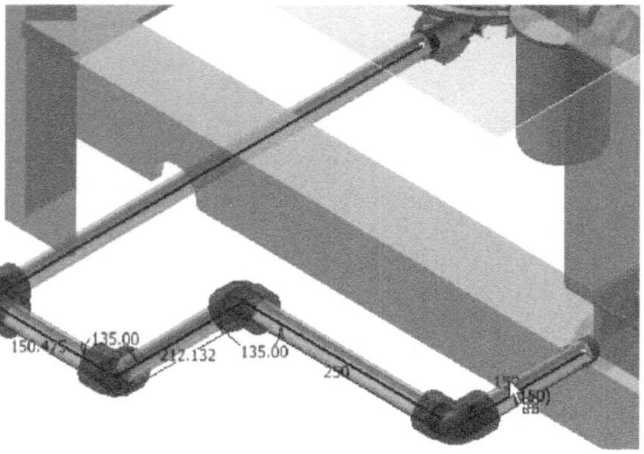

3. Review the updated route based on the revised dimension. The other sketched route segments retain their original length and orientation. A number of new route segments are added to the autorouted section.

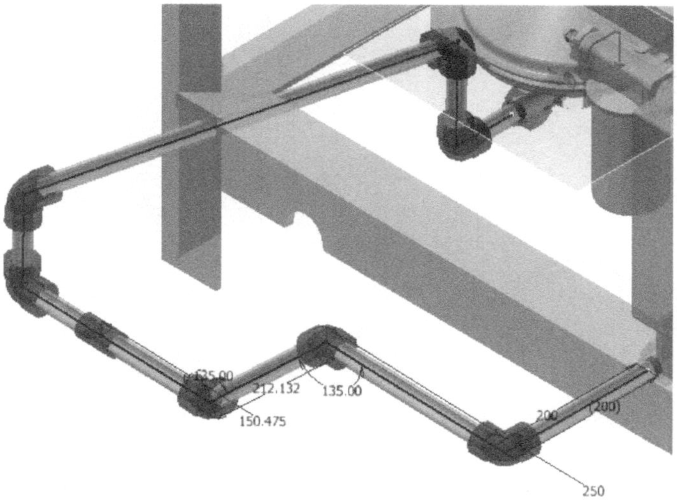

4. In the Quick Access Toolbar, click Undo.

5. To replace the autoroute section with a sketched segment, in the browser, right-click on Autoroute 1. Click Convert to Sketch.

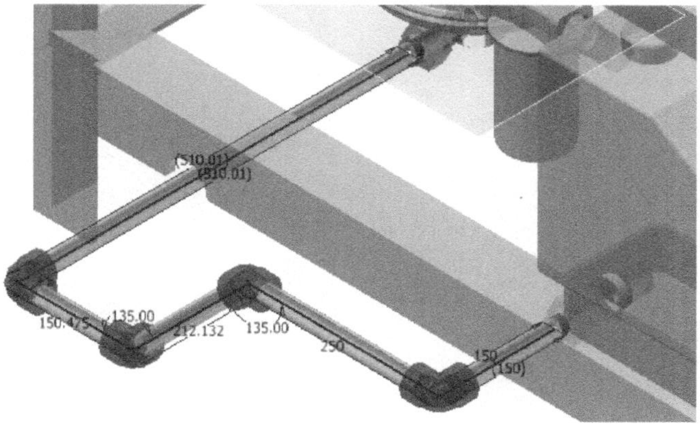

6. Edit the 150 mm dimension for the first route segment. Change the length of the segment to **200 mm**. The route updates without adding additional segments.

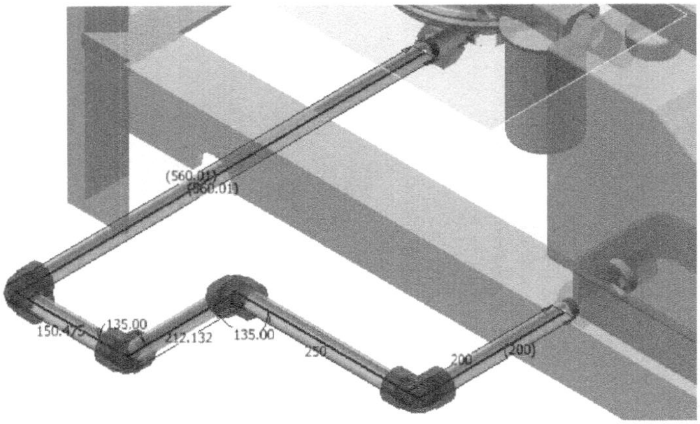

7. The route is populated automatically. In the Route tab, click Finish Route. If prompted, you can enter custom conduit file names and click OK.

8. Conduit segments and elbows are placed along the route. The fittings and pipe segments are listed under Run01 in the browser.

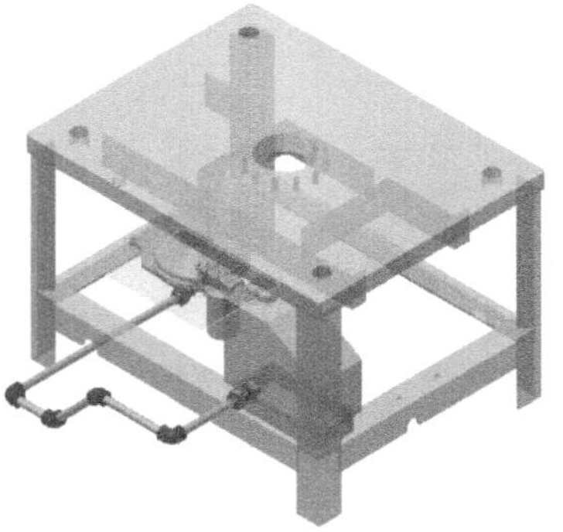

9. Close all files without saving changes.

Exercise: Create a Tube Route

In this exercise, you will create a rigid tube route from a pump to the valve on a hydraulic panel. You will use the 3D ORTHOgonal Route tool to place route nodes relative to component geometry. You will complete a precise route definition using a construction line, and Point and Rotation Snap with the 3D ORTHOgonal Route tool.

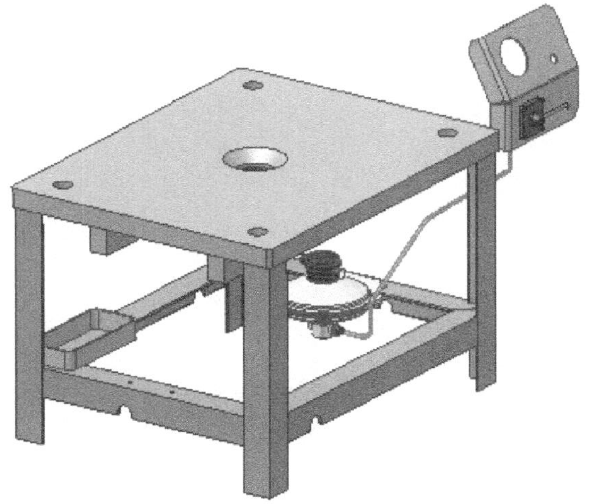

The completed exercise

Start a Tube Route

In this portion of the exercise, you will start a rigid tube route and place the first two nodes along the route.

1. Open *Tube Route.iam*.

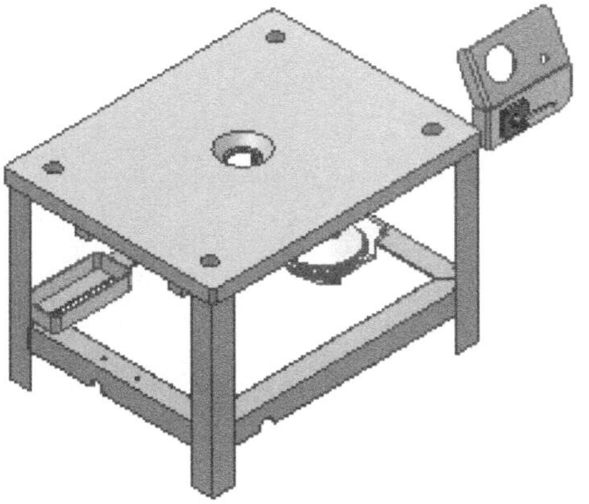

2. In the browser, expand Tube & Pipe Runs. Double-click on Run01.
3. In the Pipe Run tab, in the Manage panel, from the style list, select Steel Hydraulic Tubing 3/8".

4. In the Pipe Run tab, in the Route panel, click New Route. Click OK to accept the default route name and file location.

5. In the Route tab, in the Create panel, click Route. Reorient your view so that you can see the fitting at the pump outlet.

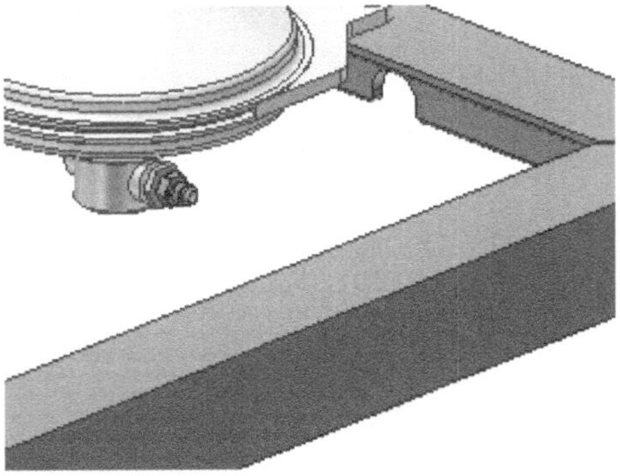

6. Click the connection point on the outlet fitting.

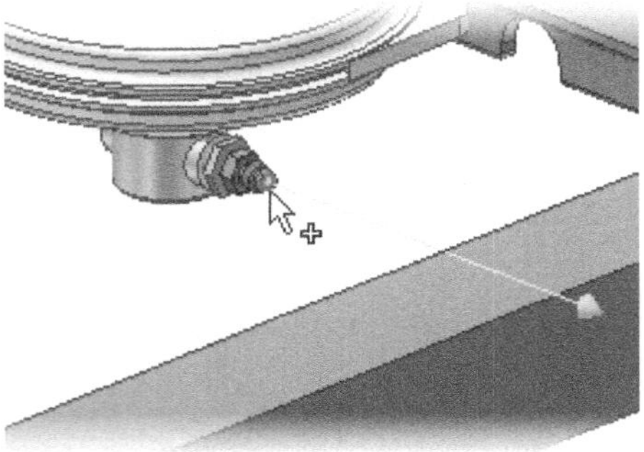

7. To place a second node along the route axis:
   - Move the cursor over the route axis.
   - Enter **75 mm**.
   - In the Enter Distance dialog box, click to accept the distance value.

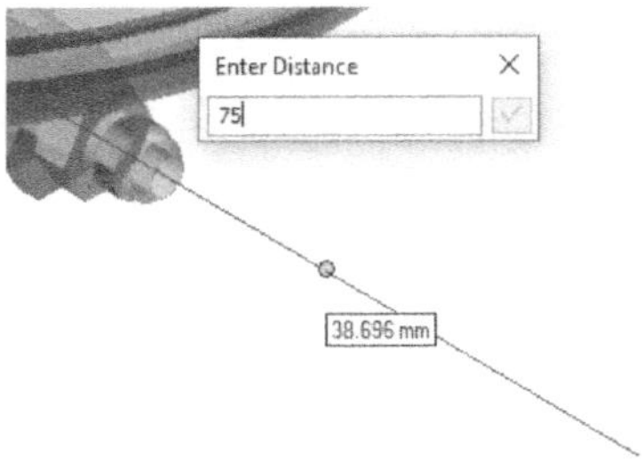

8. To activate point snaps during route creation, right-click in the graphics window and click Point Snap. Alternatively, you can select the Point Snap option () under Tool Settings in the Route palette.

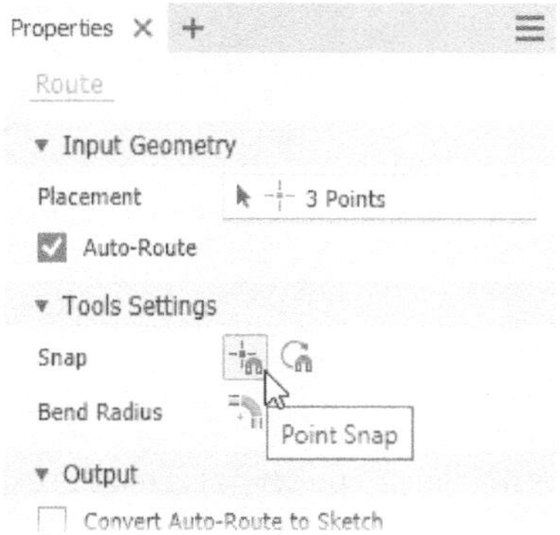

9. To create a node 25 mm above a specific planar face:
   - Move the cursor over the horizontal face of the adjacent frame brace (1).
   - When the intersection of the extended plane and the route axis is highlighted (2), enter **25 mm**.
   - In the Enter Distance dialog box, click to accept the distance value.

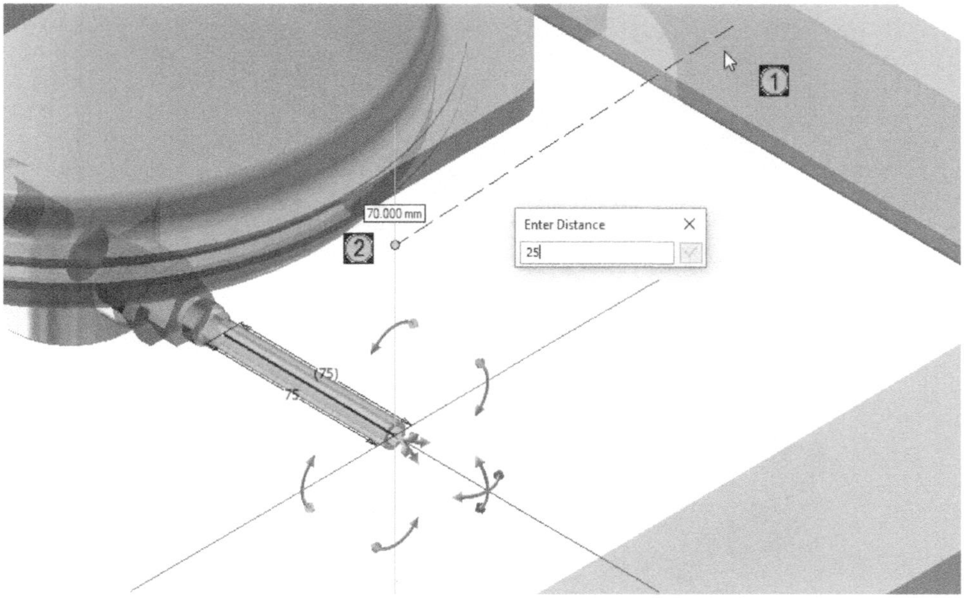

10. Right-click in the graphics window background. Click Done.

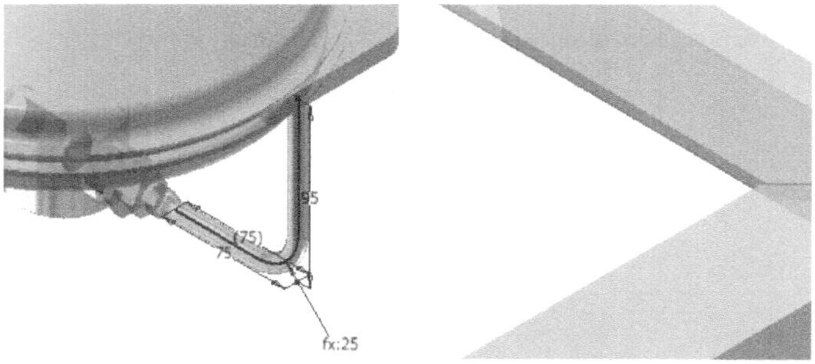

Complete the Tube Route

In this portion of the exercise, you will create a construction line along the intended route path. You route from the hydraulic panel and use the construction line to precisely match the existing route segments.

1. In the browser, right-click on Route Point 3. Click Draw Construction Line.

2. Click and drag the angle handle highlighted in the following image. When the tooltip indicates a 60° bend angle, release the mouse button.

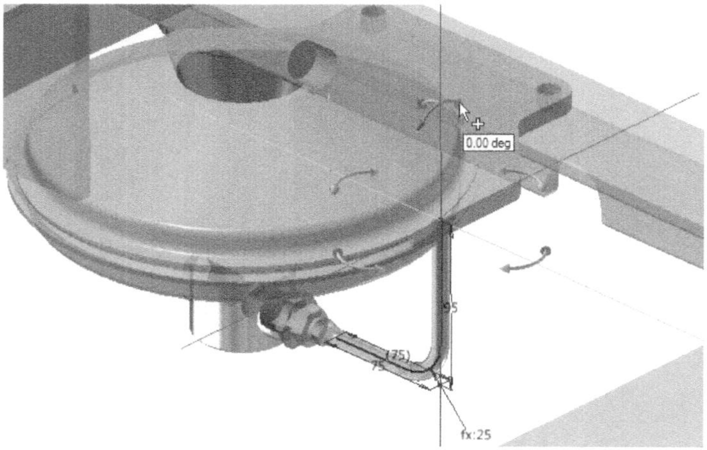

3. Move the cursor over the line extender (red axis) and then enter **500 mm**.

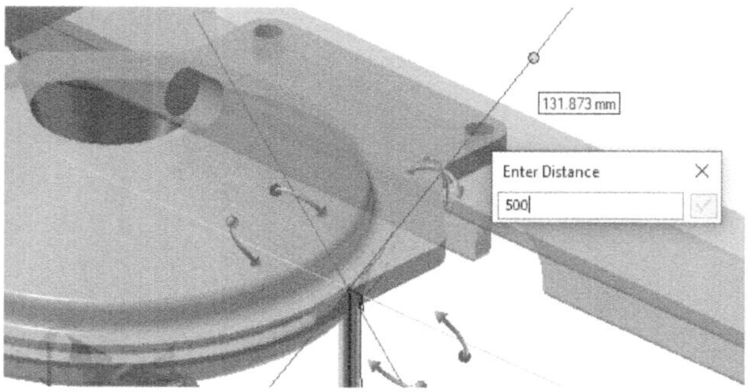

4. In the Enter Distance dialog box, click to accept the distance value. A construction line extends from the route node in the specified direction.

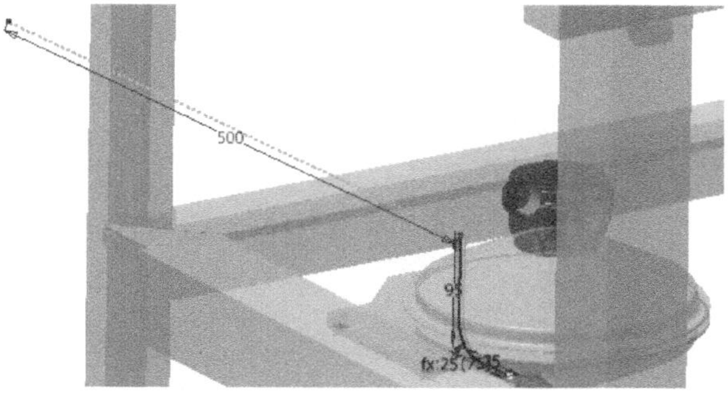

5. In the Route tab, in the Create panel, click Route.

6. Move the cursor over the end of the fitting on the valve. If the route direction arrow points up, press SPACEBAR to flip the direction. Click to place a route node at the fitting.

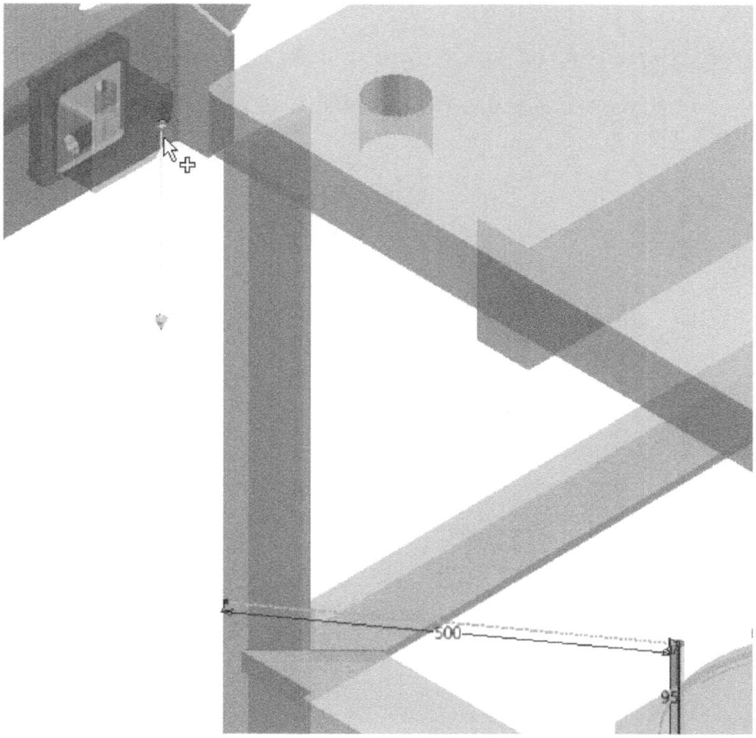

7. Place a second node 100 mm along the route axis, below the valve.

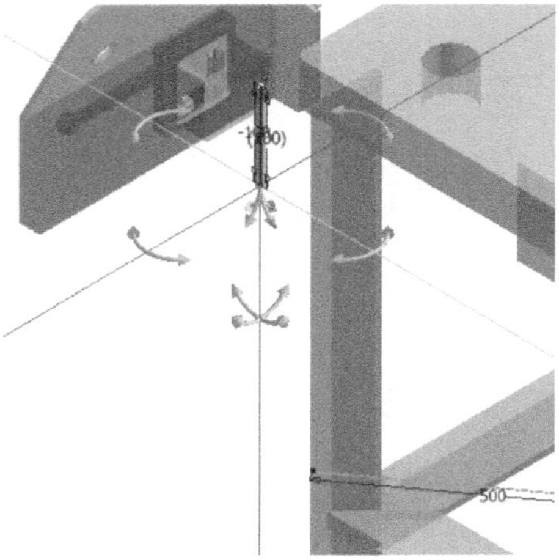

8. Right-click in the graphics window background. Click Rotation Snap to toggle it on.

   Alternatively, you can turn on Rotation Snap ( ) in the Route palette, under Tool Settings.

9. To begin rotating the axis direction, click and drag the identified angle handle toward the construction line.

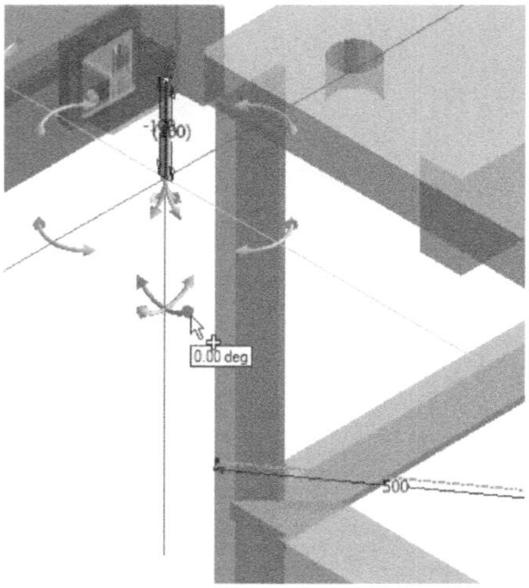

10. When the line extender snaps to the construction line, release the mouse button.

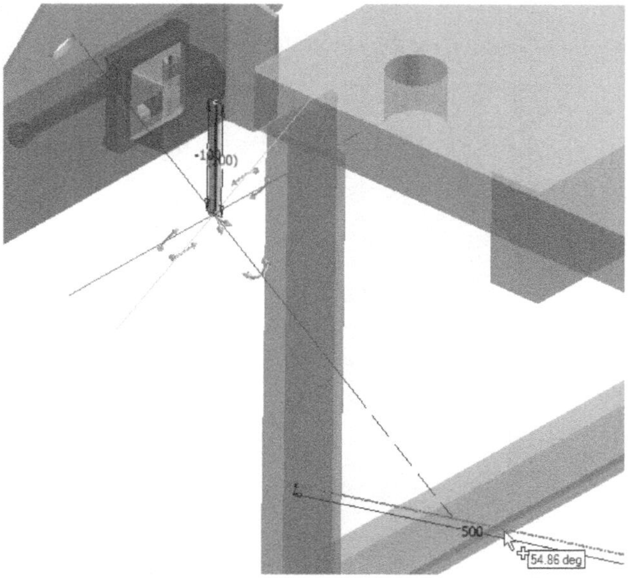

11. Move the cursor over the construction line near the intersection with the line extender. When the connection line is highlighted, click to place a route node at the intersection.

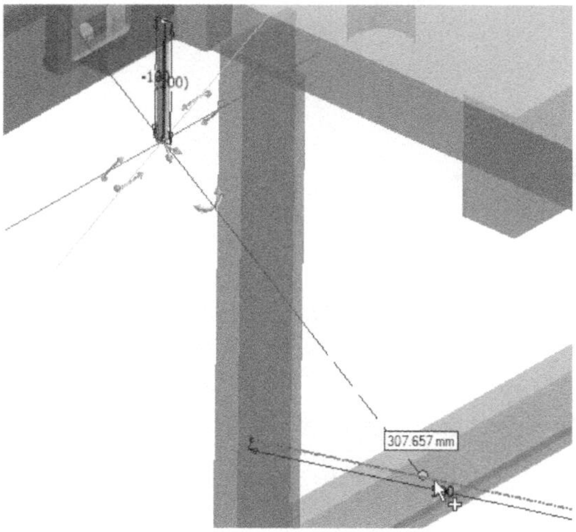

12. To complete a continuous route by adding a segment between the separate routes:
   - Click the open route node near the valve that is at the start of the construction line.
   - Accept the one segment solution for the autoroute section.

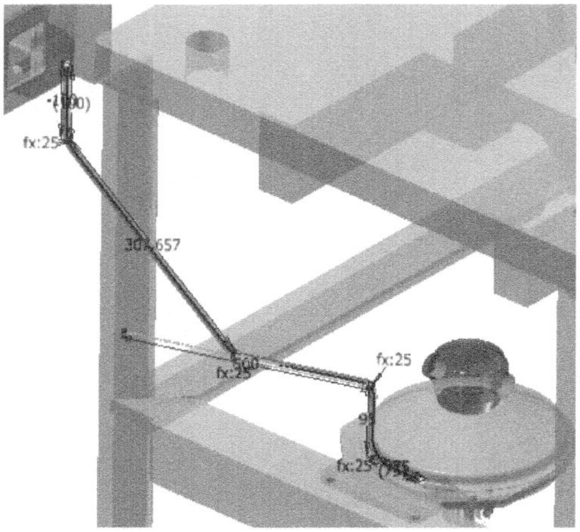

13. To replace the autoroute segment with a fully parametric segment, in the browser, right-click on Autoroute 1. Click Convert to Sketch.
14. In the graphics window, right-click on the construction line. Click Delete.

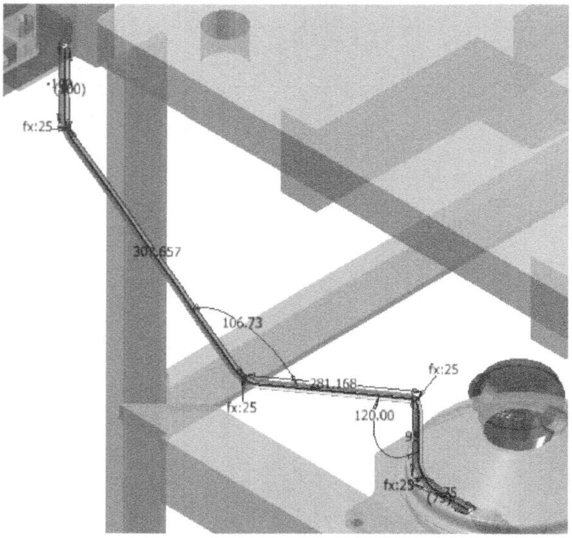

15. In the Route tab, click Finish Route. The route is populated automatically.

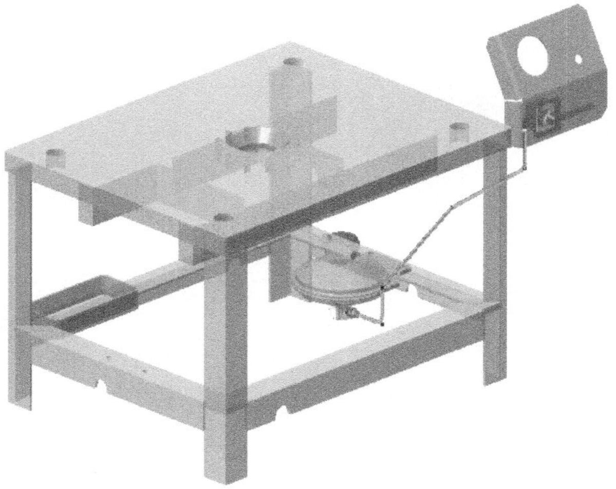

16. Close all files without saving changes.

Exercise: Create a Self-Draining Pipe Run

In this exercise, you will create self-draining pipe routes.

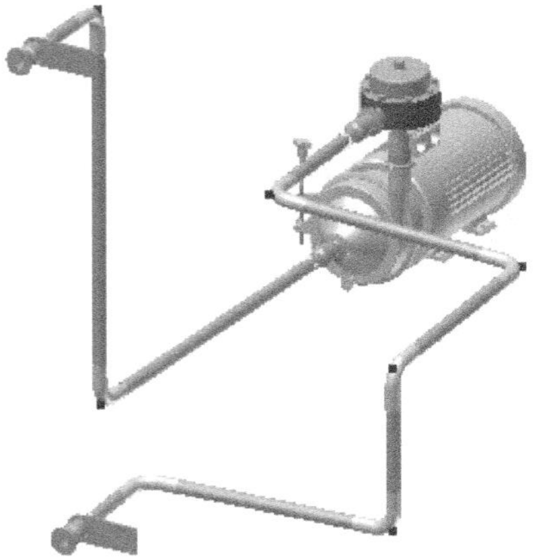

The completed exercise

1. Open *Self Draining Routes.iam.*

2. Under Representations folder > View, double-click on Default view to set it as the active view. To set Tube & Pipe Runs as active, in the browser, double-click on Tube & Pipe Runs.

3. To verify that the custom style is current:

   - In the Tube and Pipe tab, in the Run panel, review the current style.
   - If required, click 25mm Self Draining.

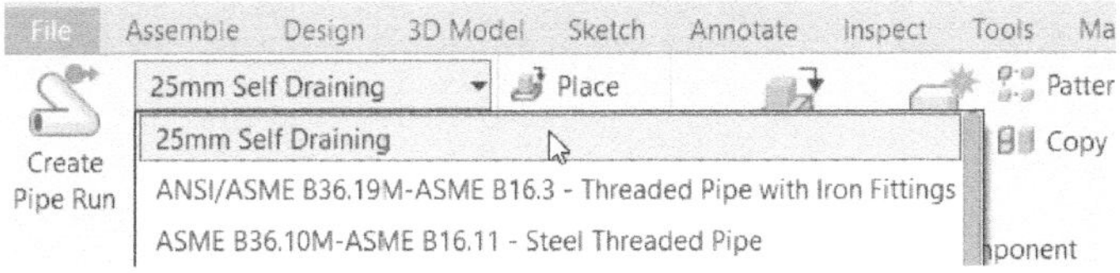

4. To set the gravity direction:
   - In the Tube and Pipe tab, in the Run panel, click Define Gravity.
   - Expand the Origin for Tube & Pipe Runs.
   - Click Z Axis.

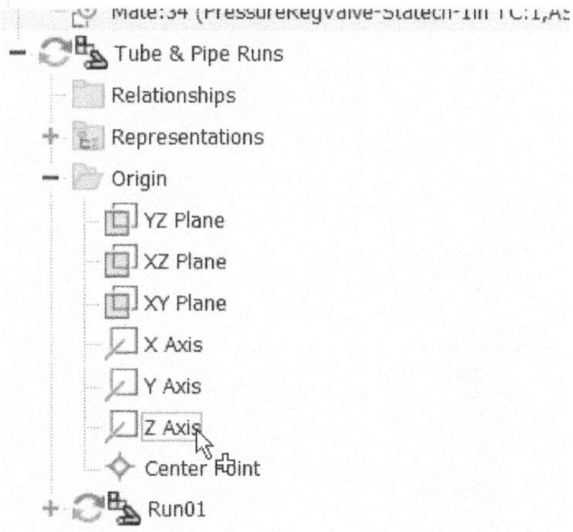

5. The required gravity direction for this assembly is down. If required, in the Gravity dialog box, click Invert Normal. Click OK.

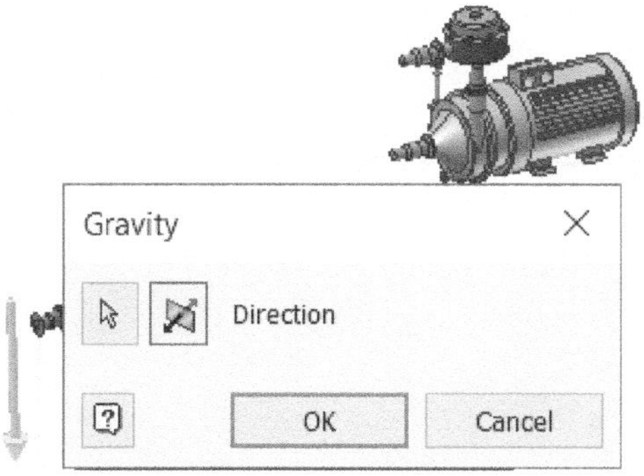

6. In the browser, double-click on Run01 to activate the pipe run.

7. To create a new route:
   - In the Pipe Run tab, in the Route panel, click New Route.
   - In the Create Route dialog box, click OK.

8. View the pump side of the top fitting.

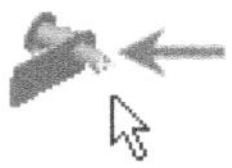

9. To define the start of the route:

- In the Route tab, in the Create panel, click Route.
- Move the cursor to the pump side of the fitting.
- When the arrow and green dot display, press SPACEBAR to flip the vector direction.
- When the arrow is pointing in the correct direction, select the start point.

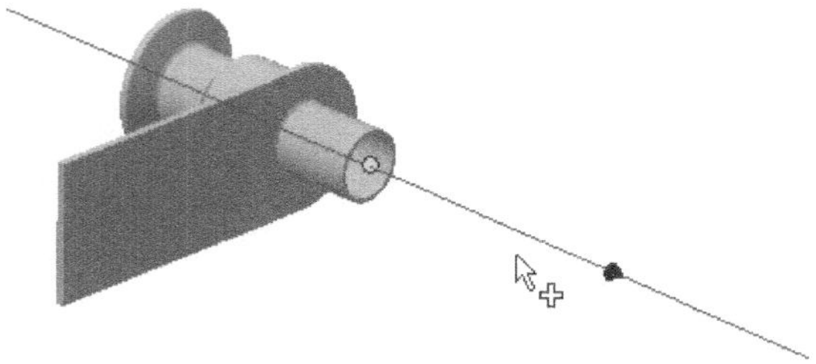

10. Rotate the view to the front of the pump.

11. To define the end of the route:

- Move the cursor to the pump fitting.
- When the arrow and green dot display, press SPACEBAR to flip the vector direction.
- Click in the graphics window to accept the point and direction.

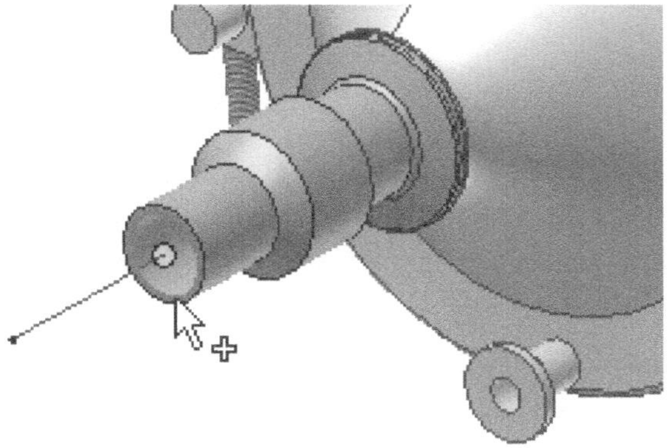

12. To accept the pipe run, click the checkmark in the Select Other tool. Click OK to close the Route palette.

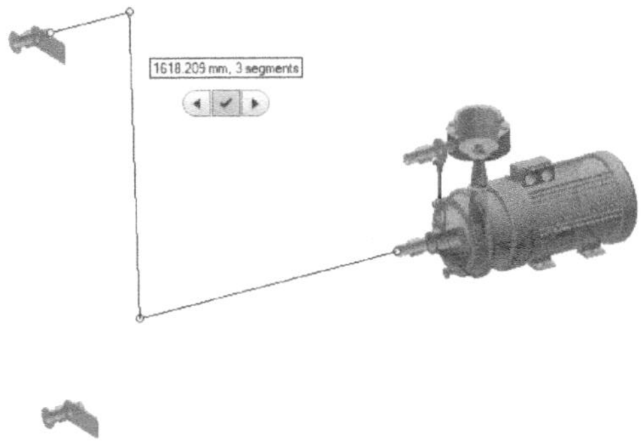

13. The route is populated automatically. In the Route tab, in the Exit panel, click Finish Route.

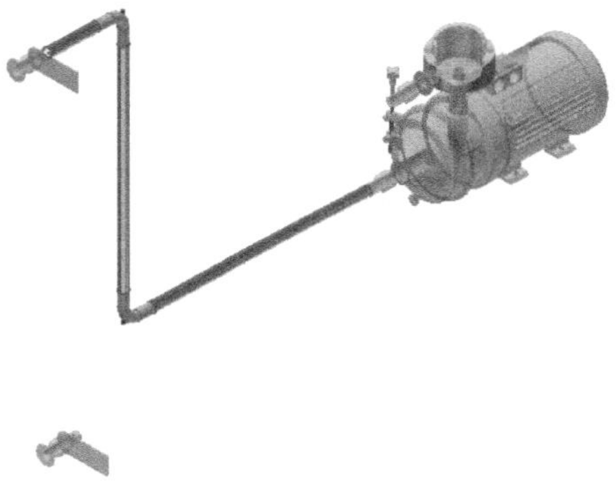

14. To view the Z axis:
    - In the browser, under Tube & Pipe Runs, expand the Origin.
    - Right-click on Z Axis. Click Visibility.
    - Right-click on Z Axis. Click Auto-Resize.
15. To reorient the view, on the ViewCube, click Left.

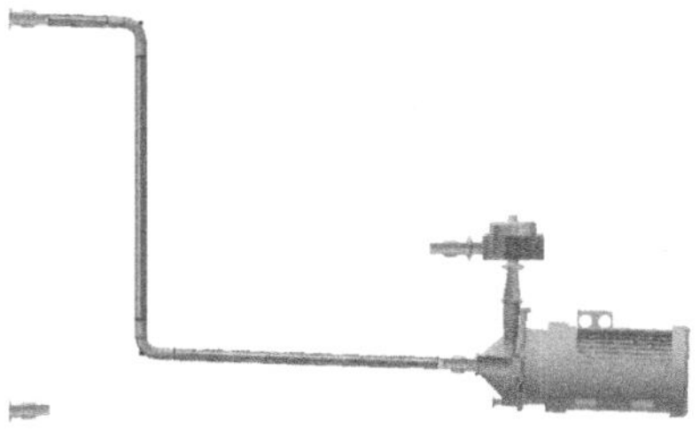

16. To measure the angle of the pipes:
    - In the ribbon, in the Inspect tab, in the Measure panel, click Measure.
    - Click the Z axis.
    - Click the vertical pipe.

    Note the 0 deg value.

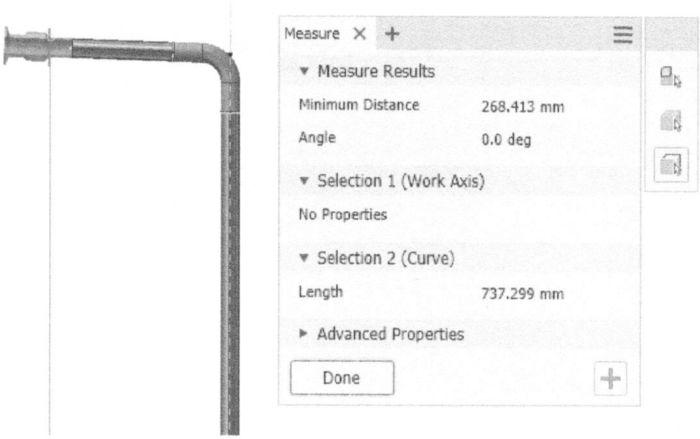

17. Measure the angle between the pipe components. Close the Measure dialog box.

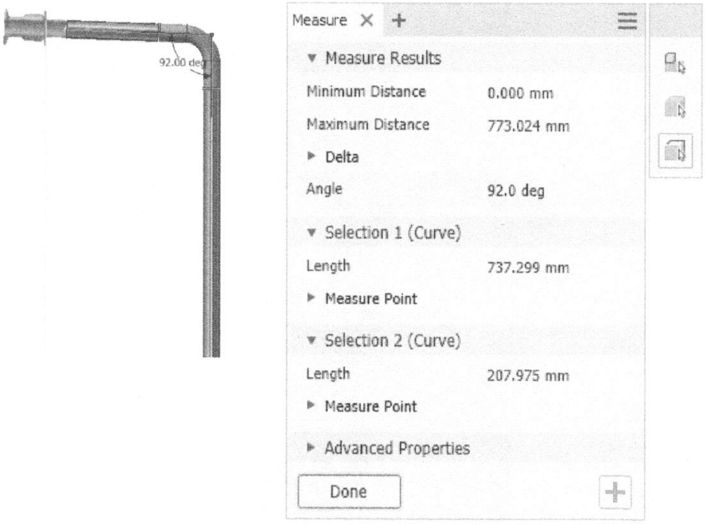

18. To create a manual pipe route:
    - On the ViewCube, click Home.
    - In the Pipe Run tab, in the Route panel, click New Route.
    - In the Create Route dialog box, click OK.

19. To define the manual route:

- In the Route tab, in the Create panel, click Route.
- Start the route at the pump outlet. Set the direction away from the pump.

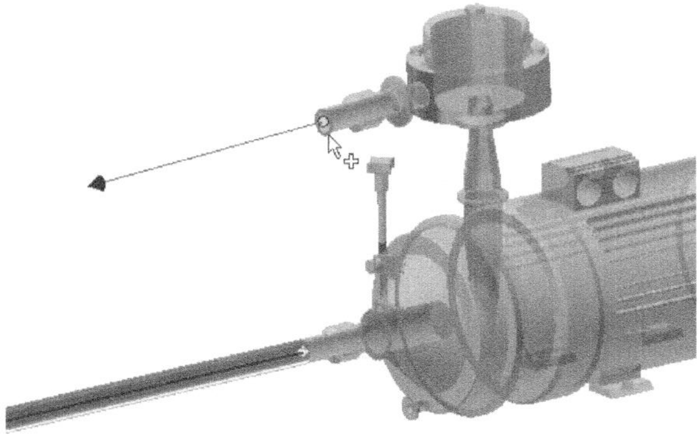

20. To define the first segment:

- Move the cursor along the axis away from the pump inlet.
- Right-click on the green dot that displays. Click Enter Distance.
- In the Enter Distance Dialog box, enter **250 mm**. Click the green checkmark.

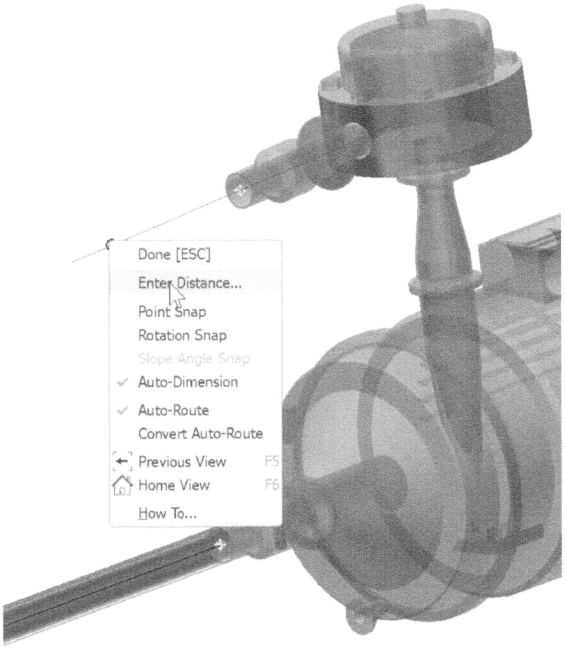

21. Note the directional indicators for the route (Arrows).

22. If the slope of the axis is not correct, click the arrow to change the slope.

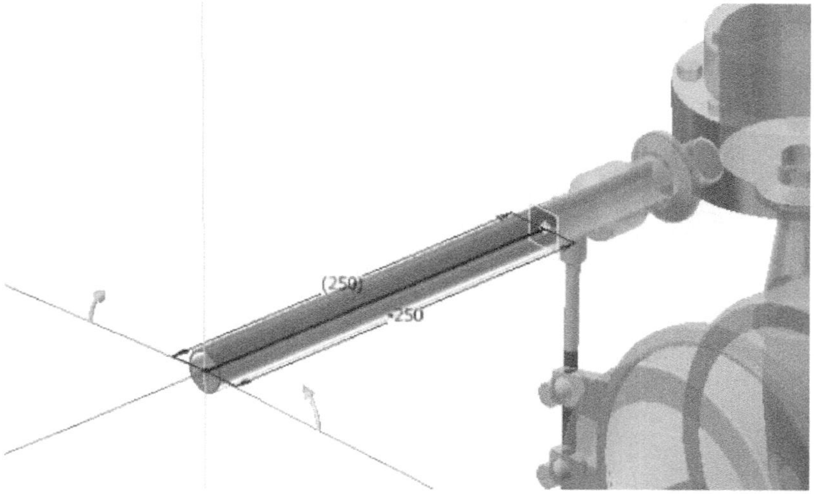

23. To define the next segment of the run:
    - Move the cursor along the axis as shown in the following image.
    - Right-click on the axis. Click Enter Distance.
    - In the Enter Distance dialog box, enter **500 mm**.
    - Click the green checkmark.

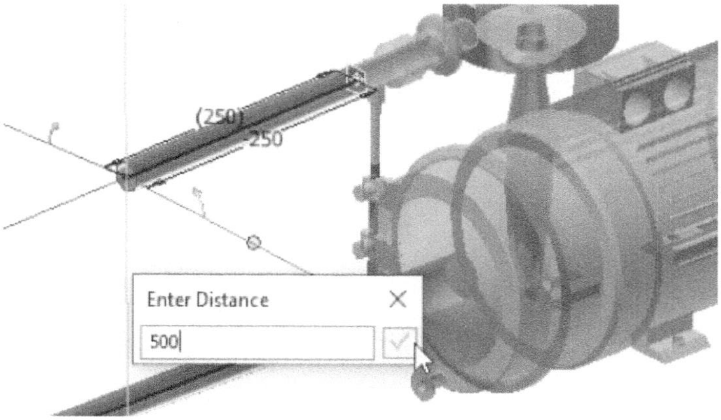

24. To complete the route:

- Reorient your view as shown in the following image.
- Move the cursor to the remaining fitting.
- Set the direction towards the pump.
- Click OK to close the Route palette.

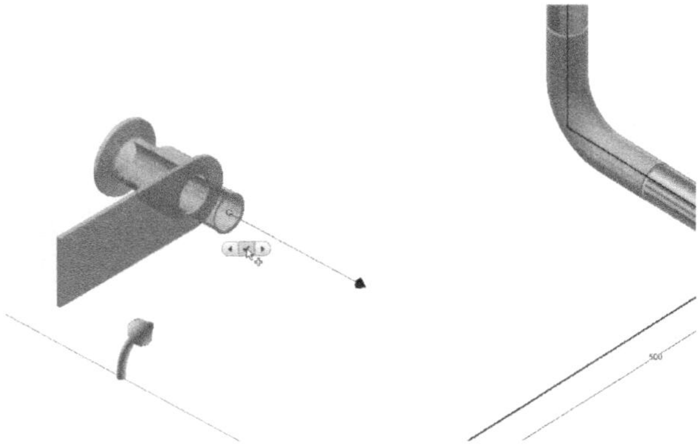

25. The route is populated automatically. In the Route tab, in the Exit panel, click Finish Route.

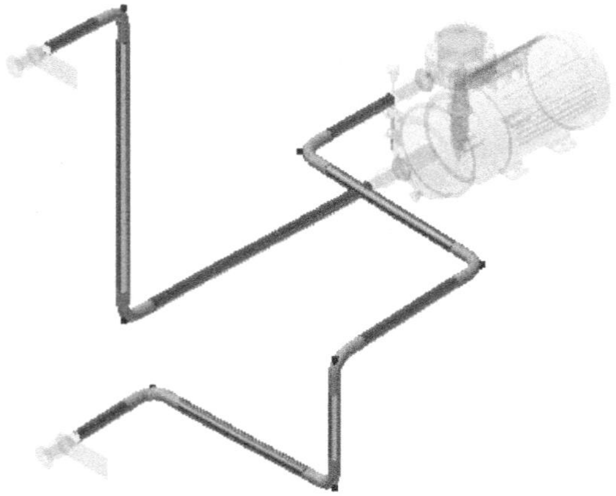

26. Use the Measure tool to verify the self-draining route.

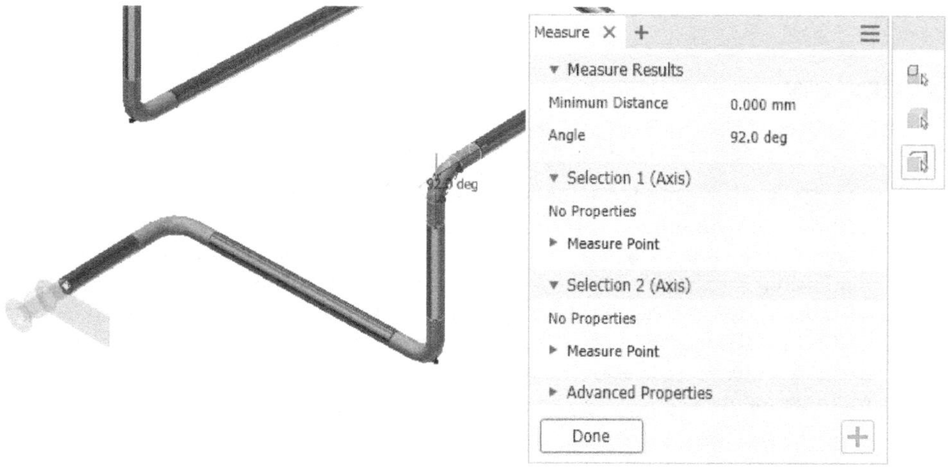

27. Close all files without saving.

Lesson: Editing Rigid Routes

Overview

This lesson describes how to edit rigid pipe and tube routes.

As a design evolves and components in the assembly change, you might need to reposition rigid pipe or tube segments around or through those components. There are numerous ways you can edit a route. You can edit sketched route segments by adding, deleting, or modifying the constraints and dimensions associated with the segments. You can reposition some nodes and segments in autoroute sections by dynamically dragging segments, or by specifying distances and orientations with the 3D ORTHOgonal Route tool. You can add new nodes or segments at the end of, or in the middle of, an existing route. You can also delete nodes or segments, and convert autoroute sections to sketched route segments.

In the following image, the route is shown before and after making a number of changes including moving, deleting, and adding segments.

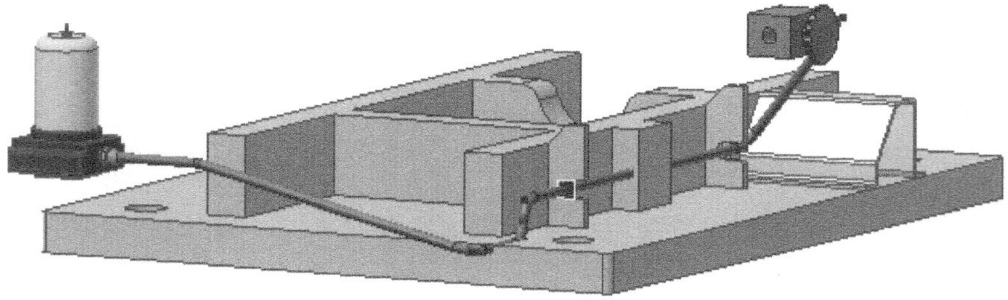

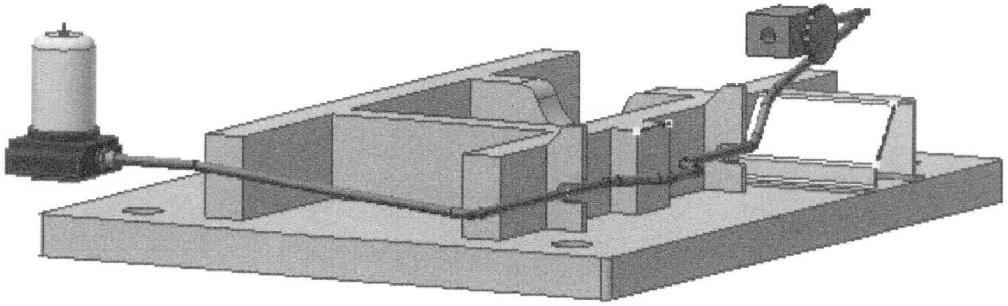

Objectives

After completing this lesson, you will be able to:

- Describe the overall process for editing rigid tube and pipe routes.
- Edit nodes and route segments in a sketched route.
- Edit an autoroute region by moving segments, moving nodes, and selecting alternate routes, and then convert it to a sketch.
- Describe how to make edits to a route derived from a 3D sketch.
- Trim or extend the length of rigid pipe or tube segments at an open route node.
- List methods to defer updates to tube and pipe components during edits.

Editing Rigid Routes

The tools and techniques you use to edit rigid pipe and rigid tube routes are almost identical. Rigid pipe routes are less flexible because of their 45° and 90° elbows. The underlying routes for both styles can contain both autoroute and parametric sections. The editing rules for autoroute and parametric route sections are the same for both rigid pipe and rigid tube routes.

In the following image, an autorouted route is converted into a parametric route controlled by constraints and dimensions.

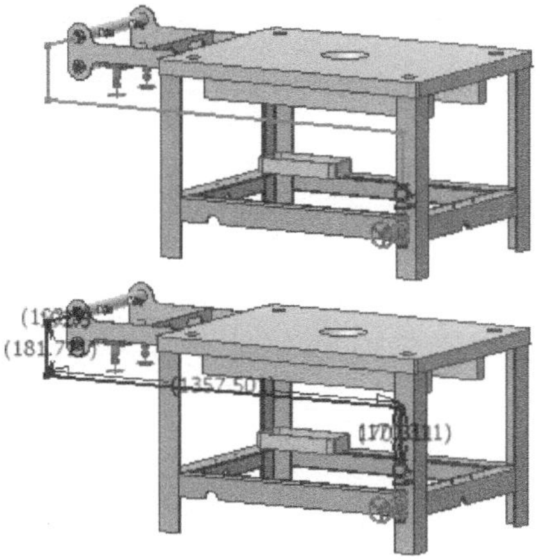

Definition of Editing Rigid Routes

The allowable edits to a rigid route depend on the type of route section containing the node or segment to be edited and the location of the node or segment in the route. Autoroute regions enable interactive drag edits of some nodes and segments, while parametric regions require you to modify constraints and dimensions to edit the route. Consider using autoroute regions in areas where you expect significant design changes. When your design stabilizes, you can convert the autoroute region to a parametric region and constrain the route to the adjacent geometry.

You access the tools and options for editing a route after you activate the route for in-place editing in the context of the overall assembly design. The tools are selected from the ribbon or the shortcut menu. The shortcut menu options are available after selecting a segment or node.

In the following image, a route segment is dragged to a new position.

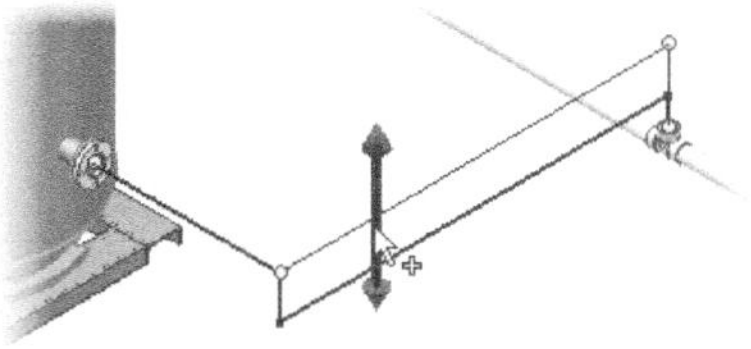

> Along with changing the path and segments of a route, when you are editing a route, you can select a different style to use for the route.

Process: Editing a Route

The following steps give an overview of editing a populated or unpopulated route.

1. In an open assembly design, activate the pipe route you need to change for in-place editing.
2. Use the tools available for that type of route to make the changes you require.

Allowable Edits in Route Regions

The following table outlines the edits that you can make to nodes and segments in autoroute and parametric route regions.

Editing Action	Autoroute Region	Parametric Region
Reference Included Geometry - Dimension or constrain nodes or segments to geometry included in the route.	No	Yes
Insert Node - Insert a new node into a route segment.	Yes	Yes
Move Node - Drag an existing coupling node. Note that you cannot drag nodes placed with the Insert Node tool.	Yes	No
3D Move/Rotate - Use the 3D Move/Rotate tool to reposition a node not associated with a fitting, circular edge, or vertex.	No	Under constrained directions only
Move Segment - Drag a route segment that is not adjacent to a node at a fitting, circular edge, or vertex.	Yes	No
Create Construction Lines - Use the 3D ORTHOgonal Route tool to draw a construction line from a route node.	No	Yes
Delete Region - Delete entire region.	Yes	No
Convert Region - Convert entire region to a different type.	Yes	No
Continue Route - Continue the route from an open node.	Yes	Yes

Disjointed Routes

Large changes to your assembly can often invalidate significant portions of a route, especially if the route is not associative to included geometry. It is often more practical to delete sections of the route and then connect the disjointed sections either with autoroute or parametric sections. You can restart the route from any open node.

The following image shows before, during, and after the editing of a route. In this design, a component in the assembly had a design change that caused it to intersect the tube route. By adding nodes to the route on both sides of the interfering area, the section of the route between those points could be deleted. New route segments were then added to complete the change.

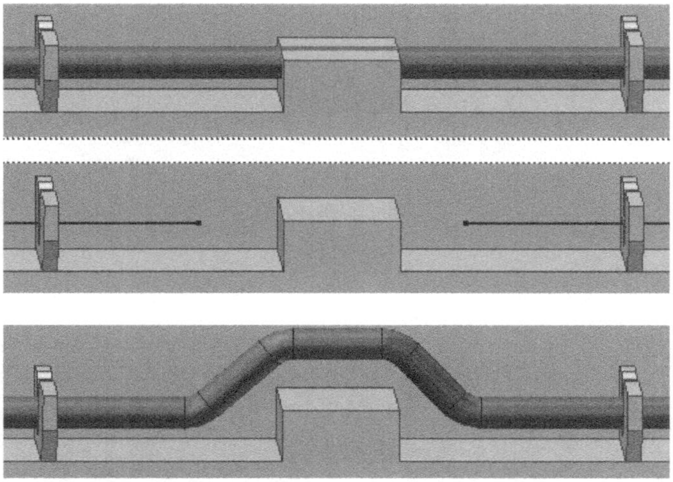

Editing Couplings

By default, a coupling is placed at the intersection of two colinear route segments. If you want to use the node as a control point to guide the route toward or away from other components and you do not require a coupling, right-click on the node and click Fitting to toggle it off. The node remains associated to the component, but the coupling is removed.

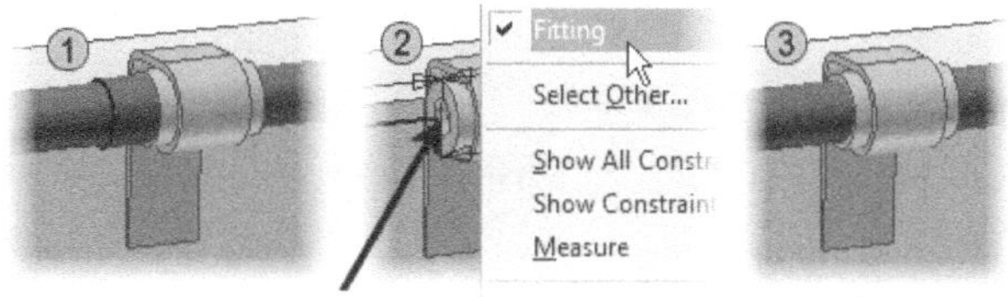

1 Coupling placed at selected circular edge of a hanger.

2 Fitting removed from route node.

3 The coupling is removed and the node remains associative to the edge.

Editing Sketched Routes

Route segments that were sketched using the 3D ORTHOgonal Route tool are partially constrained automatically with geometric and dimensional constraints. You can edit the route to further control the location and size of the route segments. The geometric and dimensional constraints can be between route segments, between segments and construction geometry, or between segments and included geometry. If you need to add or remove route segments, change the path of the route, or modify the constraining method, you need to understand the methods and options available for editing a sketched route.

In the following image, the assembly is shown before and after making changes to two routes. The changes were required because after creating the individual routes, it was determined that two of the routes interfered with each other and additional changes were required.

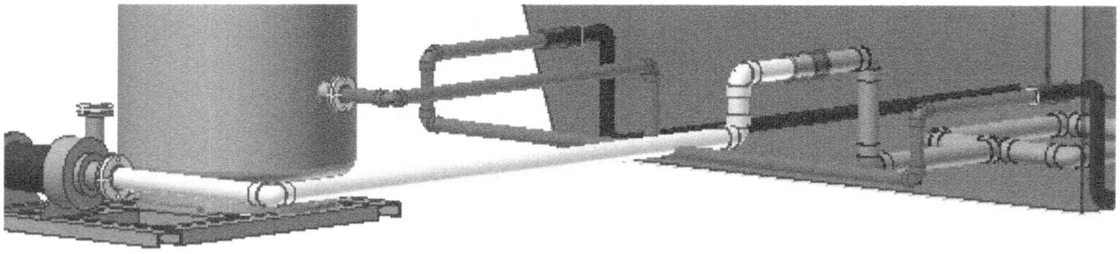

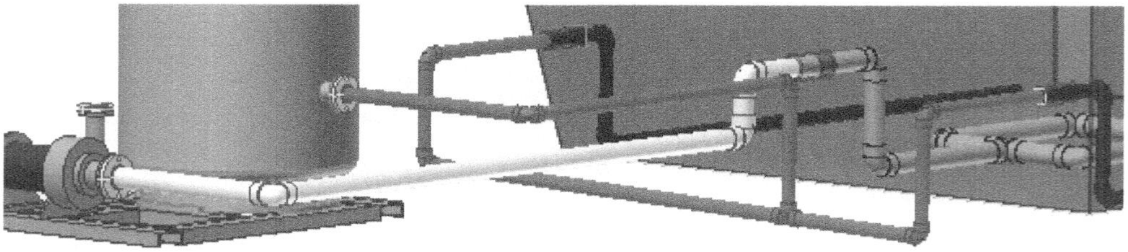

Description of Editing a Sketched Route

A series of continuous sketched route segments form a parametric section of a rigid route. You can complete the route from start node to end node before returning to edit the route, or you can stop creation of a partially completed route to make various types of edits.

The edits you can make to a sketched parametric section are:

- Add, edit, or delete dimensions, including switching dimensions between driving and driven.
- Add or delete geometric constraints.
- Insert or delete route nodes.
- Add or delete route segments.
- Reposition a node using 3D Move/Rotate.
- Include model geometry into the route.
- Delete work features and reference geometry from the Included Geometry folder.
- Add construction geometry.
- Toggle the inclusion of fittings.

Process: Editing Sketched Routes

The following steps give an overview of editing sketched routes.

1. Activate the route for in-place editing.
2. Use the available tools and options for editing sketched routes in any order and as required to make the edits you require.

Geometric and Dimensional Constraints

As you sketch a rigid route, by default the resulting segments are geometrically and dimensionally constrained to control the position and orientation of the route segments and nodes. The dimensions and constraints that are automatically added do not fully constrain the route segments. For some designs, you might also find the constraints that were automatically added are not what you require. You add and edit geometric and dimensional constraints to a route sketch in the same manner you do for sketched features in a part model.

The following image shows the sketch constraints and dimensions added to sketched route segments.

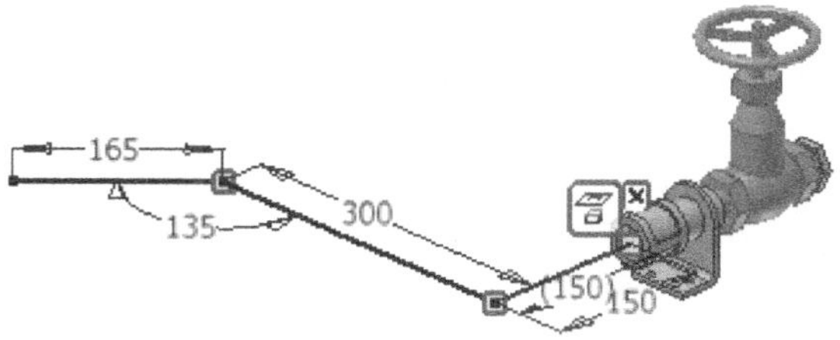

> You can place angle dimensions only between geometry that is coplanar. This applies to route segments, construction lines, and included geometry.

In the following image, the dimensioned sketch route includes construction lines to help control the orientation of the segments.

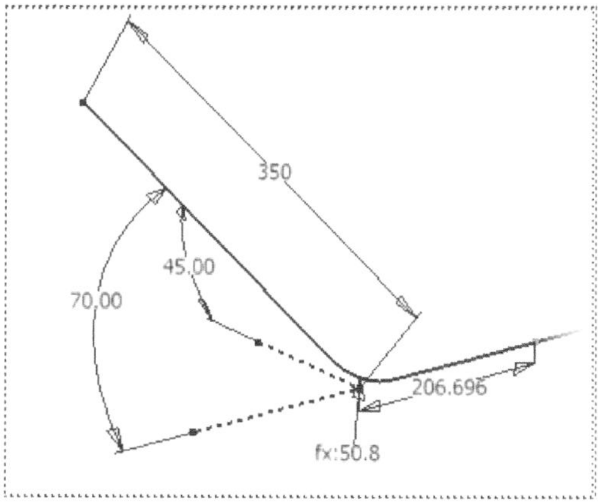

Including Geometry in a Route

To establish precise positioning of the route relative to components in your assembly, you include existing geometry in the route sketch and then dimension or constrain sketch segments or nodes to the included geometry. The constraining to included geometry can occur during the creation of the route or as an edit after the route has been created. If you know the route requires constraints to specific geometry, include the geometry before you begin creating the route segments. By including the geometry before creating the route, you can directly reference that geometry while creating the route, and not have to edit it later.

When you want to dimension the location of a node relative to a work plane from an included face, to create the dimension, you must select the node first and then the included work plane. It is important to note that you can dimension only between route nodes and included geometry. You cannot dimension between a linear or arc route segment and included geometry. You can however place geometric constraints between route segments and the included geometry. Because the route is a 3D sketch, you can place a parallel or perpendicular geometric constraint between a route segment and the adaptive work plane associated with an included face.

You use the Include Geometry tool to manually include any existing vertex, linear edge, planar face, or work feature in the route. When you select geometry to be included in the route, one or more adaptive work features are added as references in the route. The work features are placed in the Included Geometry folder below the route node in the browser. For example, if you include a planar part face in the route, an adaptive work plane is added to the route. The work plane remains associative to the planar face and updates to match any changes in position or orientation of the face in the assembly.

In the following image, on the left, the adaptive work plane is shown in the route after selecting to include the face of the channel. On the right, an additional segment was created and edited to have its end node dimensionally located a specific amount above the included geometry. The automatically created 450 mm dimension on the vertical route segment was changed to a driven dimension to enable the dimension to the included geometry to drive the position of the route node.

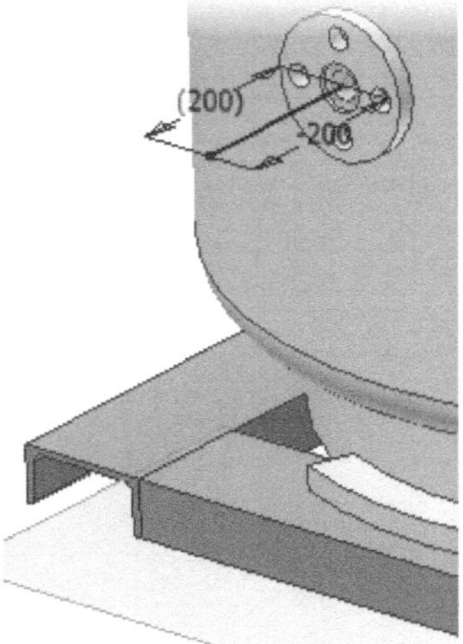

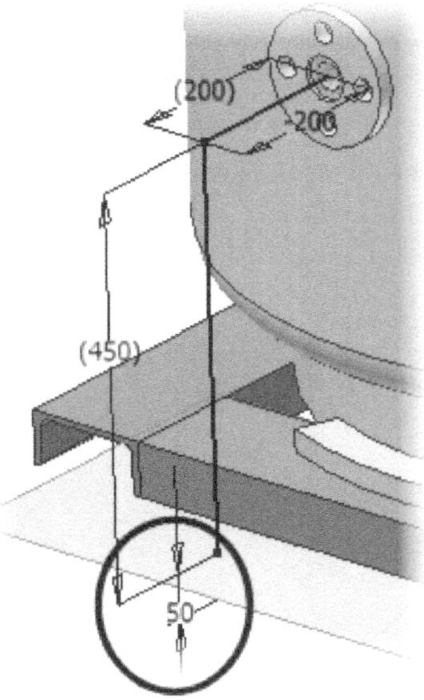

Using 3D Move/Rotate

You can use the 3D Move/Rotate tool to reposition nodes in a parametric region of a rigid route. Edits to a node position with the 3D Move/Rotate tool do not override constraints or dimensions in the route. You might need to delete some constraints and change some driving dimensions to driven dimensions to enable the 3D Move/Rotate tool to change the position of a route node. To access this tool, right-click on the node in the browser and click 3D Move/Rotate.

In the following image, a node in a rigid tube route is moved with the 3D Move/Rotate tool. The highlighted dimension must be a driven dimension to enable the node to move.

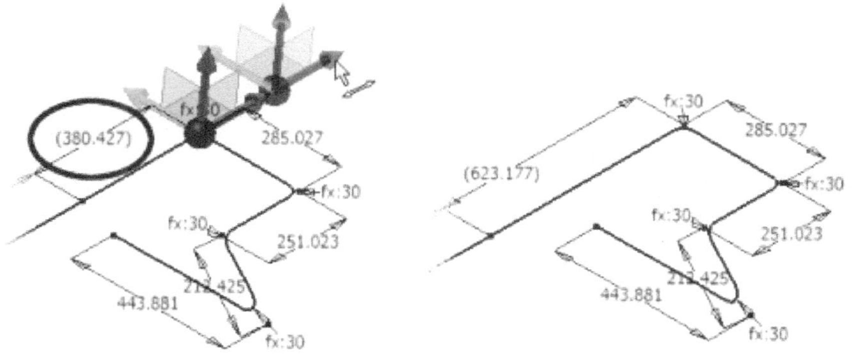

Guidelines for Editing Parametric Route Regions

- Include appropriate geometry in the route and dimension, and constrain key nodes and segments to the included geometry.
- Add only the required dimensions and constraints to meet design requirements. A fully constrained or poorly constrained route can fail to update, or update in an unexpected fashion.
- Add construction lines from route nodes to help dimension or constrain route segments. You can add multiple construction lines from one point to help orient adjacent segments in 3D space. Angle dimensions between construction lines and route segments are a good method to add parametric control for tube route segments.
- Use the 3D Move/Rotate tool to reposition nodes in a parametric region of a rigid route.

Editing Autoroute Regions

You can modify the number and position of nodes in each autoroute region when making changes that affect nodes adjacent to the autoroute regions. To make changes to an autoroute region and have those changes match your requirements, you need to know how to move segments, move nodes, select alternate routes, and convert the autoroute region to a sketch.

The following image shows the drag handles for a route segment in an autoroute region.

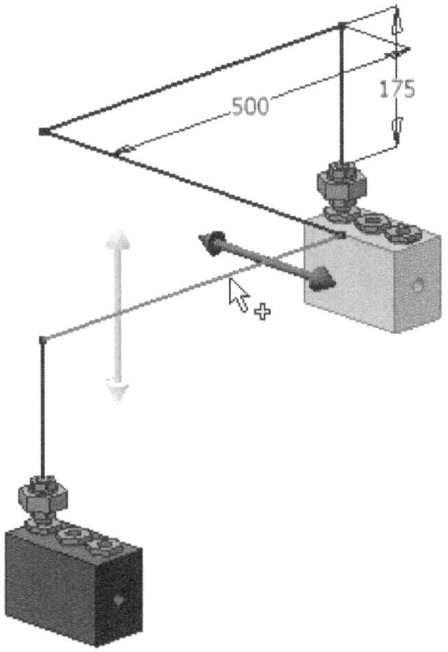

Description of Editing Autoroute Regions

Because of the nature of automatically generated routes, the edits you can make to autoroute regions are restricted to specific types. The nodes at the start and end of the autoroute section and the segments associated with these two nodes cannot be moved. When you edit an autoroute region you can:

- Move a segment in a defined open direction.
- Rotate the direction of movement and move a segment a specific distance.
- Move the node that was automatically added for connection fittings.
- Select an alternate automatically generated solution.
- Convert the autoroute region to sketched route segments.

> You can review and select from alternate autoroute solutions when you are in the route edit mode. Right-click on the Autoroute node in the browser and click Alternate Route Solution. You can use this workflow to remove edits to an autoroute region.

Move Segments

There are two tools you can use to move an autoroute segment. The Move Segment tool is accessed in the ribbon, while the Edit Position tool is accessed in the shortcut menu.

You can move segments only when the nodes at both ends of the segment are free to move. You must activate the route in place in the assembly before you can edit route nodes and segments.

Process: Moving Segments in an Autoroute Region

The following steps give an overview of moving a segment in an autoroute region using the Move Segment tool.

1. Activate the route for in place editing.
2. Start the Move Segment tool.
3. Move the cursor over a segment in an autoroute region. If the segment can be moved, two drag handles display.

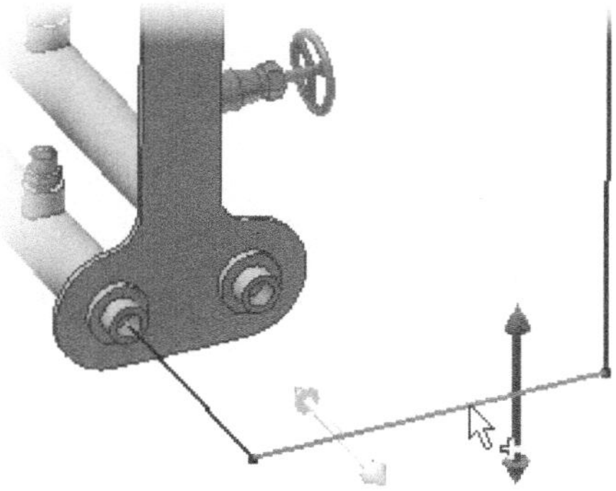

4. Click the segment near one of the handles, or a drag handle to set the allowable drag directions.
5. Drag the segment or arrow. A preview of the revised autoroute region opens. Release the mouse button to move the segment.

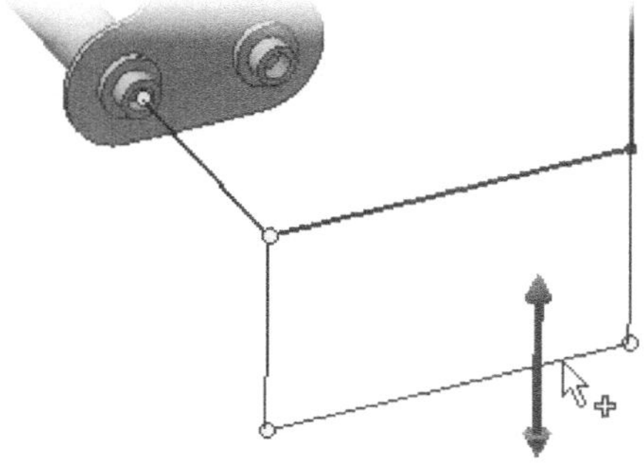

6. After moving a segment, use the Select Other tool to cycle through the route solutions. If the move results in changes to the autoroute region on both ends of the segment, use the Select Other tool to cycle through the solutions at the other end of the moved segment.

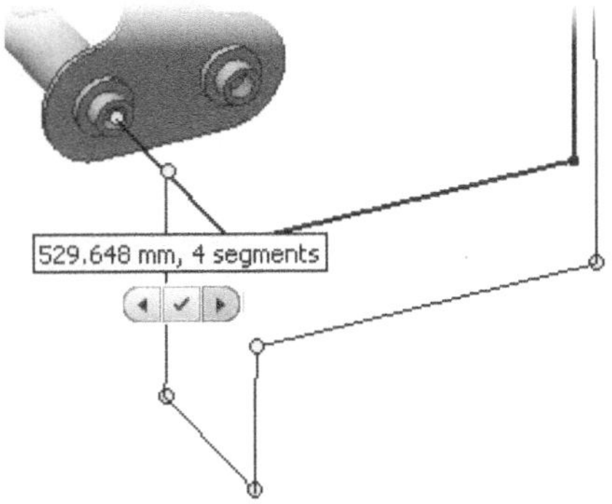

Process: Editing the Position of an Autoroute Segment

The following steps give an overview of moving the position of a segment in an autoroute region at any rotation angle, and at a precise distance using the Edit Position tool.

1. Activate the route for in-place editing.
2. To move a route segment a precise distance, right-click on the segment. Click Edit Position.
3. If required, rotate the axes of the 3D ORTHOgonal Route tool. You can use Rotation Snap to align the axes with points or edges in the assembly.

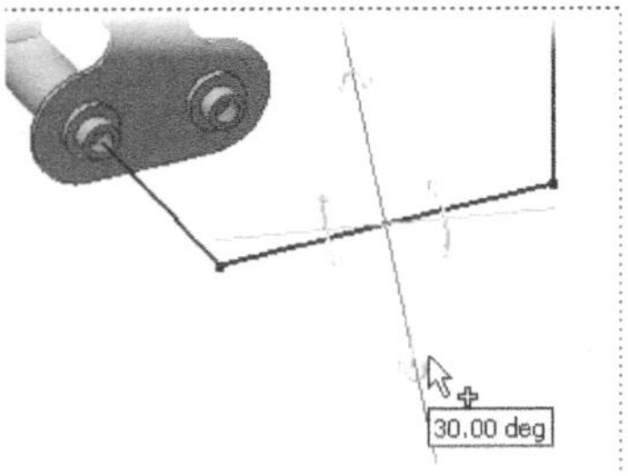

4. Move the cursor over an axis of the 3D ORTHOgonal Route tool. Enter a precise distance to move the segment.

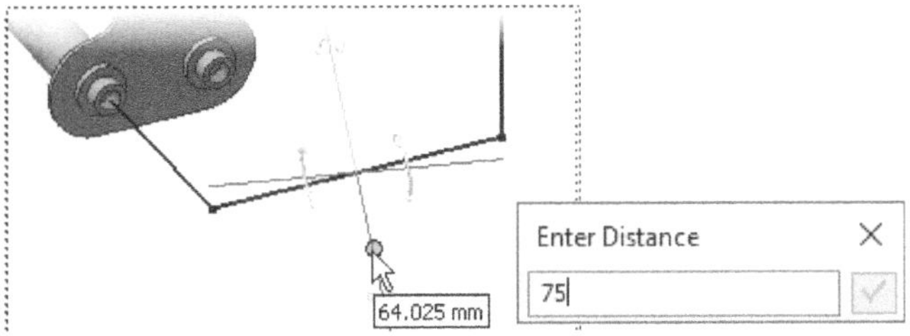

5. After moving a segment, use the Select Other tool to cycle through the route solutions. If the move results in changes to the autoroute region on both ends of the segment, use the Select Other tool to cycle through the solutions at the other end of the moved segment.

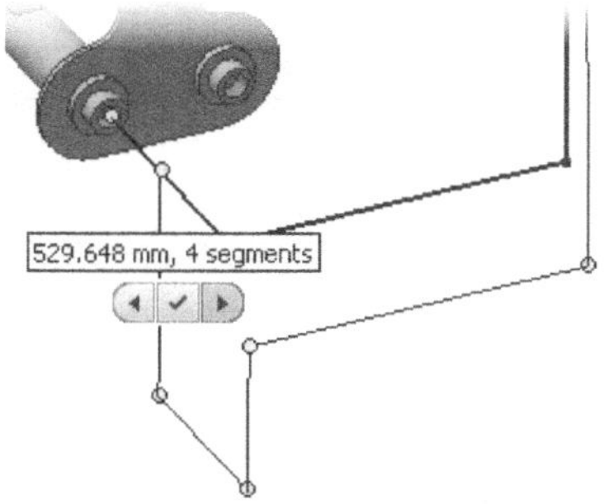

Process: Moving Route Nodes

The following steps give an overview of moving a node in an autoroute region. You can use the following process only to move coupling nodes generated by the tube and pipe environment. You cannot move coupling nodes placed with the Insert Node tool or nodes at direction changes. You must activate the route in place in the assembly before you can edit route nodes and segments.

1. To drag a coupling node, start the Move Node tool.
2. Click and drag the node. You can drag the node only along the two adjacent segments. Release the mouse button to move the node.

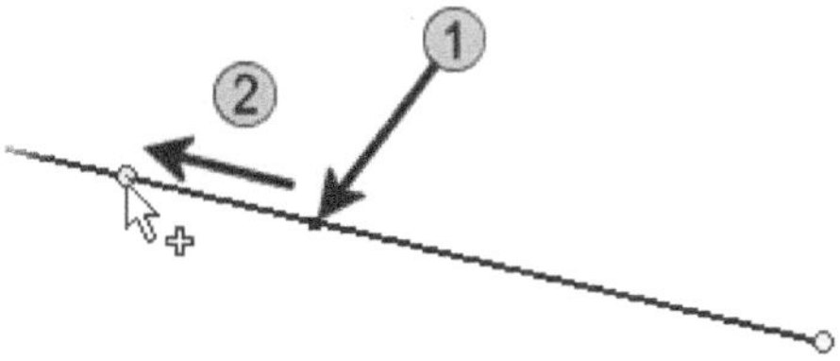

1 Original coupling node location

2 Drag node along segment

3. To move a coupling node a precise distance, right-click on the node. Click Edit Position.
4. Move the cursor over the route axis on one side of the node. Enter a precise distance to move the node.

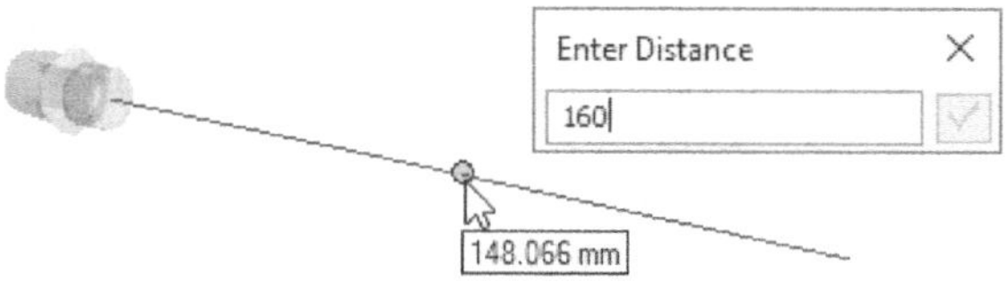

5. If moving the node results in changes to the autoroute solution, use the Select Other tool to cycle through the solutions.

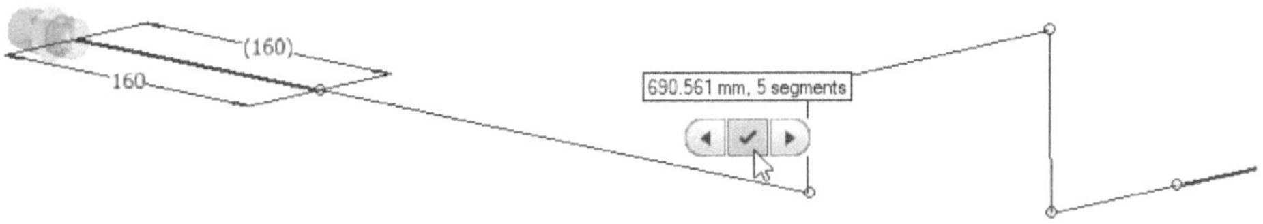

Process: Converting to a Sketch

The following steps give an overview of converting an autoroute region of segments to sketched route segments.

1. Activate the route for in-place editing.
2. In the browser, right-click on the autoroute region. Click Convert to Sketch.

Guidelines for Editing Nodes and Segments

- Use the Move Segment tool to remove unwanted route segments. Drag a segment so that one of its endpoints becomes coincident with an adjacent segment. Any segments between the two are removed.
- Use the Edit Position tool to set an angular direction to move a segment and to move the segment a precise distance.
- New solutions for the autoroute region are often generated when you move a segment in a rigid pipe route. The 45° and 90° elbow rules often cause new autoroute solutions to be generated.
- When you move a segment in a rigid tube route and there are no invalid segments in the preview, no nodes are added to the route. The bends at either end of the dragged segment change orientation and included angle to match the new segment location.

Editing Derived Routes

When you create a route that is derived from a 3D sketch, you cannot edit that route as you would for sketched or autoroute segments. To make the edits to a route derived from a 3D sketch so the route matches your requirements, you need to know where to make the changes, what types of changes you can make, and the process for making changes.

Description of Editing Derived Routes

For a rigid route derived from a 3D sketch, you must edit the 3D sketch to change position of existing nodes or segments or to add or delete route segments. Edits to the 3D sketch affect the derived route. If you change the positions of points in the 3D sketch or delete line segments, the route automatically reflects the changes. If an edit to the sketch results in an angle between two adjacent pipe segments that violates the elbow angles defined in the active style, the elbow is removed from the run.

You cannot edit a rigid route derived from a 3D sketch with the 3D ORTHOgonal Route tool or by dragging segments and nodes. You first edit the 3D sketch to add or remove segments and reposition nodes, and then update the route.

If you add line segments to the 3D sketch or add a bend to represent a custom bend in a rigid pipe route, the route does not automatically include the new segments or custom bends. You can add the new segments or bends after returning to the route environment.

You cannot directly add nodes to a derived route. You must edit the base 3D sketch and add a point at the location where you want to add the node. Because you cannot place a point along an existing line segment in a 3D sketch, you must delete the existing line and rebuild the sketch to include the new point. After you have completed the edits to the 3D sketch, you use the Derived Route tool to add the new lines and arcs to the derived route.

The following image shows the editing of a route that has derived its route from a 3D sketch. The initial populated route stopped at the bottom of the fitting. Two lines were added to the 3D sketch and then added to the derived route. The right side of the image shows the updated populated route with the additional segments.

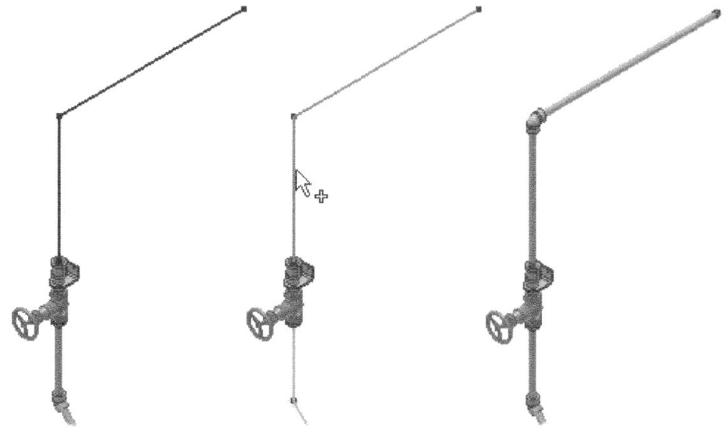

When you derive a 3D sketch for a tube route, if two lines are connected without a bend, a default radius bend is added to the route. If you edit the 3D sketch and add a bend at this location, the default radius bend is deleted from the route. You must manually add the custom bend to the derived route.

In the following image, the default bend radius of the active tube style is 200 mm. All bends in the derived route match the default bend radius. In the middle image, a 100 mm bend is added to the 3D sketch. The resulting derived route is broken at the custom bend.

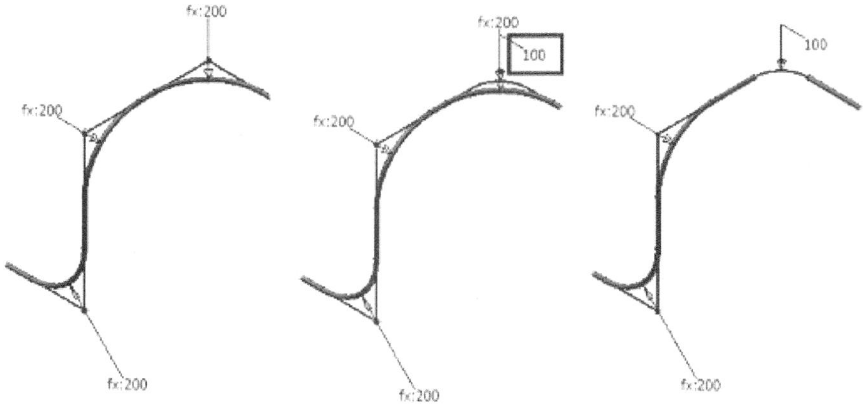

Process: Editing Derived Routes

The following steps give an overview of editing a derived route.

1. Open or activate for editing the part where the 3D sketch exists.
2. Edit the 3D sketch to match your current requirements.
3. If you added geometry to the 3D sketch, edit the route and derive that geometry into the route.

Trimming or Extending Segments

When a tube or pipe route ends at a selected point or circular edge, the length the tube or pipe engages that location might not match your final requirements. To shorten or lengthen the tube or pipe relative to that end location, you need to know how to trim or extend the length of a rigid pipe or tube segment at that open route node.

In the following image, the pipe segment was initially bottomed out in the fitting. To ensure the pipe and end flange fitting could be joined without adding to the overall length of the run, the pipe was shortened to add a bit of clearance.

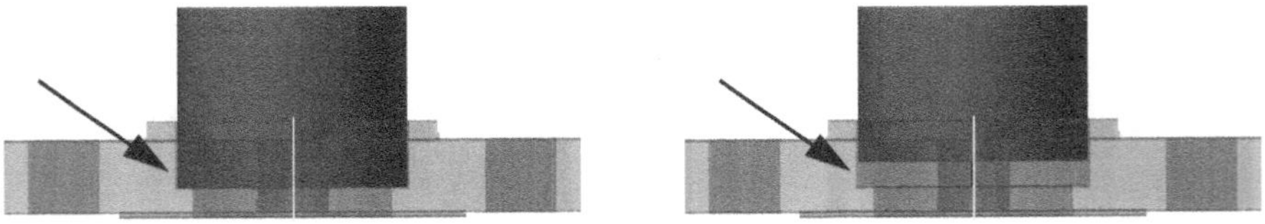

Trim/Extend Pipe Tool

You can use the Trim/Extend Pipe tool to adjust the length of rigid pipe or tube segments at an open route node. You can modify both standard and derived routes with this tool, but you most commonly use it to adjust the length of pipe or tube segments in a derived route to ensure a correct fitting engagement.

You access the Trim/Extend Pipe tool from the shortcut menu after right-clicking on a node at an open end of a conduit segment. You switch between trimming and extending by selecting the corresponding option in the Trim/Extend Pipe dialog box.

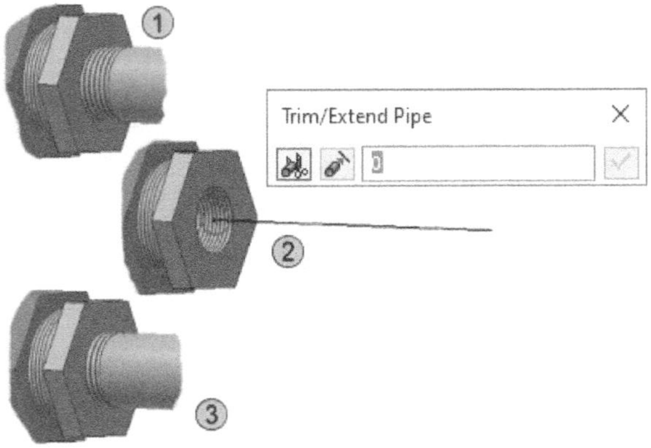

1 Pipe segment ends at fitting

2 Extend Pipe tool

3 Pipe segment engages fitting

> The node is not repositioned when you use the Trim/Extend Pipe tool. The associated segment is lengthened or shortened by the value that you enter. You must populate the route to see the results.

Procedure: Trimming or Extending a Pipe or Tube Segment

The following steps outline how to trim or extend a rigid pipe or tube segment.

1. Set the active style to a rigid pipe or tube style.
2. Create a route with the 3D ORTHOgonal Route tool or derive the route from a valid 3D sketch.
3. Populate the route.
4. Edit the route.
5. Right-click on a node at an open end of a conduit segment. Click Trim/Extend Pipe. In the Trim/Extend dialog box, click either Trim Pipe or Extend Pipe. Enter a value.
6. Click the green checkmark or press ENTER to complete the edit.
7. Return to the run. The associated conduit segment reflects the change.

Controlling Tube and Pipe Updates

When you edit nodes and segments in a route, or edit the position of components in the top-level assembly, the number, length, and position of conduit parts, and the number of fittings, can change. The number of components involved can affect update performance. To increase performance, you can disable updates to all routes and runs or limit the automatic updates to specific runs or routes. To achieve the performance benefits, you must understand the methods and procedures for deferring updates to tube and pipe components during edits.

Description of Controlling Tube and Pipe Updates

There are two methods for deferring tube and pipe updates. You can globally disable updates to all routes and runs in the Tube & Pipe Runs primary assembly, or you can select specific runs or routes to defer updates. Consider disabling all updates when you need to edit the position of assembly components that affect the position of associated route nodes. Disable updates for individual runs or routes to have conduit parts and default fittings along the route hidden and not update as you edit the route.

To globally disable updates for all routes and runs, in the Tube & Pipe Settings dialog box, you select the Defer All Tube & Pipe Updates option. You access the Tube & Pipe Settings dialog box by right-clicking on the Tube & Pipe Runs browser entry and then clicking Tube & Pipe Settings.

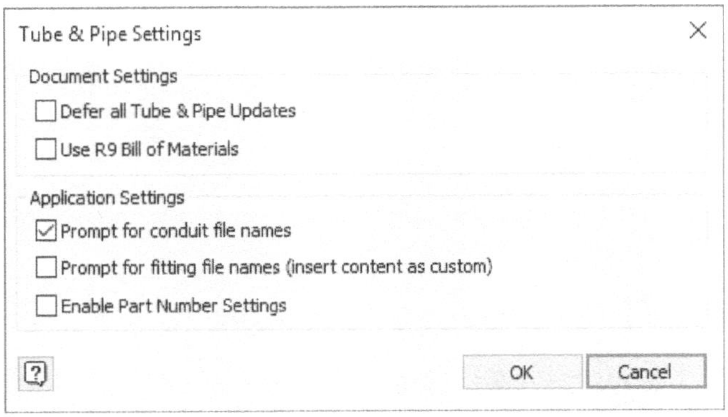

You can also toggle the deferring and updating of individual runs or routes by selecting the option Display All Objects or Defer Update And Hide All Objects. When you set the option Defer Update And Hide All Objects as active, updates are deferred and the conduit parts and fittings are hidden. When set to Display All Objects, all updates are processed. You access these options in the shortcut menu or in the Tube and Pipe tab>Manage panel as shown in the following image. The Display/Update Settings list in the shortcut menu displays when either the Tube & Pipe Runs subassembly or a run subassembly is active. The list is not available when a route is the active edit object, but it can be accessed from the Manage panel under the Route tab, as shown in the image below.

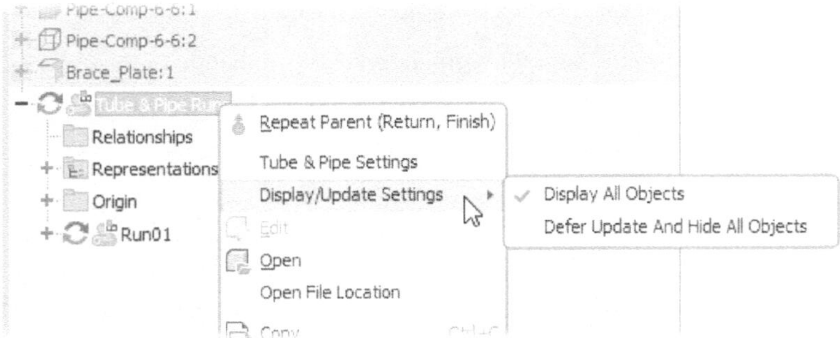

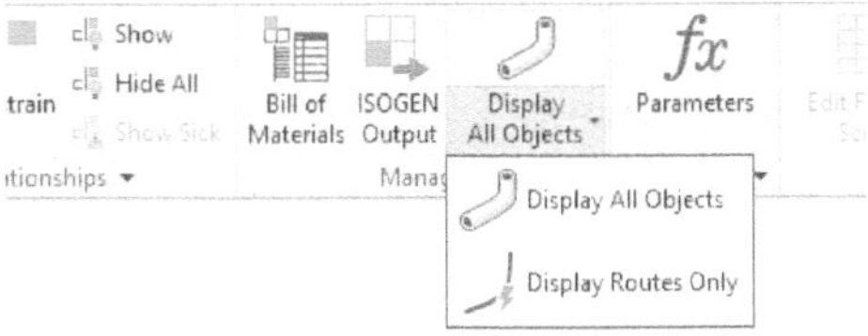

Any content that is set to defer updates has a lightning bolt icon preceding its browser icon. In the following image, the browser entries in a run are shown when the Display/Settings options are set to Display All Objects, as seen on the left, and Defer Update And Hide All Objects, as seen on the right.

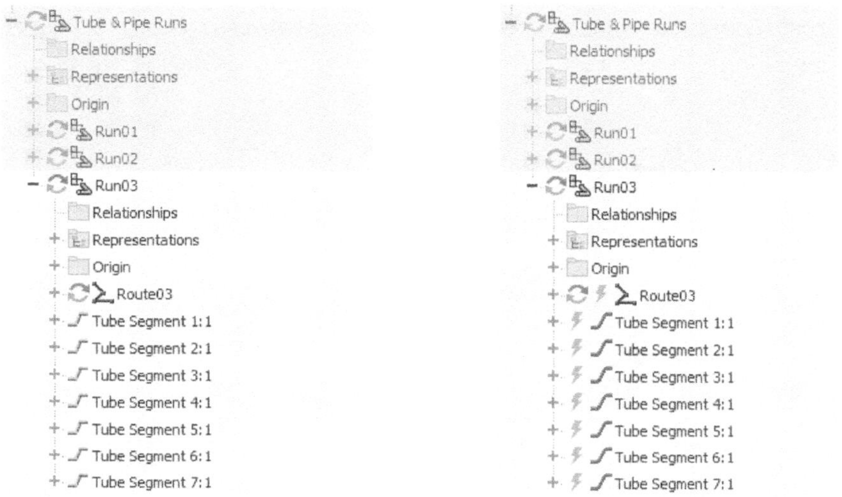

> The Defer Updates assembly setting (Tools tab>Options panel>Application Options>Assembly tab) has no effect on the update of routes and runs in the Tube & Pipe Runs subassembly. You can control updates for routes and runs only with Display/Update Settings.

Procedure: Deferring All Tube and Pipe Updates

The following steps give an overview of deferring all route and run updates.

1. Activate the top-level assembly or the Tube & Pipe Runs subassembly.
2. In the browser, right-click on the Tube & Pipe Runs subassembly and click Tube & Pipe Settings.
3. In the Tube & Pipe Settings dialog box, select the Defer All Tube & Pipe Updates check box.

Procedure: Changing Between the Updating Options

The following steps give an overview of toggling the setting between limiting automatic updates from Display All Objects to Defer Update And Hide All Objects.

1. To change the setting for the Tube & Pipe Runs primary assembly, ensure the overall assembly or the Tube & Pipe Runs primary assembly is active for editing. To change the setting for a run or route, ensure the Tube & Pipe Runs primary assembly or the run is active for editing.
2. In the browser, right-click on the Tube & Pipe Runs primary assembly, a run subassembly, or a route for which you want to change the setting. Click Display/Update Settings>Defer Update And Hide All Objects or click Display/Update Settings>Display All Objects.

Exercise: Edit Rigid Pipe Routes

In this exercise, you will edit rigid pipe routes to a filter and cooling tower assembly. You will edit the position of route nodes and segments to remove interference between pipe segments.

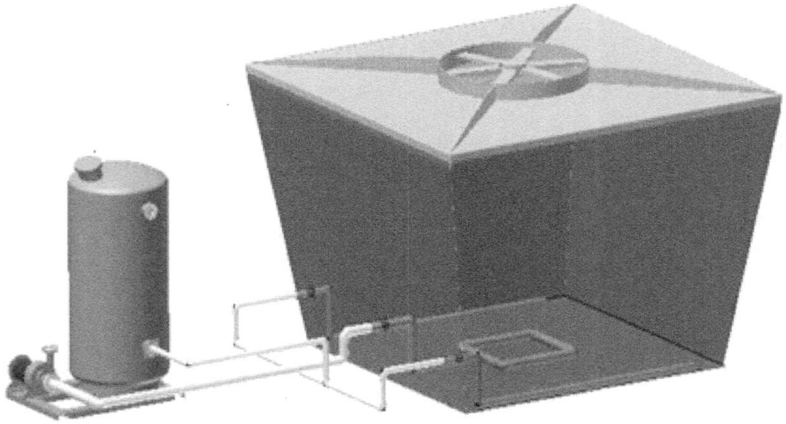

The completed exercise

Edit Sketched and Autoroute Sections

In this portion of the exercise, you will edit a sketched route and convert autoroute sections to sketched route sections.

1. Open *Edit Rigid Pipe.iam*.

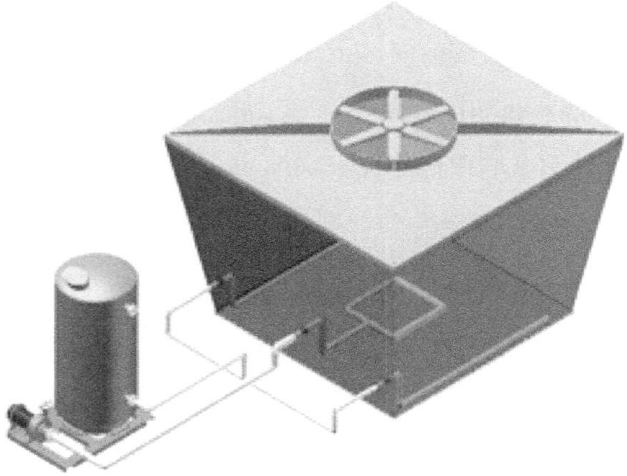

2. Use the Rotate and Zoom tools to examine the runs in the assembly. The 2" cross pipe with the tee interferes with the 3" run from the center of the tank.

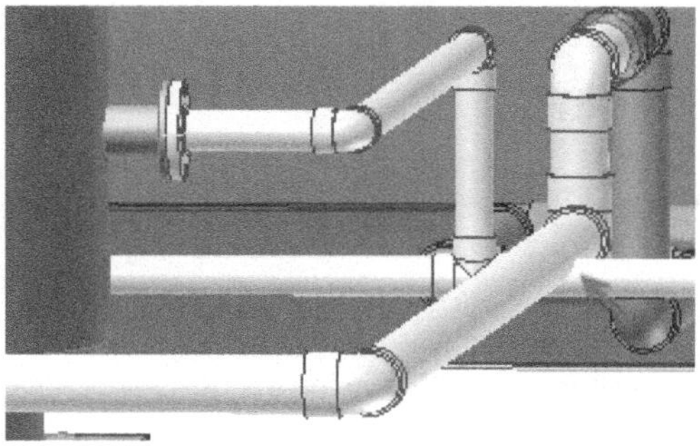

3. In the browser, double-click on Tube & Pipe Runs to activate it for editing.

4. To set Run02 to have the pipe segments and elbows in the two routes contained in the run hidden and not update during route edits, in the browser, right-click on Run02. Click Display/Update Settings>Defer Update And Hide All Objects.

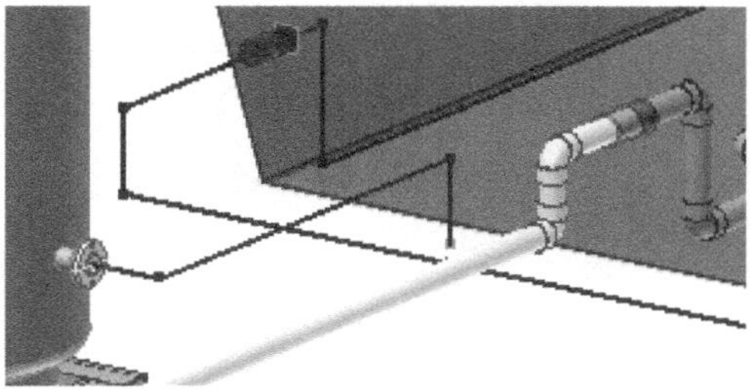

5. To edit Route2, that has both sketched and autoroute sections, in the browser, under Run02, right-click on Route02. Click Edit.

6. To edit a route sketch dimension to see how the autoroute section updates:

   - In the graphics window, double-click on the 286.671 vertical dimension. In the Edit Dimension dialog box, enter **350 mm**.
   - Note how that dimension is now an intermediate node on the vertical route segment and the autoroute changed in an undesirable fashion.

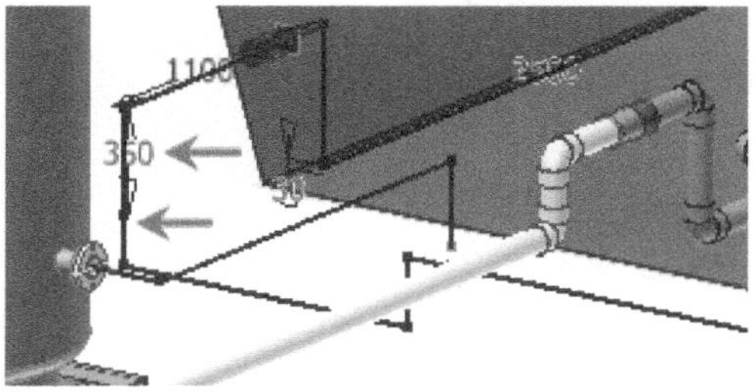

7. In the Quick Access Toolbar, click Undo.

8. In the browser, right-click on Autoroute 3. Click Convert to Sketch.

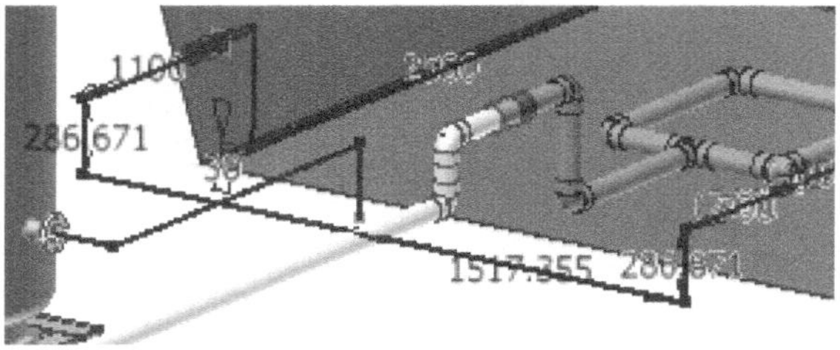

9. In the graphics window, change the new vertical dimension that was added to the converted segment to a reference dimension as shown in the following image. (Select the dimension. In the 3D Sketch tab, in the Format panel, click Driven Dimension.)

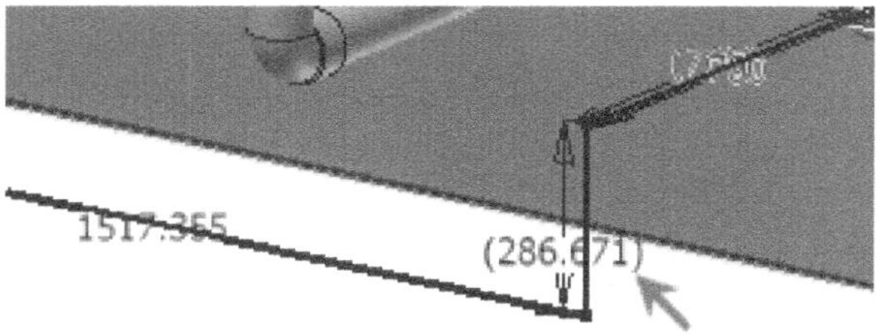

10. In the browser, right-click on Autoroute 1. Click Convert to Sketch.

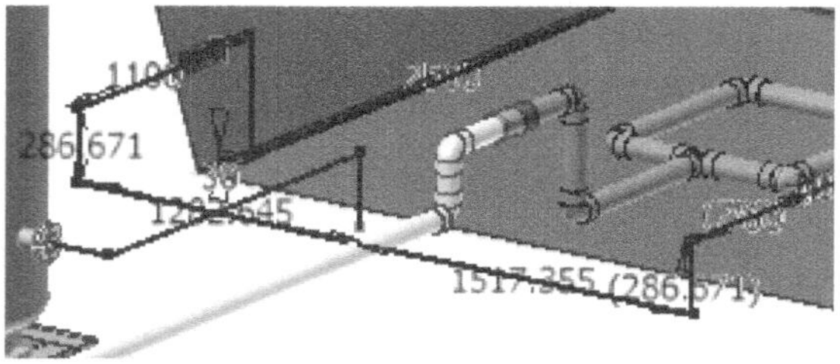

11. Change the 286.671 mm vertical dimension to **350 mm** as shown in the following image.

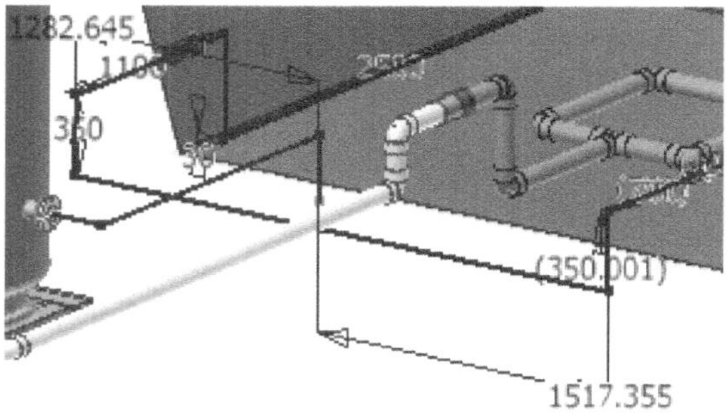

Edit Autoroute Sections

In this portion of the exercise, you will relocate the tee to the other side of the 3-inch route and edit segments in an autoroute section.

1. In the graphics window, delete the two dimensions that locate the position of the tee node.

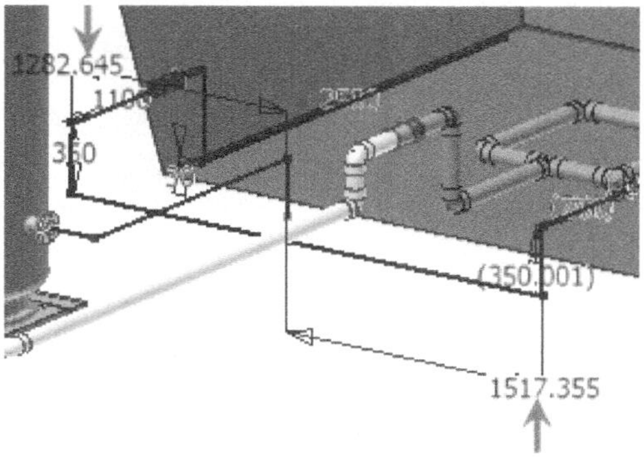

2. To include the location of the flange face in the route as a coplanar work plane:
   - In the Route tab, in the Create panel, click Include Geometry.
   - In the graphics window, click the circular flange face.
   - Press ESC.

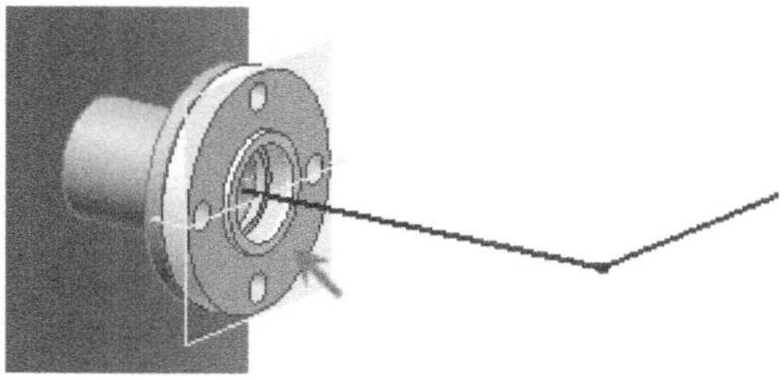

3. In the browser, right-click on Run01. Click Visibility to clear the checkmark and hide the run.

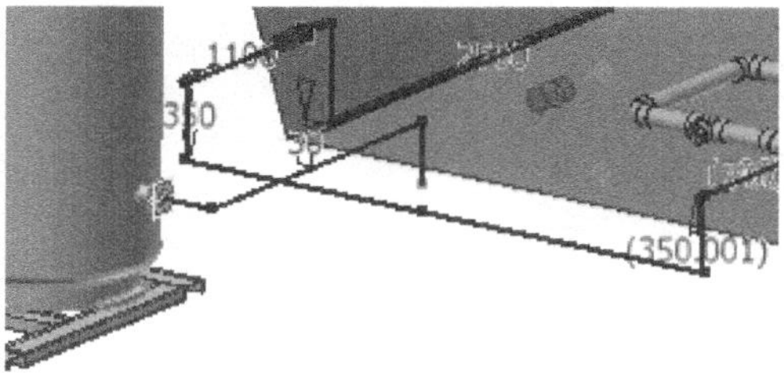

4. To dimension the location of the tee relative to the included work plane, in the Route tab, in the Constrain panel, click Dimension.

5. To specify the geometry to dimension, in the graphics window:
   - Be sure that Driven Dimension is not toggle on.
   - Click the node for the tee.
   - Click the work plane on the flange.

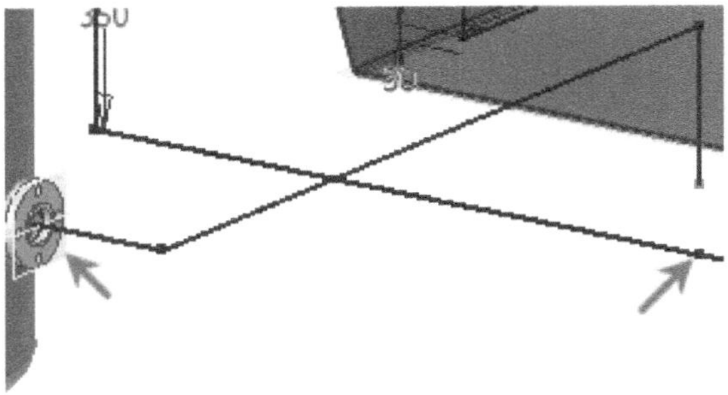

6. To complete the creation of the dimension:
   - Click to place the dimension.
   - For the dimension value, enter **700 mm**, and click the green checkmark.
   - Press ESC.

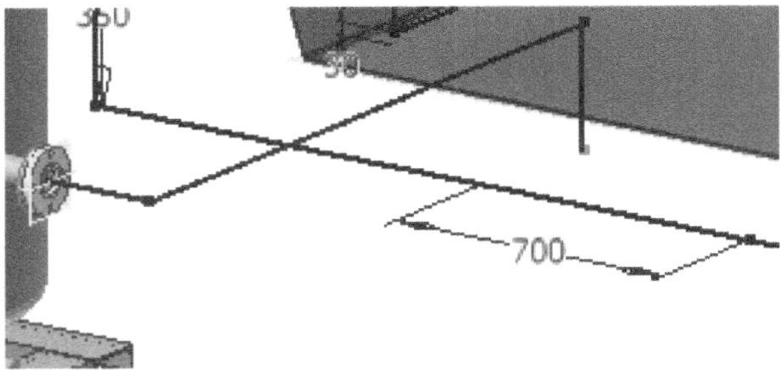

7. In the Route tab, in the Exit panel, click Finish Route. The route segments update. The fittings and conduit segments have not updated at this point.

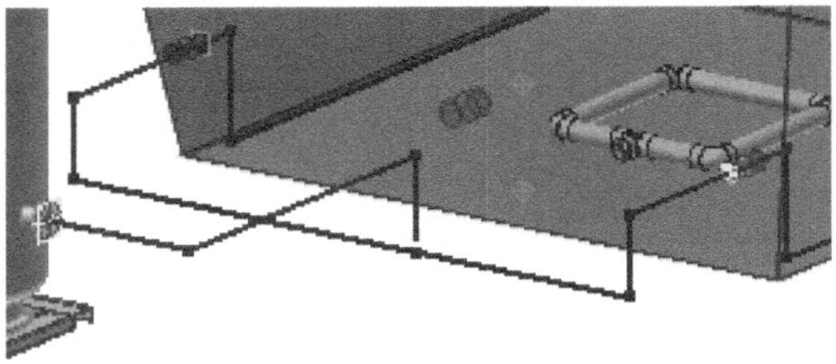

8. In the browser under Run02, right-click on Route03. Click Edit.

9. To cycle through the different solutions of the autoroute:
   - In the graphics window, right-click on one of the route segments from the supply tank to the tee. Click Alternate Route Solution.
   - Use the Select Other tool to cycle through the alternate route solutions. Accept the route solution as shown in the following image.

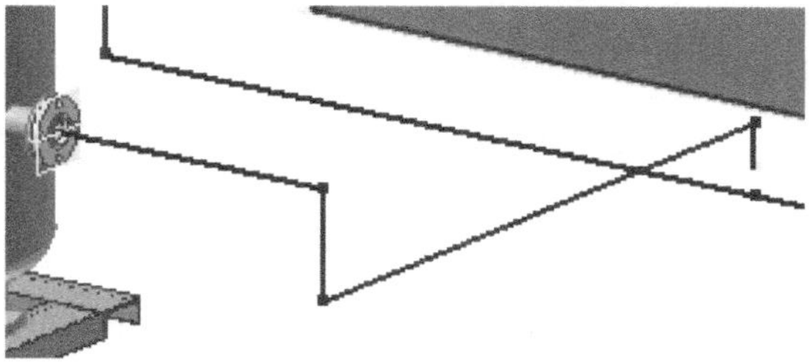

10. To move the long horizontal route segment:
    - In the Route tab, in the Create panel, click Move Segment.
    - Position the cursor over the long horizontal route segment.
    - Click and drag the segment up until the left endpoint of the route segment is coincident with the end point of the segment from the flange as shown in the following image.

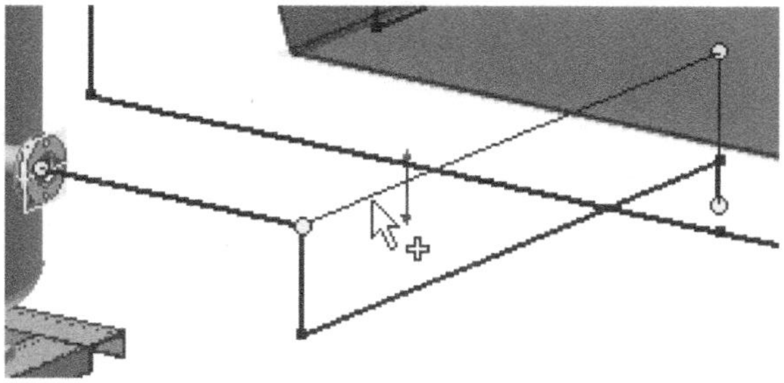

11. Right-click and select Continue, then press ESC to exit the command.

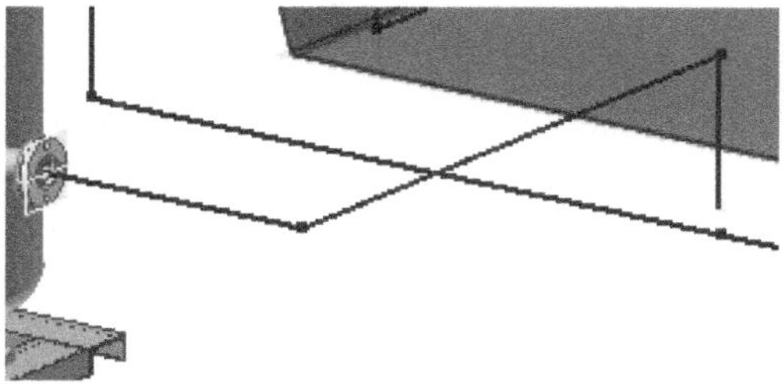

12. In the Route tab, in the Exit panel, click Finish Route.

13. In the browser, right-click on Run01. Click Visibility.

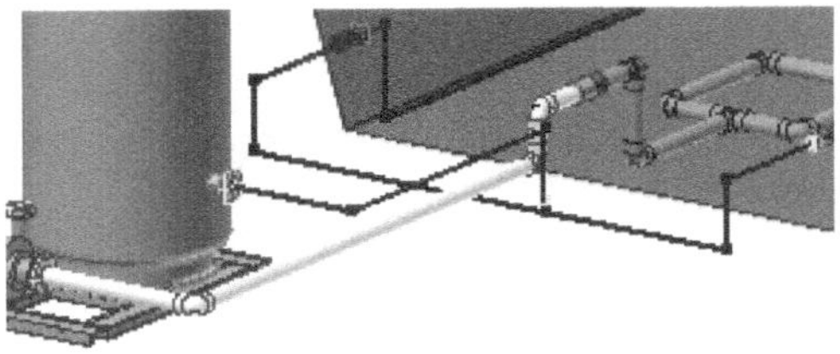

14. To update all conduit segments and fittings to match the routes, in the browser, right-click on Run02. Click Display/Update Settings>Display All Objects.

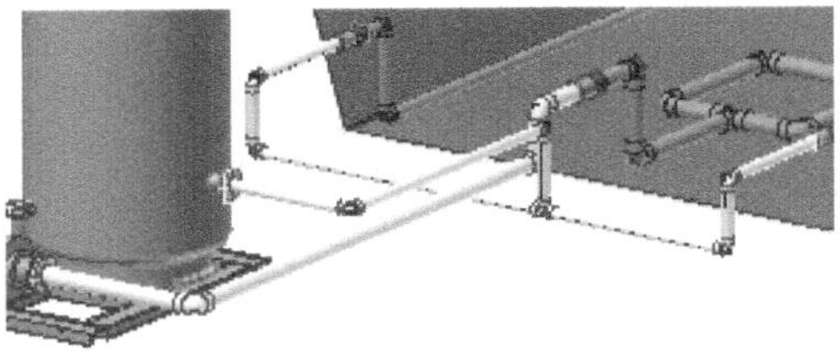

15. Close all files without saving changes.

Exercise: Edit Tube Routes

In this exercise, you will modify an existing tube route to match geometry in the assembly. You will create sketched route segments using the 3D ORTHOgonal Route tool and references to geometry in the assembly.

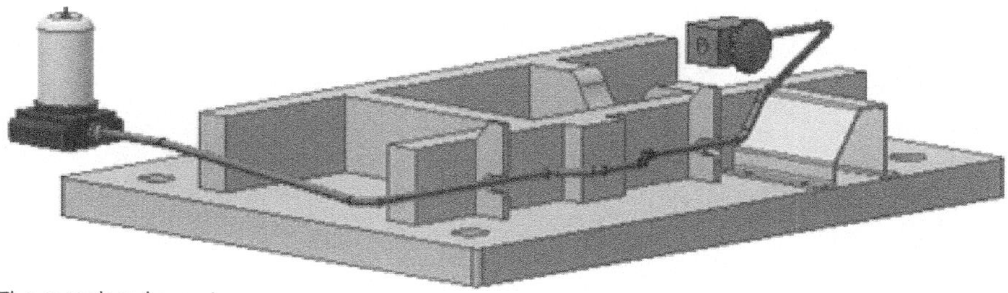

The completed exercise

Edit Route Node and Segments

In this portion of the exercise, you will edit an autoroute segment in a rigid tube route, add nodes to a route segment, and delete a route segment.

1. Open *Edit Tube.iam*.

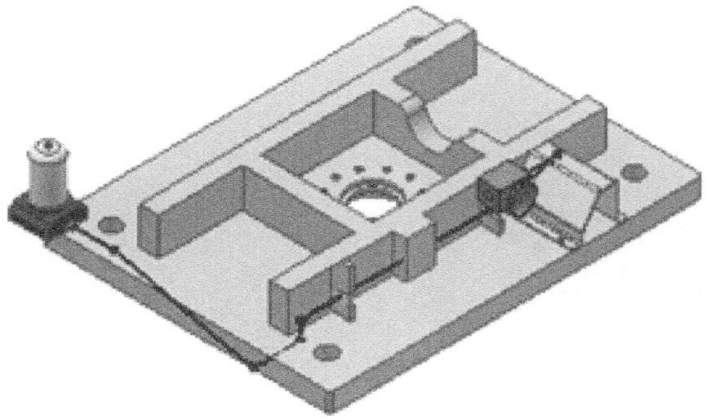

2. In the browser, expand Tube & Pipe Runs. Expand Run01. Double-click on Route01.

   The route consists of two autoroute sections connected by a single line sketched section.

3. To begin moving the segment that passes into the bottom plate up to be colinear with a segment to its right:
   - In the ribbon, click Route tab, in the Create panel, click Move Segment.
   - Position the cursor over the segment as shown in the following image.

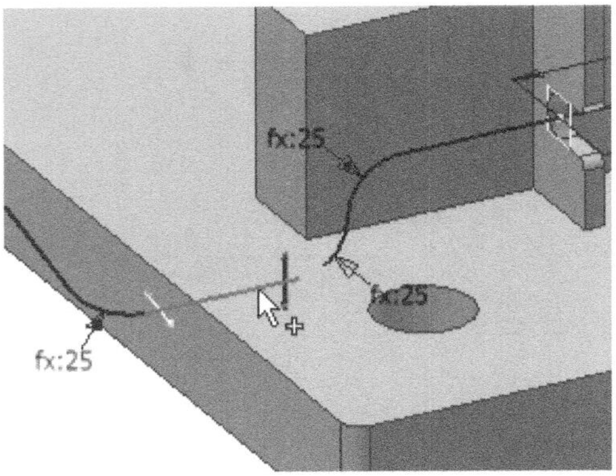

4. While the vertical arrow displays in red:
   - Click and drag the segment away from the base plate.
   - When the preview indicates a new colinear segment as shown in the following image, release the mouse button.
   - Right-click and select Continue, then press ESC.

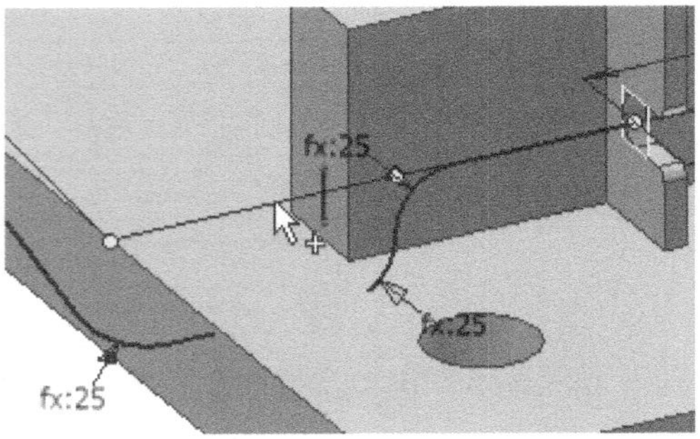

5. In the graphics window, right-click on the node between the colinear segments. Click Delete.

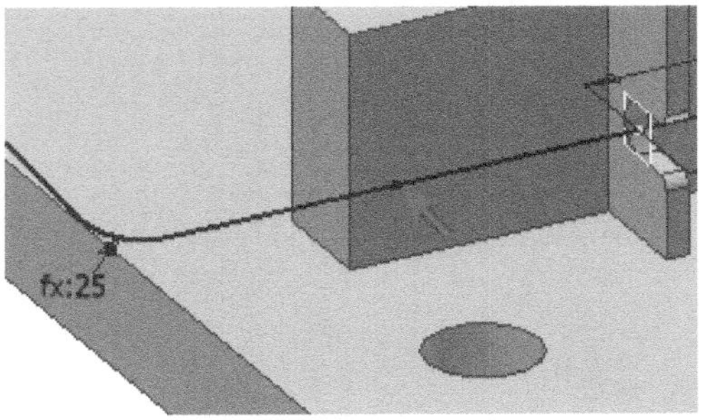

6. To add nodes to a segment so the section between the points can be deleted later:
   - In the ribbon, in the Route tab, in the Create panel, click Insert Node. Click near the identified location.
   - In the Route tab, in the Create panel, click Insert Node. Click near the other identified location.

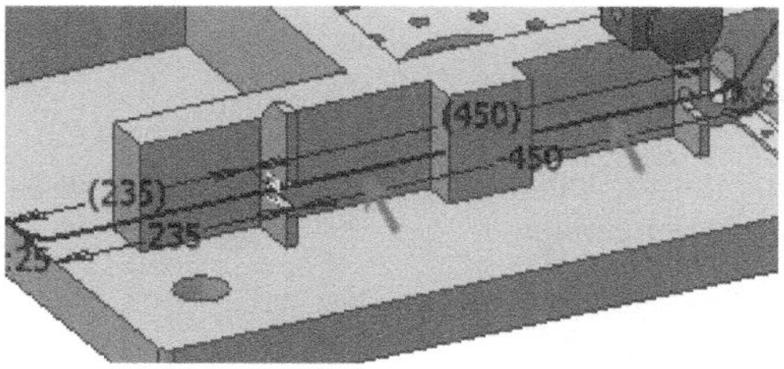

7. Right-click on the route segment located between the inserted points. Click Delete.

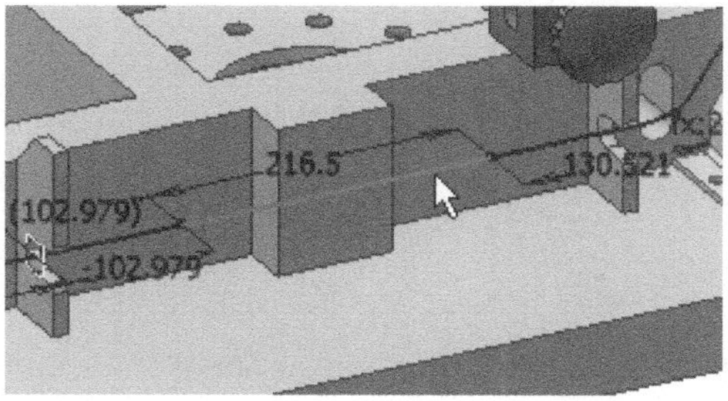

8. To include faces in the route as work planes:
   - In the ribbon, in the Route tab, in the Create panel, click Include Geometry.
   - Click the three faces of the rectangular center as shown in the following image.
   - Press ESC.

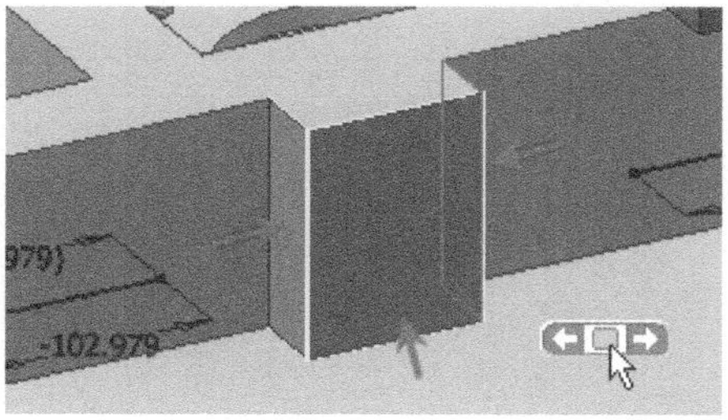

9. Select and delete the dimensions controlling the length of the identified segments.

10. Use the Dimension tool to add a dimension with a value of **50 mm** between the node and the side work plane as shown in the following image.

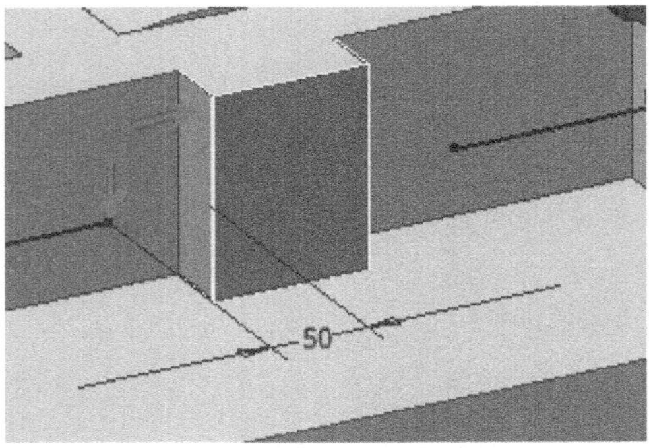

11. Add a second dimension between the other open node and the opposite work plane as shown in the following image. Set the value for this dimension to be an equation (equal) to the previous dimension. Press ESC.

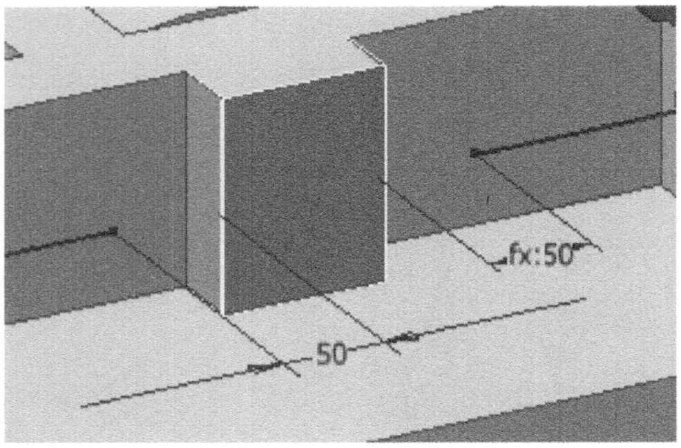

Add Interior Route Segments

In this portion of the exercise, you will create sketched route segments to reconnect a split route.

1. To create route segments to connect the opening, in the graphics window, right-click on the open node on the near side of the center extrusion. Click Route, and click the node again if required to display the direction axis.

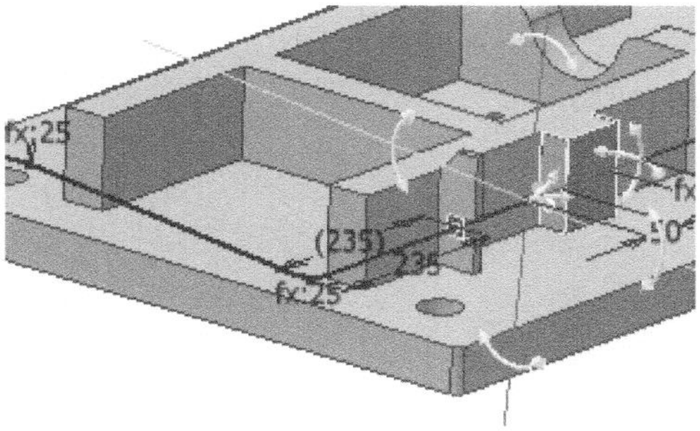

2. To align the blue direction axis perpendicular to the large face on the bottom plate:
   - Right-click on the bottom half of the blue direction axis. Click Perpendicular to Face.
   - Click the large face on the bottom plate.
   - Review the new alignment of the 3D ORTHOgonal Route tool. It displays as shown in the following image.

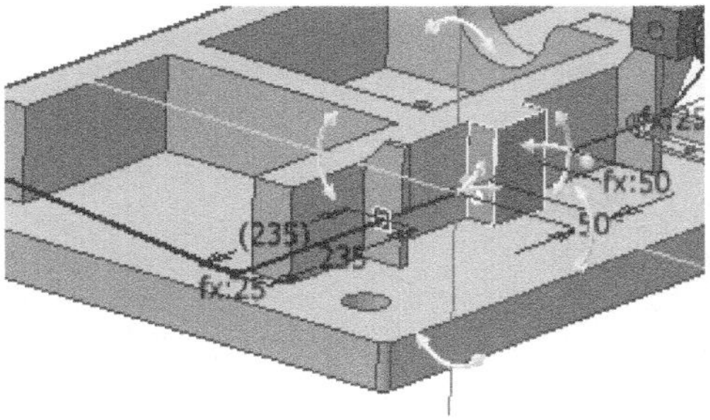

3. To change the route angle to go around the center section, click and drag the identified angle handle until the tooltip indicates a 45° degree angle bend.

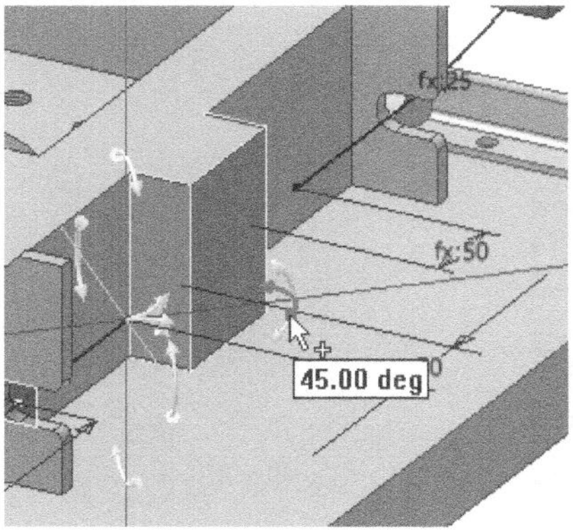

4. Right-click in the graphics window background. Ensure that the Point Snap option is selected.

5. To create a route node at the intersection of the line extender axis and the work plane, click the work plane as shown in the following image.

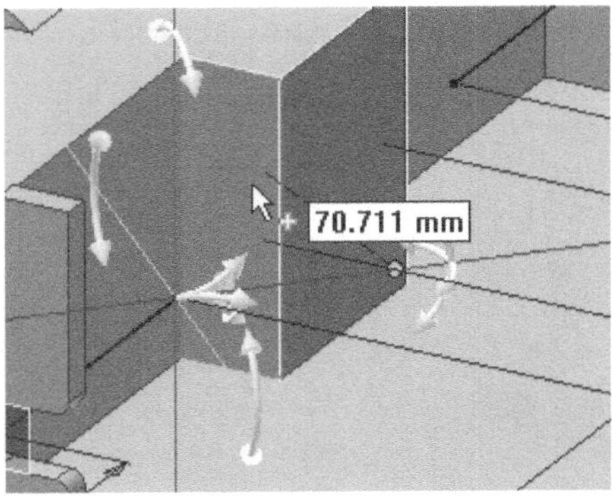

6. To realign the axes of the 3D ORTHOgonal Route tool:
   - Right-click on the red line extender axis. Click Parallel with Edge.
   - Click the edge as shown in the following image.

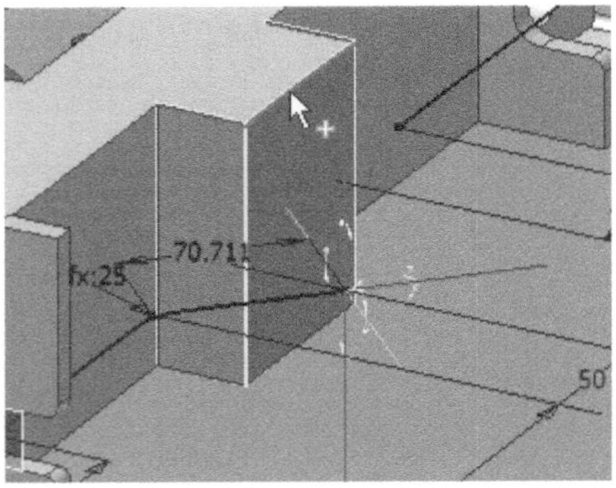

7. Click the other side work plane of the center extrusion to create a route node at the intersection of the work plane and the route axis.

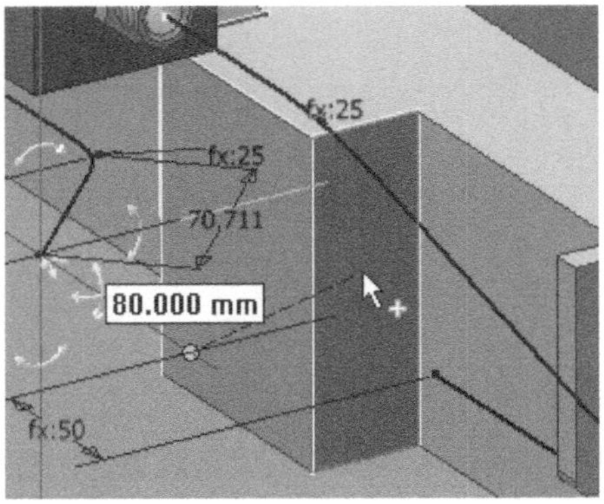

8. Click the open route node on the other side of the center extrusion. Accept the route solution with one segment.

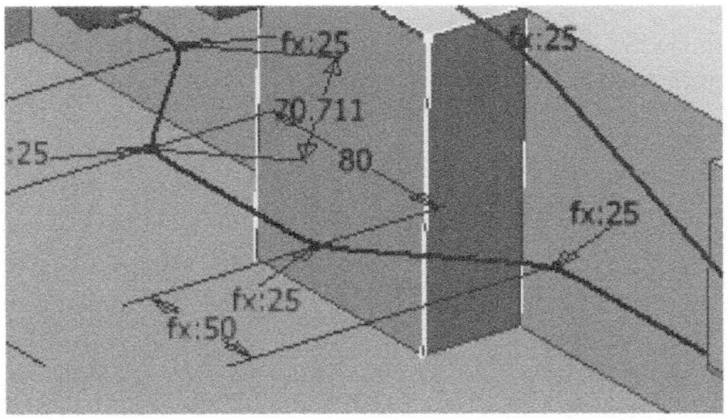

9. In the browser, right-click on Autoroute 3. Click Convert to Sketch.

10. To begin changing the constraining scheme, delete the four identified dimensions in the route: the two 135 angles and two 70.711 mm dimensions.

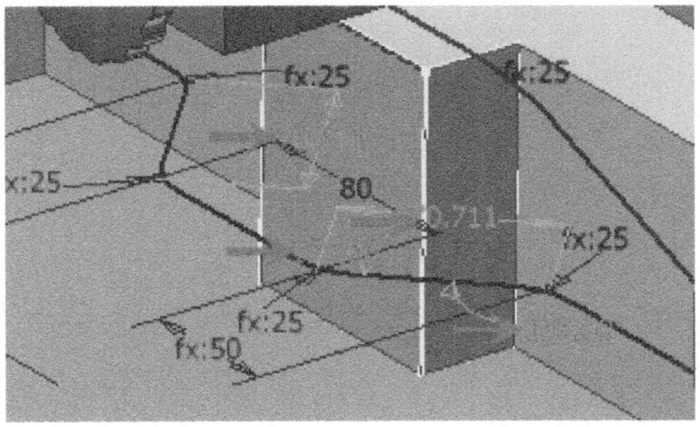

11. Use the Dimension tool to add a dimension with a value of **40 mm** between a node on the front segment and the front work plane as shown in the following image.

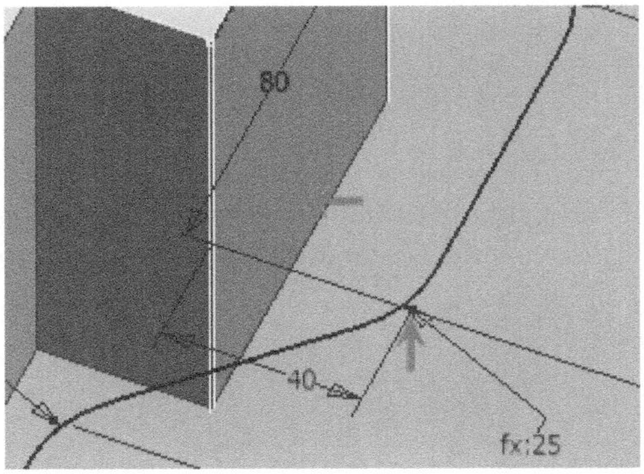

12. In the View tab, in the Navigate panel, click Look At, then click the large face on the bottom plate to reorient your view to match as shown in the following image.

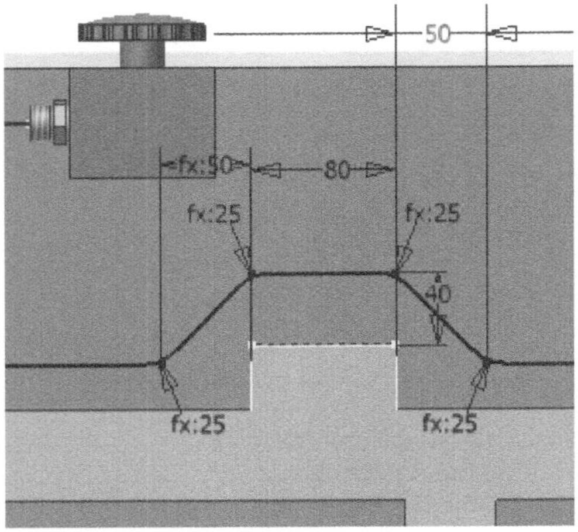

13. To constrain the two sides of the route to be colinear:
    - In the ribbon, in the Route tab, in the Constrain panel, click Collinear.
    - Click the two identified route segments.
    - Right-click in the graphics window background. Click OK.

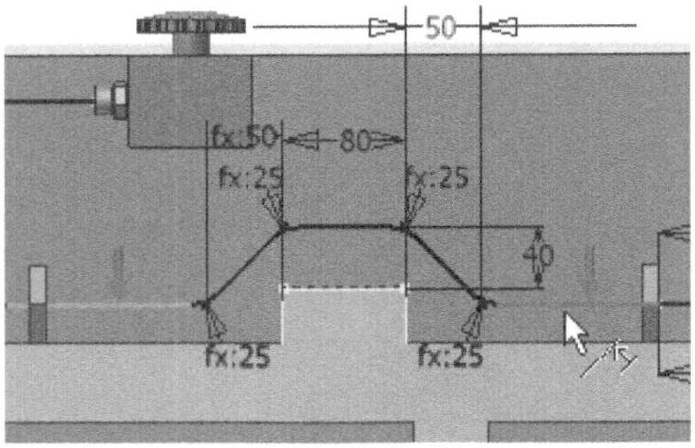

14. To change the offset distance from the center extrusion and view the symmetrical update on the route, double-click on the 40 mm dimension. Enter **30**. Review the change to the route.

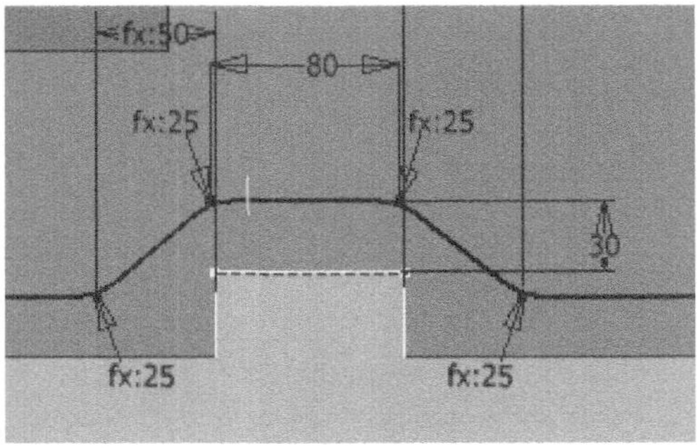

Replace Route Sections

In this portion of the exercise, you will delete and recreate a portion of a rigid tube route using sketched and autorouted sections.

1. Zoom in on the portion of the route near the angled bracket.

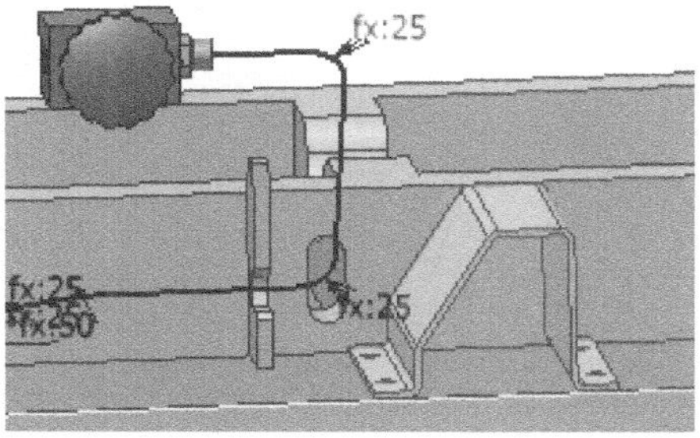

2. In the browser, right-click on Autoroute 2. Click Delete.
3. To include a face on the bracket as a work plane:
   - In the Route tab, in the Create panel, click Include Geometry.
   - Click the angled face on the bracket.
   - Press ESC.

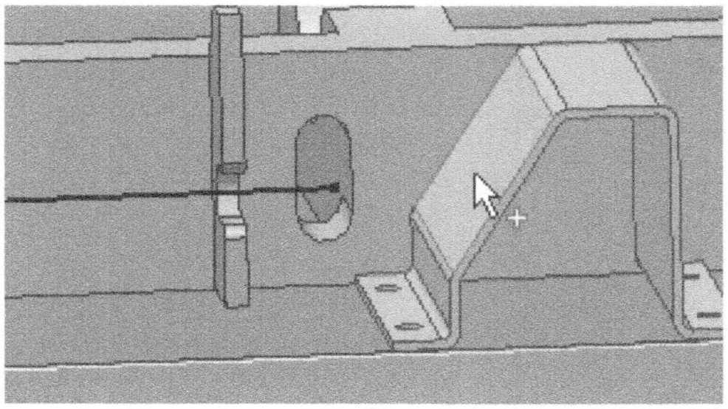

4. Use the Dimension tool to add a dimension with a value of **15 mm** between the open route node and the angled work plane as shown in the following image. Press ESC.

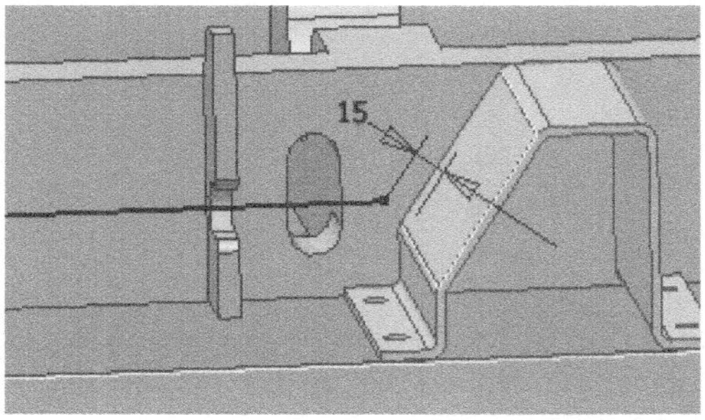

5. To add route segments to the route, right-click on the open route node. Click Route, and click the node again if required to display the direction axis.

6. To align the line extender axis with the angled face:
   - Right-click on the red line extender axis. Click Parallel with Edge.
   - Click the identified edge of the angled face on the bracket.

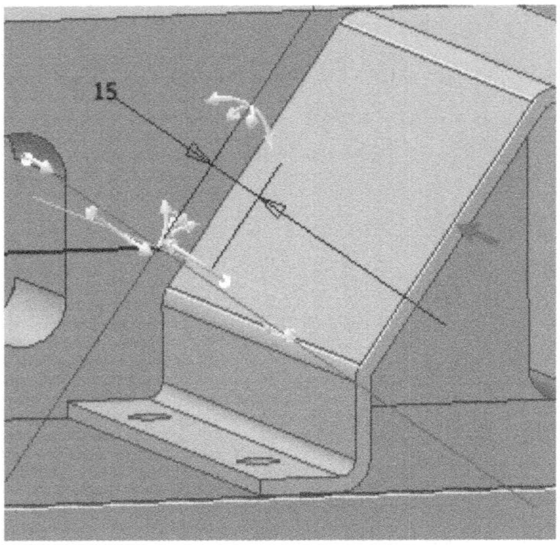

7. To add the next route point while using Point Snap, click the top face of the angle bracket as shown in the following image.

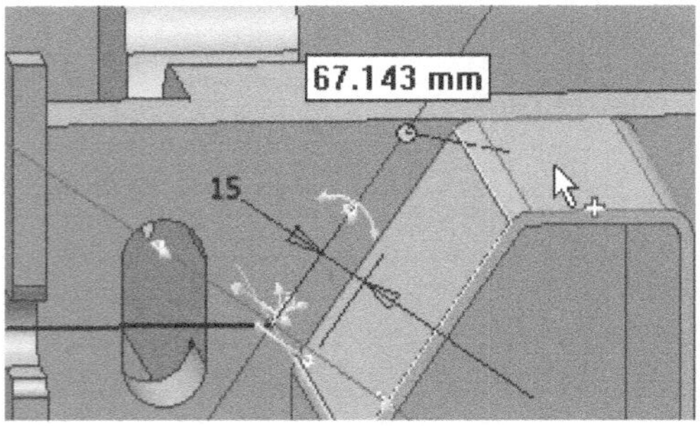

8. Click the connection point on the fitting at the control valve.

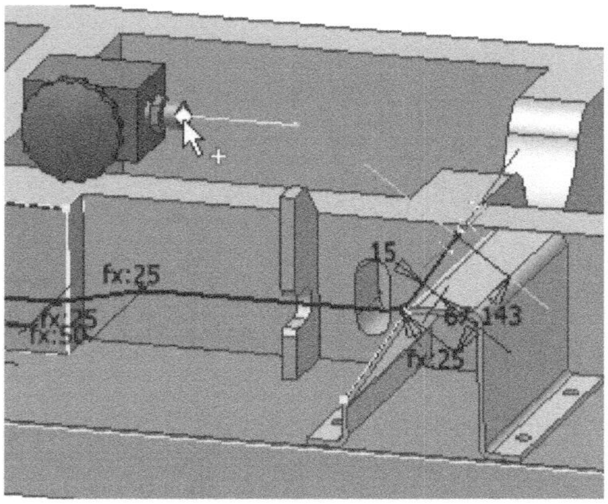

9. Cycle through the route solutions and accept the two segment solution shown in the following image.

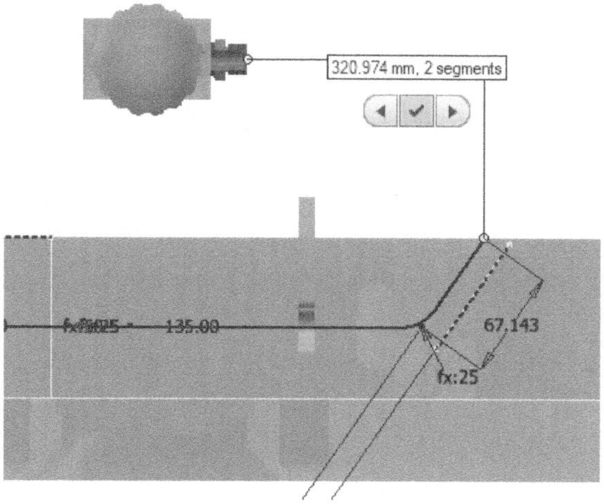

10. To eliminate the coupling from the route, right-click on the route node at the center of the arc edge as shown in the following image. Click Fitting to clear the checkmark.

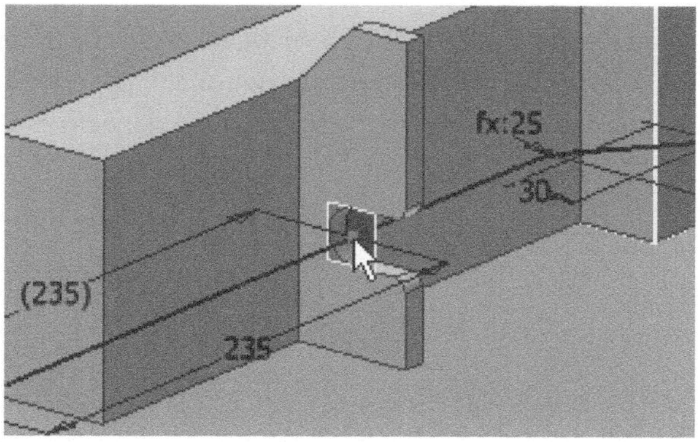

11. In the browser, double-click on Run01.

12. In the Pipe Run tab, in the Route panel, click Populate Route.

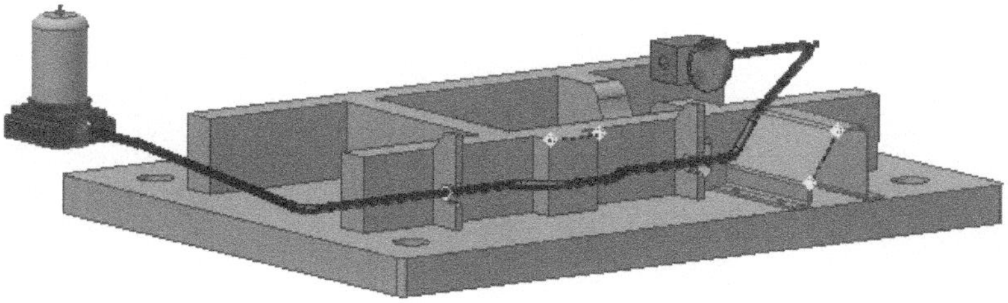

13. Close all files without saving changes.

Lesson: Working with Fittings in Rigid Routes

Overview

This lesson describes working with fittings in rigid routes.

In addition to placing and connecting fittings before creating routes, you often need to add fittings to existing runs. To achieve the edits you require in your designs, you need to know how to change or add fittings and how to apply a different style.

The following image shows an elbow fitting replaced by a tee. A new route is started from the open connection of the replacement fitting.

Objectives

After completing this lesson, you will be able to:

- Describe the process for editing or adding fittings to a rigid route and edit the route style.
- Add Content Center and authored fittings to existing populated and unpopulated routes.
- Change a fitting in a route by replacing it, deleting or restoring it, or changing its size or orientation.
- Apply a new style to a route.
- Delete routes and runs in a tube or pipe run subassembly.

Editing Route Fittings and Styles

A run does not always consist of a single path from a single start point to an endpoint. In many designs, you need to create a run with one or more branches to the path. After you complete a design, you might decide to change the diameter of the pipe or tube used in one branch of the run. To add the fittings to a route and to make the edits you require, you need to know the process for editing or adding fittings to a rigid route and how to change the style used by a route.

The following image shows a run with multiple routes and multiple fittings in the path of the routes.

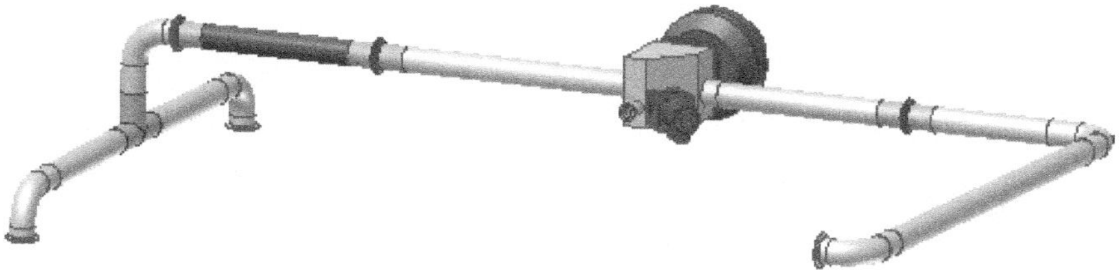

Fitting and Style Changes for a Route

You can insert library and authored fittings into either populated or unpopulated routes, replace fittings, and edit connections and the size of individual fittings in a route. You can place fittings from the supplied tube and pipe libraries in the Content Center, place custom fittings or content that you published to the Content Center, or place authored components that are stored outside of the Content Center libraries. While you can include a standard Autodesk Inventor part or subassembly in a pipe, tube, or flexible hose run, you cannot insert it directly into an existing pipe route. To add the part to a route, the component requires connection information. You can author standard part and iParts with the Publishing wizard and publish them to a custom library in the Content Center.

To facilitate route branching, you can place a fitting such as a tee or wye to provide a start point for the additional route. You can insert the fitting as a new fitting in the route or replace an existing fitting. For example, you can replace an elbow with a tee so that you can add a route from the branch of the tee.

To move a fitting, you must edit the route before you can reposition the underlying route node or segment.

You can delete and reapply fitting connections to change the position of components in the run. You can also update library fittings in a run to a different diameter before or after changing a style to change the diameter of a route.

> You can reposition fittings that have no connections with the 3D Move/Rotate tool. Enter precise values or drag the 3D Move/Rotate triad components to position the fitting.

Process: Editing Route Fittings and Styles

The following diagram gives an overview of editing the fittings and style for a route.

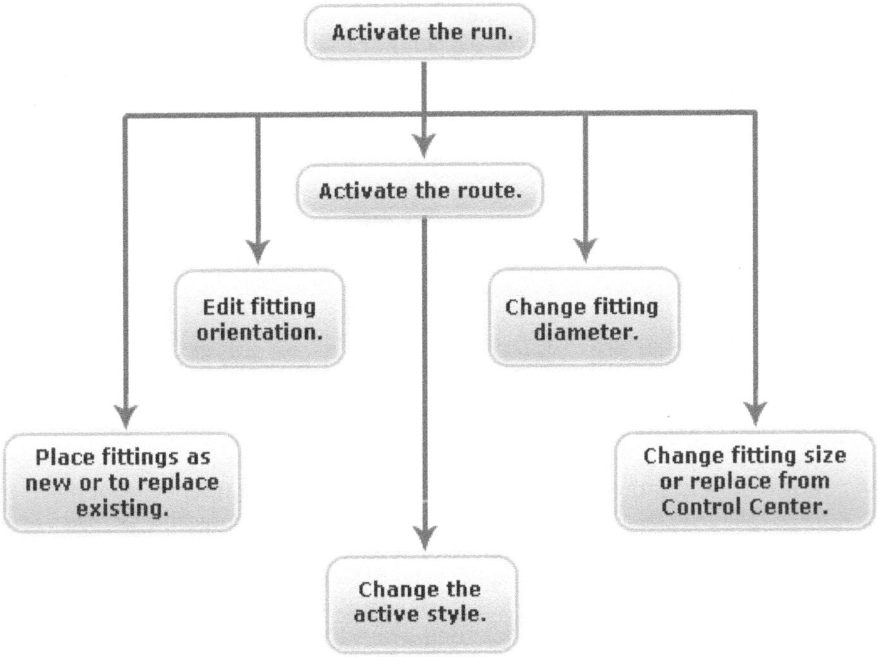

Process: Changing Route Diameter and Fittings

The following steps give an overview of changing the diameter of a route and then editing the fitting connections to account for this change.

1. Edit the run that contains the fitting

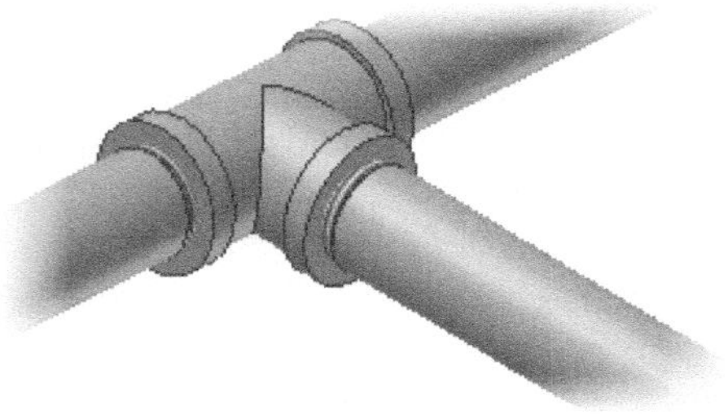

2. Activate the route to receive the new diameter. Activate the new style to apply it to the active route. Return to the run.

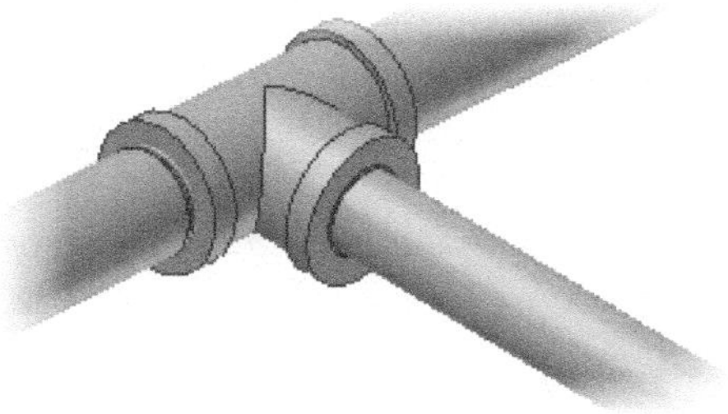

3. Delete the connection on the fitting, attaching it to the conduit segment. This can be done by right-clicking and selecting Edit Fitting Connections or Delete all connections.

4. Place appropriate fitting(s) and connect them to the open fitting node.

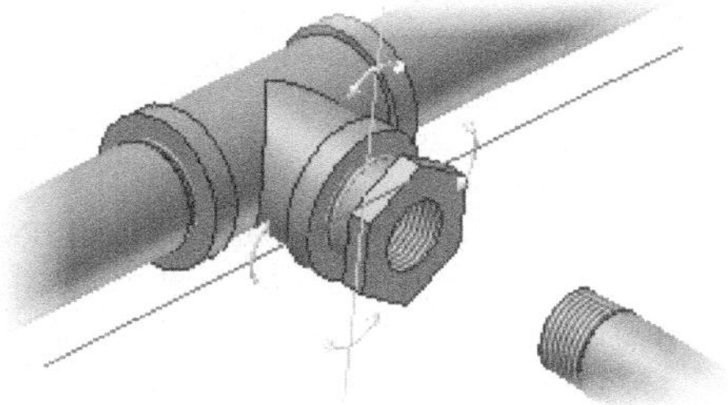

5. Connect the conduit to the new fitting

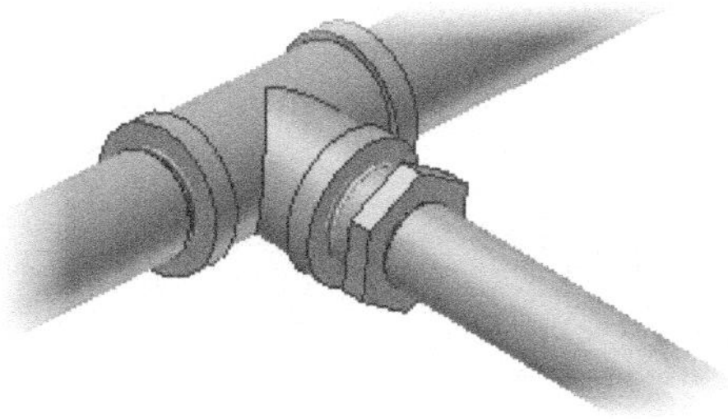

Adding Fittings to a Route

Before starting a route, you add fittings to a run to specify where a route starts and stops in the run. After you have created a route, you can add fittings to the run by selecting locations on the route. This enables you to add gauges, add valves, and split the path into multiple directions. To edit a run and add the content you require, you need to know how to add fittings to a populated or unpopulated route.

In the following image, the populated run is shown before and after adding an authored valve to the route.

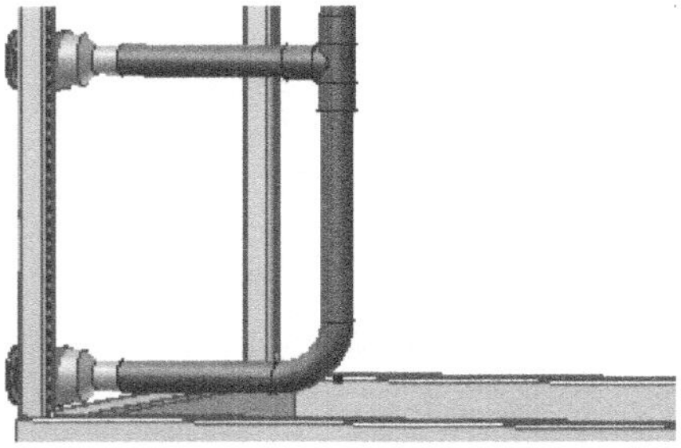

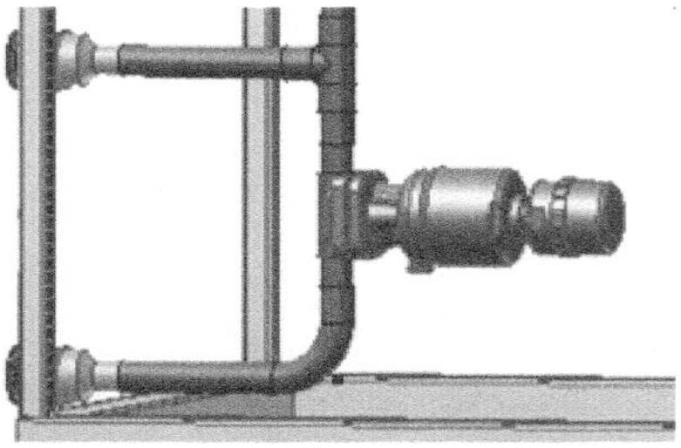

Content Center Fittings

You can insert fittings from the Content Center into a populated or unpopulated rigid route. When you insert the fitting, you drag over segments, nodes, or existing fittings in a populated route. The fitting snaps to the segment, node, or existing fitting to preview its placement.

When you insert a fitting into an existing route, the fitting's nominal size, end treatment, and gender (male or female connection) settings are checked to see if they match the current route's settings. For example, you can replace a 90° elbow with a tee, because both fittings contain connections that are 90° apart. However, a coupling cannot replace a 90° elbow, because the two connections on the coupling are in line and the elbow connections are not. When the settings of a fitting or component do not match the settings of the existing run, a warning message opens in a tooltip, but you can continue to place the fitting. Additional fittings or changes to the route or route style might be required to ensure a valid route.

The following image shows a tee fitting placed from the Content Center. Although the nominal diameter of the tee is larger than the pipe segment, the placed tee splits the route segment into two segments. You can add bushings or other fittings to create valid connections between the pipe segments and the tee.

When you insert or replace a fitting, checks are made on the basic connection information. Checks are not made for other attributes, such as piping standard or pressure rating.

When you place a fitting from the Content Center, the generated part is stored in the Content Center Files location specified in the active project file.

Placing an Authored Fitting

If you have authored a fitting or component for use in the tube and pipe environment and saved it outside the Content Center, you use the Place Fitting tool to open the part and place it in the active run or one of the routes in the active run. The workflow to place the fitting in a segment or on a node is identical to placing a fitting from the Content Center. Drag the previewed fitting over any of the routes in the active run and click to place it in a route. Click when the cursor is not over a route node or segment to place the fitting in the run. The Place Fitting tool is located on the Pipe Run tab. By default, the Place Fitting tool is available only when an individual run is the active edit object.

When you insert an authored fitting into a route, you can specify both its orientation and its angle. To specify the orientation of a fitting during placement, either press SPACEBAR to switch between permitted orientations, or right-click and click Select Orientation. After placement in a route segment, you can drag the angle-control arrows or specify a precise rotation to rotate the fitting about the segment.

In the following image, an authored fitting is placed in a populated route.

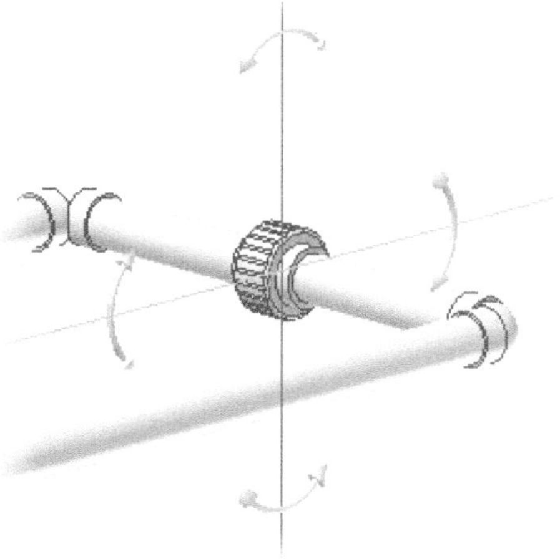

To change the orientation or angle of a fitting after you place it, edit the run. Right-click on the fitting in the graphics window or browser and click Edit Orientation.

Access

Place from Content Center

Ribbon: Assemble tab>Component panel

Ribbon: Tube and Pipe tab>Content panel

Ribbon: Pipe Run tab>Content panel

Access

Place Fitting

Ribbon: Pipe Run tab>Route panel

Procedure: Adding Fittings to a Route

The following steps give an overview of placing Content Center library fittings and authored fittings into an existing run.

1. Activate the run for in-place editing.
2. In the Content Center or Place Fitting dialog box, navigate to and select the fitting or component that you want to place.
3. If placing from the Content Center, select the nominal diameter or diameters for the fitting.

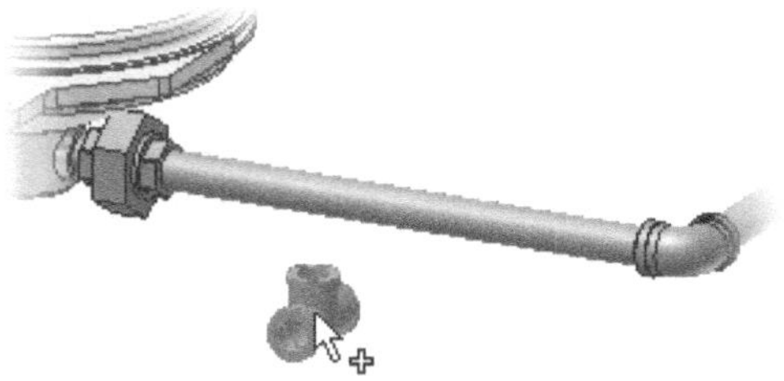

4. Position the fitting over route segments and nodes to position it in the route. Press SPACEBAR to cycle through valid orientations when the fitting snaps to a route node.

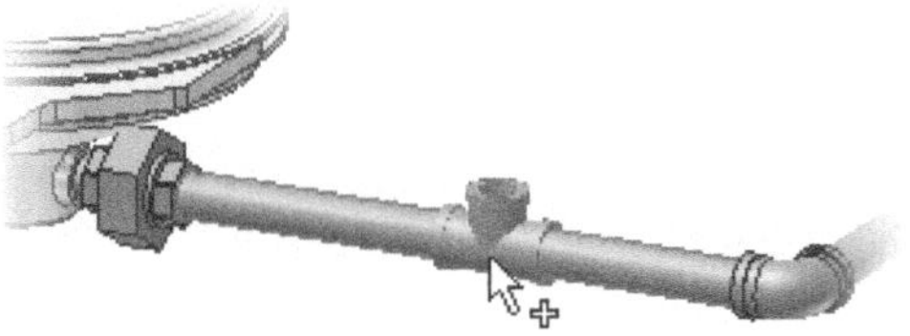

5. Click to place the fitting and activate the Select Orientation tool.

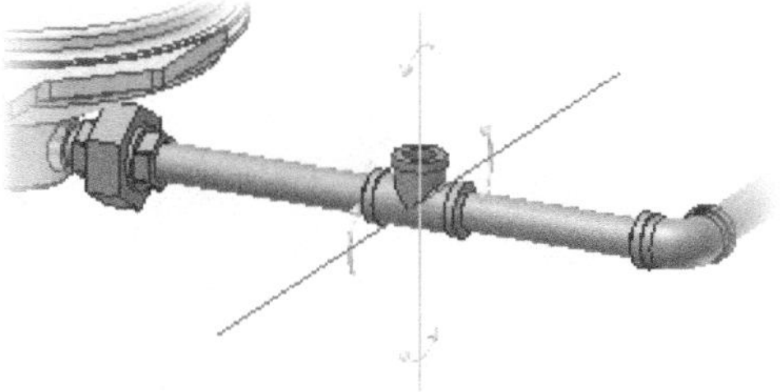

6. Set the orientation using the drag handles or entering a precise orientation angle. You can use the Point Snap and Rotation Snap tools to precisely align the fitting with other geometry.

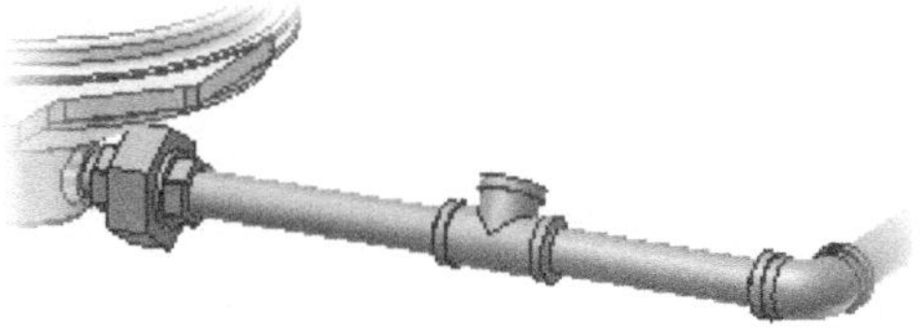

7. Prior to finalizing the placement, you can right-click and use the context menu options to change the size and diameter of the fitting or edit the connections of the fittings.

8. Right-click and select Done to finalize placement.

> You can place a library fitting anywhere in a rigid route as long as its placement does not violate any of the current style rules, such as minimum segment length. You can also place library fittings anywhere in an assembly, just as you place standard parts. However, avoid placing library or authored fittings or components outside of a pipe run, because you cannot restructure their position in the assembly after placement.

Changing a Fitting

After you have positioned a fitting along a route, you might need to change it in some manner. Knowing what types of changes you can make and how to make the changes means you can achieve the final design that you require.

In the following image, a change to the height of the welded frame caused a fitting to extend beyond the top. To correct the problem with minimal impact on the existing design, the orientation of the fitting was changed.

Description of Changing a Fitting

You can make the following types of changes to an existing fitting:

- Replace it with another fitting.
- Change its size.
- Change its orientation.
- Edit its connections.
- Delete it.
- Restore it.

When you replace a fitting, you can replace a library or authored fitting with another library or authored fitting. The new fitting must be a valid replacement. You can replace an elbow with a tee, but a coupling cannot replace an elbow. If the new fitting does not match the gender or size of the original fitting, a warning opens, but the replacement is not blocked.

You can change the diameter of an existing Content Center library fitting regardless of its current connections and the sizes of any connected fittings or segments. Fittings and routes associated with the fitting are not updated to match the new diameter. You must manually update any fittings and routes to match the new fitting.

In the following image, the tee fitting in the left-side image is replaced with a welded branch fitting in the right-side image. A single conduit segment replaces the two segments on either side of the tee. The connection to the bushing is retained.

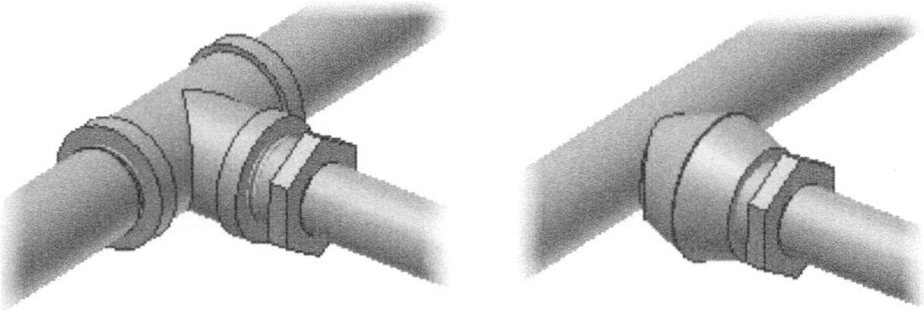

Access

You can change a fitting in two ways:

1. Use the Place from Content Center or Place Fitting tools to place a new fitting on the existing fitting and have it automatically replaced with the new fitting.

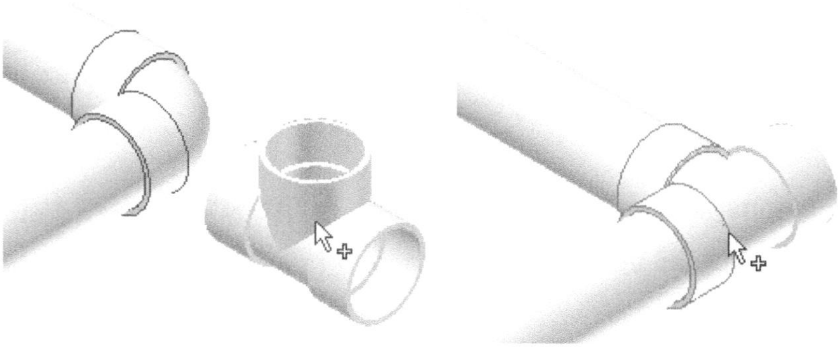

2. Right-click on the fitting in the browser or graphics window and then click the edit option appropriate for the fitting and the required change.

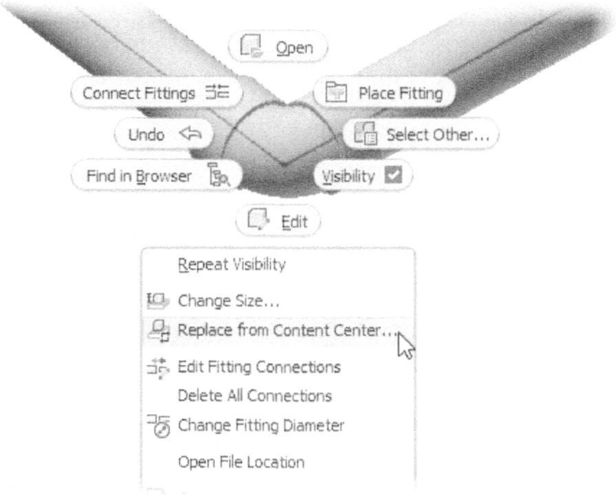

The shortcut menu options for changing a fitting vary depending on whether the fitting is from the Content Center or if it is a placed authored fitting. The options that might be listed for changing a fitting are:

- Change Size
- Replace from Content Center
- Edit Fitting Orientation
- Delete
- Restore Fitting
- Change Fitting Diameter

Procedure: Replacing with a New Placed Fitting

The following steps give an overview of replacing a fitting in a rigid route when placing a fitting into a run.

1. Activate the run containing the fitting to be replaced.
2. Select the new fitting. You can select a new fitting from the Content Center, or a different authored fitting.
3. Insert the fitting. Position the new fitting on the existing fitting.
4. Press SPACEBAR to cycle through available fitting orientations. Drag a rotation handle or enter a precise rotation value to rotate the new fitting.

Procedure: Replacing Content Center Library Fittings

The following steps give an overview of replacing a single or all instances of a Content Center library fitting in a run.

1. Activate the run containing the fitting or fittings to be replaced.
2. Right-click on the fitting in the active run. Click Replace from Content Center.
3. In the Content Center, select the replacement fitting family. Click OK.
4. In the Content Center family dialog box, specify the nominal size or sizes for the replacement fitting. To replace all instances of the fitting in the active run, select Replace All.
5. Click OK to replace the fitting(s). The orientation and angle of the replacement fittings match the original fittings.

Procedure: Restoring Elbows or Couplings

The following steps give an overview of restoring an elbow or coupling that you previously replaced with another fitting.

1. Right-click on the replacement fitting. Click Restore Fitting.
2. You might need to make additional edits to routes or fittings to create valid routes.

Applying a New Style

When you create a run, typically all of the routes in the run are the same style of tube or pipe. In some situations, you might want to change the style for a specific route in a run. For example, you might want to have a route be a different diameter tube or pipe from the other routes. To apply a new style to a route, you need to know where and how this is done.

In the following image, the bypass route was changed from using the diameter of the main line to a smaller diameter by selecting a different style defined with a smaller diameter. Additional fittings were inserted to transition the diameters from one value to the other.

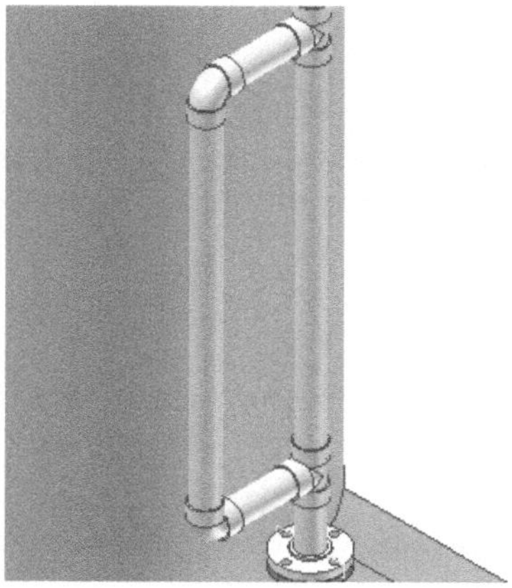

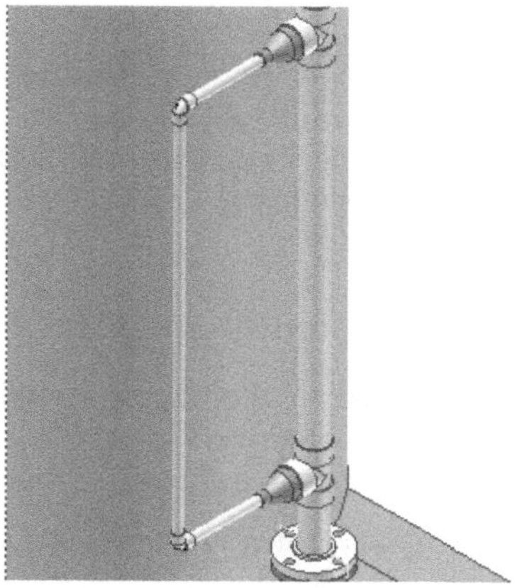

Changing the Style for a Route

The most common reasons that you change the style for a route are to set a different nominal diameter for the route or to change the rules for creating the route. When you change the style of a route, elbows and couplings are automatically updated to match the new size. Fittings placed from the Content Center or as authored fittings require manual edits of their diameters. When you change the style of a route, you can select styles only for rigid pipes or tubes. You cannot switch from a style for a rigid pipe or tube to a style for a flexible hose. So for example, if the route's initial style is for a rigid pipe, you can select a different style for a rigid pipe or a rigid tube.

To change a route from one style to another, the style you want the route to use must first exist. For every style variation you want to use in a design, you must have a unique style created. So if you want to use the same type of pipe but in different diameters, you need a style for each diameter.

> Use caution if you are going to make changes to a style. A change to a style affects all routes defined by the style. Instead of directly editing an existing style, copy the existing style and make changes to the new style.

Procedure: Changing Styles for a Route

The following steps give an overview of changing the active style for a specific route in a run.

1. Activate the route for editing in place.
2. In the Route tab, in the Manage panel, in the styles list, select the style to be active for the route.

Deleting Routes and Runs

As you create a design, you might decide that a route, a run, or the entire Tube & Pipe Runs subassembly does not reflect your design intentions. Instead of editing what you have already created, you might want to delete the route, run, or primary tube and pipe assembly. To delete the content as you intend, you need to know what environment needs to be active and where to initiate the delete.

Description of Deleting Routes and Runs

To delete a run, you edit the Tube & Pipe Runs subassembly and delete the run subassembly. To delete the entire Tube & Pipe Runs subassembly, delete it from the top-level assembly. A new Tube & Pipe Runs subassembly is generated when you create a new run.

You can also delete individual routes in a run. To delete a route, edit the run that contains the route. In the browser, right-click on the route and click Delete Route. You can delete the route segments and all fittings in the route, or you can delete the route segments but leave the fittings. If you delete the segments only, the fittings remain in the parent run.

Exercise: Place and Edit Fittings

In this exercise, you will place fittings from the Content Center into existing routes. You will build a route between placed fittings and replace a fitting in a route.

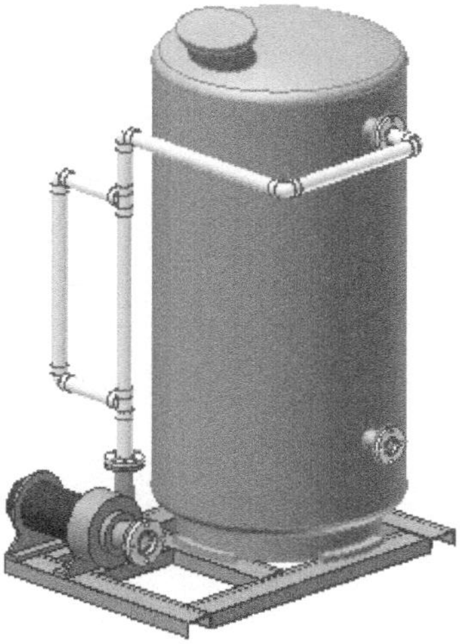

The completed exercise

Place Fittings

In this portion of the exercise, you will place library fittings in both populated and unpopulated routes. You will create a new route between the placed fittings.

1. Open *Edit Fittings.iam*.

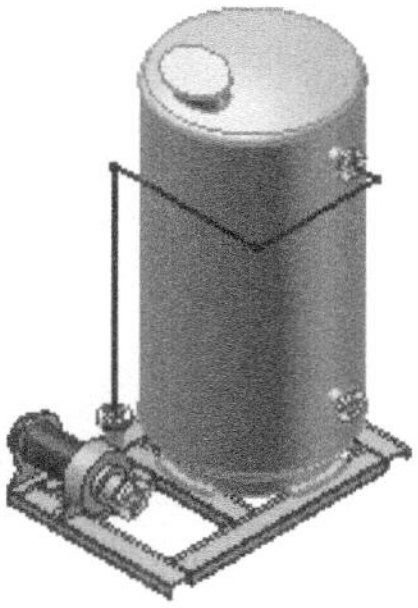

2. In the browser, expand Tube & Pipe Runs. Double-click on Run01 to activate it.
3. To begin adding a fitting to the run, in Pipe Run tab, in the Content panel, click Place.

4. In the Place from Content Center dialog box, under Category View:
   - Expand Tube & Pipe.
   - Expand Fittings.
   - Under Fittings, click Tees.

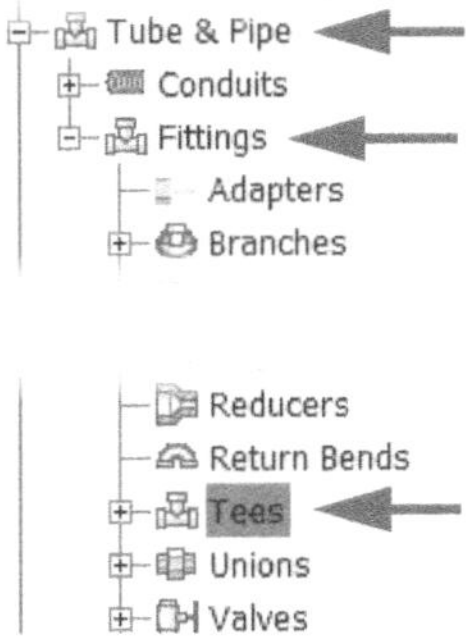

5. In the Tees pane, double-click on ASTM D 2466 Tee Socket Type - Schedule 40.
6. In the ASTM D 2466 Tee Socket-Type – Schedule 40 dialog box:
   - In the ND list, select 2.
   - Click OK.
7. Move over the vertical route segment adjacent to the pump. Click to place the fitting near the top of the segment.

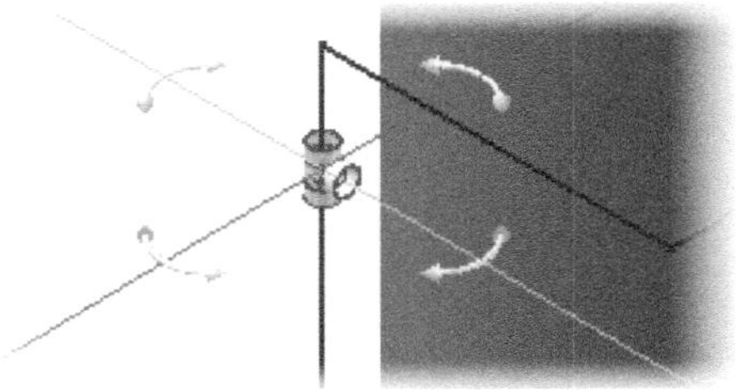

8. To set the rotation of the fitting in the route:
   - Move the cursor over one of the orientation arrows.
   - Enter **180** to rotate the tee about the route axis.
   - In the Enter Angle dialog box, click the green checkmark.
9. Right-click on the graphics window. Click Done.

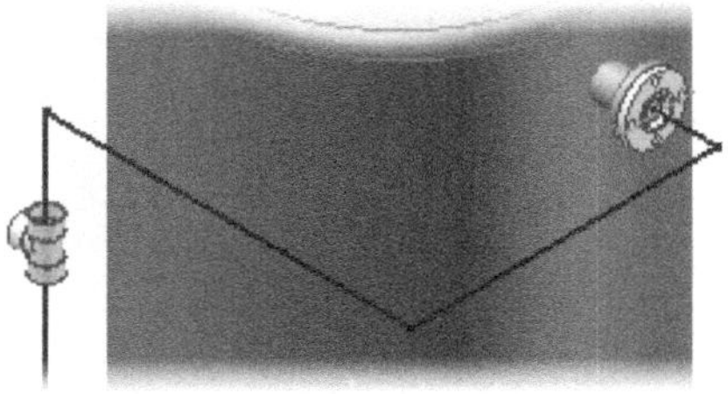

10. To add conduit segments and elbows along the route, in the Pipe Run tab, in the Route panel, click Populate Route. Note how the separate pipe segments are connected to the tee.

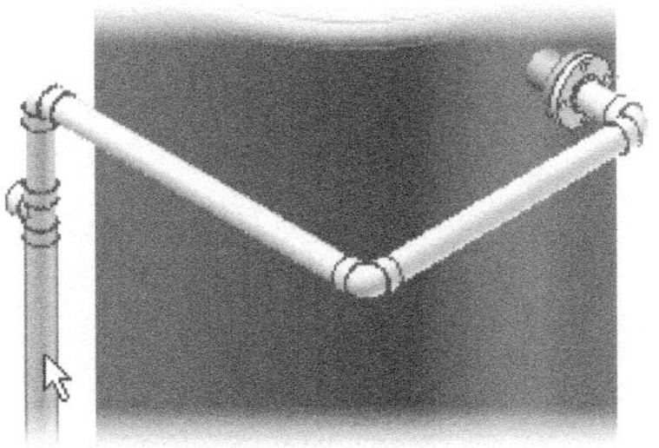

11. To begin adding another fitting to the route:
    - In the Pipe Run tab, in the Content panel, click Place.
    - In the Tees pane, double- click ASTM D 2466 Tee Socket-Type – Schedule 40.
12. In the ASTM D 2466 Tee Socket-Type - Schedule 40 dialog box, select 2 from the ND list. Click OK.
13. Move over the vertical route segment adjacent to the pump. Click to place the fitting near the bottom of the segment.

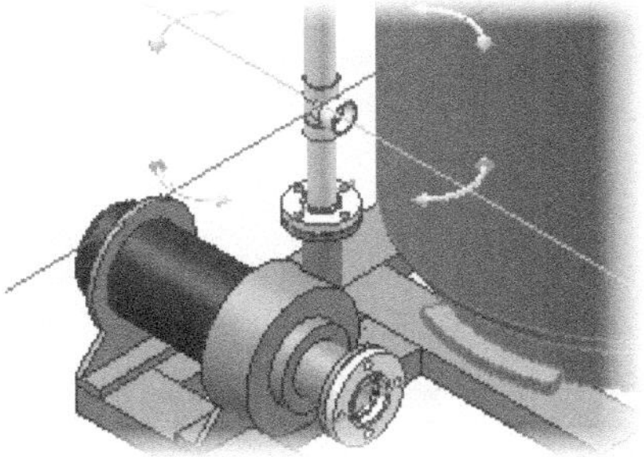

14. Rotate the tee 180°. Right-click in the graphics window. Click Done.
15. To begin creating a new route:
    - In the Pipe Run tab, in the Route panel, click New Route.
    - In the Create New Route dialog box, click OK.
    - In the Route tab, in the Create panel, click Route.
16. Click the connection point on the opening in the lower tee.

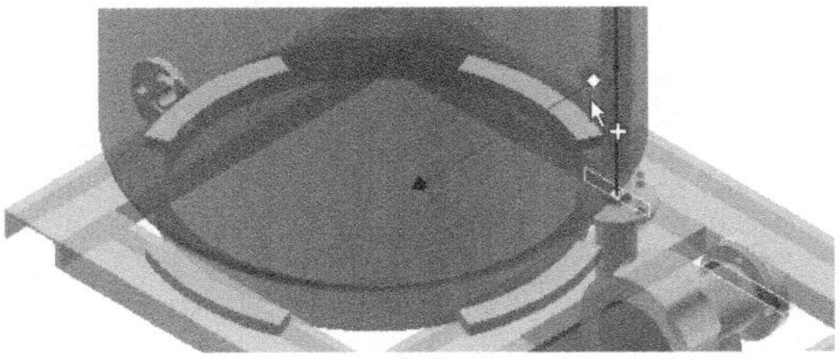

17. Move the cursor over the direction axis, away from the tee opening. Enter **300 mm** to place a second node.

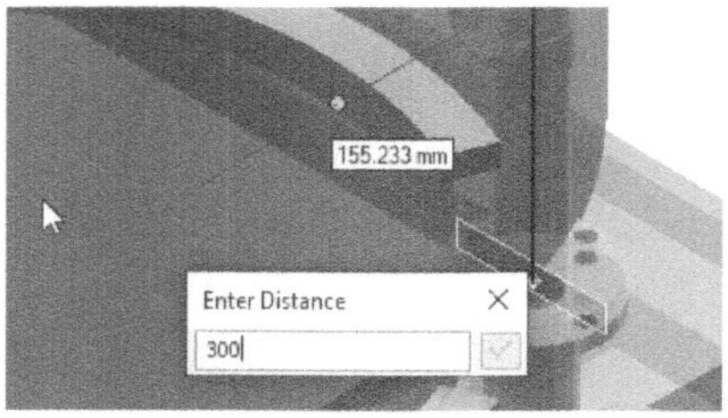

18. To set the route endpoint and number of autoroute segments:
    - Click the connection point on the upper tee opening.
    - Click the checkmark on the Select Other tool to accept the default solution.

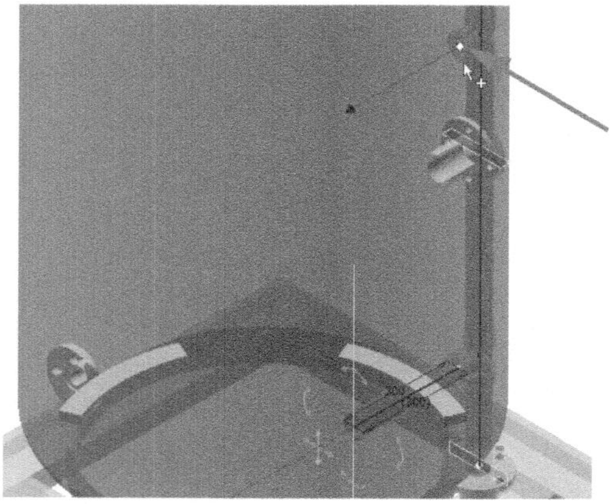

19. Right-click in the graphics window. Click Finish Edit. The route is populated automatically.

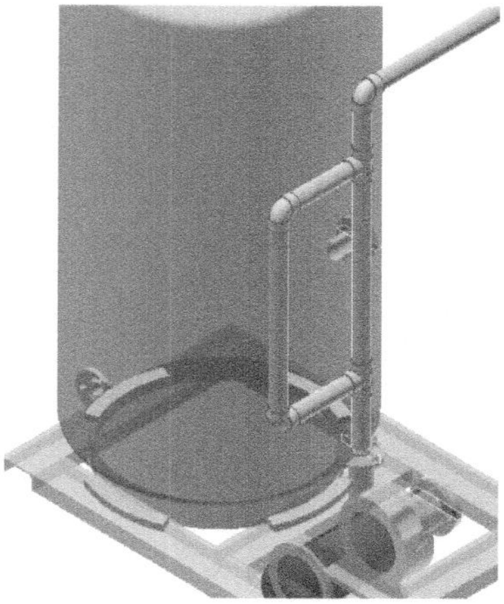

Place and Edit Fittings

In this portion of the exercise, you will replace an elbow with a library fitting.

1. In the browser under Run01, review the fitting components that are listed. Note that between Route01 and Route02, there are two tee socket fittings and three 90° elbow fittings.

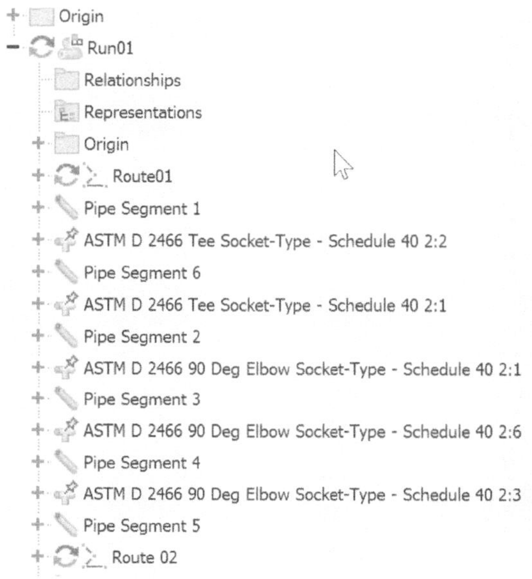

2. To begin selecting the fitting:
   - In the Pipe Run tab, in the Content panel, click Place.
   - In the Category View pane, browse to Tube & Pipe>Fittings>Tees.
3. In the Tees pane, double-click on ASTM D 2466 Tee Socket-Type - Schedule 40.
4. In the ASTM D 2466 Tee Socket-Type - Schedule 40 dialog box, select 2 from the ND list. Click OK.
5. Position the cursor over the elbow adjacent to the tank. The tee preview snaps to the elbow node.

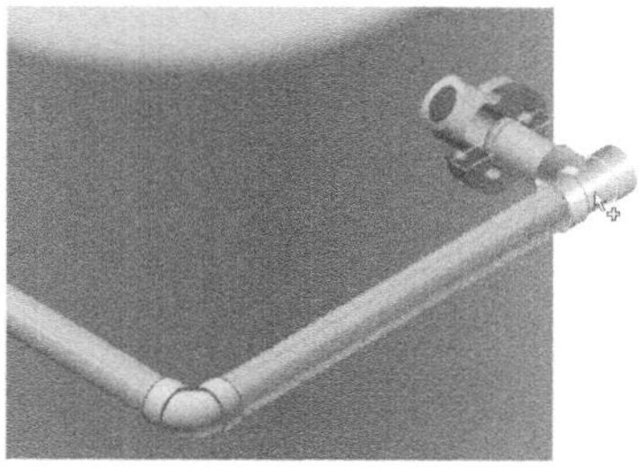

6. To set a different orientation and replace the elbow with the tee fitting:
   - Press SPACEBAR so the preview displays as shown in the following image.
   - Click at the previewed location.

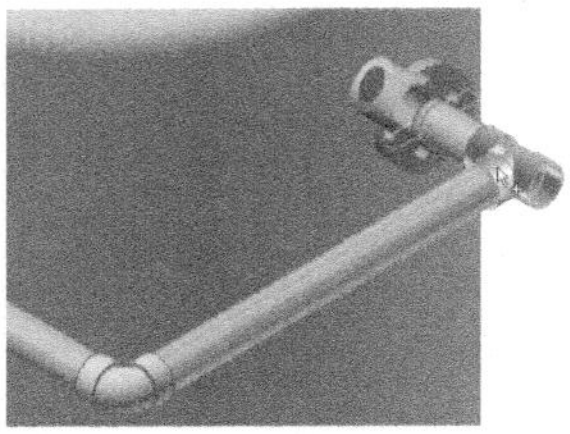

7. Right-click in the graphics window. Click Done.

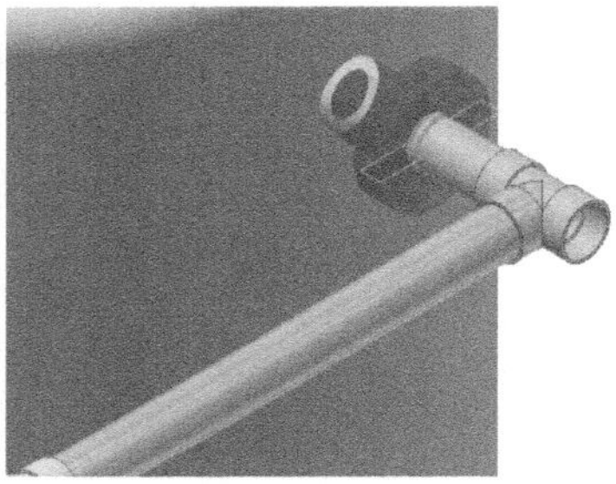

8. In the browser under Run01, review the fitting components that are listed. Note that one elbow was replaced with a tee fitting.

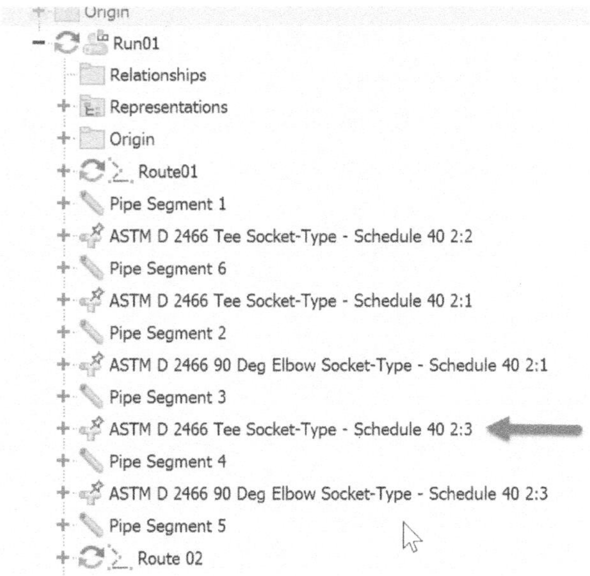

9. To restore the replaced fitting, right-click on the tee that replaced the elbow. Click Restore Fitting.

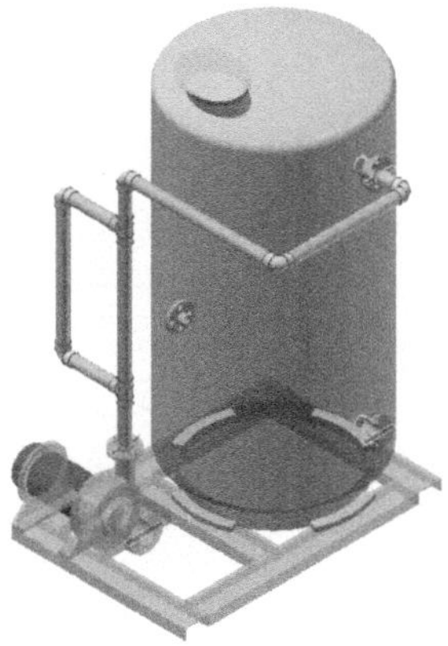

10. Close all files without saving changes.

Exercise: Edit Routes and Fittings

In this exercise, you will edit styles and fittings to change the diameter of a route branch. You will delete fitting connections, apply a new style to a route branch, place and connect fittings, and then reconnect the route branch.

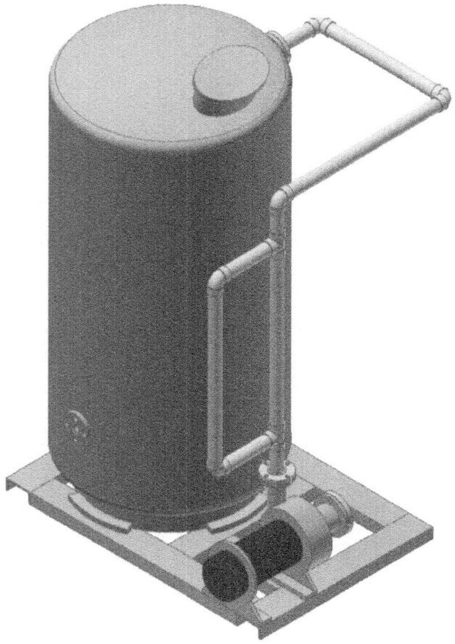

The completed exercise

1. Open *Edit Routes and Fittings.iam*.

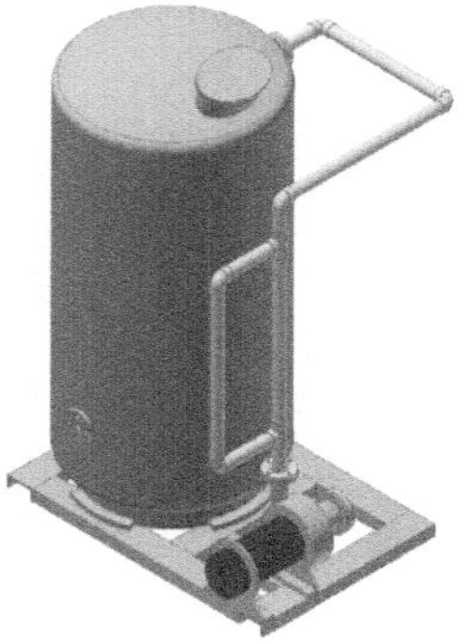

2. In the browser, expand Tube & Pipe Runs. Double-click on Run01 to activate it.

3. To edit the connection at a fitting, in the graphics window, right-click on the tee near the pump. Click Edit Fitting Connections.

4. To delete the connection to the bypass route, in the Edit Connections dialog box:
   - Select the last connection in the list.
   - Click Delete.
   - Click OK.

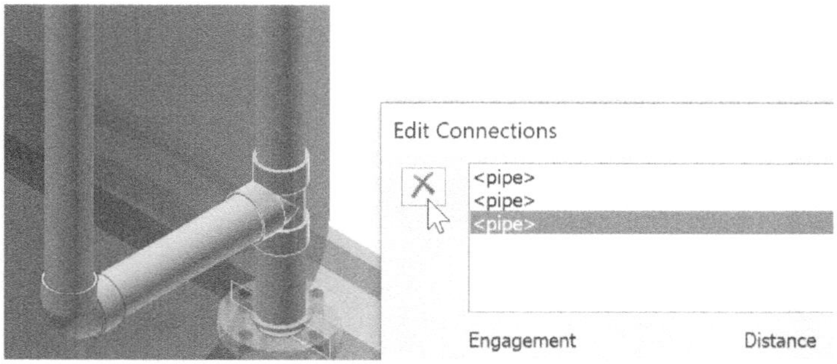

5. Right-click on the upper tee. Click Edit Fitting Connections. Delete the connection to the horizontal pipe segment. Click OK.

6. To begin changing the start and end point and the style for the bypass route, in the browser, under Run01, right-click on Route02. Click Edit.

7. Right-click on the browser node (Route Point 4) that was create at the opening of the upper tee.
   - Click 3D Move/Rotate.
   - Click the green arrowhead on the 3D triad.
   - In the 3D Move/Rotate mini-toolbar, for Y, enter **-100 mm**.
   - Click the green checkmark.

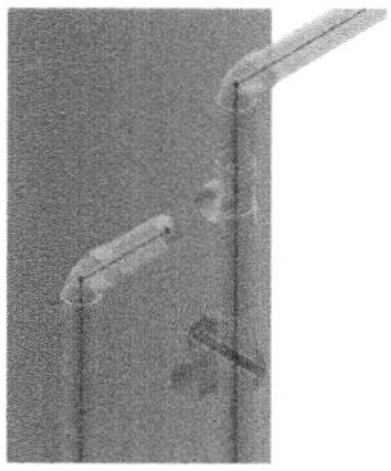

8. Use the 3D Move/Rotate tool to move the node at the opening of the lower tee. Move the node 100 mm away from tee opening.

9. To change the style for the active route, in the style list in the Route tab, in the Manage panel, select ASTM D 1785-ASTM D 2466 - Jointed PVC Pipe and Fittings 1 1/4".

10. Right-click in the graphics window. Click Finish Edit. The conduit and elbows in Route02 update to match the new style.

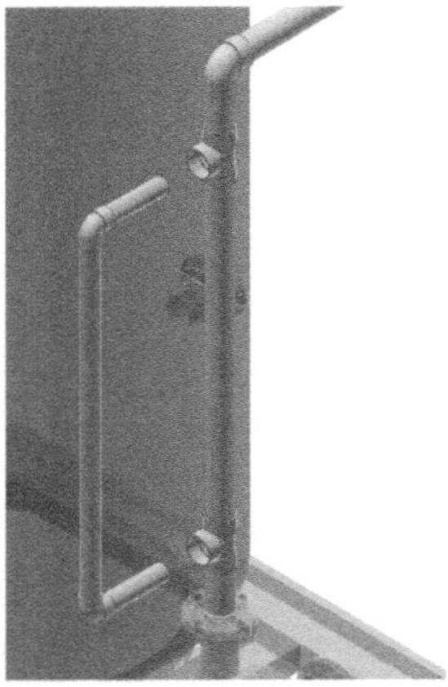

11. To begin adding a reducing fitting:
    - In the Pipe Run tab, in the Content panel, click Place.
    - In the Category View list, click Tube & Pipe>Fittings>Bushings.

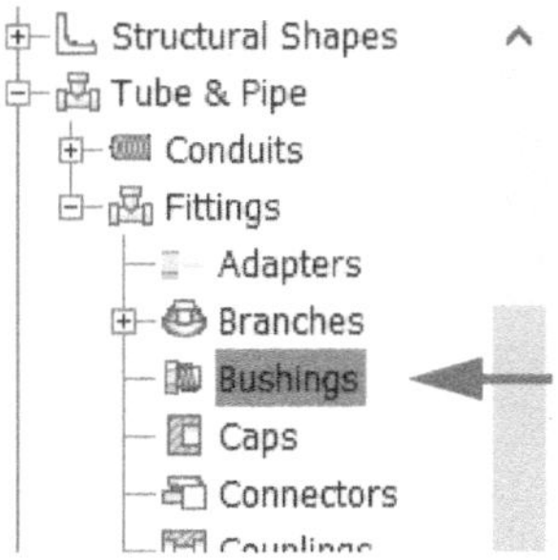

12. In the Bushings pane, double-click on ASTM D 2466 Reducer Bushing Socket-Type 1 - Schedule 40.
13. In the ASTM D 2466 Reduced Bushing Socket-Type 1 - Schedule 40 dialog box:
    - In the ND1 list, select 2.
    - In the ND2 list, select 1 1/4.
    - Click OK.
14. To place and connect the first reducer fitting:
    - Right-click in the graphics window background. Click Connect Fitting.
    - Click the open connection point on the lower tee.
    - Right-click in the graphics window. Click Continue.

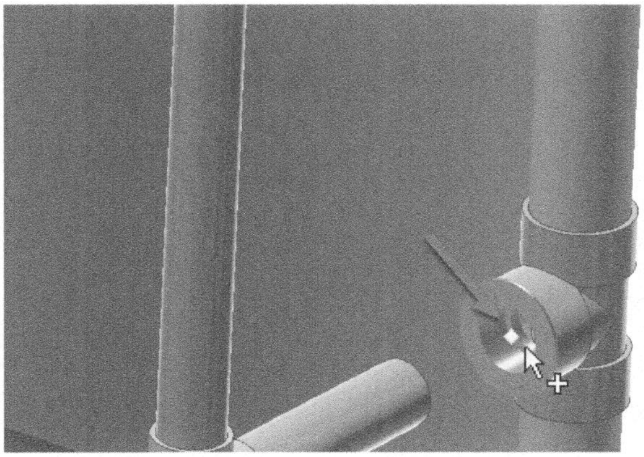

15. Click the open connection on the upper tee to add a second reducer fitting.
16. Right-click in the graphics window and click Done.
17. To reconnect the pipe segments:
    - In the Pipe Run tab, in the Route panel, click Connect Fittings.
    - Click the open connection point on the pipe segment adjacent to the upper tee.

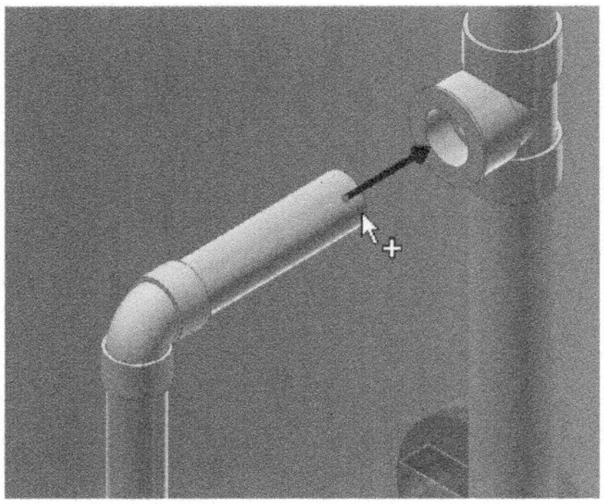

18. Click the open connection point on the upper tee. In the Connect Fittings dialog box, click Apply. A new route segment connects to the tee.

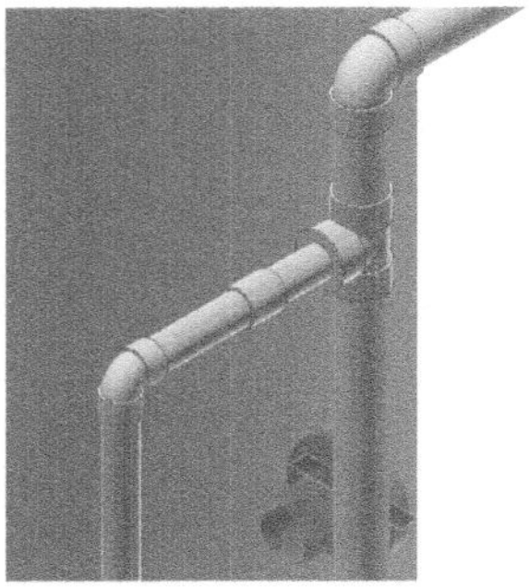

19. Click the open connection point on the pipe segment adjacent to the lower tee.

   - Click the open connection on the lower tee.
   - In the Connect Fittings dialog box, click OK.

20. To delete the coupling connection nodes from the modified route:

   - In the browser, double-click on Route02.
   - Right-click on a coupling node. Click Delete.
   - Right-click on the other coupling node. Click Delete.

21. Right-click in the graphics window background. Click Finish Edit.

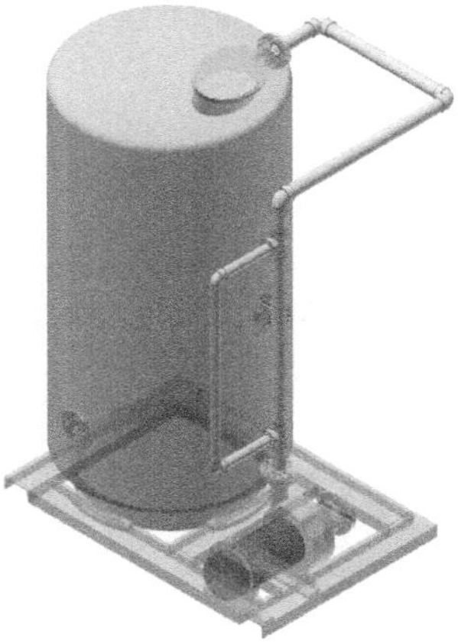

22. Close all files without saving changes.

Lesson: Flexible Hose Routes

Overview

This lesson describes the creation and editing of flexible hose routes.

Because of the fundamental differences between flexible hose routes and rigid pipe or tube routes, you have an additional set of tools and workflows to use and follow to create flexible hose routes. To create and edit flexible hose routes that meet your design requirements, you must know what tools to use and understand the workflow to follow for their use.

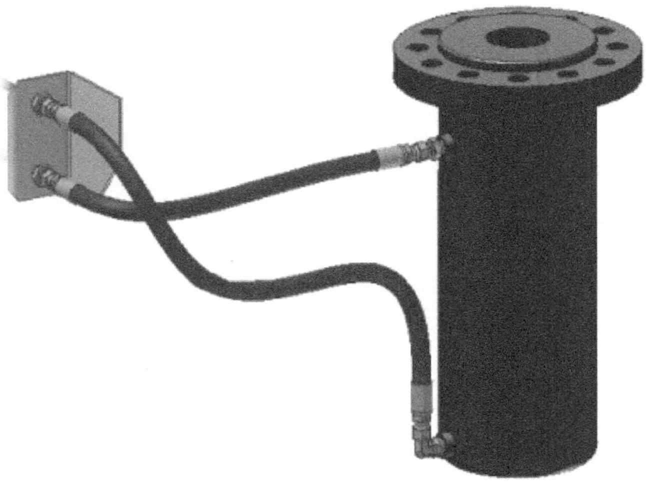

Objectives

After completing this lesson, you will be able to:

- Describe the characteristics of flexible hose routes and the process to create them.
- Insert nodes into an existing flexible hose route.
- Edit the nodes of a flexible hose route.
- Change the length of a hose route.
- List the ways you can edit the start and end fittings in a flexible hose route.
- Check the minimum bend radius of flexible hoses.

Creating Flexible Hose Routes

There are many uses of flexible hoses in a design. Flexible hoses are often used because they are the easiest means to establish the pneumatic or hydraulic line without having to use multiple pipe segments and elbows or establish complex bends in a tube. Because a flexible hose is flexible, it is the best solution to use when the components that the flexible hose connects to move dynamically in the assembly. To create flexible hose routes to meet your design criteria, you must know the process and options for their creation.

In the following image, the route for the flexible hose changed as the position of the screw gun changed from its top position to its bottom position.

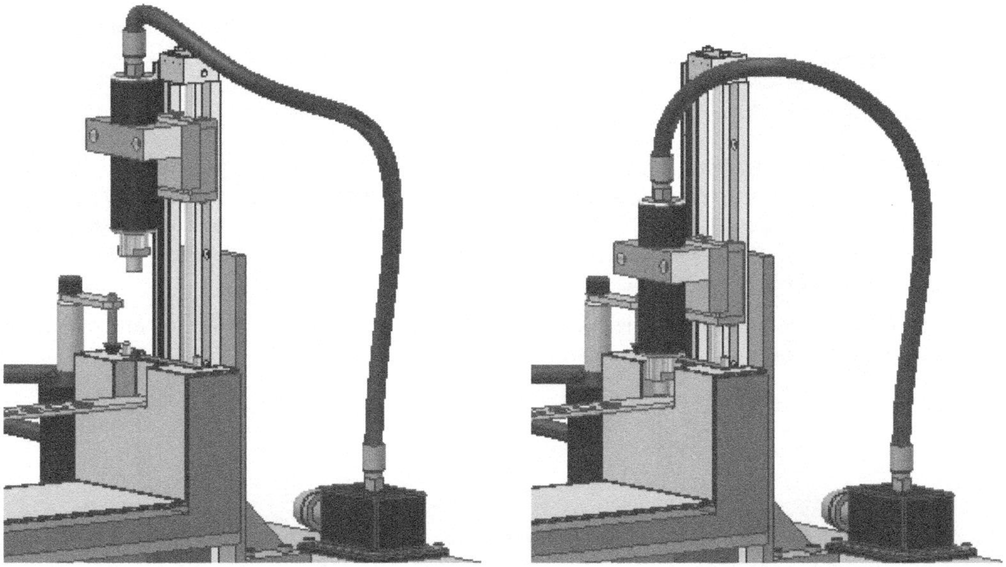

Description of Creating Flexible Hose Routes

A flexible hose route defines a path between two fittings or points that control where it starts and ends. Between the start and end fittings or points, you can have additional points to control the exact path of the hose. The resulting hose route is a 3D spline path.

Depending on what flexible hose style is active when you create the route, the flexible hose route might contain up to three parts: a start fitting, an end fitting, and the flexible hose segment that connects them. A style can include both start and end fittings, one fitting only, or no fittings. When fittings are included in the style, you place the fittings in the design as part of the process for defining the route.

Things to consider before and during the creation of a flexible hose route include:

- In what assembly or subassembly do you add the fittings if the fittings are not part of the hose style? Place the fittings in the pipe run subassembly when they are assembled before adding to the overall assembly. Place the fittings in the overall assembly if they all come together at that point in the assembly process.
- What is the required path for the hose, and what is the minimum number of control points required to define and control that path?
- How and where are the parts in the assembly design going to be moving and impacting the path of the hose?
- Are you going to use work points, vertex points, or offset distances from other geometry to position the control points for the hose route? Route points based on work points and vertex points are associative to model changes. Route points based on offsets from a face or the 3D ORTHOgonal Route tool are not associative to model changes.

Flexible Hose Route with Fittings

When the active flexible hose style has both a start and an end fitting, you define the route by first specifying the insertion location of the start fitting and then the end fitting. After you specify these two nodes, a preview of the spline path opens. You can then complete the creation of the route by just using those two points, by placing intermediate nodes through vertices and points, or by specifying points offset from a selected face.

The following image shows a flexible hose route between a hydraulic cylinder and a valve body. The unpopulated route is a 3D spline path.

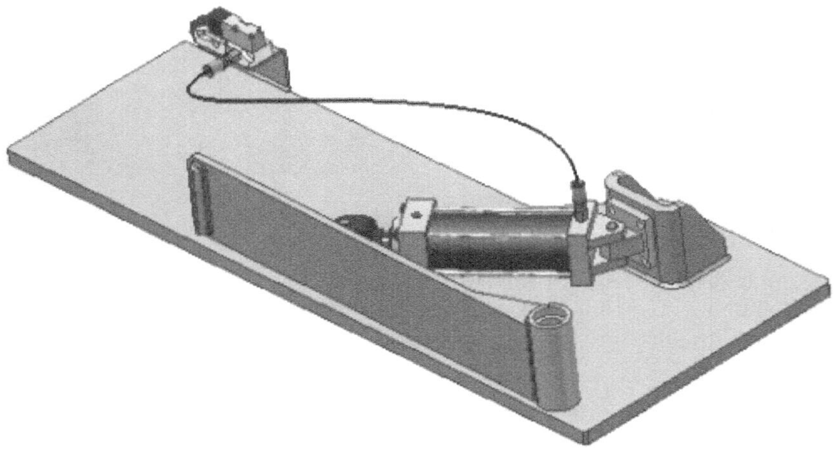

Intermediate and Offset Points

Once the start and end points for the route are selected the route displays. You can add additional points along the route prior to completing the route. This is done using the Intermediate Point and Offset Point commands in the context menu. An intermediate point enables you to locate the point along the axes of the triad. Note that you can also rotate an axis as required. Selection begins from the start point of the route. The Offset Point command enables you to place a new point along the route's spine by offsetting it a set distance from a plane or work plane. Before adding the node to the route, you can change the offset distance by accessing the Edit Offset option from the shortcut menu. All nodes added after that continue to use that offset value. To place another node with a different value, change the value before placing that new point.

In the following image a new route node is offset from the mounting plate (top image) using the Offset Point option. The route updates to pass through the new point (bottom image).

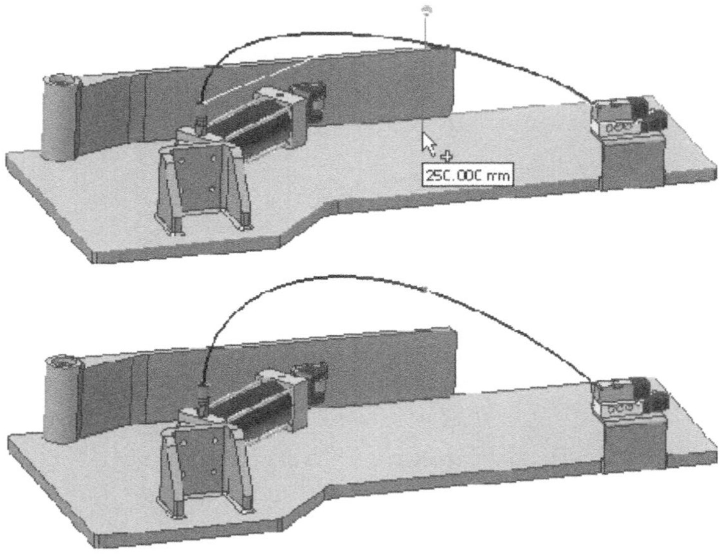

Intermediate Route Nodes at Circular Edges

You can also select a circular or arc edge to define a node using the Intermediate Point command in the context menu. An arrow indicates the side of the containing plane from which the spline approaches. To change the direction of the approach arrow, you can either press SPACEBAR, or you can right-click on the edge and click Select Other Direction to cycle through the solutions with the Select Other tool. You can also specify an offset distance along the axis through the edge. To do this, select the edge and enter a value to offset the node in the direction indicated by the arrow. Nodes placed at or offset from circular or arc edges are associative to the edge.

The following image shows the placement of an intermediate node at a circulate edge in a flexible hose route. The resulting route depends on the selected route approach direction.

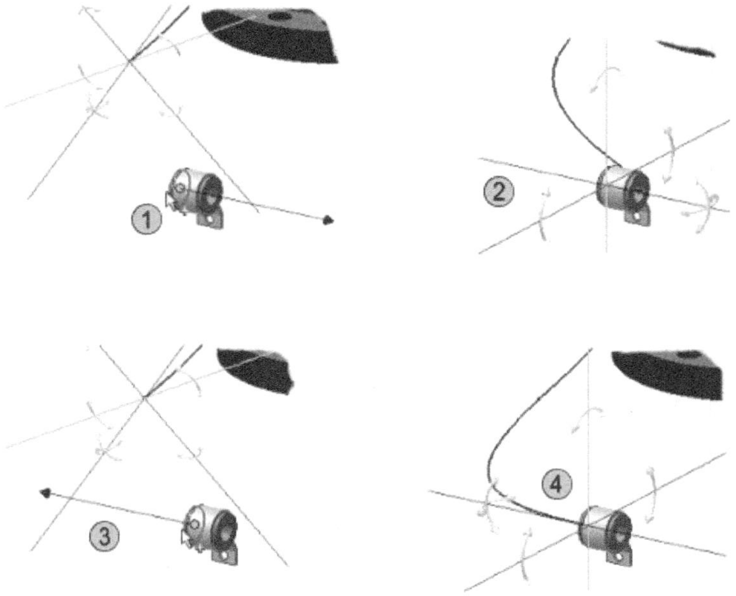

1. Circular edge selected to position an intermediate route node. The route approach direction is previewed with an arrow.
2. The resulting hose route approaches the node from right side. The hanger interferes with the route.
3. The same circular edge selected and the route approach direction flipped.
4. The resulting route approaches the node from the correct side.

Flexible Hose Route without Fittings

If the active flexible hose style has no fittings or if the end fitting is suppressed, you can use the 3D ORTHOgonal Route tool to place intermediate nodes. The tool displays angle handles similar to those used for tube routes, but there are no radius handles. Nodes placed in a flexible hose route are not joined with straight segments and bends. The spline path for the route passes through all of the nodes placed along the route.

The following image shows the creation of a route where the active style has no start or end fittings. A number of route nodes are placed with the 3D ORTHOgonal Route tool. The spline-based route passes through all nodes.

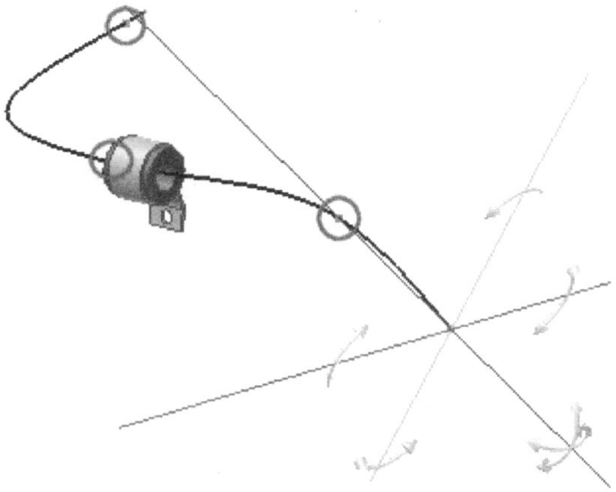

Process: Creating Flexible Hose Routes

The following diagram gives an overview of creating a flexible hose route.

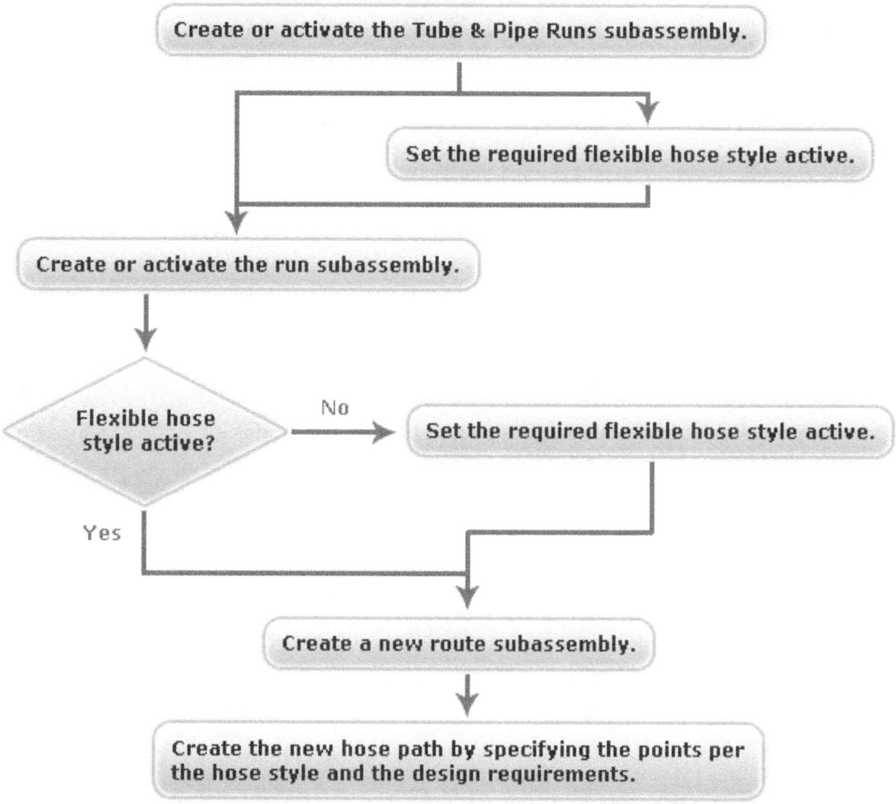

Inserting Nodes

After creating the route for a flexible hose, changes to the overall assembly design or refinement in the path can dictate that you need to add another node to the route. To insert nodes in a route so that the route meets your design requirements, you need to know the procedure for adding nodes to an existing flexible hose route.

In the following image, the initial route for the flexible hose had only a start and end node (1). After inserting an intermediate node, that inserted node was edited to be offset a specific distance from the face of a part in the design (2). The flexible hose updated to reflect the new path through the new node and edited path (3).

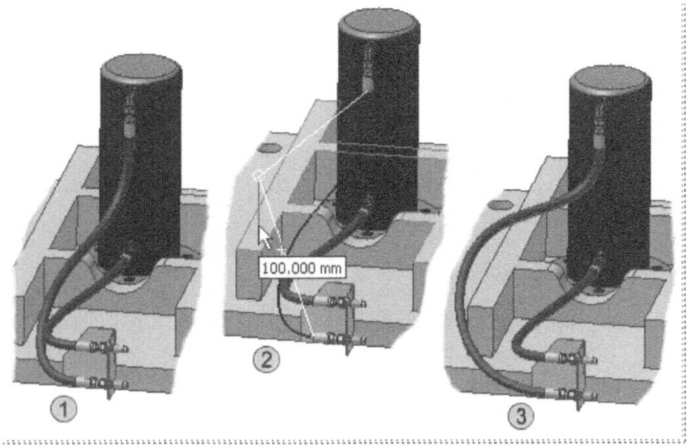

Access

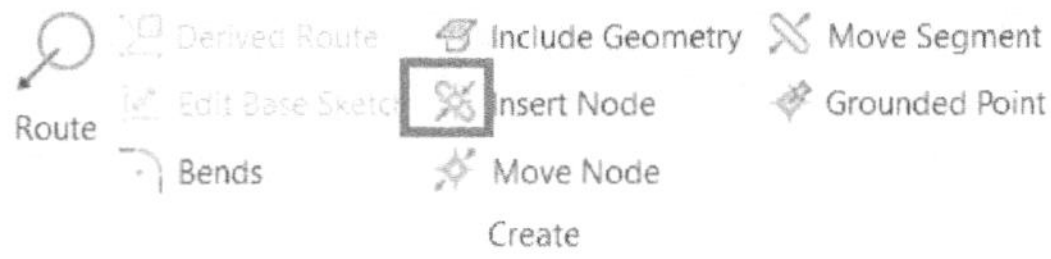

Ribbon: Route tab>Create panel

Procedure: Inserting Nodes

The following steps give an overview of inserting intermediate nodes into a flexible hose route.

1. Activate the hose route for edit.
2. Start the Insert Node tool.
3. Click the location on the route where you want the node inserted.

Editing Hose Route Nodes

Just like any aspect of a design, the route of a flexible hose is subject to change. To modify an existing flexible hose route so it adheres to your current design requirements, you need to know the different methods and options for editing the nodes in a flexible hose route.

In the following image, the route for the flexible hose was edited to have intermediate nodes associate to work points so that the route passes through the center of the hose clamp.

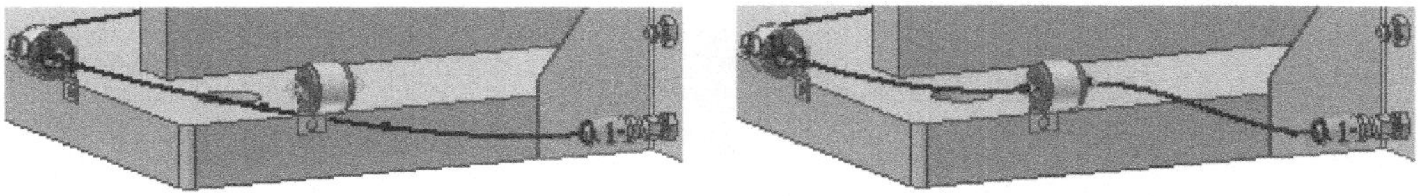

Hose Route Node Edits

The nodes in a flexible hose route that are not the start or end nodes are referred to as intermediate nodes. You can edit an intermediate node by redefining it, moving it using the 3D Move/Rotate tool, or deleting it. You access these three edit options from the shortcut menu after selecting an intermediate node while editing the route.

Edit Option	Description
Redefine	Select to set the node a specified distance offset from a point on a selected face or through a selected work point of vertex in the assembly. A node offset from a face is not associative to the face, while a node set based on a selected work point or geometry vertex is associative to that work point or vertex. Associative nodes update their position if the work point or vertex changes in position.
3D Move/ Rotate	Use to change the position of the node through the manipulation of the 3D Move/ Rotate triad. Enter precise distances, or drag the 3D Move/Rotate triad components in the graphics window to reposition a node. This edit option is available only for intermediate nodes not associated to a work point or vertex.
Delete	Select to remove the selected node from the 3D route spline.

In the following image, an intermediate node is being repositioned with the use of the 3D Move/Rotate tool. The node is being moved along one axis because the arrowhead for the one access was clicked to drag.

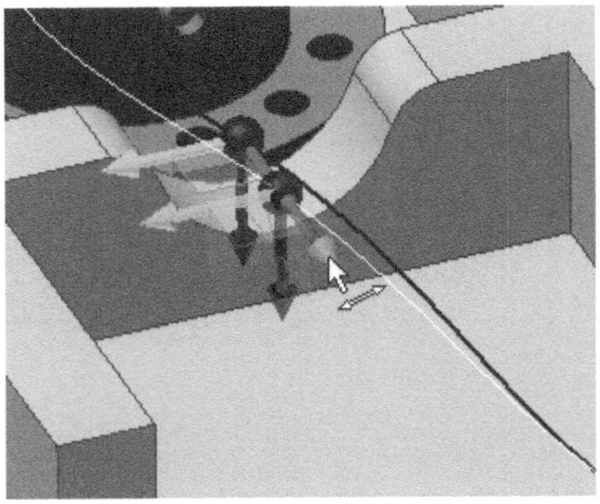

Edit of a Start or End Node

The editing methods and options for start and end nodes depend on the active style for the flexible hose style. When a flexible hose route style does not have a fitting at one or both ends of the route, you can disassociate the node on that end. After disassociating it from the start or end work point, you can edit it just like you can nonassociative intermediate nodes. This includes moving it to a new position, redefining it to a new location, or redefining it to be associated to other geometry or to a fitting. When you select to associate it to a fitting, that node is associated to the fitting as if it is part of that hose style. This means you can no longer edit the position of that point without editing the position of the fitting or deleting the fitting all together.

You disassociate the start or end node by deleting the work point it is associated to. First, ensure that you don't have a style that uses fittings as the active style. You then delete the work point by selecting the Delete option in the shortcut menu for the selected work point. To locate the work point to delete, in the Included Geometry folder listed in the browser below the route being edited, select the different work points to have them highlight in the graphics window. You can also locate the point by hovering the cursor over the start or end node in the graphics window and then using the Select Other option to cycle the active selection until the work point is selected.

> To have the Redefine option after disassociating a start or end node, you must first either access the 3D Move/Rotate tool or exit editing the route.

Procedure: Editing Hose Route Nodes

The following diagram gives an overview of the options and steps to edit nodes in a flexible hose route.

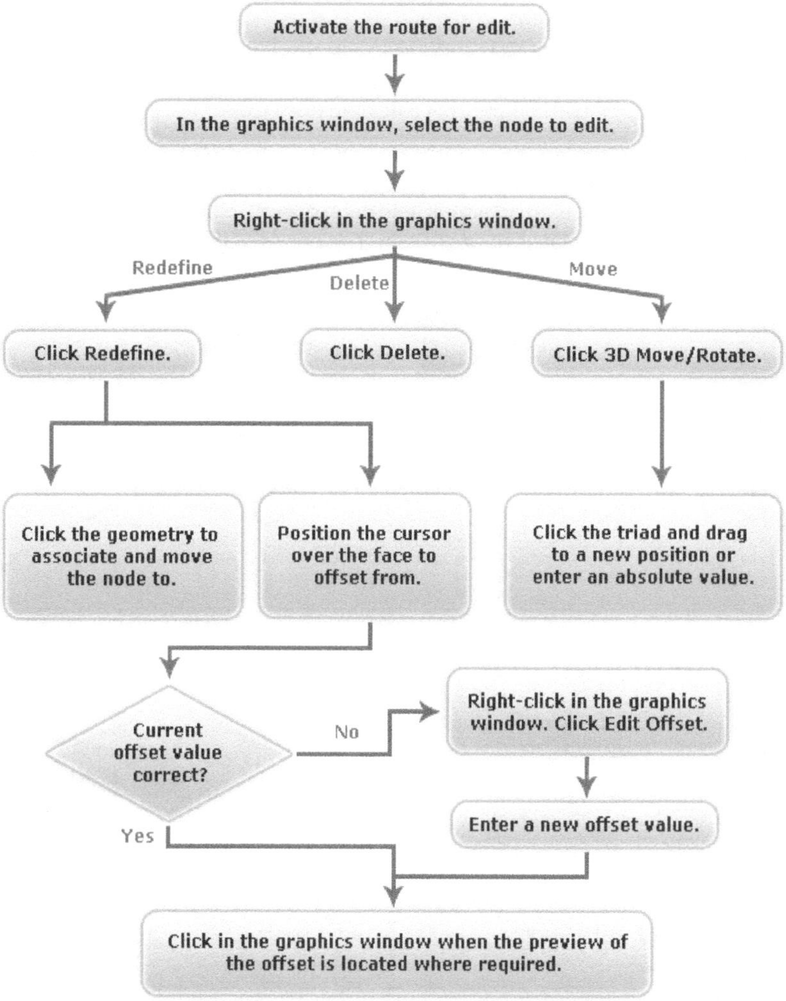

Editing Hose Length

When you create a hose route, its actual length is based on the default spline path that goes through the specified route nodes. The length of the flexible hose that is used when manufacturing the design is either set based on its length when purchased or its custom cut length during assembly. A purchased hose with end fittings is often a fixed length so the available lengths dictate the length of the hose in your design. When the length is cut during assembly, it is cut in an incremental value that is rounded up from the exact design size. To create flexible hosing with the correct length, you need to know where and how to change the length of a flexible hose route.

In the following image, the actual length of the flexible hose in the initial design was 462.085 mm. Because the roundup value was set to 10 mm, the reported rounded length for this hose was 470 mm. After editing the length of the route to an actual length greater than 500 mm and less than or equal to 510 mm, the rounded length value is now 510 mm. The preview of the new path with the new length is shown relative to the original path.

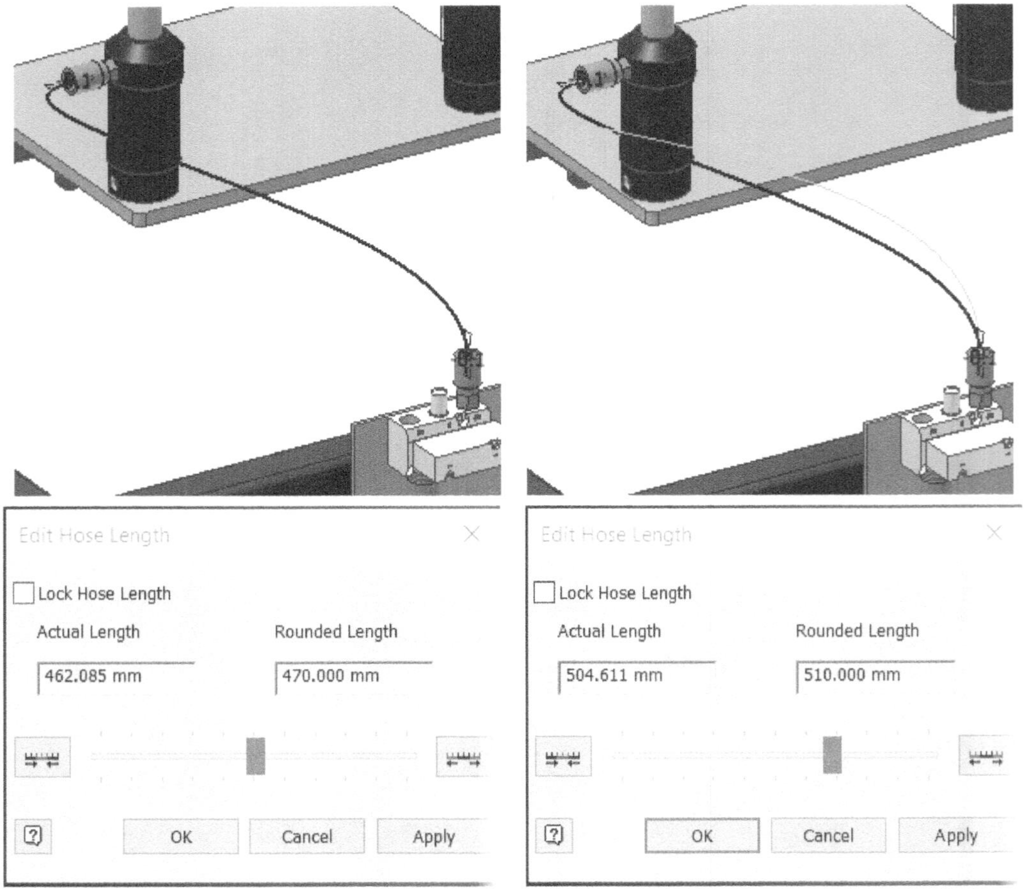

The Lock Hose Length option allows you to calculate the exact sum of hose length. If components move or shift, this option prevents the length of the hose from changing. The flexible hose will adapt, as needed, to maintain the length. This can be used as an alternative to assigning a dimension to the hose length.

Editing the Length of Hoses

You can edit the length of a flexible hose route when the route in the flexible hose subassembly in the run is active for edit.

The length of a hose is increased or decreased by increasing or decreasing the path of the spline while maintaining its path through the defined nodes. When you increase the length, the spline arc increases from one node to another. When you decrease the length, the spline path becomes flatter and more direct from one node to the next.

You can think of the spline path as having tension on it. The longer the length, the less tension as it passes from one node to the next, thereby having bigger curves. With a shorter length, there is more tension on the path as it goes between the nodes, thereby creating straighter segments.

The value that a hose is rounded as it is lengthened or shortened is controlled by the round up value that is set in that hose's style. You change the round up value in the Tube & Pipe Styles dialog box, Rules tab by entering a new value in the Hose Round Up Value field. To enter a new value, you must first select and set the style to be edited. You activate the style for edit by selecting the hose style in the list of styles and clicking Edit in the shortcut menu or in the dialog box.

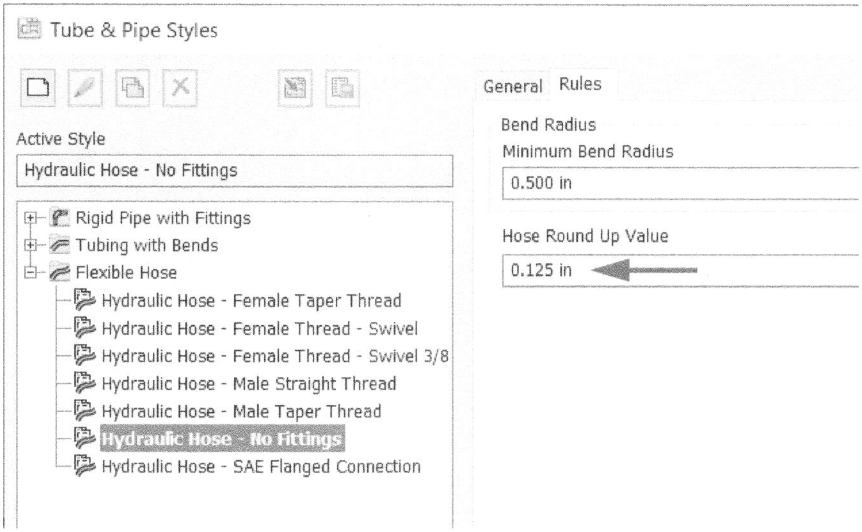

> If you have not selected to edit the style, the Hose Round Up Value field is grayed out and the values cannot be changed.

Access

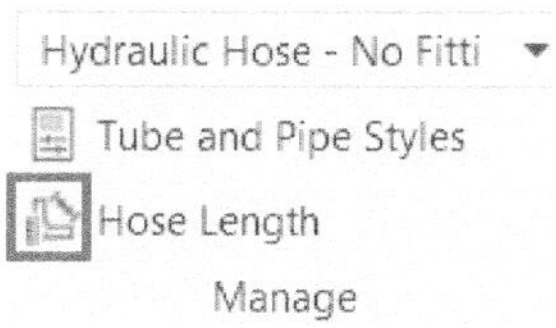

Ribbon: Route tab>Manage panel

Procedure: Editing Hose Length

The following steps give an overview of adjusting the length of a hose route.

1. Start the Hose Length tool

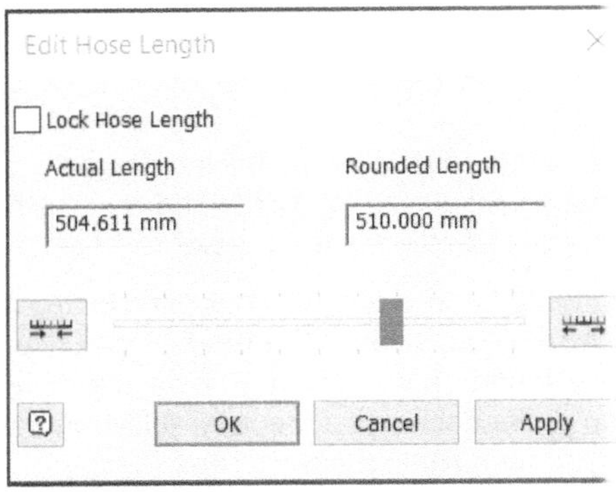

2. In the Edit Hose Length dialog box, drag the slider to the right to increase the length of the hose or to the left to reduce the length. The actual and rounded lengths are displayed.

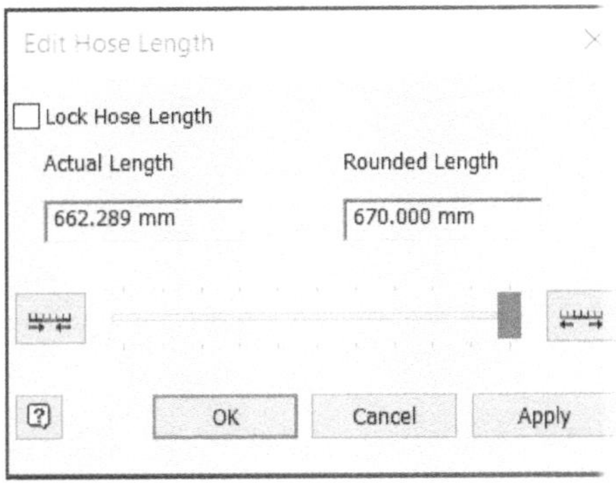

3. To make length adjustments beyond the range provided by the slider, click the button closest to the slider position to recenter the slider without changing the route length. Drag the slider to continue the length adjustment.

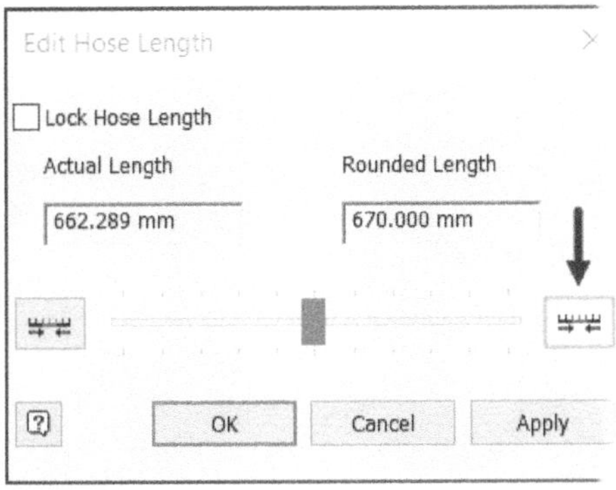

4. Enable the Lock Hose Length option to prevent the length of hose from changing when components move. This option also allows you to calculate an exact sum of hose length.

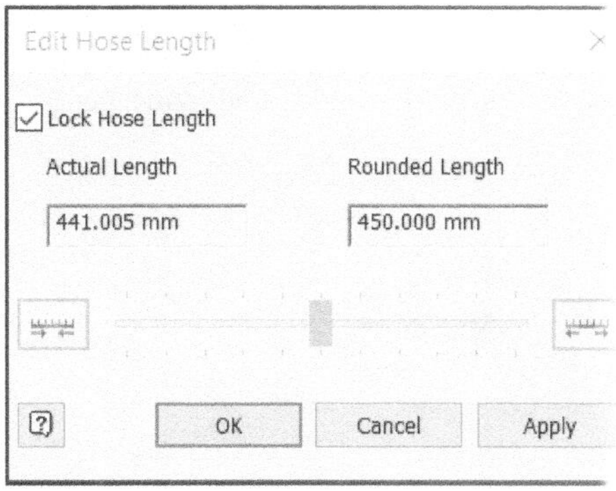

Edits for Hose Fittings

After you add a flexible hose to your design, you might need to change the type of fitting on the hose or change the engagement condition of the fitting to the selected connection. To make the changes to the hose fittings as you require, you need to know the different ways you can edit the start and end fittings in a flexible hose route.

In the following image, the end fitting for the hose was changed from one fitting type to another, and the rotation orientation of that new fitting was changed to match a different set of design requirements. Note how the one fitting was changed and the others remained the same.

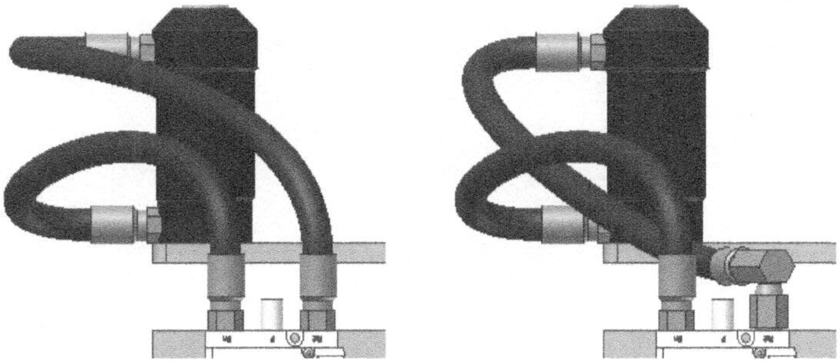

Hose Fitting Edit Options

When you change the hose style, the fittings on the hose automatically change to match what is set in that style. The fittings update to the current style even if a different fitting type was previously set for a single fitting. If no fittings are defined in the style, the fittings in the route are automatically removed from the design. Switching to a hose style that does have fittings defined will add the fittings back into the route.

You edit the start or end fitting associated with a flexible hose style when the flexible hose route subassembly is active for editing. You access the options for editing a hose fitting from the shortcut menu after right-clicking on the fitting in the browser or graphics window.

Your options for editing a fitting on a hose that is based on the hose style are:

<table>
<tr><th>Option</th><th>Description</th></tr>
<tr><td>Change Size</td><td>Use to select a different size for the same type. This is the same basic workflow and option as when you are editing any Design Accelerator-created content. One example of using this option is changing the size of a bolt in a bolted connection.

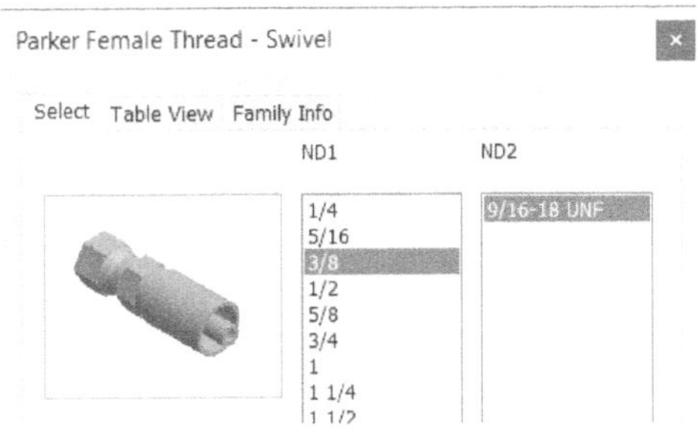

</td></tr>
<tr><td>Change Fitting Diameter</td><td>Use to assign a new diameter from this list of available diameters.</td></tr>
<tr><td>Replace from Content Center</td><td>Use to select a different fitting type from the Content Center. This is the same basic workflow and options as when editing any Design Accelerator- created content. One example of using this option is changing a bolt in a bolted connection from a hex head to a socket head.

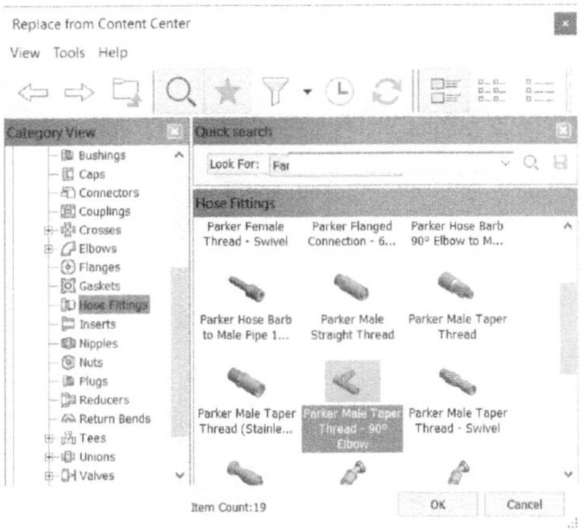

</td></tr>
<tr><td>Edit Fitting Orientation</td><td>Use to rotate the fitting about the center axis of the path. This option is required for fittings such as elbows that go in a direction other than straight back from the connection location.

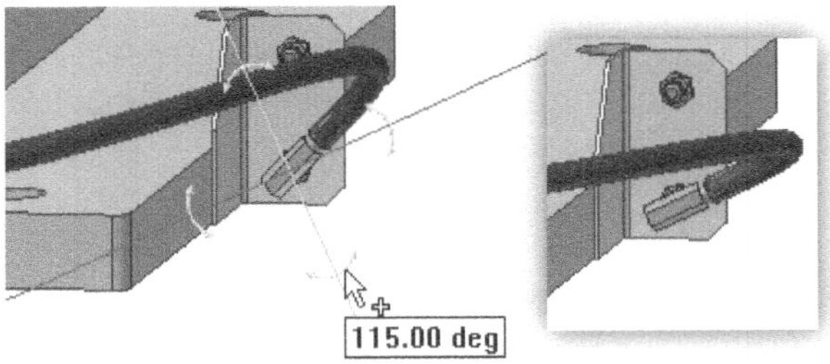

</td></tr>
</table>

Option	Description
Edit Fitting Connections	Use to change the engagement offset condition and value or to delete the connection between the fitting and its location. 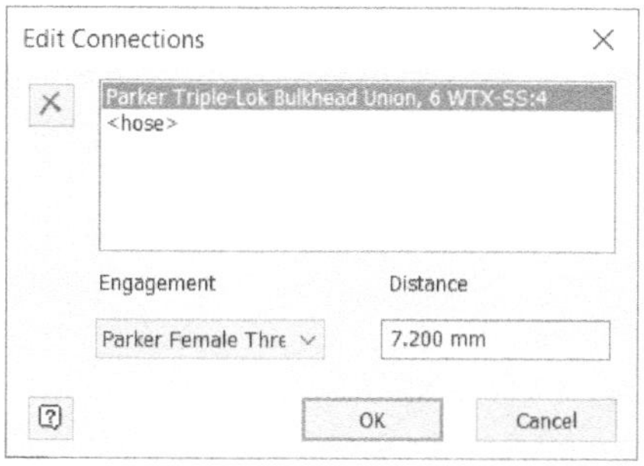
Delete All Connections	Use to delete the connections associated with a fitting to disassociate it from its assigned location.
3D Move / Rotate Fitting	Use to change the position of the fitting. For this option to be available, the hose fitting can no longer be associated to a location.

Check Minimum Bend Radius

To ensure correct fluid flow through a flexible hose, you need to ensure that no bend in the hose causes a restriction. You ensure a restriction does not occur by having all bends greater than or equal to the minimum bend radius for that hose material and style. To check for violations to the minimum bends, you need to learn about the command and options for checking the minimum bend radius of flexible hoses.

Check for Minimum Bend Radius Violations

When you check a route for minimum bend radius violations, the bends in the route are checked against the value set in the flexible hose style for that route. Before running a check, you should ensure that the value set in the style matches your current requirements. You set the minimum bend radius value in the Tube & Pipe Styles dialog box, Rules tab.

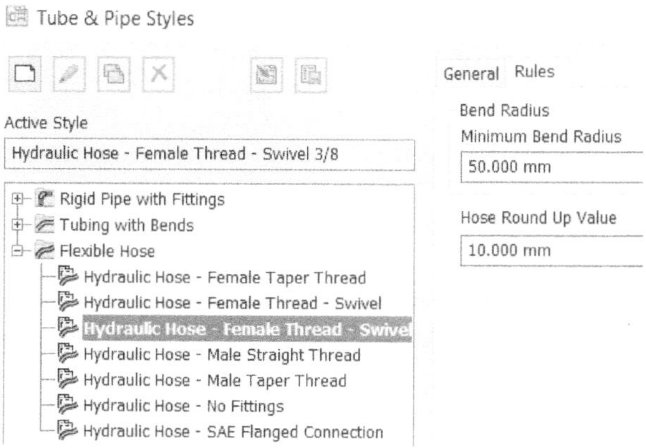

You access the option to check for minimum bend radius violations by first activating the run or route. After activating the run with the route to check or activating the specific route, in the browser, right-click on the route and then click Bend Radius>Check. When a minimum bend radius violation is discovered, the route is marked in the browser.

The following images show how a flexible hose route displays in the browser when it violates the minimum bend radius rule specified in the style (shown on the top), and how it displays when it meets the minimum bend radius rule (shown on the bottom).

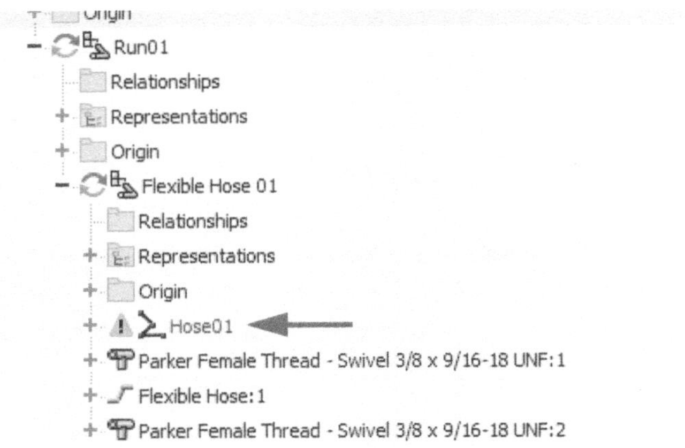

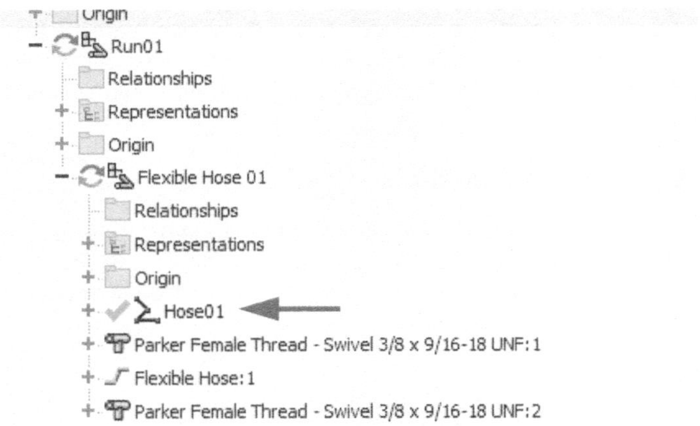

To eliminate violations of the minimum bend radius, you must edit the route and add or move nodes or edit the hose length. After editing the route, check the bend radius again. When the edit has corrected the violation, the notification in the browser is cleared.

To clear the browser notification without fixing the violation, in the browser, right-click on the route with the violation. Click Bend Radius>Clear Violation. The violation at this point is not eliminated, the violation will display the next time you check for minimum radius violations on that route.

Exercise: Create a Flexible Hose Route

In this exercise, you will create a flexible hose route from a bulkhead to a cylinder. You will create a new run and place fittings and intermediate nodes to control the shape of the spline path. You will also edit the length of the route to improve clearance between the hose and assembly components.

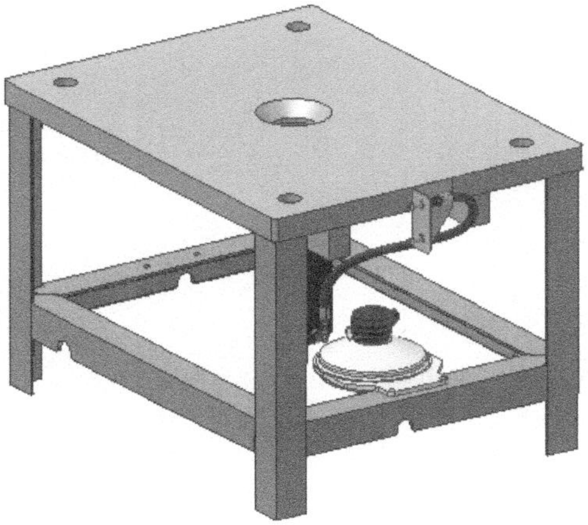

The completed exercise

1. Open *Flexible Hose Route.iam*.

2. In the browser, in the Tube & Pipe Runs subassembly, double-click on Run01 to activate the run subassembly.
3. To set the active style, in the Pipe Run tab>Manage panel, from the Style list, select Hydraulic Hose - Female Thread - Swivel 3/8.
4. To begin creating a new route subassembly:
   - In the Pipe Run tab, in the Route panel, click New Route.
   - Click OK to accept the default name and location for the flexible hose subassembly.
5. In the Route tab, in the Create panel, click Route.

6. To position the start fitting defined in the style:
   - Move the cursor over the end of the upper bulkhead fitting.
   - When the preview of the fitting displays snapped to the bulkhead fitting, click to connect it.

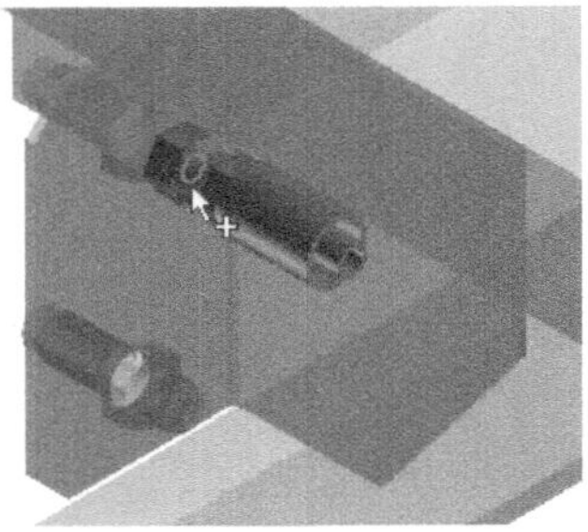

7. To position the end fitting of the hose:
   - Move the cursor to the top edge of the 90° fitting located near the bottom of the cylinder.
   - Click to place the end fitting.

   Note: If the fitting snaps to the wrong orientation, press SPACEBAR to change the orientation.

8. Examine the route.

   A spline path preview displays between the two fittings, and it intersects the table plate near the bulkhead.

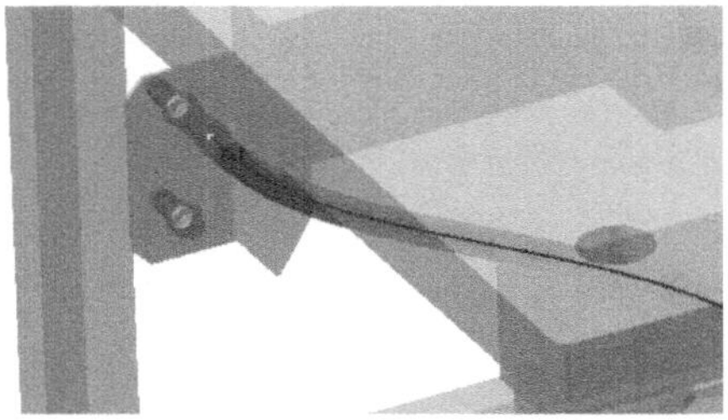

9. Reorient your view as shown in the following image.

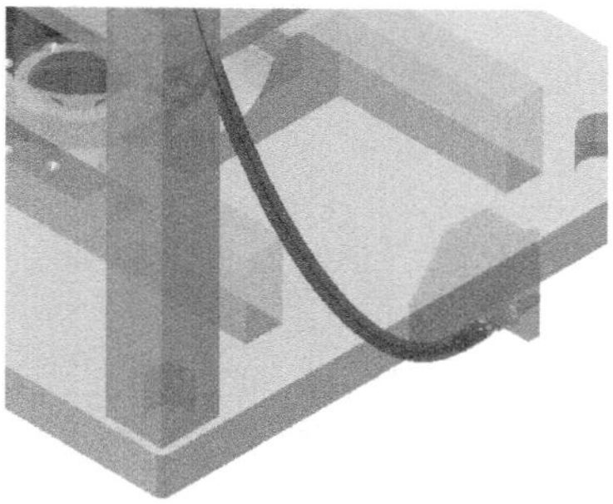

10. Right-click and select Offset Point to create another point on the route.

11. Move the cursor over the table plate, adjacent to the bulkhead.

    The face is highlighted and a straight-line preview of the route opens. A vertex is previewed offset from the face at the cursor.

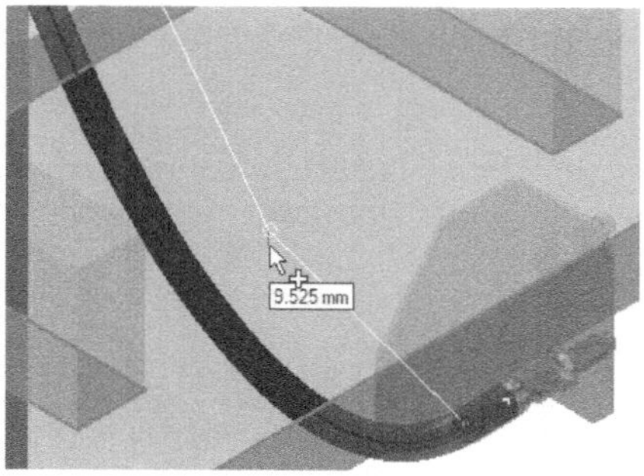

12. To change the offset distance:

    - Right-click on the face and click Edit Offset.
    - In the Edit Offset dialog box, enter **75**.
    - Click OK.

13. Move the cursor over the same face. Click near the location on the face as shown in the following image.

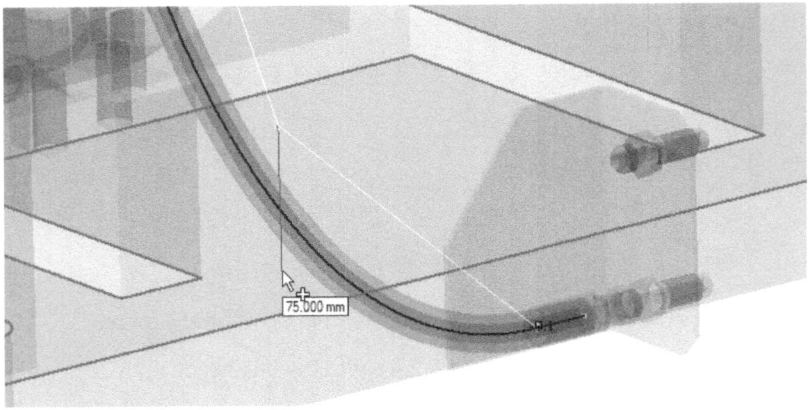

14. Right-click in the graphics window. Click Done.

15. In the ribbon, in the Route tab, in the Manage panel, click Hose Length.

16. In the Edit Hose Length dialog box:

    - Drag the length slider and release the slider when the Actual Length reports approximately **655 mm**. **Note:** The length rounds to the next 10 mm increment, as defined in the style.

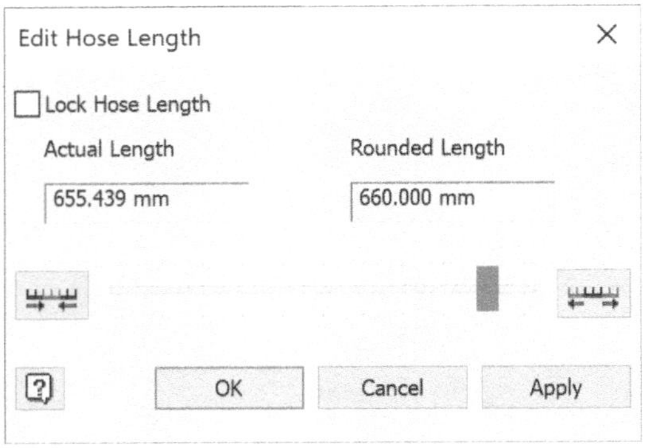

    - Click OK to update the route.

17. Right-click in the graphics window. Click Finish Edit. The route is populated automatically and a flexible hose is routed along the spline path similar to that shown below. The hose location may vary depending on the location reference selected for the offset point.

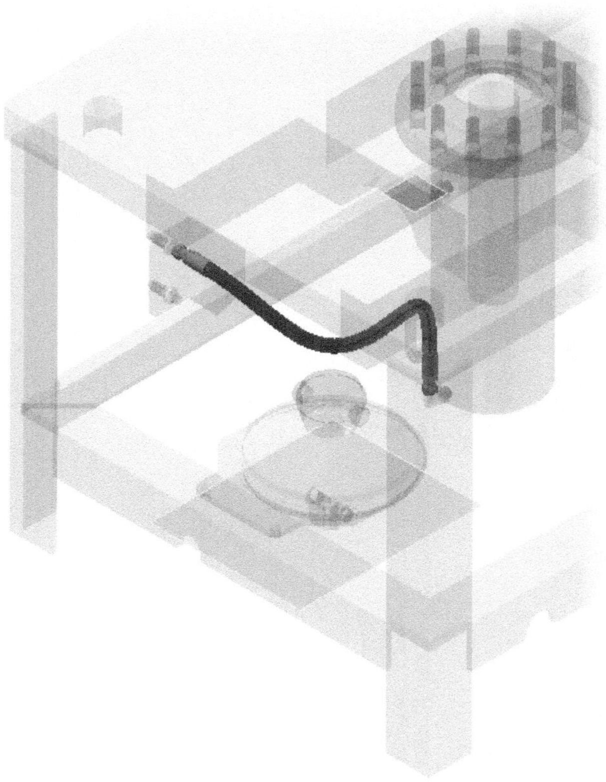

18. Close all files without saving.

Exercise: Edit a Flexible Hose Route

In this exercise, you will edit a flexible hose route. You will add, redefine, and move route nodes, adjust the hose length, and check the minimum bend radius.

The completed exercise

1. Open *Flexible Hose Edit.iam*.

2. Rotate the model and examine the flexible hose route. The hose has obvious interferences with the plate, at the arc opening and adjacent to the bulkhead bracket.

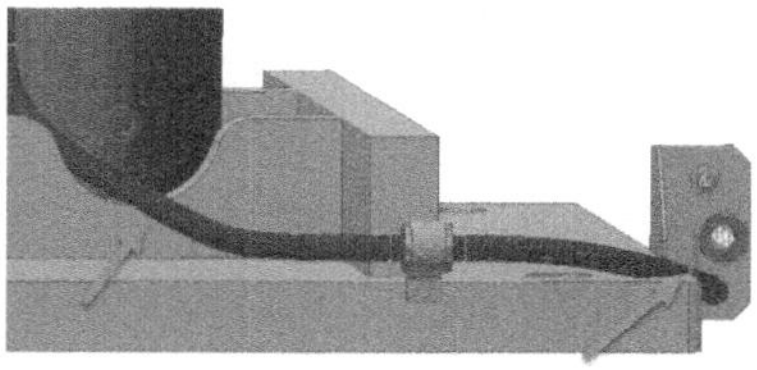

3. In the browser:
   - Expand Tube & Pipe Runs.
   - Expand Run01.
   - Expand Flexible Hose 01.
   - Right-click on Hose01. Click Edit.
4. Rotate the model to the view as shown in the following image. To turn off the display of the tubing, click Display Routes Only in the Manage panel.

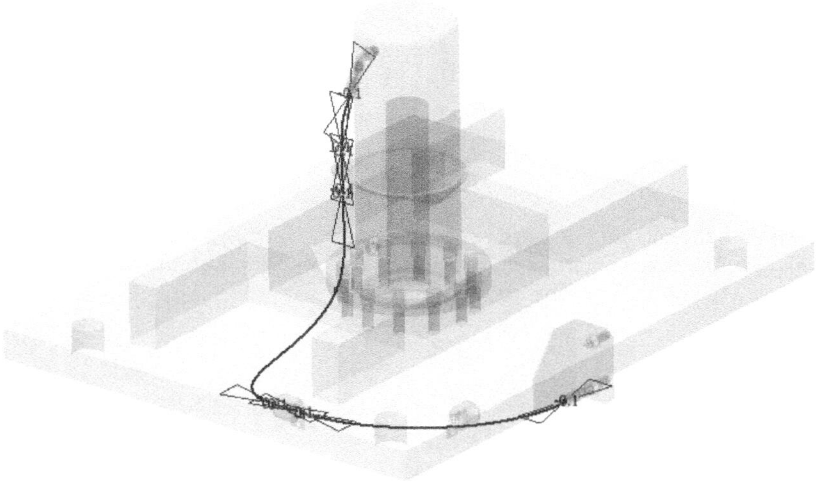

5. To begin adding nodes to the route so it passes through the second hanger, in the ribbon, in the Route tab, in the Create panel, click Insert Node.
6. Click the route near the second hanger as shown in the following image.

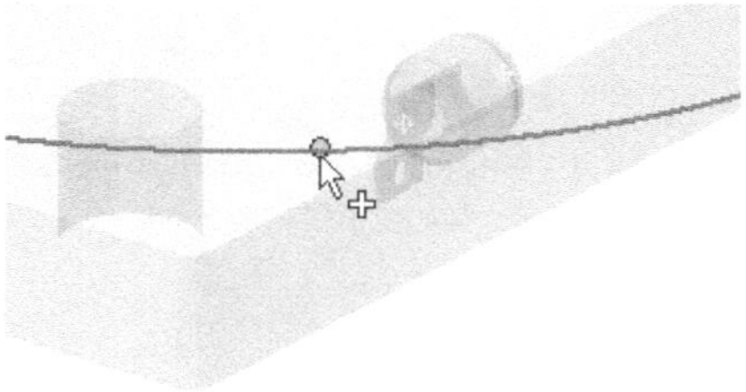

7. Repeat the previous two steps to insert a second node on the other side of the hanger.

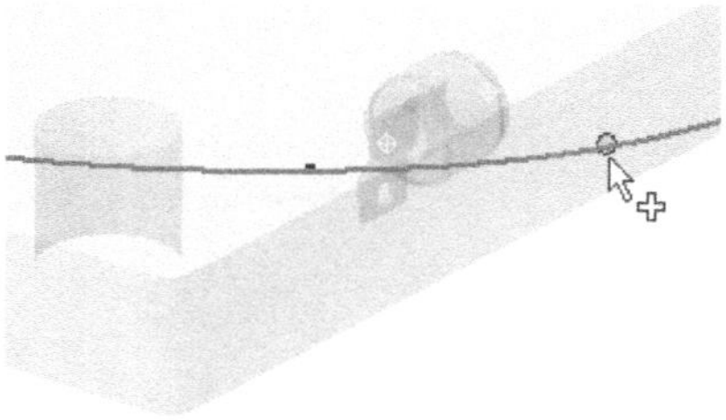

8. Right-click on the first node that you added. Click Redefine.

9. To set a new position for this node:

   - Move the cursor over the work point to the left of the hanger.
   - Ensure that the arrow is pointing away from the hanger. If the arrow points through the hanger, press SPACEBAR to change the direction.
   - Click to place the node on the work point.

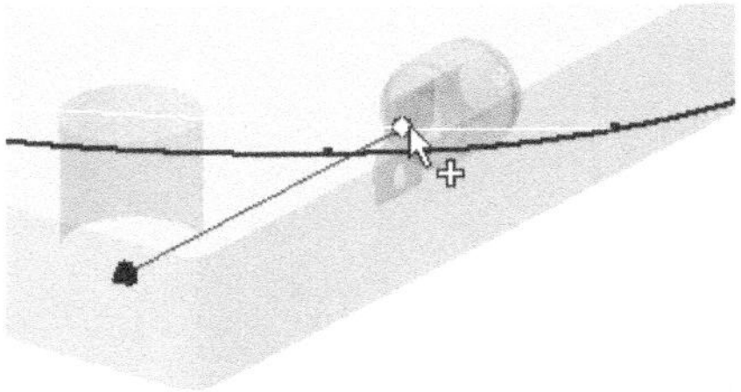

10. Redefine the second node to be coincident with the work point on the other side of the hanger. The direction arrow for this node must point through the hanger. Press SPACEBAR to change the direction of the arrow.

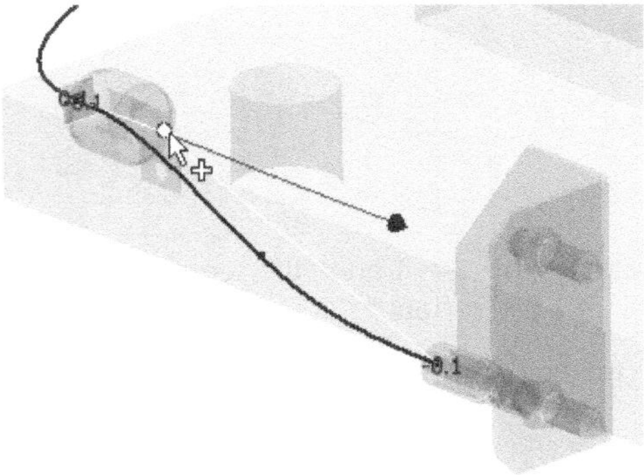

11. To begin moving the node in the plate opening to eliminate the second interference, right-click on the node near the plate saddle. Click 3D Move/Rotate.

12. To move the node a set amount:

- Click the blue arrowhead on the triad.
- For the Z value in the mini-toolbar, enter **-25**.
- Click the green checkmark in the mini-toolbar to raise the node.

13. To dynamically reposition the node:

- Right-click on the same node. Click 3D Move/ Rotate.
- Click and drag the red arrowhead just over **100 mm** as shown in the following image.
- Click the green checkmark in the mini-toolbar.

14. Turn on the display of all objects.

- On the Route tab, in the Manage panel, click Display all objects.

15. Right-click in the graphics window. Click Finish Edit. The route is updated and the hose does not intersect the plate.

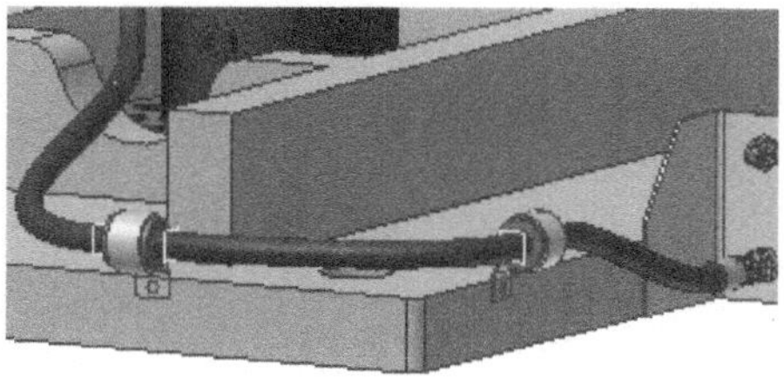

16. To begin editing the hose so its length matches the stock length of a purchased 1400 mm hose with fittings, in the browser, right-click on Hose01. Click Edit.

17. In the Route tab, in the Manage panel, click Hose Length.

18. In the Edit Hose Length dialog box:

    - Drag the slider to the right until the rounded length is reported as **1420 mm**.
    - Click OK.

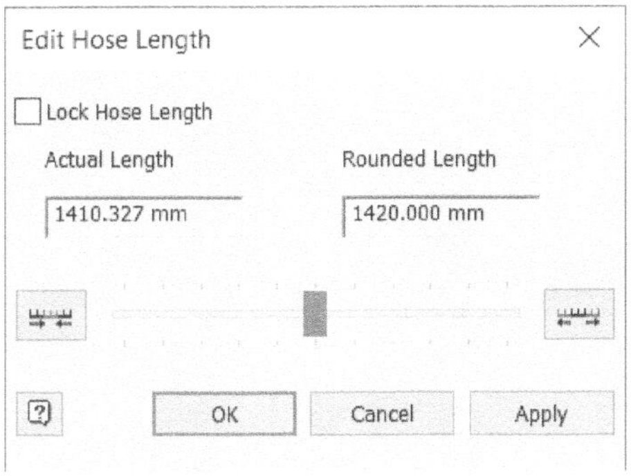

19. In the Route tab, in the Exit panel, click Finish Route. Review the results of the design changes.

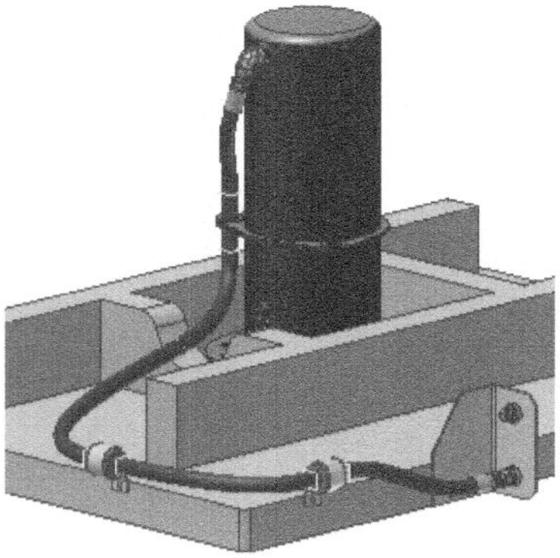

20. Ensure that Run01 is active. In the browser, right-click on Hose01. Click Bend Radius>Check.

    The browser icon for Hose01 changes to a green checkmark. The hose does not violate the minimum bend radius of the active style.

21. Close all files without saving.

Lesson: Leveraging Routes and Runs

Overview

This lesson describes how you can reuse tube and pipe routes and runs, and how to configure tube and pipe run subassemblies in different versions of an iAssembly.

Being able to reuse tube and pipe routes and runs means you can complete your designs in less time when the design requires similar routes or runs. It also means you have a technique that you can use to create a route or run and use it as a template to easily create unique routes or runs in different designs. Understanding how to configure iAssembly members so they include the correct tube and pipe run content for that member means you can achieve the configurations that completely represent the variations of your designs.

In the following image, the same assembly containing tube and pipe content is shown in three different configurations. For the bottom left configuration, the route for the flexible hoses had to be copied as a unique route so the configuration could be created with longer hoses.

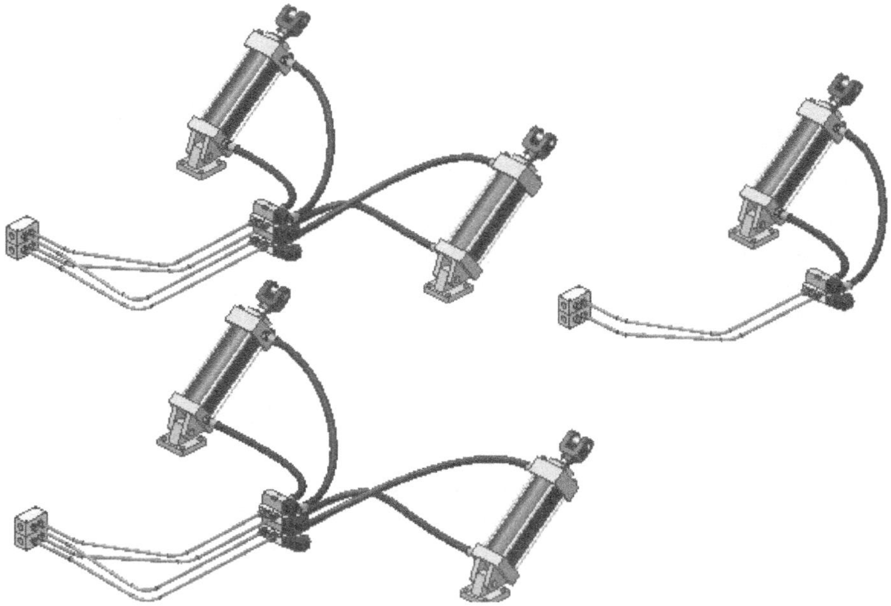

Objectives

After completing this lesson, you will be able to:

- Reduce the time required to complete routed system designs by reusing existing routes, runs, and tube and pipe runs assemblies.
- Manage tube and pipe components in iAssemblies.

Reuse of Routes and Runs

Machines often require similar or exact routes or runs spaced or patterned across the design. To reduce the time required to complete your routed system designs, you need to know when and how to reuse existing routes, runs, and tube and pipe runs assemblies.

In the following image, a run is patterned to complete a symmetrical design.

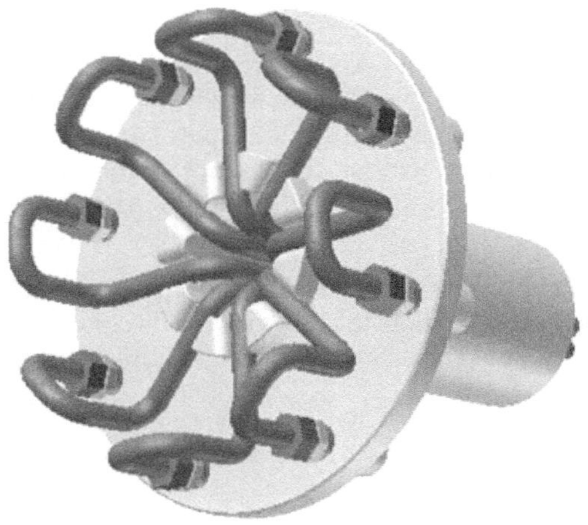

Definition of Reusing Routes and Runs

The reuse of a route or run means you have added a secondary occurrence of the route or run to the same assembly design or to another design. Initially a secondary occurrence of a run or route is much like any other occurrence of a subassembly. The secondary occurrence is driven by changes to the initial adaptive route or run. If the copied route or run must be modified to meet design requirements in its new role, you must convert the secondary occurrence to a new adaptive component.

When you set a secondary occurrence to be adaptive, it becomes independent of the original route or run. During the conversion, new files are generated for the copied component and all of the components below it.

Because you can copy and reuse routes and runs at many levels of your design, if you intend to modify the copied components, you must be sure to copy them to an appropriate level of the tube and pipe hierarchy. The type of components to be reused, and the intended use of the copied components, determine the workflow to reuse the original tube and pipe components.

In the following image, a copied run is converted to a new adaptive run in the primary runs subassembly. The new run is connected to other fittings in the assembly.

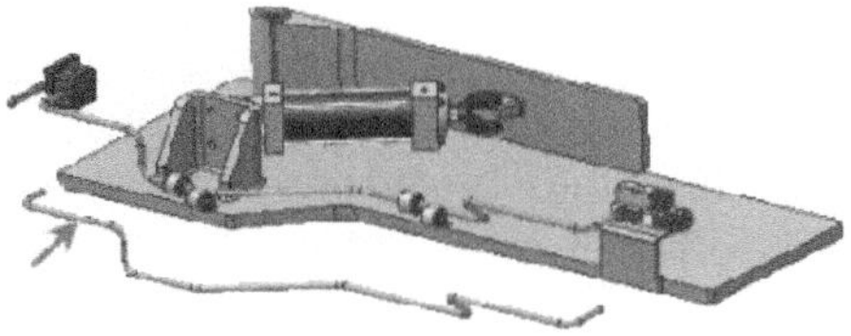

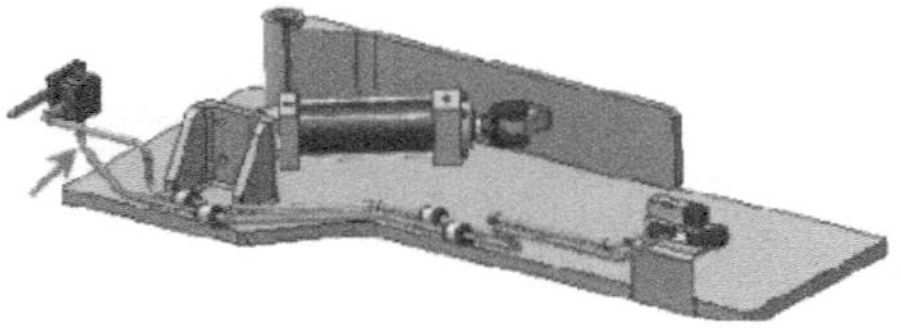

Common Copy and Reuse Scenarios

The following list outlines some common copy and reuse scenarios for tube and pipe components. You can copy within the same document or between documents if the appropriate tube and pipe hierarchy is available. You can also use the Pattern Component tool on the primary runs subassembly, runs, or routes to pattern multiple occurrences.

- Copy the primary runs subassembly to the same top-level assembly: A copied secondary occurrence of the primary runs subassembly cannot be made adaptive in the same top-level assembly. You can position the secondary occurrences with assembly constraints. Any changes to the original primary runs subassembly are reflected in any secondary occurrences. You can also use the Pattern Component tool to generate patterned secondary occurrences of the primary runs subassembly.
- Copy the primary runs subassembly to a different top-level assembly that currently does not contain a primary runs subassembly: The copied subassembly is initially placed as a nonadaptive occurrence of the original primary runs subassembly. You can convert the copied occurrence into a new, adaptive primary runs subassembly in the new design.
- Copy a run within the same primary runs subassembly: You should always paste copied runs at the same level of the tube and pipe hierarchy. You can leave the copied run as a secondary occurrence, or convert the run to a new adaptive run in the primary runs subassembly.
- Copy a run to the primary runs subassembly in another design: Although you can leave the copied run as a secondary occurrence of the original run subassembly, you typically convert the copied run to a new, adaptive run in the new design.
- Copy a route to the same run or another run in the same primary runs subassembly: Copied routes are typically less practical than copied runs. Most routes contain only path information, no conduit segments of fittings are included. The exception is a flexible hose route where the active style specifies the hose and fittings stored in a subassembly below the route. You can convert copied routes into new adaptive routes in the run.

> Combine routes that you want to copy or reuse in a single run. You can then copy the single run to efficiently replicate the populated routes.

Managing Tube and Pipe Components in iAssemblies

You create iAssembly configurations when you have a design that has multiple variations that are based on a core design. In each iAssembly configuration, variations can be the inclusion or exclusion of components and constraints, changing of constraint values, modifying properties and parameters, or making a variety of any other types of changes. To achieve the tube and pipe variations you require in different iAssembly members, you must understand the unique settings and options for tube and pipe runs.

The following image shows two configurations of an iAssembly. The takeout route is removed in the configuration shown on the right.

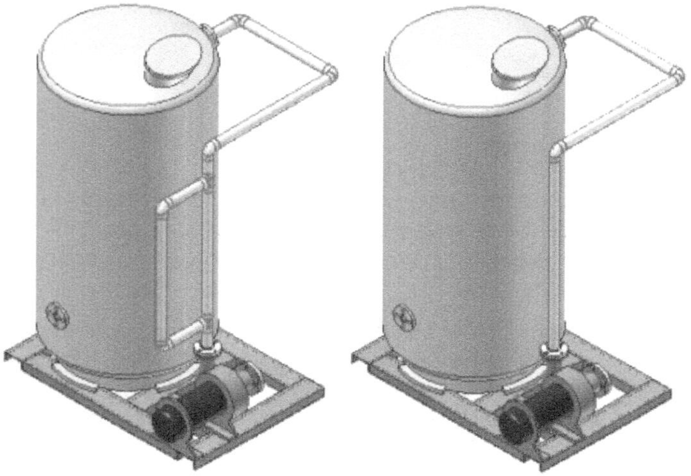

Tube and Pipe Configurations

When you create an iAssembly factory from a top-level assembly containing a primary runs subassembly, the primary runs subassembly becomes the tube and pipe configuration for the initial iAssembly member. The primary runs subassembly in the initial member is marked as adaptive. When you add a configuration member to the iAssembly, the primary runs subassembly for those new members is initially a nonadaptive secondary occurrence.

If the primary runs subassembly does not require changes in the iAssembly member, it can remain a secondary occurrence. These secondary occurrences update when the primary adaptive run updates.

If you need to make changes to routes and runs in an iAssembly member, you must convert the primary runs subassembly in the member to a unique, adaptive version. Each new adaptive primary runs subassembly is added to the iAssembly factory. You convert a secondary occurrence to a unique adaptive occurrence by right-clicking on the run in the browser or graphics window and then clicking Make Adaptive.

In the following image, the iAssembly contains only three configuration members. The first member has a primary adaptive run, and the second member has a secondary occurrence of the primary run. The third member has a unique run because it was set as adaptive.

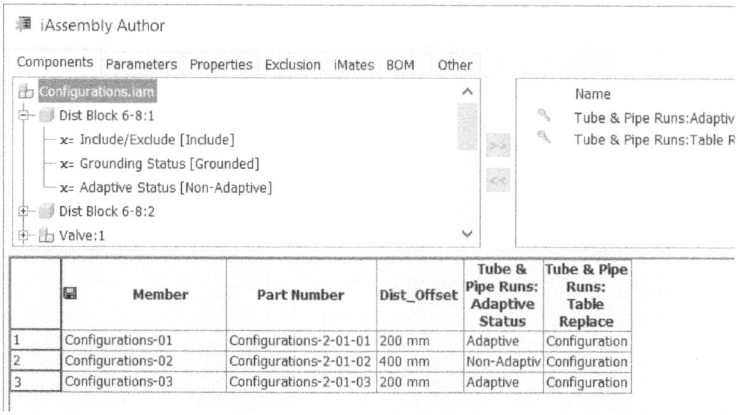

	Member	Part Number	Dist_Offset	Tube & Pipe Runs: Adaptive Status	Tube & Pipe Runs: Table Replace
1	Configurations-01	Configurations-2-01-01	200 mm	Adaptive	Configuration
2	Configurations-02	Configurations-2-01-02	400 mm	Non-Adaptiv	Configuration
3	Configurations-03	Configurations-2-01-03	200 mm	Adaptive	Configuration

Key points to remember when creating iAssembly configurations with tube and pipe runs include:

- A run can be set adaptive only in one iAssembly member.
- Any number of iAssembly members can use the secondary occurrence of a run.
- Any nonadaptive primary runs subassembly can be converted to a unique adaptive primary runs assembly. All adaptive primary runs subassemblies are added to the iAssembly.

> Group routes that you want to include or exclude in an iAssembly member in a common run. You can delete the run in the iAssembly member to control tube and pipe components.

Process: Managing Tube and Pipe Configurations

The following steps give an overview of creating and managing tube and pipe configurations in an iAssembly factory.

1. Create all routes and runs required for all versions of the iAssembly. Place and constrain all components required in all versions.

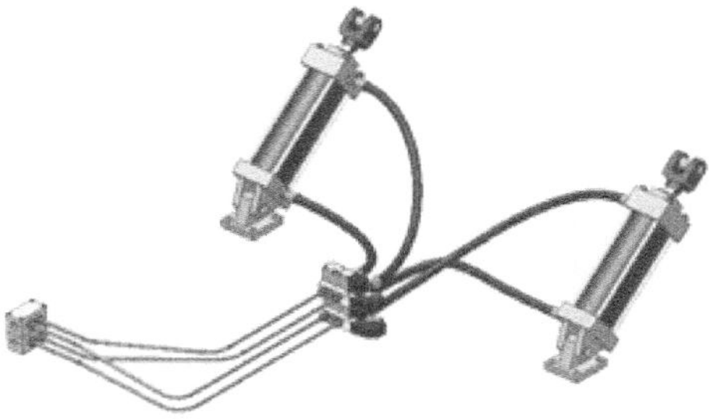

2. Create the iAssembly factory. Add a row for each required iAssembly member. Close the iAssembly Author.

	Member	Part Number	Cyl_Offset	Tube & Pipe Runs: Adaptive Status
1	Configuration	Configurati	-400 mm	Adaptive
2	Configuration	Configurati	-500 mm	Non-Adaptive
3	Configuration	Configurati	-400 mm	Non-Adaptive

3. In the browser, activate each iAssembly member.

4. If the active iAssembly member requires changes to tube and pipe components, use the Make Adaptive tool to create a unique, adaptive primary runs subassembly. The new primary runs subassembly is added to the Tube and Pipe Interchangeability set for the iAssembly factory.

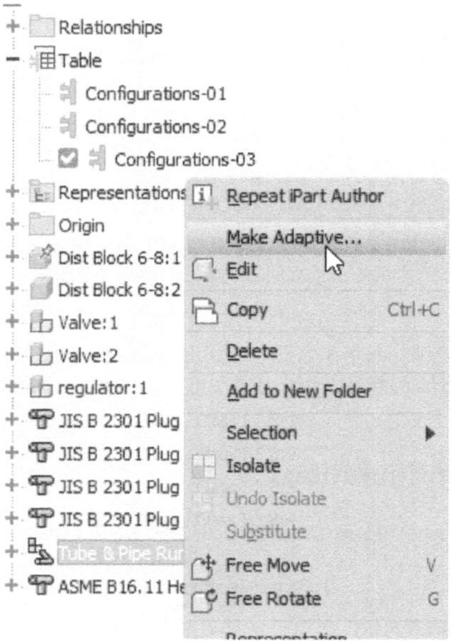

In the Make Adaptive dialog box, you can enter new unique file names in the New Name column. Note the visual color of the tube and pipe file row during editing until the file name check is satisfied:

- Cyan: Indicates the active row you are currently editing.
- White: Indicates the new file name is valid.
- Yellow: Indicates the file name is duplicated with another conduit part in the File Name list.
- Red: Indicates the file name is duplicated with an existing file in the parent location.

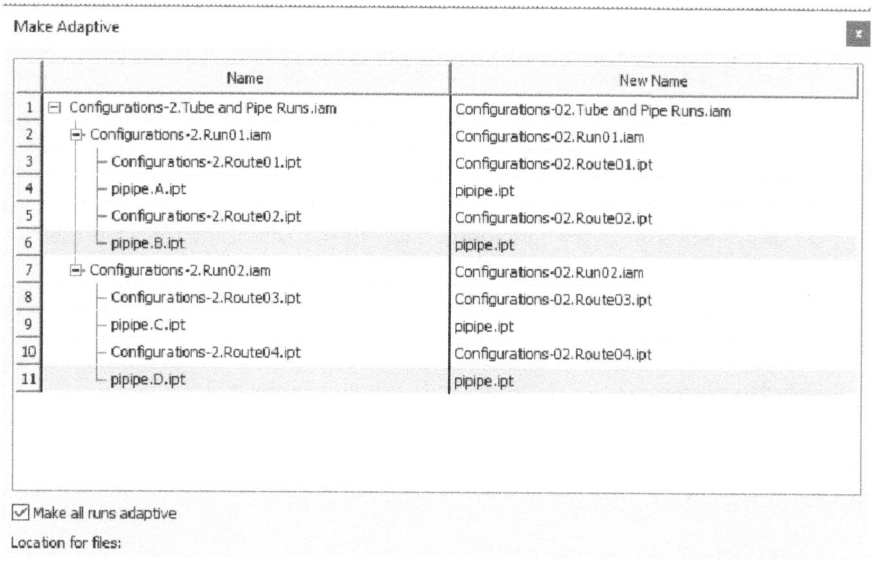

If you are making a secondary occurrence of a primary runs assembly adaptive, do any of the following:

- Select or clear the Mark all runs adaptive check box.
- If the default file location is not satisfactory, enter or browse to the file location for the new primary runs assembly.

5. Activate the adaptive primary runs subassembly. Delete any routes or runs that are not required for the active iAssembly member.

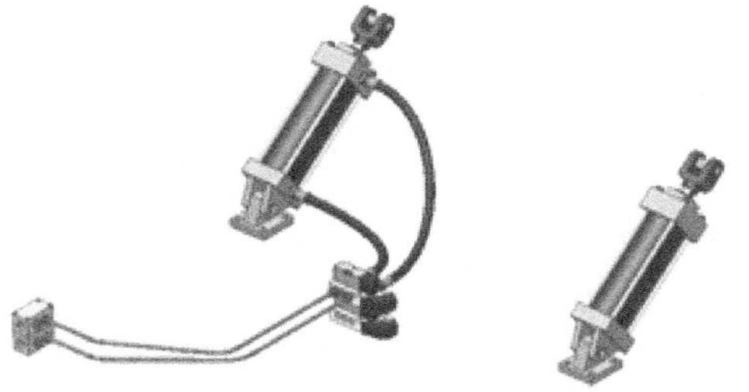

6. Complete the other changes required for the specific iAssembly member.

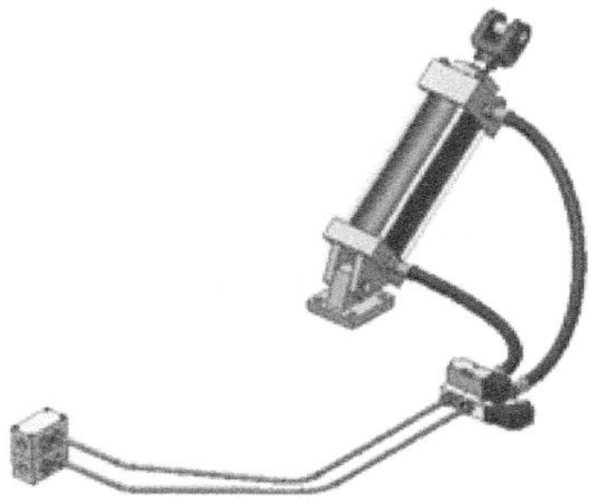

Guidelines for Tube and Pipe Configurations

- Group routes that you want to include or exclude in an iAssembly member in a common run. You can delete the run in the iAssembly member to control tube and pipe components.
- To reduce complexity in excluding components in a configuration, avoid placing components as first-level children of the Tube & Pipe Runs subassembly. Place common components either outside the Tube & Pipe Runs subassembly, or in runs inside the Tube & Pipe Runs subassembly.
- It is good practice to maintain a version of the primary runs subassembly that contains all tube and pipe components for all configurations. Name the occurrence to reflect its role because it might not describe a valid set of routes and runs.
- If the primary runs subassembly for an iAssembly member requires changes, make it adaptive before editing routes and runs in other iAssembly members. If you delete a tube and pipe component in the adaptive occurrence of the primary runs subassembly, the components are deleted in all secondary occurrences and cannot be opened.
- Model States can be used to suppress tube and pipe components in model states.

File Naming Conventions

File naming conventions can be determined in the File Naming Defaults dialog box, found under Application Options>File tab. The following are the conventions for the Tube & Pipe tab:

- Click on the + button to add attributes.

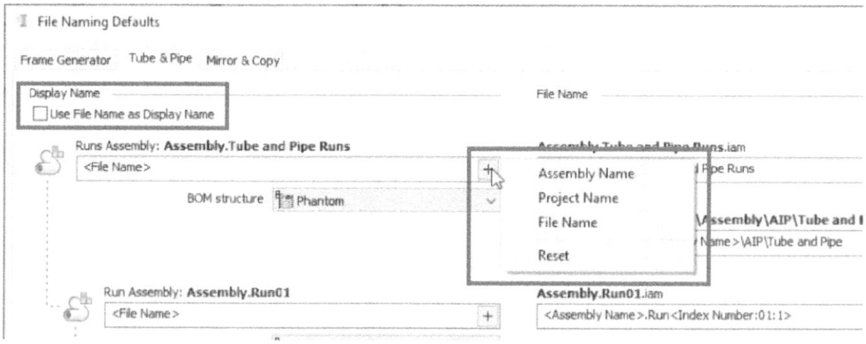

- The BOM structure of assemblies is added through a drop-down list.

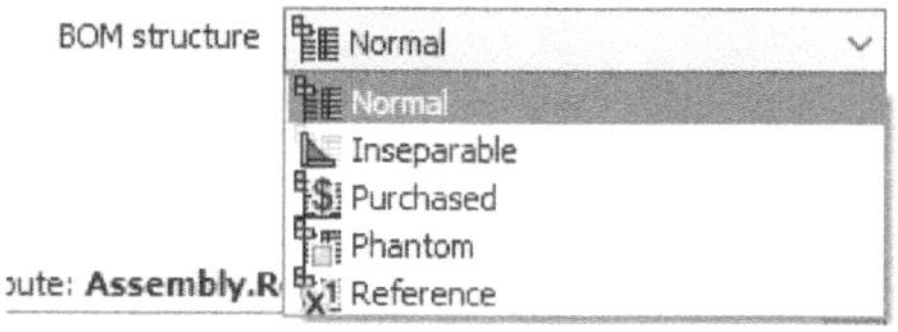

- You can add the date and other project attributes, as shown in image below.

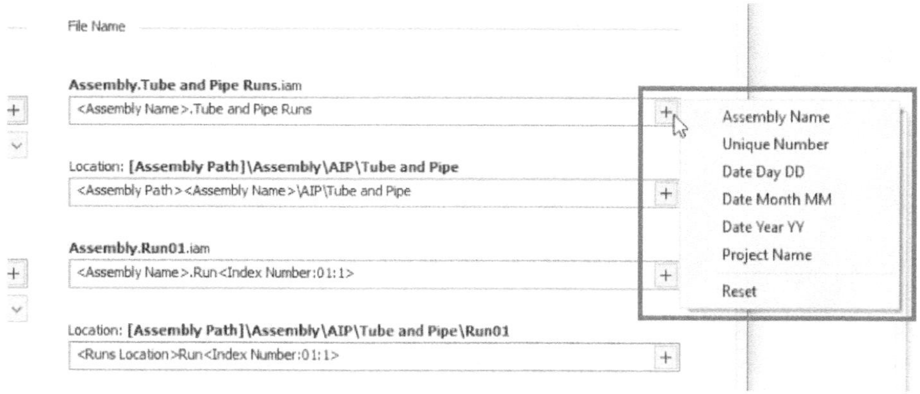

- Different folder types are available: Pipe Segment, Pipe Bend Segment, Pipe Sweep Segment, Hose Assembly, etc.

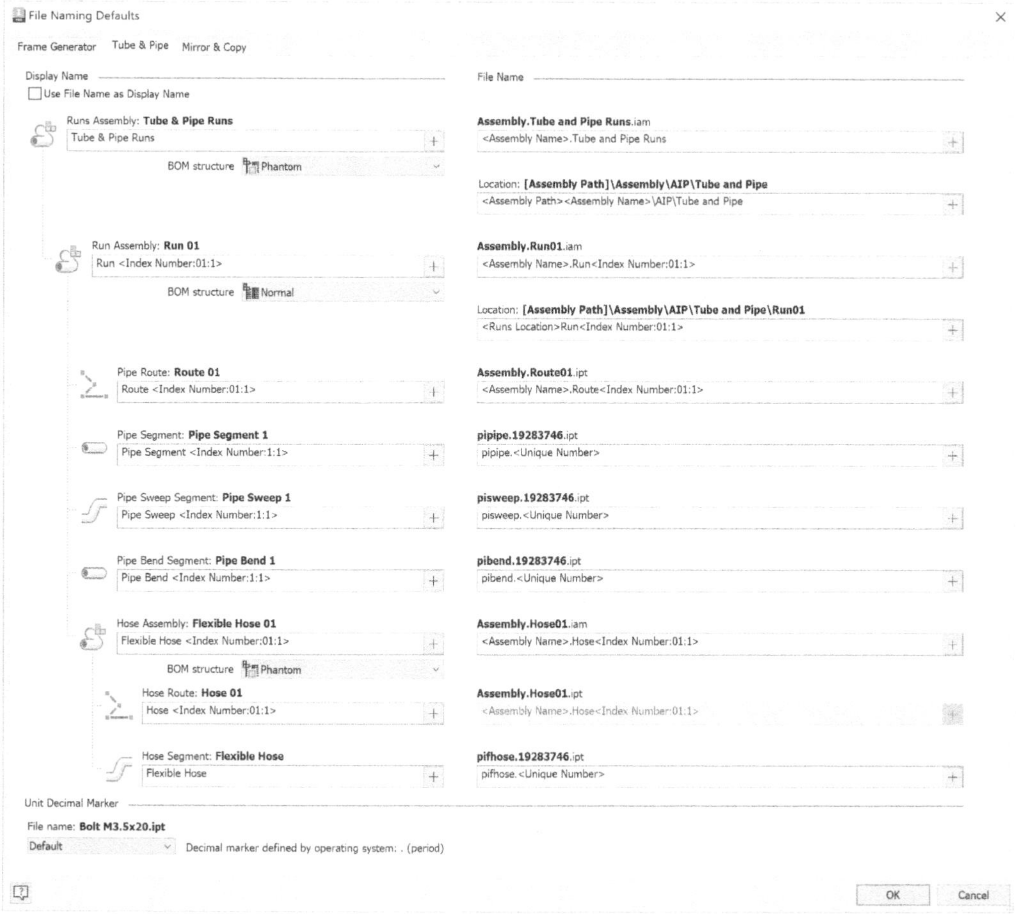

Exercise: Reuse a Run

In this exercise, you will copy an existing run and reuse it in the same assembly. You will examine the dependence of the copied run on the original run. You will then make the new run adaptive and edit one of the runs to verify their independence.

The completed exercise

1. Open *Copy a Run.iam*.

2. In the browser, double-click on Tube & Pipe Runs to activate it.

3. In the browser, drag Run01 and drop it into the graphics window. A run assembly is added and listed as a nonadaptive occurrence in the browser.

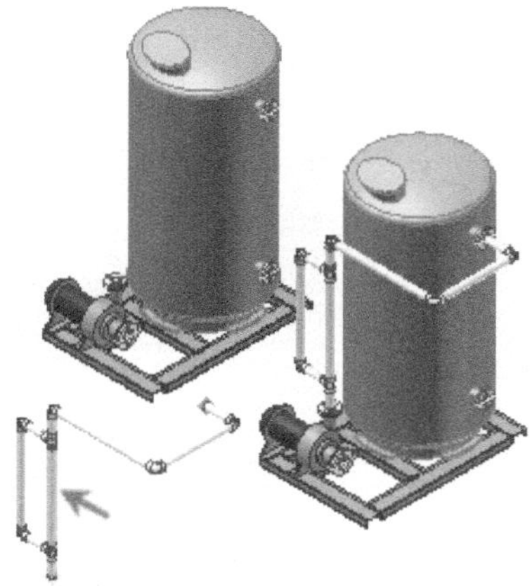

4. In the Tube and Pipe tab, in the Exit panel, click Finish Tube and Pipe to return to the top-level assembly.

5. To begin assembling the run assembly:
   - In the Assemble tab, in the Relationships panel, click Constrain.
   - Select the axis of the vertical pipe segment below the lower tee in the new run.

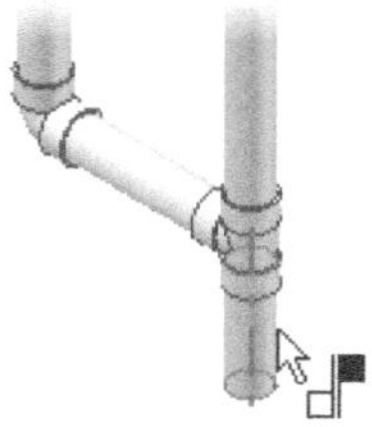

6. Click the cylindrical outlet on the rear pump. Right-click in the graphics window background and click Apply or click Apply in the Place Constraint dialog box.

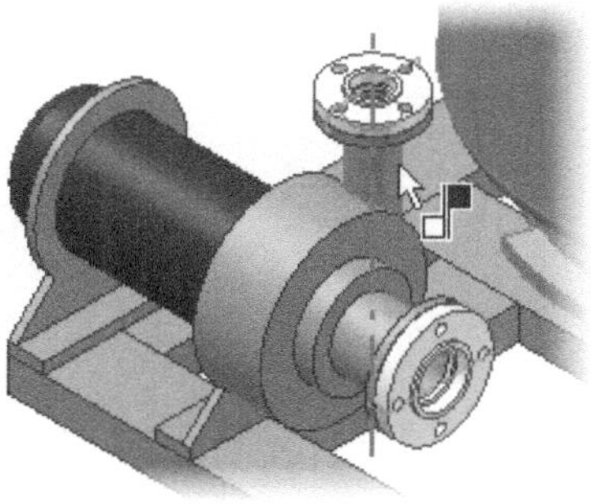

7. Place a second axis/axis mate constraint between the horizontal outlet on the rear tank and the adjacent pipe segment in the new run.
   - Right-click in the graphics window background and click Apply.
   - Press ESC.

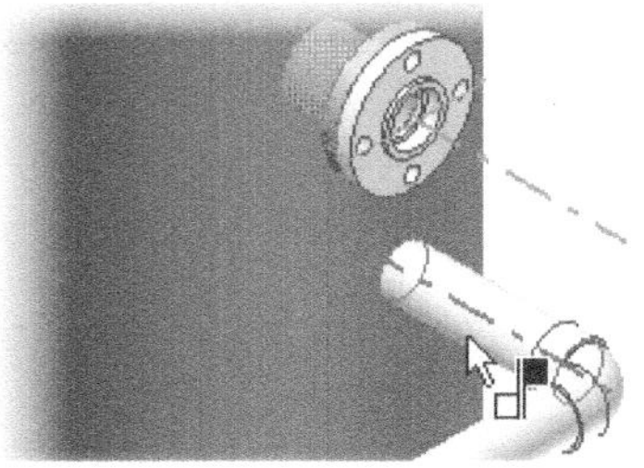

8. In the browser, expand Run01. Under Run01, double-click on Route02 to activate it.

9. In the Route tab, in the Create panel, click Move Segment. Click and drag the vertical takeout segment a short distance away from the adjacent vertical segment.

10. Right-click in the graphics window background and click Done.

11. In the browser, double-click on Tube & Pipe Runs. The takeout route updates in both instances of the run.

12. Right-click on Tube & Pipe Runs and select Tube & Pipe Settings. Make sure that Prompt for conduit file names and Prompt for fitting file names are selected. Click OK.

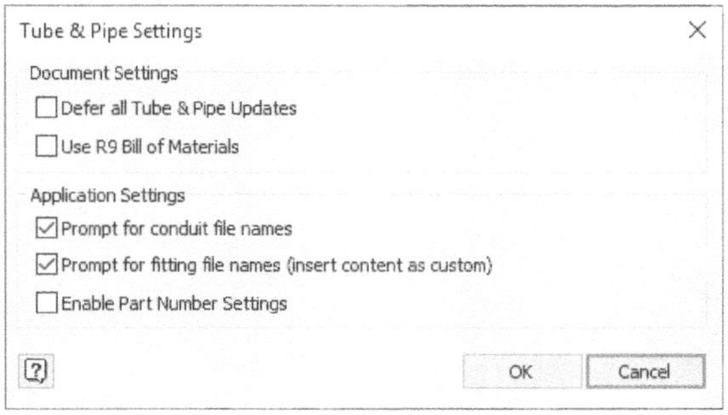

13. To begin making the second occurrence a unique run assembly, in the browser, right-click on Copy Run.Run01:2. Click Make Adaptive.

14. To save the run and all its components as unique documents, do the following:

- In the message dialog box, click Yes.
- In the Save dialog box, click OK.
- In the Make Adaptive dialog box, click in the New Name column and enter unique file names (e.g., pipipe001, pipipe002, etc.). If it does not allow you to change the file names, make sure Step 12 was completed. Once you have entered the new names, click OK.

Run02 is now a unique adaptive subassembly in the Tube & Pipe Runs subassembly. Click global update, if required.

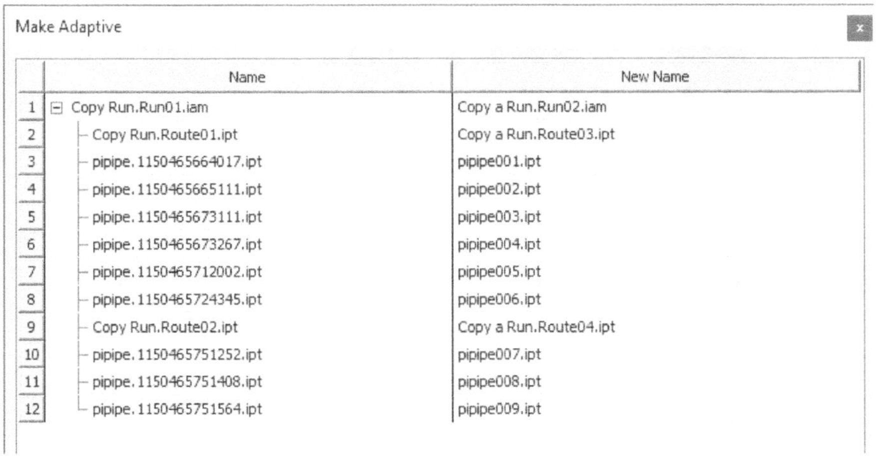
Make Adaptive

	Name	New Name
1	Copy Run.Run01.iam	Copy a Run.Run02.iam
2	Copy Run.Route01.ipt	Copy a Run.Route03.ipt
3	pipipe.1150465664017.ipt	pipipe001.ipt
4	pipipe.1150465665111.ipt	pipipe002.ipt
5	pipipe.1150465673111.ipt	pipipe003.ipt
6	pipipe.1150465673267.ipt	pipipe004.ipt
7	pipipe.1150465712002.ipt	pipipe005.ipt
8	pipipe.1150465724345.ipt	pipipe006.ipt
9	Copy Run.Route02.ipt	Copy a Run.Route04.ipt
10	pipipe.1150465751252.ipt	pipipe007.ipt
11	pipipe.1150465751408.ipt	pipipe008.ipt
12	pipipe.1150465751564.ipt	pipipe009.ipt

Note that the visual color of the rows may display in the following colors during editing until the file name check is satisfied:

- Cyan: Indicates the active row you are currently editing.
- White: Indicates the new file name is valid.
- Yellow: Indicates the file name is duplicated with another conduit part in the File Name list.
- Red: Indicates the file name is duplicated with an existing file in the parent location.

15. Under Run01, double-click on Route02 to activate it.

16. In the Route tab, in the Create panel, click Move Segment. Click and drag the vertical takeout segment toward the adjacent vertical segment.

17. Right-click in the graphics window background. Click Done.

18. In the browser, double-click on Tube & Pipe Runs. The takeout route updates in Run01 but not in Run02.

19. Close all files without saving.

Chapter Summary

In this chapter, you learned how to create and edit rigid pipe and tube routes, and how to identify and use different fittings in rigid routes. You also learned how to create and edit flexible hose routes, and how to successfully manage routes and runs.

Having completed this chapter, you can:

- Create rigid routes for tube and pipe designs.
- Create rigid routes by using the sketching tools and techniques.
- Edit rigid tube and pipe routes.
- Edit fittings and modify styles.
- Create and edit flexible hose routes.
- Reuse tube and pipe routes and runs, and configure tube and pipe run subassemblies in different versions of an iAssembly.

Chapter 4

Fittings and Components

You use the tools and features introduced in this chapter to manage your library of parts. Taking advantage of custom libraries, custom parts, and custom iParts saves you time and helps you to maintain an efficient design process. Using the Content Center to store and reuse your custom parts provides for a consistent and effective interface. You also create and use custom tube and pipe styles in order to increase your drawing productivity.

Objectives

After completing this chapter, you will be able to:

- Manage the libraries that are included in the Content Center as well as your own libraries of tube and pipe components.
- Author and publish your own tube and pipe content.
- Manage the properties and settings of published tube and pipe content.
- Create new styles using published content.

Lesson: Managing Libraries

Overview

This lesson describes the use and configuration of the Content Center Libraries.

By understanding how to use and configure the Content Center, not only do you benefit from reusing the industry-standard-based fittings, piping, tubes, and hose components, you also benefit from the Content Center by using it to manage and access all of your company-specific tube and pipe library content.

In the following image, a custom valve that was published to a custom Content Center library is in the process of being added to a design.

Objectives

After completing this lesson, you will be able to:

- Describe the purpose and functionalities of the Content Center.
- Explain the difference between a Desktop install and an Autodesk® Vault® Server based install.
- Add a custom library to the Content Center.
- Configure the path for saving and accessing Content Center files.
- Copy content from an industry library to a custom Content Center library.
- Transfer a custom library between Autodesk Vault Server and Autodesk® Inventor® Desktop Content.

About the Content Center

To benefit from the use and creation of Content Center data, you must first understand the purpose and functionalities of the Content Center.

The following image shows just a few of the many possible parts that are available in the Content Center for use in your designs.

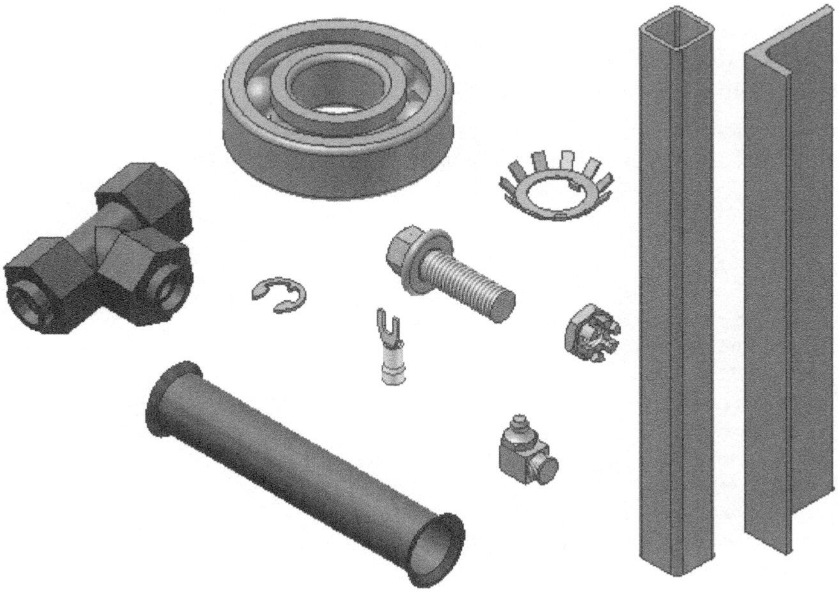

Definition of the Content Center

The Content Center is a central storage location for library data consisting of features and parts that you can select and insert into your part or assembly designs. The data in the Content Center is stored in different library databases. The location of the library database files depend on your work environment.

When you install the Content Center, you have the option of selecting one or more libraries that contain parts based on common industry standards. Along with these supplied industry-standard libraries, you can create your own custom libraries and publish your own parts or features to those libraries. By publishing your library content to custom Content Center libraries, everyone has access to the same published version of the data. Not only does reusing Content Center published data help you create a design more efficiently, it also helps establish consistency between designs and among designers.

The parts that you select and use from a common industry library are either fully defined by an industry standard, or defined by a standard along with the values you enter. In addition to directly selecting and inserting data from the Content Center, some of the tools that you use also reference and use data from the Content Center. For example, when you use the Bolted Connection Generator to add a bolted connection to your assembly, the bolts, washers, and nuts that you select are based on the content in the Content Center.

Content Center Access Options

The way you install Content Center library content depends on your work environment. The two different ways that Content Center content libraries can be installed and accessed are:

- Autodesk Inventor Desktop Content
- Autodesk Vault Server

In a Desktop Content installation the Content Center libraries are individual files that are stored and accessed on your computer. When utilizing Desktop Content, you do not need to install additional software or services to access and use the Content Center content. In a Vault Server installation the Content Center libraries are stored and accessible only through Vault Server.

In the following image, the content libraries are shown listed in Autodesk Vault Server and as individual Desktop Content library files. The list of the Desktop Content library files is being viewed in Windows Explorer.

Autodesk Vault Server Libraries

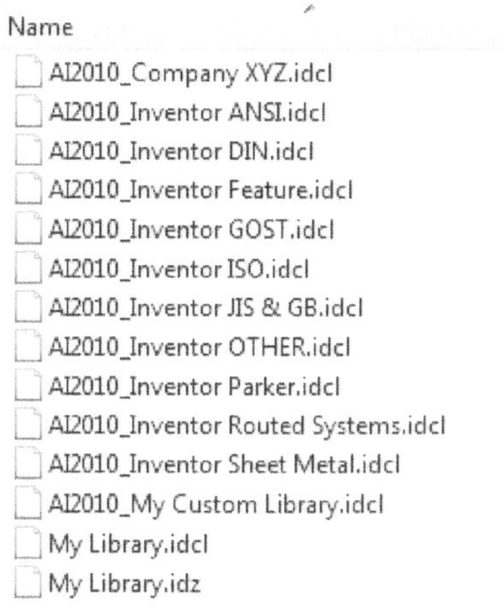

Inventor Desktop Content Libraries

If you are a stand-alone user or work using a laptop computer that might or might not always have access to the Autodesk Vault Server and your custom libraries, you will want to install using Desktop Content. If you are working as a member of a work group where multiple people access the same custom library content, then you will want to use Vault Server.

For More Information

Additional information on the options and settings for installing and configuring Content Center libraries is available in the Autodesk Inventor Help system. In the Help system, visit the Inventor Help Topics>Assembly Component Generators>Content Center.

Structure and Contents of a Library

You can think of a Content Center library as having three related aspects. The first aspect is the categories of library data. The second aspect is the families of parts or features in the category. The third aspect is the family members in the part family or feature family.

1. Categories in a library establish an organization to the content. Categories also define which parameters are optional or required in any subcategory, part family, or feature family. The categories display in a hierarchy structure similar to that of the folders in Windows Explorer. With logical names and a logical grouping of categories, it is easy to navigate through the available categories to the intended content.
2. A part family or feature family is the overall master model or template for the specific content. This master model is used to create the required variations of that part or feature. With the parametric model geometry, the family defines and stores parameter and image data.
3. Each of the defined variations for a part or feature family is referred to as a family member. The variations could be things like length, diameter, material, or part number.

Model geometry does not exist in the Content Center for every possible variation. Instead, only one set of model geometry is defined for a family, and the variations are based on the parameter values of the family members. The model geometry for the family member is added to your part or created as a part file when you require it. This enables you to have efficient storage and selection of library content.

Thus when you define or use Content Center content, you follow the order of creating or selecting a category, then a family, and then the family member. It is the family member that is ultimately added to your part or assembly design.

In the following image, the Category View pane on the left lists the organizational categories for Tube & Pipe type parts. By selecting the Bushings category, the preview on the right lists and shows the families of parts defined in that category. By selecting the ASME B16.11 Flush Bushing part family, all of the defined members for that part family list in the lower right table.

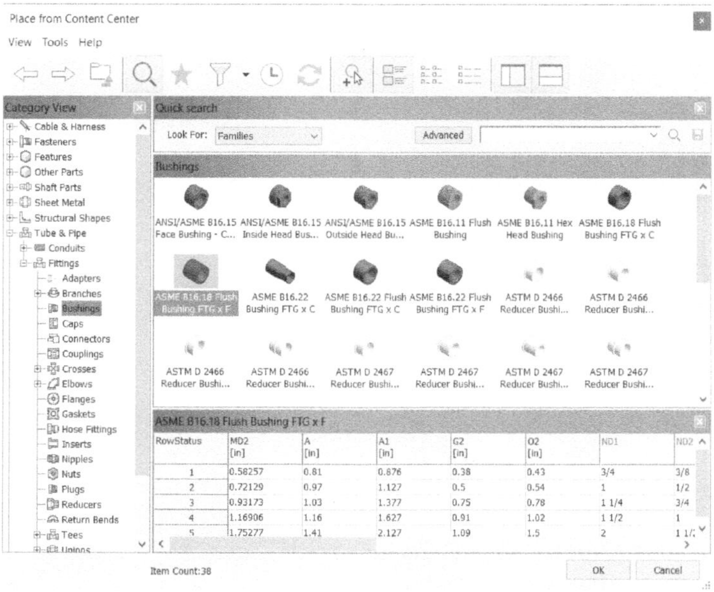

Content Center Roles

When you work with Content Center data, you either work with it as a consumer or as an editor. As a consumer, you access the libraries and use the stored parts or features in your design. As an editor, you can define the categories in a library and the required parameters for the categories, publish parts or features to the library categories, or define the published part or feature iterations that a consumer can select to reuse.

- **Content Center consumer** - When you reuse content from the Content Center to include it in your designs.
- **Content Center editor** - When you add parts or features to a library either one at a time or in a batch; when you add family members to a family; or, when you edit the parameters and properties of families or family members.

Example of Content Center Libraries and Content

As part of the Content Center, multiple libraries of preexisting content are available, which are based on industry standards. By accessing this Content Center content, you save yourself significant time researching possible sizes and modeling geometry to represent it in your design.

In the following image, multiple categories of part content are listed in the dialog box. In this case, an ISO 49 Male and Female Union Flat Seat U2 union has been selected for reuse. All of the different defined variations for this part are listed in the family preview pane. By clicking OK, this part is created and ready for you to use.

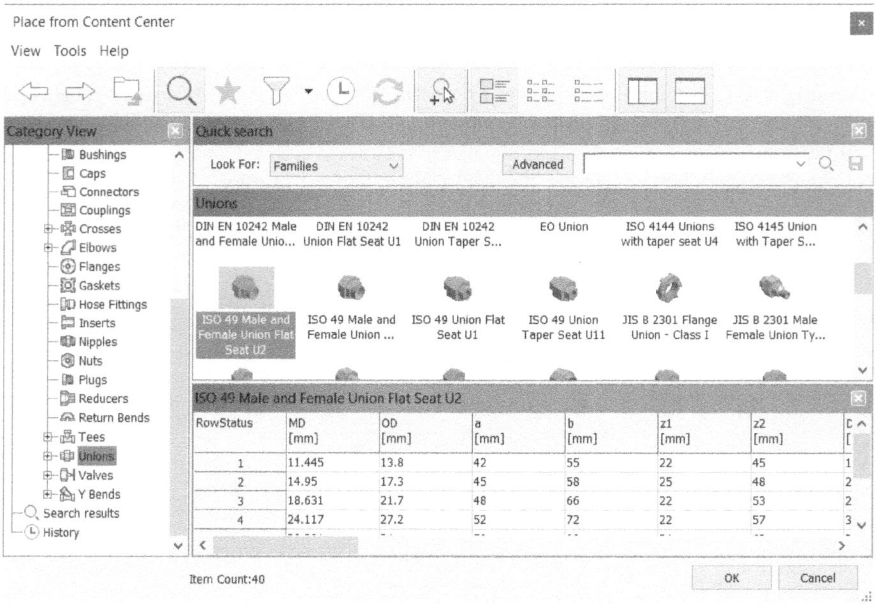

The following image shows an example of the Content Center being used to access a part to place in the assembly.

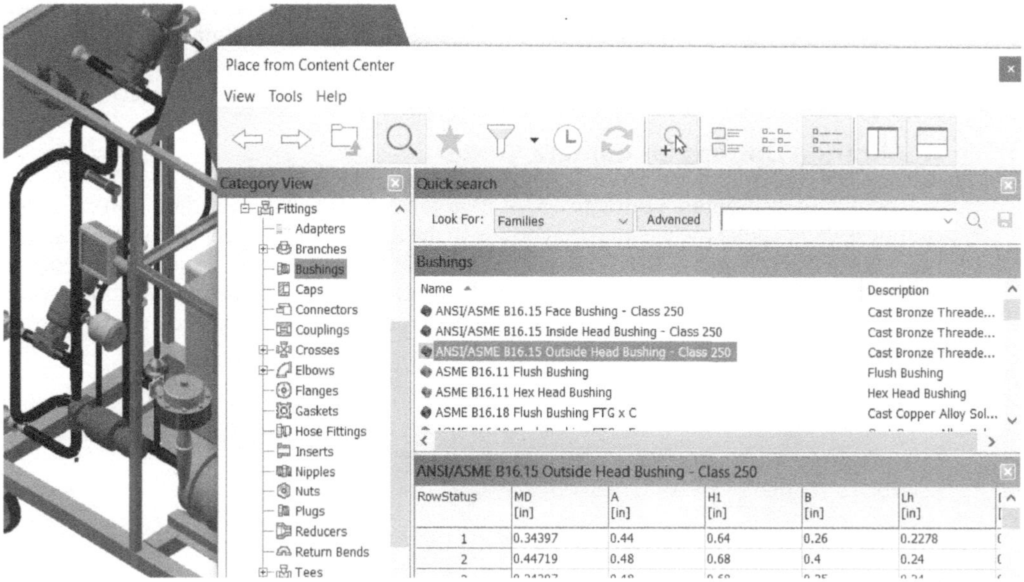

Installation Options

You have the option of configuring how you want Content Center to access libraries and what libraries are available for use. To configure the Content Center library access to match your design environment, you need to know where the configuration settings are located. You also need to understand where to configure the available desktop content libraries per project.

Application Options for Content Center

You configure the Content Center to access its libraries from either Inventor Desktop Content or Autodesk Vault Server by selecting that option in the Application Options dialog box, Content Center tab, Access Options area. When you have the Inventor Desktop Content option selected, you can specify the folder location where the content libraries reside. When you have Autodesk Vault Server selected, the list of available libraries and where you access them depends on the server you log into at a later time.

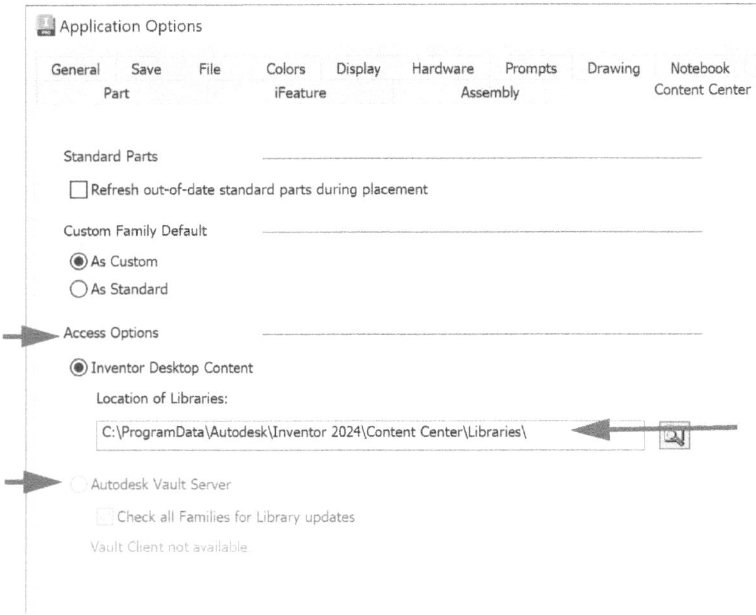

When you are configured to use Autodesk Vault Server, the access and use of library content is accomplished after logging in to Vault Server. The importing or creation of libraries occurs in the Autodesk Data Management Server Console (ADMS Console). The console is a separate application that you start by clicking ADMS Console on the desktop or from the Windows programs list. The console is also where user accounts, access permissions, and user groups are created and managed. Before a library can be used or you can modify the contents of a library, the library must exist in the Autodesk Data Management Server, and a user with correct permissions must be available for you.

This lesson focuses its information on the use of Desktop Content.

Configure Libraries per Project

To consume or publish content to a library, your active project file must be configured to access the content in that library.

Of all the libraries that might be available in Autodesk Inventor Desktop Content or Autodesk Vault Server, you can limit which libraries are available in Content Center. You specify which libraries are available on the basis of the active project file. If you have different project files, each project file can be configured to access different libraries. You specify which libraries are available in a project file in the Configure Libraries dialog box. You access the Configure Libraries dialog box from the Projects dialog box by selecting the project file, expanding the Configure Content Center Libraries drop-down list, and then clicking Configure Content Center Libraries.

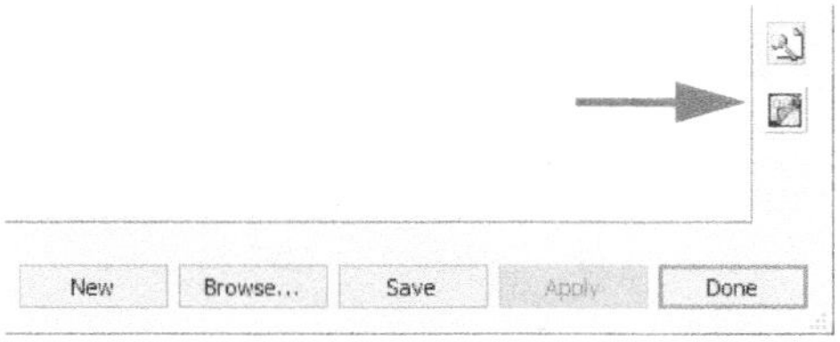

When configured to use Desktop Content, the libraries that are available for use in the active project file have their In Use check box selected in the Configure Libraries dialog box. Only the content that is defined in the selected libraries is available for reuse in your designs. Libraries that have an access value of read/write are the only libraries that can have content published to them, or property and parameter values changed. To remove a library from being used, clear the check box in the row for that library and save the changes to the project file.

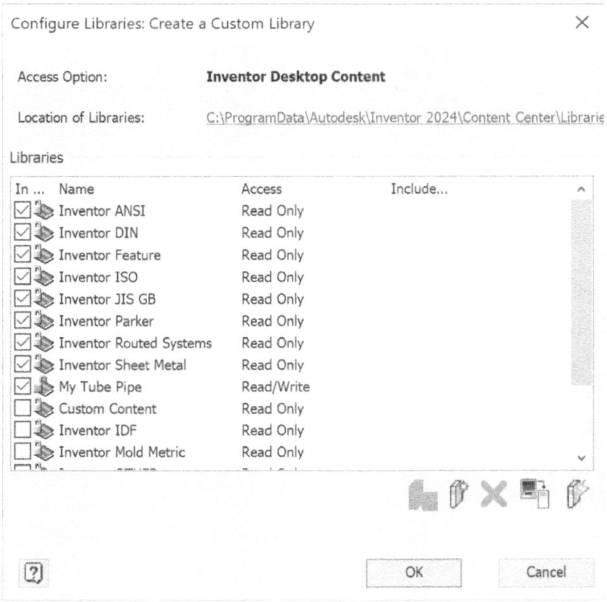

Select only the libraries that have the content you require for a project. That way only the content you require is listed in the Content Center and locating content is easier.

You can change the display name for a library. In the Configure Libraries dialog box, right-click on the library. Click Library Properties. Then, in the Library Properties dialog box, enter a new name.

Adding a Custom Library

When Autodesk Inventor is configured to use Desktop Content libraries and you want to use custom libraries, you use the Configure Libraries dialog box to create a custom read/write library. After you have included a custom library you can copy component families and standard parts to the library in order to customize them to your specifications. You also can create your own standard parts and then publish them to your custom library for reuse.

In the following image, the Content Center Editor dialog box displays showing a custom Tube and Pipe library and a custom connector that has been published to the library.

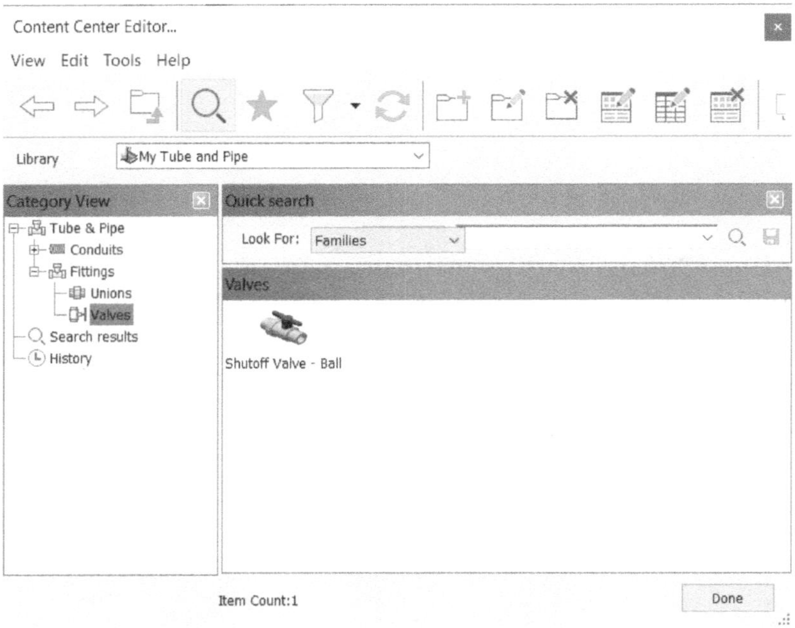

Purpose and Benefits of a Custom Library

The following list identifies the main purposes and benefits of creating custom libraries:

- Placing your custom components in the Content Center for reuse.
- Copying existing content from standard libraries, and modifying its properties to match your specific requirements.
- Increasing performance by decreasing the footprint of Content Center libraries. You copy just the component families that you will use from standard libraries to your custom library, and then detach the standard libraries that are loaded.

Custom Library Access

You initiate the creation of a custom desktop content library from in the Configure Libraries dialog box. After clicking the Create Library button in the Configure Libraries dialog box, the Create Library dialog box displays. In the Create Library dialog box, you enter the display name for the new custom library and the name for the library database file. The display name is used as the library identifier in the Content Center. The new file is saved in the Desktop Content location.

In the following image, the Create Library option in the Configure Libraries dialog box is shown being accessed to create a new custom desktop content library. Observe the existing custom library in the list, My Tube Pipe, and the difference in the glyph between read only libraries and read/write libraries. One glyph contains a lock (Read Only) and one doesn't (Read/Write).

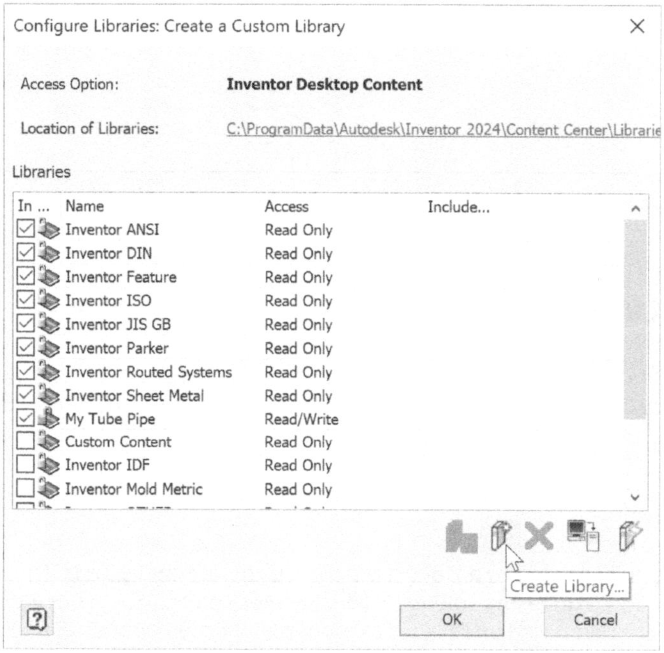

Procedure: Adding a Custom Library

The following steps give an overview of creating a custom desktop content read/write library.

1. In the Get Started tab, in the Launch panel, click Projects.
2. In the Projects dialog box, ensure the correct project file is selected, select Configure Content Center Libraries.

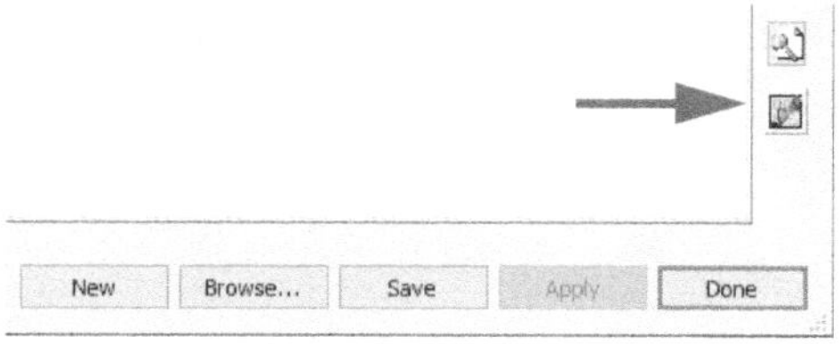

3. In the Configure Libraries dialog box, click Create Library.

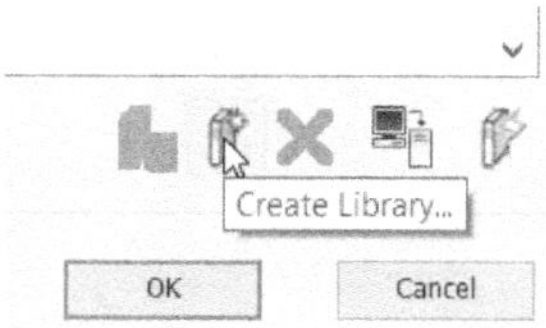

4. In the Create Library dialog box, enter the display name and file name. Click OK.

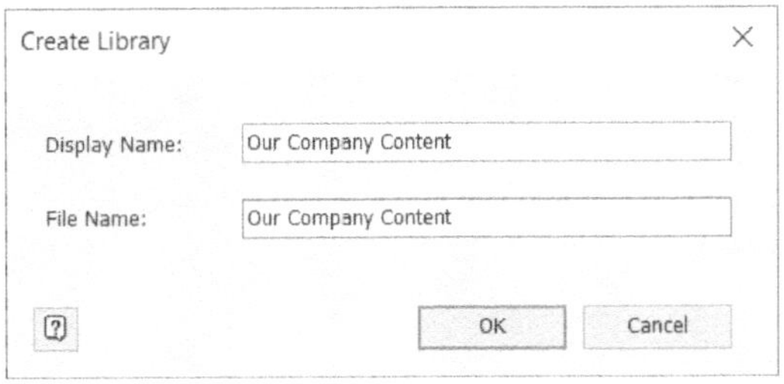

5. Close the dialog boxes and save the changes to the project file.

Configuring the Content Center File Path

When you use parts from the Content Center that are fully defined by an industry standard, those files are created and saved in a file location configured in your Autodesk Inventor. To have the files saved where you prefer them, you need to know where and how to configure the path for Content Center files.

Purpose of the File Path

Content Center parts that are fully defined by an industry standard are true library parts. They are true library parts because they do not require any editing by you. For these parts, you do not enter any unique values, you only select a part based on set sizes or properties. Because you need them only as library parts, these parts are created and saved in a library path. For easier management and performance, the library path location for these Content Center parts is a unique and independent setting.

The path that you have set for the Content Center files also becomes a search location any time you place or open additional parts from the Content Center. After you select what you need in the Content Center, the Content Center searches the path location to see whether the exact same part already exists as a file. If one is found in the path, then that file is used instead of creating a new file. By doing this, the performance for accessing and using content is better and more efficient. To minimize the amount of time to search the path for an exact match, each part from the Content Center is created in a subfolder to the defined path. The name of the folder is a key because it identifies the part family.

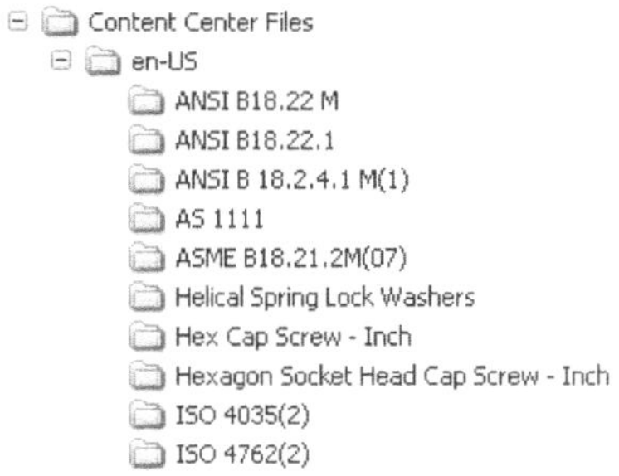

You cannot modify a Content Center library part that you are using if it resides in a library path. To have it not reside in a library path, you can either save the part to a location outside of the path, or activate a different project file that does not have that location defined as a library path.

Content Center Files Location

The path for the automatic saving and referencing of Content Center files is based on the current settings in the Application Options dialog box and the active project file.

You specify the default path for Content Center files on an Autodesk Inventor installation in the Application Options dialog box, File tab, Default Content Center Files field.

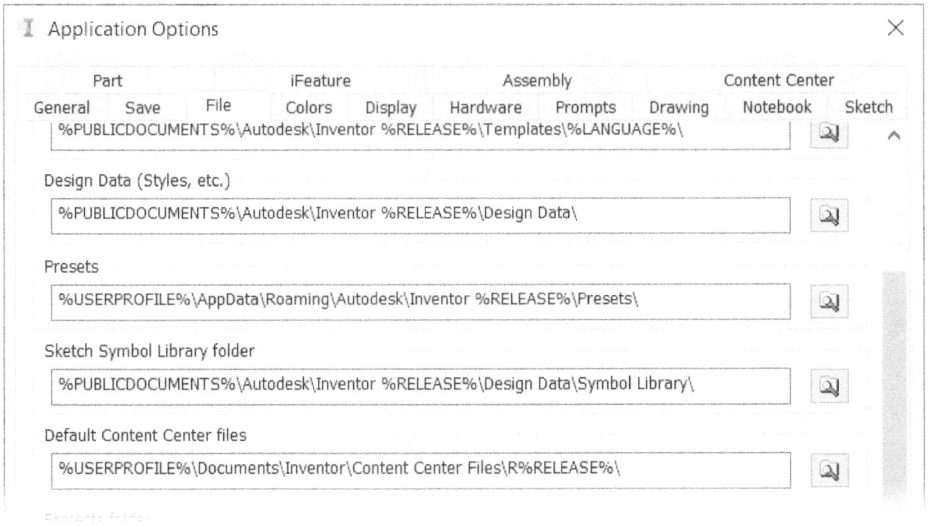

To use the default path specified in Application Options, the Content Center Files path under Folder Options in the active project file must be set to [Default] as shown in the following image. If you want the active project file to use a different path other than the default, you can enter or select a different path. To return the Content Center Files to [Default] after specifying a different path, you must right-click on Content Center Files and click Use Default Folder.

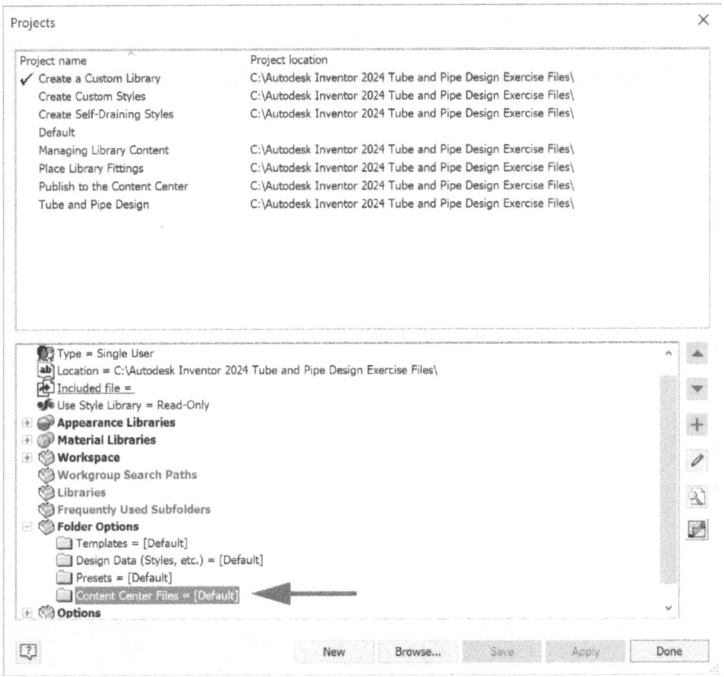

Process: Configuring the Default Content Center Files Path

The following steps give an overview of setting the default Content Center files path and having the active project use that default path.

1. In the Application Options dialog box, File tab, in the Default Content Center Files field, enter the required file path.
2. In the Projects dialog box, Folder Options, ensure the path for the Content Center Files option is set to [Default]. If it is not, right-click on Content Center Files and then click Use Default Folder.

Guidelines for Configuring the Content Center Files Path

Follow these guidelines when configuring the path for your Content Center files.

- Configure the default path to the required location instead of changing each path file. By doing this you have one set of Content Center files that all projects can reference.
- When working in a group environment, change the default path in each team member's Inventor installation to point to a shared server location. The content files are then available for everyone, even when opening an assembly file created by a team member that contains references to Content Center parts.

Copying Content to a Custom Library

You copy existing content to a custom library in order to modify its properties to match your specific requirements, reduce the number of parts available in the Content Center, and to share the copied components with all designers.

In the following image, on the left, a merged library view shows Parker Hydraulic Hose. The Copy To tool is used to copy the component family to My Tube and Pipe. On the right, the library view is set to My Tube and Pipe where the same Parker Hydraulic Hose family displays.

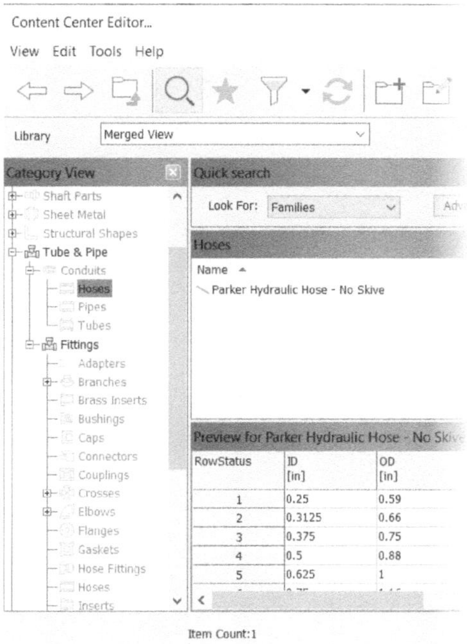

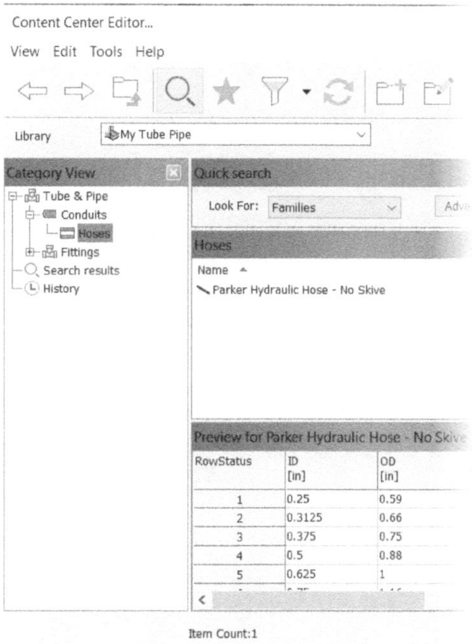

Content Center Editor

You use the Content Center Editor to complete a number of tasks associated with populating and defining the properties of content in your custom library. Tasks you can accomplish in a custom read/write library include:

- Copying content from an industry library to the custom library.
- Copying the category structure of an industry library so you can publish custom content to the same structure but in a different library.
- Creating new category structures to identify where content can be published.
- Creating and defining all the family member variations of a part.
- Defining a file naming scheme for part family content.

Access

Ribbon: Tools tab>Content Center panel

Copy To>Custom Library

Use the Copy To tool to copy a component family to a custom library.

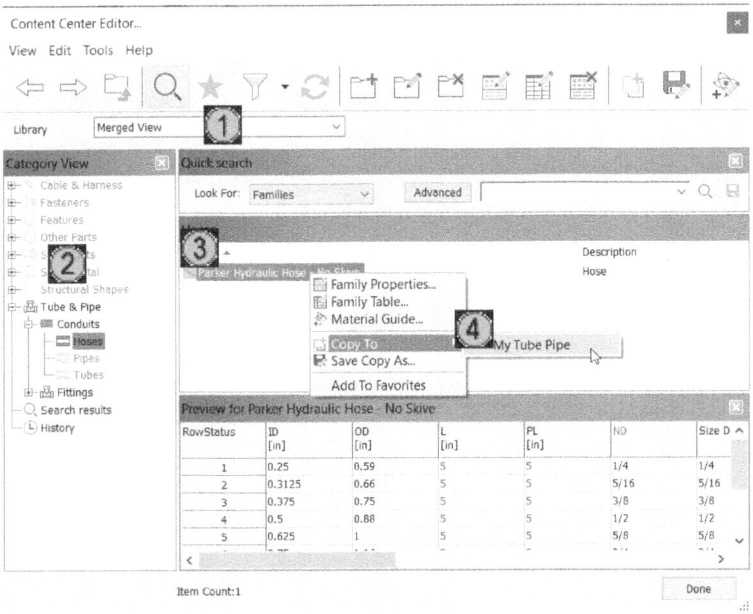

1 **Library View -** Display components from a single library or select Merged View to display a specific component family from all libraries at the same time.

2 **Category View -** Select the type of component that you want to copy to your custom library.

3 **Component Families -** Select the component family to copy to your custom library.

4 **Shortcut Menu -** Right-click on the component family and click the custom library to copy to.

Tools in the Content Center Editor

Once you display the Content Center Editor, you have a number of tools available to you for creating and modifying categories and content. Unless otherwise specified, you access each tool in the Content Center Editor by selecting a category or part family and clicking that tool name from the toolbar, shortcut menu, or Edit menu.

Option	Description
Library View	Use to specify what content displays in the tree view pane and the category and family collection pane. By selecting a specific library, you can create new categories and subcategories. Selecting Merged View displays all the filtered content for the configured libraries.
Create Category	Use to create a new subcategory to the selected category. Displays the Create Category dialog box where you specify a category name, small and large icon images, and parameters. When adding parameters, you specify a unique name, the type of data, its units, and if it is required or optional to map a value into that parameter during the process of publishing content into that category.
Delete Category	Use to permanently remove a category from the library. The category to delete cannot have any subcategories or part families defined within it. Access it after selecting the category.
Category Properties	Use to display the Category Properties dialog box and review the configured parameters and their properties.
Copy To	Use to copy part families and the category structure it resides in from one library to a read/write library. Once they are copied, you can modify the family member properties and values or use Replace Family Template to have a slightly different version of the part. Access it after selecting a category or part family.
Copy Category Structure To	Use to copy an existing category structure and its parameter settings from one library to a read/write library. Access it by selecting the category and clicking Copy Category Structure To from the shortcut menu.
Family Properties	Use to display the Family Properties dialog box to change the family name and description, industry standard it is based on, and thumbnail image. Access it after selecting the part family.
Family Table	Use to display the Family Table dialog box to add part family members, add or remove property columns, select key columns, or change the properties for a family member. Access it after selecting the part family.
Replace Family Template	Use to substitute a different version of the part for the one that was initially published. Use Open From Content Center and select the part to establish your beginning point for the different version you use for replacement. Access it by selecting the part family and clicking Replace Family Template from the shortcut menu.
Delete Family	Use to permanently remove a part family from the library. Access it after selecting the part family.
File Naming	Use to set the file naming scheme so placed members of a part family have unique file names when placed in an assembly and saved in the library path. You can use static values, parameter values, or a combination of both. Access it after selecting a category or part family.
Publish Part	Use to batch publish parts into Content Center libraries without having to exit and come back to create the family members. Access it by clicking Edit>Publish Part.

Procedure: Copying Content to a Custom Library

The following steps give an overview of copying a component family to a custom library.

1. Start the Content Center Editor in the Manage tab.

2. In the Content Center Editor dialog box, select the category view and right-click on the component family to copy. Click Copy To and select the custom library to copy to.

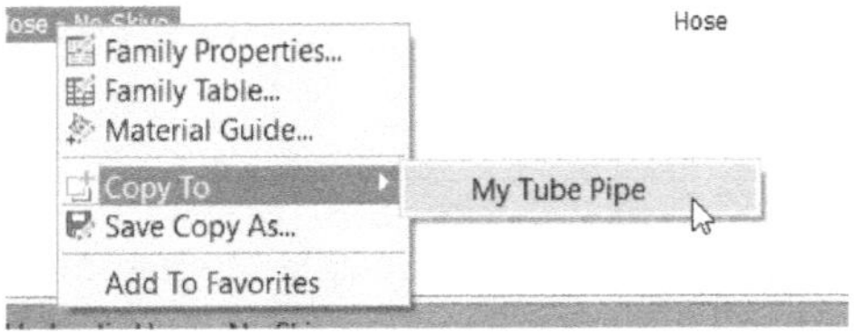

3. In the Library View list, click the custom library. Navigate to the category that you copied from, select the copied family and review the preview.

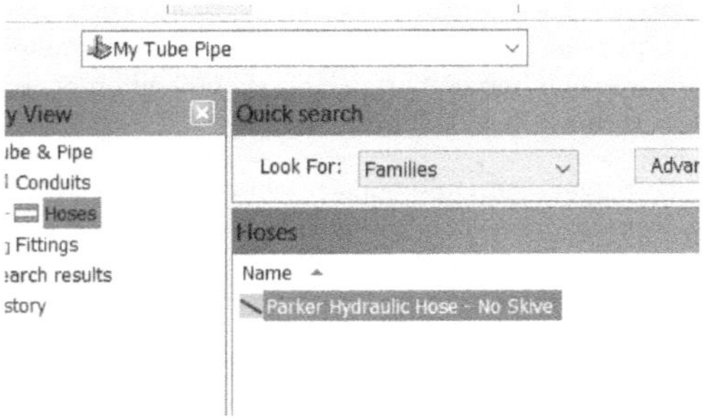

Transferring Library Content

Depending on your work environment, you might have custom libraries configured in one library configuration and you want them available in the other type of configuration. To have a custom library configured for one type of installation and make it available in another installation type, you need to know how to transfer a custom library between Inventor Desktop Content and Autodesk Vault Server.

Transfer of Libraries

If your computer has a previous release of Autodesk Data Management Server with custom libraries defined and you install Autodesk Inventor to use Desktop Content, the first time you run Inventor, you are given the option to transfer the legacy libraries to the Desktop Content location. If you do not transfer the libraries at that time and you want them available at a later time, you will need to manually transfer the libraries.

When you manually transfer custom content libraries, you can select to transfer them from Autodesk Vault Server to Inventor Desktop Content or vice versa. You transfer custom content libraries when you want to:

- Move from using ADMS to using Desktop Content.
- Move from Desktop Content to using Vault Server.
- Make Vault Server content available to you when in a stand-alone mode.
- Make a custom library created in Desktop Content available in Vault Server.

Accessing the Library Transfer Guide

You transfer a custom Content Center library from Autodesk Vault Server to Inventor Desktop Content or vice versa in the Library Transfer Guide dialog box. You access the Library Transfer Guide option in the Configure Libraries dialog box. You display the Configure Libraries dialog box by selecting the project file to edit in the Projects dialog box and then clicking Configure Content Center Libraries.

The following image shows the access location for Configure Content Center Libraries in the Projects dialog box and Library Transfer Guide in the Configure Libraries dialog box.

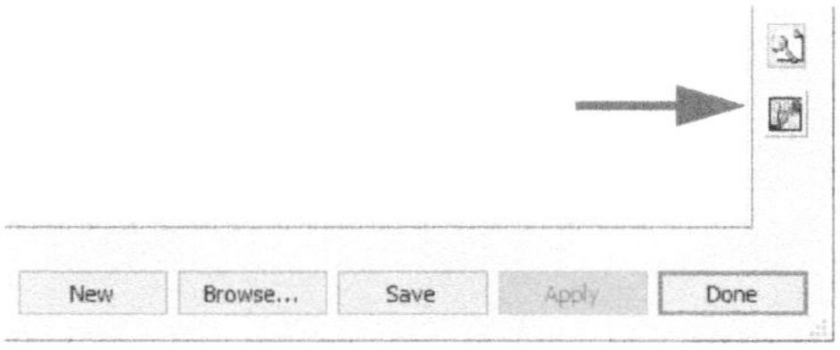

Configure Content Center

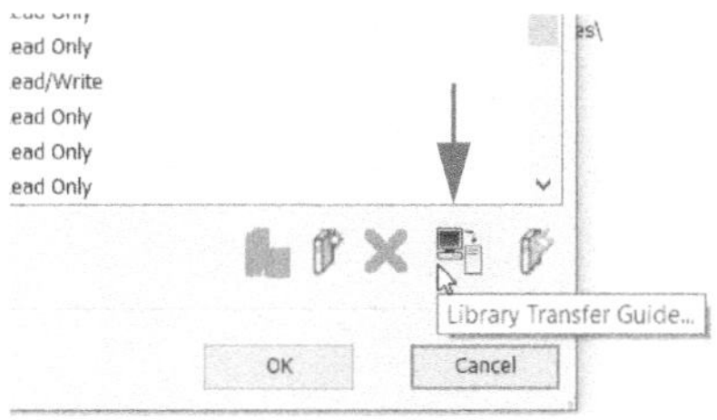

Library Transfer Guide

Process: Transferring Library Content

The following steps give an overview of transferring a custom content library to or from Inventor Desktop Content.

1. In the Projects dialog box, select the project file to configure.
2. In the Project dialog box, select Configure Content Center Libraries.
3. In the Configure Libraries dialog box, click Library Transfer Guide.
4. Select if you want to transfer custom libraries from Autodesk Vault Server to Inventor Desktop Content or from Inventor Desktop Content to Autodesk Vault Server.
5. Specify the server, database, username, and password to log into Vault Server.
6. Select the libraries to transfer.
7. If transferring the library to Desktop Content and the library is identified as needing migration, select and update the transferred library.

Exercise: Create a Custom Library

In this exercise, you will create a new library for custom tube and pipe components. You will copy a family from one of the read-only libraries to the new custom library and edit a version in the family.

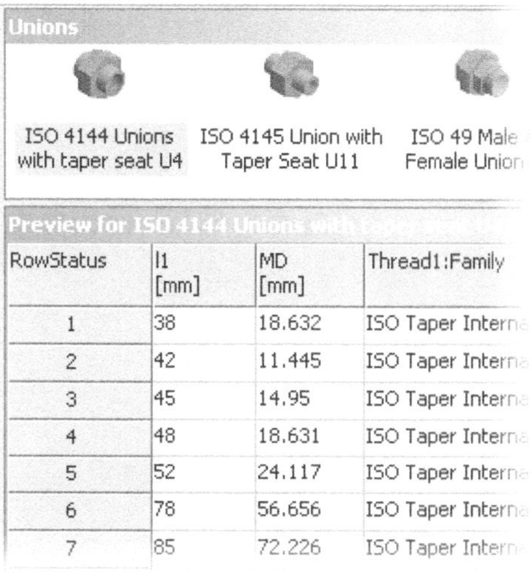

The completed exercise

Create a Custom Library

In this portion of the exercise, you will create a custom read/write library in the Content Center.

1. Start the Autodesk Inventor software but do not open any files. Close any open files.
2. In the Get Started tab, in the Launch panel, click Projects.
3. To add this exercise's project file to Inventor:
   - In the Projects dialog box, click Browse.
   - In the Choose Project File dialog box, navigate to the directory with the exercise files and open *Create a Custom Library.ipj*.

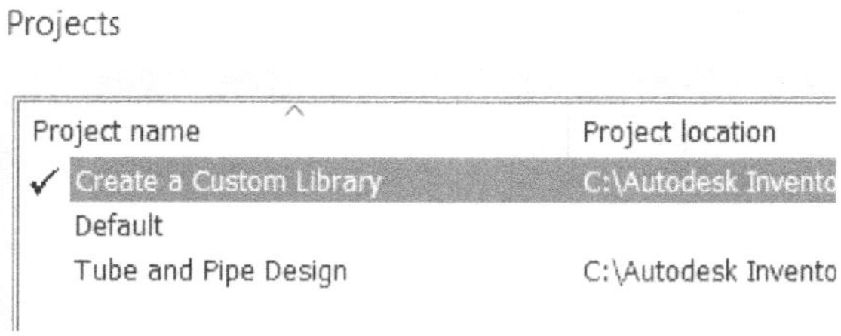

4. To create a new read/write library:
   - In the Projects dialog box, select Configure Content Center Libraries.
   - In the Configure Libraries: Create a Custom Library dialog box, click Create Library.

5. In the Create Library dialog box, for Display Name, enter **My Tube Pipe**. Click OK.

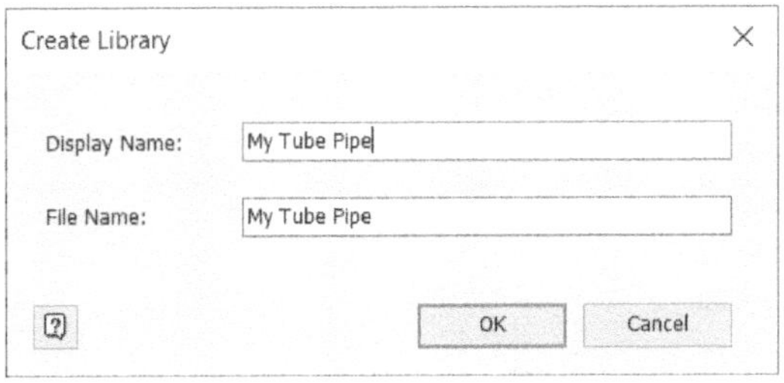

6. Verify that the custom Read/Write library is In Use. Click OK.

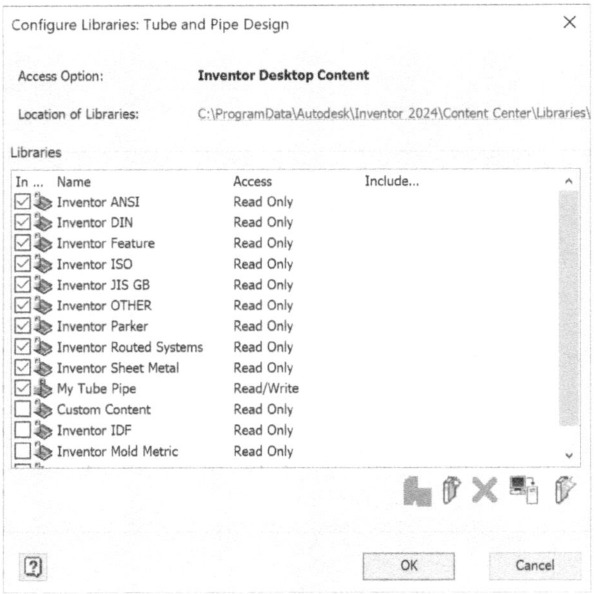

7. In the Projects dialog box, click Save. Click Done.

Populate and Use the Library

In this portion of the exercise, you will copy a family of fittings to the new library and edit some of the members.

1. In the Tools tab, in the Content Center panel, click Editor.
2. In the Category View, expand Tube & Pipe>Fittings. Click Unions.
3. Right-click on ISO 4144 Unions with Taper Seat U4. Click Copy To>My Tube Pipe.

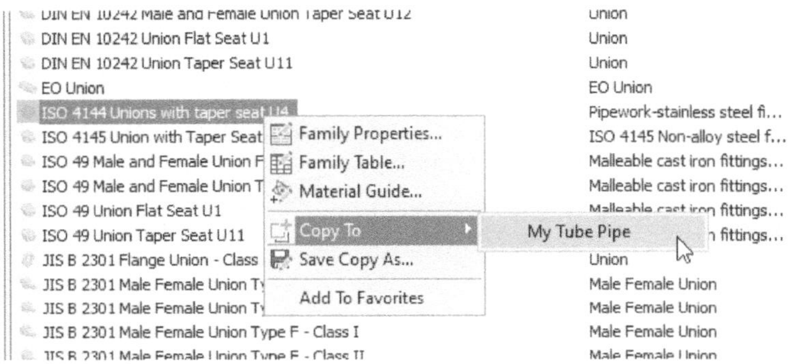

4. The image of the union is no longer grayed out because the family can be edited.
5. Right-click on ISO 4144 Unions with Taper Seat U4. Click Family Table.
6. In the filter list, select All Columns.
7. In the MD column, double-click on the cell in row 1. Enter **18.632** and press ENTER.

   The cell is highlighted and the row icon indicates that the part has changed.

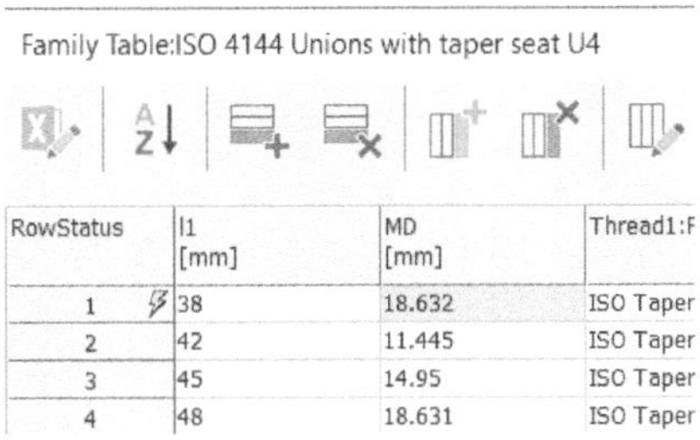

8. Select rows 6, 7, and 8. Right-click on the row number for one of the rows. Click Delete Row. Click Yes to confirm the delete.

   Note: You suppress or delete rows containing members that you don't use.

9. To complete the change:
   - Click OK.
   - Click OK to close the Publish Result dialog box.
   - Click Done to close the Content Center Editor.

10. Start a new assembly file.

11. In the Assemble tab, in the Component panel, click Place from Content Center.

12. Expand Tube & Pipe>Fittings>Unions.

13. Select ISO 4144 Unions with Taper Seat U4 that you edited.

14. If the table of members is not displayed, in the ribbon, click View menu>Table View to toggle it on. Confirm that the edits you made display.

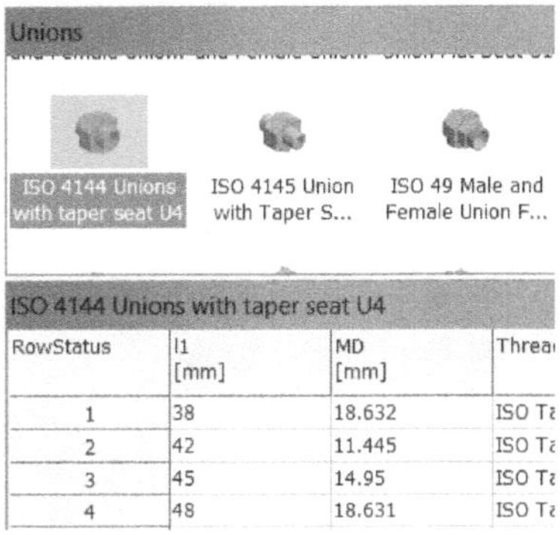

15. Click Cancel to close the Place from Content Center dialog box.

16. Close all files without saving.

Lesson: Creating Library Content

Overview

This lesson describes how to author and publish your own tube and pipe content.

Autodesk Inventor has multiple industry standards, and substantial part content within those standards that you can load and use in your designs. However, you probably require only certain parts and sizes within those standards. For those parts that you require, you might also require specific values for their properties such as their part numbers or stock numbers. In addition, you might have custom tube, pipe, and hose fittings that you have developed specific to your applications. By understanding how to access and include these components in your library data, and modify the values and properties of library content, you can access and use Content Center data more efficiently in your designs.

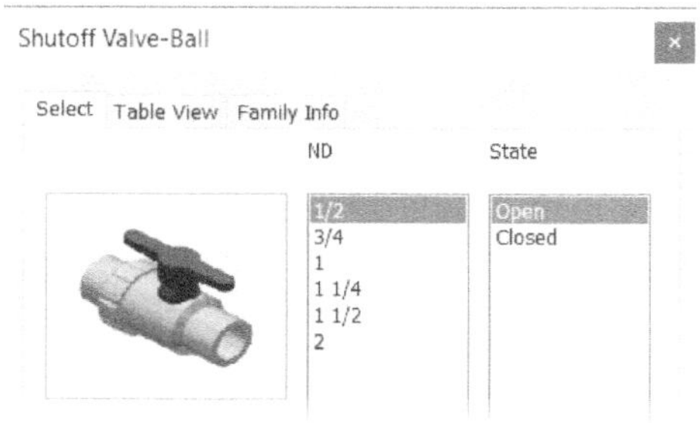

Objectives

After completing this lesson, you will be able to:

- Describe how to create custom content.
- Author tube and pipe content to add connection and engagement information.
- Publish tube and pipe content to a Content Center library.

Creating Custom Content

The supplied content libraries contain a limited number of components. You can supplement the standard libraries by adding fittings and other components to one or more custom libraries. In addition to new conduit parts and fittings, you can add components that you use in your tube and pipe designs such as filters, gauges, pumps, and other specialized components.

The following image shows some sample content that you can create and add to the Content Center libraries.

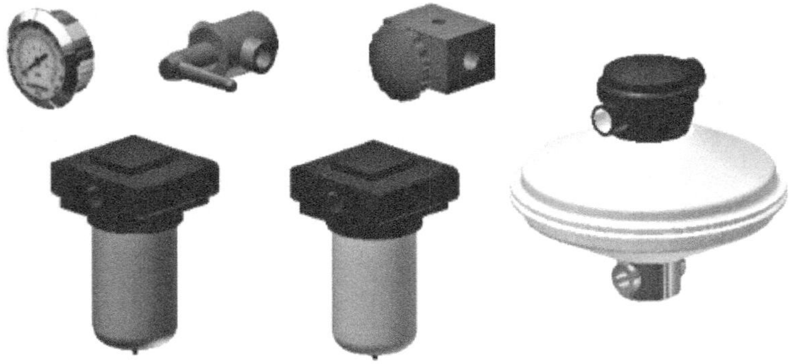

Process: Creating Custom Tube and Pipe Content

The following steps outline the process for creating custom tube and pipe content.

1. Create the component as a standard Autodesk Inventor part. If you have several variations (sizes) of the component, create an iPart.
2. Use the Tube and Pipe Authoring tool to add connection information to the part. The connection information is used when you place the fitting or conduit (pipe, hose, tube) in a run.
3. Save the part file. The part is unchanged except that the tube and pipe connection information is now stored in the part file. If the component is a regular part (not an iPart), you can place the component into tube and pipe runs using the Place Fitting tool.
4. If the component is an iPart factory or conduit, you must publish the part to a custom library in order to use the component in tube and pipe runs. The publishing guide adds extra family and category information and stores the part definition in a library. You can also publish a regular part to a custom library although there is just one variation of the part.

Authoring Tube and Pipe Content

The authoring process adds intelligent connection information to a part. You can author standard Autodesk Inventor parts and place the authored parts in a run using the Place Fitting tool. You can also author iPart factory parts and publish the iPart variations to a custom library in the Content Center. The connection information added in the authoring process is applied to all variations of the published fitting. The authoring process is the same for both standard parts and iParts.

In the following image, an authored union is shown with the browser demonstrating the included connection information.

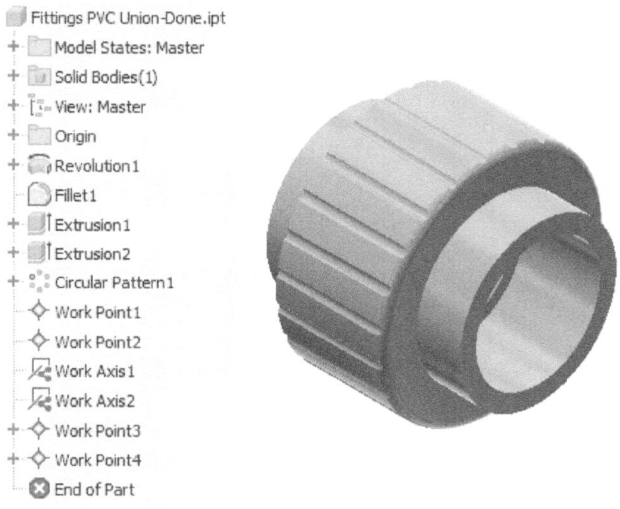

Connections and Engagement

When you author a part, you specify a connection point, connection axis, and minimum and maximum engagement length.

The connection point is typically a point on the outer edge of the connection. It is the point where conduits connect and is the starting point for the engagement distance.

The engagement is the amount that the conduit (tube, pipe, or hose) is inserted into or onto the fitting. You specify a range of engagement values by specifying a maximum and a minimum value. The maximum engagement is the maximum amount that the conduit (tube, pipe, or hose) can be inserted onto or into the fitting. The minimum engagement is the minimum amount the conduit must be inserted onto or into the fitting for a correct connection. The minimum engagement is specified as a percent of the maximum.

When you populate a route or add a fitting to a run, the adjacent conduit is inserted into the fitting so that the end of the segment lies within the engagement zone specified for the connection, and the length of the segment is an even multiple of the increment value that is specified in the style.

When you author a part, the connection point, connection axis, and engagement zone display on the part as shown in the following image.

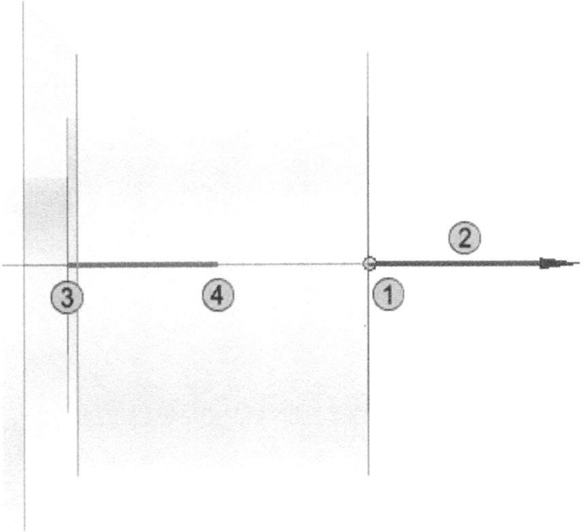

1 The connection point.

2 The connection axis. Must point away from the connection.

3 The maximum engagement. The maximum distance the connecting conduit will be inserted into the connection. Measured from the connection point.

4 The minimum engagement. The minimum amount the connecting conduit is inserted into the connection. Specified as a percentage of the maximum distance.

You can specify the maximum engagement length in one of the following ways:

- As a percentage of the Nominal Size parameter: Use this option when the maximum engagement length varies linearly, or approximately linearly, with the nominal diameter, and there is no face or work feature that defines the engagement length.
- As a fixed distance from the engagement point: Use this option when authoring a standard part or when all variations in the iPart table have a fixed engagement length. Pipe, hose, and tubing do not use the engagement values, but you should specify a fixed engagement distance of zero for these parts.
- By selecting features on the part: You can select either a work point that is coincident to the connection axis, or a planar face or work plane that intersects the connection axis. A work point is generated at the selected point or at the intersection of the selected plane and connection axis. The maximum engagement length extends from the connection point to this work point for each variation of the library part. This definition provides the most flexibility for defining engagement length. Use it whenever possible.

Access

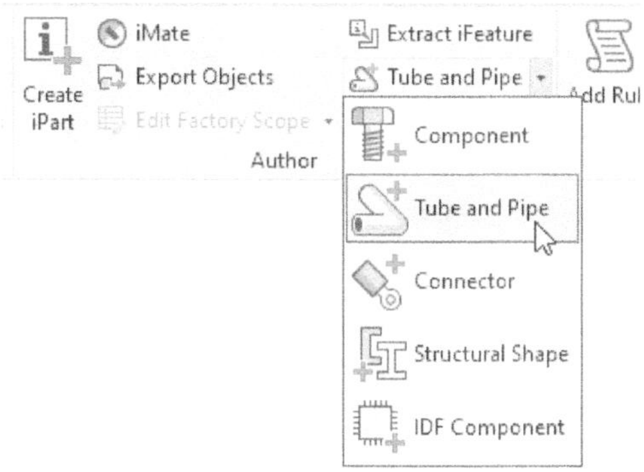

Ribbon: Manage tab>Author panel

Tube & Pipe Authoring Dialog Box

When you author a part using the Tube & Pipe Authoring dialog box, you should follow specific steps to specify the required parameters to complete the process.

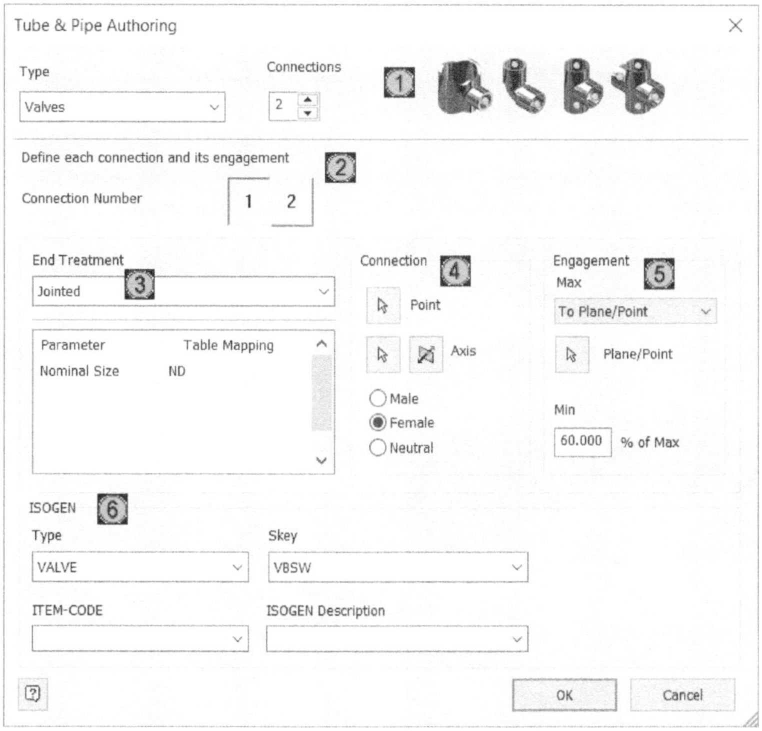

1. Specify the type of part that you are publishing and the number of connections that are required in the assembly.
2. For each connection, you must define its End Treatment, Connection, and Engagement.
3. Select your required end treatment from the list and specify the parameter mapping.
4. Select a connection point, axis, and type of connection. Use the flip direction button to reverse the axis direction.
5. Select the type of engagement and how the pipe is inserted into a fitting.
6. Specify ISOGEN properties if this component will be used with a tube and pipe application with ISOGEN properties. The ISOGEN properties are written to a PCF file, which can be used to automatically generate isometric drawings for use by manufacturing.

Tube and Pipe Authoring Tool Custom Angle

If the pipe route designs that you create use fittings at angles other than 45° and 90°, you need to author those custom angle fittings so they are available for downstream consumption. Use the Tube and Pipe Authoring tool to create custom angled fittings.

When you author a tube and pipe fitting, you can author both common and custom angled fittings. Custom angle support in the Tube and Pipe Authoring tool enables you to publish fittings with nonstandard angles.

In the case of elbows, the authoring tool determines the angle from the two connection vectors. In the case of tees, the angle is calculated from the three connection vectors. The calculated angle displays in the dialog box as a read-only value when the fitting type is set to Elbows or Tees.

In the following image, a custom elbow to be authored uses a non-traditional angle of 88°.

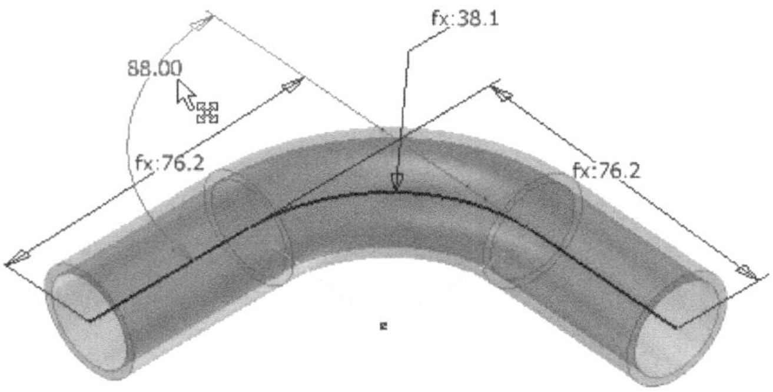

Procedure: Authoring Content

The following steps show how to author a fitting to add connection and engagement information. The steps are the same for normal Autodesk Inventor parts and for iParts.

1. Start the Tube and Pipe Authoring tool.

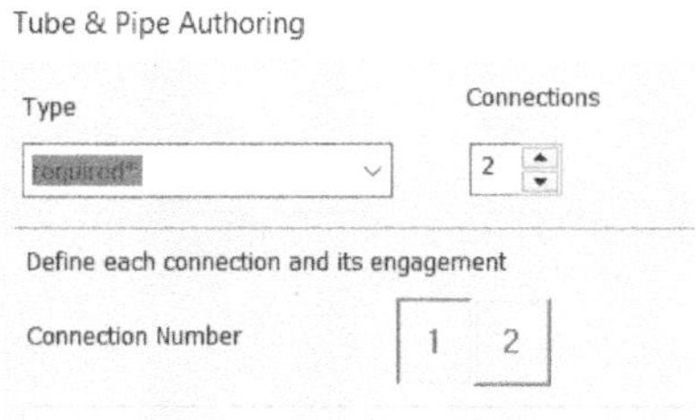

2. Select a fitting type. The list includes all fitting categories in the Content Center. You can select Other if the fitting or component is not described by any of the listed fitting types.

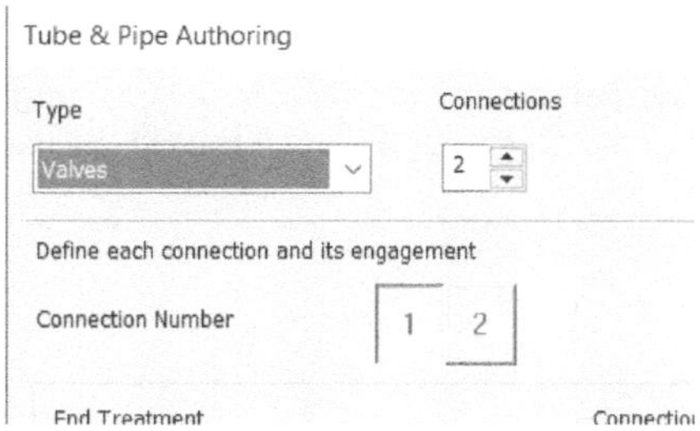

3. Specify the number of connections. Many fittings have two connections, but some have three or more. Click a connection number to define that connection.

4. For each connection, select an end treatment. For fittings and other content, the connection must match the end treatment of the conduit (pipe) segments.

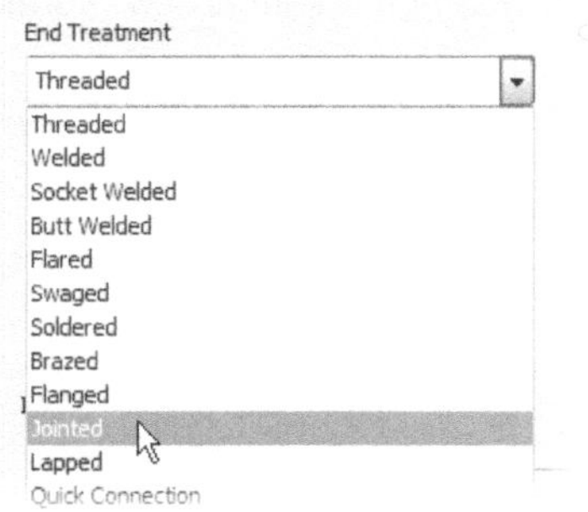

5. For iParts that define a family of fittings, map the Nominal Size parameter to the corresponding key column in the iPart table. For standard Autodesk Inventor parts, enter a value for the nominal size. This value is checked against the nominal diameter of the route when the authored part is placed in a route using the Place Fitting tool.

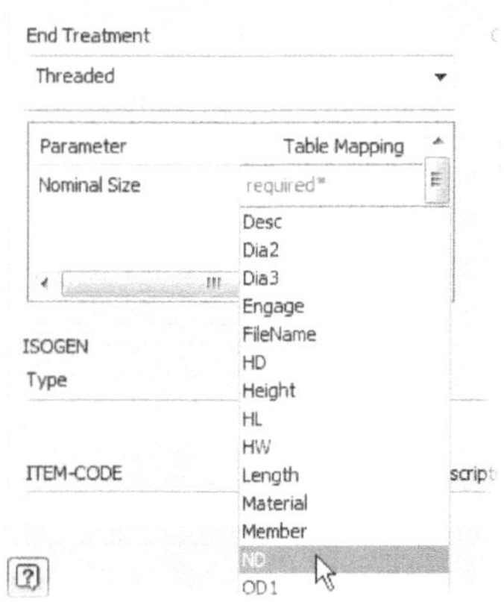

Note: For conduit parts, you must map five parameters (Nominal Size, Pipe Length, Schedule, Outside Diameter, and Inside Diameter) to the corresponding columns in the iPart table.

6. Define a connection point and axis for each connection.

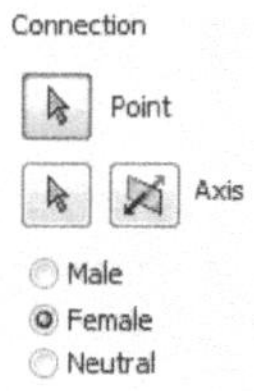

- The connection point is typically centered at the outer edge of the connection opening. The axis points away from the fitting. You typically define connection information by selecting circular edges.

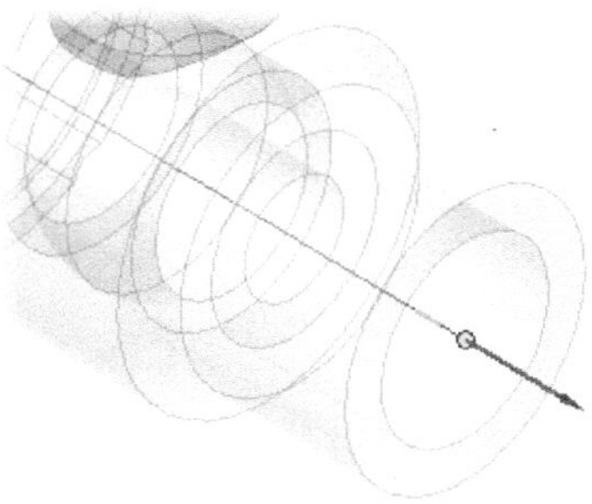

- A work point is placed at the center point of the edge. Information about the connection is attached to the work point feature.

7. Specify the engagement for each connection. The engagement zone is previewed on the model.

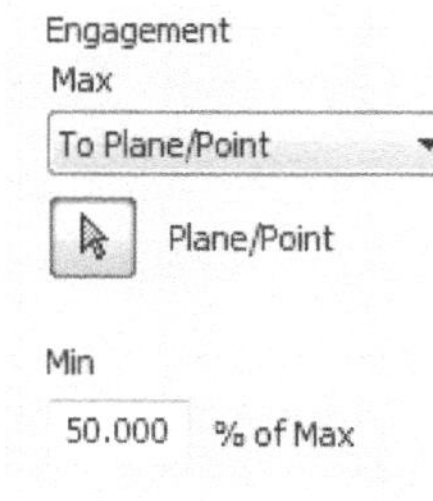

8. If required for documentation, add ISOGEN data.

9. Save the part. If the fitting is a regular part, the fitting is ready to be placed in a run using the Place Fitting tool. If the fitting is an iPart, it is ready for publishing to a custom library.

Requirements for Tube and Pipe iParts

Because multiple versions of a fitting or component are required to match the nominal diameters available in a rigid pipe, tube, or hose style, you typically create an iPart factory before you publish custom tube and pipe content. The iPart table must define all versions of the part. You cannot use custom iPart factories to generate tube and pipe content.

The parameters required in the iPart table depend on the type of content you create. A conduit (pipe, tube, or hose) iPart requires more parameters than an iPart fitting. When you author the part, you map the parameters from the iPart table to special tube and pipe parameters. When you publish the iPart to a library, each column is mapped to parameters stored in the library. You use these parameters to generate the selected version from the library when you place content from the library into a tube or pipe run.

Requirements for All Tube and Pipe Parts

The primary key for all tube and pipe library components is a nominal diameter designation for the part. The recommended column name is ND, but you can use any name without spaces. Imperial unit content uses a fractional inch value to describe the nominal diameter (1/4, 1/2, 1, 1 1/2, and so on). Metric content uses the measurement in millimeters, preceded by the letter M (M8, M10, M20, and so on).

Additional Requirements for Fittings

If the fitting or component has multiple connections with different nominal diameters, such as a reducer or reducing tee, you must supply additional key columns for the other nominal diameters. The suggested naming convention for a fitting with a single nominal diameter key is ND. For fittings with multiple keys, use ND1, ND2, and so on.

Additional Requirements for Conduit

Define both a nominal diameter (ND) key column and a second key column named SN that contains the conduit schedule (30, 40, and so on). Define internal diameter (ID) and outer diameter (OD) parameters in the conduit iPart. In the Tube and Pipe Styles dialog box, in the Size tab, you can select either Nominal Diameter and Schedule, or OD and ID values. Therefore, you must also include the ID and OD parameters in the iPart definition. These parameters are not key values.

Define a pipe length column (recommended name PL). Enter a nominal pipe length (10 in or 100 mm) for each row in the table. The actual value does not matter because the pipe is sized to fit in the run when the route is populated. Because the thumbnail image for the Content Center is generated from the pipe image, assign a length that results in a reasonable looking graphic display of the pipe.

Add the Stock Number property to the iPart table and assign unique stock numbers to each member. The Stock Number is used in the parts list for length rollup.

Publishing Tube and Pipe Content

When you have finished authoring a part, you can publish the part to a custom read/write Content Center library. To publish parts as content to a library, you need to know which tools to use and the procedure for publishing a part.

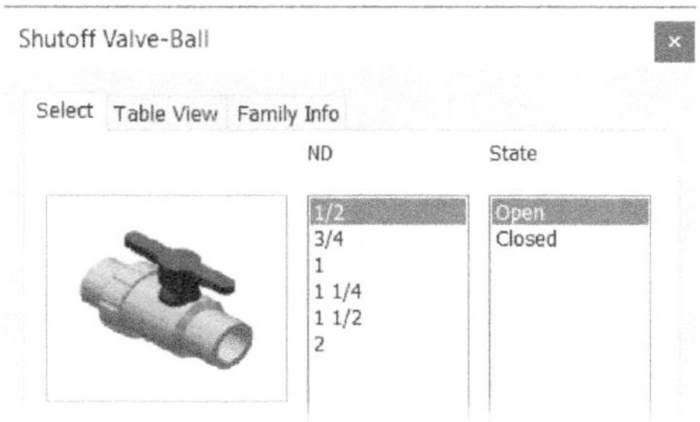

Publishing Parts

When publishing parts, you either publish multiple parts in a batch or publish one part at a time. To publish parts in a batch, you access the tool from the Content Center Editor, an assembly file, or a part file. To publish a single part, you must access the tool while the part is open.

Access

Ribbon: Manage tab>Content Center panel

Ribbon: Manage tab>Content Center panel

Options When Publishing a Part

After you start the process for publishing a single part, you specify multiple items in multiple pages of the Publish Guide dialog box. The first thing you do is select which library to publish the part to and the language to publish it in. The next task is to select which library category the part should be published in. Based on the selected library category, you then map the defined parameters in the category to parameters in the part. After mapping the parameters, you identify which category parameters are key columns of data. The next task is to enter the naming and industry standard information for this new part family. The last task is to specify what image to use for the part family thumbnail image, the default image or an alternate BMP or JPG file.

When prompted to map the category parameters to the part parameters, you can click the list arrow and select the required iProperty or parameter as shown in the following image. The required mappings display with a yellow background. They were already defined during the authoring process. The other, undefined mappings are for branch fittings and are optional.

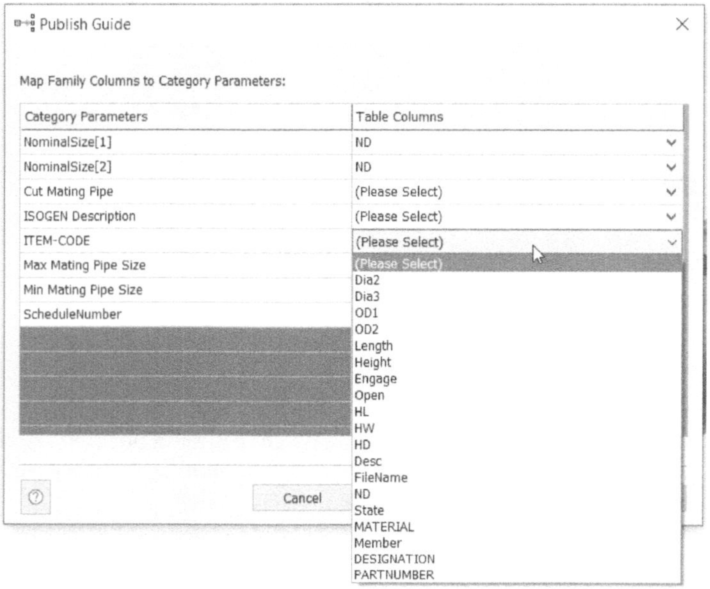

During the placement of a part, you need to differentiate which family member to insert into your design. To help select which family member you want to include in your design, you identify category parameter columns as key columns. You can then select values in these key columns during the placement of a part family member. Along with identifying which columns of values you want to select from, at this publishing step, you also specify the order in which the columns display. Their order of selection and thus importance are based on the order they are listed in the Key Columns list as shown in the following image.

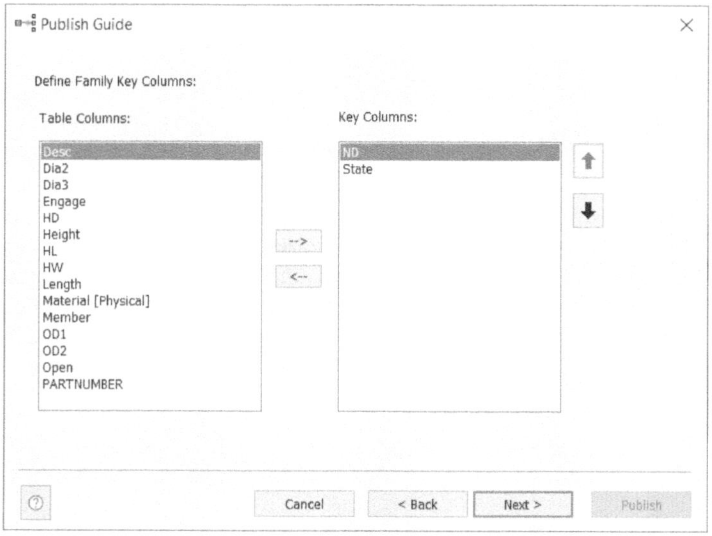

The name you enter in the Name field in the Family Naming area sets the Content Center part family name. This name must be unique from all the other part family names in that category. By entering a description and selecting standard information, you help identify information about the part.

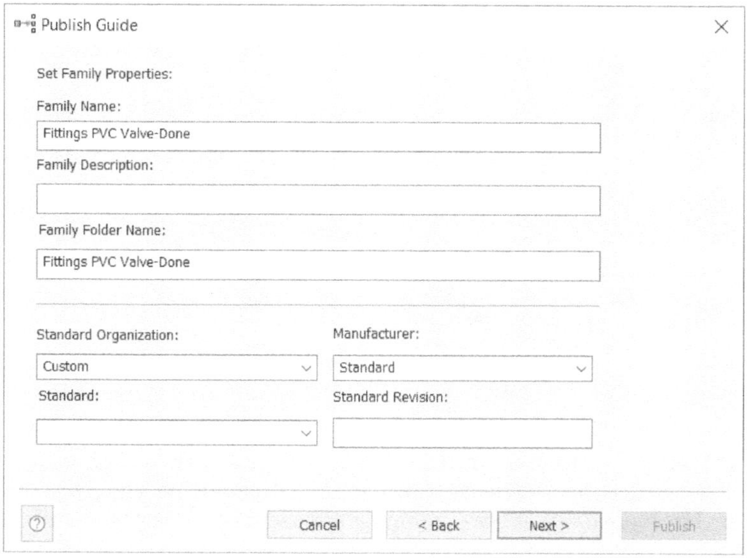

After publishing the part family, you can change the family name values, standard settings, parameter mapping, and thumbnail image by using the Family Properties option in the Content Center Editor. You also can add columns to the part family and map those added column values to the part's parameters.

If you are publishing a part to a custom category and you want to map category parameters to part parameters, the parameter names in the part file must be in all uppercase letters.

Key Category Parameter Fields

The category parameter fields you specify for a part family are the value fields you select when placing the library part in your assembly design. When placing a part and the Select tab is active, the order the fields are shown left to right is based on the key field list order you set. After you have published a part family, you can change the order and columns of parameters that are key fields. You change the key fields after publishing in the Content Center Editor.

Category parameters can be configured to contain a set value for each family member or permit for a range of values. By default they are configured to have a set value.

Key fields display in red text when viewed in the table view during placement or in the Content Center Editor. When viewing a part family in table view that contains many defined members, it can be difficult or time-consuming to locate the exact configuration you require. This is one reason why you identify key columns of properties.

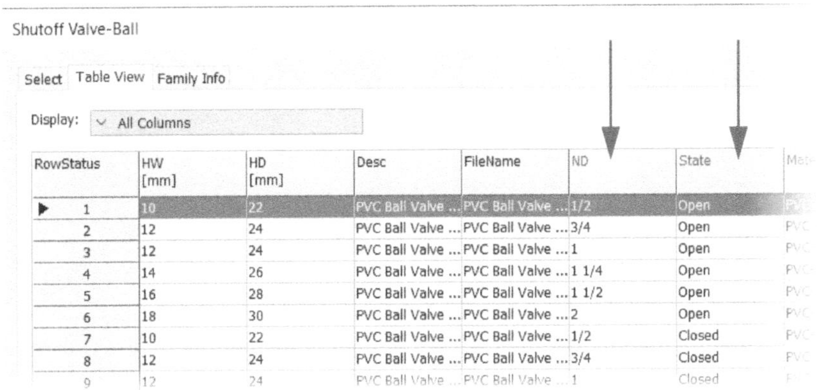

RowStatus	HW [mm]	HD [mm]	Desc	FileName	ND	State
1	10	22	PVC Ball Valve ...	PVC Ball Valve ...	1/2	Open
2	12	24	PVC Ball Valve ...	PVC Ball Valve ...	3/4	Open
3	12	24	PVC Ball Valve ...	PVC Ball Valve ...	1	Open
4	14	26	PVC Ball Valve ...	PVC Ball Valve ...	1 1/4	Open
5	16	28	PVC Ball Valve ...	PVC Ball Valve ...	1 1/2	Open
6	18	30	PVC Ball Valve ...	PVC Ball Valve ...	2	Open
7	10	22	PVC Ball Valve ...	PVC Ball Valve ...	1/2	Closed
8	12	24	PVC Ball Valve ...	PVC Ball Valve ...	3/4	Closed
9	12	24	PVC Ball Valve ...	PVC Ball Valve ...	1	Closed

By defining key fields of category properties, you can identify the family member you want to include in your assembly design in a quick and efficient manner. In the Select tab, the left-to-right order of properties in the dialog box for placement of a Content Center part is based on the identification and order of the key fields.

In the following image, the category parameter column ND is the first key field followed by State. If non-required parameters are listed, selection of all the different possibilities is simple because the values listed in the subsequent columns to the right are dependent on what was selected for placement in the column to its left. In the following example, there are six ND values defined that have a state of either Open or Closed.

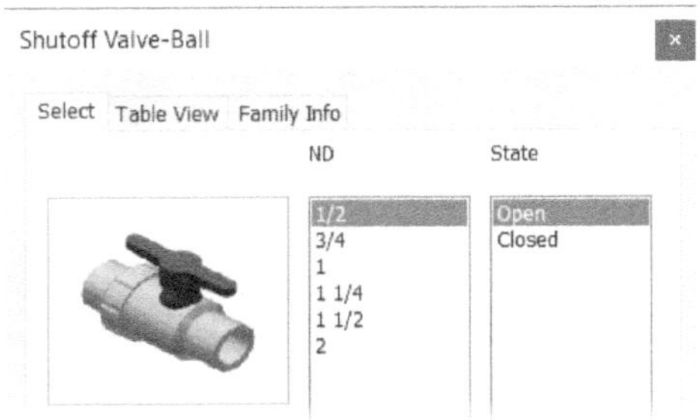

Procedure: Publishing Tube and Pipe Content

The following steps give an overview of publishing a fitting to a library.

1. Start the Publishing Tool.
2. Specify the library and language.

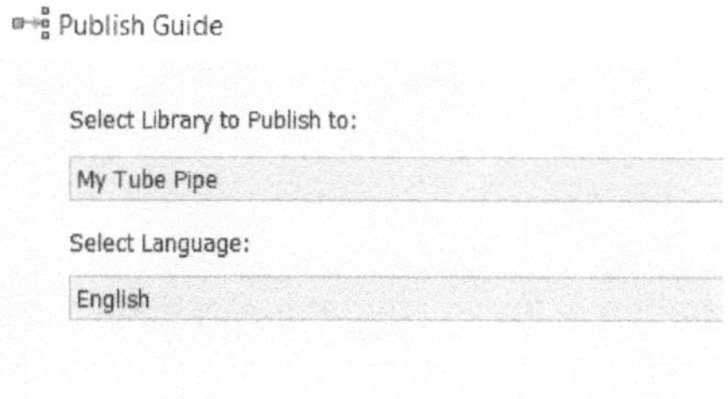

3. The category is automatically selected for you based on the type that you specified in the authoring tool.

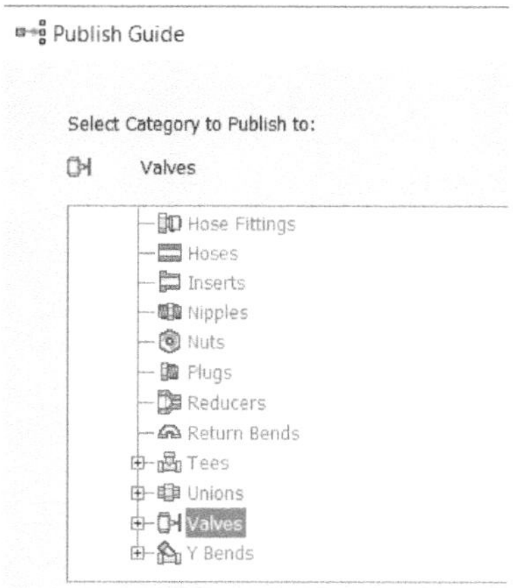

4. Confirm that the mapping is correct. The parameters are mapped automatically based on the information that you supplied when you authored the part. Required parameters display with a different background color.

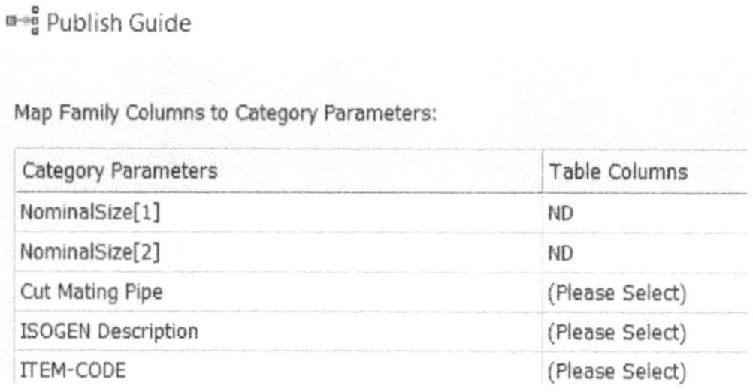

5. Define key columns. The selected key columns are the variations that display when you select the part from the Content Center. Typically, these are mapped automatically based on the information you provided when you created the iPart factory.

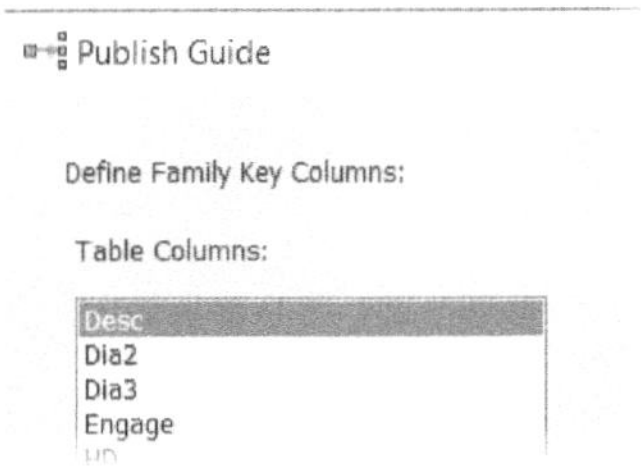

6. Specify the family properties. The information helps you find the part in the Content Center when you apply filters or use the search tool.

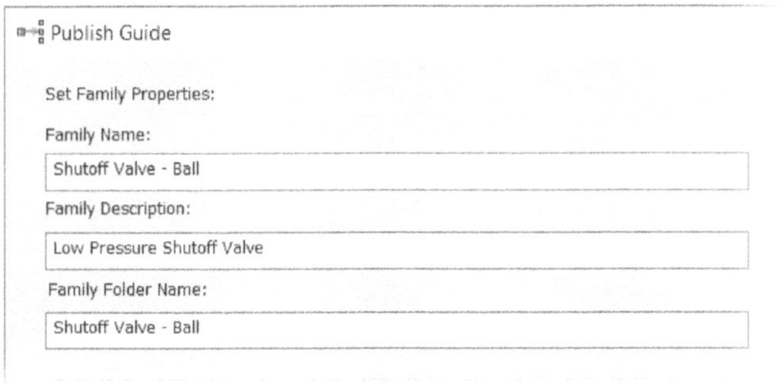

7. Accept the default thumbnail image or specify another.

Guidelines for Publishing Part Content

Follow these guidelines when publishing part content to a Content Center library.

- Export part parameters that you want to map to category parameters before publishing the part.
- Parameters that you mark as key fields display in the dialog box for value selection when you are placing a published part.
- When setting the key fields, select the category parameters that help you identify the unique differences between the family members that you require in your assemblies.
- Set the order of the key fields based on the importance of the parameter values, or based on which values help categorize the differences among family members.

Publishing a Hose

You can use the same part to publish a rigid pipe, tube, or flexible hose. However, the part must be an iPart.

Exercise: Author a Fitting

In this exercise, you will use the Tube and Pipe Authoring tool to add connection information to a standard Autodesk Inventor part and to an iPart.

The completed exercise

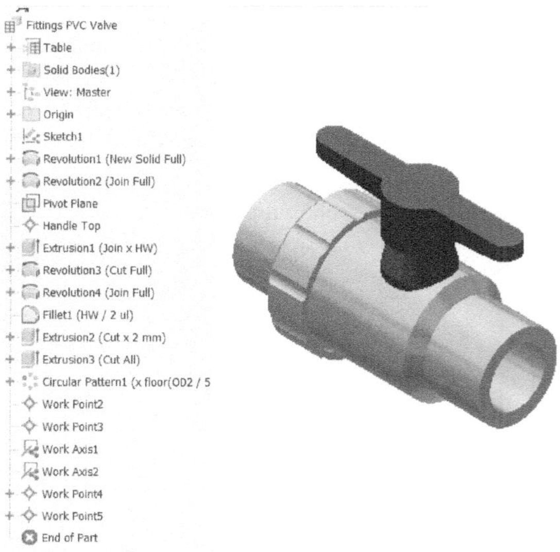

Author a Standard Part

In this portion of the exercise, you will use the Tube and Pipe Authoring tool to add connection information to a standard Autodesk Inventor part.

1. Open *Fittings PVC Union.ipt* from the Workspace folder.

2. In the ribbon, in the Manage tab, in the Author panel, click Tube and Pipe.

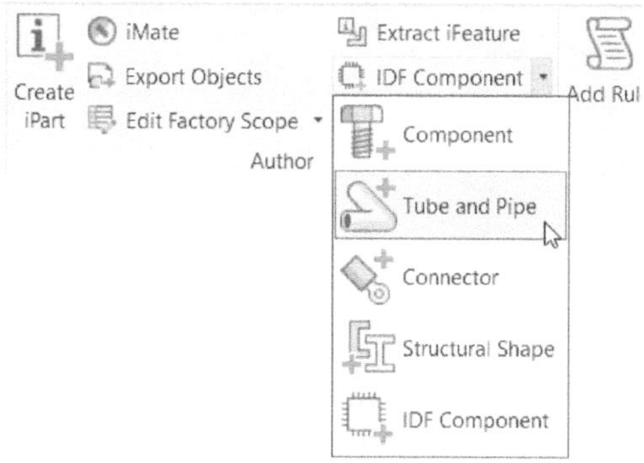

3. In the Tube & Pipe Authoring dialog box, from the Type list, select Unions. Set the number of connections to **2**.

4. From the End Treatment list, select Jointed.

   This setting matches the end treatment of the existing PVC pipe segments in the Content Center.

5. In Nominal Size, enter **2**.

6. In Connection, the Point button is already depressed when you open the dialog box.

   Click a circular edge of the near opening in the part.

   A connection point displays at the center of the opening.

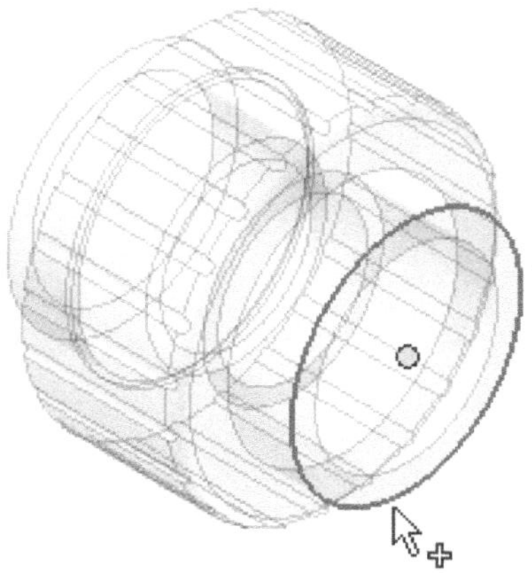

7. In the Tube & Pipe Authoring dialog box, under Connection, click Select Axis. Click the same circular edge.

   A connection axis and direction vector display.

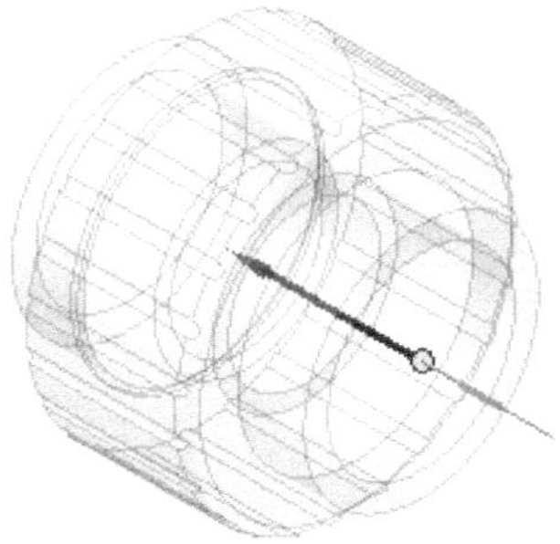

8. If the direction vector is pointing into the part, in the Tube & Pipe Authoring dialog box, click Flip Direction.

   The direction arrow points away from the part as required.

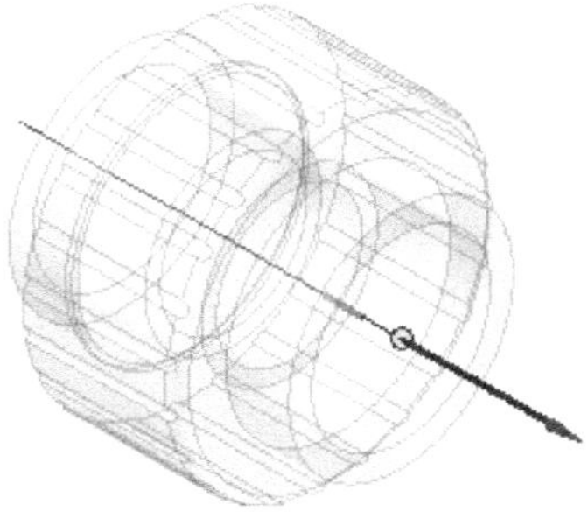

9. In the Tube & Pipe Authoring dialog box, under Engagement, select To Plane/Point. Click the face at the bottom of the opening.

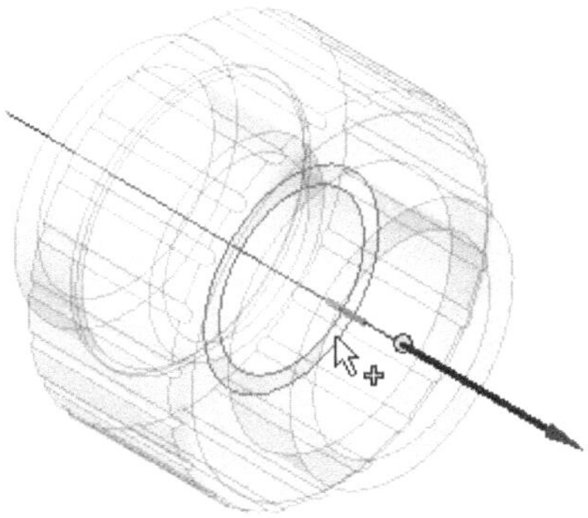

10. On the ViewCube, click Front.

    The engagement zone extends from the selected face to 50% of the maximum engagement length.

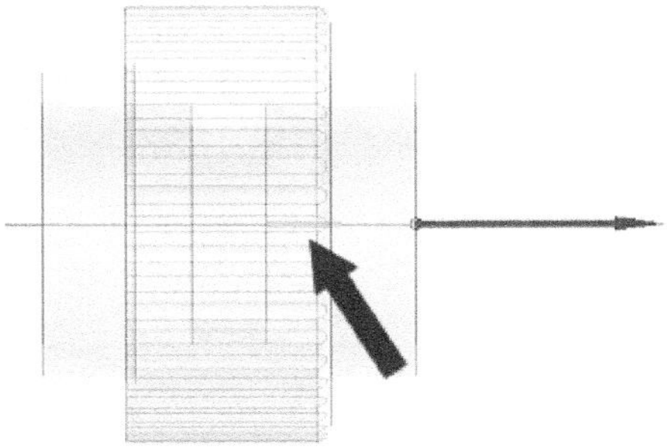

11. In the Tube & Pipe Authoring dialog box, click the Connection Number 2 button.
12. From the End Treatment list, select Jointed.
13. Add a connection point, connection axis, and a similar engagement length to the opening on the other end of the part.

    The completed connection matches the one in the following image.

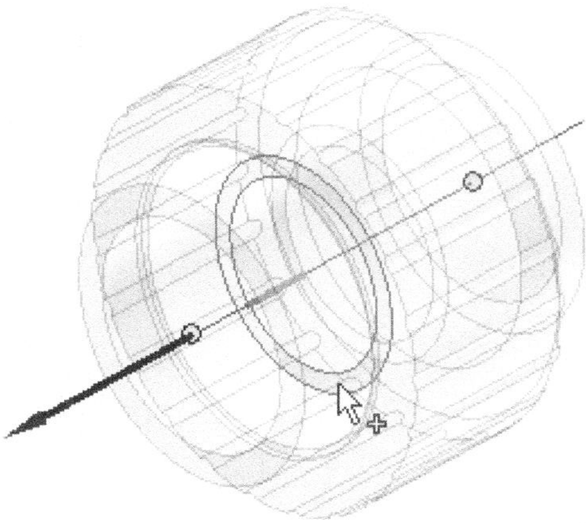

14. Click OK to author the part. Click OK to close the Authoring Result dialog box.

15. Examine the browser. The added work features at the bottom of the browser contain the connection information.

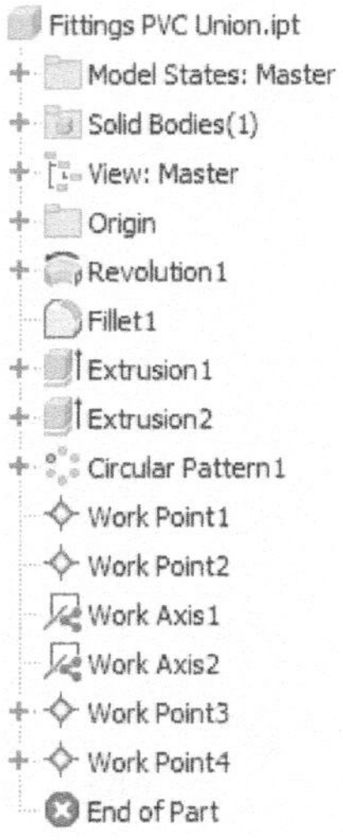

16. Close all files without saving changes. You will learn to publish parts in the next exercise.

Author an iPart

In this portion of the exercise, you will add connection information to an iPart for publishing to the Content Center.

1. Open *Fittings PVC Valve.ipt*.

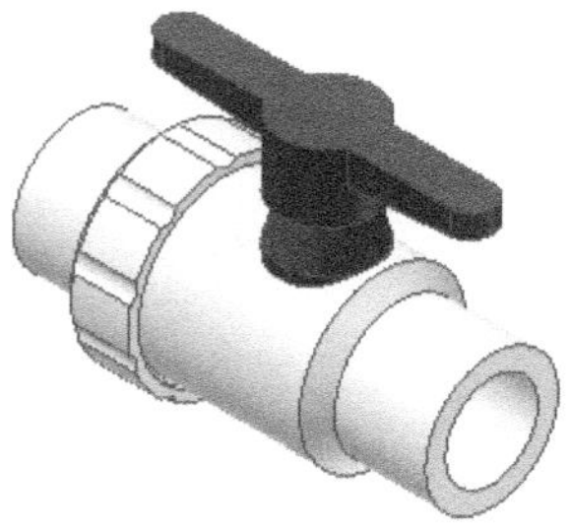

2. Expand the Table node in the browser. Expand ND = 1/2.

   Note: If the keys are not displayed, right-click on the Table node. Click List by Keys.

3. In the browser, right-click on Table and click Edit Table. Examine the data in the iPart Author dialog box. The ND value is the primary key, and the State value is the secondary key for the iPart.

   Note: The open or closed state of the valve controls the angle of a workplane (0° or 90°). This method is more reliable than suppressing and not suppressing features to represent the different states.

4. Click Cancel to close the iPart Author dialog box.

5. In the Manage tab, in the Author panel, click Tube and Pipe.

6. From the Type list, select Valves. From the End Treatment list, select Jointed.

7. Under Table Mapping, select the cell containing required*. From the Table Mapping list, select ND.

   The ND values in the iPart table are mapped to the nominal size key in the library table when you publish the part later in the exercise.

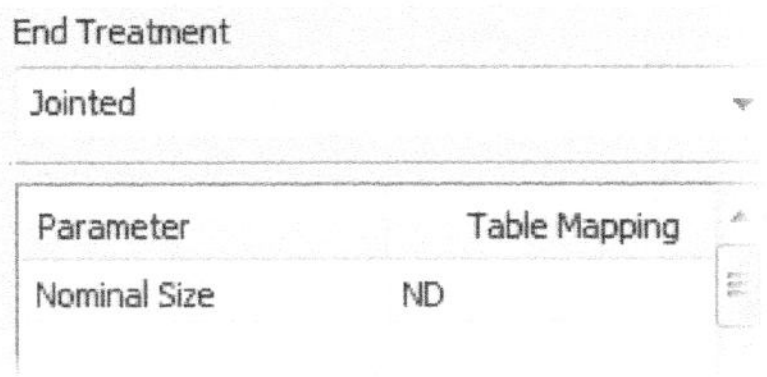

8. Use the same techniques that you used in the previous exercise to add connection information to the near opening in the part. Specify the maximum engagement length using the To Plane/Point option. Select the face highlighted in the following image. Enter **60** for Minimum Engagement Length.

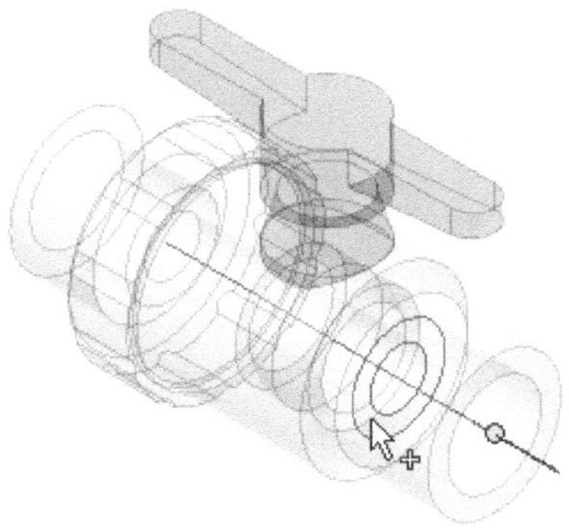

9. Click the Connection Number 2 button. From the End Treatment list, select Jointed.

10. Define the remainder of the connection information to match the other end.

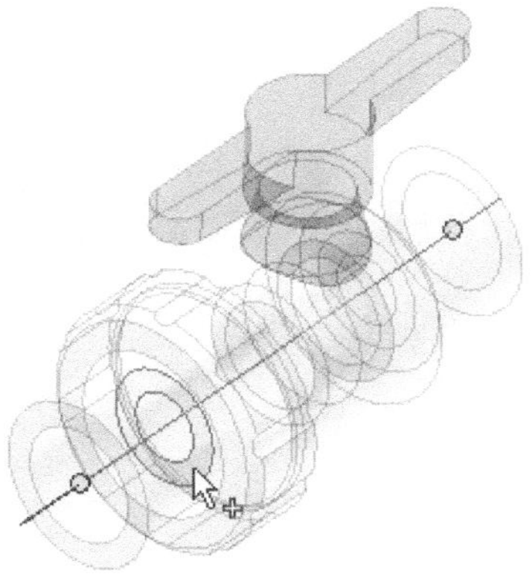

11. Under ISOGEN, from the Type list, select VALVE.

    Note: Although you do not export an ISOGEN PCF file in this exercise, add ISOGEN properties to the valve for possible future use.

12. From the Skey list, select VB** Valve - Ball.

    Because the third and fourth characters in the key are **, you must specify a second key value.

13. From the '**'= list, select SW Socket Weld.

    If a tube and pipe assembly containing the valve is exported to a PCF file, the ISOGEN software recognizes the valve.

14. In the Tube & Pipe Authoring dialog box, click OK.

15. Click OK to close the Authoring Result dialog box.

16. Close all files without saving changes. You will learn to publish parts in the next exercise.

Exercise: Publish to the Content Center

In this exercise, you will prepare a valve with the Tube and Pipe Authoring tool and publish the valve to the Content Center. You will place a union and different versions of the valve into an existing pipe run.

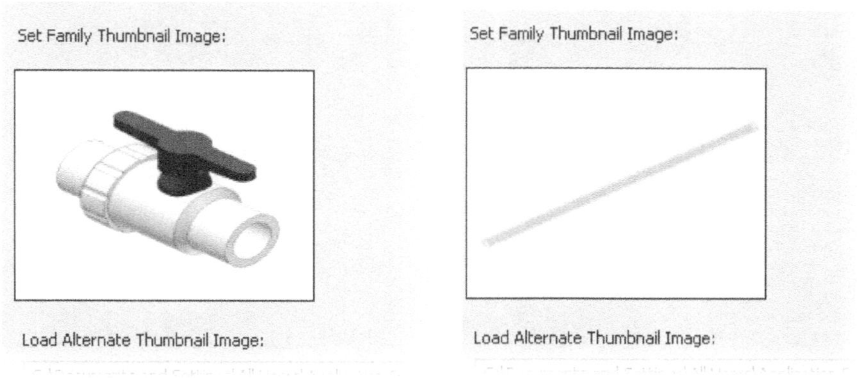

The completed exercise

Setup and Load Library

In this section of the exercise, you will set up Autodesk Inventor so you can complete the exercise steps of preparing a valve with the Tube and Pipe Authoring tool and publishing the valve to the Content Center. You will load a custom library and set a project file current.

1. Start Inventor but do not open any files. Close any open files.
2. In the Get Started tab, in the Launch panel, click Projects.

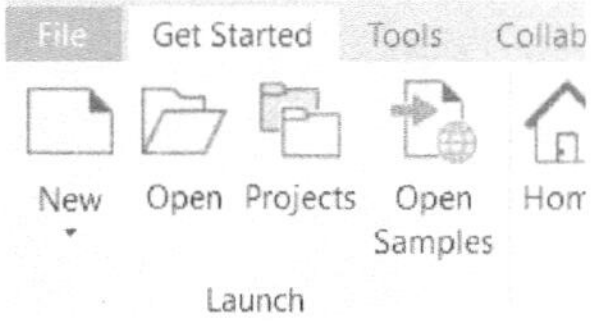

3. In the Projects dialog box, select Configure Content Center Libraries.

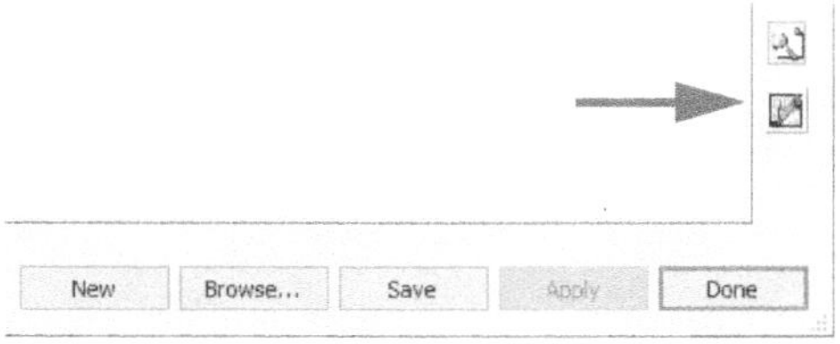

4. In the Configure Libraries dialog box:
   - Click the hyperlink text for Location of Libraries to open a Windows Explorer window viewing that folder.
   - Click Cancel to close the Configure Libraries dialog box.

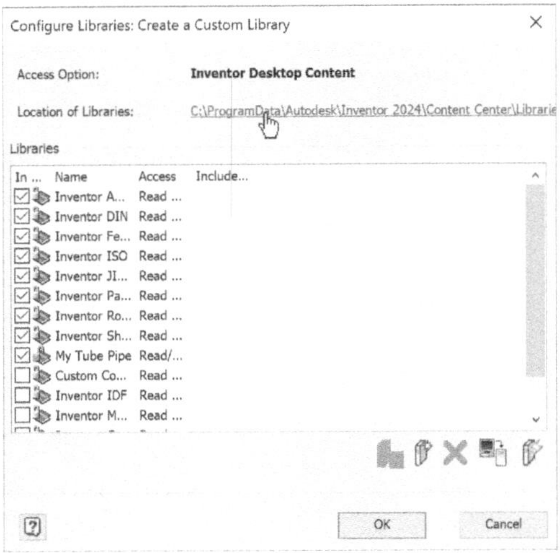

5. Open another session of Windows Explorer.
   - Navigate to the install directory of the exercise files (*C:\Autodesk Inventor 2024 Tube and Pipe Design Exercise Files*).
   - Click to open the Libraries folder in the exercise files directory.
   - Click to open the Publish to the Content Center folder in the exercise directory.
6. Copy *My Tube and Pipe.idcl* from the Publish to the Content Center folder to the window opened by the hyperlink in a previous step.
7. Close the Windows Explorer windows.
8. To add this exercise's project file to Autodesk Inventor:
   - In the Projects dialog box, click Browse.
   - In the Choose Project File dialog box, navigate to the directory with the exercise files and open *Publish to the Content Center.ipj.*

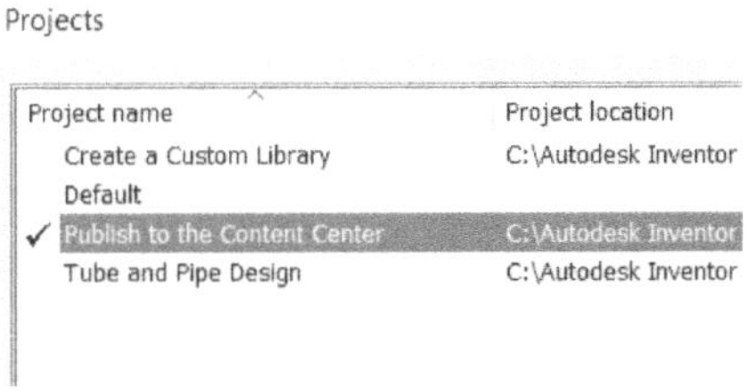

9. In the Projects dialog box, select Configure Content Center Libraries.

10. In the Configure Libraries dialog box, review the list of libraries that are set to be in use when this project file is active. Ensure that My Tube and Pipe is set to In Use.

11. Close the Configure Libraries dialog box and the Projects dialog box.

Publish the Valve

In this portion of the exercise, you will publish the authored valve to the Content Center.

1. Open *Fittings PVC Valve-Done.ipt*.
2. To display the Publish Guide dialog box, in the ribbon, in the Manage tab, in the Content Center, click Publish Part.
3. In the list of libraries, ensure that My Tube and Pipe is selected.

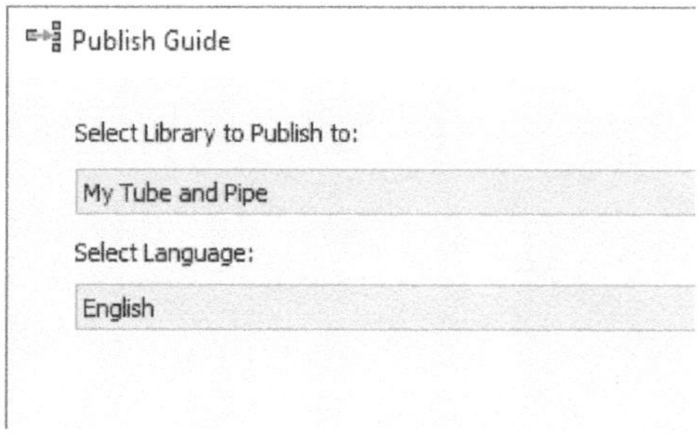

4. Click Next. In the category list, ensure that Valves is selected.

5. Click Next. The required mappings are displayed with a yellow background. They were already defined during the authoring process. The other undefined mappings are for branch fittings.

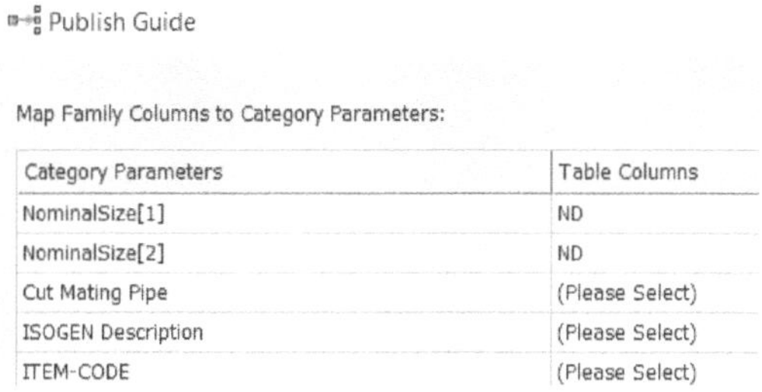

6. Click Next. The key columns should be already defined.

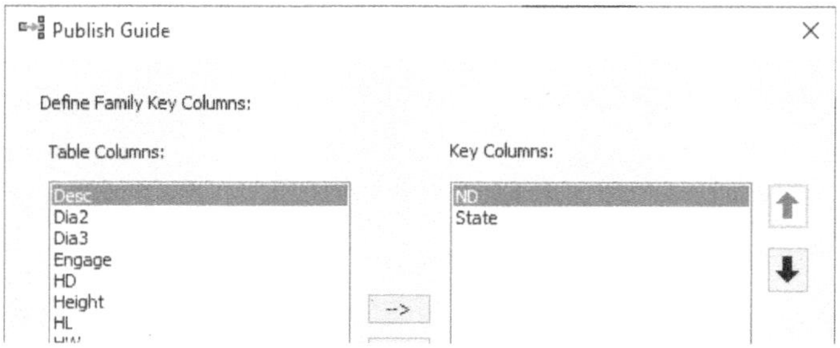

7. Click Next. Enter the following information:
   - For Family Name, enter **Shutoff Valve - Ball**.
   - For Family Description, enter **Low Pressure Shutoff Valve**.
   - From the Standard Organization list, select ANSI.
   - From the Standard list, select ASTM D 2466.
   - For Manufacturer, enter **Apollo**.

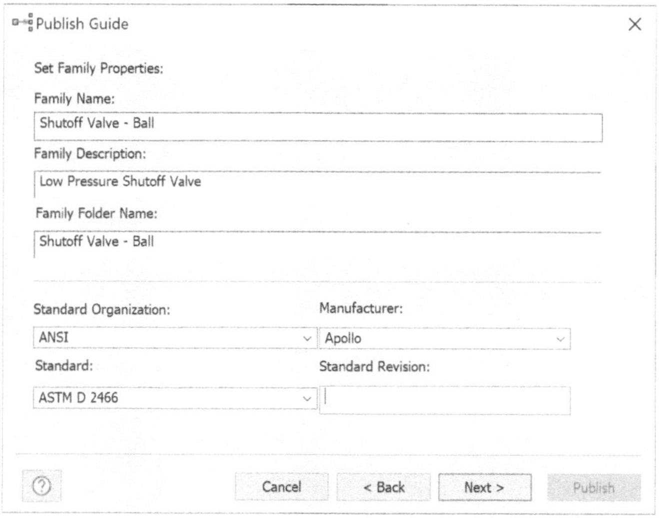

8. Click Next. Review the thumbnail image.

9. Click Publish. Click OK to close the message that confirms the part was successfully published to the library.

10. Close all files without saving changes.

Publish Hose

In this portion of the exercise, you will add connection information to a fitting and conduit part. You then publish them to the Content Center.

1. Open *Fittings Hose.ipt*.

Note: You can use the same part to publish a rigid pipe, tube, or flexible hose.

2. In the browser, right-click on Table. Click Edit Table.

3. In the iPart Author dialog box, click the Other tab.

   The nominal diameter is the only key required for a pipe, tube, or hose. Although there is no schedule value associated with hose, a schedule parameter is still required. In this file, the schedule column (SN) is mapped to the outer diameter value as indicated by the formula in the SN column.

4. Click the Properties tab. Expand Project. Click Stock Number. Click >> to add the Stock Number property to the table.

5. In the Stock Number column, enter the following:
   - For the 3/8" hose, enter 10143.
   - For the 1/2" hose, enter 10144.

	ID	OD	PL	SN	ND	Material	Member	Stock Number
1	0.375in	0.63in	15 in	OD=0.63in	3/8	Polycarbonate, Smoke	Fittings Hose-01	10143
2	0.5 in	0.78in	15 in	OD=0.78in	1/2	Polycarbonate, Smoke	Fittings Hose-02	10144

6. Click OK.
7. In the Manage tab, in the Author panel, click Tube and Pipe.
8. In the Tube and Pipe Authoring dialog box,:
   - From the Type list, select Hoses.
   - The connection count is fixed at two.
9. From the End Treatment list, select Hose - Permanent.
10. Map the parameters to the table columns as shown in the following image. To select a table column, select the cell and click the arrow to the right of the cell.

Parameter	Table Mapping
Nominal Size	ND
Schedule Number	SN
Inside Diameter	ID
Outside Diameter	OD
Pipe Length	PL

11. Add a connection point and connection axis at the near end of the pipe.

    Note: The direction arrow must point away from the pipe.

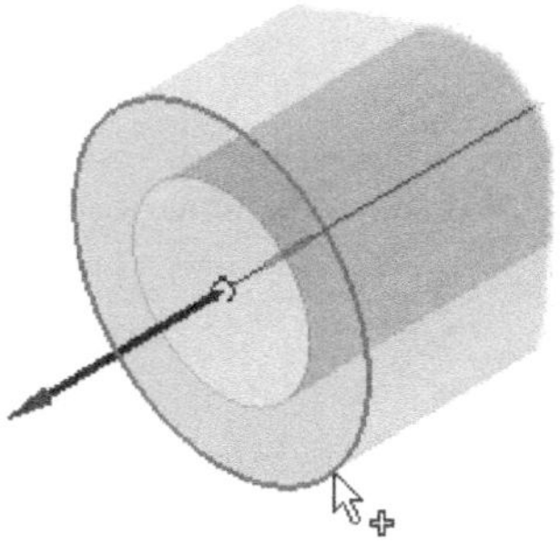

12. Under Connection, select Male.

13. Under Engagement, from the Max list, select Distance. Keep the default settings.

    Note: Although engagement is ignored for conduit, it is recommended that you set the minimum and maximum engagement to 0.

14. Click the Connection Number 2 button. From the End Treatment list, select Hose - Permanent.
15. Define a connection point and axis at the other end of the pipe. The direction arrow must point away from the pipe.
16. Under Connection, select Male.
17. Set the same Engagement distance as it was done for the other end.
18. In the Tube & Pipe Authoring dialog box, click OK. Click OK to close the message box.
19. In the Manage tab, in the Content Center panel, click Publish Part.
20. In the list of libraries, ensure that My Tube and Pipe is selected. Click Next.
21. In the category list, ensure that Hoses is selected. Click Next.
22. In the Mapping page, click Next.
23. In the Key Columns page, click Next.
24. In the Family Properties page:
    - For Family Name, enter **Clear Hose**.
    - For Family Description, enter **Water Hose**.
    - For Manufacturer, enter **Parker.**
    - For Standard, enter **Parker**.
    - Click Next.
25. In the Set Family Thumbnail page, click Publish. Click OK to close the message box.
26. Close all files without saving changes.

Exercise: Place Library Fittings

In this exercise, you place custom fittings and place library fittings from Content Center.

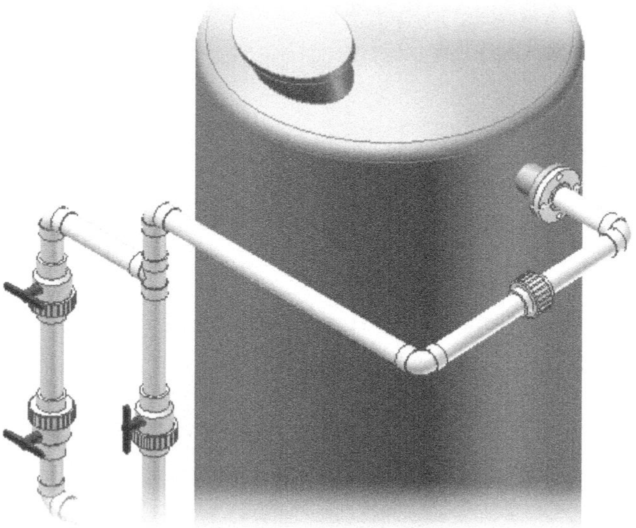

The completed exercise

Setup and Load Library

In this section of the exercise, you will set up Autodesk Inventor so you can complete the exercise steps of placing library fittings using the Place Fitting command and the Place from Content Center command. You will load a custom library and set a project file current.

1. Start the Autodesk Inventor software but do not open any files. Close any open files.
2. In the Get Started tab, in the Launch panel, click Projects.

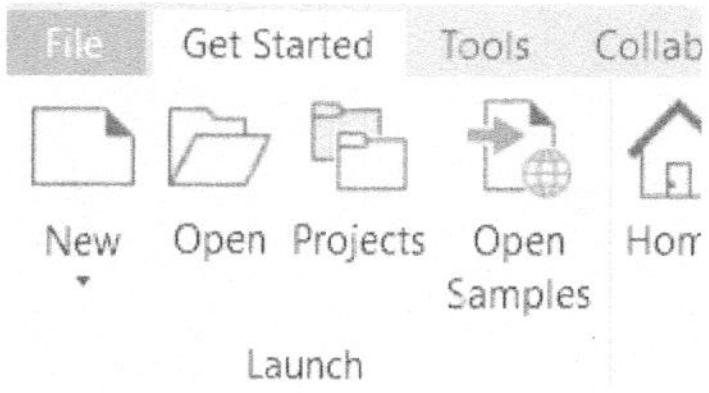

3. In the Projects dialog box, select Configure Content Center Libraries.

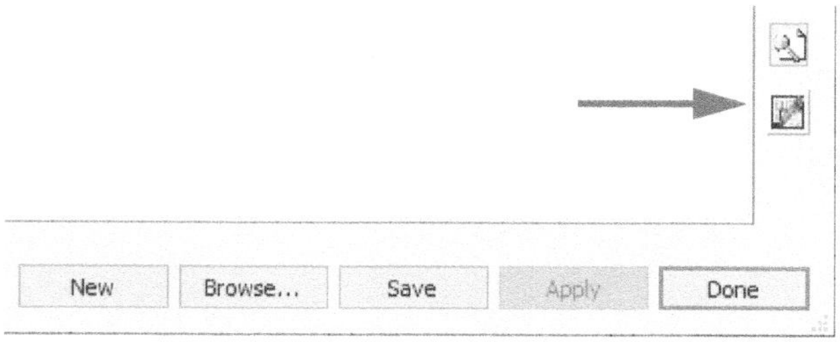

4. In the Configure Libraries dialog box:

   - Click the hyperlink text for Location of Libraries to open a Windows Explorer window viewing that folder.
   - Click Cancel to close the Configure Libraries dialog box.

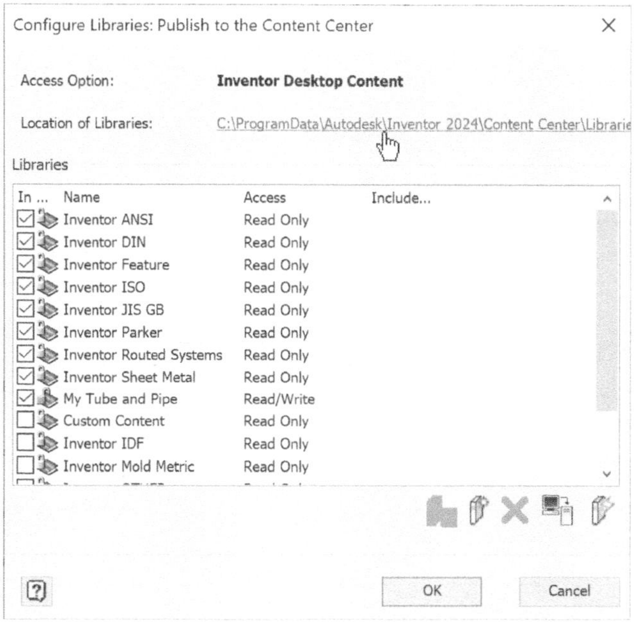

5. Open another session of Windows Explorer.

   - Navigate to the install directory of the exercise files (*C:\Autodesk Inventor 2024 Tube and Pipe Design Exercise Files*).
   - Click to open the Libraries folder in the exercise files directory.
   - Click to open the Place Library Fittings folder in the Library folder.

6. If the library My Tube and Pipe already exists in the ProgramData folder, go to the next step. Otherwise, copy *My Tube and Pipe.idcl* from the Place Library Fittings folder to the window opened by the hyperlink in a previous step.

7. Close the Windows Explorer windows.

8. To add this exercise's project file to Inventor:
   - In the Projects dialog box, click Browse.
   - In the Choose Project File dialog box, navigate to the directory with the exercise files and open *Place Library Fittings.ipj*.

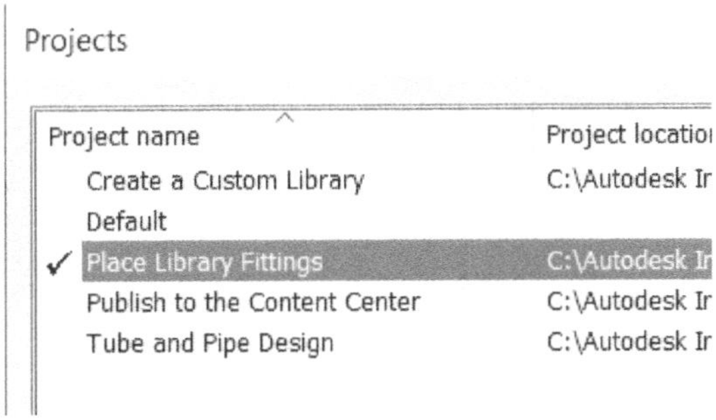

9. In the Projects dialog box, select Configure Content Center Libraries.
10. In the Configure Libraries dialog box, review the list of libraries that are set to be in use when this project file is active.

11. Close the Configure Libraries dialog box and the Projects dialog box.

Use Library Fittings

In this portion of the exercise, you will place an authored fitting and the published valve in an existing route.

1. Open *Fittings Takeout.iam*.

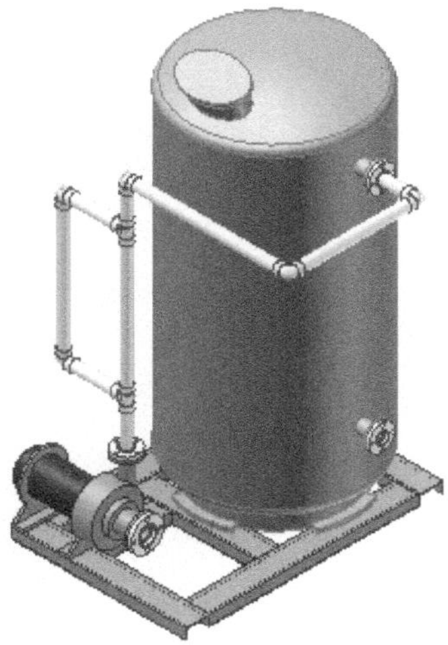

2. In the browser, expand the Tube & Pipe Runs subassembly. Double-click on Run01.
3. In the ribbon, in the Pipe Run tab, in the Route panel, click Place Fitting.
4. Open *Fittings PVC Union-Done.ipt*.
5. Move the cursor over the horizontal pipe segment that is highlighted in the following image. Click near the center of the segment.

   The union is placed in the run. The segment is replaced with two segments that engage the union.

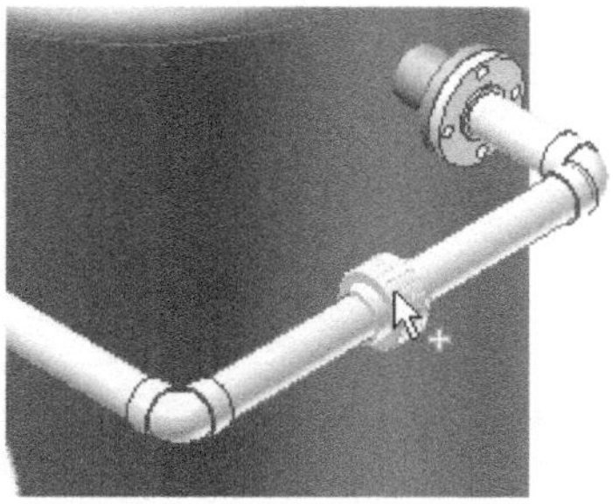

6. Right-click in the graphics window and click Done.
7. In the ribbon, in the Pipe Run tab, in the Content panel, click Place.
8. In the Place from Content Center dialog box, browse to Tube & Pipe>Fittings>Valves.
9. In the family pane, double-click on Shutoff Valve - Ball.

10. In the Shutoff Valve - Ball dialog box, under ND, select 2. Under State, select Closed. Click Apply.

    The valve is generated and is attached to the cursor.

11. Move the cursor over the middle of the vertical pipe segment in the takeout. Drag the fitting down close to the bottom of the segment. Click to place the fitting.

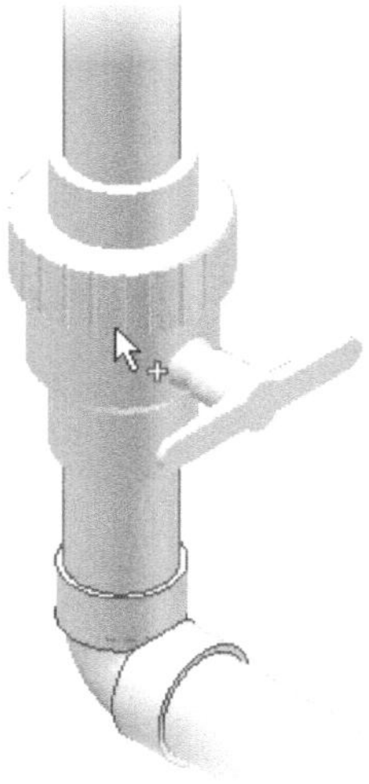

12. Rotate the valve 90° to match the following image.

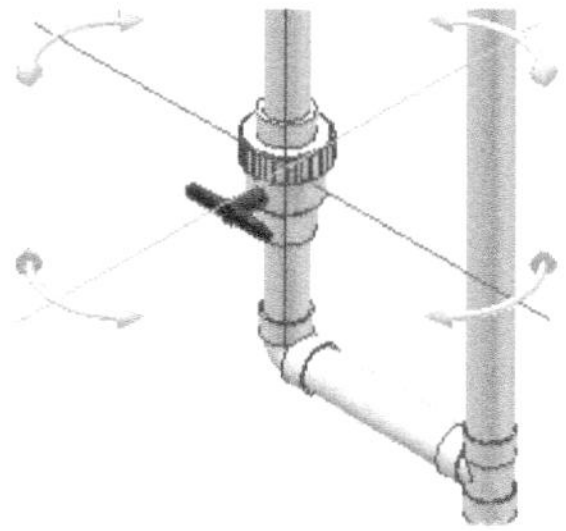

13. Right-click in the graphics window background. Click Continue.

14. Place the second valve in the segment above the first valve. Rotate the second valve to match the first valve that you inserted in the segment.

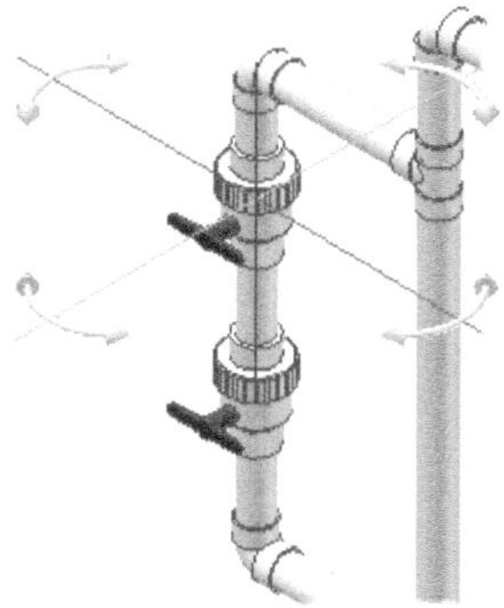

15. Right-click in the graphics window background. Click Done.
16. Insert a 2" open state valve in the adjacent segment. Rotate the valve to match the first two.

17. Right-click in the graphics window background. Click Done.
18. Finish the Tube and Pipe run.
19. Close the file and do not save changes.

Lesson: Managing Library Content

Overview

This lesson describes the management and editing of settings for your published tube and pipe content.

You need to understand how published Content Center parts have their document setting values and file property values set in order to ensure that your published content has the document settings you require and the property values that reflect your company requirements. When a change is required, you need to know how to edit a published part family using the Content Center Editor.

Objectives

After completing this lesson, you will be able to:

- Explain the document setting values of published Content Center parts.
- Add and edit the columns of values for a library part family so that they map to an Inventor property.
- Add a property to a published part to set its browser display name.

Document Settings for Published Parts

Parts published to the Content Center not only contain the 3D geometry for the parts, the published parts also contain information that describes, identifies, and defines the parts. Some of that published information includes the values for the parts' document settings. To ensure that your published content has the document settings you require, you need to understand how published Content Center parts have their document setting values set.

BOM Document Settings

When you publish a custom part to a Content Center library, the template that is created contains the same document settings as the part file that was used as the basis of the publication. While some properties for the part family like Name and Description can be modified in the Content Center Editor, other properties are set within the template at the time the part was published to the Content Center.

Bill of Material (BOM) document setting values are some of the document properties that are set in the template only during the time of publication. The bill of material values that are set in the document settings include the values for:

- Default BOM Structure
- Base Quantity
- Base Unit

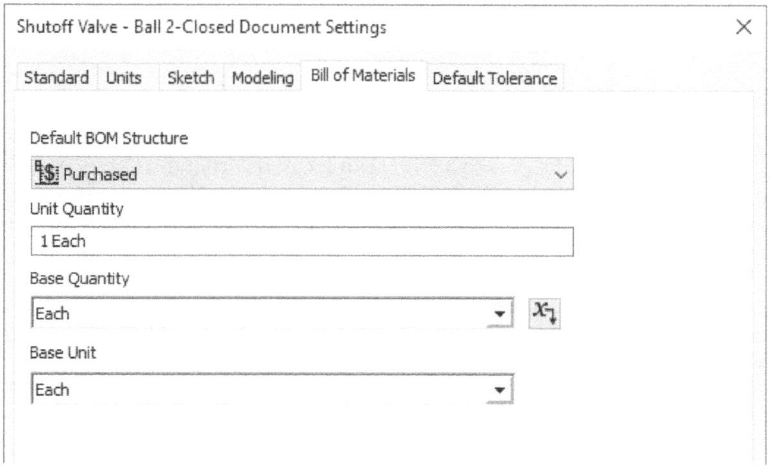

Replace Family Template Option

You can change the document settings for parts already published to the Content Center by replacing the family template with a modified part.

The Replace Family Template option is a shortcut menu option available in the Content Center Editor. To access this option, you right-click on the family part after selecting the corresponding read/write library in the Library View list.

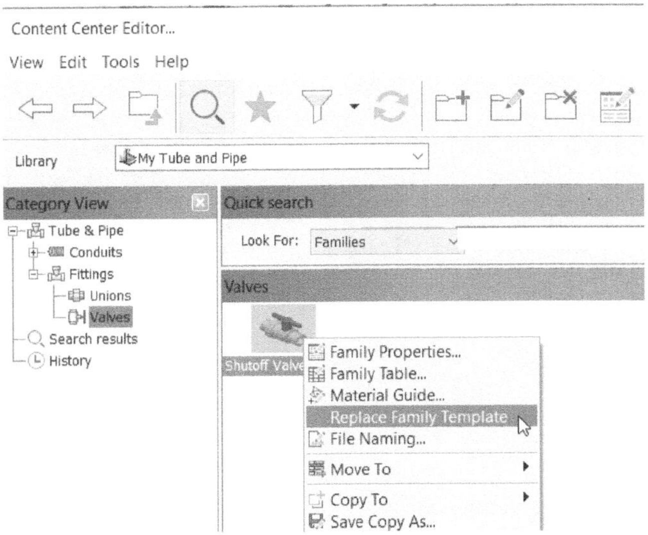

To obtain a version of the library part that you can modify and use to republish, in the ribbon, click Open from Content Center and save the part to a folder not located within the library path. With the part saved outside the library path, you can make and save your required changes. After saving the changes, you select the modified part after selecting the Replace Family Template shortcut menu option.

> Changes made to the part family template in the Content Center do not automatically update library parts that are being referenced in assemblies. To have the assemblies reference a part that contains the new document values, the library part saved on your computer or the server must be overwritten by a new version of the part. Use Refresh Standard Components from the Tools menu to overwrite existing standard part files with new versions in the Content Center.

Adding and Editing Family Column Values

A key aspect of any part is the additional information available about that part. For Autodesk Inventor files, this additional part information is stored in the files property fields.

Because individual library family members can have unique property information for different iterations of the part, the file property values for a library part must be written at the time that the part is instanced into an assembly. To have these property values automatically reflect your company requirements, you must know how to add and edit the columns of values for a library part family so that they map to an Inventor property.

In the following image, the project properties for this library part are automatically entered based on the values for that content family member, as assigned in the Content Center Editor. With the value set correctly for the family member, every time that the part is added to an assembly by any user, the correct values are automatically entered. These values can then be listed in the parts list or exported for use by other applications.

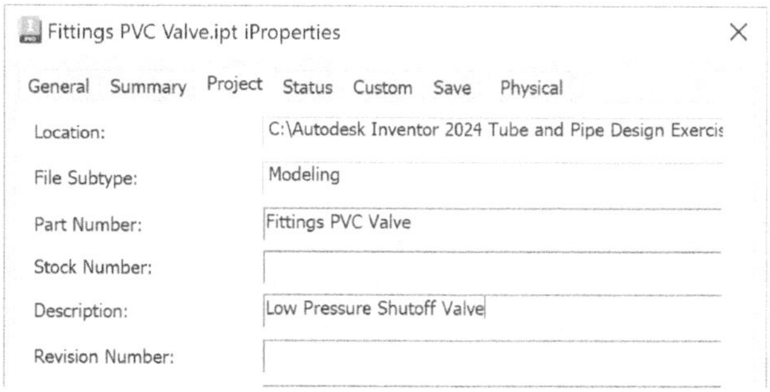

Access Family Table

You access the table of properties for a part family from within the Content Center Editor. After selecting the part family, you can click Family Table from the shortcut menu, toolbar, or Edit menu.

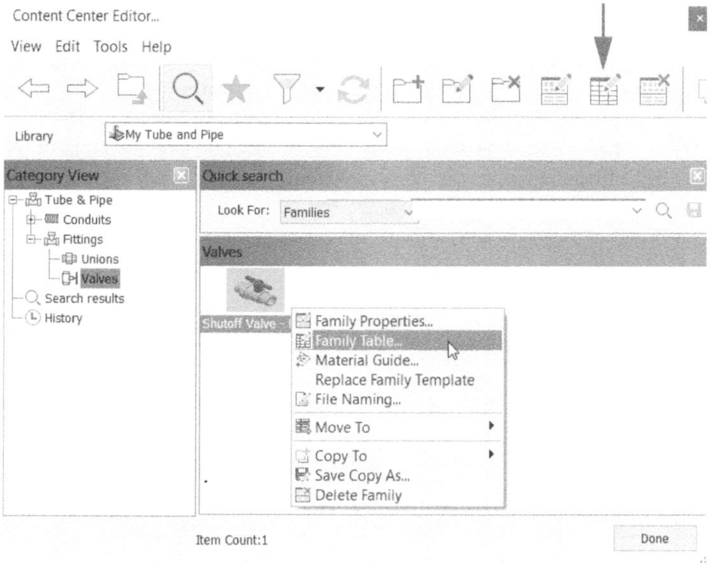

Access to Add or Edit Columns

After you open the Family Table dialog box, you can add columns by right-clicking on the row for the column headers and then clicking Add Column, or by clicking Add Column in the toolbar. By clicking a column header before clicking Add Column, the new column is added directly after the selected column.

To open the Column Properties dialog box to edit the properties of an existing column, you can double-click on the column header or right-click on the column header, and then click Column Properties. You can also click the column header and click Column Properties in the toolbar.

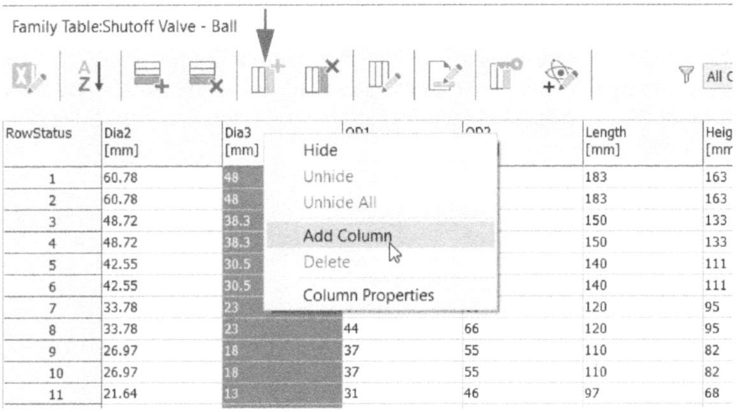

Column Properties

After you select Add Column or Column Properties, the Column Properties dialog box opens, enabling you to enter properties for the column and column fields.

When you are adding a new column, the Column Name field is an empty editable field. After the column has been created, this field is a read-only field. Within the Column Properties dialog box, you set values for the type of data being stored in the cells of that column. You also set units if applicable for the data type, the heading caption for the column, an expression that can reference values from other columns, and mapping for the property value to a predefined or custom file property.

Depending on the data types of the columns, an expression can be a mathematical formula that calculates a new value, or it can concatenate values into a single string. To reference the value in a different column, you can enter the column name in all capitals encased in brackets ({ }), or by clicking the browse button to the right of the expression field and selecting the column name from the list. If you are entering the column name manually, remember to enter the column name and not the column caption.

When you add or change an expression in the Column Properties dialog box, all of the cells in that column are automatically edited to have the same value or expression. If you need to, you can enter values and expressions directly into the individual cells.

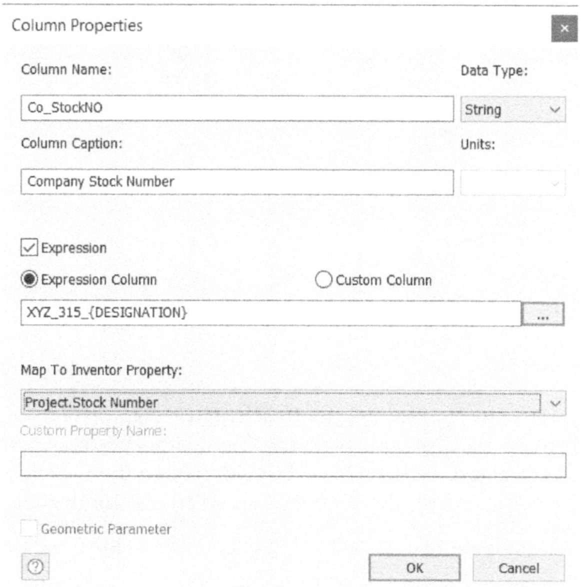

By mapping the value of a column to a file property field, the value for that family member is then available for use by the assembly where the part is instanced. For example, it can be included as information in the assembly's BOM and parts list. Some of the property fields include but are not limited to:

- Summary Information.Revision Number
- Project.Part Number
- Project.Stock Number
- Project.Material
- Project.Size Description

If you want to map a column value to a file property and an appropriate property does not currently exist, you select Custom from the list and then enter a new custom property name. This property is then automatically added to the part template as a custom property.

Parameters with a Range

Parameter values can be set by the individual family member, or you can configure the family members to permit for an entered value. You configure a parameter to accept a range of values by selecting the Expression option of Custom Column and then specifying the range criteria. When you specify a family table column to accept a range of values, when the part is being placed in an assembly, you have a value field to enter a value.

In the following image, because the custom part was configured with a range of values for the Length table column parameter, a value must be entered during placement of the part.

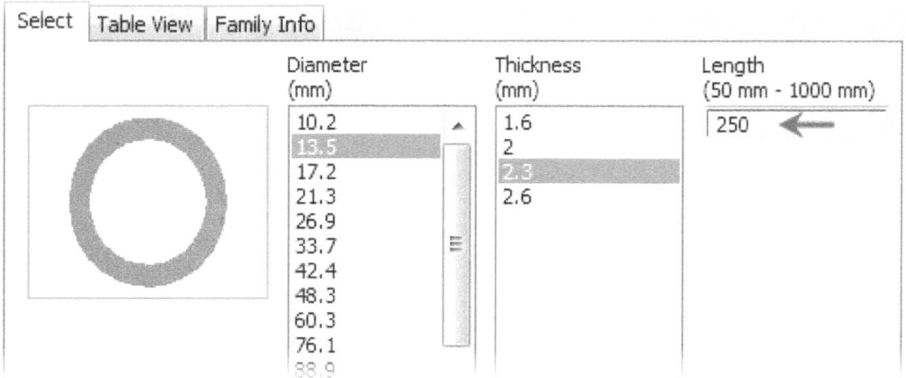

To configure a table column family to be a range of values, right-click on the column label and click Column Properties. In the Column Properties dialog box, select the Expression check box and then click Custom Column. With those items selected, click the More button to open the Specify Range dialog box. With the Specify Range dialog box open, specify the required criteria for the value.

In the following image, the Length column is set to a default value of 250. The value must be greater than 50 but not more than 1000.

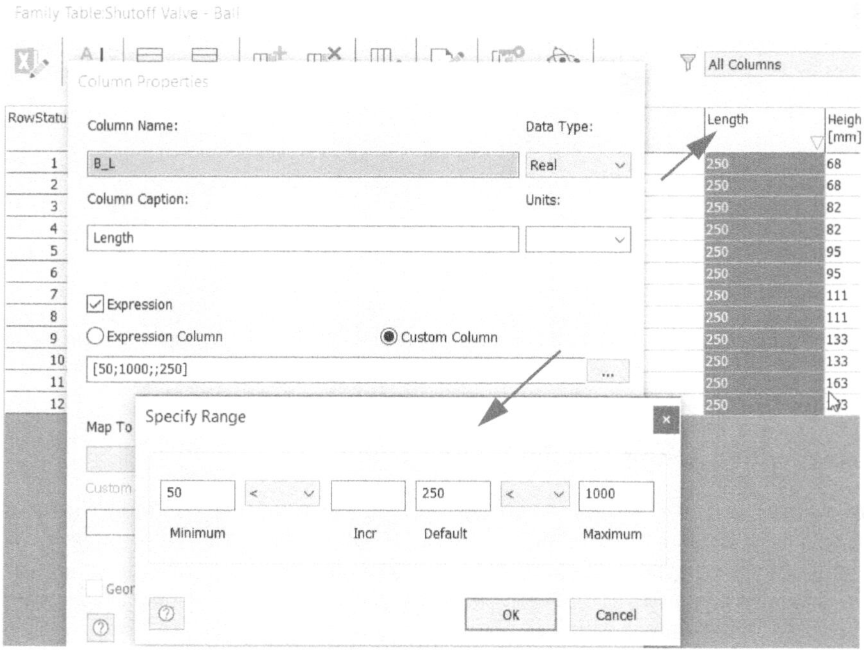

Process: Adding and Editing Column Values

The following diagram gives an overview of adding and editing column values for a library part family.

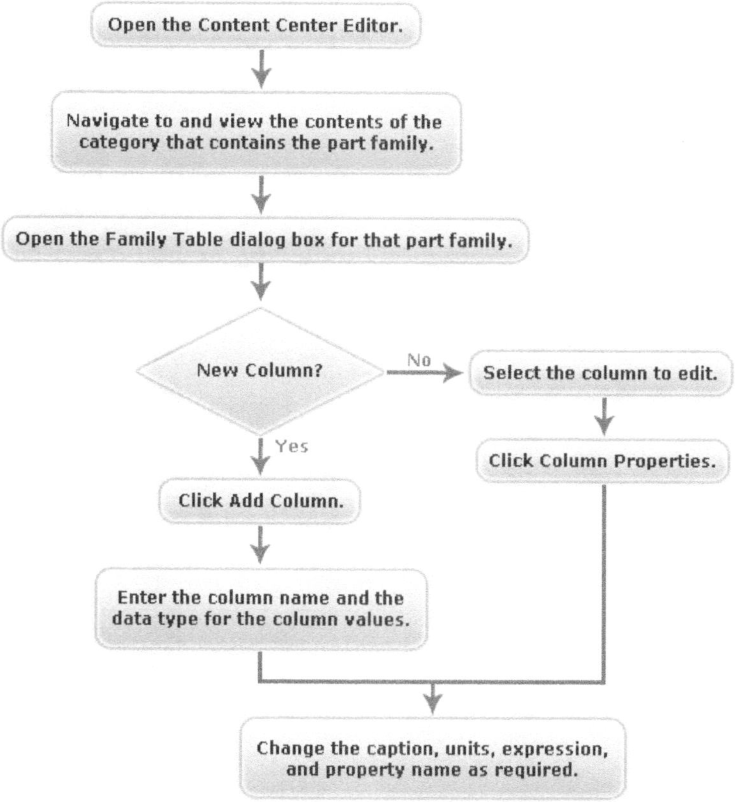

Adding a Custom Display Name

After you publish a part to the Content Center, you can edit the table in the Content Center Editor. You can edit values, add or delete members, or add additional columns and map their values to Inventor iProperties.

One typical change is to customize the browser display name for parts generated from the family. When you place a fitting from the Content Center, the name displayed in the browser is a concatenation of the family name and the designation. To use another display name, you can either edit the values or expression for the Designation column, or create a new column in the Content Center table and map the new column to Inventor's Display Name property.

If you plan to revise any information in the Content Center table, make the changes before placing parts from the family in a run. If you edit the table after you place parts in a run, you are notified that the parts are out of date. You can use the Refresh Standard Components tool to update the placed components with the revised data from the table.

In the following image, the ball shutoff valve displays in the browser using a custom name, which was assigned using the Content Center Editor.

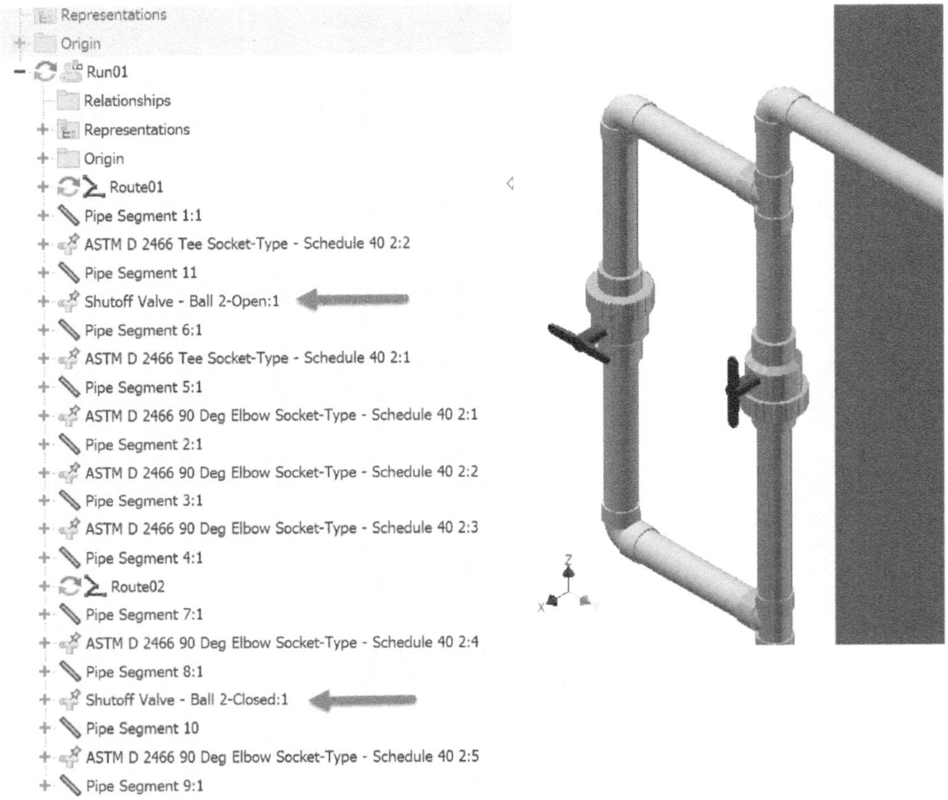

Procedure: Adding a Custom Display Name

You can edit a published part to add additional columns and map those columns to Inventor properties. The following steps outline how to add a custom display name for library parts.

1. Start the Content Center Editor.
2. Display the family table for the member you want to edit.
3. Add a new column.
4. In the Column Properties dialog box, enter values for Column Name (no spaces) and Column Caption.
5. Select the Expression check box. For Expression, enter an expression using fixed text and selected parameters. To add a parameter to the expression, click the Browse button to the right of the Expression box.

6. Under Map to Autodesk Inventor Property, select Member.Display Name. The completed dialog box displays in the following image.

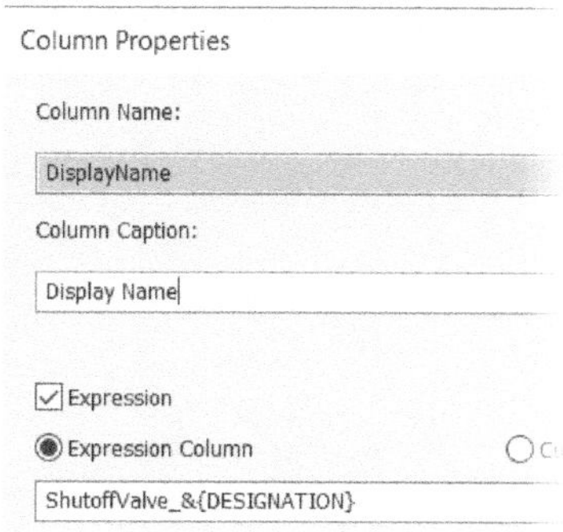

7. The family table is updated to include the new column. Note that the Display Name column is a concatenation of a fixed string and the contents of the Designation column.

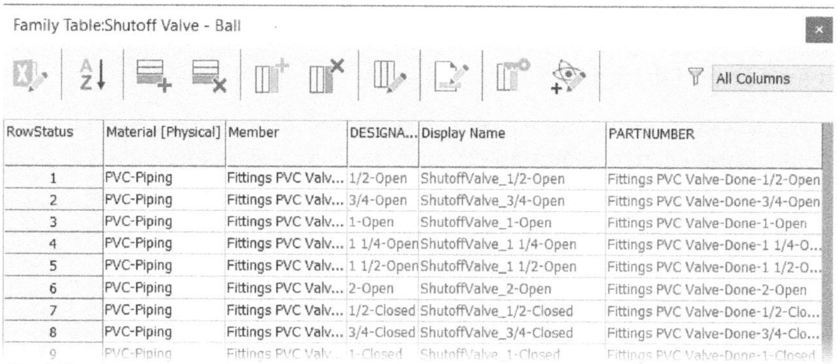

RowStatus	Material [Physical]	Member	DESIGNA...	Display Name	PARTNUMBER
1	PVC-Piping	Fittings PVC Valv...	1/2-Open	ShutoffValve_1/2-Open	Fittings PVC Valve-Done-1/2-Open
2	PVC-Piping	Fittings PVC Valv...	3/4-Open	ShutoffValve_3/4-Open	Fittings PVC Valve-Done-3/4-Open
3	PVC-Piping	Fittings PVC Valv...	1-Open	ShutoffValve_1-Open	Fittings PVC Valve-Done-1-Open
4	PVC-Piping	Fittings PVC Valv...	1 1/4-Open	ShutoffValve_1 1/4-Open	Fittings PVC Valve-Done-1 1/4-O...
5	PVC-Piping	Fittings PVC Valv...	1 1/2-Open	ShutoffValve_1 1/2-Open	Fittings PVC Valve-Done-1 1/2-O...
6	PVC-Piping	Fittings PVC Valv...	2-Open	ShutoffValve_2-Open	Fittings PVC Valve-Done-2-Open
7	PVC-Piping	Fittings PVC Valv...	1/2-Closed	ShutoffValve_1/2-Closed	Fittings PVC Valve-Done-1/2-Clo...
8	PVC-Piping	Fittings PVC Valv...	3/4-Closed	ShutoffValve_3/4-Closed	Fittings PVC Valve-Done-3/4-Clo...
9	PVC-Piping	Fittings PVC Valv...	1-Closed	ShutoffValve_1-Closed	Fittings PVC Valve-Done-1-Closed

8. Apply the changes to the Content Center and then exit the Content Center Editor.

Exercise: Add a Column to a Part Family

In this exercise, you will add a custom property column to a part family and assign its value to the Part Name file property field.

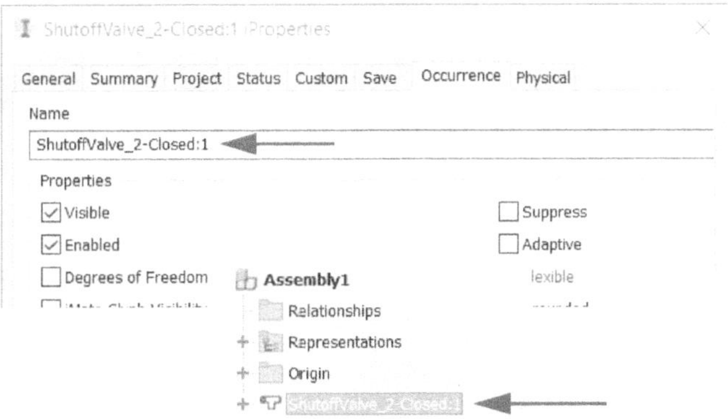

The completed exercise

Setup and Load Library

In this section of the exercise, you will set up Autodesk Inventor so you can complete the exercise steps of adding a column to a part family. You will load a custom library and set a project file current.

1. Start the Autodesk Inventor software but do not open any files. Close any open files.
2. In the Get Started tab, in the Launch panel, click Projects.

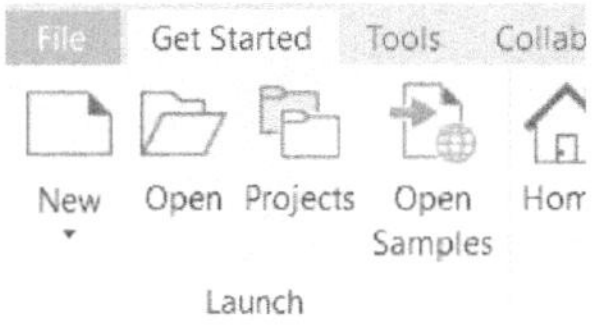

3. In the Projects dialog box, select Configure Content Center Libraries.

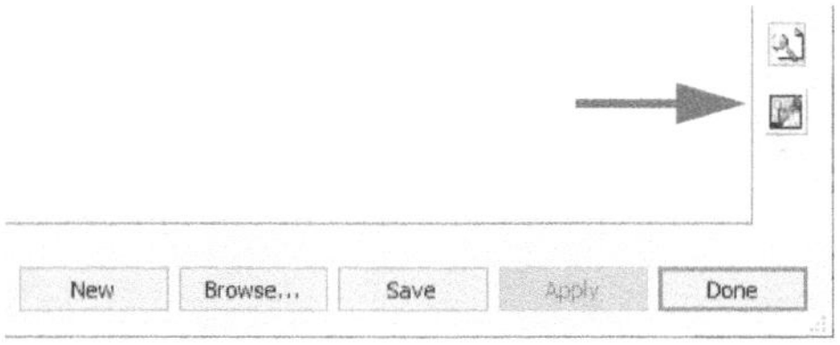

4. In the Configure Libraries dialog box:
   - Click the hyperlink text for Location of Libraries to open a Windows Explorer window viewing that folder.
   - Click Cancel to close the Configure Libraries dialog box.

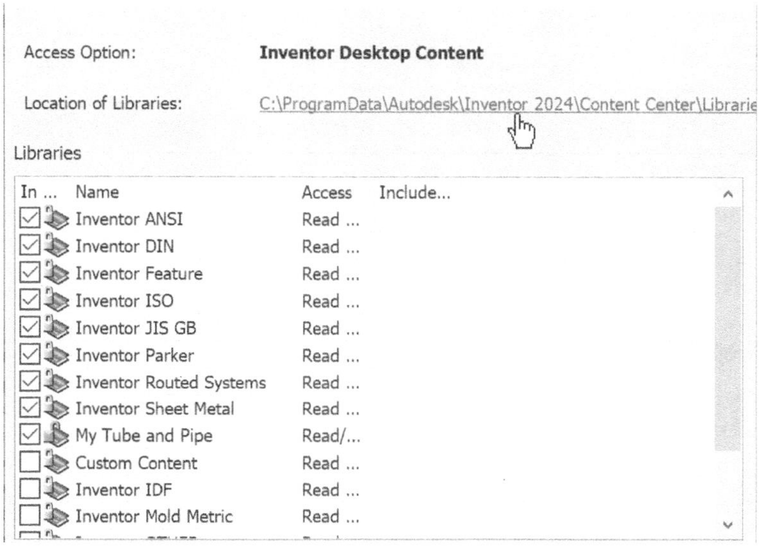

5. Open another session of Windows Explorer.
   - Navigate to the install directory of the exercise files.
   - Click to open the Libraries folder in the exercise directory.
   - Click to open the Add a Column to a Part Family folder in the exercise Libraries folder.
6. If the library My Tube and Pipe already exists in the ProgramData folder, go to the next step. Otherwise, copy *My Tube and Pipe.idcl* from the Add a Column to a Part Family folder to the window opened by the hyperlink in a previous step.
7. Close the Windows Explorer windows.

8. To add this exercise's project file to Autodesk Inventor:
   - In the Projects dialog box, click Browse.
   - In the Choose Project File dialog box, navigate to the directory with the exercise files and open *Managing Library Content.ipj*.

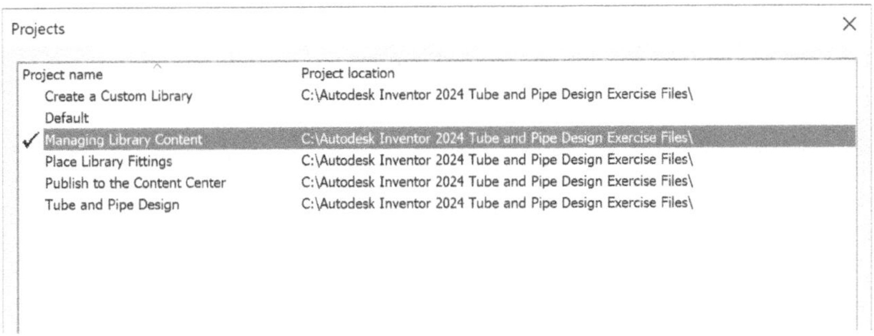

9. In the Projects dialog box, select Configure Content Center Libraries.
10. In the Configure Libraries dialog box, review the list of libraries that are set to be in use when this project file is active.

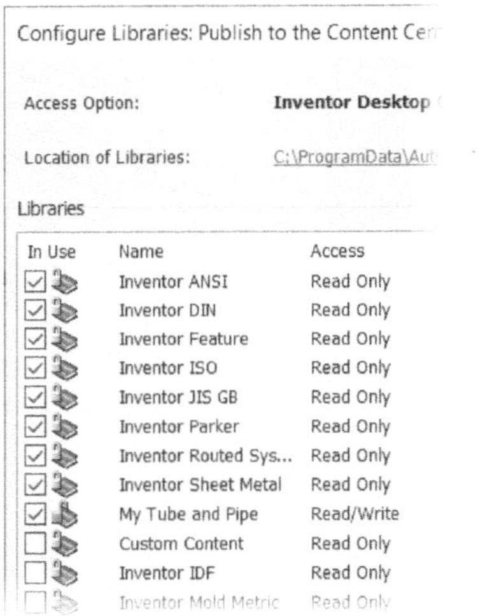

11. Close the Configure Libraries dialog box and the Projects dialog box.

Add a Column to a Part Family

1. In the Tools tab, in the Content Center panel, click Editor.

2. To access the family table information for the Shutoff Valve - Ball:
   - In the Library View list, select My Tube and Pipe.
   - In the Category View pane, under Tube & Pipe, under Fittings, click Valves.
   - In the family pane for Valves, right-click on Shutoff Valve - Ball. Click Family Table.

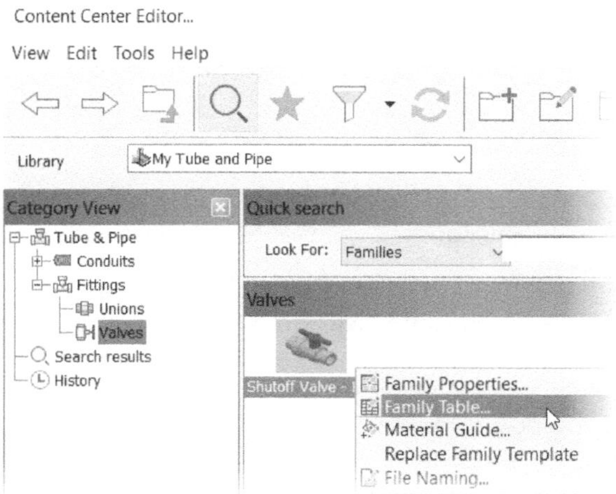

3. To begin adding a new custom column after the Designation column:
   - Click the Designation column header.
   - Right-click on the heading. Click Add Column.

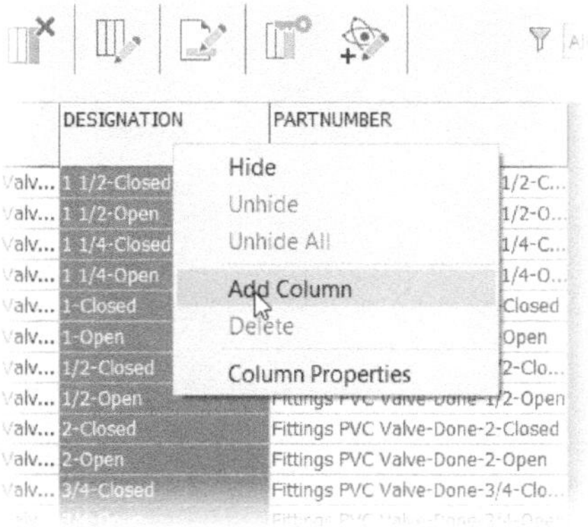

4. In the Column Properties dialog box:
   - For Column Name, enter **DisplayName** (no space).
   - For Column Caption, enter **Display Name**.

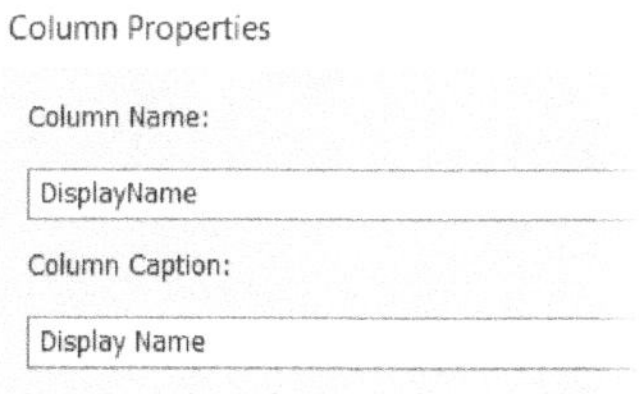

5. To begin setting the values in the column:
   - Select the Expression check box.
   - Under Expression Column, enter **Shutoff Valve_**.

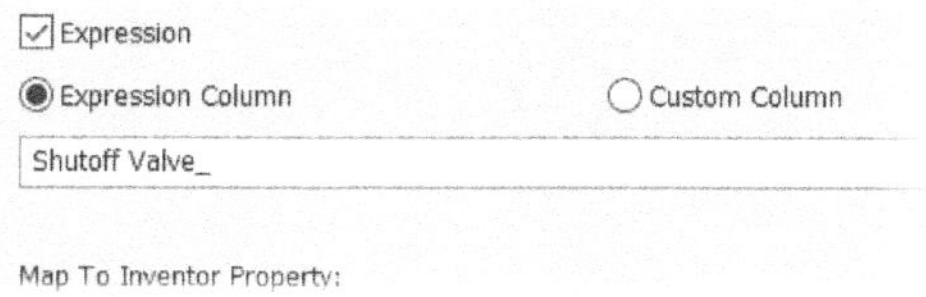

6. To have the current value in another column display in the expression:
   - Click the Browse button to the right of the expression field.
   - In the Parameter Name column, double- click DESIGNATION.

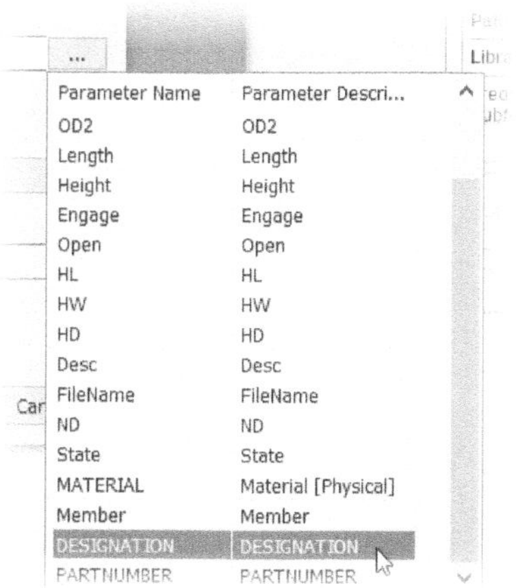

7. In the Map to Inventor Property drop-down list, select Member.Display Name.

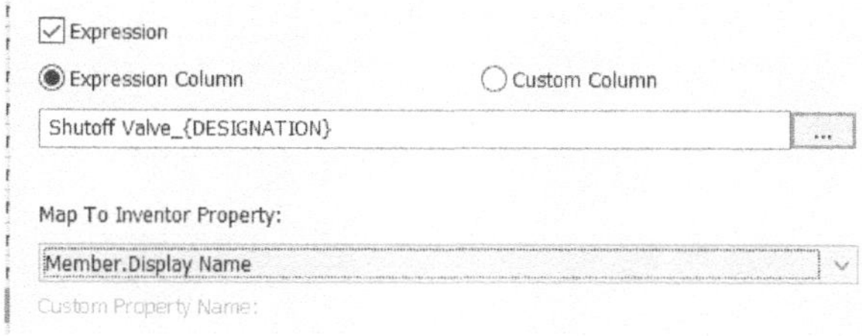

8. Click OK. The Family Table dialog box now displays with the custom column.

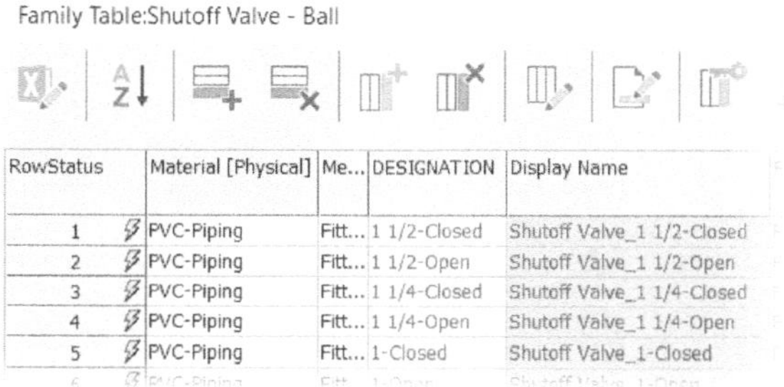

9. To complete the change:

- In the Family Table dialog box, click OK to close the dialog box and write the information to the Content Center for this part family.
- Click OK when informed the information was published successfully.
- Click Done to close the Content Center Editor.

10. Start a new assembly file.

11. To begin adding a PVC valve to the assembly:

- In the Assemble tab, in the Component panel, click Place from Content Center.
- In the Category View list, under Tube & Pipe, under Fittings, click Valves.
- In the family pane, double-click on Shutoff Valve - Ball.

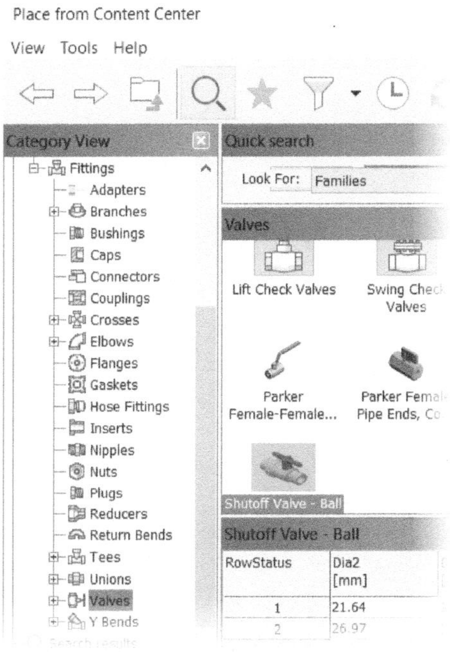

12. To add an instance of the shutoff valve:

- In the part family dialog box, ND list, select 2.
- In the State list, select Closed.
- Click OK.

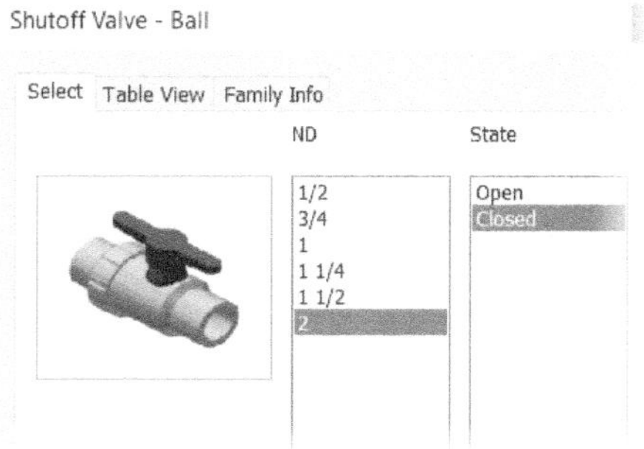

13. In the graphics window, click to place an instance of the part. Press ESC.

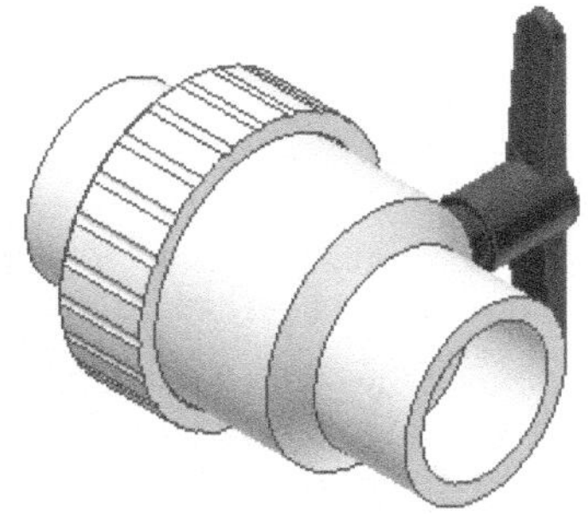

14. In the browser or graphics window, right-click on the Shutoff Valve - Ball and click iProperties.

15. To observe the results of the added column:

    - In the iProperties dialog box, Occurrence tab, review the Part Name value for the placed instance of the shutoff valve.
    - Review the part file name in the browser.
    - Observe that both names match the added column from the part family.
    - Click Close.

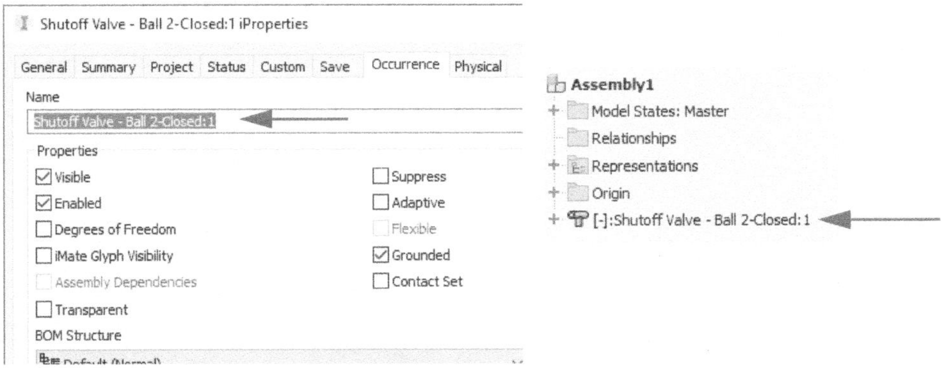

16. Close all files without saving changes.

Lesson: Creating Tube and Pipe Styles

Overview

This lesson describes how to create new styles using published content. Styles use library components for segments and for basic fittings such as elbows, couplings, and flexible hose end fittings.

You can create new styles for your own parts by first publishing the conduit (pipe, tube, or hose) and related fittings to a custom library and then specifying these components when you create the new style. You can select components from any library when you create or edit a style as long as the components have been authored using the Tube and Pipe authoring tool.

Valid components for the current style are filtered based on the standard that you select. You can publish related components using one of the standards in the default libraries or create your own standard to group your components together.

Objectives

After completing this lesson, you will be able to:

- Create a new tube or pipe style.
- Create and configure a new style as a self-draining style.
- Configure tube and pipe styles in a template file.

Creating a New Style

You create a new rigid pipe, tube, or hose style in the same way as you do for other Autodesk Inventor styles. Clicking the New button clears the settings so that you can define a new style. The most common reason for creating a new style is to specify a new pipe, tube, or hose diameter.

The following image demonstrates three different styles for flexible hose routes.

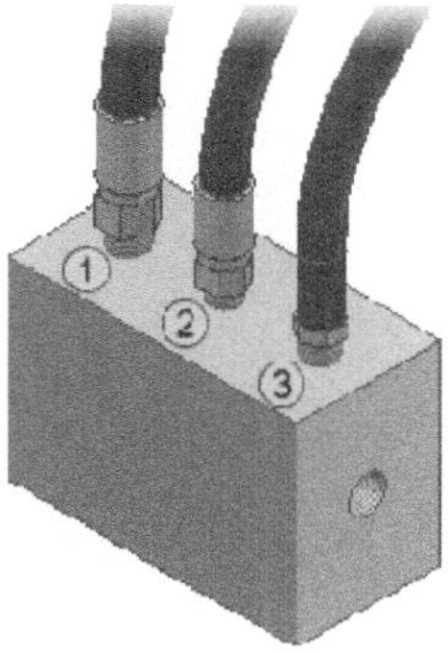

1. Flexible hose style, 1/2" nominal diameter.

2. Flexible hose style, 3/8" nominal diameter.

3. Flexible hose style, 3/8" nominal diameter. This style has no start or end fittings. The hose is connected to preplaced fittings.

Creating a Tube, Pipe, or Hose Style

You can create a new tube and pipe style, or edit an existing style from any level of the tube and pipe assembly, but not when the top-level assembly containing the Tube & Pipe Runs subassembly is active. The Tube & Pipe Styles dialog box contains settings to control both route and run properties.

Access

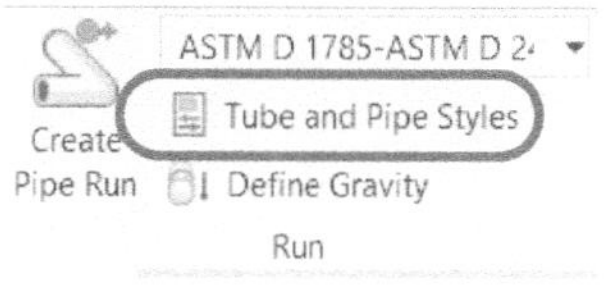

Ribbon: Tube and Pipe tab>Run panel

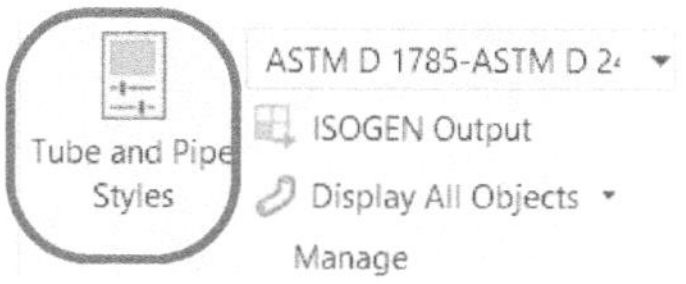

Ribbon: Pipe Run tab>Manage panel

Tube & Pipe Styles Dialog Box: Create New

To create a new tube and pipe style, click the New button in the Tube & Pipe Styles dialog box.

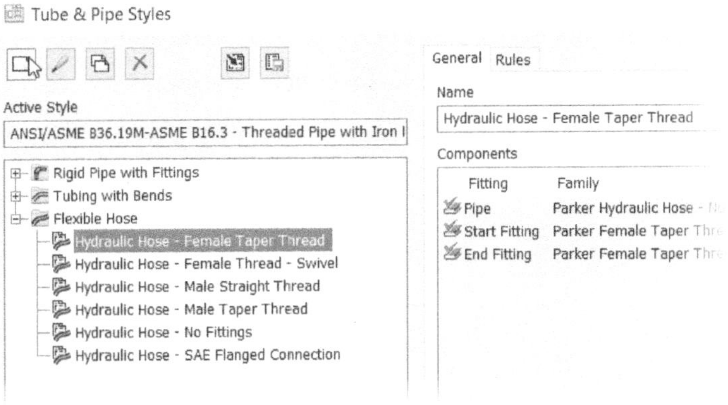

> **Copy an Existing Tube and Pipe Style**
>
> To use an existing tube and pipe style as the basis for a new style, first make the existing style the active style. In the Tube & Pipe Styles dialog box, select Copy. The copy is named the same as the original style with _Copy(#) following the name. Right- click the copy and select Edit to change the name and modify the components and other parameters for the new style.

Tube & Pipe Styles Dialog Box: General Tab

The following options are available in the Tube & Pipe Styles dialog box, in the General tab.

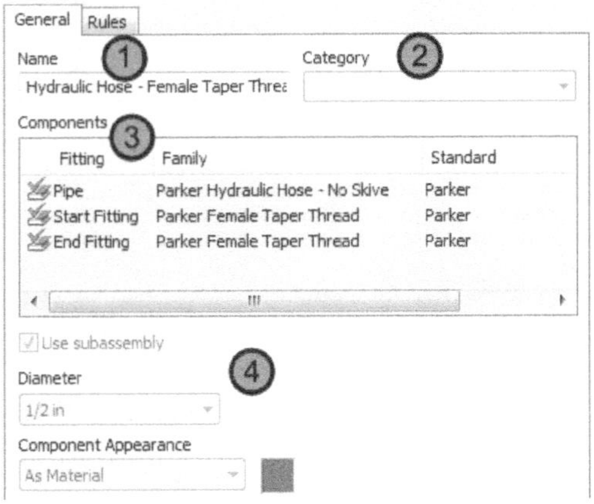

1. **Name -** Enter a name for your custom tube and pipe style.

2. **Category -** Set the category in which the style definition is organized. Leave this parameter blank to have the new style placed in the same category as the active style.

3. **Components -** Determine the fittings and other components that are used at connections when creating a tube and pipe run. Double-click on a row, or right-click and click Browse to select a component from a list of library parts matching your criteria.

4 Use these settings to override the settings that are established when selecting components and setting their standards in the components area.

Components Area

For components, you can select the conduit and default fittings for the current style. Both the conduit and fittings are generated from the Content Center libraries. You can select components from any library when you create or edit a style as long as the components have been authored using the Tube and Pipe authoring tool. The available components are filtered by the other parameters in the Tube & Pipe Styles dialog box.

- For a rigid pipe style, select pipe, coupling, 90° elbows, and 45° elbows if you specified 45° elbows in the General tab. Flanged and welded rigid pipe styles do not require a coupling.
- For a tube style, select pipe and coupling components.
- For a flexible hose style, select a hose, start fittings, and end fittings. You can suppress either or both fittings. You can specify whether or not each flexible hose with fittings is treated as a flat set of components or as a subassembly in the active run.
- All styles in the default template include appropriate conduit and fitting selections.

The following image demonstrates that both standard components and your custom published components are selectable in the library browser when searching for components.

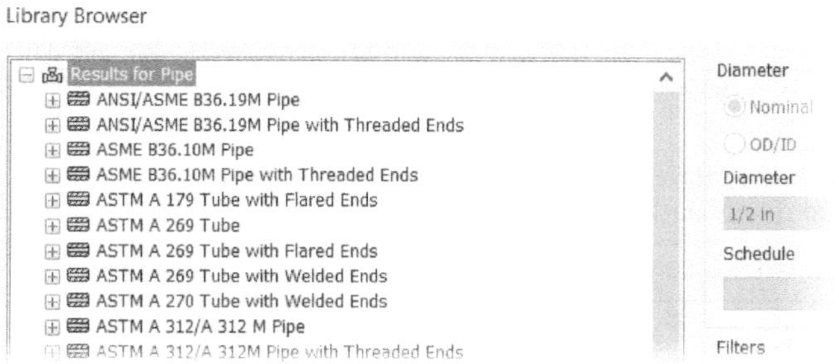

Diameter Parameter

The setting for the Diameter controls the diameter of the conduit in the active style.

Setting	Description
Diameter	Specifies the conduit (pipe, tube, or hose) dimensions. You can specify either a nominal diameter and schedule, or inner and outer diameter values. These values are opened from the published conduit part selected in the Fittings tab.

Rules Tab

Settings in the Rules tab control the minimum and maximum lengths for rigid pipe or tube segments in a run and the smallest length increment for segments. If the route type is tubing with bends, you must also specify a default radius for tube bends. When you populate a route, elbows and couplings are placed at the route node points, and pipe or tube segments connect these fittings. The minimum and maximum lengths prevent you from creating segments that cannot be manufactured. When the length of a segment is adjusted to engage the adjacent fittings, its length is changed by the increment setting so the ends of the segment fall in the engagement zones of the fittings.

Flexible hose styles permit for unlimited lengths. Rules define the minimum allowable bend radius and a round-up value for hose length in the assembly bill of materials.

The following image shows the Rules tab of the Tube & Pipe Styles dialog box.

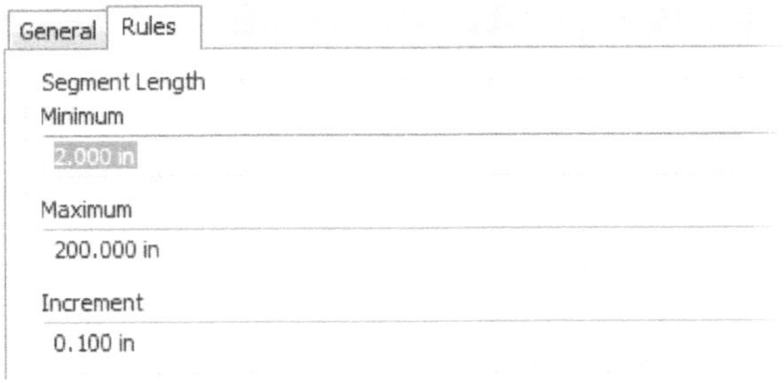

Flexible Hose Requirements

A style definition for a flexible hose includes the hose and optional start and end fittings. You can specify a start and an end fitting, just a start fitting, or no fittings. The number of fittings you specify in the style affects how you place the hose in your model as described in the table below:

Fittings Defined in the Style	Placement Procedure
Start and End	Specify the location of the start and end fittings. The route is automatically created. You do not have to add any route points; however, you can add points to refine the route.
Start Only	Specify the location of the start fitting and then select any number of additional points to specify the hose route.
None	Select a start point and any number of additional points to specify the hose route.

A flexible hose with fittings is often identified as a single component in an assembly and not as a separate hose part and fittings. In the style definition, you can specify to place each flexible hose route in a subassembly below the active run rather than as separate components in the run itself. You can use the subassembly to help organize and identify the flexible hose in a parts list or BOM.

Process: Creating a New Tube and Pipe Style

The following steps describe how to create a new tube and pipe style.

1. Start the Tube and Pipe Styles tool.
2. In the Tube & Pipe Styles dialog box, select New.
3. Enter a name for the new style, and specify other parameters as required in the General tab including the fittings to be used.
4. Specify rules in the Rules tab.
5. Save the new style in the default category, or specify a new category in the General tab.
6. Right-click on the new style and click Active. Close the Tube & Pipe Styles dialog box and create your route.

Configuring a Self-Draining Style

In your design work, you need to be able to create self-draining tube and pipe designs. You can author tube and pipe components with angles other than 45° and 90°. You need the option and capability to define a style as self-draining and to edit a tube and pipe style's custom angle. These options and capabilities are part of the Tube and Pipe Style Editor.

The following image shows the Tube & Pipe Styles dialog box where a new style is being defined.

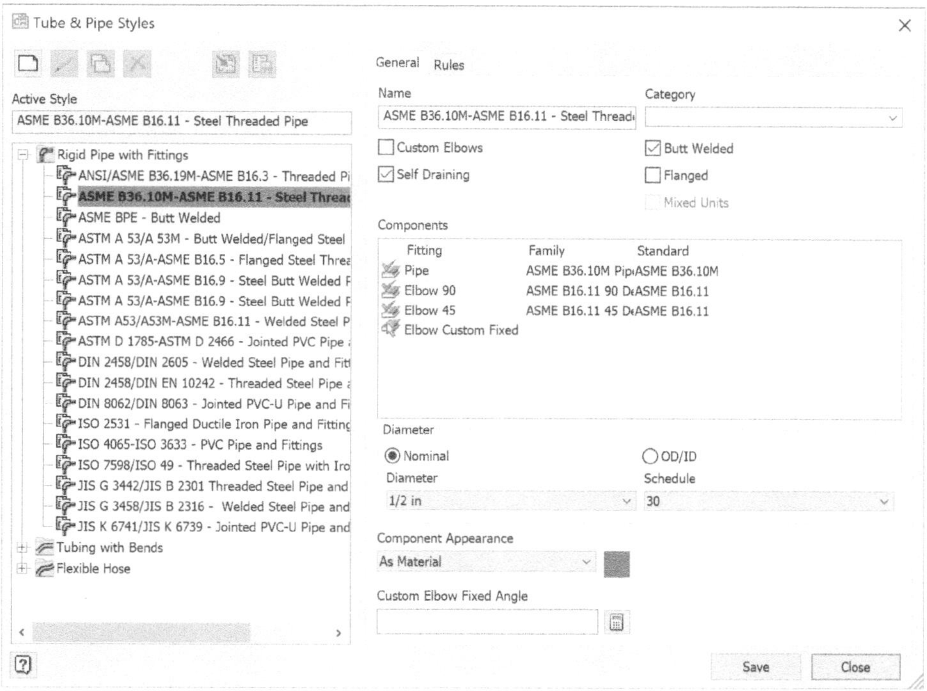

Tube and Pipe Styles

The Tube & Pipe Styles dialog box enables you to define a self-draining style when creating a new style. In the General tab, when Self Draining (1) is selected, a new option - Elbow Custom (2) - displays in the Fitting column. You right-click on Elbow Custom and then browse the available custom fittings previously published to the Content Center. In addition to the new elbow option, the Self Draining option enables the display of the Custom Elbow Angle field, and access to the Tube and Pipe Calculator. Clicking the Calculate the Slope angle button (3), located to the right of the Custom Elbow Angle field, displays the calculator.

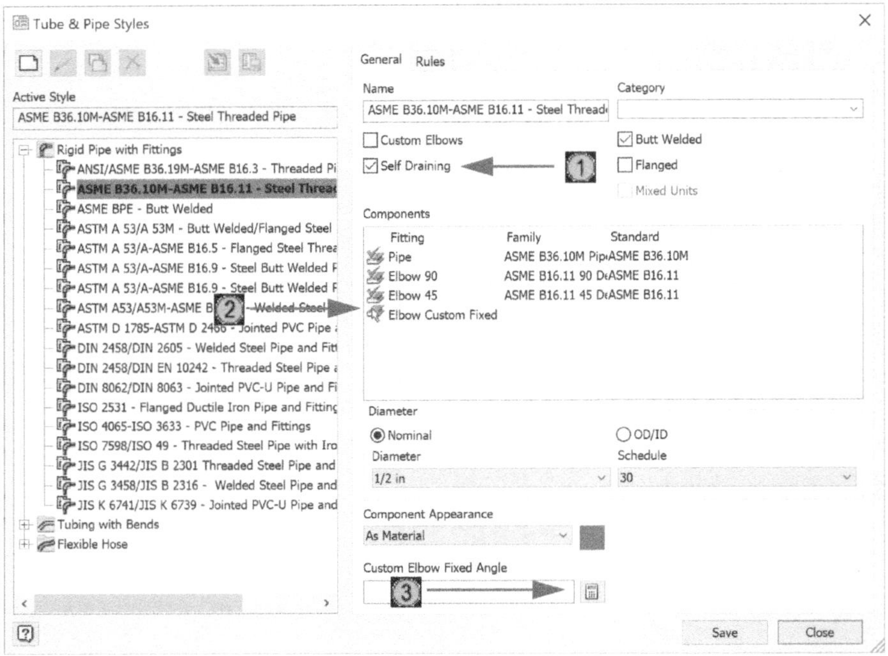

Library Browser

When you are defining the components in a new tube and pipe style, you can browse and search through the library by right-clicking on the fitting listed under Components, and then clicking Browse in the shortcut menu.

The Filters area in the Library Browser dialog box enables you to filter the list by an exact angle or a range of angles. These filter tools and options are oriented vertically on the right side of the dialog box. You use the Angle Calculator to calculate angle and slope based on other parameters.

In the following image, the Tube & Pipe Angle Calculator dialog box is shown displayed over the Library Browser dialog box after being accessed by clicking the identified calculator.

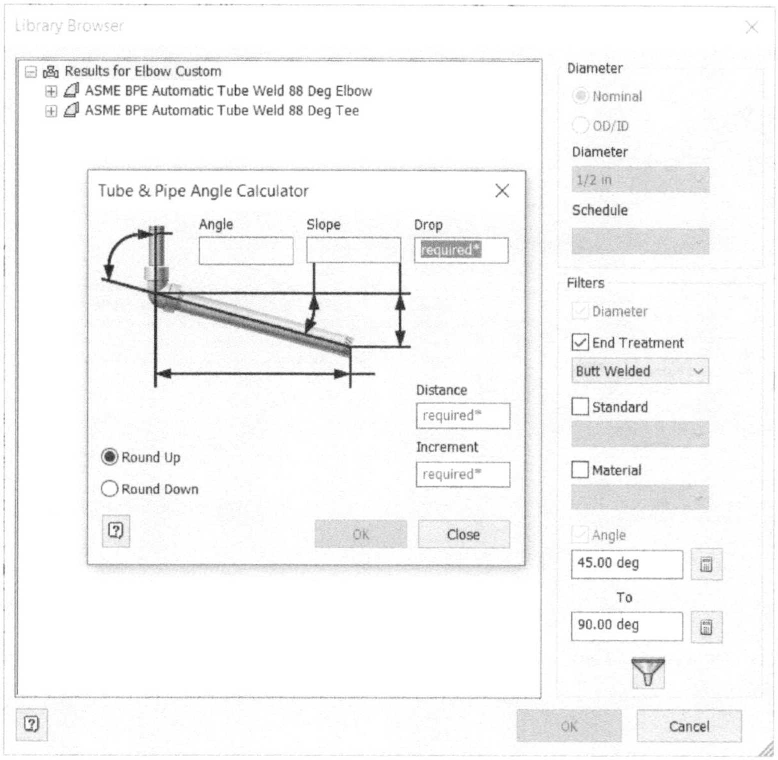

Process: Configuring a Self-Draining Style

The following steps describe how to configure a self-draining tube and pipe style.

1. Start the Tube and Pipe Styles tool.
2. In the Tube & Pipe Styles dialog box, select New.
3. Enter a name for the new style, and specify Self Draining and other parameters as required in the General tab including the pipe and fitting components to be used.
4. Define the self-draining elbow fitting, Elbow Custom. You can browse the available custom fittings previously published to Content Center, or use the Tube and Pipe Calculator to calculate the slope angle interactively.
5. Specify rules in the Rules tab.
6. Save the new style in the default category, or specify a new category in the General tab.
7. Right-click on the new style and click Active. Close the Tube& Pipe Styles dialog box, and create your self-draining route.

Custom Elbow Styles

The styles which support the use of custom elbows (Custom Elbow 45 and Custom Angle 90) are available in the Tube and Pipe Styles dialog box.

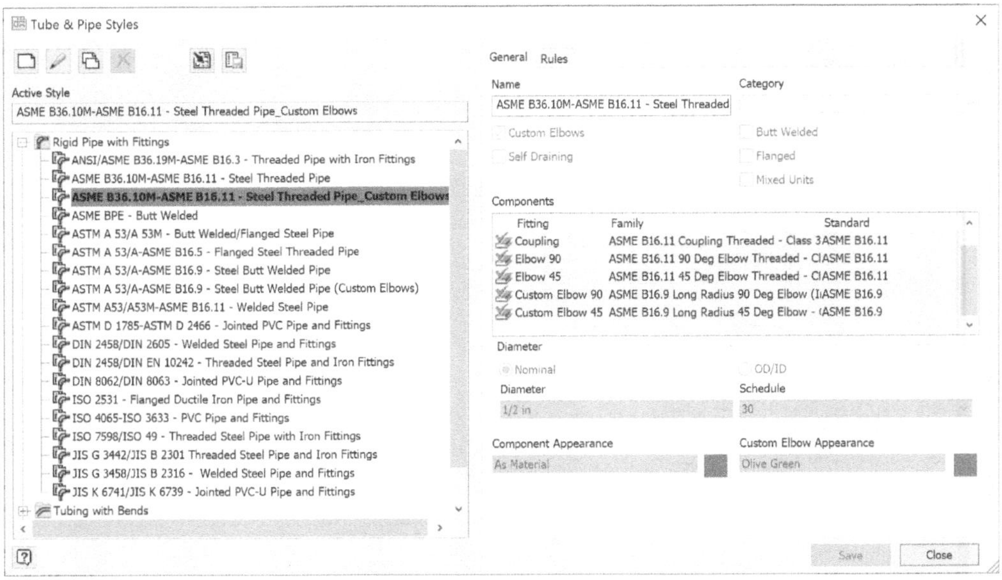

To highlight which elbows need to be custom made, you can change the Custom Elbow Appearance under General settings.

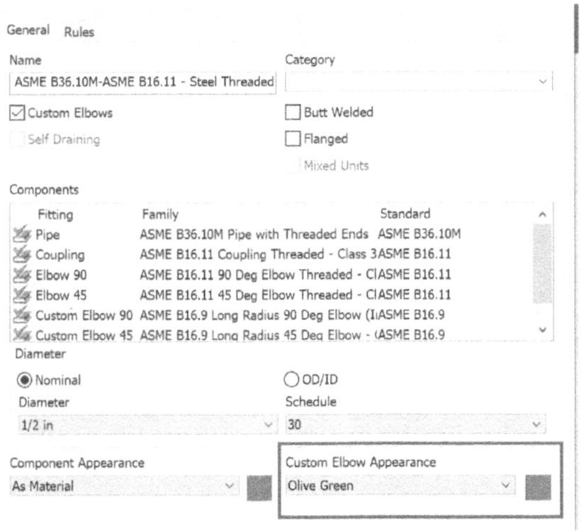

The Custom Elbows library and the Custom Return Bends library are present in the Content Center. Parts from both libraries are supported and can be authored and published.

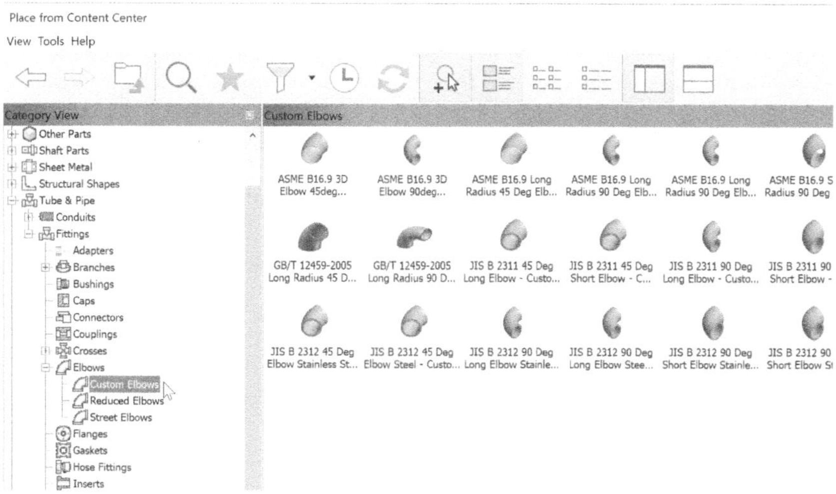

Place from Content Center
View Tools Help
Category View
Custom Elbows
Other Parts
Shaft Parts
Sheet Metal
Structural Shapes
Tube & Pipe
Conduits
Fittings
Adapters
Branches
Bushings
Caps
Connectors
Couplings
Crosses
Elbows
Custom Elbows
Reduced Elbows
Street Elbows
Flanges
Gaskets
Hose Fittings
Inserts
ASME B16.9 3D Elbow 45deg...
ASME B16.9 3D Elbow 90deg...
ASME B16.9 Long Radius 45 Deg Elb...
ASME B16.9 Long Radius 90 Deg Elb...
ASME B16.9 Long Radius 90 Deg Elb...
GB/T 12459-2005 Long Radius 45 D...
GB/T 12459-2005 Long Radius 90 D...
JIS B 2311 45 Deg Long Elbow - Custo...
JIS B 2311 45 Deg Short Elbow - C...
JIS B 2311 90 Deg Long Elbow - Custo...
JIS B 2312 45 Deg Elbow Stainless St...
JIS B 2312 45 Deg Elbow Steel - Custo...
JIS B 2312 90 Deg Long Elbow Stainle...
JIS B 2312 90 Deg Long Elbow Stee...
JIS B 2312 90 Deg Short Elbow Stainle...

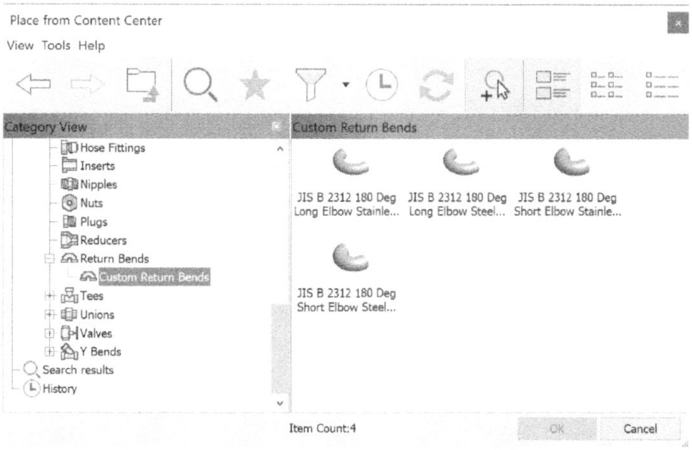

Place from Content Center
View Tools Help
Category View
Custom Return Bends
Hose Fittings
Inserts
Nipples
Nuts
Plugs
Reducers
Return Bends
Custom Return Bends
Tees
Unions
Valves
Y Bends
Search results
History
JIS B 2312 180 Deg Long Elbow Stainle...
JIS B 2312 180 Deg Long Elbow Steel...
JIS B 2312 180 Deg Short Elbow Stainle...
JIS B 2312 180 Deg Short Elbow Steel...
Item Count:4
OK
Cancel

Configuring Styles in Templates

The Tube & Pipe Runs subassembly is created from the default template file piping runs.iam. The template defines the available styles. Because you can open the Tube & Pipe Styles dialog box only after you create the Tube & Pipe Runs subassembly, adding and modifying styles in the template follows a different workflow from that used to modify other Autodesk Inventor templates. You cannot save a tube and pipe style to an external library. Styles are stored only in the template assembly file.

In the following image, the 25mm Self Draining style is shown in the Custom category of the Tube & Pipe Styles dialog box.

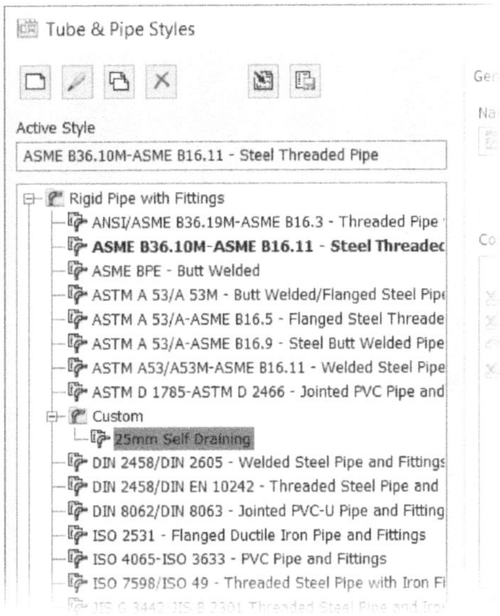

Process: Adding and Modifying Styles in the Default Template

The following steps give an overview of adding new styles or changing existing styles in the default template.

1. Create a new standard Autodesk Inventor assembly.
2. In the Environments tab, in the Begin panel, click Tube and Pipe.
3. Save the pipe run using the default names. In the Create Tube and Pipe Run dialog box, note the location of the Tube & Pipe Runs subassembly.
4. Activate the Tube & Pipe Runs subassembly. In the browser, right-click on Run01 and click Delete Run.
5. Make any edits to existing styles or add new styles to the Tube & Pipe Runs subassembly. Select a style from the Style list to be the default style when you create new Tube & Pipe Runs subassemblies.
6. Return to the top-level assembly. In the browser, right-click on the Tube & Pipe Runs subassembly. Click iProperties. In the Occurrence tab, clear the Adaptive check box.

7. Save the top-level assembly. Close the application.

8. Rename the existing *piping runs.iam* file to *piping runs_ORIGINAL.iam* (or similar) in the Design Data/Tube and Pipe folder under the Autodesk Inventor installation folder. Renaming the file keeps it in the folder, which enables you to easily return to it if required.

9. Rename the Tube & Pipe Runs subassembly as *piping runs.iam*. Copy or move the file to the Design Data/Tube and Pipe folder.

> Back up the default *piping runs.iam* template file before you create a new template.

Exercise: Create Custom Styles

In this exercise, you will create a new flexible hose style from parts published to a custom library.

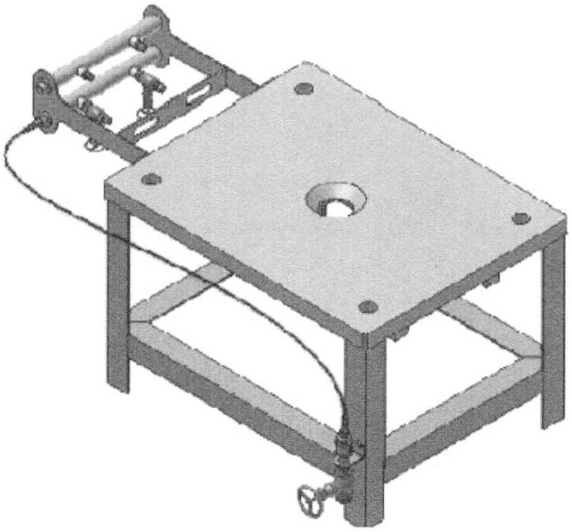

The completed exercise

Note: If you have completed the Publish to The Content Center exercise in the Creating Library Content lesson in this chapter, you can skip the exercise steps in Setup and Load Library and use what you have already created.

Setup and Load Library

In this section of the exercise, you will set up Autodesk Inventor so you can complete the exercise steps of creating a new flexible hose style. You will load a custom library and set a project file current.

1. Start the Autodesk Inventor software but do not open any files. Close any open files.
2. In the Get Started tab, in the Launch panel, click Projects.

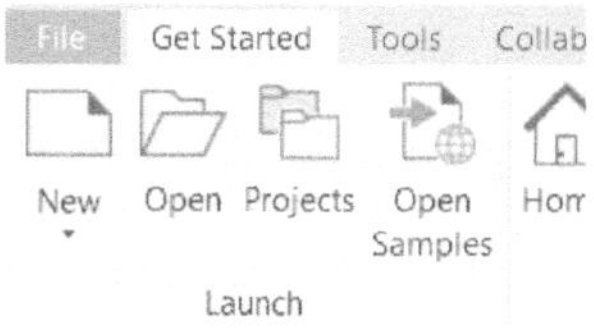

3. In the Projects dialog box, select Configure Content Center Libraries.

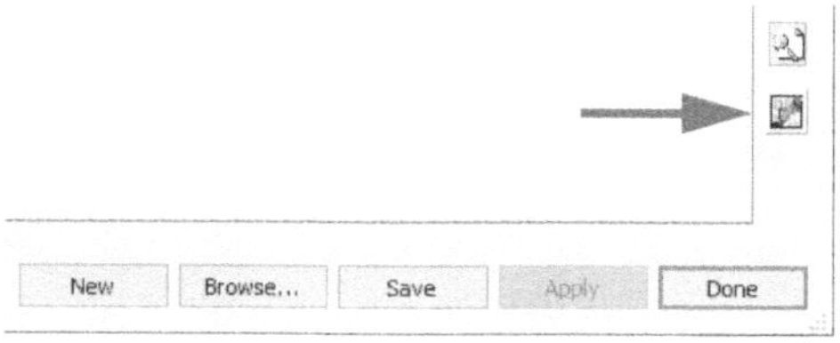

4. In the Configure Libraries dialog box:
   - Click the hyperlink text for Location of Libraries to open a Windows Explorer window viewing that folder.
   - Click Cancel to close the Configure Libraries dialog box.

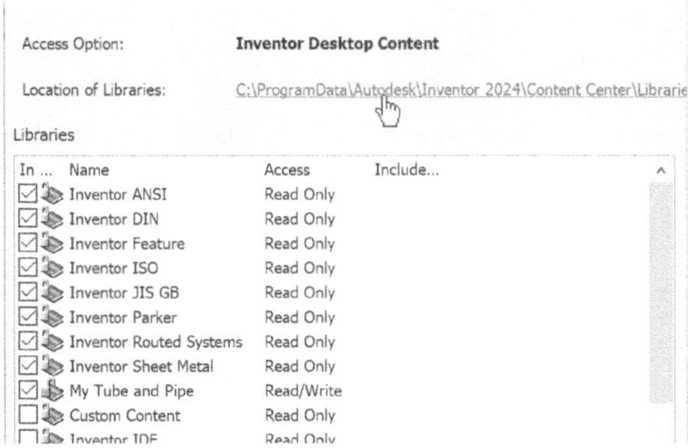

5. Open another session of Windows Explorer.
   - Navigate to the install directory of the exercise files.
   - Click to open the Libraries folder in the exercise directory.
   - Click to open the Create Custom Styles folder in the exercise Libraries folder.
6. If the library My Tube and Pipe already exists in the ProgramData folder, go to the next step. Otherwise, copy *My Tube and Pipe.idcl* from the Create Custom Styles folder to the window opened by the hyperlink in a previous step.
7. Close the Windows Explorer windows.
8. To add this exercise's project file to Autodesk Inventor:
   - In the Projects dialog box, click Browse.
   - In the Choose Project File dialog box, navigate to the directory with the exercise files and open *Create Custom Styles.ipj*.

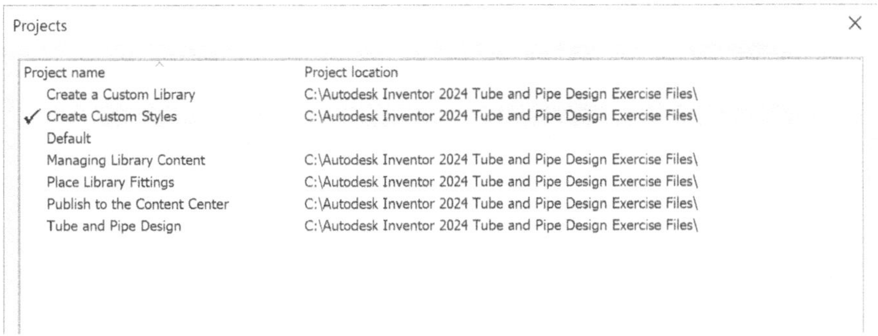

9. In the Projects dialog box click Configure Content Center Libraries.

10. In the Configure Libraries dialog box, review the list of libraries that are set to be in use when this project file is active.

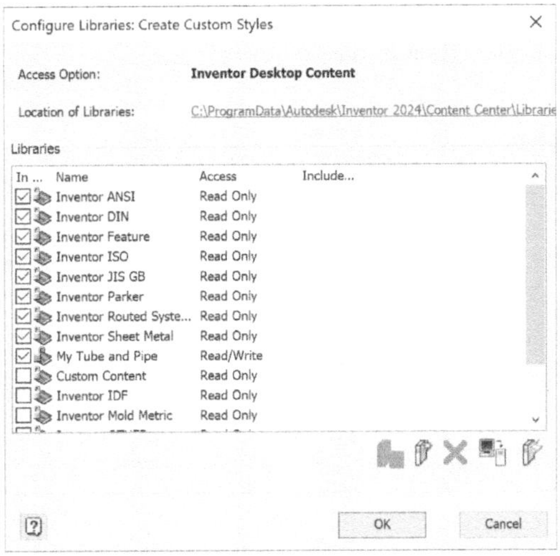

11. Close the Configure Libraries dialog box and the Projects dialog box.

Create a Style

In this portion of the exercise, you will create a new style based on your published components. You will use the style to complete a route.

1. Open *Fittings Custom Style.iam*.

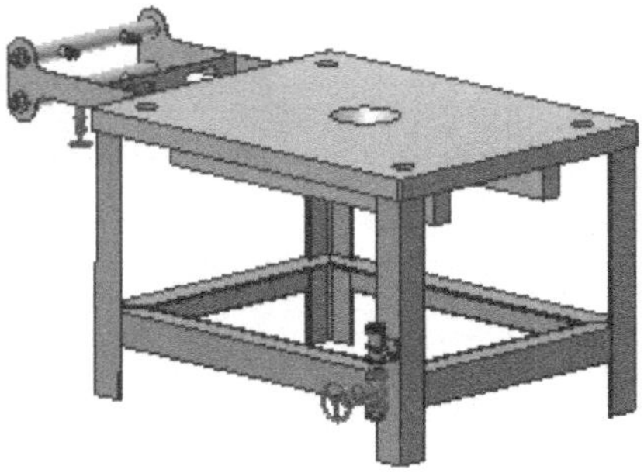

2. In the Environments tab, in the Begin panel, click Tube and Pipe. Click OK to accept the default names and locations.

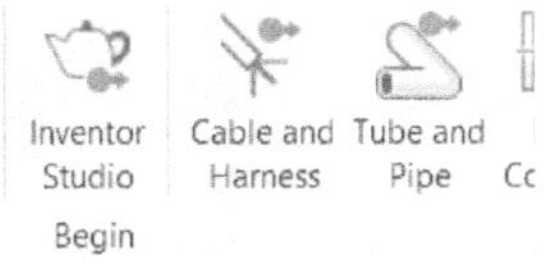

3. In the ribbon, in the Pipe Run tab, in the Manage panel, click Tube and Pipe Styles.

4. In the Tube & Pipe Styles dialog box, from the Style list, expand Flexible Hose, select Hydraulic Hose - Male Taper Thread.
   - Click Copy.
   - From the Style List, right click Hydraulic Hose - Male Taper Thread_Copy(1), and click Edit.

5. In the General tab, for Name, enter **Flexible Water Line - 1/2"**.

6. Under Components, for Pipe, right-click in the Standard column. Click Browse.

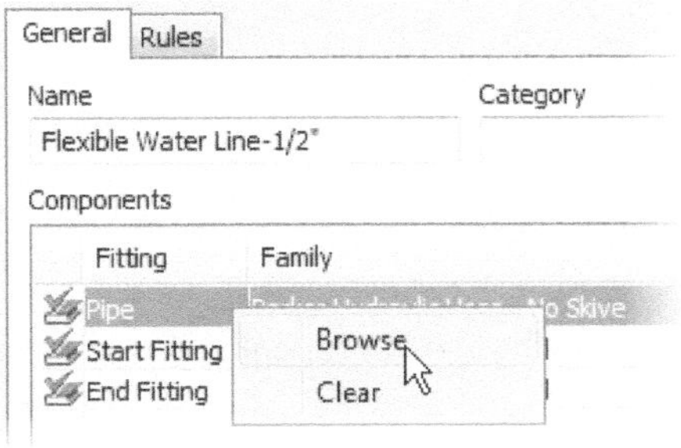

7. In the Library Browser, expand Clear Hose. Select 10144. Click OK.

8. In the Tube & Pipe Styles dialog box, click Save.

9. In the Active Style list, right-click on Flexible Water Line - 1/2". Click Active. Close the Tube & Pipe Styles dialog box.

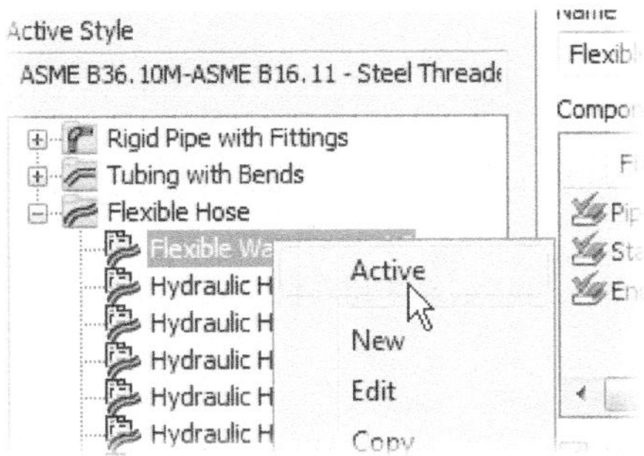

10. In the Pipe Run tab, in the Route panel, click New Route. Click OK to accept the default file names and locations.

11. In the Route tab, in the Create panel, click Route.

12. Connect the pipe thread end (default connection) of the start fitting to the connection point on the bushing on the inlet valve.

13. Connect the end fitting to the circular edge on the manifold opening that is highlighted in the following image.

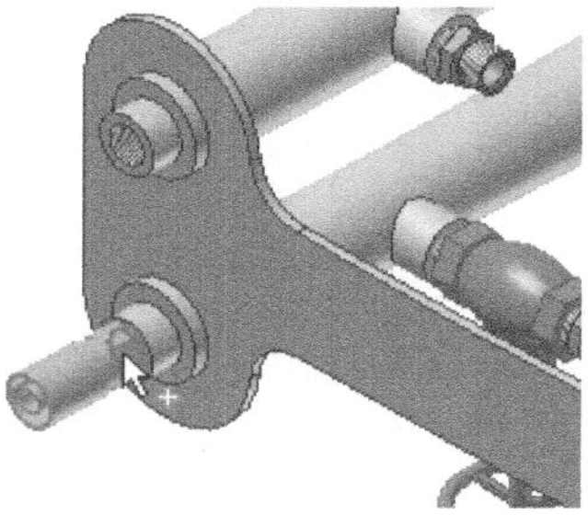

14. The route is populated automatically. Right-click in the graphics window background. Click Done.

15. Right-click in the graphics window background. Click Finish Edit.

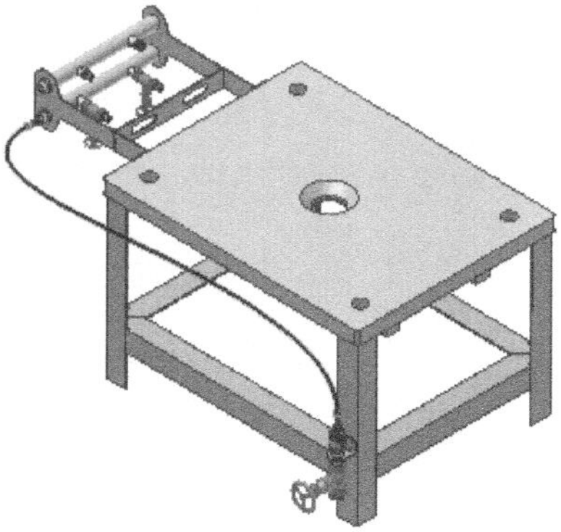

16. If prompted, click OK to accept the default name for the conduit file names.

Note: If you right-click on the main Tube & Pipe Runs and open Tube & Pipe Settings, you can turn on Prompt for conduit file names under Application Settings to be able to enter custom conduit file names.

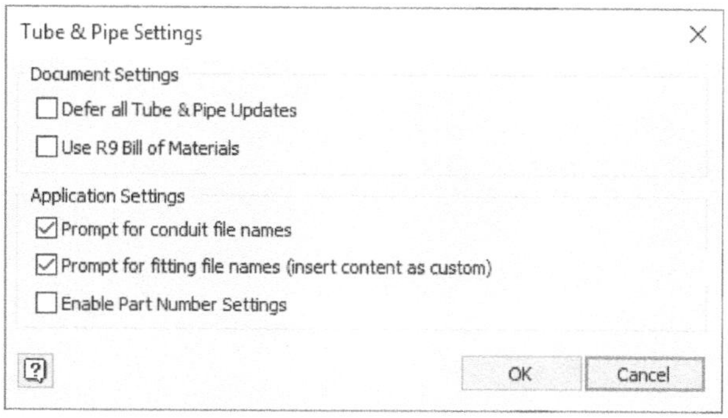

17. Close all files without saving changes.

Exercise: Create Self-Draining Styles

In this exercise, you author and then publish a custom elbow component to a custom library and then create a new self-draining tube and pipe style.

The completed exercise

Setup and Load Library

In this section of the exercise, you will set up Autodesk Inventor so you can complete the exercise steps of authoring and then publishing a custom elbow component to a custom library and then creating a new self-draining tube and pipe style. You will load a custom library and set a project file current.

1. Start the Autodesk Inventor software but do not open any files. Close any open files.

2. In the Get Started tab, in the Launch panel, click Projects.

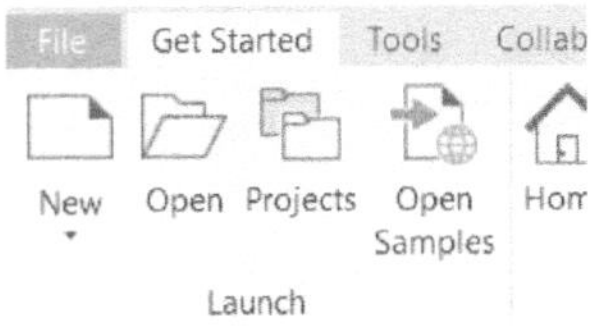

3. In the Projects dialog box, select Configure Content Center Libraries.

4. In the Configure Libraries dialog box:
   - Click the hyperlink text for Location of Libraries to open a Windows Explorer window viewing that folder.
   - Click Cancel to close the Configure Libraries dialog box.

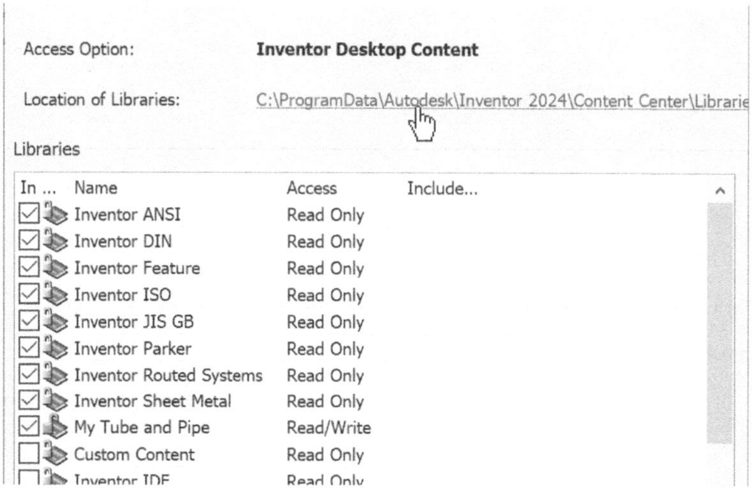

5. Open another session of Windows Explorer.
   - Navigate to the install directory of the exercise files.
   - Click to open the Libraries folder in the exercise directory.
6. Copy *Self-Draining.idcl* from the Library folder to the window opened by the hyperlink in a previous step.
7. Close the Windows Explorer windows.
8. To add this exercise's project file to Autodesk Inventor:
   - In the Projects dialog box, click Browse.
   - In the Choose Project File dialog box, navigate to the directory with the exercise files and open *Create Self-Draining Styles.ipj.*

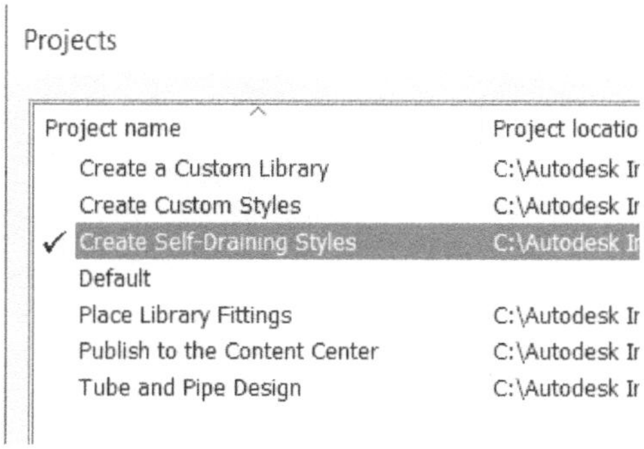

9. In the Projects dialog box, select Configure Content Center Libraries.

10. In the Configure Libraries dialog box, review the list of libraries that are set to be in use when this project file is active.

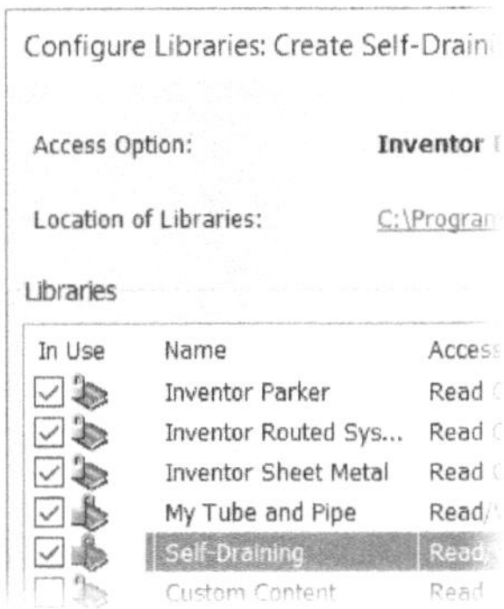

11. Close the Configure Libraries dialog box and the Projects dialog box.

Author a Custom Elbow

In this section of the exercise, you will author a custom elbow for a self-draining system.

1. Open *Self Draining Elbow.ipt*.

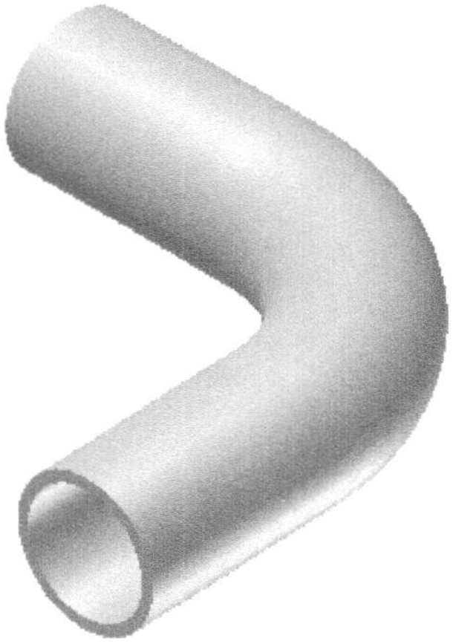

2. To view the values of the sketch:

- In the browser, expand Sweep1.
- Under Sweep1, click Sketch1.
- Review the values of the sketch.

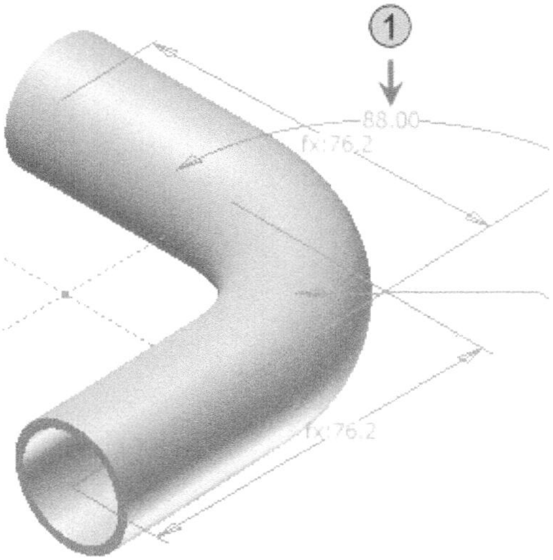

3. To start the authoring process:

- In the Manage tab, in the Author panel, click Tube and Pipe.
- In the Tube & Pipe Authoring dialog box, under Type, select Elbows (1).
- For End Treatment, select Butt Welded (2).
- For Parameter, under Table Mapping, select Nominal Size (3).

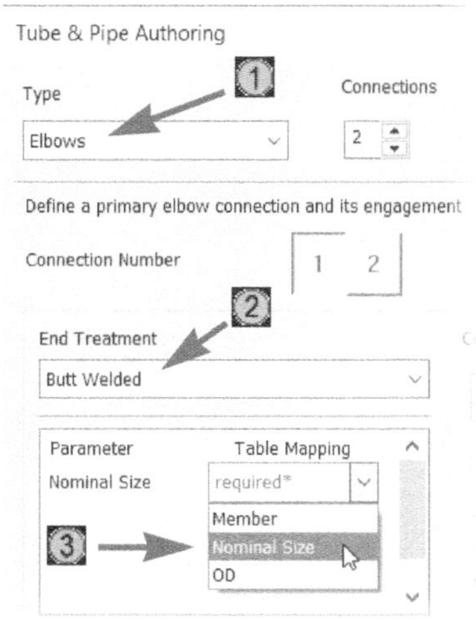

4. To define the connection point:
   - In the Tube & Pipe Authoring dialog box, under Connection, click Point (1).
   - In the graphics window, select the end diameter of the elbow (2).

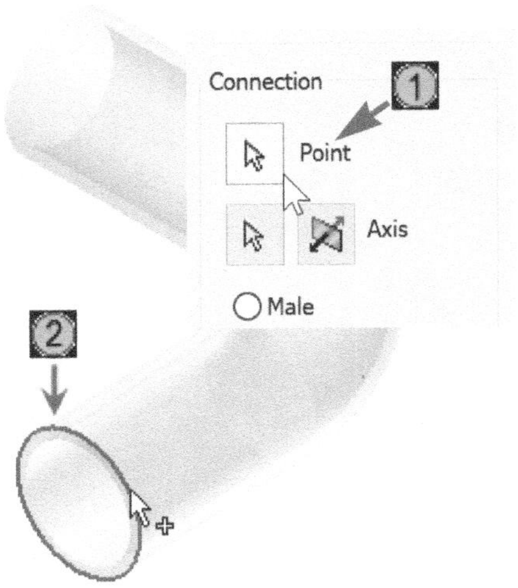

5. To define the axis of the connection:
   - Under Connection, click Neutral (1).
   - Click Selects a work axis or circular edge to define the connection axis (2).
   - Select the inside diameter of the elbow (3).
   - If required, reverse the direction of the connection so the arrow is pointing away from the elbow (4).

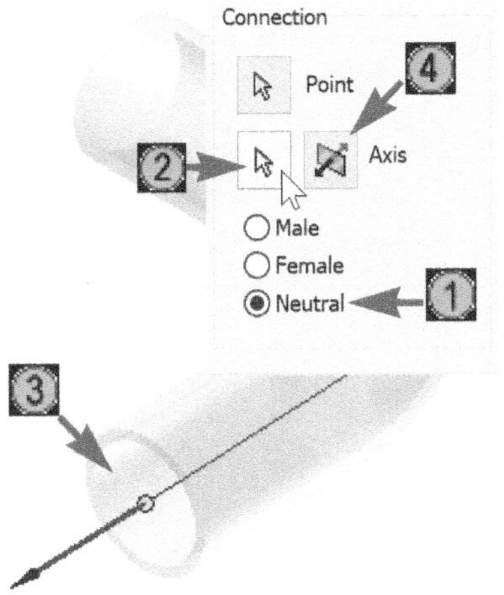

6. To define the second connection:
   - In the Tube & Pipe Authoring dialog box, for Connection Number, click 2.
   - Select Butt Welded in the End Treatment list.
   - Repeat the previous two steps to define the second connection, but on the other end.
7. To complete the authoring process:
   - In the Tube & Pipe Authoring dialog box, click OK.
   - The Authoring Result dialog box displays.
   - Click OK.

Publish a Custom Elbow

In this section of the exercise, you will publish the custom elbow to the Content Center.

1. To start to publish the custom elbow:
   - In the Manage tab, in the Content Center panel, click Publish Part.
   - In the Publish Guide dialog box, under Select Library to Publish to, select Self- Draining.
   - Click Next.

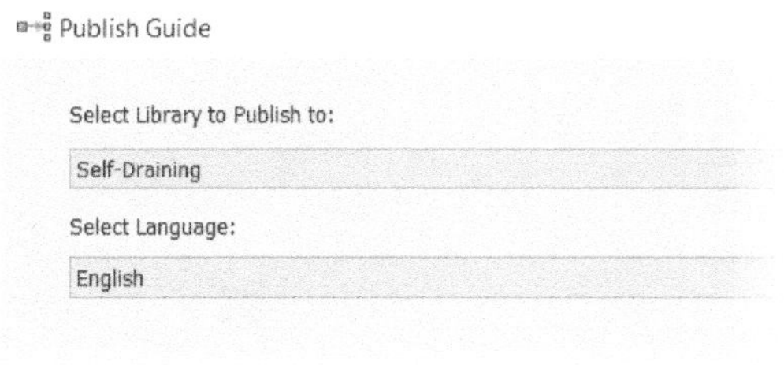

2. In the Publish Guide dialog box:
   - Verify that Elbows is selected.
   - Click Next.
3. In the Publish Guide dialog box, under Map Family Columns to Category Parameters:
   - For NominalSize[1], under Table Columns, select Nominal Size if it is not already selected.
   - For NominalSize[2], under Table Columns, select Nominal Size if it is not already selected.
   - Click Next.

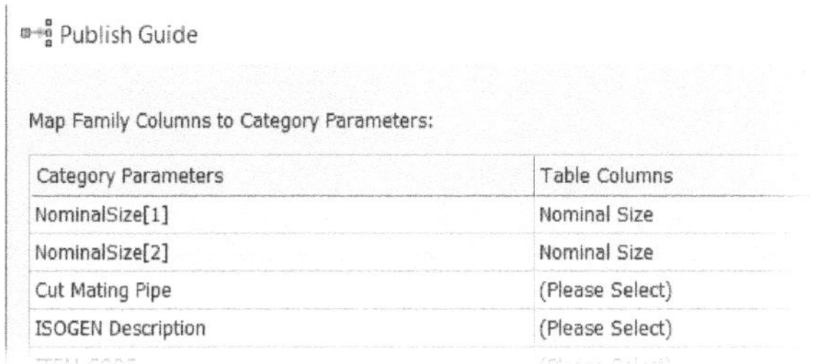

4. To Define Family Key Columns:
   - If Nominal Size is already configured as a Key Column, click Next to continue.
   - If Nominal Size is not configured as a Key Column, in Table Columns, select Nominal Size.
   - Click the arrow to place in Key Columns.
   - Click Next.
5. To set family properties:
   - Under Family Name, enter **88 deg Self Draining Elbow**.
   - For Family Description, enter **Custom Self Draining Elbow**.
   - For Standard Organization, enter **Custom**.
   - Click Next.

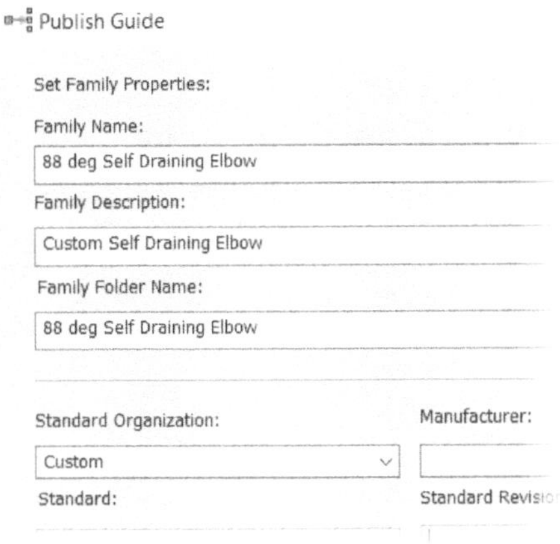

6. In the Publish Guide:
   - Click Publish.
   - In the Publish dialog box, click OK.

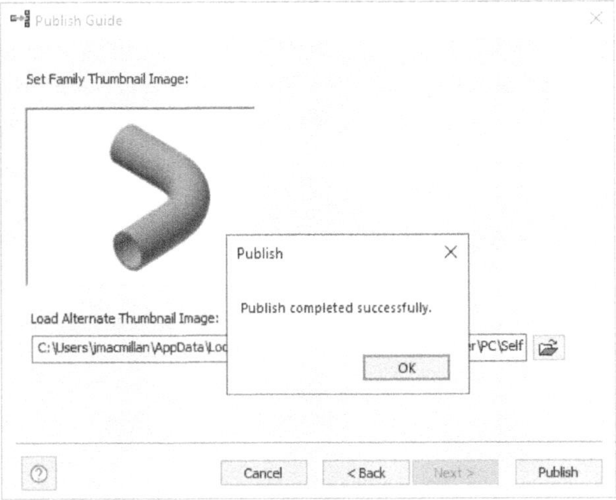

7. To verify publication to the Content Center:

- In the Manage tab, in the Content Center panel, click Editor.
- In the Content Center dialog box, for Library View, select Self-Draining.
- Under Category View, expand Tube & Pipe.
- Expand Fittings and select Elbows.
- Select the 88 deg Self Draining Elbow to preview the family table.
- Click Done to close the Content Center Editor.

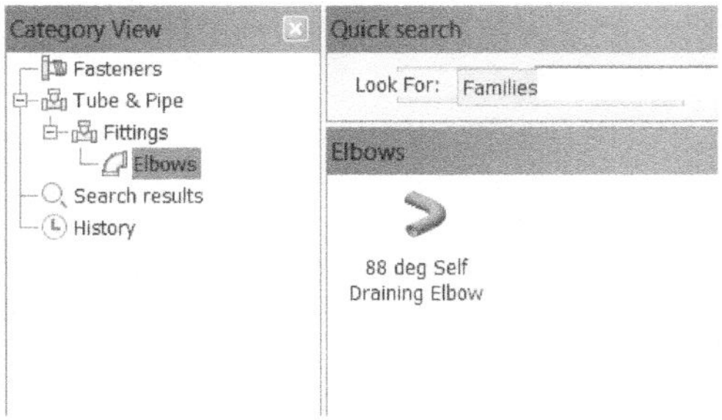

8. Close all files without saving.

Create a Custom Self-Draining Style

In this section of the exercise, you will create a new self-draining tube and pipe style.

1. Open *Self Draining Styles.iam.*

2. To create a pipe run:

- In the Environments tab, in the Begin panel, click Tube and Pipe.
- In the Create Tube & Pipe Run dialog box, click OK.

3. To start to create a self-draining style:
   - In the Pipe Run tab, in the Manage panel, click Tube and Pipe Styles.
   - In the Tube & Pipe Styles dialog box, click New.

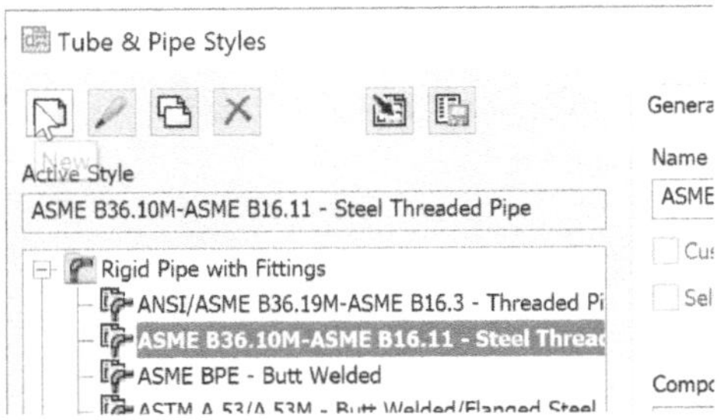

4. To define settings for the new self-draining style:
   - In the Tube & Pipe Styles dialog box, in the General Tab, in the Name field, enter **25mm Self Draining**.
   - For Category, enter **Custom**.
   - Select Butt Welded.
   - Select Self Draining.

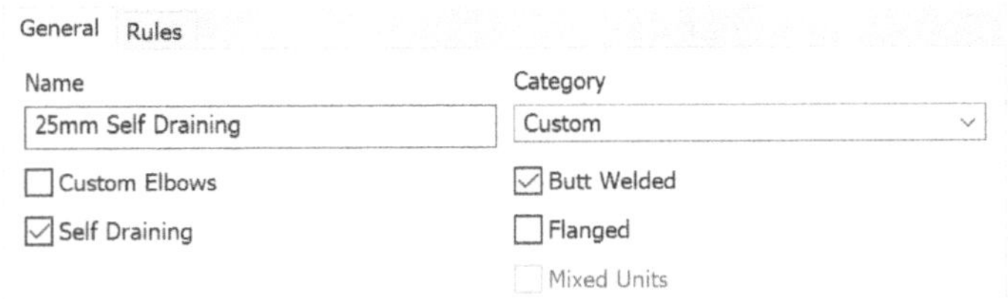

5. To define the pipe component of the style:
   - Under Components, in the Fitting column, right-click on Pipe and click Browse.
   - In the Library Browser, expand Results for Pipe.
   - Select DIN 2458 Pipe. Click OK.

6. To set the diameter of the pipe:
   - In the Tube & Pipe Styles dialog box, under Diameter, in the Diameter drop-down list, select 25 mm.

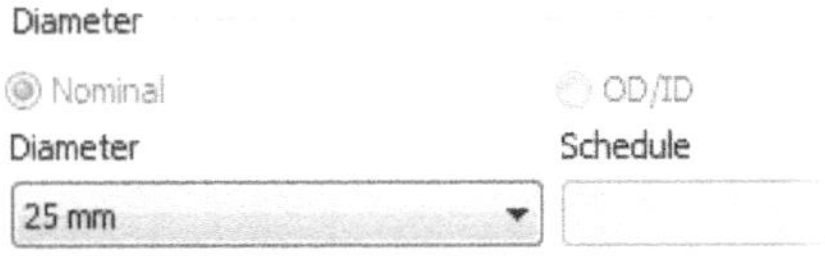

7. To define the Elbow 90 component:

- In the Fitting column, double-click on Elbow 90.
- In the Library Browser, click DIN 2605 90 Deg Elbow Type 3.
- Click OK.

8. To define the self-draining elbow:

- In the Fitting column, double-click on Elbow Custom.
- View the options in the Library Browser.

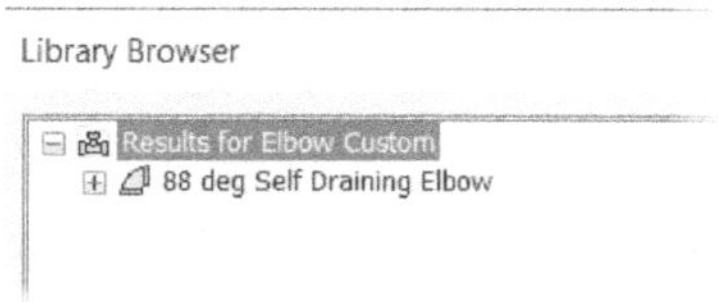

9. Select 88 deg Self Draining Elbow and click OK.

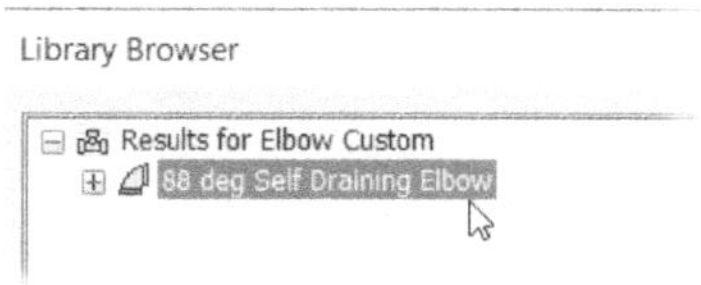

10. To define the rules for the Pipe style:

- In the Tube & Pipe Styles dialog box, click the Rules tab.
- Under Segment Length, for Minimum, enter **20mm**.
- For Maximum, enter **6m**.
- For Gap, enter **2mm**.
- Clear the checkmark for Display Gap.

11. To save the style, in the Tube & Pipe Styles dialog box, click Save.

12. In the Tube & Pipe Styles dialog box, under Active Style, verify the Custom folder and new pipe style are present. Click Close.

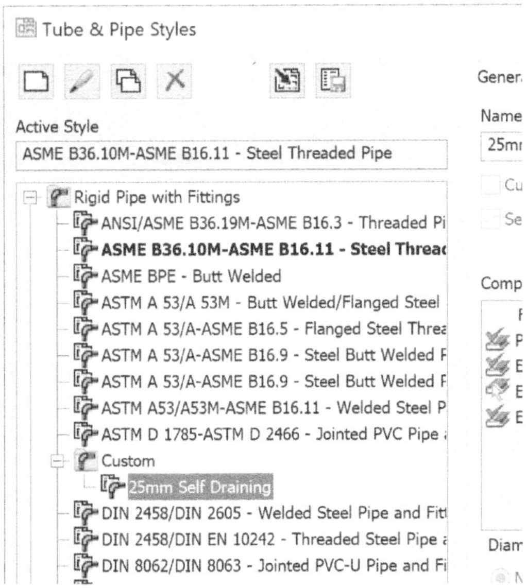

13. To set the custom style current:

- In the Pipe Run tab, in the Manage panel, review the current style.
- In the list, select 25mm Self Draining.

14. Close all files without saving changes.

Chapter Summary

In this chapter, you learned the tools and features to manage your library of parts. This included taking advantage of custom libraries, custom parts, and custom iParts to save time and help you to maintain an efficient design process. You also learned how to use the Content Center to store and reuse your custom parts, and how to create and use custom tube and pipe styles in order to increase your drawing productivity.

Having completed this chapter, you can:

- Manage the libraries that are included in the Content Center as well as your own libraries of tube and pipe components.
- Author and publish your own tube and pipe content.
- Manage the properties and settings of published tube and pipe content.
- Create new styles using published content.

Chapter 5

Documenting Tube and Pipe Assemblies

In this chapter, you learn how to document tube and pipe assemblies in drawings. You also learn how tube and pipe runs are represented in the assembly bill of materials, how to structure tube and pipe parts lists, and how to create bending machine or ISOGEN output files.

Objectives

After completing this chapter, you will be able to:

- Manage the amount of assembly data that gets loaded into memory and is visible in drawing views through the use of model state representations.
- Document tube and pipe assemblies with assembly design view representations and drawings.
- Export tube and pipe design data to create bending machine or ISOGEN files.

Lesson: Representing Tube and Pipe Designs

Overview

This lesson describes the tools and techniques for managing the amount of assembly data that is loaded into memory, and establishing what is visible in drawing views of tube and pipe designs.

When you work on large or complex assembly designs, you do not want your productivity to be compromised when the assembly file loads a large number of parts into memory that are not relevant to your immediate tasks or to the drawing view. By learning how to set and change an assembly's level of detail, you free up memory on your computer so it is available for your essential creation and manipulation tasks. You can also benefit from the use of different levels of detail configurations for the generation of drawing views.

Through learning how to represent parts as simple bounding shapes by substituting a derived assembly, you can simplify your design and free up memory. You simplify the less relevant components around the design area of focus. These simplified representations are helpful both during the process of design creation and during the process of creating drawing documentation.

In the following set of images, different piping aspects of a set of processing equipment are currently being designed. While the intent is to create, validate, and document the entire design, there are many areas of the design that do not require other aspects of the design to be visible when creating or documenting that area. Other areas of the design need to be visible, but a simplified outline of the parts is all that is required. The various tools and techniques for working in assemblies make switching back and forth between different degrees of detail quick and easy.

In the following image of the assembly, all aspects of the assembly are loaded and set to display their assigned materials. In this case, 1,442 occurrences of components display after opening 443 different files. In the second image, because a specific area of the design is being worked on, representation of the assembly was changed so that only 329 occurrences of components display after having to open only 231 files. Not only do these representations improve performance, they also change the material display to make visual identification easier.

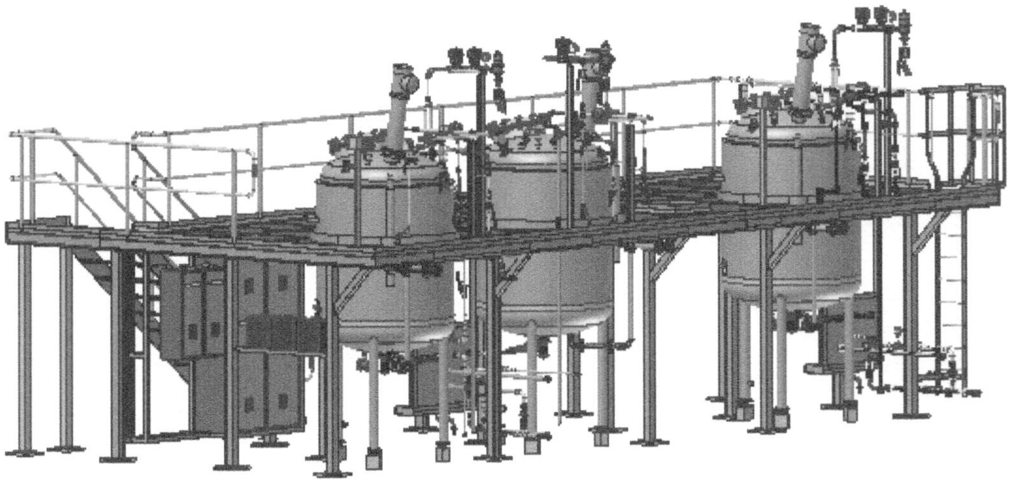

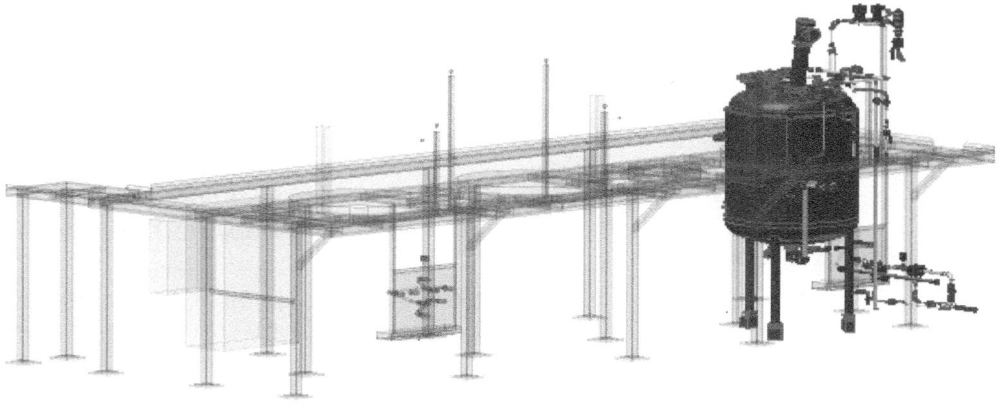

Objectives

After completing this lesson, you will be able to:

- Describe the purpose, types, and location of representations.
- Explain the purpose and characteristics of model states.
- Create, save, and activate your own custom model states.
- Explain the purpose of a substitute model state.
- Describe the process for creating a substitute model state.

About Representations

In the assembly modeling process, the number of unique parts and part instances can easily reach hundreds or thousands. As an assembly progresses, the amount of information displayed in the graphics window can become cluttered and make it difficult to work on the design. When the time comes to document your design, the sheer number of parts can make your views so crowded that they are difficult to decipher. To simplify your design to complete modeling tasks or to document the design, you need to learn about the types of representations in an assembly, their purposes, and where they are located.

Every assembly has two different types of representations that you can create to assist you in managing what and how the assembly content displays. You use these different representation types for visual clarity and to show positional variations in the design. These two types of representations are called design view representations and positional representations. Every assembly can also leverage the use of Model States to help show variations in a design and to improve performance in the assembly. All three of these can be used to help document the design in drawing views based on the assembly. Model states will be discussed further in the next topic.

Representations are stored and organized within the Representations browser node and model states are organized within the Model States node. To activate a specific representations or model states, you double-click on the required name, or right-click on it and click Activate in the shortcut menu.

In the following image, the browser on the left shows the default nodes that contain the assembly representations and on the right the nodes have been expanded and the representations are shown. In both representations, the Primary is active.

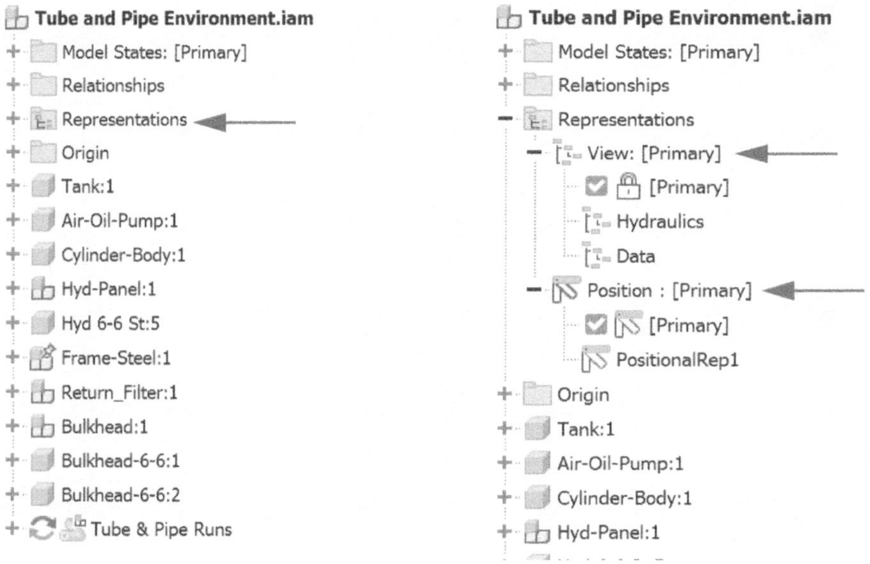

Design View Representations

A design view representation is a saved display of the assembly file. The display settings saved in the design view include component visibility, component colors, components enabled or not enabled, view magnification, and viewing angle. When an assembly's viewing properties are set to your satisfaction, you save the display as a view representation. The view representation can be locked to prevent changes, copied as the starting point for a new view representation, and used in 2D drawings to set the component visibility for drawing views.

You can include tube and pipe components in any top-level design view representation. You cannot create design view representations in the Tube & Pipe Runs subassembly, or in any run subassembly.

A common use for design view representations in assemblies with a primary runs subassembly is to isolate groups of associated routes, runs, and the components they connect.

In the following image, a design view representation isolates the flexible routes in the right-hand image by controlling visibility.

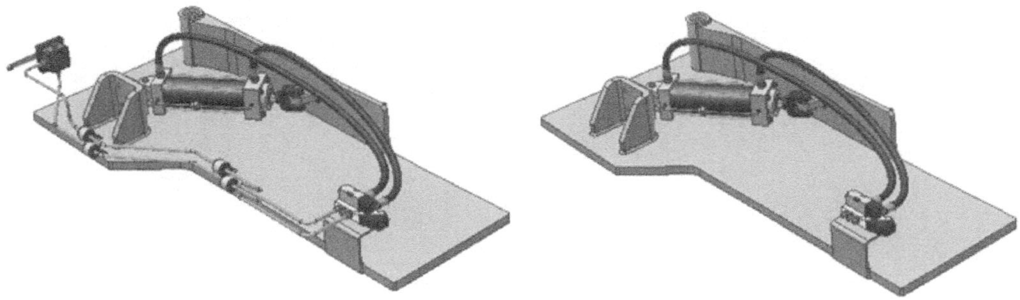

The following image shows how design view representations can be used to show the components of interest in an assembly with multiple tube and pipe runs and changing the visibility of the tank.

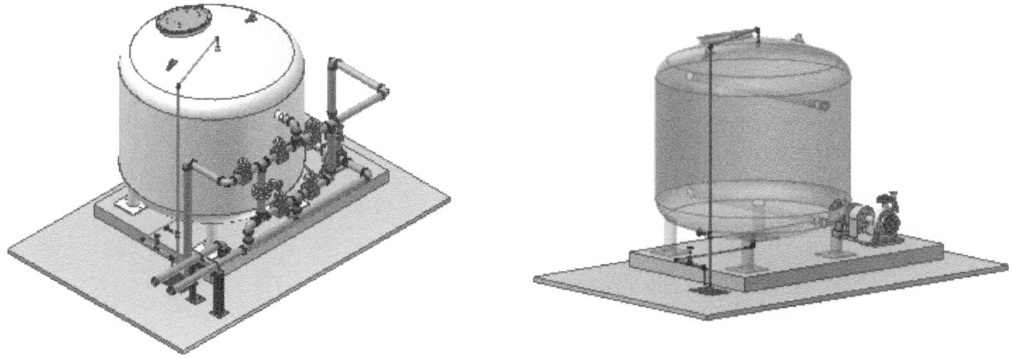

Positional Representations

Positional representations are captured snapshots of an assembly's available movements that can be used for motion studies, to confirm clearances to nearby components, to create overlay drawing views, and to provide key points for Autodesk® Inventor® Studio animations.

Rigid and flexible tube and pipe routes respond differently to positional representations applied at the top-level assembly. Flexible hose segments update their length to match any change in the position of the start or end fittings, or the position of any nodes that are associative to moved geometry. Rigid pipe and tube routes move with repositioned components only if the entire route can move with the component. You must activate the Primary positional representation to enable editing of any tube and pipe components.

The following image shows an assembly in both closed and open positional representations. The flexible hose routes update to match the position of the end fittings. The small rigid route on the cylinder moves with the cylinder.

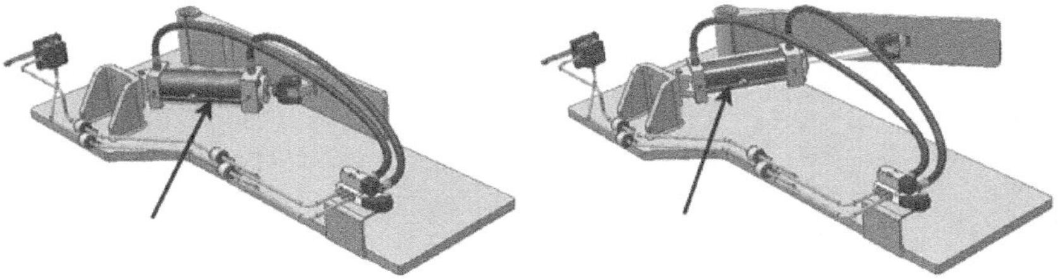

> You cannot create positional representations in the Tube & Pipe Runs subassembly, or in any run subassembly. Create all positional representations in the top-level assembly.

Determine Maximum Hose Length

Because flexible hose routes adjust in length based on the position of their start and end, you can use positional representations to determine the required hose lengths as you create your designs. You can quickly compare the reported lengths at different positional representations. The following image shows how the flexible hose routes automatically updated when different positional representations were activated.

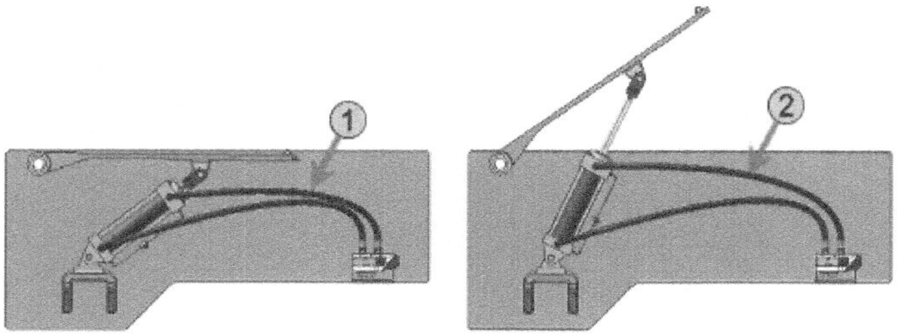

1 Closed positional representation. Hose length = 800 mm.

2 Open positional representation. Hose length = 950 mm.

About Model States

You use model state to change the suppression status of components in an assembly. By suppressing components, you simplify an assembly, show configurations of the design, and reduce the number of active components in the assembly. Additionally, drawing views can be created using model states. Model states are stored and organized within the Model State browser node. To activate a specific representation or model state, you double-click on the required name, or right-click on it and click Activate in the shortcut menu.

In the following images, the browser and model on the left shows the default Primary model state that contains the entire assembly representation. On the right, the browser and model show that the Frame Suppressed model state is active. In this model state, the steel frame is suppressed to help with clarity and can be used in a drawing view.

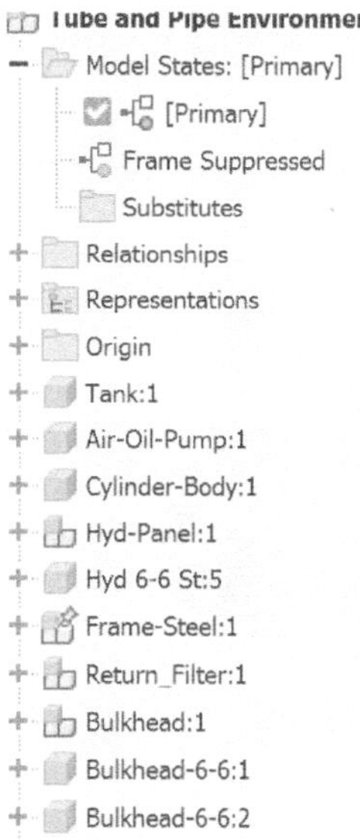

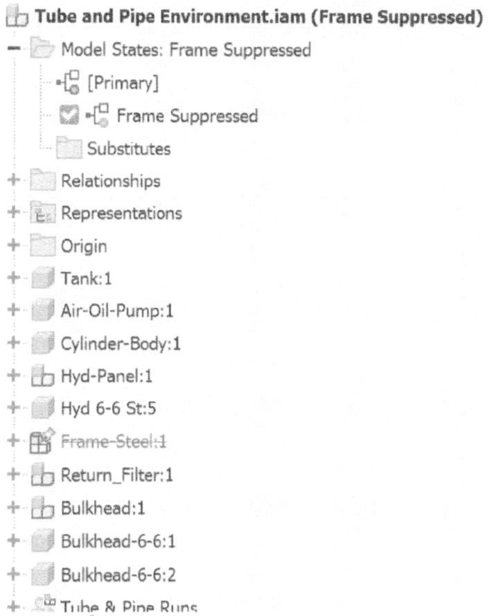

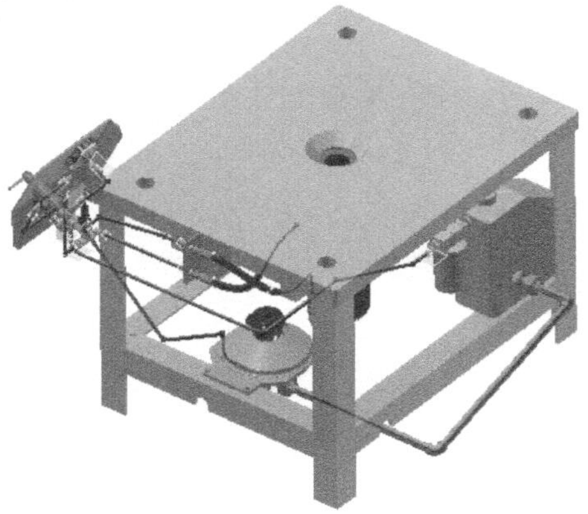

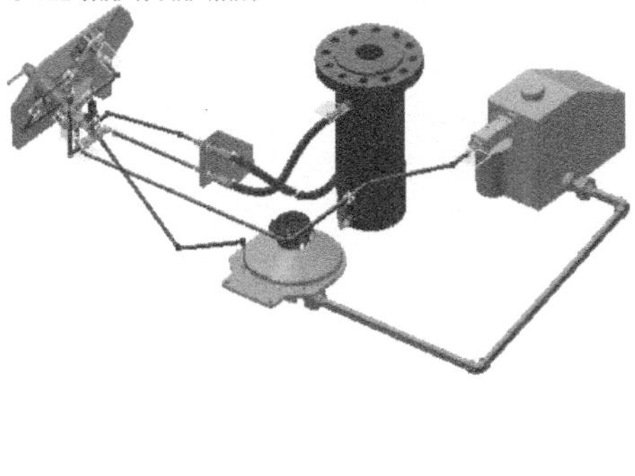

> When model states are active, routes and runs cannot be created. You must be in the Primary model state to use the tube and pipe functionality. Model states are recommended for documenting your designs; however, can't be used to control routes and runs.

When working on an overall assembly that has subassemblies, you can activate model states in any level subassembly using model state that exist at the subassembly level. The model state you have set active in the subassembly is then saved in the model state for the overall assembly. Using this technique, you can quickly change suppression of components nested in multiple levels by activating a model state at the upper level assembly.

You can also save a lot of time by directly opening a file with a selected model states. In that way, the components are never loaded into memory while the assembly is loading. To select a model state during opening, click Options in the Open dialog box after clicking the assembly once. You can also select a model state during the creation of derived parts, presentation files, and drawing views.

Procedure: Creating, Saving, and Activating Model States

The following steps give an overview of creating, saving, and activating different model states.

1. In the browser, right-click on the Model State node. Create a new model state by selecting New in the shortcut menu.

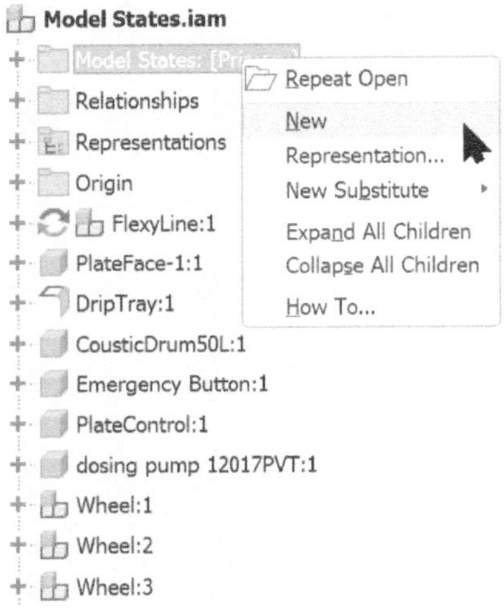

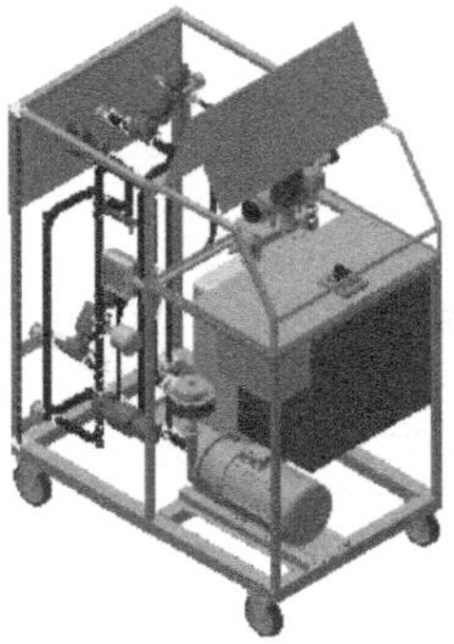

2. Ensure the model state is active and select and suppress the components to complete the model state so that the model appears as shown.

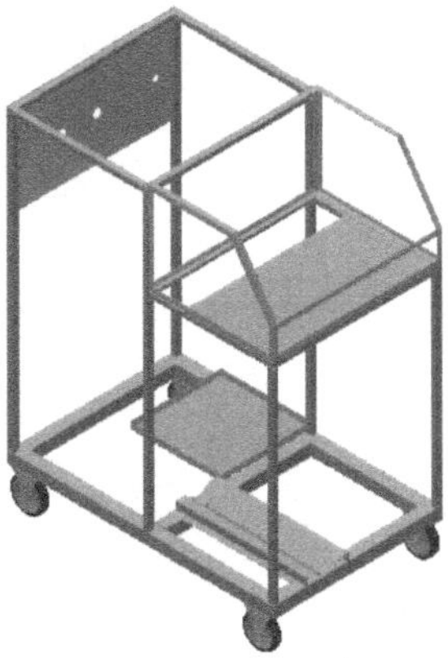

3. Change the name of the new Model State from Model State # to a name that reflects the purpose of the model state, for example, which components are suppressed or why.

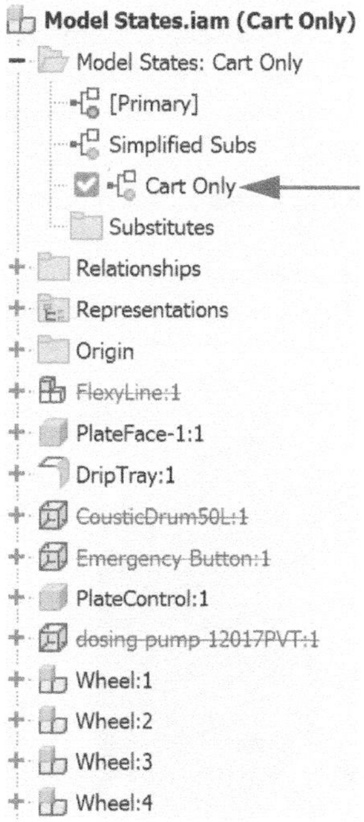

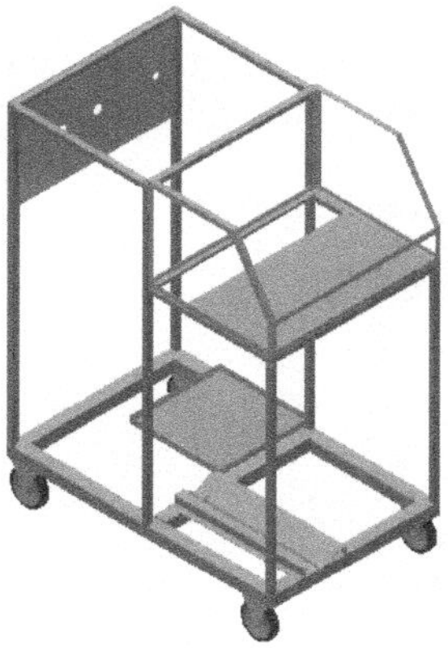

4. Save the assembly file.

5. In the browser, in the Model States node, double-click on the model state you want to make active. Or, right-click on it and click Activate.

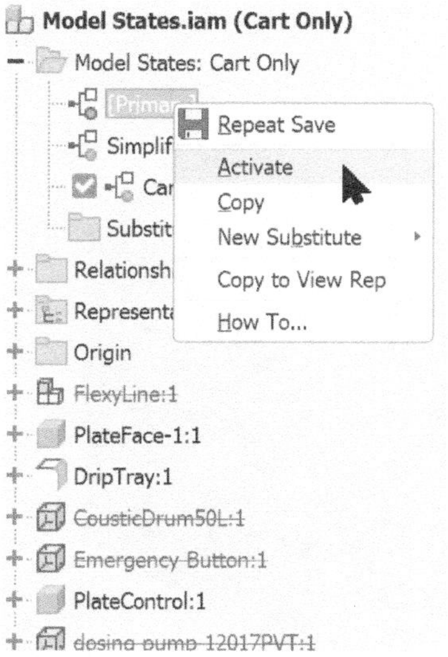

About Substitute Model States

When working in a large assembly, there are times when suppressing components removes too much visual information. Often in those cases, you do not need to view all the detail of the design, just some aspect or degree of it. You can simplify your designs and reduce the resource footprint of large assemblies or of detailed parts in an assembly through the use of substitute model states. Substitute model states are created by leveraging substitute geometry by deriving it (Derive Assembly), simplifying it (Simplify), or by selecting a replacement part (Select Part File).

In the following image, the top model state is the primary for this assembly and contains all components as initially assembled. The bottom image is a substitute model state that was created by substituting derived geometry from the assembly. The derived assembly replaced components in the assembly with bounding geometry to simplify it and reduce the number of active documents.

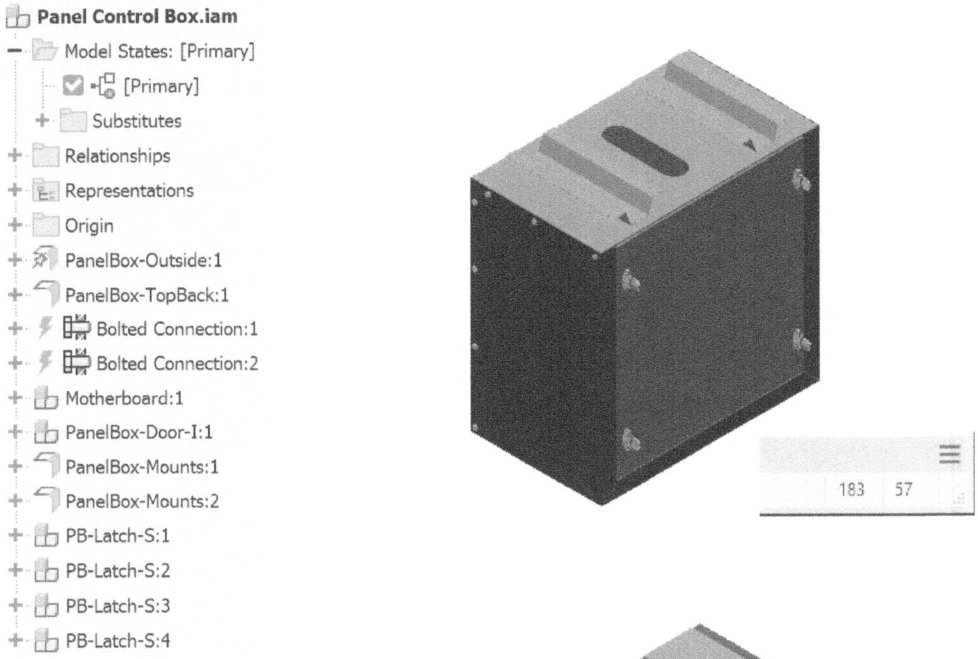

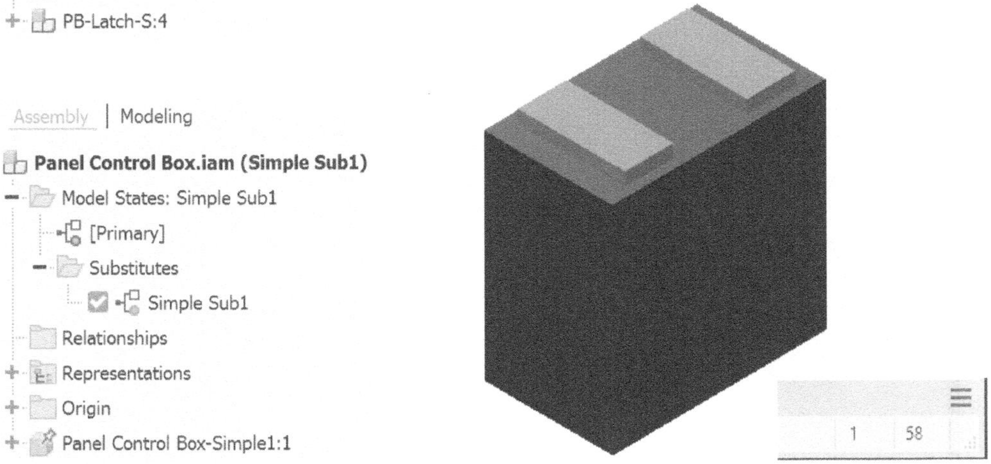

Once a substitute model state is created in a subassembly, it can be used in the top-level assembly. In the following image, the overall assembly is shown using different substitute model states for two of its subassemblies. The impact of these substitute model states on open files is shown in the occurrence information below the assembly images.

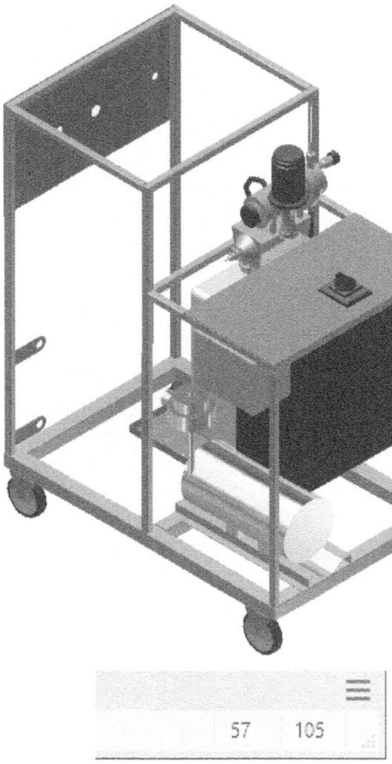

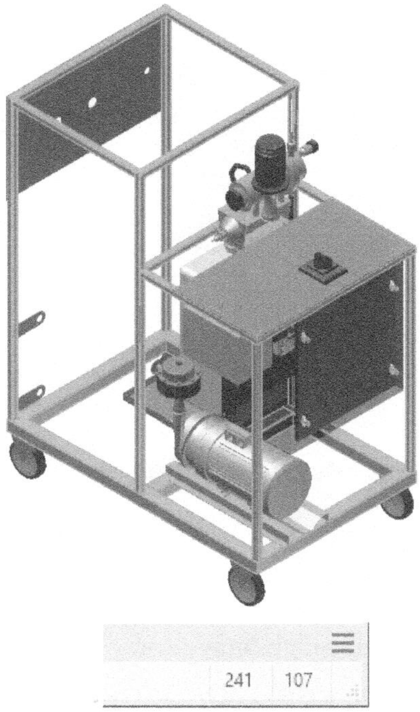

In the following image, the left-hand model is the primary with all of the components loaded and visible, and the right-hand image shows the results of creating a simplified substitute model state that derives only some of the parts and geometry in the assembly to create a simplified substitute. With the substitute model state saved in the assembly, you have the option of selecting which model state you want to load and have displayed when you use this assembly or use it in other designs or drawings. The Simplify tool gives you a large decrease in file size and can maintain some of your original properties like component colors and mass properties.

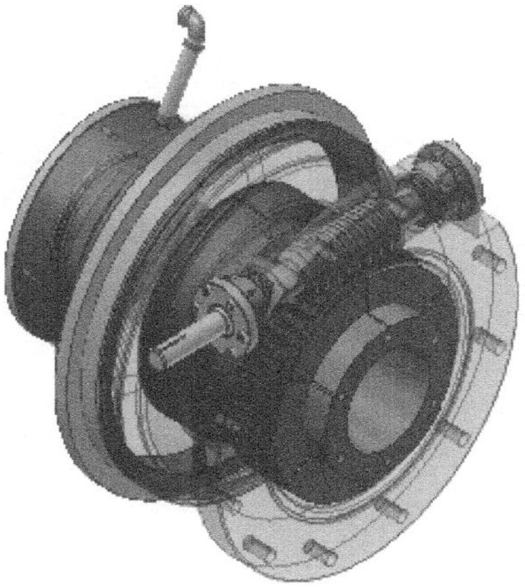

In the following image, the full assembly is shown on the left and an existing substitute part file for the assembly is shown on the right. This simplified single part file can be used in the creation of a substitute model state for the assembly. For the substituting part to correctly represent the assembly, the replacing part's coordinate system and the assembly's coordinate system must align and have the same relative distance to the model geometry. If the coordinate systems do not align, the substituting part will display in a different position than the assembly when that substitute model state is active.

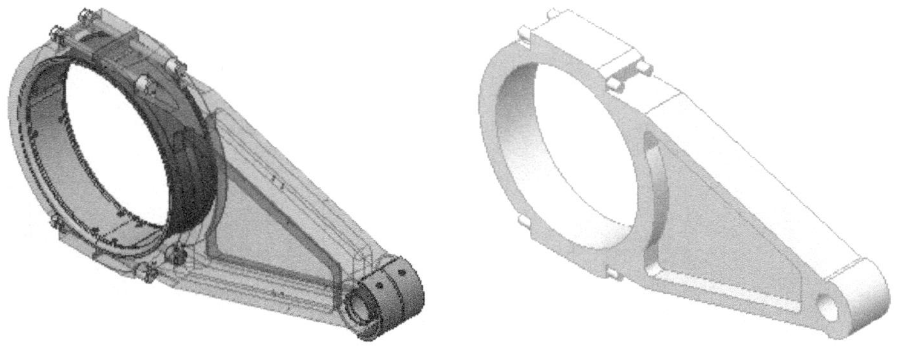

Procedure: Creating a Substitute Model State

1. Open the assembly file that you want the substitute model state to be created in.
2. In the browser, expand the Model States node, right-click on the Substitutes folder. Create a new model state by selecting New Substitute in the shortcut menu and selecting one of the three substitute creation methods.

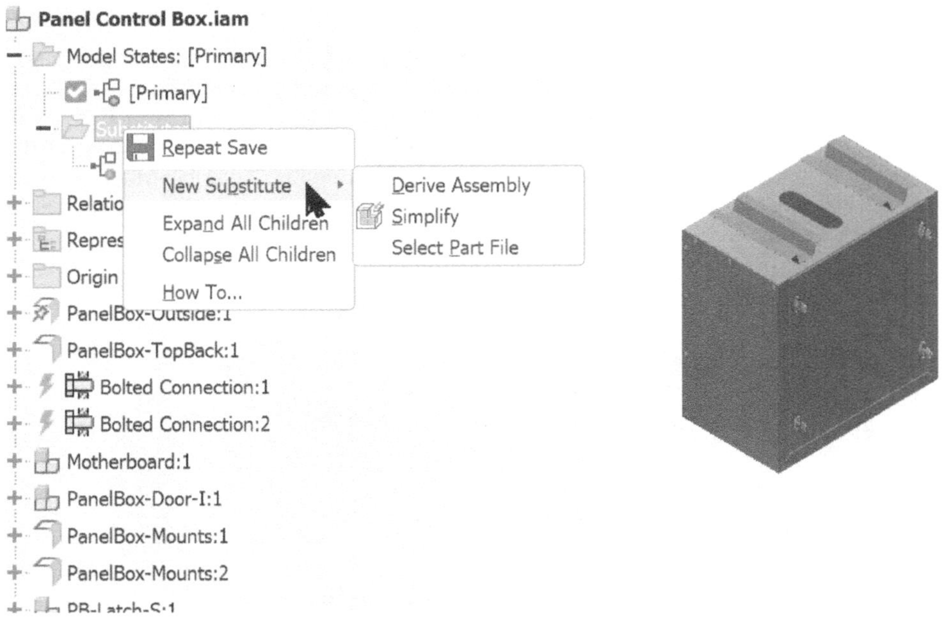

3. Define the substitute part geometry based on the substitute creation method selected:
   - Derive Assembly - Assign the part name, template, and file location and use the Derived Assembly dialog box to define the derive style and which components to include, exclude, subtract or intersect, or include as bounding box.
   - Simplify - Define the simplified substitute part file using the Properties panel to simplify the assembly to a single part file. Leverage existing model states, or view and positional reps, replace components with envelopes, simplify features, and exclude components to generate the required substitute geometry.
   - Select Part File - Substitute the existing assembly by selecting an existing part file.
4. Change the name of the new Substitute Model State from Substitute # to a name that reflects the purpose of the substitute model state.

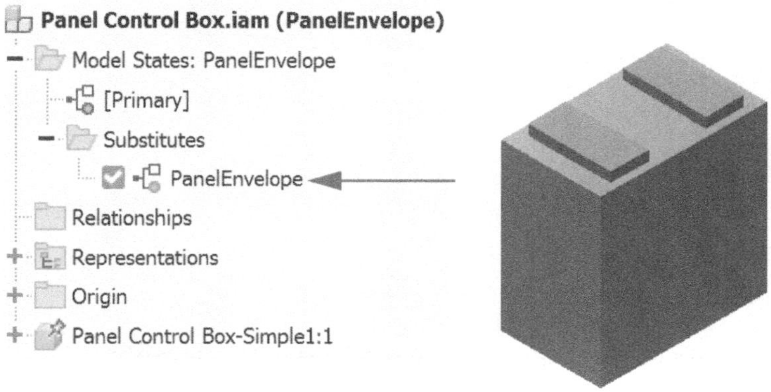

5. Save the assembly file.
6. In the browser, in the Model States node, double-click on the model state you want to make active. Or, right-click on it and click Activate.

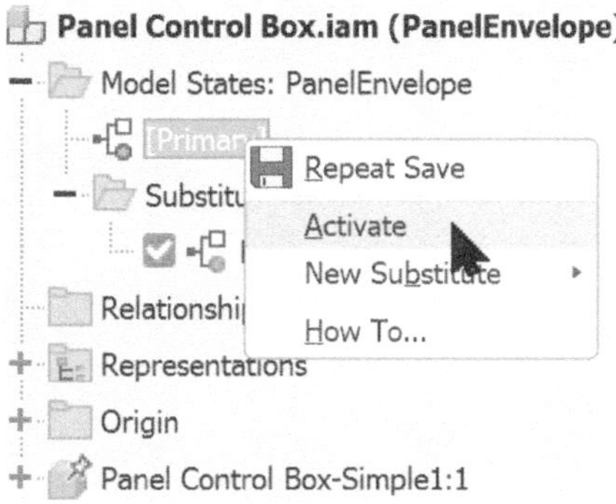

Exercise: Create Model States

In this exercise, you will create model states that control the geometry that is displayed in the top-level assembly.

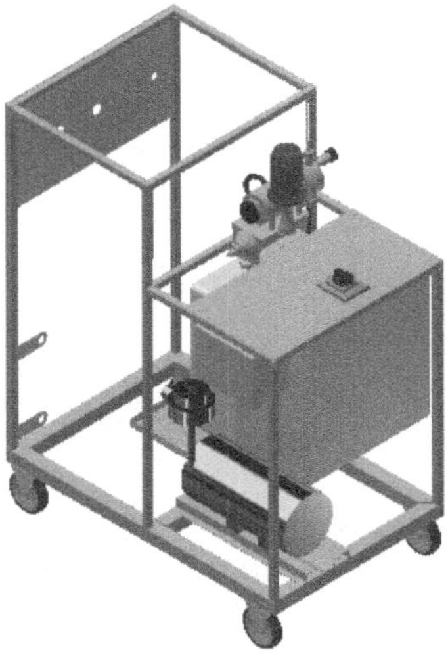

The completed exercise

Create a Substitute Model State Through a Derived Assembly

In this section of the exercise, you will create a substitute model state by deriving an assembly. You will then use that substitute model state in the overall assembly.

1. Open *Model States.iam*.

2. In the browser, right-click on Panel Control Box. Click Open.

3. To begin creating a substitute model state by deriving this assembly into a new part:
   - In the browser under Model States, right-click on Substitutes.
   - Click New Substitute>Derive Assembly.

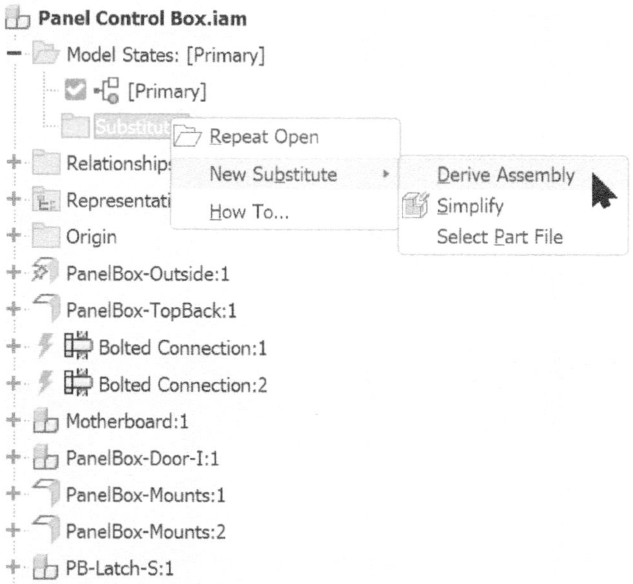

4. In the New Derived Substitute Part dialog box:
   - In the New Component Name field, enter **Panel Control Box-Simple1**.
   - Click OK.

5. In the Derived Assembly dialog box:
   - In the Bodies tab, set the Derive style to Single solid body merging out seams between planar faces.
   - Change the status of the components in the assembly as shown in the following image. This represents the three components as bounding boxes.
   - Click OK.

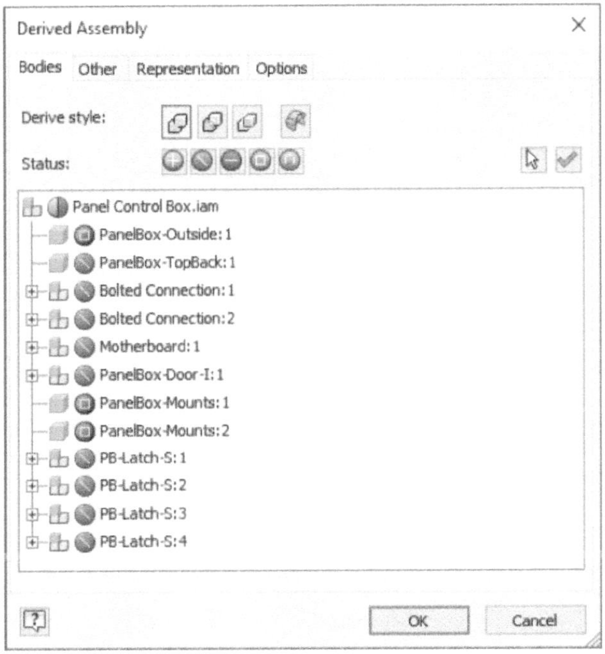

6. Review the results in the browser and graphics window.

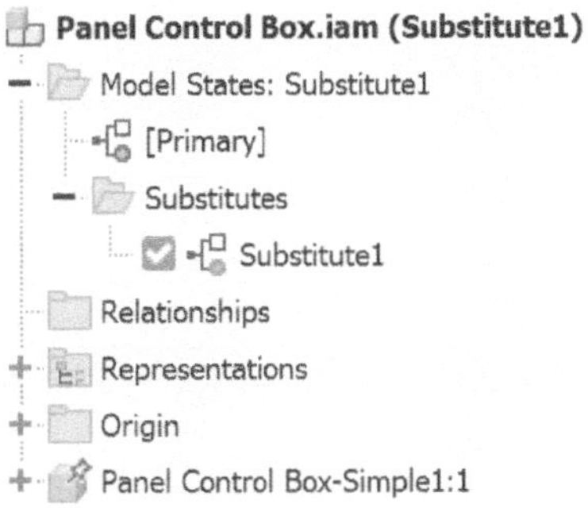

7. In the Model States node, double-click on Primary to activate it. Notice how all the components in the assembly are now displayed again.

8. In the browser, rename Substitute1 in the Substitutes folder to **Simple Sub1**.

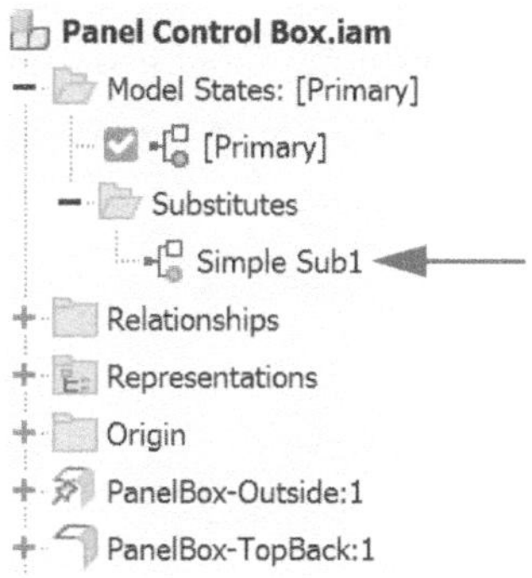

9. To open the derived part and review its configuration:
   - Double-click Simple Sub1 to activate the model state.
   - In the browser, right-click on Panel Control Box-Simple1:1. Click Open.
   - Notice how the part has been simplified to a single body.
   - Save and close the derived part, *Panel Control Box-Simple1.ipt*.

10. In the browser in the Model States node for *Panel Control Box.iam*, double-click on Primary to set it active.

11. Save and close *Panel Control Box.iam*. When prompted to save changes to the assembly and its dependents, click OK.

12. To create and name a new model state for the overall *Model State.iam* assembly, in the browser:
   - Right-click on the Model States: Primary node and click New.
   - Rename the new level of detail to Simplified Subs.

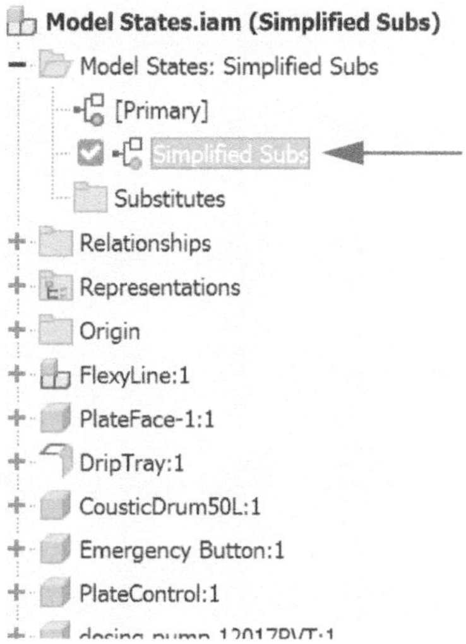

13. In the Occurrence Meter, review the current values for Total Occurrences in Active Document and Open Documents in this Session.

14. To have the panel control box display with its simple substitute model, in the browser:

- Expand the tree display for Panel Control Box, Model States >Substitutes.
- Double-click on Simple Sub1 as shown in the following image.

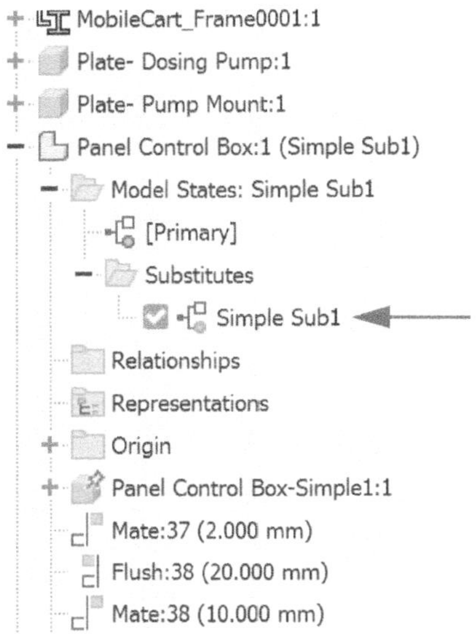

15. Review the changes in the graphics window and Occurrence Meter. The assembly design now displays as shown in the following image with a simplified single body panel control box.

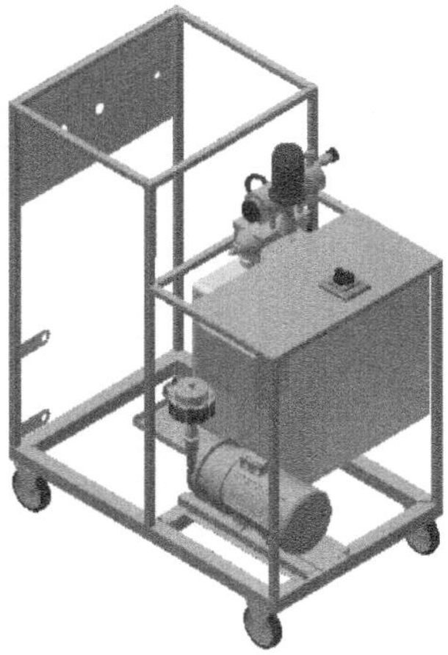

Create a Substitute Model State by Selecting a Part File

In this section of the exercise, you will create a substitute model state by selecting an existing simplified part file. You will then use that substitute model state in the overall assembly.

1. To begin substituting a simplified part file for the MobilePump assembly, in the browser right-click on MobilePump. Click Open.

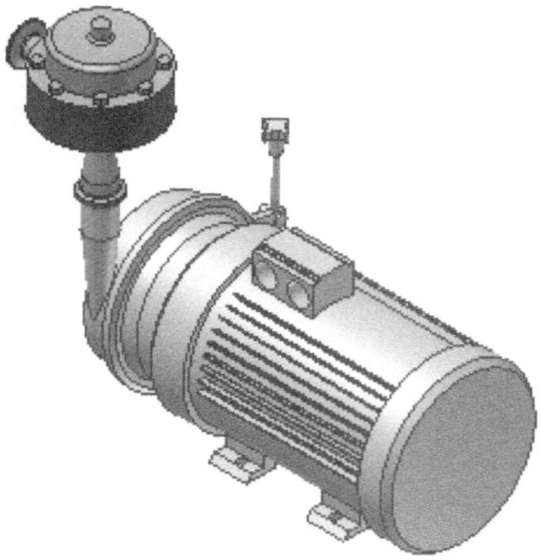

2. In the browser under the Model States node, right-click on Substitutes. Click New Substitute>Select Part File.

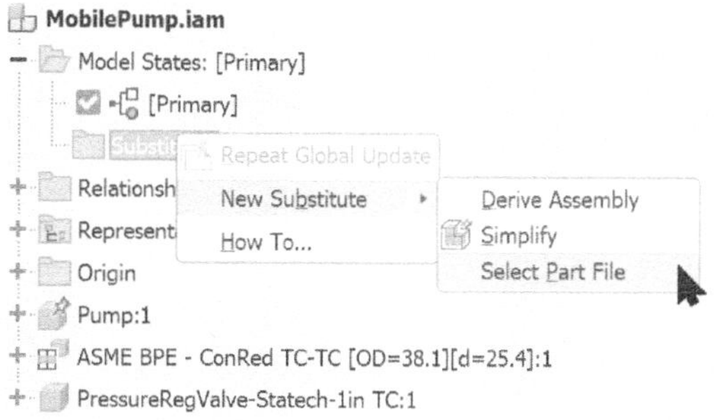

3. To substitute the assembly with a part:
   - In the Place Component dialog box, select *MobilePump-Simple.ipt*. Click Open.

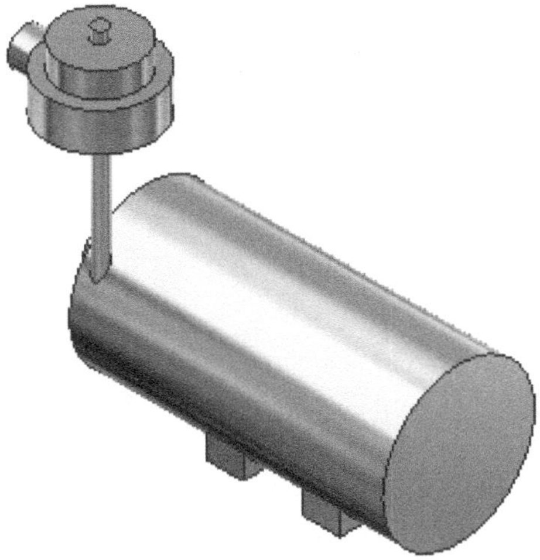

4. Save and close *MobilePump.iam*. If prompted to save changes to the part and its dependents, click OK.
5. To have the pump display with its simple substitute model, in the browser:
   - Ensure that the Simplified Subs model state is active in the top-level assembly.
   - Expand the tree display for MobilePump, Model States, and Substitutes.
   - Double-click on Substitute1 as shown in the following image.

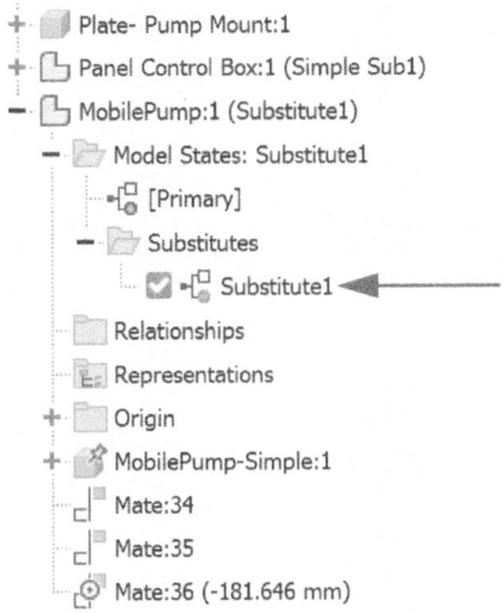

6. Review the changes in the graphics window and Occurence Meter. The assembly design now displays as shown in the following image.

7. To switch the assembly back to displaying all the detail of the subassemblies, in the browser under Model States, double-click on the Primary model state.

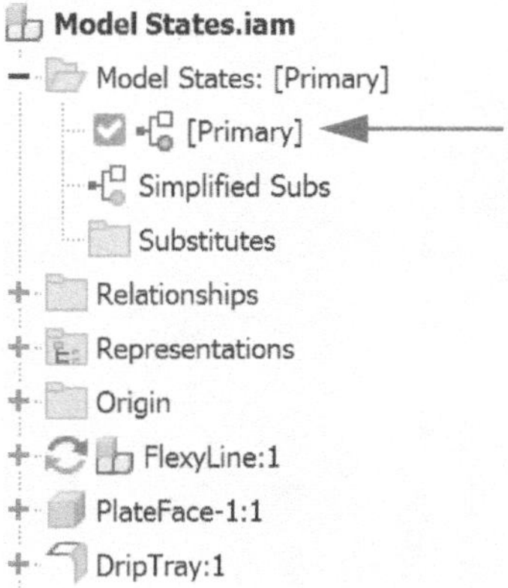

Create a Model State to represent only the components of the Cart

In this section of the exercise, you will create a model state by simply suppressing assembly components.

1. Right-click on Model States: Primary node and select New.

2. Rename the model state as Cart Only.

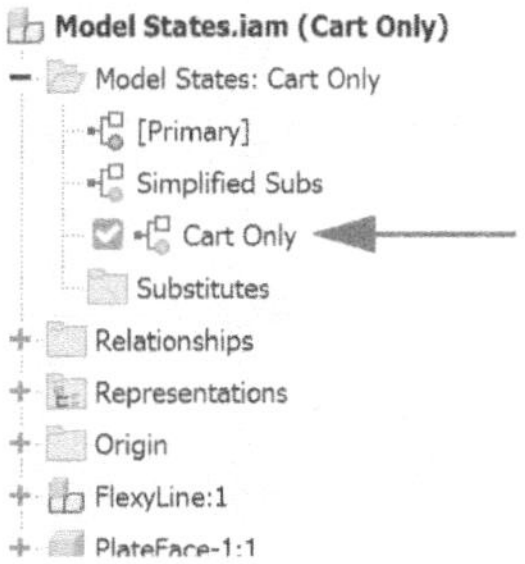

3. In the browser, suppress the components as shown in the following image. Only the components that are used for the cart remain. Click OK when reminded that the components will be removed from the Bill of Materials.

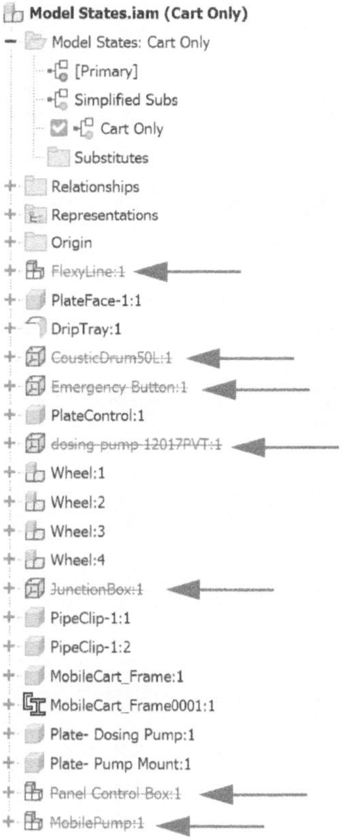

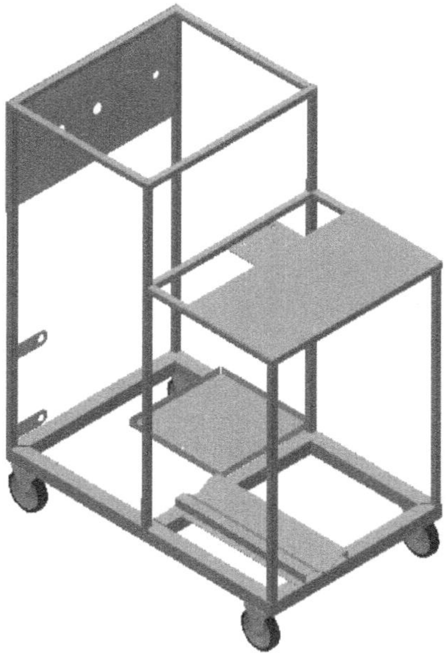

4. Return the assembly to the Primary model state and save the assembly file. When prompted to save changes to the assembly and its dependents, click OK. Any of the model states can be used in an assembly drawing.

Lesson: Documenting Routes and Runs

Overview

This lesson describes how to document tube and pipe assemblies through the creation of drawings. Piping assemblies can range from a single-run tube with start and end fittings to a complex design with multiple branching runs, and many fittings and other components from the Tube and Pipe library. Pipe documentation typically includes one or more dimensioned assembly views to describe the positioning of pipes and fittings in the parent assembly. A complex tube or pipe assembly with multiple runs might require a separate drawing or drawing views for each run or group of related runs.

After you create design view representations in the assembly file to isolate related runs and the assembly components that are important to those runs, you create drawing views based on those design view representations. The selected design view controls which components display in the drawing views.

After completing your designs, you need to document the tube and pipe sections of the design as you would for any other design. The ability to create drawing views, add centerlines to your pipe runs, and control component display in the parts list enables you to efficiently document tube and pipe designs.

In the following image, a simple run is documented in a drawing file. The general length of the different segments can be determined by quickly viewing the dimensions. For cumulative values, you can refer to the parts list that contains information specific to the run.

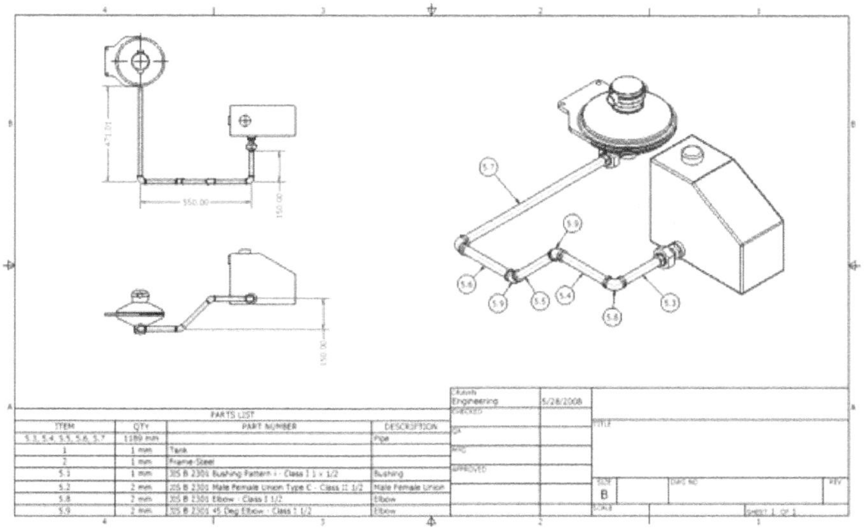

Objectives

After completing this lesson, you will be able to:

- Create drawing views of tube and pipe designs using different representations.
- Add centerlines to the center of a drawing with routes.
- Customize a parts list to merge pipe, hose, or tubing.

Creating Drawing Views

Tube and pipe designs require documentation just as any other design does. However, documenting routes and runs has requirements unique to the tube and pipe environment. Adding centerlines to pipe runs enables you to efficiently dimension your design. Controlling the parts list display enables you to document individual and cumulative pipe run lengths. Effective use of these techniques enables you to quickly document your tube and pipe designs.

The following image shows a drawing view based on a level of detail representation. The parts list for the drawing is configured to show both individual and cumulative values for the member lengths.

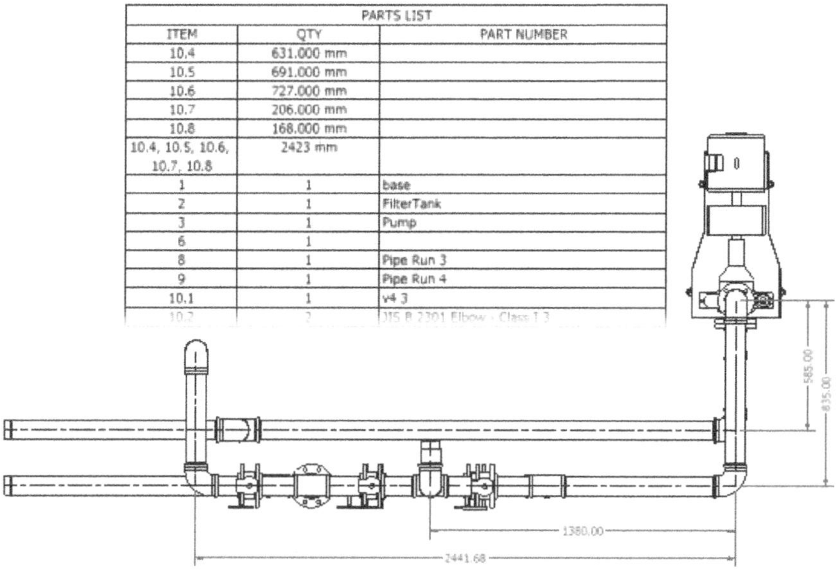

PARTS LIST		
ITEM	QTY	PART NUMBER
10.4	631.000 mm	
10.5	691.000 mm	
10.6	727.000 mm	
10.7	206.000 mm	
10.8	168.000 mm	
10.4, 10.5, 10.6, 10.7, 10.8	2423 mm	
1	1	base
2	1	FilterTank
3	1	Pump
6	1	
8	1	Pipe Run 3
9	1	Pipe Run 4
10.1	1	v4 3
10.2	2	JIS B 2301 Elbow - Class 1 3

Options to Document Tube and Pipe Designs

When you create drawing views to document routes and runs, you can incorporate many Autodesk Inventor tools into your design that can enhance the documentation of your design. While you use standard techniques to create your drawing views, you can create design view, position, and level of detail (LOD) representations to isolate related runs and apply the representations to your assembly drawing views to document portions of your pipe designs.

You can also create routes and runs drawing views based on presentation files. However, to create an exploded view, the route segments would have to be done manually. You cannot create standard piping schematics and piping and instrumentation diagrams (P&ID) from a tube, pipe, or hose assembly in Autodesk Inventor.

The following image shows three level of detail variations on the same piping design. On the right, the complete assembly is shown. In the middle, a level of detail representation showing only the piping components of the design was created. On the left, another level of detail representation was created and used to create a presentation file. In the presentation file, the piping components of the supply line were exploded, and the drawing view created.

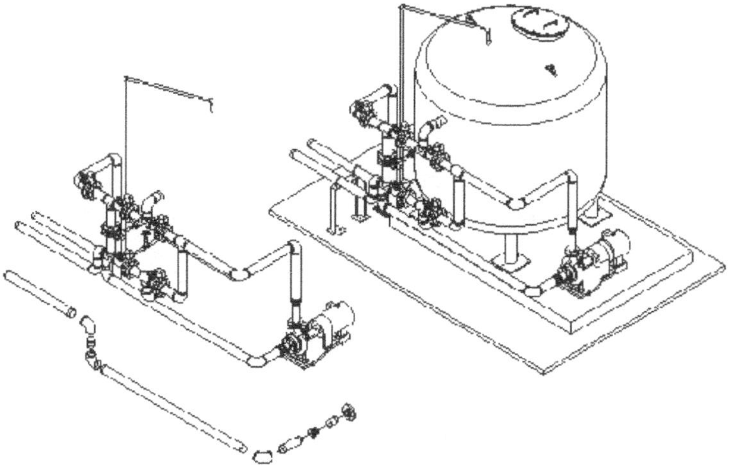

Creating and using a template file for drawings ensures that the view geometry, title block information, and other iProperty information is configured and matches your company standards

Drawing View Creation Options

The following image shows the Drawing View dialog box. You use the Drawing View dialog box to create drawings based on representations created in the assembly file. After determining the assembly file, you can create drawing views based on model states (1), design view representations (2), or positional view representations (3).

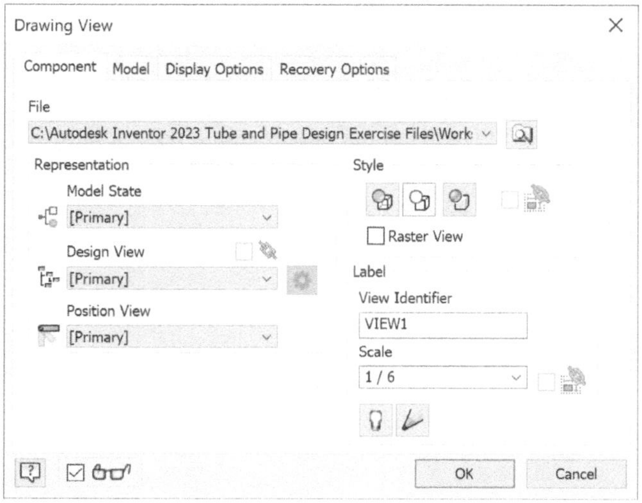

Procedure: Creating Pipe Drawing Views

The following steps give an overview of generating two-dimensional drawing views of a pipe assembly.

1. In a drawing file, create the required assembly drawing views. Use design view representations or level of detail representations to limit components or to isolate runs.
2. Include centerlines for some or all routes.
3. Add dimensions as required. Dimension to centerlines in orthographic views or display component work points for dimensioning.
4. Create a parts list to tabulate pipe components. The tube and pipe drawing templates include parts list formatting to merge similar pipe segments into a single row.

Including Route Centerlines

You include centerlines on a route so you can dimension the pipe components to their centerlines in order to obtain a true distance or angle. You can include centerlines for an individual route, all routes in a run, or all routes in the Tube & Pipe Runs subassembly. If you create a new view based on a view that already has centerlines included, the new view also includes centerlines.

In the following image, the route centerlines display for the hydraulic lines to a cylinder housing. On the left, the view is shown as it displays when created. On the right, the view is shown with route centerlines included.

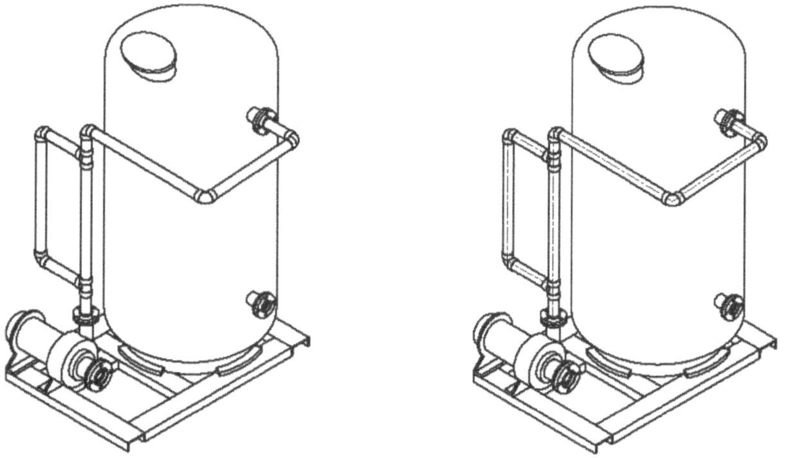

Including Route Centerlines Access

You access route centerline display by locating the run in the browser under the view where you want to display the centerlines. In the browser, right-click on the Run and click Include Route Centerlines.

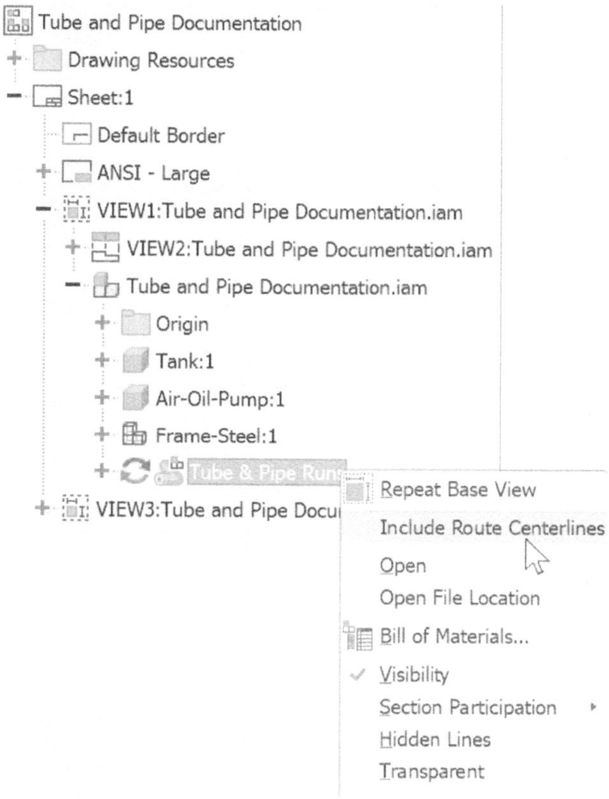

Route centerline display is not controlled by the Automated Centerlines settings for standard Autodesk Inventor components.

Properties for Included Route Centerlines are edited using the 3D Sketch Geometry Layer.

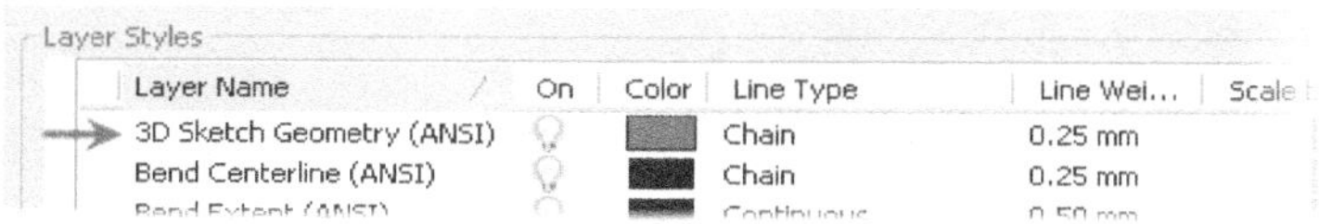

Procedure: Including Route Centerlines in Drawing Views

The following steps give an overview of including route centerlines in drawing views of tube and pipe designs.

1. Open or create a drawing file with a drawing view containing at least one tube and pipe run.

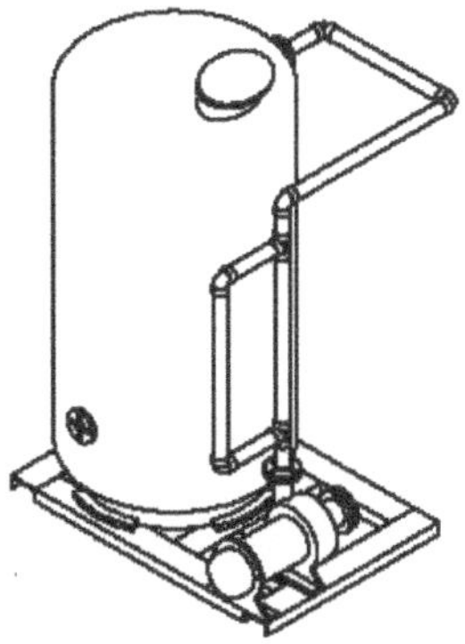

2. Locate the drawing view in the browser.

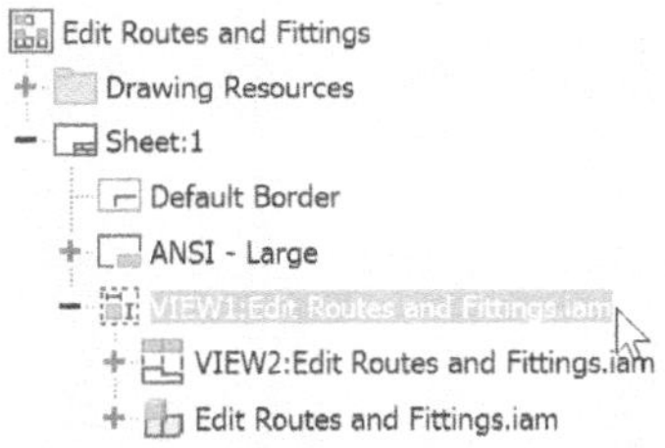

3. Expand the contents of the view until the run is exposed.

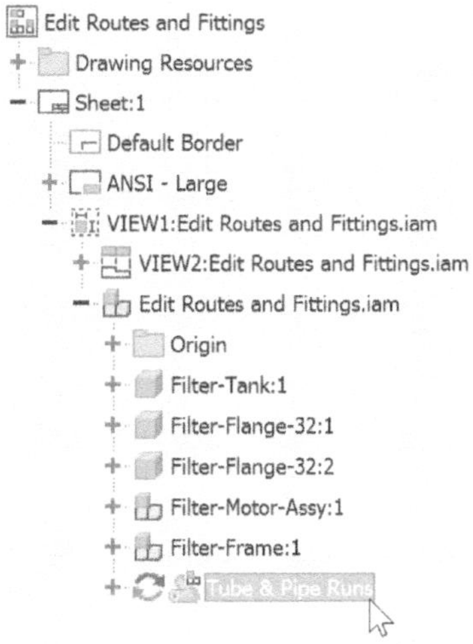

4. Right-click on the run and click Include Route Centerlines.

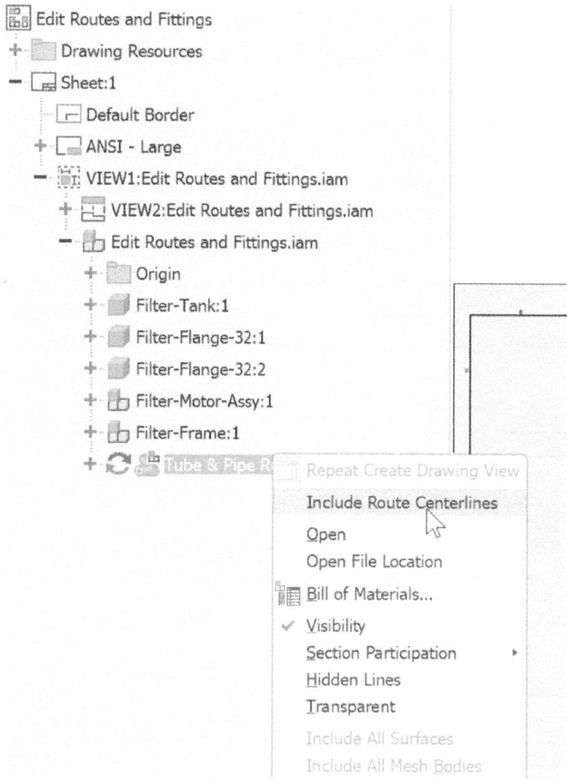

5. The centerlines display in the drawing view.

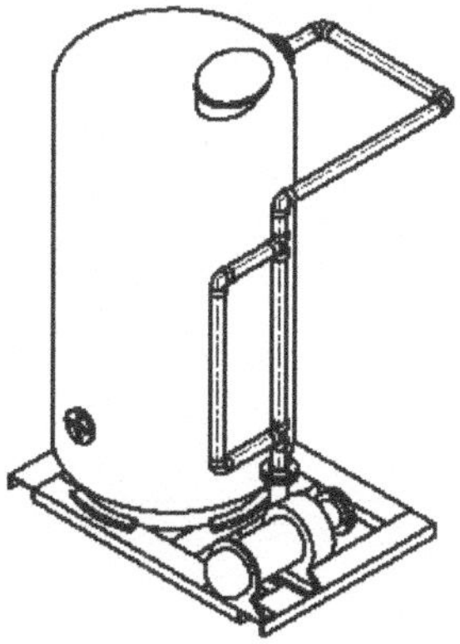

Customizing a Parts List

A parts list documents the components in an assembly and is based on the assembly's bill of materials. You can create a flattened list of all the parts in the assembly, or you can create a parts list that matches the structured BOM of the assembly.

If you select a drawing view as the source for the parts list, the bill of materials from the assembly in the view is used to generate the parts list. Phantom components in the BOM are not displayed in a parts list, and their children are promoted to the level of the parent assembly. Because the Tube and Pipe Runs subassembly has a Phantom BOM structure, all pipe run subassemblies display as first-level children in a parts list that is based on the BOM of the top-level assembly.

The following image shows two versions of a parts list created from a tube and pipe drawing view. On the left, the parts list is shown with no modifications. On the right, the same parts list is modified to group common components and display both the group and the group participants.

PARTS LIST		
ITEM	QTY	PART NUMBER
1	1	base
2	1	FilterTank
3	1	Pump
4	1	ISO 7005-1 Hubbed Threaded Flange
5	1	ISO 7005-1 Hubbed Threaded Flange
6	1	
8	1	Pipe Run 3
9	1	Pipe Run 4
10	1	Pipe Run 6
11	1	Pipe Run 7
12	1	Pipe Run 9
13	1	Pipe Run 11
14	1	Pipe Run 12
15	1	Pipe Run 14
16	1	Pipe Run 18
17	1	Pipe Run 19
18	1	Pipe Run 20
19	1	Pipe Run 21
21	1	Tank Lid
22	12	ANSI B18.2.3.5M - M12 x 1.75 x 25

Unmodified Parts List

PARTS LIST		
ITEM	QTY	PART NUMBER
10.4	631.000 mm	
10.5	691.000 mm	
10.6	727.000 mm	
10.7	206.000 mm	
10.8	168.000 mm	
10.4, 10.5, 10.6, 10.7, 10.8	2423 mm	
1	1	base
2	1	FilterTank
3	1	Pump
4	1	ISO 7005-1 Hubbed Threaded Flange
5	1	ISO 7005-1 Hubbed Threaded Flange
6	1	
8	1	Pipe Run 3
9	1	Pipe Run 4

Modified Parts List

Tube and Pipe BOM Structure

The structure of the bill of materials (BOM) determines how parts lists display and what is included in the bill of materials for downstream applications.

The following image shows the default BOM structure for an assembly that includes one flexible hose run and one rigid pipe run.

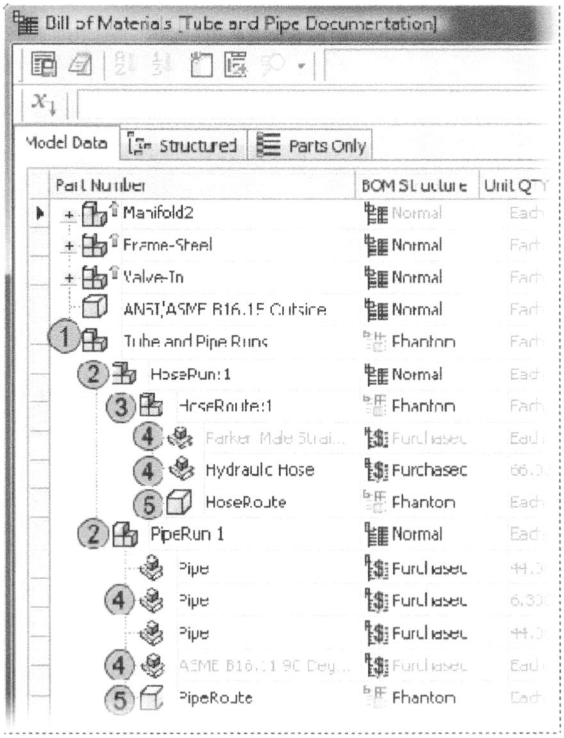

1 **Tube and Pipe Runs Subassembly** — The top-level assembly is a container for the underlying runs and should not be included in the BOM. By default, it is assigned a Phantom BOM structure.

2 **Hose or Pipe Run Subassembly** — Normal BOM structure. Included in the BOM and parts list.

3 **Flexible Hose Route Subassembly** — In the style for a flexible hose route, you can select to store the hose and its fittings in a subassembly. The resulting subassembly is assigned a Phantom BOM structure by default and its hose and fittings are promoted one level. If you want to display the flexible hose as an item in the BOM or parts list, change the structure to Inseparable.

4 **Pipe, Tube, Hose, or Fittings** — Purchased BOM structure. Display in the BOM.

5 **Hose or Pipe Route** — These parts contain the route points and do not represent physical components. They are assigned Phantom BOM structures.

In the following image, on the left, a drawing parts list is edited to group common pipe components and display both the individual and combined components. On the right, the resulting parts list displays showing both configurations of the components.

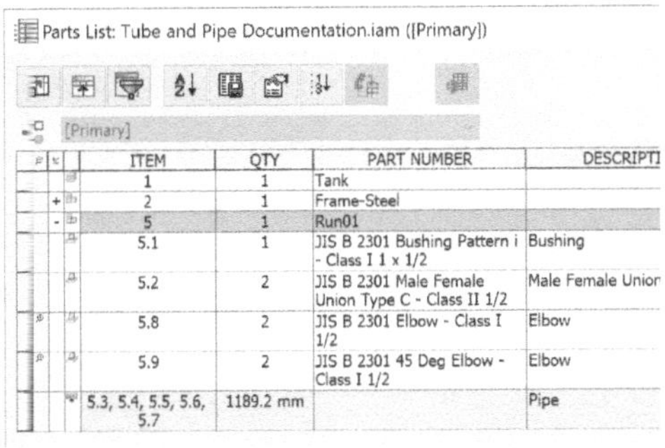
Parts List: Tube and Pipe Documentation.iam ([Primary])

[Primary]

ITEM	QTY	PART NUMBER	DESCRIPTI
1	1	Tank	
2	1	Frame-Steel	
5	1	Run01	
5.1	1	JIS B 2301 Bushing Pattern i - Class I 1 x 1/2	Bushing
5.2	2	JIS B 2301 Male Female Union Type C - Class II 1/2	Male Female Unior
5.8	2	JIS B 2301 Elbow - Class I 1/2	Elbow
5.9	2	JIS B 2301 45 Deg Elbow - Class I 1/2	Elbow
5.3, 5.4, 5.5, 5.6, 5.7	1189.2 mm		Pipe

PARTS LIST		
ITEM	QTY	PART NUMBER
1	1	Tank
2	1	Frame-Steel
5.1	1	JIS B 2301 Bushing Pattern i - Class I 1 x 1/2
5.2	2	JIS B 2301 Male Female Union Type C - Class II 1/2
5.8	2	JIS B 2301 Elbow - Class I 1/2
5.9	2	JIS B 2301 45 Deg Elbow - Class I 1/2
5.3, 5.4, 5.5, 5.6, 5.7	1189.2 mm	

BOM Structure and Flexible Hoses

Depending on your needs for manufacturing and purchasing tube and pipe components, you can display flexible routes in the BOM as individual components or as a single unit. Managing your BOM structure in this manner enables you to define and export your BOM data in the most efficient manner.

The following images show a tube and pipe assembly with different configurations in the BOM. On the top left, the BOM is edited to change the displayed configuration of a parts list. On the top right, the default configuration is shown. The BOM structure for the flexible hose is set to Phantom, and the assembly structure is collapsed.

On the bottom left, the BOM structure is still Phantom, but the assembly structure has been expanded to show individual components of the flexible hose. You might use this method if you were to purchase the fittings and hose in bulk, and complete an assembly. On the bottom right, the BOM structure is set to Purchased. Note the balloons to both the fittings and hose are the same numbers, just as if you purchased the flexible hose as a single unit, ready to install.

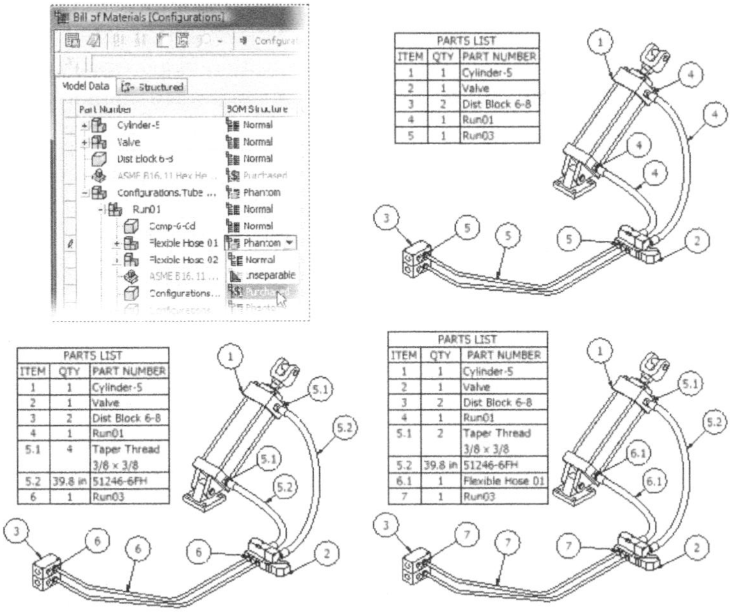

ITEM	QTY	PART NUMBER
1	1	Cylinder-5
2	1	Valve
3	2	Dist Block 6-8
4	1	Run01
5	1	Run03

ITEM	QTY	PART NUMBER
1	1	Cylinder-5
2	1	Valve
3	2	Dist Block 6-8
4	1	Run01
5.1	4	Taper Thread 3/8 x 3/8
5.2	39.8 in	51246-6FH
6	1	Run03

ITEM	QTY	PART NUMBER
1	1	Cylinder-5
2	1	Valve
3	2	Dist Block 6-8
4	1	Run01
5.1	2	Taper Thread 3/8 x 3/8
5.2	39.8 in	51246-6FH
6.1	1	Flexible Hose 01
7	1	Run03

Customizing a Parts List

You can customize the display of data in a parts list in the following ways:

- Merge rows that contain the same value in one or more columns.
- Control the visibility of individual rows that are combined in a merged row.
- Format columns with numerical values.
- Substitute values in a column with values from a selected iProperty.

To customize parts list columns in a template, edit the styles in the template drawing. Use the Style Editor to add a new parts list style or edit an existing parts list style. You can edit the style to merge rows for similar conduit segments and display the summed length of the segments. You can also format column values for most columns, with the following exceptions:

- Item
- File Name
- Material
- Any date column

The quantity property for a conduit segment reflects the length of the segment. Segments of the same style are often merged in a single row, and the sum of the segment lengths is shown in the quantity column.

Merging Rows

To show the summed length of segments, you must first merge the parts list rows containing segments. The degree to which you can merge segments depends on the BOM view setting for the parts list.

- If you place the parts list using the Parts Only BOM view, you can merge conduit segments of the same style from all runs into a single row.
- If you place the parts list using the Structured BOM view option, the conduit segments display one level below the run subassembly. You can merge the rows for conduit segments in each run.

Parts list rows with the same value for at least one key iProperty are merged. You can specify from one to three key iProperties to determine how rows merge. Rows with the same values for all keys are merged. Because all conduit parts generated from a tube and pipe style share the same stock number, you can specify this single key to merge conduit rows. You can also display each segment in its own row in addition to the merged row.

You merge rows by accessing the Group Settings dialog box and enabling Grouping. You access the Group Settings dialog box from the Parts List dialog box when editing a parts list.

The following image shows the settings required in the Group Settings dialog box to group all conduits of the same stock number.

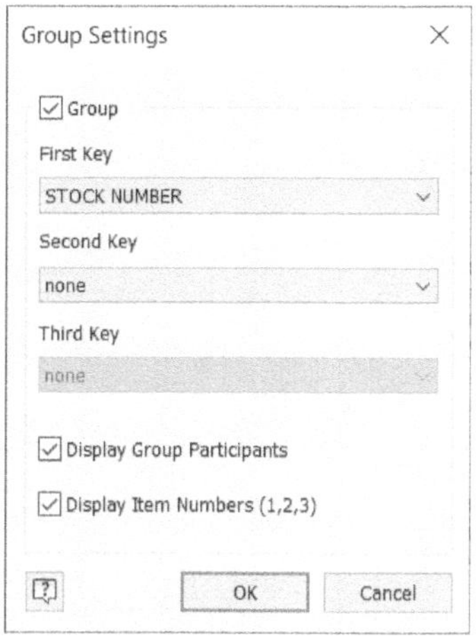

> Parts list rows with the same nonblank value for their part numbers are automatically merged. Each tube and pipe component generated has a unique part number. To avoid unexpected row merges, ensure that either all components in the assembly have a unique part number, or that the Part Number property is left blank.

Procedure: Modifying a Parts List

The following steps give an overview of modifying a standard parts list to merge conduit segments and report the summed length in a single row.

1. Edit a parts list.

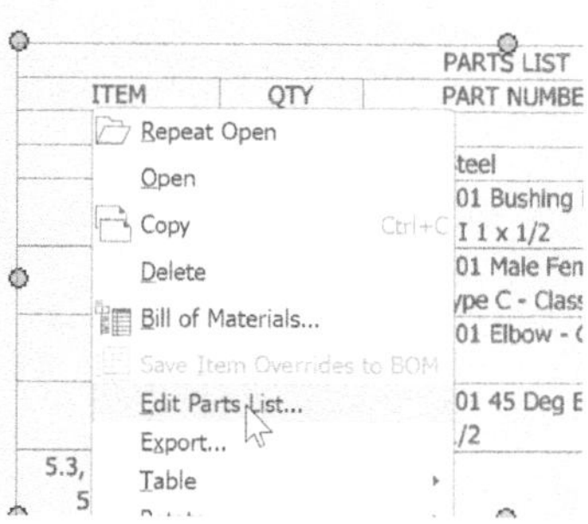

2. Expand the assembly to review the values.

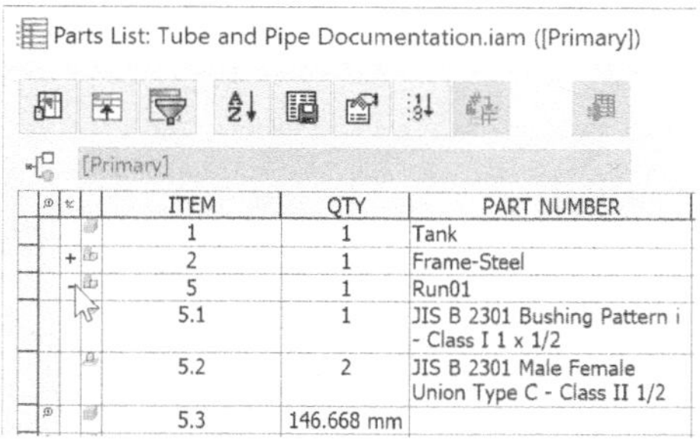

3. In the Parts List dialog box, click Group Settings.

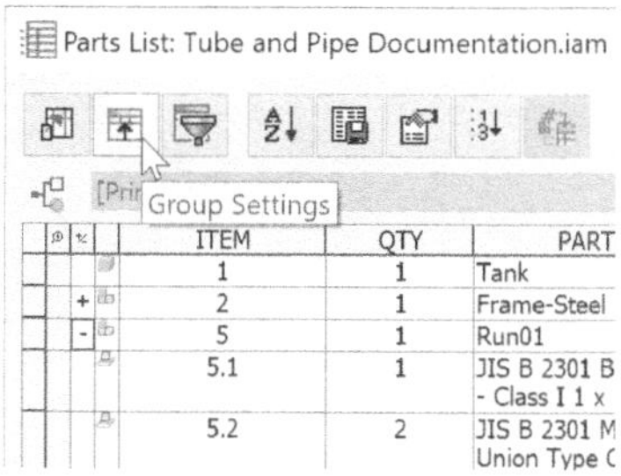

4. In the Group Settings for the parts list, click Group to merge rows that have a common value in the Stock Number property.

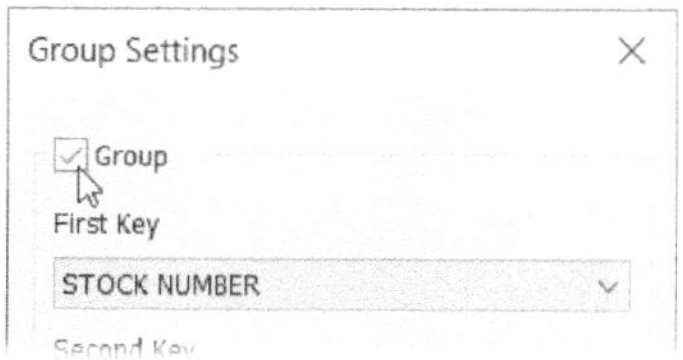

5. The segments are included in a single row, and the values summed.

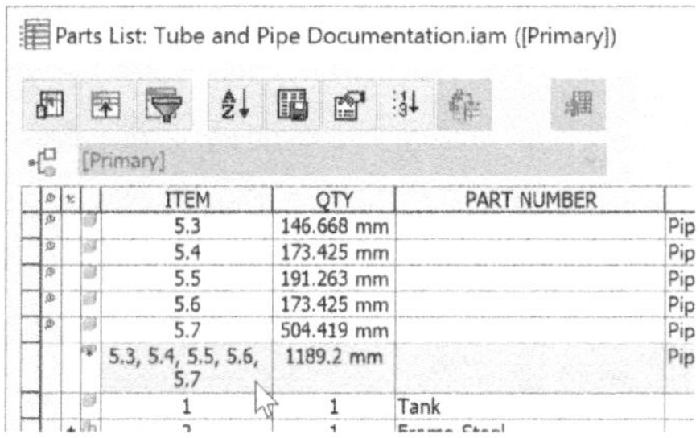

6. To remove the individual entries in the parts list, clear the checkmark for Display Group Participants.

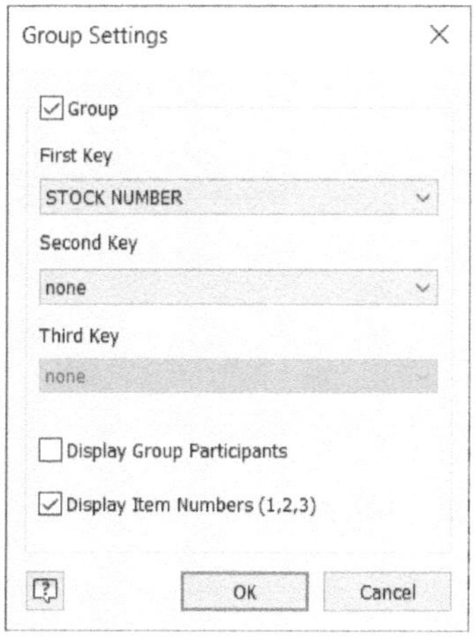

7. The changes are reflected in the Parts List dialog box and the parts list.

PARTS LIST			
ITEM	QTY	PART NUMBER	DESCRIPTION
1	1	Tank	
2	1	Frame-Steel	
5.1	1	JIS B 2301 Bushing Pattern i - Class I 1 x 1/2	Bushing
5.2	2	JIS B 2301 Male Female Union Type C - Class II 1/2	Male Female Union
5.8	2	JIS B 2301 Elbow - Class I 1/2	Elbow
5.9	2	JIS B 2301 45 Deg Elbow - Class I 1/2	Elbow
5.3, 5.4, 5.5, 5.6, 5.7	1189.2 mm		Pipe

Exercise: Document Routes and Runs

In this exercise, you will document a tube and pipe assembly in the drawing environment. You will create the views required to display the design. You will then add centerlines and dimension to the pipe runs. Finally, you will create and edit a parts list to complete the documentation.

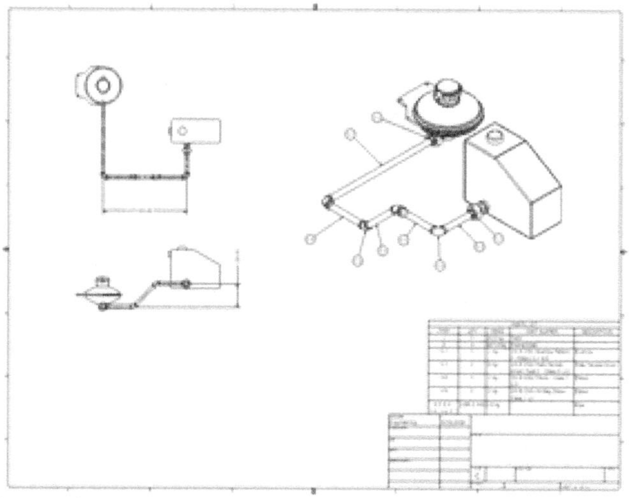

The completed exercise

Document a Pipe Run

In this portion of the exercise, you will place views of a rigid pipe route and add annotations to document the design.

1. Open *Tube and Pipe Documentation.iam*.

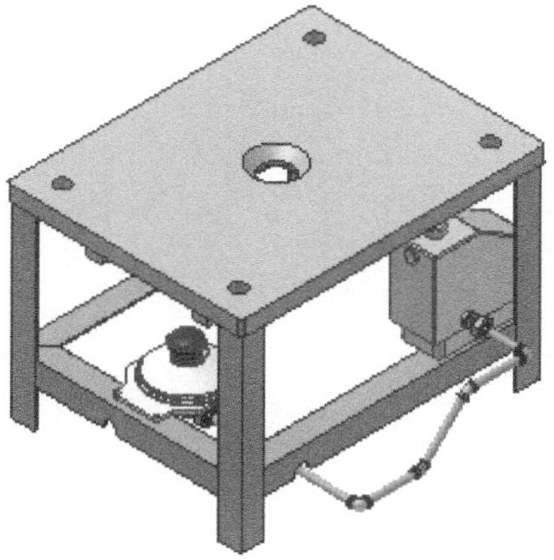

2. To create a new drawing file:
   - At the top of the browser, right-click on *Tube and Pipe Documentation.iam* and select Create Drawing View.
   - In the Create New File dialog box, expand Templates>en-US>Metric .
   - Select *ANSI(mm).idw.*
   - Click Create.
3. Use the Drawing View dialog box to create the base and projected view:
   - Under Representation, select **Feed Line** in the Design View drop-down list.
   - Under Style, ensure that only Hidden Line Removed is selected.
   - Under Scale, enter **0.2**.
   - Drag the view near the top-left corner of the sheet.
   - Select the FRONT view on the ViewCube to orient into a 2D orientation.
   - Use the arrows in the top-right corner of the ViewCube to rotate the view as shown.
   - Before you click OK in the Drawing view dialog box, you can continue to create projected views. Click below the existing view to place a projected view.
   - Click OK to complete the views. Your views should match the following image.

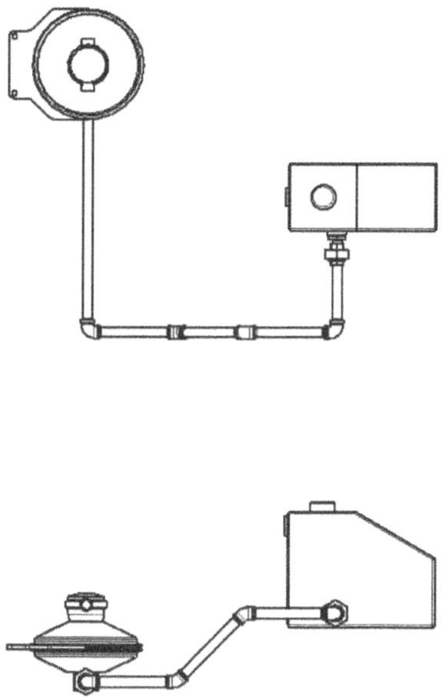

4. Create an isometric view:
   - In the Place Views tab, click Base.
   - Create a new base view that uses the **Feed Line** Design View representation.
   - Assign a scale value of **0.3**.
   - Under Style, ensure that only Hidden Line Removed is selected.
   - Relocate the view to the top-right corner of the drawing.
   - Use the ViewCube that displays adjacent to the view to display it in the isometric orientation, as shown in the following image.
   - Click OK.

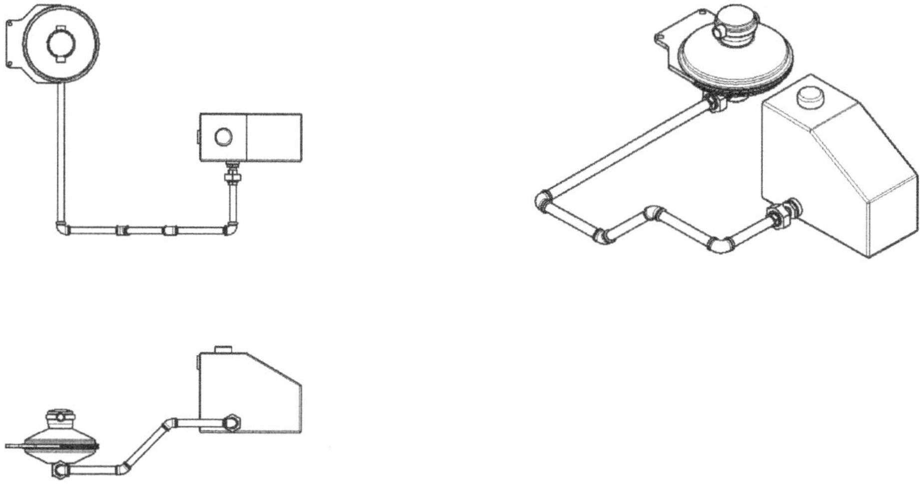

5. If the isometric view is missing lines in it, double-click on isometric view, go to the Display options tab, and select Tangent Edges, then click OK. Missing lines will appear on the view.

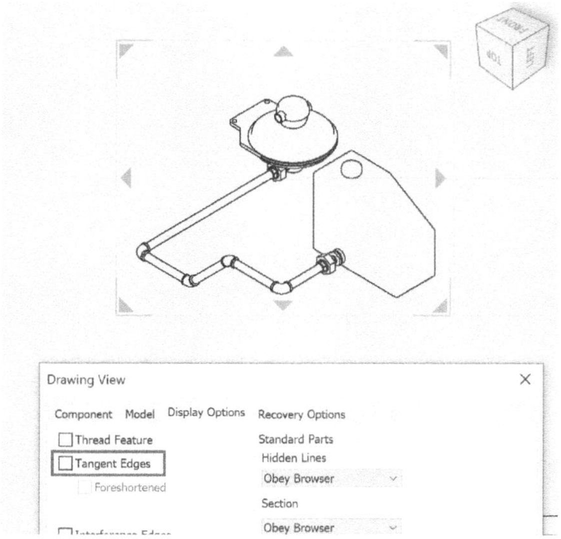

6. If required, drag the view borders to separate the views on the sheet.

7. To display route centerlines:
   - In the browser, expand VIEW1:*Tube and Pipe Documentation.iam*.
   - Expand *Tube and Pipe Documentation.iam*.
   - Right-click on Tube & Pipe Runs.
   - Click Include Route Centerlines.

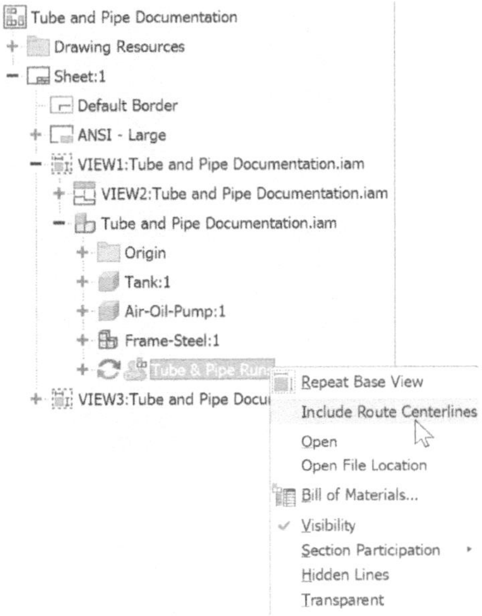

8. Display route centerlines in the projected view.

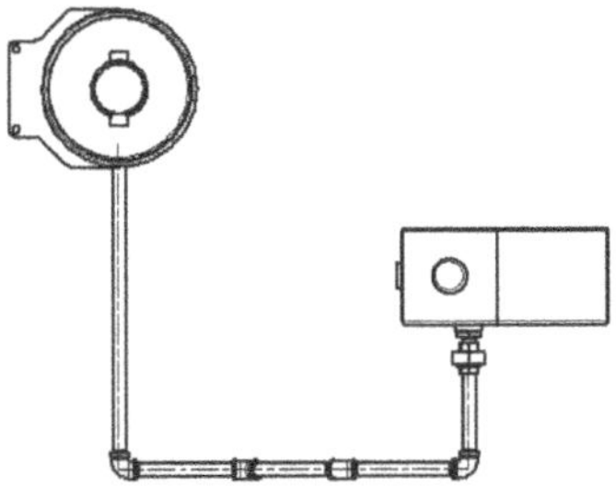

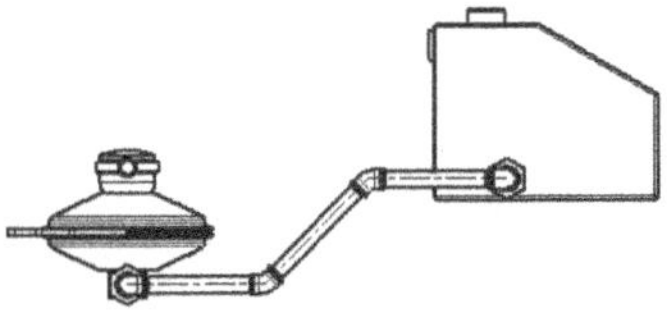

9. To add dimension to the views:

- In the Annotate tab, in the Dimension panel, click Dimension.
- Place dimensions between the centerlines, as shown in the following image.

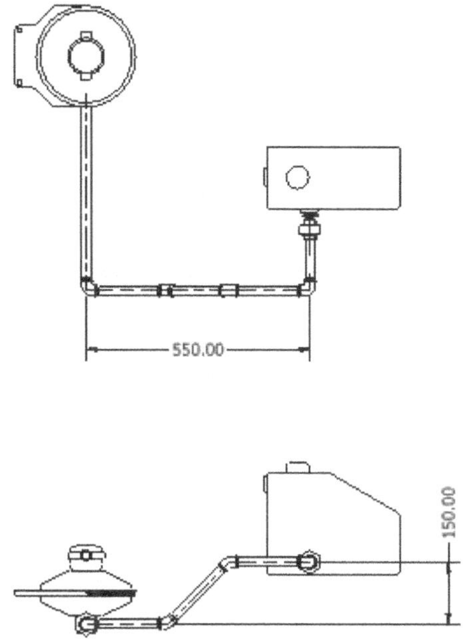

Add a Parts List and Balloons

In this portion of the exercise, you will place and modify a parts list to document the design.

1. To add a parts list:
   - In the Annotate tab, in the Table panel, click Parts List. Select the isometric view.
   - In the Parts List dialog box, under BOM Settings and Properties, for BOM View, verify that Structured is selected.
   - Click OK. Place the parts list above the title block.

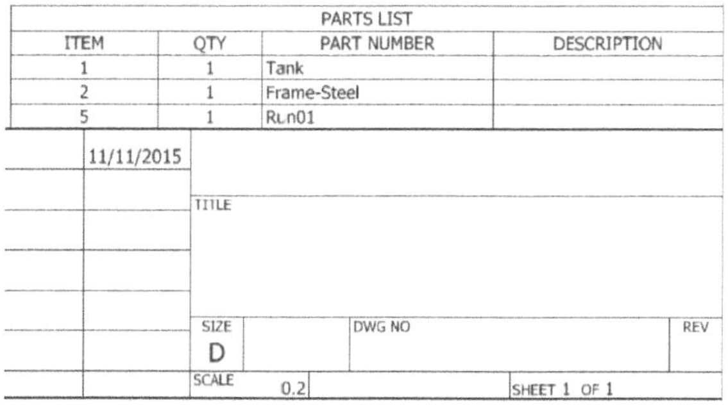

2. To access the view properties for the BOM:
   - Right-click on the parts list. Click Bill of Materials.
   - In the Bill of Materials dialog box, click the Structured Tab (1).
   - In the toolbar, click View Options (2).
   - Click View Properties (3).

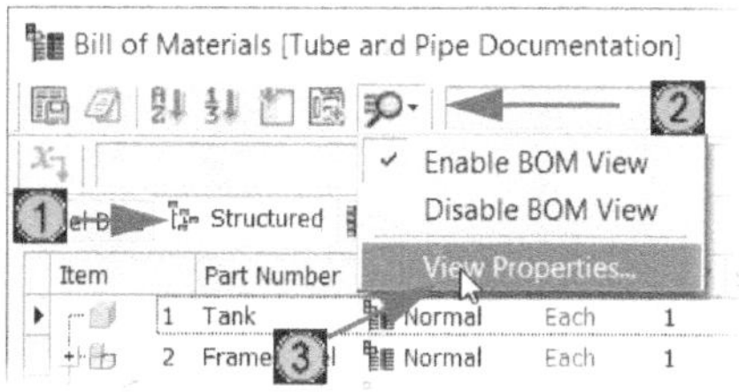

3. To change the display level:
   - In the Structured Properties dialog box, under Level, select All Levels.
   - Click OK.
   - In the Bill of Materials dialog box, click Done.

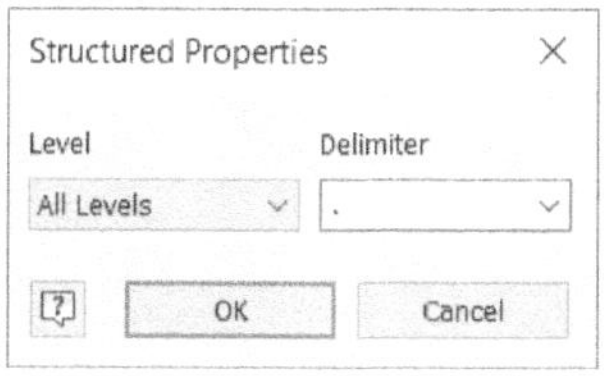

4. To begin to edit the parts list:

- Right-click on the parts list.
- Click Edit Parts List.
- In the Parts List dialog box, expand the assembly Run01.

Note the individual lengths of each segment.

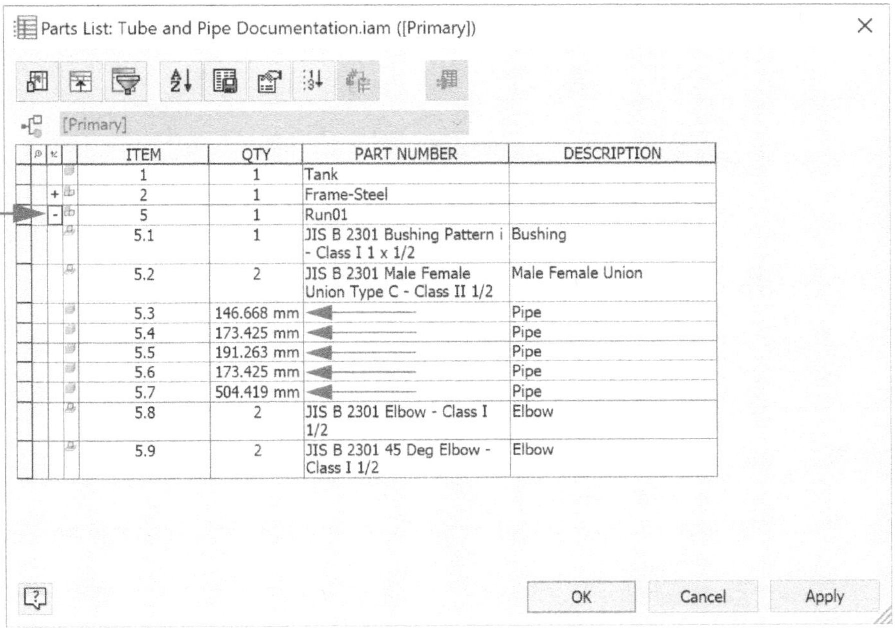

ITEM	QTY	PART NUMBER	DESCRIPTION
1	1	Tank	
2	1	Frame-Steel	
5	1	Run01	
5.1	1	JIS B 2301 Bushing Pattern i - Class I 1 x 1/2	Bushing
5.2	2	JIS B 2301 Male Female Union Type C - Class II 1/2	Male Female Union
5.3	146.668 mm		Pipe
5.4	173.425 mm		Pipe
5.5	191.263 mm		Pipe
5.6	173.425 mm		Pipe
5.7	504.419 mm		Pipe
5.8	2	JIS B 2301 Elbow - Class I 1/2	Elbow
5.9	2	JIS B 2301 45 Deg Elbow - Class I 1/2	Elbow

5. To apply group settings:

- In the Parts List dialog box, in the toolbar, click Group Settings.
- Click Group.
- Note that the default setting is to merge rows with the same Stock Number property.
- Click OK.

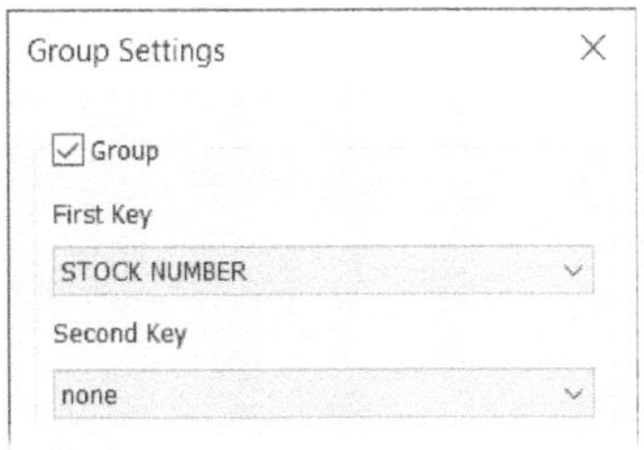

6. In the Parts List dialog box, QTY column, note the individual and combined lengths display.

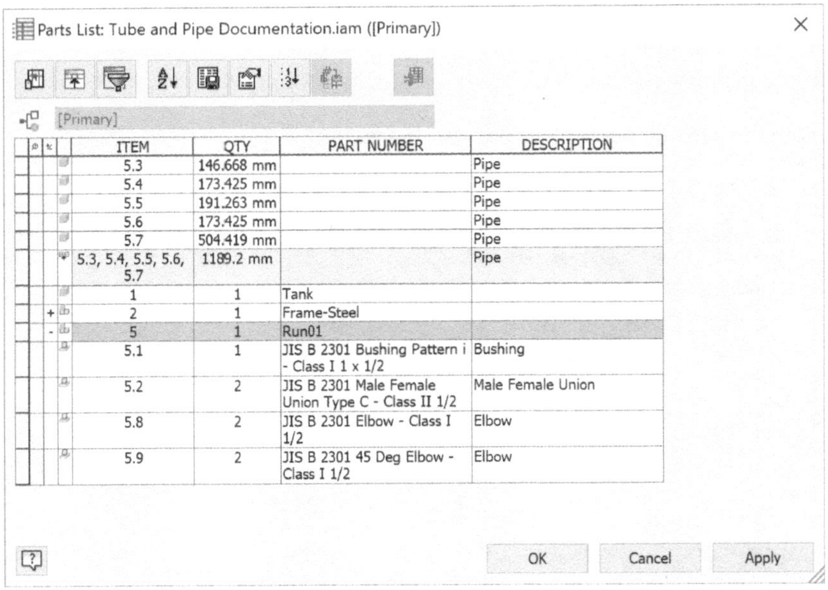

ITEM	QTY	PART NUMBER	DESCRIPTION
5.3	146.668 mm		Pipe
5.4	173.425 mm		Pipe
5.5	191.263 mm		Pipe
5.6	173.425 mm		Pipe
5.7	504.419 mm		Pipe
5.3, 5.4, 5.5, 5.6, 5.7	1189.2 mm		Pipe
1	1	Tank	
2	1	Frame-Steel	
5	1	Run01	
5.1	1	JIS B 2301 Bushing Pattern i - Class I 1 x 1/2	Bushing
5.2	2	JIS B 2301 Male Female Union Type C - Class II 1/2	Male Female Union
5.8	2	JIS B 2301 Elbow - Class I 1/2	Elbow
5.9	2	JIS B 2301 45 Deg Elbow - Class I 1/2	Elbow

7. To remove the individual entries:
   - Click Group Settings.
   - In the Group Settings dialog box, under Group, for Display Group Participants, clear the checkmark.
   - Click OK.

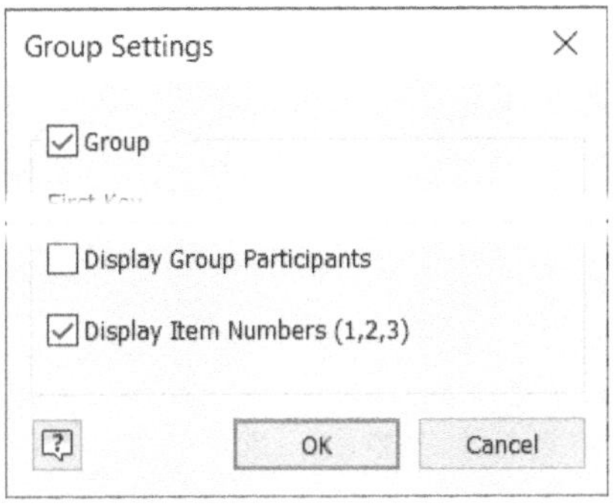

8. In the Parts List dialog box, QTY column, note only the combined length displays.

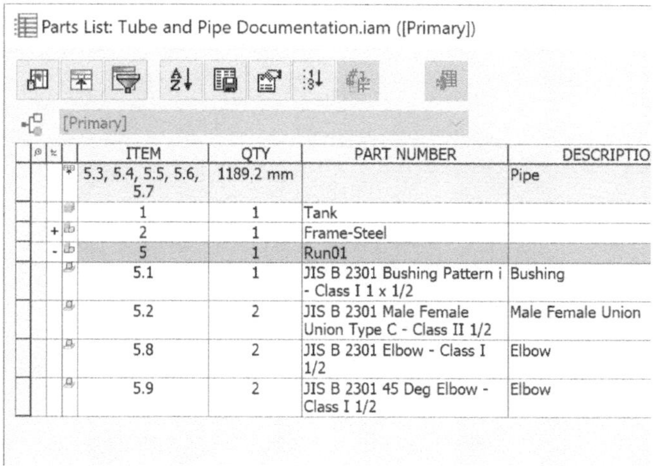

ITEM	QTY	PART NUMBER	DESCRIPTIO
5.3, 5.4, 5.5, 5.6, 5.7	1189.2 mm		Pipe
1	1	Tank	
2	1	Frame-Steel	
5	1	Run01	
5.1	1	JIS B 2301 Bushing Pattern i - Class I 1 x 1/2	Bushing
5.2	2	JIS B 2301 Male Female Union Type C - Class II 1/2	Male Female Union
5.8	2	JIS B 2301 Elbow - Class I 1/2	Elbow
5.9	2	JIS B 2301 45 Deg Elbow - Class I 1/2	Elbow

9. To add a column to the Parts List:

- In the Parts List dialog box, click Column Chooser.
- In the Parts List Column Chooser dialog box, under Available Properties, select Mass.
- Click Add.

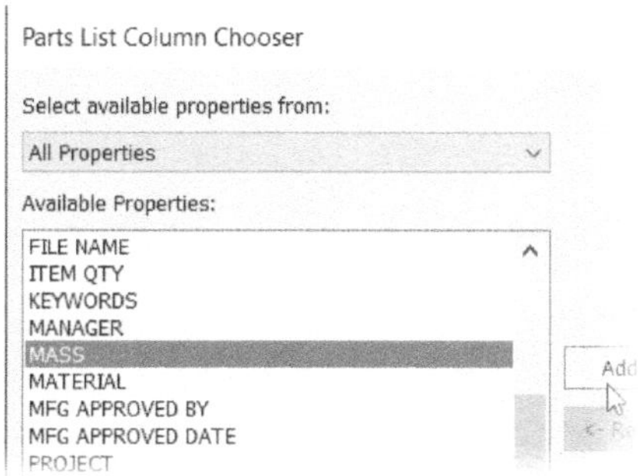

10. To reorder the Parts List columns:

- Under Selected Properties, Select Mass.
- Click Move Up, until the Mass column is below the QTY column.
- Click OK.

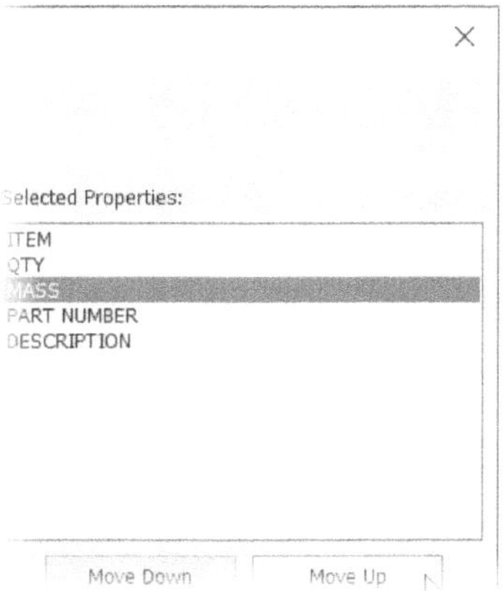

11. To begin to format the Mass column:

- Select the Mass column header.
- Right-click and select Format Column.

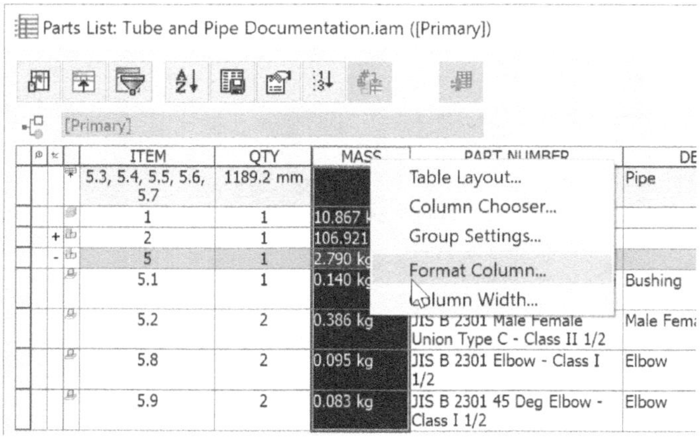

12. To enable Value Substitution:
- In the Format Column: MASS dialog box, click the Substitution tab.
- Click Enable Value Substitution.
- Under When exists, use value of, select Browse Properties.

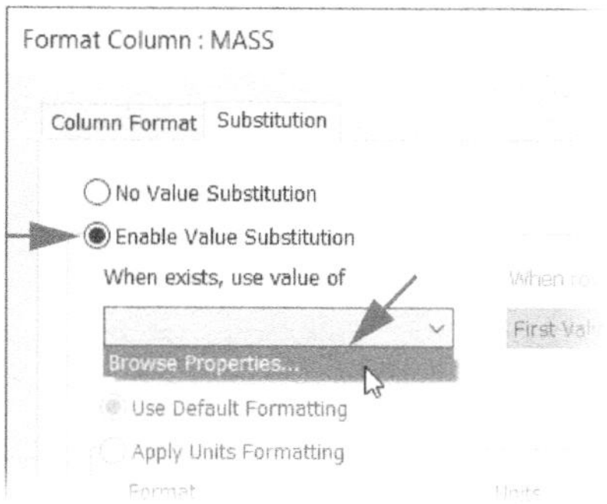

13. To select a column:
- In the Parts List Column Chooser dialog box, under Available Properties, select MASS.
- Click OK.

14. Under When rows are merged, value used is, select Sum of Values.

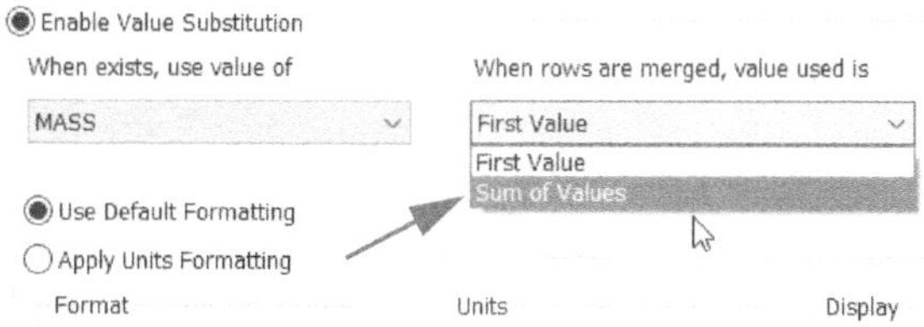

15. To format the units for the Mass column:

- In the Format Column: MASS dialog box, click the Column Format tab.
- Click Apply Units Formatting.
- Under Precision, select 1.1.
- Click OK.

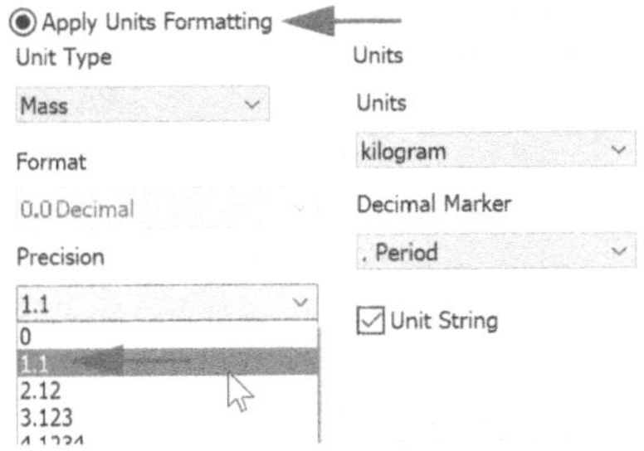

16. To reorder the parts list:

- In the Parts List dialog box, click the gray box at the left of the first row.
- Click and drag the same box to the bottom of the list.
- Click OK.

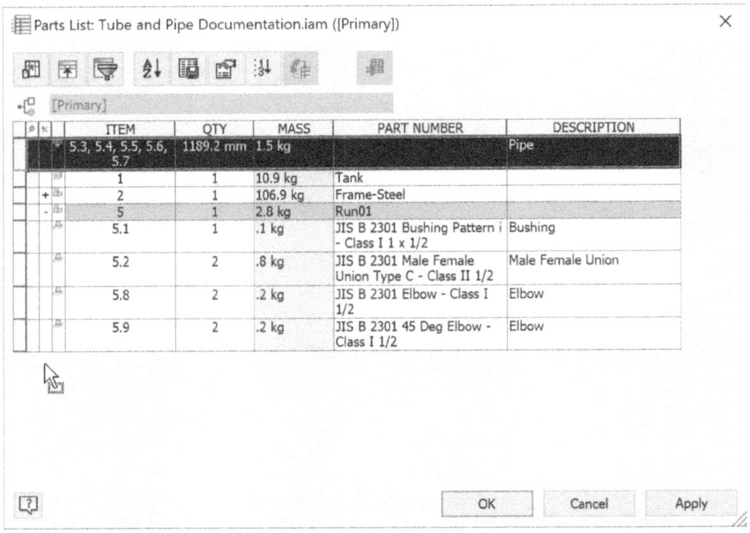

17. Reposition the Parts List over the Title Block.

PARTS LIST				
ITEM	QTY	MASS	PART NUMBER	DESCRIPTION
1	1	10.9 kg	Tank	
2	1	106.9 kg	Frame-Steel	
5.1	1	.1 kg	JIS B 2301 Bushing Pattern i - Class I 1 x 1/2	Bushing
5.2	2	.8 kg	JIS B 2301 Male Female Union Type C - Class II 1/2	Male Female Union
5.8	2	.2 kg	JIS B 2301 Elbow - Class I 1/2	Elbow
5.9	2	.2 kg	JIS B 2301 45 Deg Elbow - Class I 1/2	Elbow
5.3, 5.4, 5.5, 5.6, 5.7	1189.2 mm	1.5 kg		Pipe

18. To add balloons to the isometric view:

- In the ribbon, in the Annotate tab, in the Table panel, click Balloon.
- Add balloons to the segments and fittings as shown in the following image.

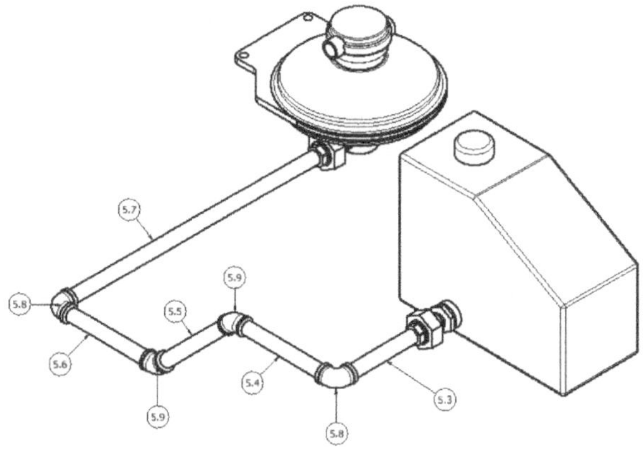

19. Close all files without saving changes.

Lesson: Exporting Tube and Pipe Design Data

Overview

This lesson describes how to export tube and pipe design data to NC bending machine output files and ISOGEN files.

When you create a design, to achieve efficiency and the highest possible quality, you want to leverage your existing design data in as many locations and in as many ways as possible. For a design composed of tubes and pipes, this existing design data might be the bending information for bent tubes, or the design data for use in other applications. Knowing how to export tube and pipe design data to control the bending of a tube, or for use elsewhere, means you can achieve that additional leverage.

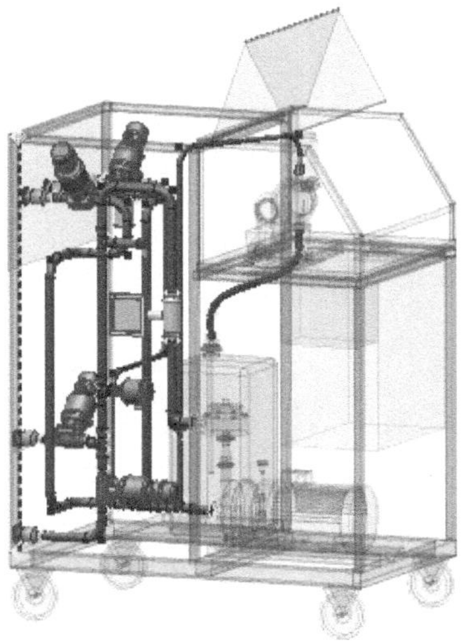

Objectives

After completing this lesson, you will be able to:

- Create NC bending machine output files.
- Create ISOGEN files.

Creating Bending Machine Files

Bent tubes are often manufactured by numerically controlled (NC) tube bending machines. To use the design data of your bent tube runs to control an NC bending machine, you need to know where and how to export the data.

In the following image, the run for a tube requires multiple bends in different directions. By exporting the bend data, all of the direction, length, and radius information is available to control the machine to create the required final part.

Bending Machine Output

You can save your tube routes in two common bending machine formats: XYZ and YBC. The output file extension for XYZ is *filename.xyz*. The output file extension for YBC is *filename.lra* (which stands for length, rotation, and angle) or *filename.ybc*. The files are ASCII text files that describe the route to be manufactured. You can view and edit the files in a text editor.

You access the Bending Machine Output option from the shortcut menu after right-clicking on a tube segment that is created for a populated run. The bending machine output option is available only for tube segments.

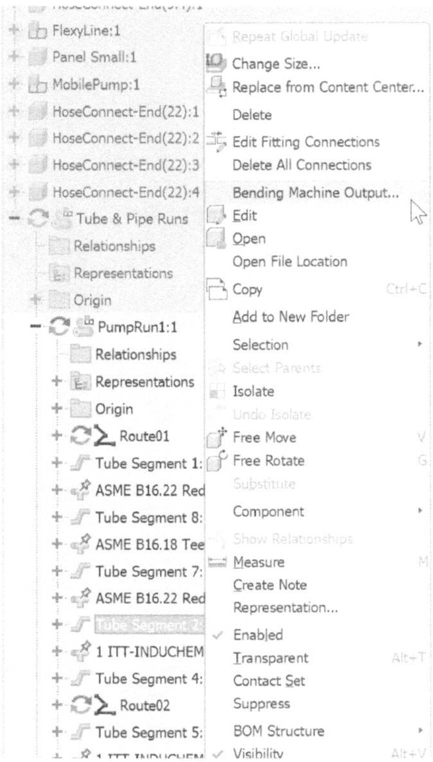

Managing Files

Bending machine output files are not associated with the model. If you use Pack and Go or the Autodesk® Vault® software, you must manually include the bending machine output files.

Bending machine files are not automatically updated when you make changes to the model. You must manually create new bending output files if you change the tube run. Bending machine data that is pasted into drawing files is also not associative to the model data and requires a manual update. Establish a manual process for updating files that fits your workflows.

The exported files are text files that you can edit in a text editor. The following image is an example of YBC output.

Export TP Design Data_PumpRun1_1_Tube Se

File Edit Format View Help

MASTER/YBC:
Number of points = 6
Number of Straights = 7
Unit of Length = millimeter
Unit of Angle = degree

Point		Y	
0	54.1	0	90
1	78.4	90.00	90
2	628.4	0.00	90
3	80.1	-90.00	90
4	62.4	-90.13	90
5	48.4	0.00	90
6	24.8	0	

Developed Length: 1455.4

Procedure: Creating Bending Machine Output Files

The following steps give an overview of creating a bending machine output file.

1. Edit the tube run where the segment to be exported is located.
2. Either in the browser or the graphics window, right-click on the tube segment to be exported. Click Bending Machine Output.
3. In the Save dialog box:
   - Select a folder and edit the file name to match your requirements.
   - Select the type of file to output.
   - Click Save.

Exporting ISOGEN Files

Centerline isometric drawings are often required to document tube and pipe designs. In Autodesk Inventor, you can output ISOGEN data that can be read into an ISOGEN-capable application to generate detailed isometric piping drawings.

ISOGEN files are not associative to changes to runs in the model. If you make changes to an assembly, you must manually export the ISOGEN output data again to reflect the changes.

Access

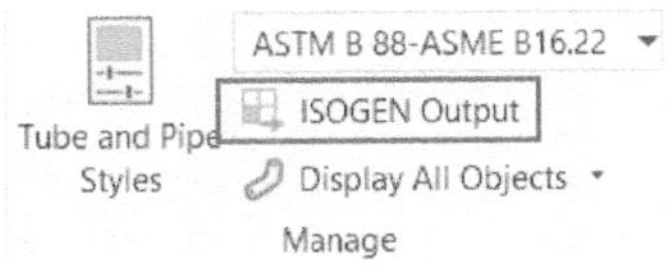

Ribbon: Pipe Run tab>Manage panel

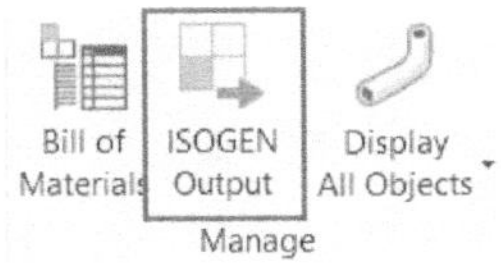

Ribbon: Tube and Pipe tab>Manage panel

ISOGEN Output Options

When you start the ISOGEN Output tool when a run is active for edit, the file you create contains only the exported data from that run. If you start the tool when the Tube & Pipe Runs primary assembly is active, then you can click Options in the ISOGEN Output dialog box to display the ISOGEN Output Options dialog box. In the ISOGEN Output Options dialog box, you select which runs to output, and whether you want to combine the data to a single output file or a separate file for each run.

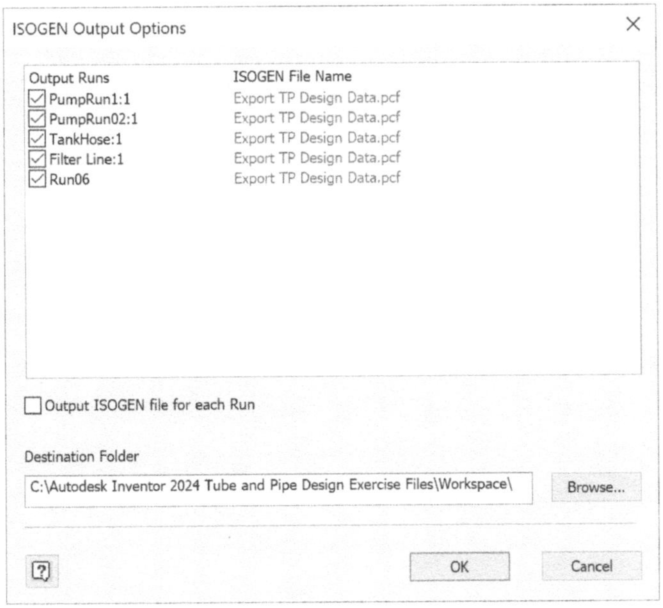

Adding ISOGEN Properties to Fittings and Conduit Parts

ISOGEN properties are required for all components in the active run when you save the run in ISOGEN format. Fittings and conduit parts in the supplied libraries include ISOGEN properties. If you create your own custom tube and pipe components, you can add ISOGEN properties when you author the parts.

Procedure: Creating ISOGEN Files

The following steps give an overview of exporting data to an ISOGEN PCF file.

1. Determine the output level for the ISOGEN data. To export data from a single run, edit the run in the assembly.
2. Start the ISOGEN Output tool.
3. In the Save dialog box, select a folder. If required, rename the output file. If you want to save data for multiple runs, click Options to select the runs to output and to either save to a single file or a separate file for each run.
4. Click OK. The data is saved to the specified file.

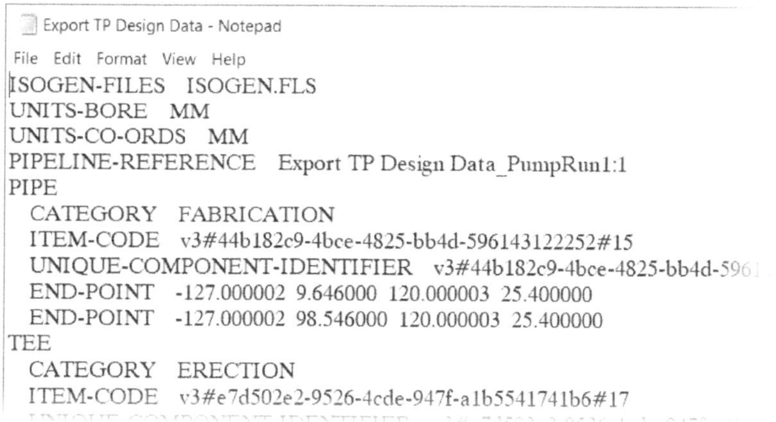
Export TP Design Data - Notepad

File Edit Format View Help

```
ISOGEN-FILES   ISOGEN.FLS
UNITS-BORE   MM
UNITS-CO-ORDS   MM
PIPELINE-REFERENCE   Export TP Design Data_PumpRun1:1
PIPE
   CATEGORY   FABRICATION
   ITEM-CODE   v3#44b182c9-4bce-4825-bb4d-596143122252#15
   UNIQUE-COMPONENT-IDENTIFIER   v3#44b182c9-4bce-4825-bb4d-596
   END-POINT   -127.000002  9.646000  120.000003  25.400000
   END-POINT   -127.000002  98.546000  120.000003  25.400000
TEE
   CATEGORY   ERECTION
   ITEM-CODE   v3#e7d502e2-9526-4cde-947f-a1b5541741b6#17
```

Exercise: Export Tube and Pipe Design Data

In this exercise, you will create a bending machine file for a bent tube segment, and you will also export all the run data to an ISOGEN file.

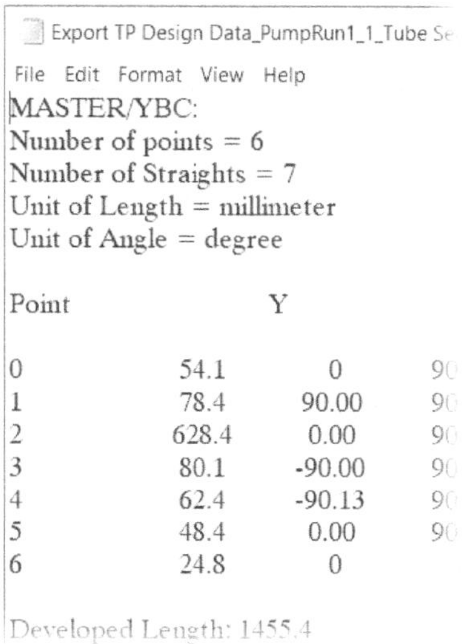
Export TP Design Data_PumpRun1_1_Tube Se

File Edit Format View Help

MASTER/YBC:
Number of points = 6
Number of Straights = 7
Unit of Length = millimeter
Unit of Angle = degree

Point		Y	
0	54.1	0	90
1	78.4	90.00	90
2	628.4	0.00	90
3	80.1	-90.00	90
4	62.4	-90.13	90
5	48.4	0.00	90
6	24.8	0	

Developed Length: 1455.4

The completed exercise

1. Open *Export TP Design Data.iam.*

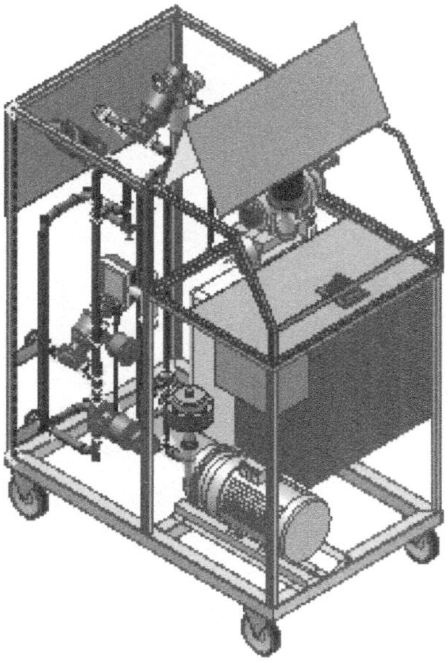

2. In the browser under Tube & Pipe Runs, double-click on PumpRun1:1 to activate it for editing in place.

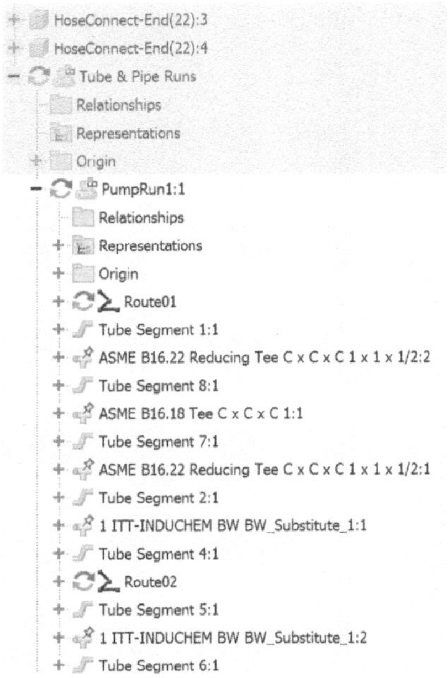

3. In the browser, right-click on Tube Segment 2:1. Click Bending Machine Output.

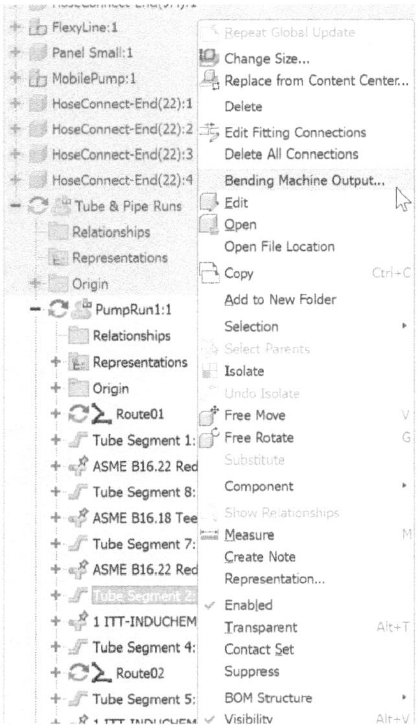

4. In the Save Bending Machine Output File dialog box, click Save to create an LRA (or YBC) file with the default name.

5. To begin exporting all of the data for the run, in the ribbon, in the Pipe Run tab, in the Manage panel, click ISOGEN Output.

6. In the ISOGEN Output dialog box, click Save to create a PCF file with the default name.

7. In the browser, double-click on Tube & Pipe Runs to activate it for editing.

8. To export the data for multiple runs, in the Tube and Pipe tab, in the Manage panel, click ISOGEN Output.

9. In the ISOGEN Output dialog box, click Options.

10. In the ISOGEN Output Options dialog box:
    - In the Output Runs list, clear the check box for TankHose:1.
    - Click OK.

11. In the ISOGEN Output dialog box, click Save.

12. In the ISOGEN Properties Required dialog box:
    - In the ISOGEN SKey column for the coupling, select COSW Coupling - Socket Weld.
    - Click OK.

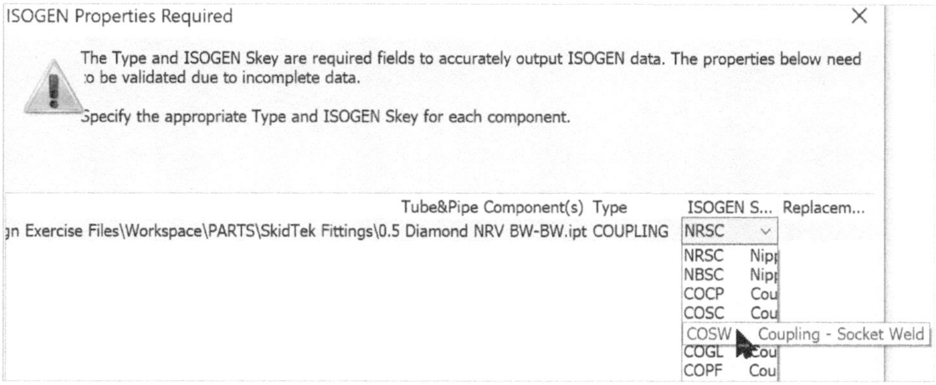

13. To review the data in the exported files, open the generated files in Notepad.

14. Close all files without saving changes.

Chapter Summary

In this chapter, you learned how to document tube and pipe assemblies with assembly design view and positional representations and model states and how to use them in drawings. You also learned how tube and pipe runs are represented in the assembly bill of materials, how to structure tube and pipe parts lists, and how to create bending machine or ISOGEN output files.

Having completed this chapter, you can:

- Manage the amount of assembly data that gets loaded into memory and is visible in drawing views through the use of model states.
- Document tube and pipe assemblies in drawings.
- Export tube and pipe design data to create bending machine or ISOGEN files.

Made in United States
Cleveland, OH
05 November 2026

47656820R00226